BY: D.J. DIRKSEN & R.A. REEVES

Recreation Sales Publishing, Inc.
P.O. Box 4024
Burbank, CA 91503-4024
Phone (818) 843-3616

NINTH EDITION

ISBN 0-943798-15-9

CREDITS
MAPS BY RENEE REEVES
COVER DESIGN AND CARTOONS BY GREG DIRKSEN

COVER PHOTOGRAPHS:
CLEAR LAKE, LAKE COUNTY
Courtesy of TOMMY GILLIAM

P.O. BOX 995, Lakeport, CA 95453
Ph: 707-263-1231

INFORMATION IS PRESENTED
AS IT APPEARS WHEN LAKES
ARE AT FULL CAPACITY.
WEATHER CONDITIONS
MUST BE CONSIDERED

ALL FEES AND INFORMATION
ARE SUBJECT TO CHANGE

MAPS ARE NOT TO SCALE

Printing by: DELTA LITHOGRAPH, Valencia
Typography by: IMAGE COMMUNICATIONS, Torrance

Library of Congress 89-064190

GUIDEBOOKS FROM RECREATION SALES PUBLISHING

RECREATION LAKES OF CALIFORNIA
Ninth Edition

Current information and detailed *maps* on over *420 lakes* throughout California. A MUST for *campers, R.V.ers, fishermen, boaters and hunters*. The BEST guidebook available for any outdoor enthusiast—**Over 600,000 Copies Sold.**

WINTER RECREATION IN CALIFORNIA
Third Edition

Downhill and cross country skiing, snow play areas and snowmobiling, resorts and campgrounds. Maps and information for every area that offers winter sports. Lots of little known places as well as all the *major ski resorts* throughout the State.

RECREATION ON THE COLORADO RIVER

Everything you need to know about this spectacular River from the *headwaters* high in the Colorado Rockies to the *Gulf of California*. Maps of every recreation site including *Lakes Powell, Mead and Havasu*.

L.A. GOLF
The Public Courses of Los Angeles and Ventura Counties

The first comprehensive Guide to these *golf courses* ever published. All the *public 18 HOLE and PAR 3 COURSES* with detailed maps of each location. *Fees, starter phone numbers* and what's available plus a description of each course.

ORDER FORM

	Price	Sales Tax	Total Price	Quantity	Total Amount
Recreation Lakes of California	16.95	1.14	18.09	______	______
Winter Recreation in California	12.95	.87	13.82	______	______
Recreation on the Colorado River	9.95	.67	10.62	______	______
L.A. Golf—The Public Courses of Los Angeles and Ventura Counties	14.95	1.01	15.96	______	______
				Shipping	$1.50

* NO SHIPPING CHARGES on any combination of 2 books or more

CHECK ENCLOSED $ ______

NAME: ____________________

ADDRESS: ____________________

____

SEND ORDER TO:

Recreation Sales Publishing, Inc.
P.O. Box 4024
Burbank, CA 91503-4024
Phone (818) 843-3616

INTRODUCTION

We are pleased to introduce our Ninth Edition of RECREATION LAKES OF CALIFORNIA. As in previous editions, this guide presents in a clear concise manner the location, facilities, and recreational opportunities at California's many Lakes.

California is blessed with an abundance and variety of recreation lakes. From a quiet alpine setting at 10,000 feet in the Sierra, an urban lake at sea level in San Francisco or a large inland sea 228 feet below sea level near the desert, each of California's lakes are unique in their own way. No matter where you are in the State, there is a lake nearby awaiting you.

Each lake is described according to location, elevation size, facilities and type of fish. The book is divided into three sections which are marked by black bleedoffs at the bottom of the page; the left is the North Section, the middle is Central and the right is the South Section. Campgrounds for tents and R.V.s, picnic areas, launch ramps, marinas and other facilities are located on each map as well as hiking, bicycle and equestrian trails. The maps also show important recreation areas near each lake, such as State and National Parks, Wilderness Areas, the Pacific Crest Trail and the California Aqueduct Bikeway.

While boating, fishing, and camping are basic to most lakes, we have also included swimming, hiking, backpacking and equestrian information. Waterslides, boat tours, golf courses and other specific attractions are mentioned. Name your interest, a ferry ride at Edison Lake leading to the John Muir Wilderness Trailhead or dragboat racing at Ming Lake, RECREATION LAKES OF CALIFORNIA will fill your need.

In compiling the many facts required for this Ninth Edition, we are overwhelmed by the tremendous support and cooperation of the people who completed our questionnaires and answered our numerous phone calls. The U. S. Forest Service, the Army Corps of Engineers and other Federal Agencies supplied all the necessary facts regarding their jurisdiction. The California State Park System, the California Department of Fish and Game, along with other State, County and Local Agencies were indispensable in providing many of the details required for this publication. The people operating the private facilities along with the various Chambers of Commerce and Visitor's Bureaus were equally supportive. Most of all, we want to thank you, our readers, for your timely suggestions and encouragement. RECREATION LAKES OF CALIFORNIA is a team effort which is constantly improving by the contributions of those who use it. We thank you.

GOLDEN PASSPORTS TO SELECTED FEDERAL RECREATION AREAS

Entrance Fee for You and All People in the Same Private Vehicle
GOLDEN EAGLE: $25 for One Calendar Year - Apply by Mail or in Person
GOLDEN AGE: Free to Permanent U.S. Residents 62 Years or Older
GOLDEN ACCESS: Free to Medically Blind or those with Permanent Disability

These Include 50% Discount on Camping and Other User Fees
Must Apply in Person at Most Federal Recreation Areas with Proof of Age or Disability

Write for Further Information:

National Park Service
U.S. Department of the Interior
18th & C Streets NW
Washington, DC 20240

U.S. Forest Service
U.S. Department of Agriculture
14th & Independence Ave., SW
Washington, DC 20250

Or a Regional Office

CAMP STAMPS

A Camp Stamp Program has been initiated by the U.S. Forest Service to help the public pay for their campsite fees, thereby eliminating the need to carry cash or checkbooks. These stamps are sold in denominations of 50 cents, $1, $2 or $3 at a discount of 15%. They can be used in conjunction with the Golden Age and Golden Access Passports. The stamps do not expire. Camp Stamps can be purchased at your local Forest Service Office or write to:

CAMP STAMPS
Forest Service USDA
Dept. B, P.O. Box 2417
Washington, DC 20013

CAMPGROUND RESERVATIONS

While reservations are not required or taken at some campgrounds, they are often advised. Most group campsites require reservations. For those requiring specific information on the many public and private facilities listed in this guide, there is an information phone number and address on each page.

Most U. S. Forest Service campsites are on a first-come, first-served basis. Selected National Forest campgrounds may now be reserved. We have listed these campgrounds on the map pages by the symbol M . Reservations are advised from Memorial Day to Labor Day.

For Forest Service MISTIX Reservations:

Ph: 1-800-283-CAMP.

The California State Park System also uses MISTIX for their campsite reservations.

For State Park MISTIX Reservations contact:

P.O. Box 8705
San Diego, CA 92138-5708
Phone: 1-800-444-7275
TDD (for the deaf): 1-800-274-7275
Out of State: 619-452-1950
Customer Service: 619-452-5956

MISTIX Reservations for both Forest Service and State Parks may be charged to Visa or Master Card. All Fees are Subject to Change.

INDEX

A

Abbott 132
Agua Hedionda 190
Almaden Lake Park 126
Almaden Reservoir 126
Almanor 24
Alondra 168
Alpine (Marin County) 116
Alpine (Stanislaus National Forest) 83
Amador 87
Anaheim 177
Anderson 128
Angler's 181
Antelope 26
Anza 117
Apollo Park 165
Arrowbear 173
Arrowhead 173
Atascadero 155
Avocado 146

B

Bailey 4
Barrett (Mammoth Lakes) 102
Barrett (San Diego) 193
Bass 139
Bathtub 19
Baum 12
Bear River 76
Beardsley 93
Beauty 67
Benbow 27
Berkeley Aquatic Park 117
Berryessa 86
Bethany 122
Big (Fall River Valley) 12
Big (Tahoe National Forest) 59
Big Bear (Gold Lakes Basin) 38
Big Bear (San Bernardino N.F.) 174
Big Lagoon 7
Big Sage 4
Bishop Creek Canyon 106
Black Butte 34
Black Rock 142
Blue (Alpine County) 80
Blue (Lake County) 56
Blue (Modoc National Forest) 11
Boca 45
Bon Tempe 116
Bowman 40
Bridgeport 95
Brite Valley 151
Britton 14
Buena Vista Aquatic Area 160
Bucks 30
Bullards Bar 39
Butt Valley 25
Butte 19
Butte Valley Wildlife Area 5

C

C Reservoir 4
Cachuma 158
Cahuilla 183
Calero 126
Camanche 89
Camp Far West 60
Cape 30
Caples 78
Caribou 20
Carmen 93
Carr 40
Cascade 41
Carbon Canyon 177
Casitas 159
Castaic 162
Castle 8
Cave 2
Chabot 121
Cherry 94
Chesbro 126
Clark 177
Clear (Klamath Basin) 3
Clear (Lake County) 57
Clear (Modoc National Forest) 11
Clementine 59
Cleone 28
Cogswell 167
Collins 49
Contra Loma 120
Convict 103
Copco 1
Corona 179
Courtright 142
Coyote 131
Craig 177
Coyote-Hellyer 127
Crater 20
Crowley 104
Crystal (Angeles National Forest) 167
Crystal (Fall River Valley) 12
Crystal (Mammoth Lakes) 102
Cucamonga-Guasti 178
Cull Canyon 121
Cunningham 127
Curtz 81
Cuyamaca 192

D

Dark 67
Davis 31
Delta 4
Del Valle 123
De Sabla 29
Diaz 148
Dixon 188
Doane Pond 190
Don Castro 121
Don Pedro 110
Donnells 93
Donner 47
Dorris 4
Duncan 4

E

Eagle (Lassen National Forest) 21
Eagle (Tahoe National Forest) 41
Earl 7
East Park 33
Eastman (Fall River Valley) 12
Eastman (Madera County) 137
Echo 66
Edison 145
El Capitan 193
El Dorado 169
El Estero 132
Elizabeth (Angeles National Forest) 164
Elizabeth (Fremont) 122
Elk Grove Park 74
Ellery 100
Elsinore 179
Englebright 50
Evans (Buena Vista Rec.) 160
Evans (City of Riverside) 178
Evergreen 80

F

F Reservoir 4
Fairmont 178
Fall River 12
Fallen Leaf 65
Faucherie 40
Fee 2
Feeley 40
Finney 184
Finnon 63
Fish 7
Florence 145
Folsom 72
Fordyce 41
Frazier Park 165
French Meadows 61
Frenchman 32
Freshwater Lagoon 7
Fuller 40
Fulmor 181

G

Gardisky 99
George 102
Gerle Creek 68
Gibraltar 158
Gibson Ranch 74
Glen Helen 166
Gold Lakes Basin 38
Goose (Gold Lakes Basin) 38
Goose (Modoc National Forest) 2
Granite 80
Grant (June Lake Loop) 101
Grant Park 127
Grassy 38
Graven 4
Green Valley 173
Greenstone 99
Gregory 172
Guadalupe 126
Gull 101

H

Harbor 168
Hart 151
Hartley 93
Havasu 196
Haven 38
Heenan 81
Hell Hole 62
Hemet 182
Hennessy 86
Henshaw 189
Hensley 136
Highland 91
Highland Springs 57
Hodges 193
Horseshoe (Mammoth) 102
Horseshoe (Mojave Narrows) 166
Hughes 164
Hume 147
Hummingbird 99
Huntington 144

I

Ice House 69
Independence 42
Indian Creek 81
Indian Tom 5
Indian Valley 58
Iron Canyon 13
Iron Gate 1
Irvine 177
Isabel 122
Isabella 152

J

Jackson 166
Jackson Meadow 42
Jenkinson 71
Jenks 173
Jennings 194
Jordan Pond 121
Juanita 5
Junction 70
June 101
Juniper 19

K

Kaweah 149
Kelly 53
Kent 116
Kerckhoff 140
Keswick 17
Kidd 41
Kirkwood 78
Kirman 93
Klamath Basin 3

L

Lafayette 119
Laguna Niguel 177
Laguna Seca 132
Lagunitas 116

Lake Valley 53
Lakes Basin Recreation Area 38
Leavitt 93
Legg 170
Letts 33
Levin 127
Lewiston 16
Lexington 125
Lily 2
Lindsey 40
Little Grass Valley 37
Little Medicine 6
Little Rock 165
Little Tule 20
Loch Lomond 129
Long (Gold Lakes Basin) 38
Long (Tahoe National Forest) 41
Loon 68
Lopez 156
Los Banos 135
Los Gatos Creek Park 125
Lost 138
Lost Creek 37
Lower Bear River 76
Lower Blue 80
Lower Bucks 30
Lower Klamath 3
Lower Letts Valley 33
Lower Otay 193
Lundy 98

M

Mammoth 102
Mammoth Pool 141
Manzanita 19
Martis Creek 48
Mary 102
Mc Cloud (Mammoth Lakes) 102
Mc Cloud (Shasta-Trinity) 9
Mc Clure 114
Mc Coy Flat 21
Mc Cumber 19
Mc Murray 40
Mc Swain 114
Meadow 80
Medicine 6
Meiss 5
Mendocino 55
Merced 124
Merritt 117
Mile Square 177
Millerton 138
Milton 42
Ming 151
Miramar 193
Modesto 111
Mojave Narrows Park 166
Mono 98
Morena 195
Morning Star 59
Morris 167
Mosquito 91
Mountain Meadow 24
Mud (Modoc County) 10
Mud (Gold Lakes Basin) 38
Murray 193

N

Nacimiento 154
Natoma 73
New Hogan 90
New Melones 107
Nicasio 116
North 106

O

Oakwood 112
O'Neill Forebay 134
Oroville 36
Orr 5

P

Packer 38
Palomar Park 190
Paradise 29
Pardee 88
Parkway 128
Peck Road 170
Pelican 166
Perris 176
Philbrook 29
Phoenix 116
Pillsbury 54
Pine 20
Pine Flat 146
Pinecrest 92
Pinto 130
Piru 163
Plaskett 33
Pleasant Valley 148
Portal Forebay 145
Poway 191
Prado Park 178
Prosser Creek 44
Puddingstone 175
Pyramid 161

Q

Quail 161

R

Ralphine 85
Ralston Afterbay 62
Ramer 184
Rancho Seco 74
Red 79
Redinger 140
Reflection 181
Rice 80
Rock 2
Rock Creek 105
Rollins 52
Round 38
Round Valley 23
Rucker 40
Ruth 22

S

Sabrina 106
Saddlebag 99
Salmon 38
Salt Springs 75
Salton Sea 185
San Antonio 153
San Diego City Lakes 193
San Dimas 167
San Gabriel 167
San Justo 133
San Luis 134
San Pablo 118
San Vicente 193
Santa Ana River 177
Santa Fe 170
Santa Margarita 155
Santee 191
Sardine 38
Sawmill 40
Scotts Flat 51
Sequoia 147
Serene 41
Shadow Cliffs 122
Shasta 18
Shastina 5
Shaver 143
Shoreline 124
Silver (Eldorado National Forest) 77
Silver (Gold Lakes Basin) 38
Silver (June Loop) 101
Silver (Lassen National Forest) 20
Silver (Plumas National Forest) 30
Silverwood 171
Siskiyou 8
Skinner 180
Sly Creek 37
Sly Park 71
Smith 30
Snag (Gold Lakes Basin) 38
Snag (Lassen National Forest) 29
Snag (Modoc National Forest) 2
Snake 30
Solano 86
Sonoma 84
Sotcher 102
Soulajule 116
South 106
Spaulding 46
Spicer Meadows 91
Spring 85
Stafford 116
Stampede 43
Starkweather 102
Sterling 41
Stevens 81
Stevens Creek 124
Stone Lagoon 7
Stony Gorge 35
Strawberry 92
Stumpy Meadows 63
Success 150
Sugar Pine 59
Summit (Alpine County) 81
Summit (Lassen National Park) 19
Summit (Shasta-Trinity N.F.) 14
Sunbeam 187
Sutherland 193

T

T. J. 102
Tahoe 64
Talawa 7
Tamarack 80
Temescal 117
Tenaya 100
Thermalitos Forebay-Afterbay 36
Tinemaha 148
Tioga 100
Topaz 82
Trinity 15
Trumbull 97
Tule (Fall River Valley) 12
Tule (Klamath Basin) 3
Tulloch 108
Turlock 113
Twin (Alpine County) 80
Twin (Mammoth Lakes) 102
Twin (Toiyabe Nat. Forest) 96

U

Union 91
Union Valley 70
Upper Blue 80
Utica 91
Uvas 126

V

Vasona 125
Virginia 97

W

Ward 145
Weaver 40
Webb 160
Webber 42
West Valley 10
Whale Rock 155
Whiskeytown 17
Whittier Narrows 170
Wiest 186
Wishon 142
Wister Unit 184
Wohlford 190
Woods 79
Woodward 109
Woollomes 151
Wrights 67

Y

Yorba Linda 177
Yosemite 115
Yucaipa 178

Z

Zaca 157

NORTH SECTION
LAKES 1 — 58

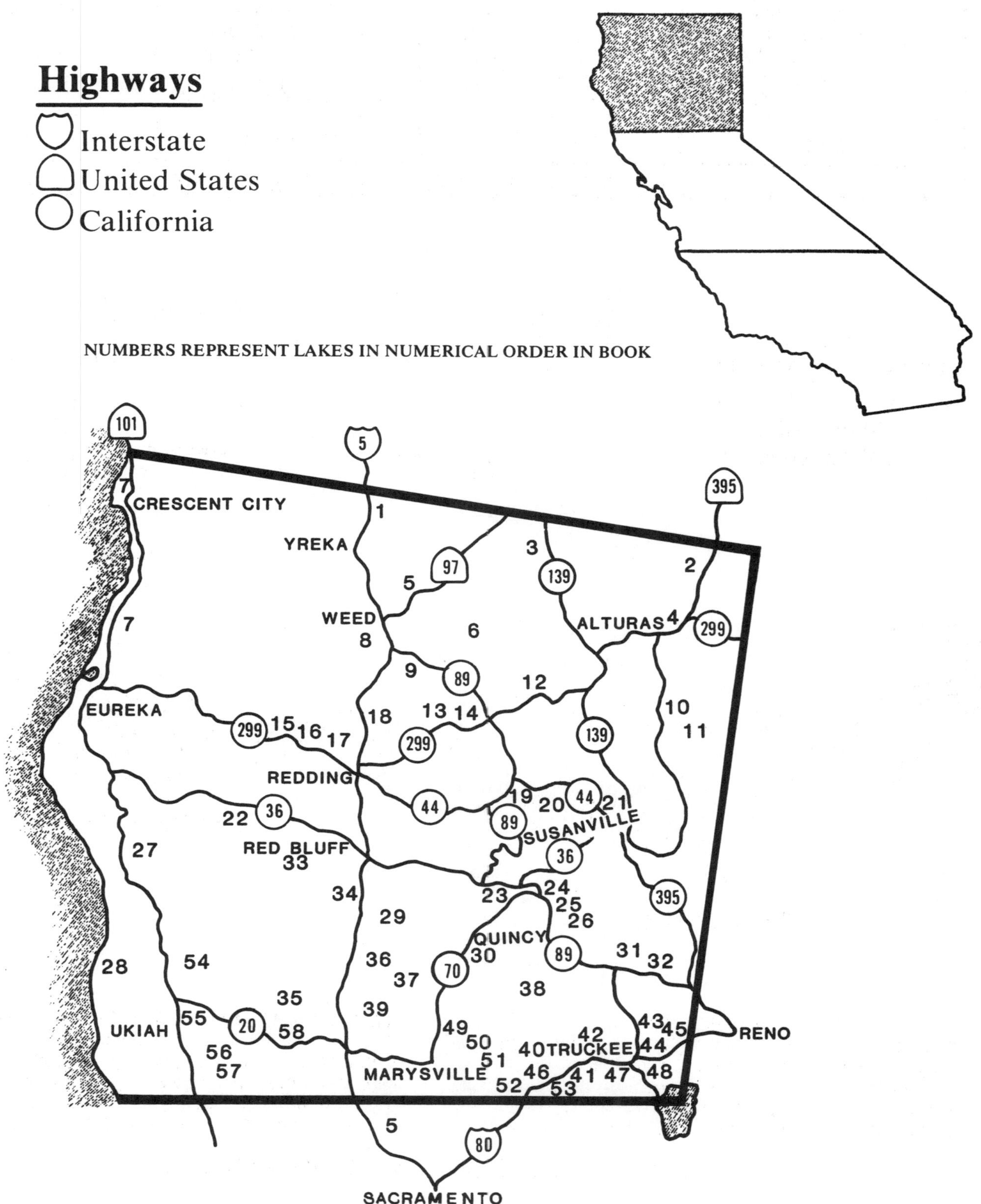

IRON GATE RESERVOIR AND COPCO LAKE

Iron Gate Reservoir and Copco Lake are located 8 miles east of Interstate 5 near the Oregon border. They are under the jurisdiction of the Pacific Power and Light Company which administers the facilities. Both Lakes are fed by the Klamath River. Copco Lake, elevation 2,613 feet, has a surface area of 1,000 acres and is 5 miles long. Iron Gate, elevation 2,343 feet, is almost 7 miles long and covers a surface area of 825 acres. Each Lake has an abundant Yellow perch fishery as well as Rainbow trout and Largemouth bass. The Klamath River provides a good salmon and steelhead crop. River guides are available from September through March. Hunting is popular in this area of abundant game.

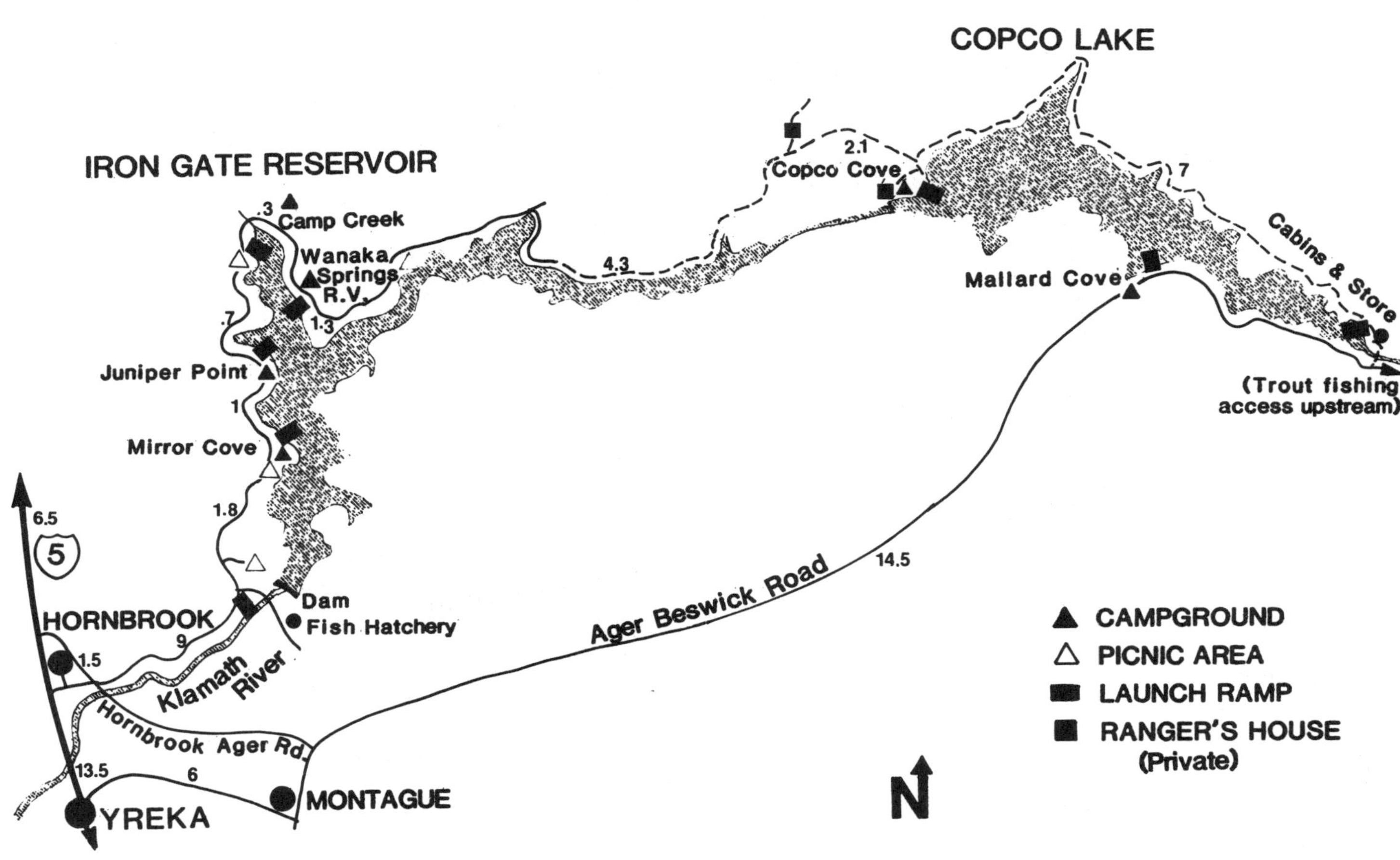

INFORMATION: Pacific Power, 300 S. Main, Yreka 96097, Ph: 916-842-3521

CAMPING	BOATING	RECREATION	OTHER
Iron Gate Reservoir: Camp Creek - 12 Sites with Water Juniper Point - 9 Sites, No Water Mirror Cove - 10 Sites, No Water Copco Lake: Copco Cove - 1 Site Mallard Cove - 1 Site	Power, Row, Canoe, Sail & Inflatable 10 MPH Speed Limit in Designated Areas Copco Lake - Upper 1\3 Set Aside for Fishing (No Wake) Launch Ramps Rentals: Fishing Boats with Motors - Copco Lake Only Docks	Fishing: Trout, Catfish, Crappie, Perch, Salmon & Steelhead-Klamath River Swimming Picnicking Hiking & Riding Trails Rafting Hunting: Deer, Quail, Dove, Waterfowl, Wild Turkey	Copco Only: Cabins - Reserve: Copco Lake Store Star Route 1, Box 188 Montague 96064 Ph: 916-459-3655 Groceries, Bait &Tackle Full Facilities at Hornbrook

GOOSE, CAVE AND LILY LAKES, FEE RESERVOIR

Goose Lake rests on the California-Oregon border at an elevation of 4,800 feet. This huge 108,800 surface acre Lake is used primarily for waterfowl hunting and boating. Trout fishing is considered poor. In contrast, nearby Cave and Lily Lakes offer excellent fishing for Brook and Rainbow trout, but boating is limited. These two small mountain Lakes are neighbors at 6,000 feet in the Modoc National Forest. Poor access roads limit the use of trailers. Fee Reservoir, at 4,000 feet, is under the jurisdiction of Modoc County, and it is known for its large Rainbow trout.

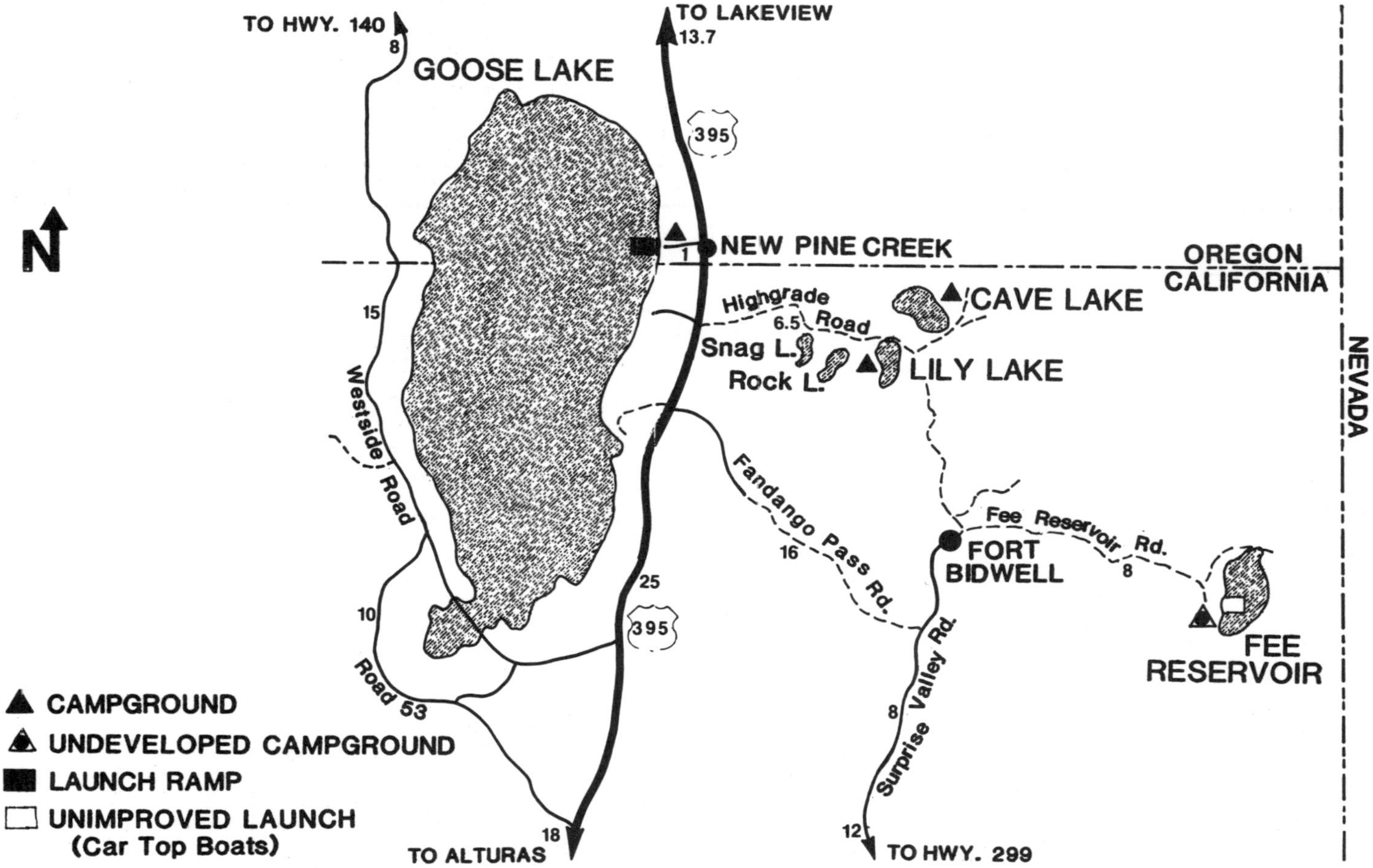

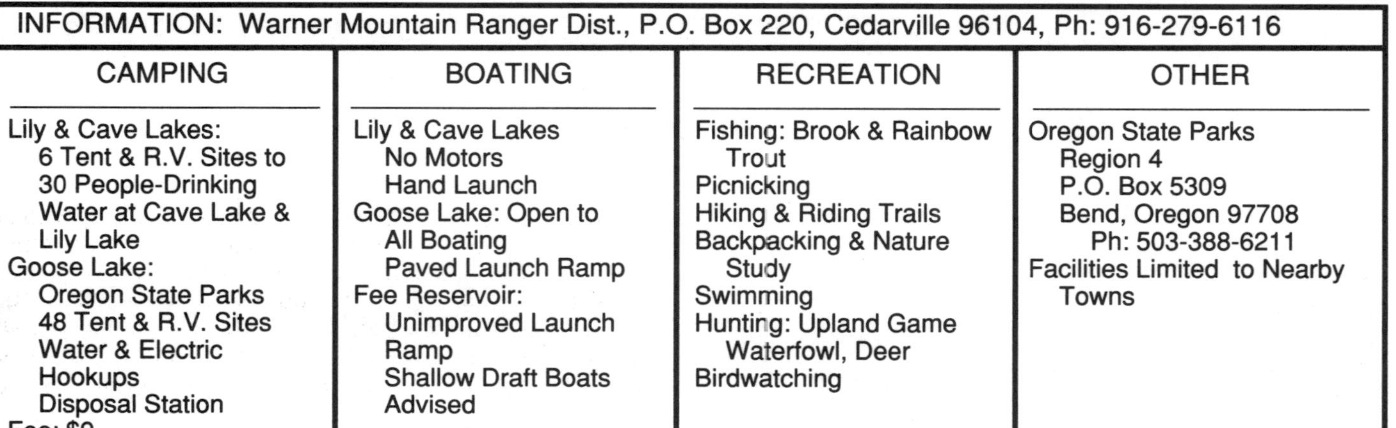

INFORMATION: Warner Mountain Ranger Dist., P.O. Box 220, Cedarville 96104, Ph: 916-279-6116

CAMPING	BOATING	RECREATION	OTHER
Lily & Cave Lakes: 6 Tent & R.V. Sites to 30 People-Drinking Water at Cave Lake & Lily Lake Goose Lake: Oregon State Parks 48 Tent & R.V. Sites Water & Electric Hookups Disposal Station Fee: $9	Lily & Cave Lakes No Motors Hand Launch Goose Lake: Open to All Boating Paved Launch Ramp Fee Reservoir: Unimproved Launch Ramp Shallow Draft Boats Advised	Fishing: Brook & Rainbow Trout Picnicking Hiking & Riding Trails Backpacking & Nature Study Swimming Hunting: Upland Game Waterfowl, Deer Birdwatching	Oregon State Parks Region 4 P.O. Box 5309 Bend, Oregon 97708 Ph: 503-388-6211 Facilities Limited to Nearby Towns

LOWER KLAMATH, TULE AND CLEAR LAKES
KLAMATH BASIN NATIONAL WILDLIFE REFUGES

This is waterfowl country! These Lakes are within the Klamath Basin National Wildlife Refuges which has one of the greatest concentrations of migratory waterfowl in the world. Photography and wildlife observation (over 270 species of birds have been identified) are popular activities. This is a hunter's paradise. Since rules and boundaries are strictly enforced, it is essential you contact the Fish and Wildlife Service for detailed information. Except for canoeing at Tulelake, boating is auxiliary to hunting. There is no fishing. Accommodations can be a problem, especially during hunting season, so plan ahead by contacting the facilities listed below or the Tulelake Chamber of Commerce, P.O. Box 592, Tulelake 96134.

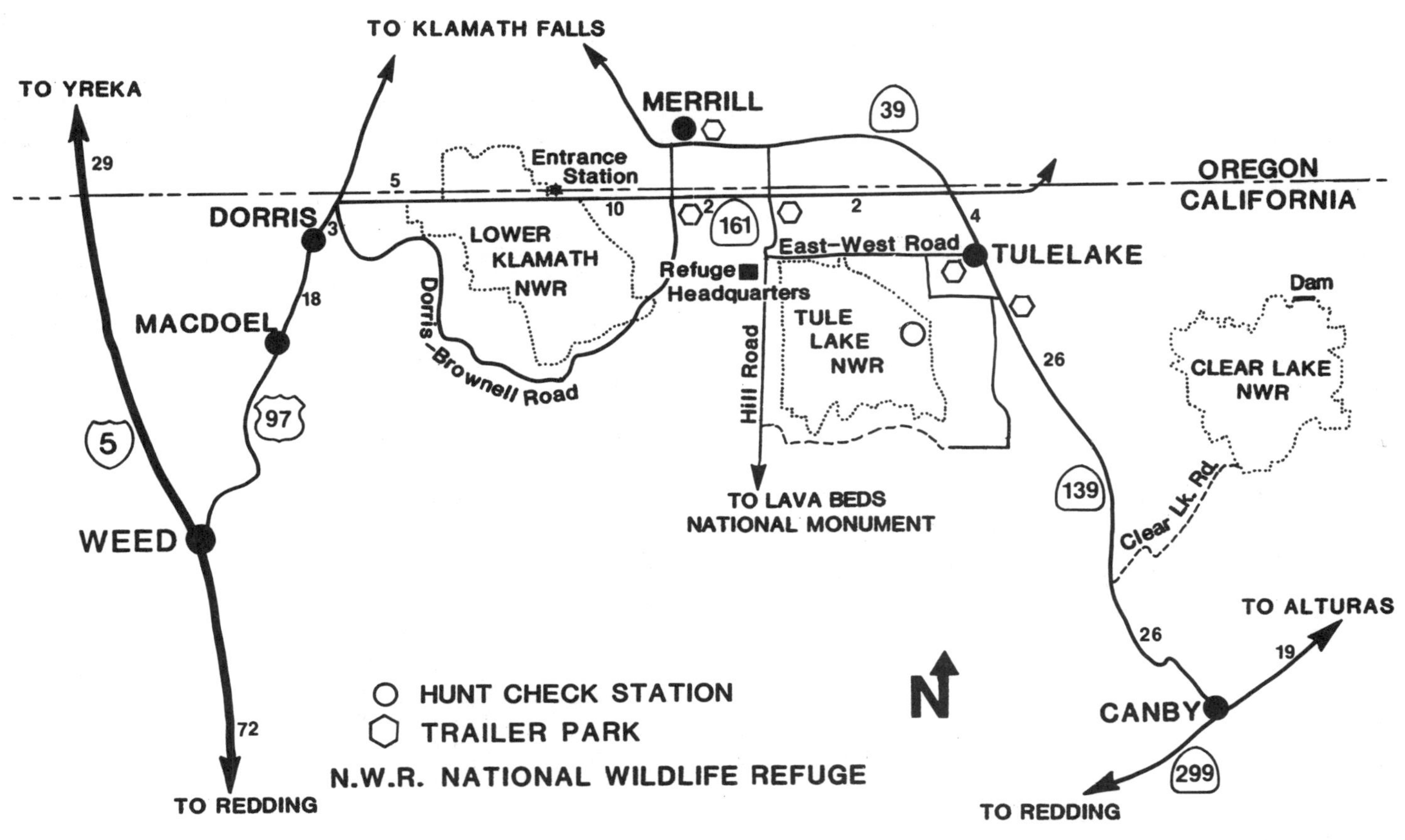

INFORMATION: Klamath Basin NWR, Rt. 1, Box 74, Tulelake 96134, Ph: 916-667-2231

CAMPING	BOATING	RECREATION	OTHER
Shady Lanes Trailer Park: P.O. Box 297 Tulelake 96134 Ph: 916-667-2617 58 R.V. Sites Full Hookups Sheepy Ridge Camp Rt. 1, Box 45-A Tulelake 96134 Ph: 916-667-5370 60 Tent/R.V. Sites Full Hookups: $10.50	Boats are Allowed Only During Hunting Season Except for Canoe Area at Tulelake NWR - Open July Through September Air Thrust & Water Thrust Boats are Prohibited	Hunting: Geese, Ducks, Coots, Snipe & Pheasants *Steel Shot is Required for Waterfowl Hunting Birdwatching Nature Study Photography	Westside Grocery & Trailer Park Rt. 1, Box 46F Tulelake 96134 Ph: 916-667-5225 14 Tent/R.V. Sites Full Hookups Fee: $9 Lava Beds National Monument 40 Tent/R.V. Sites

BIG SAGE, "C", "F", DUNCAN, GRAVEN, BAILEY AND DORRIS RESERVOIRS, DELTA LAKES

Although facilities are limited, Mother Nature has provided an abundance of recreational opportunities at these Lakes in the Modoc National Forest and Modoc County. Big Sage Reservoir rests at an elevation of 4,900 feet on a sage and juniper covered plateau. This 5,400 acre Reservoir is open to all boating and provides a warm water fishery. Nearby Reservoirs "C", and "F" and Duncan provide a good opportunity to catch the large Eagle Lake trout. Dorris Lake is in the Modoc National Wildlife Refuge. It is closed during waterfowl hunting season. The angler will find trout and a warm water fishery. Graven, Bailey and Delta are under the jurisdiction of Modoc County and are primarily known for their good catfishing.

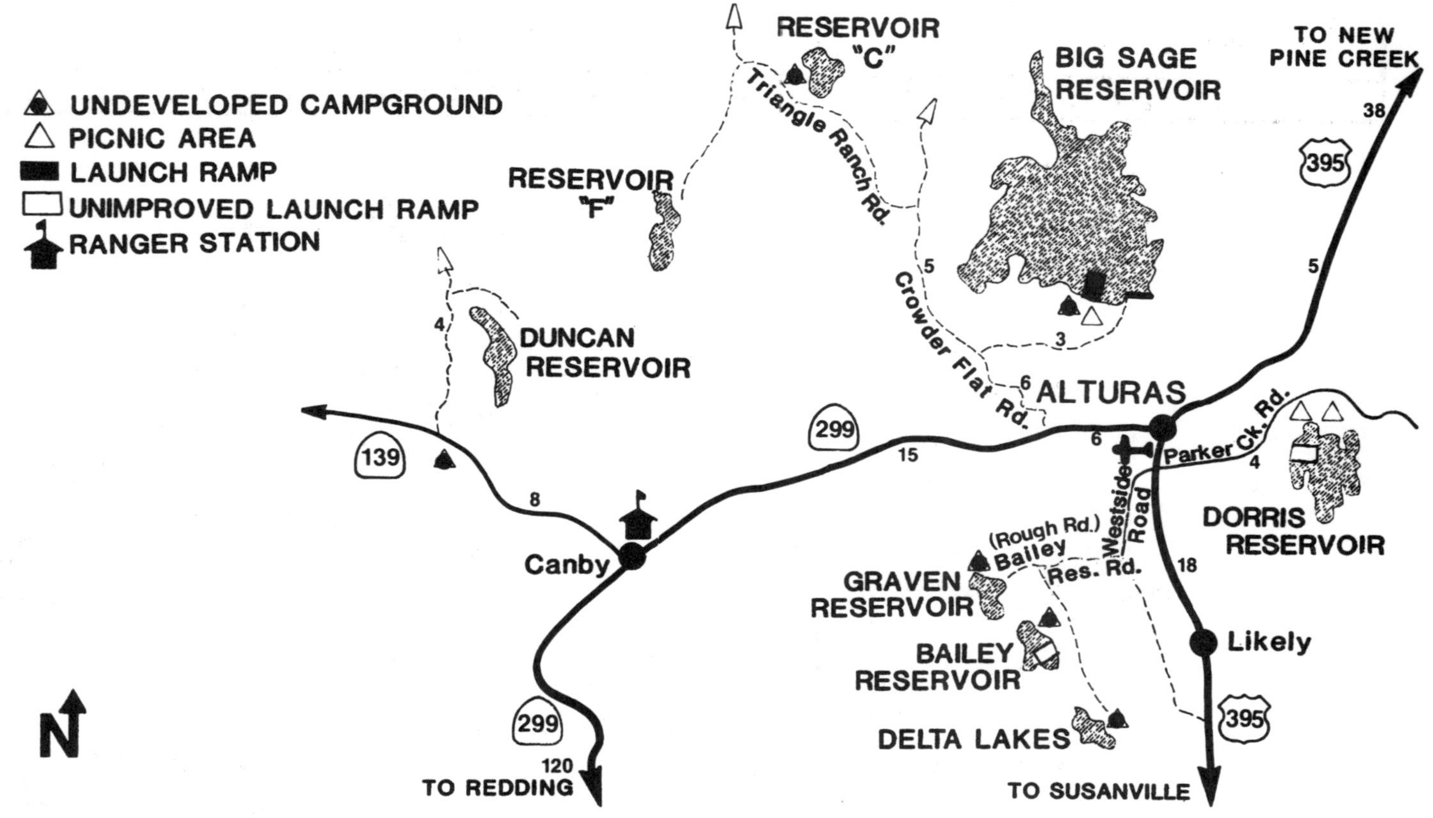

INFORMATION: Devils Garden Ranger Dist., P.O. Box 5, Canby L96015, Ph: 916-233-4611			
CAMPING	BOATING	RECREATION	OTHER
Undeveloped Campsites as Shown on Map No Drinking Water Limited Trailer Access	Big Sage: Open to All Boating Paved Launch Ramp Dorris: Open to All Boating Unimproved Ramp Underwater Hazards Other Lakes Open to Small Hand Launched Boats	Fishing: Trout, Bass, Catfish & Panfish, Eagle Lake Trout at Res. "C", Res. "F", & Duncan Hiking & Riding Trails Nature & Bird Study Hunting: Waterfowl, Upland Game, Deer & Antelope No Hunting at Dorris	Dorris Reservoir: Modoc National Wildlife Refuge P.O. Box 1610 Alturas 96101 Ph: 916-233-3572 Graven, Bailey & Delta Modoc County 202 W. 4th St. Alturas 96101 Ph: 916-233-3939

INDIAN TOM, MEISS, JUANITA, ORR AND SHASTINA LAKES

These Lakes along Highway 97 from Weed to the Oregon Border provide a variety of recreational experiences. The alkaline waters in Indian Tom support a unique Cutthroat fishery. Meiss Lake is within the Butte Valley Wildlife Area. Waterfowl hunting and wildlife observation are the primary activities. Juanita is a pretty mountain Lake resting at an elevation of 5,100 feet. There is a nice campground which provides facilities for the physically disabled. The trout fishing is good. Orr is a small private Lake open to the public for boating and fishing. Lake Shastina is a popular private facility providing good fishing and all boating. Contact the Chamber of Commerce at P.O. Box 366, Weed 96094 or phone 916-938-4624 for information.

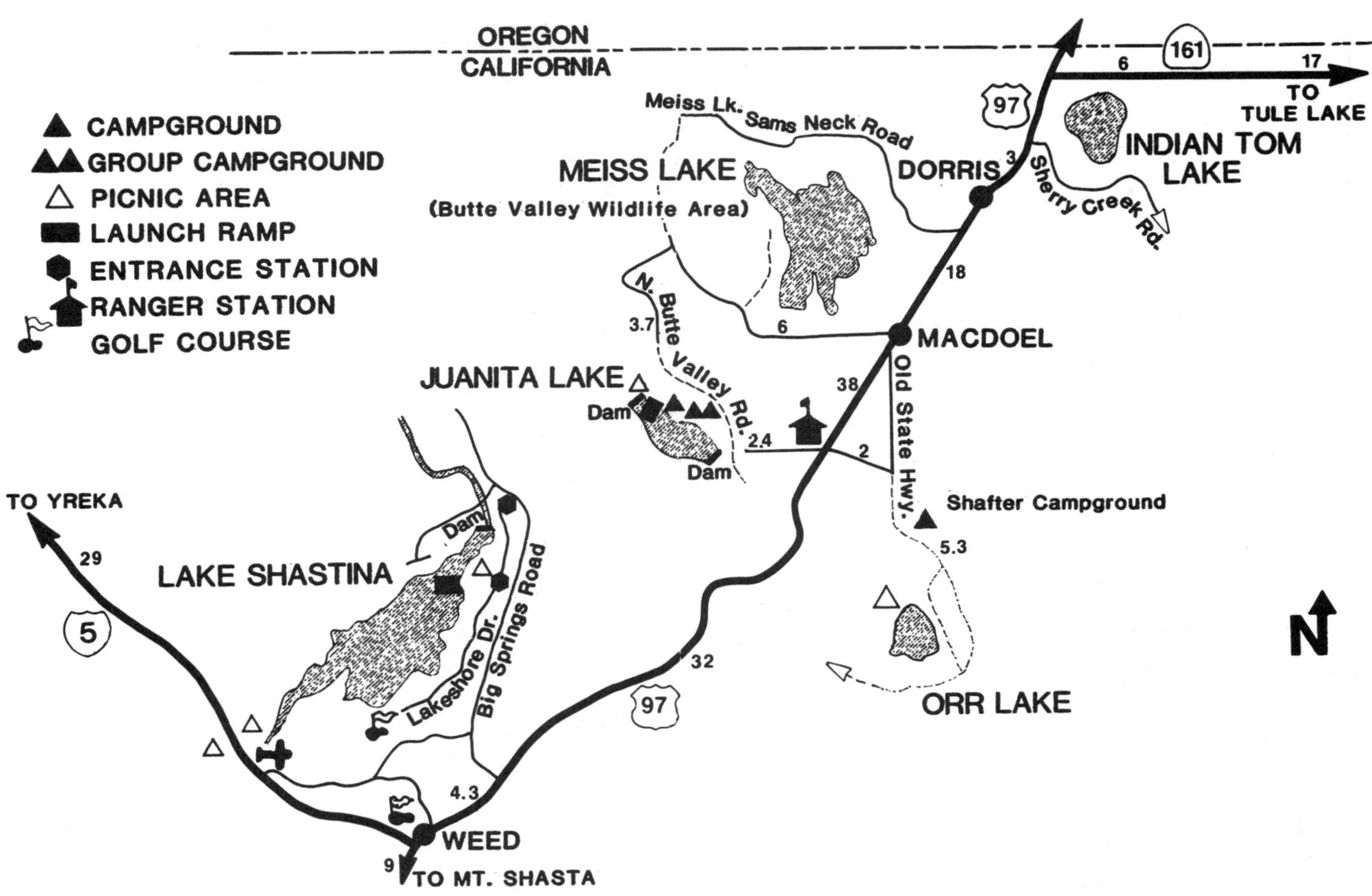

INFORMATION: Goosenest Ranger Station, 37805 Hwy. 97, Macdoel 96058, Ph: 916-398-4391

CAMPING	BOATING	RECREATION	OTHER
Juanita Lake: 23 Dev. Sites 2 Handicap Sites Fee: $4 1 Multiple Unit Site Fee: $6 No Firearms Discharged in Campground Shafter: 10 Sites - Free	Juanita: Open to All Non-powered Boating Launch Ramp Shastina: Open to All Boating Orr & Indian Tom: Small Hand Launch Craft - Max. 10 HP Meiss: Shallow Draft Non-powered Boating	Fishing: Juanita: Brown & Rainbow Trout Shastina: Trout, Silver Salmon, Bass, Catfish & Crappie Indian Tom: Cutthroat Hunting: Waterfowl, Deer & Quail Swimming & Picnicking Hiking & Backpacking	Full Facilities in Weed & Tule Lake Gas & Grocery Store at Macdoel & Mt. Hebron Butte Valley Wildlife Area P.O. Box 249 Macdoel 96058 Ph: 916-398-4627 Juanita Lake: 1-1/2 Mile Barrier Free Trail Around Lake

MEDICINE LAKE

Medicine Lake is in the Modoc National Forest at an elevation of 6,700 feet. Once the center of a volcano, this 640-acre Lake has no known outlets and is 150 feet deep in places. The pine-covered campgrounds are maintained by the U. S. Forest Service. Points of interest include Lava Beds National Monument, Glass Mountain, Burnt Lava Flow, Medicine Lake Glass Flow and Undertakers Crater. Although remote, this is a popular Lake for boating, waterskiing and sailing. The fishing is good from shore or boat. Little Medicine Lake has a population of Arctic Greyling which offers Californians a unique fishing opportunity. The small 5 acre Bullseye Lake has a Rainbow and Brook trout fishery.

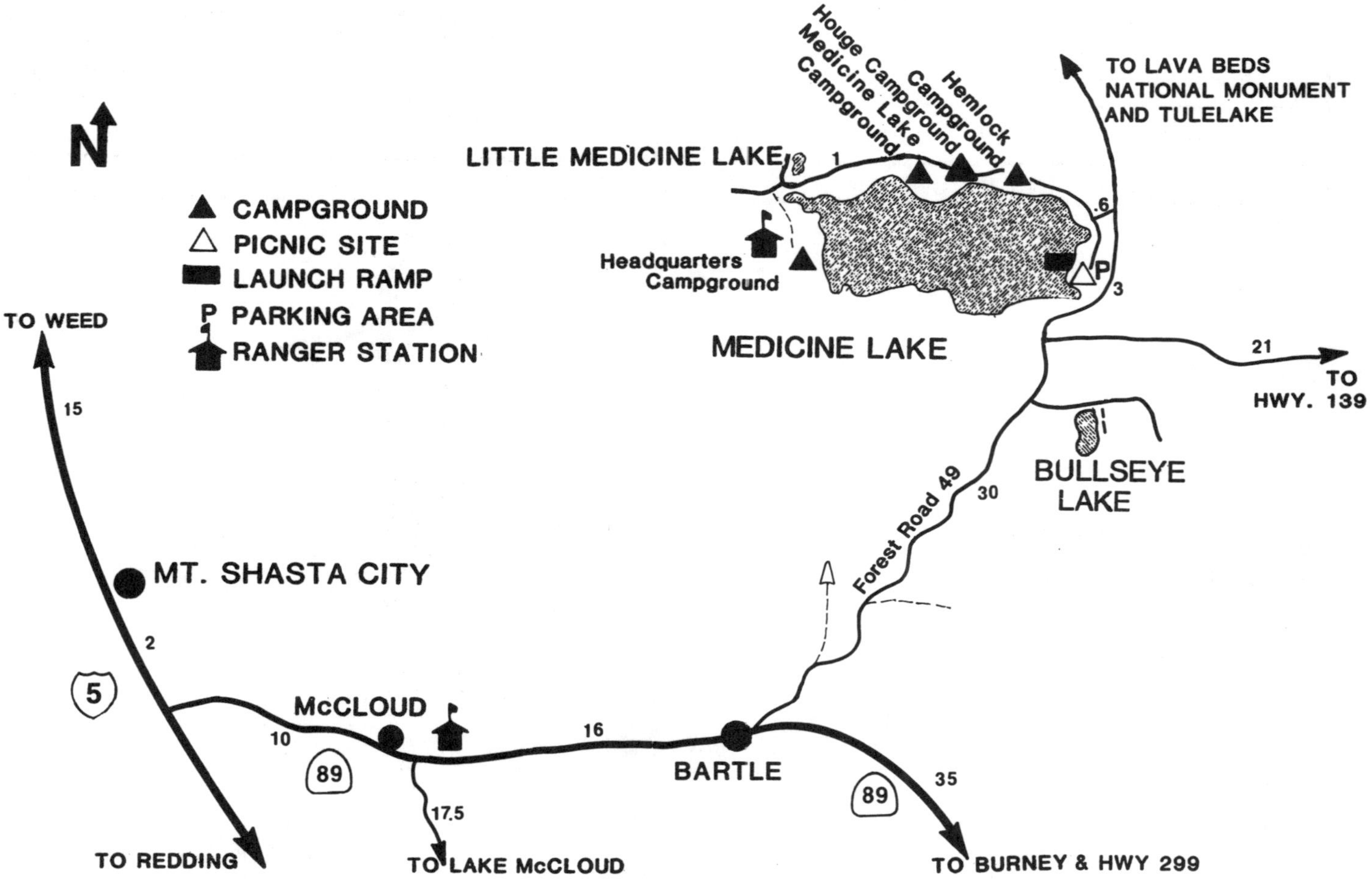

N
CAMPGROUND
PICNIC SITE
LAUNCH RAMP
P PARKING AREA
RANGER STATION
LITTLE MEDICINE LAKE
Houge Campground
Medicine Lake Campground
Hemlock Campground
Headquarters Campground
MEDICINE LAKE
TO LAVA BEDS NATIONAL MONUMENT AND TULELAKE
TO HWY. 139
BULLSEYE LAKE
Forest Road 49
MT. SHASTA CITY
McCLOUD
BARTLE
TO WEED
TO REDDING
TO LAKE McCLOUD
TO BURNEY & HWY 299
5
89
89
1
.6
3
21
30
15
2
10
16
17.5
35

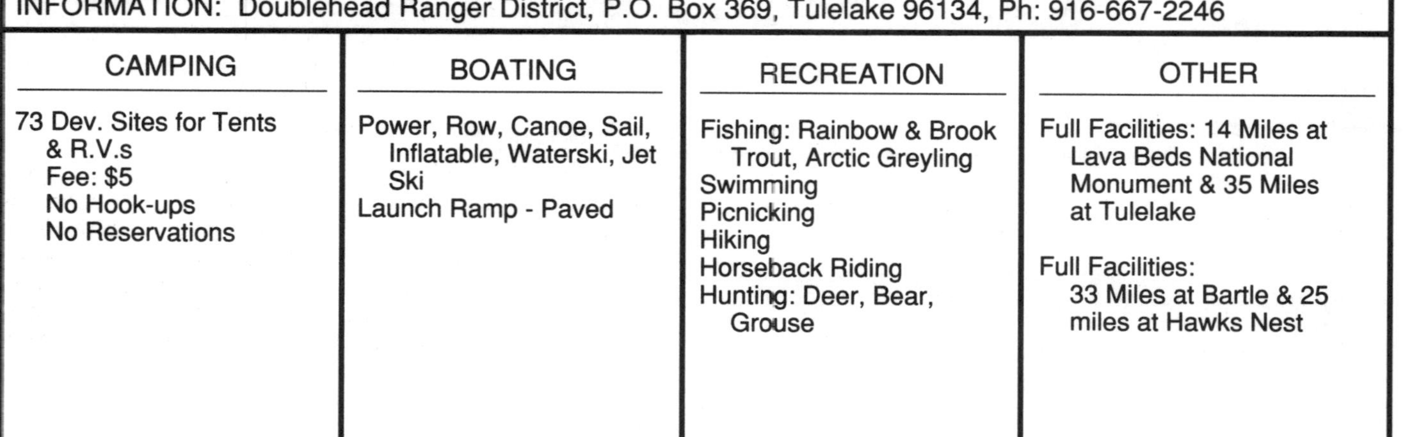

INFORMATION: Doublehead Ranger District, P.O. Box 369, Tulelake 96134, Ph: 916-667-2246

CAMPING	BOATING	RECREATION	OTHER
73 Dev. Sites for Tents & R.V.s Fee: $5 No Hook-ups No Reservations	Power, Row, Canoe, Sail, Inflatable, Waterski, Jet Ski Launch Ramp - Paved	Fishing: Rainbow & Brook Trout, Arctic Greyling Swimming Picnicking Hiking Horseback Riding Hunting: Deer, Bear, Grouse	Full Facilities: 14 Miles at Lava Beds National Monument & 35 Miles at Tulelake Full Facilities: 33 Miles at Bartle & 25 miles at Hawks Nest

LAKE EARL, FISH LAKE, FRESHWATER LAGOON, STONE LAGOON AND BIG LAGOON

Big Lagoon and its smaller neighbors, Stone and Freshwater Lagoons are three of California's most unusual Lakes. Separated from the Pacific Ocean by a narrow strip of sand, these brackish water lakes offer the angler a unique opportunity to fish for trout while a few feet away you may cast for surf perch. Lakes Earl and Talawa are part of the Lake Earl Wildlife Area. These shallow water lakes offer a variety of game fish as well as an abundance of waterfowl and animal life. Fish Lake, at an elevation of 1,800 feet, is a popular freshwater fishing spot. No motors are allowed on this small 22-acre lake. The Forest Service maintains a nice campground amid fir and huckleberries. There are a variety of trails leading to Red Mountain Lake and on to Blue Lake.

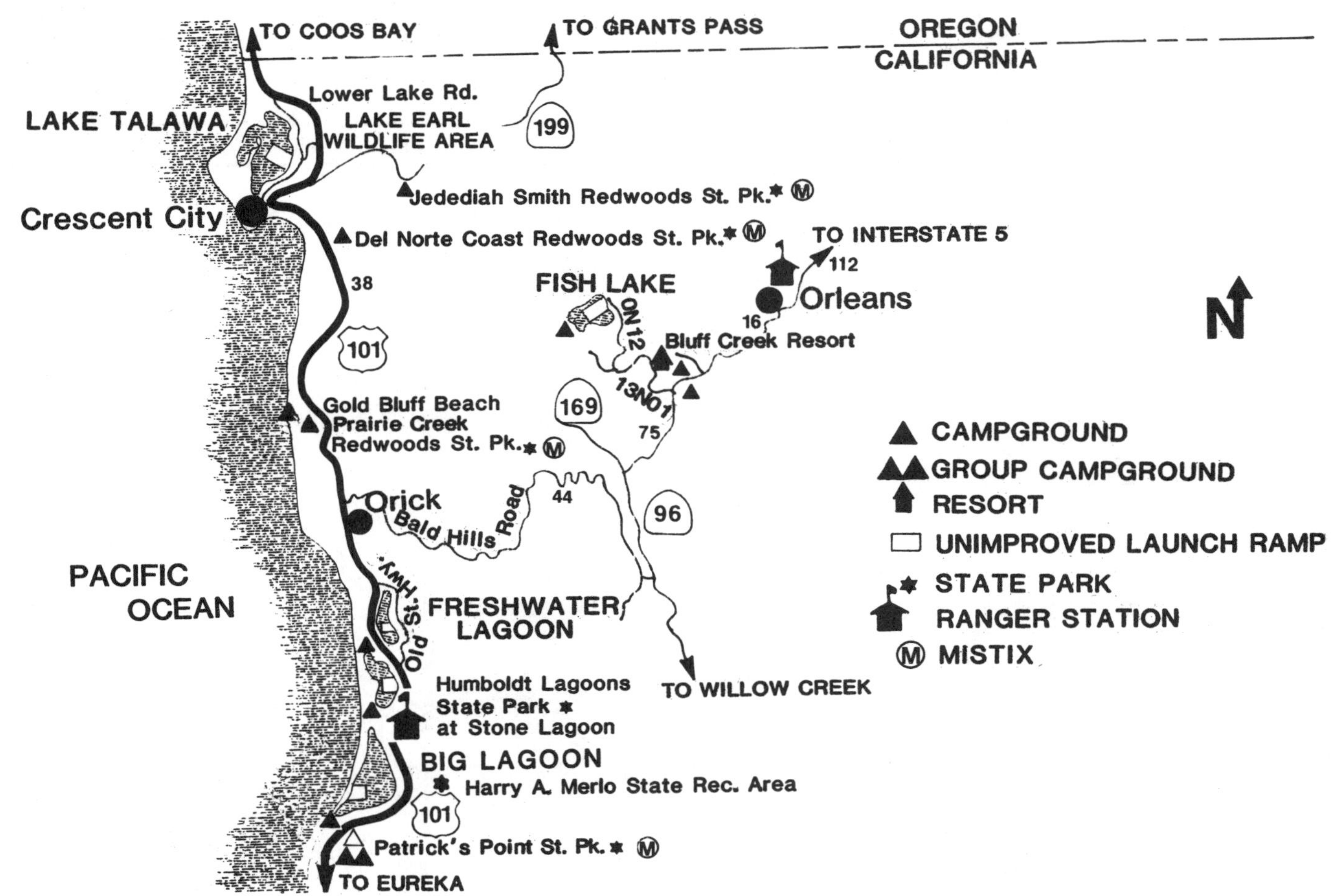

INFORMATION: Calif. State Parks, Klamath Dist. Office, 600A W. Clark, Eureka 95501, Ph: 707-445-6547

CAMPING	BOATING	RECREATION	OTHER
Redwoods State Parks: Jedediah Smith Del Norte Coast Prairie Creek Gold Bluff Beach State Parks: Humboldt Lagoons Stone Lagoon Patrick's Point Reservations: Mistix	Lake Earl: Fishing Boats—Beach Launch Freshwater Lagoon: Waterskiing Stone Lagoon: Canoes & Fishing Boats Big Lagoon: Fishing & Small Sailboats Fish Lake: Non-Power Boats Only Unimproved Ramp	Fishing: Rainbow, Brown & Cutthroat Trout Picnicking Swimming at Lagoons Hiking & Nature Trails Beach Combing Tidal Pools Redwood Groves Birdwatching Hunting: Deer, Elk, Waterfowl	Fish Lake: Orleans Ranger Sta. Orleans 95556 Ph: 916-627-3291 Store, Gas, Trailer Park at Bluff Creek Resort

LAKE SISKIYOU AND CASTLE LAKE

Lake Siskiyou is a man-made Reservoir, at an elevation of 3,181 feet, located in the morning shadows of awesome Mount Shasta. On the headwaters of the Sacramento River, the Lake has 437 surface acres with 5-1/4 shoreline miles surrounded by pine trees. The campground offers complete facilities for the varied recreational activities such as its 1,000 feet of sandy swimming beach, complete marina and store. The Pacific Crest Trail is located nearby and the fishing is good. Crystal clear Castle Lake is located just south of Lake Siskiyou. Although primarily for fishing, this pretty little lake also allows swimming. There is a small picnic area near Castle Lake and 5 campsites for tents.

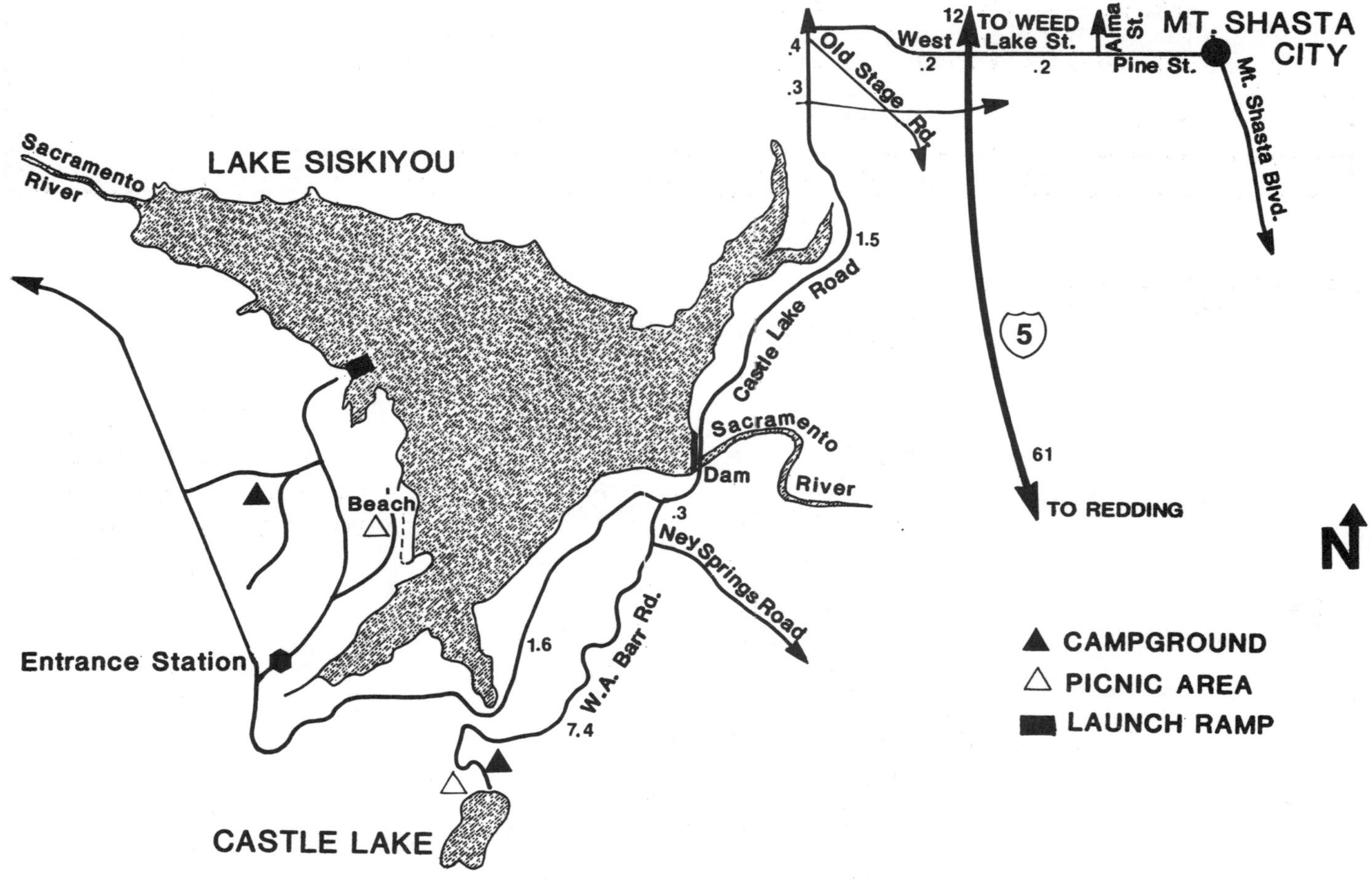

INFORMATION: Lake Siskiyou, P.O. Box 276, Mt. Shasta 96067, Ph: 916-926-2618			
CAMPING	BOATING	RECREATION	OTHER
299 Dev. Sites for Tents & R.V.s Full Hook-ups Fee: $10 - $13 Group Camps Castle Lake: Mount Shasta Ranger District - 5 Tent Sites	Power, Row, Canoe, Windsurfing, Sail, & Inflatables 10 MPH Speed Limit Marina Launch Ramp Rentals: Fishing, Canoe, Pedalboat, Pontoon Berths, Docks, Moorings, Dry Storage	Fishing: Rainbow, Kamloop, Brown, & Brook Trout, Largemouth & Smallmouth Bass Swimming Picnicking Hiking Backpacking-Parking 2 Children's Playgrounds	Snack Bar Grocery Store Bait & Tackle Laundromat Disposal Station Propane Community-Sized Barbecue Handicap Fishing Patio Full Facilities - 3.5 Miles at Mt. Shasta

LAKE MC CLOUD

The dam on the McCloud River was constructed by P. G. & E. in 1965. At an elevation of 3,000 feet, the surface area of this 520-acre Lake belongs to P. G. & E., and the surrounding land belongs to the Hearst Corporation. The U. S. Forest Service was deeded a narrow strip of land between the road and high water mark from Tarantula Gulch to Star City Creek.

The steep shoreline provides a beautiful setting for the Lake with pine trees towering above the rocky terrain. This is a popular Lake for fishing. There are no developed campsites on the Lake, but there is a small unimproved campground and picnic area at Star City Creek. A Forest Service campground is located on the McCloud River at Ah-Di-Na.

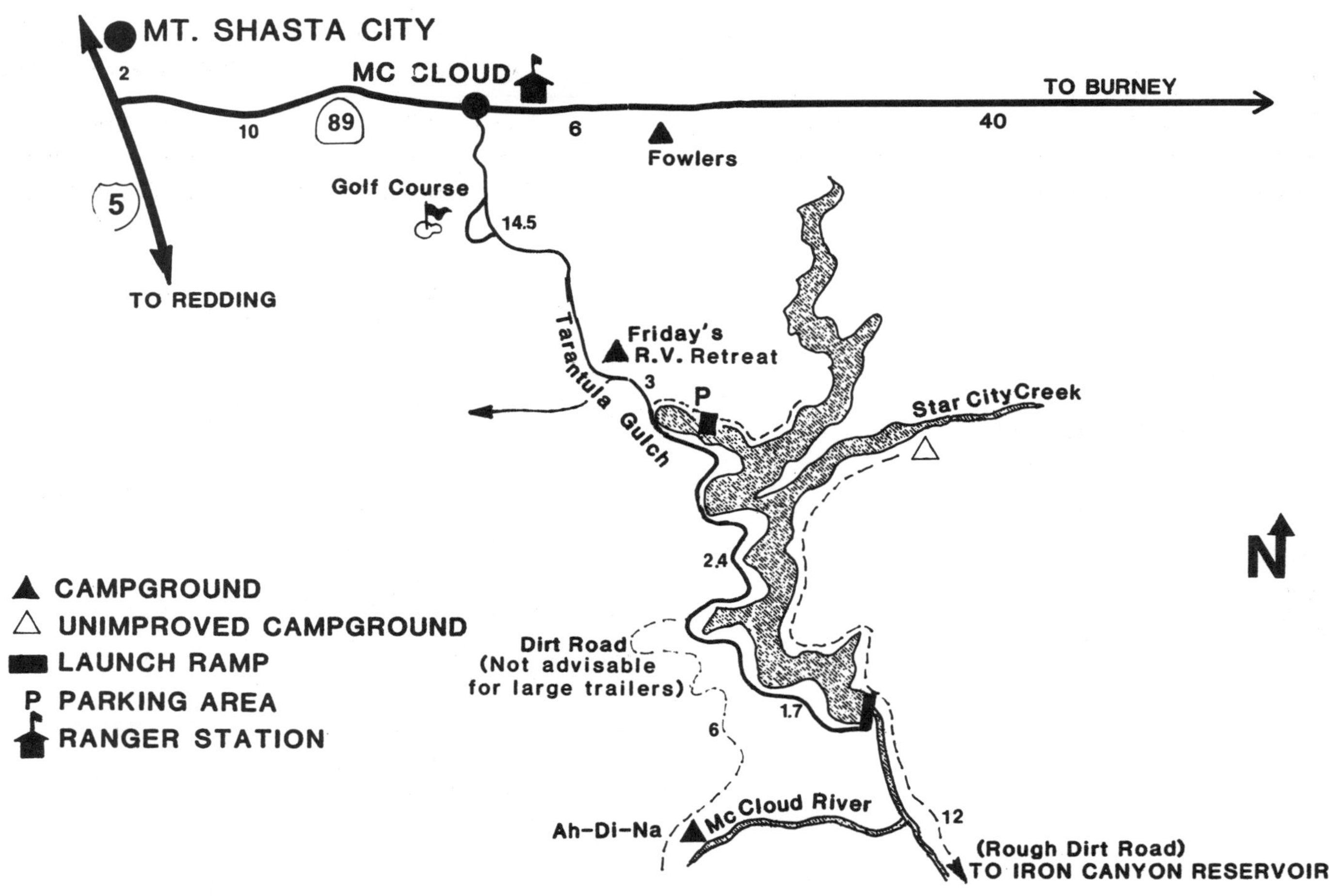

INFORMATION: McCloud Ranger Dist., Drawer I, McCloud 96057, Ph: 916-964-2184			
CAMPING	**BOATING**	**RECREATION**	**OTHER**
Star City Creek: Small Unimproved Campground with Toilets Ah-Di-Na: 16 Camper Sites Narrow Dirt Road Not Advised for Large Trailers Water, Toilets Fowlers: 40 Units Water, Toilet	Power, Row, Canoe Launch Ramp	Fishing: Rainbow & Brown Trout (All Dolly Varden Trout must be Released) Picnicking Hiking Nature Study	Full Facilities in McCloud Fridays RV Retreat 30 Full Hook-Ups Restrooms, Hot Showers, Laundromat Ph: 916-964-2878

WEST VALLEY RESERVOIR

West Valley Reservoir, 970 surface acres, is located in the northeastern corner of California, off Highway 395 just east of Likely resting at an elevation of 4,770 feet. The 7 miles of shoreline is relatively sparse with only a few clusters of small trees. All types of boating are permitted including boat camping. Waterskiing is popular. Eagle Lake trout are the primary game fish and they are often "big ones." There are also catfish and Sacramento perch. Support facilities are limited to a single lane paved ramp and primitive campsites. This is a relatively remote reservoir, but for the dedicated angler who enjoys landing the big one, give it a try. The lake is usually frozen over from December to early March.

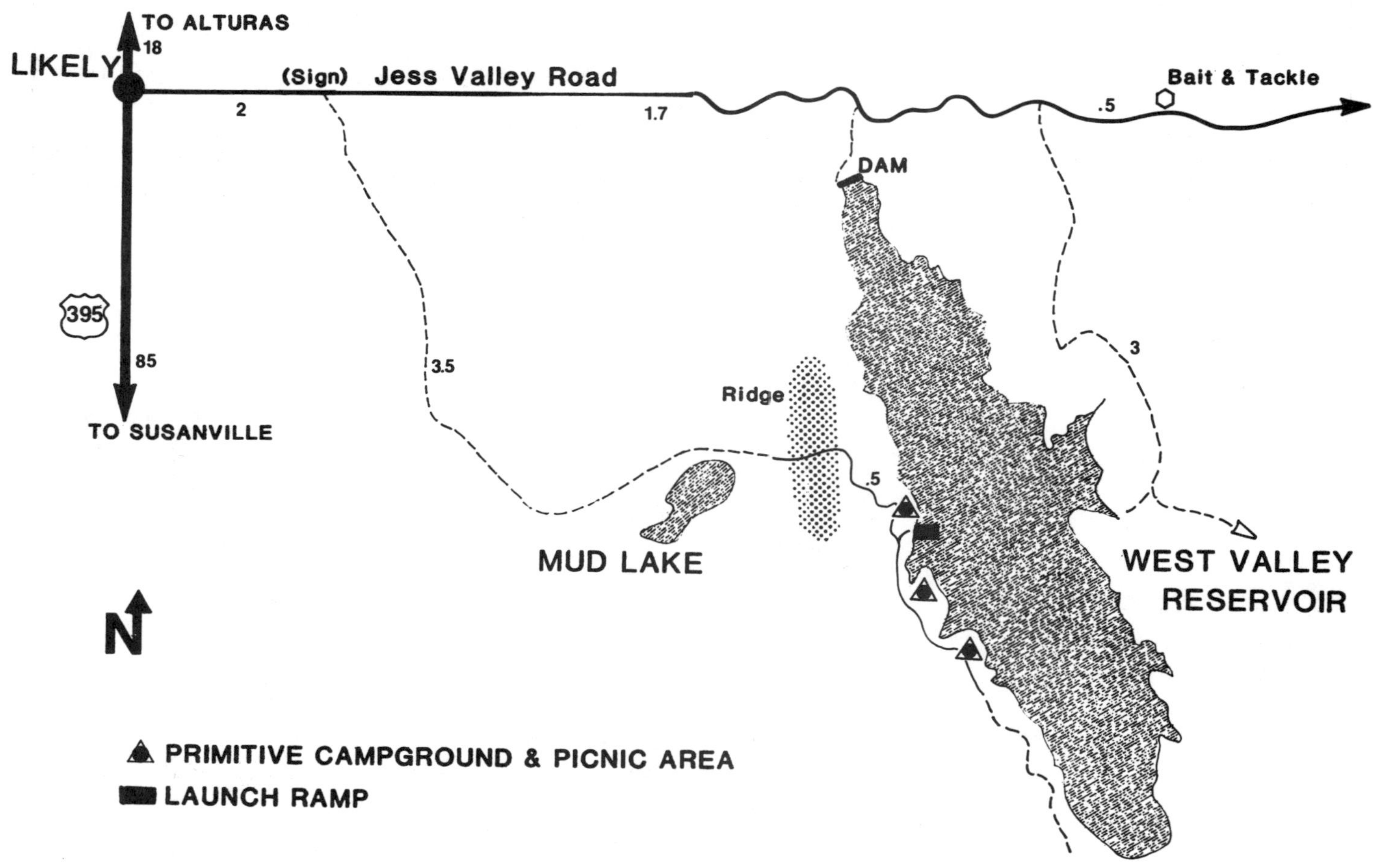

INFORMATION: Modoc County, 202 W. 4th St., Alturas 96101, Ph: 916-233-3939			
CAMPING	BOATING	RECREATION	OTHER
Primitive Camping Water & Toilets	Power, Row, Canoe, Sail, Waterski, Jet Ski, Windsurfing & Inflatable Overnight Camping In Boat Permitted Anywhere High Winds Can Be Hazardous	Fishing: Eagle Lake Trout, Catfish, Sacramento Perch Swimming Picnicking Hiking Backpacking-Parking Hunting: Deer & Rabbit	Full Facilities - 6 Miles at Likely

BLUE LAKE

Blue Lake, 28 miles southeast of Alturas, is in the Modoc National Forest. This pretty mountain Lake of 160 surface acres is surrounded by Ponderosa Pine, White Fir and meadows at an elevation of 6,000 feet. This is a popular, well-used facility near the South Warner Wilderness area. The Lake fishing is good for Rainbow and Brown trout. There are no boating facilities other than an unimproved launch ramp, but all boating is permitted. For the hiker, backpacker, horseback rider or energetic fisherman, the South Warner Wilderness offers good trails. A Wilderness Permit is not required for the South Warner Wilderness.

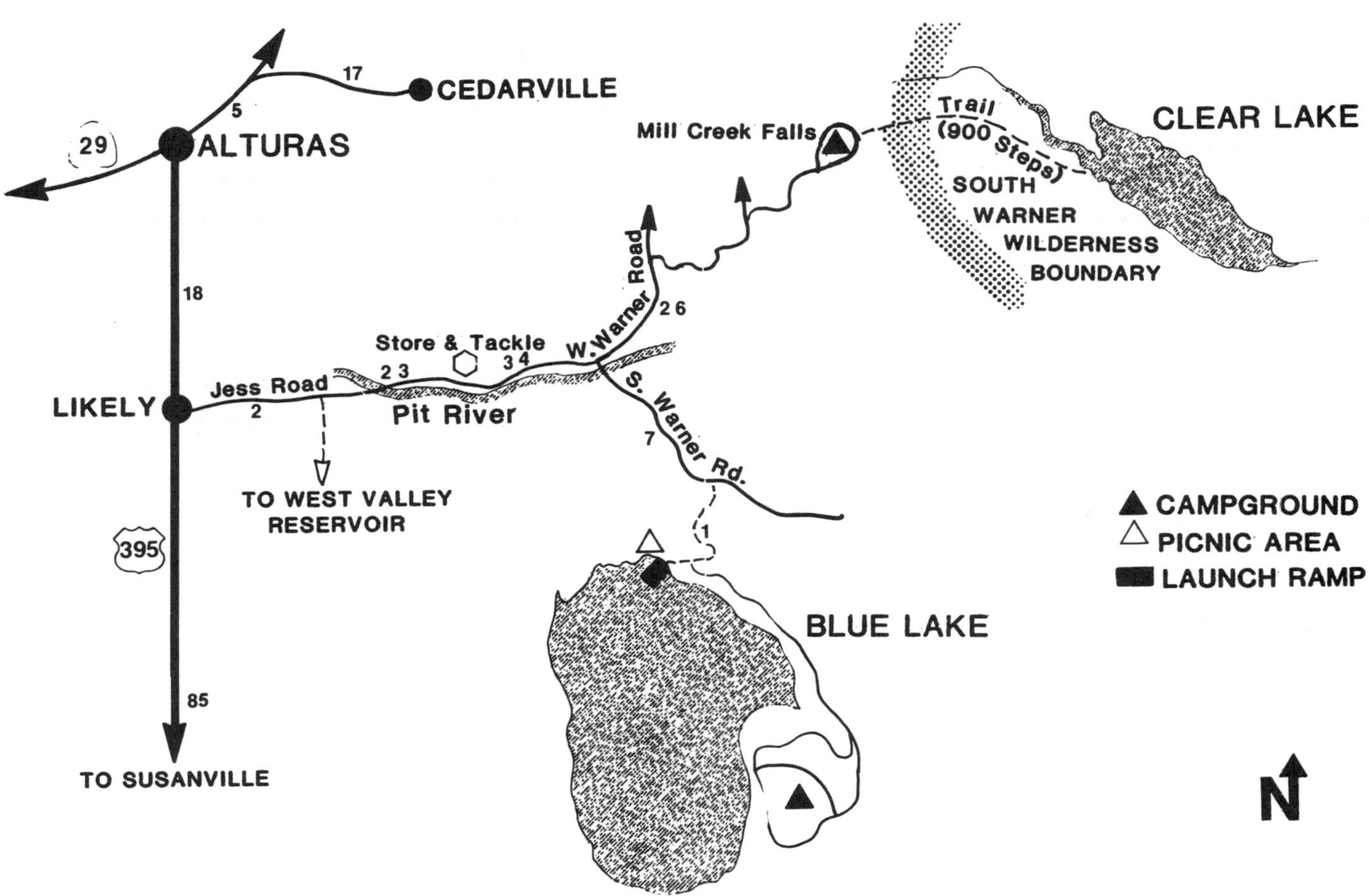

INFORMATION: Warner Mountain Ranger District, Box 220, Cedarville 96104, Ph: 916-279-6116

CAMPING	BOATING	RECREATION	OTHER
Blue Lake Camp: 48 Dev. Sites for Tents & R.V.s under 22 feet Fee: $5 Mill Creek Falls: 19 Dev. Sites for Tents & R.V.s under 22 feet Fee: $5	Power, Row, Canoe, Sail, & Inflatable Launch Ramp	Fishing: Rainbow & Brown Trout Picnicking Hiking Swimming Hunting: Deer in Vicinity	Lancaster's Store: Groceries, Bait & Tackle, Licenses Likely: Grocery Store Restaurant Gas Station Full Facilities - 28 Miles at Alturas

EASTMAN, TULE, BIG, FALL RIVER CRYSTAL AND BAUM LAKES

The Fall River Valley is an angler's paradise. Nestled between the Sierra and Cascade mountain ranges, these lakes are fed by Hat Creek, Pit and Fall Rivers. Baum has 89 surface acres and Crystal has 60 acres. Each of these lakes are connected and support trophy sized brown trout as well as rainbow and eastern brook. The warm water fisheries of Big, Tule, Eastman and Fall River Lakes are all contiguous. There are also rainbow trout up to 4 pounds. The streams and rivers offer prime fishing. Hat Creek and Fall River are designated "Wild Trout" streams which provide trophy trout. Artificial lures must be used and other special rules apply.

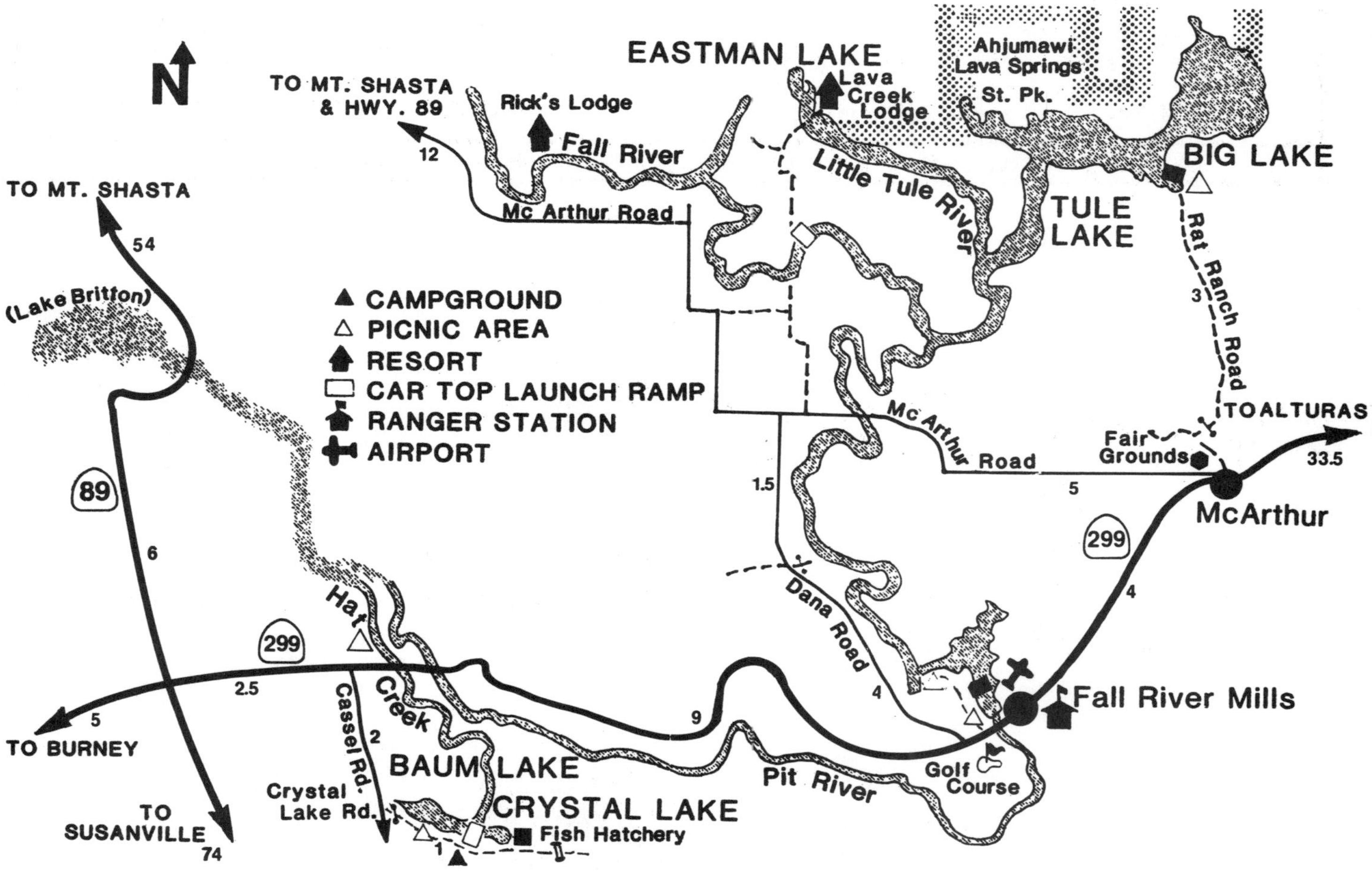

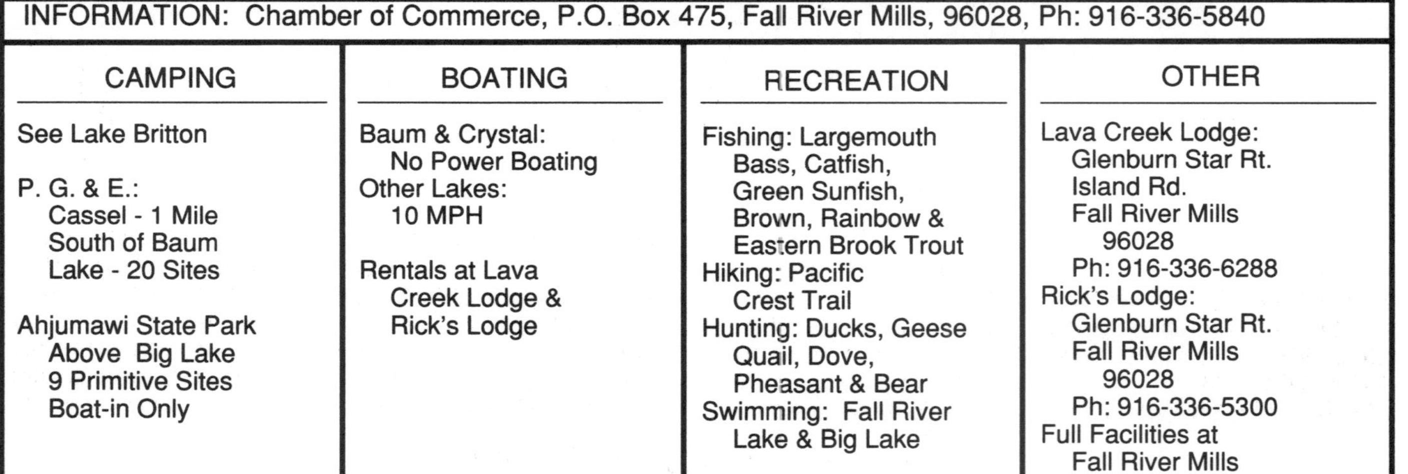

INFORMATION: Chamber of Commerce, P.O. Box 475, Fall River Mills, 96028, Ph: 916-336-5840			
CAMPING	BOATING	RECREATION	OTHER
See Lake Britton P. G. & E.: Cassel - 1 Mile South of Baum Lake - 20 Sites Ahjumawi State Park Above Big Lake 9 Primitive Sites Boat-in Only	Baum & Crystal: No Power Boating Other Lakes: 10 MPH Rentals at Lava Creek Lodge & Rick's Lodge	Fishing: Largemouth Bass, Catfish, Green Sunfish, Brown, Rainbow & Eastern Brook Trout Hiking: Pacific Crest Trail Hunting: Ducks, Geese Quail, Dove, Pheasant & Bear Swimming: Fall River Lake & Big Lake	Lava Creek Lodge: Glenburn Star Rt. Island Rd. Fall River Mills 96028 Ph: 916-336-6288 Rick's Lodge: Glenburn Star Rt. Fall River Mills 96028 Ph: 916-336-5300 Full Facilities at Fall River Mills

IRON CANYON RESERVOIR

Iron Canyon Reservoir is at an elevation of 2,700 feet in the Shasta-Trinity National Forest. This beautiful 500-surface acre Lake has 15 miles of forested shoreline. Larger boats with deep draft are not recommended due to shallow lake levels, but owners of smaller, low-speed boats find Iron Canyon ideal. The lake level varies greatly during the year depending on weather and P. G. & E. power needs. There are some big trout in the lake, and the fishing can be good. The U. S. Forest Service has a self-service campground providing a quiet atmosphere amid pine and fir trees. P. G. & E., in co-operation with U. S. F. S., has a campground and paved launch ramp at Hawkins Landing. This lake is perfect for those seeking solitude.

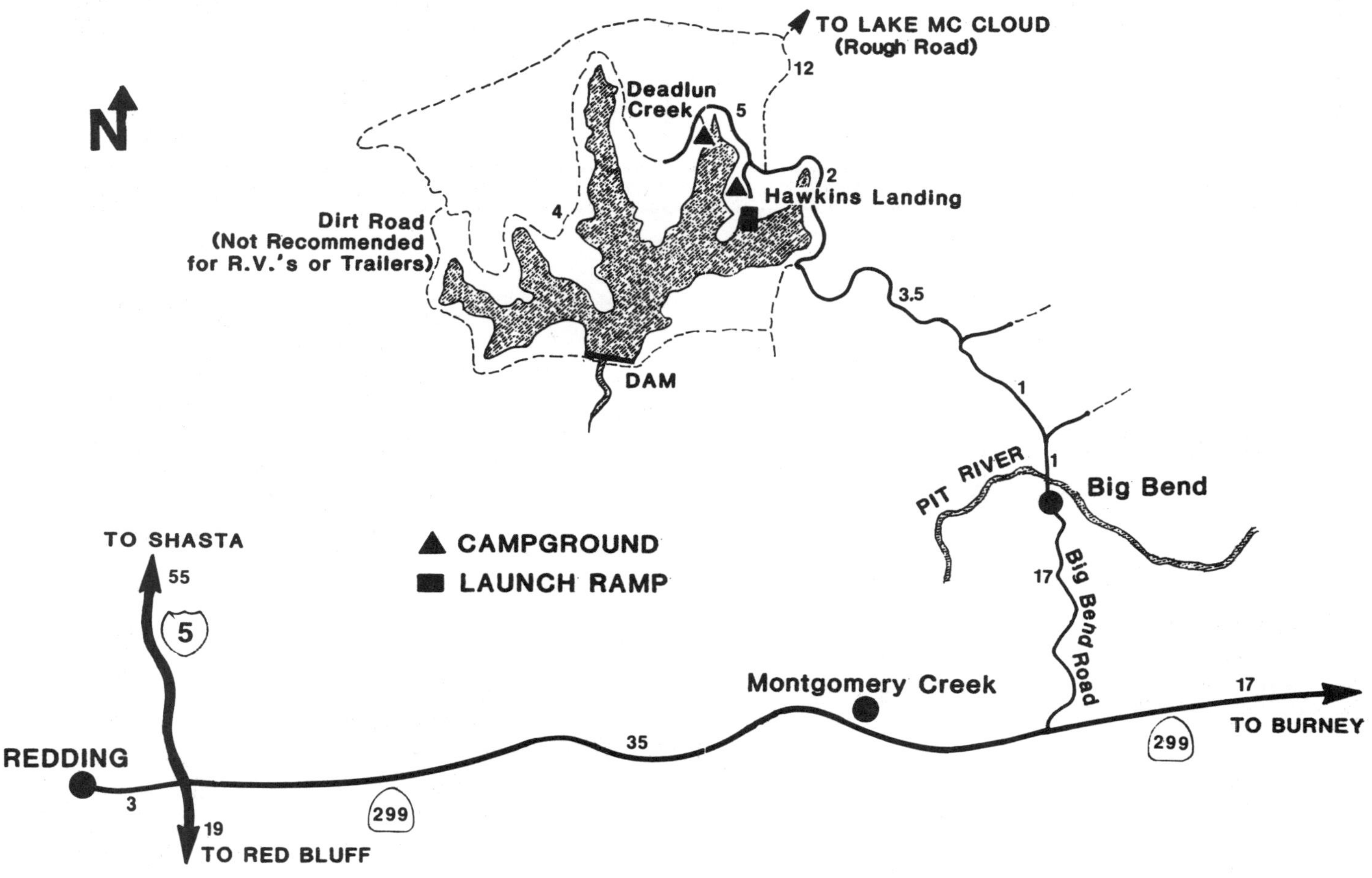

INFORMATION: Shasta Lake Ranger District, 6543 Holiday Rd., Redding 96001, Ph: 916-275-1587			
CAMPING	BOATING	RECREATION	OTHER
U. S. F. S. - Deadlun Creek: 30 Dev. Sites for Tents & R.V.s to 15 feet - No Fee U. S. F. S. and P. G. & E.- Hawkins Landing: 10 Dev. Sites for Tents & R.V.s Fee: $8	Power, Row, Canoe, & Inflatables Speedboats & Waterskiing Not Permitted Launch Ramp at Hawkins Landing Campground	Fishing: Rainbow & Brown Trout Swimming Picnicking Hiking Bird Watching Hunting: Deer	At Big Bend: Grocery Store, Bait & Tackle, Gas Station (Hours of Operation are Limited) U. S. F. S. Guard Station and Fire Station Caution: Heavy Logging Truck Traffic at Times

LAKE BRITTON

Lake Britton, located in the Shasta-Trinity National Forest, is at an elevation of 2,760 feet. This 1,600 surface acre Lake has 18 shoreline miles and is nestled amid the evergreen forests near the Pit River. The McArthur-Burney Falls Memorial State Park has 768 acres stretching from Burney Falls along Burney Creek to the shoreline of Lake Britton. Burney Creek is planted with trout weekly in season. This park, established in 1920, is not only one of the oldest in the State Park System, but one of the best facilities in Northern California. There are also U. S. Forest Service and P. G. & E. campgrounds around the Lake. Burney Falls, called by Teddy Roosevelt, "the eighth wonder of the world," is the popular attraction of the area. This is a good boating Lake although caution should be used as there can be floating debris. Fishing can be excellent in nearby streams and fair in the Lake.

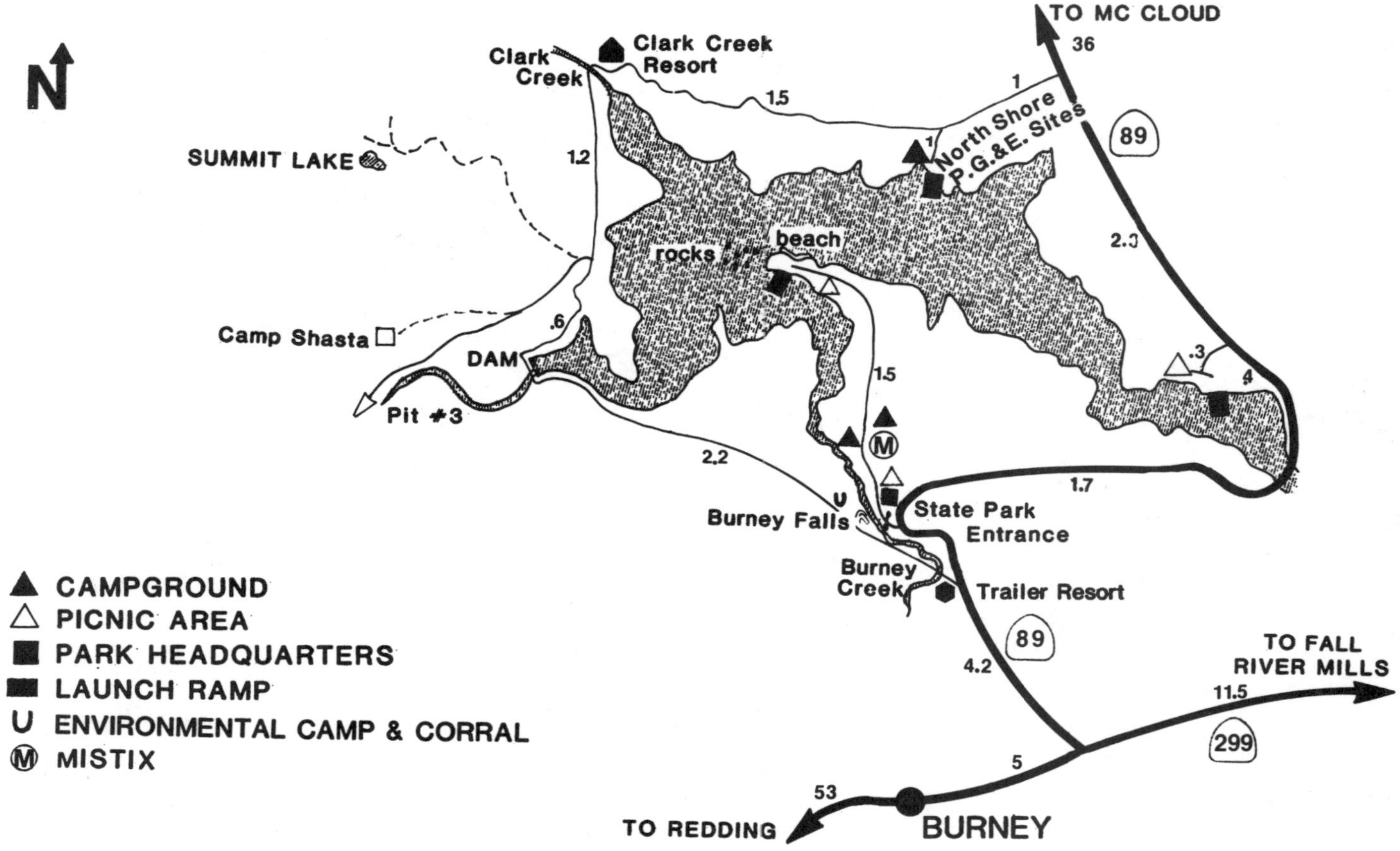

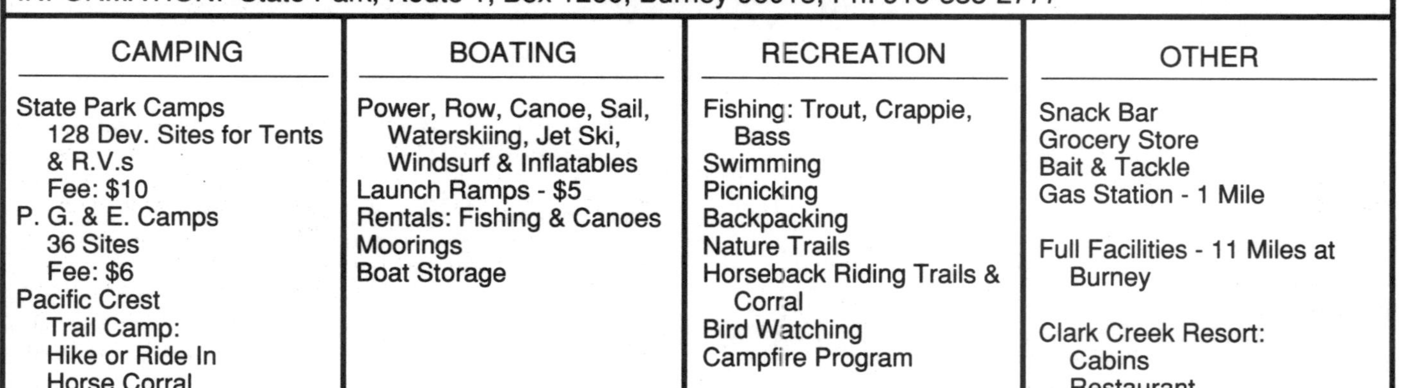

INFORMATION: State Park, Route 1, Box 1260, Burney 96013, Ph: 916-335-2777

CAMPING	BOATING	RECREATION	OTHER
State Park Camps 128 Dev. Sites for Tents & R.V.s Fee: $10 P. G. & E. Camps 36 Sites Fee: $6 Pacific Crest Trail Camp: Hike or Ride In Horse Corral Fee: $6	Power, Row, Canoe, Sail, Waterskiing, Jet Ski, Windsurf & Inflatables Launch Ramps - $5 Rentals: Fishing & Canoes Moorings Boat Storage	Fishing: Trout, Crappie, Bass Swimming Picnicking Backpacking Nature Trails Horseback Riding Trails & Corral Bird Watching Campfire Program	Snack Bar Grocery Store Bait & Tackle Gas Station - 1 Mile Full Facilities - 11 Miles at Burney Clark Creek Resort: Cabins Restaurant

TRINITY LAKE
(Clair Engle Lake)

Clair Engle Lake, more commonly called Trinity Lake, is one of California's finest recreation spots. A part of the Whiskeytowon-Shasta-Trinity National Recreation Area, this 17,000 surface acre Lake offers prime outdoor opportunities. Houseboaters and dispersed area campers find the often uncrowded 145 miles of pine, cedar and oak-covered shoreline ideal for "getting away from it all." There are hundreds of quiet coves for the angler to tie up overnight and catch his meal or better yet, catch a world record smallmouth bass. Trinity holds the State record of 9 lb. 1 oz. for smallmouth. Fishing for trout, largemouth bass or catfish is equally seductive. While water level fluctuation in late season can create hazards, boaters will always find plenty of water to ski, cruise or sail. There are ample marine support facilities including ramps, rentals and full service marinas. Trinity Lake rests at an elevation of 2,370 feet just below the rugged, granite peaks of the Trinity Alps Wilderness.

...Continued...

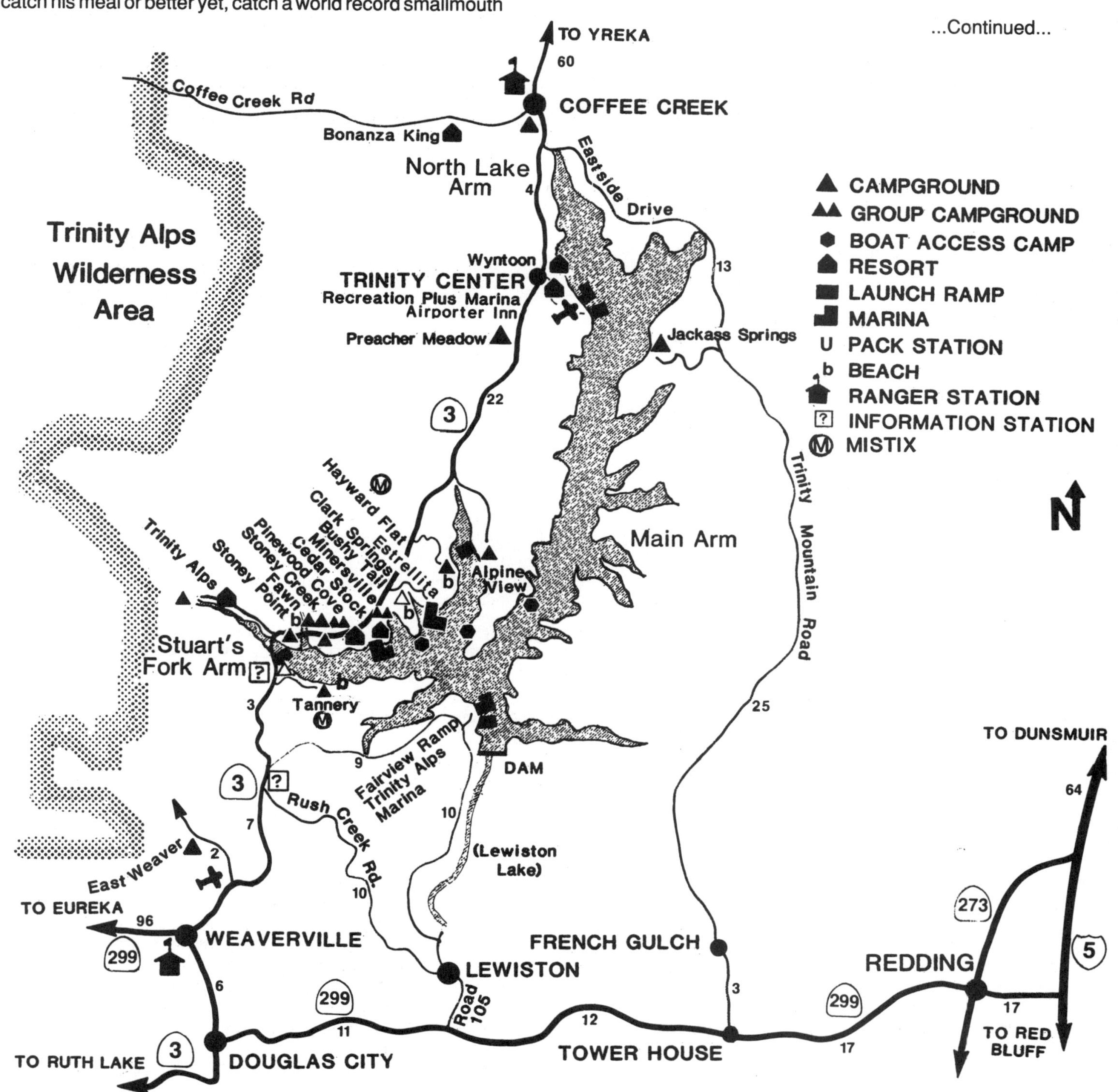

TRINITY LAKE

U.S.F.S. CAMPGROUNDS

All sites have paved parking, drinking water and flush toilets unless otherwise noted.

STUART FORK ARM:

TANNERY - 87 Sites, Launch Ramp for Campers Only, Beach, Amphitheater, Fee: $8 - Single Family Sites, $12 - Multiple Family Sites
STONEY POINT - 22 Walk-In Sites, Fee: $5
MINERSVILLE - 30 Sites, Fee: $7 - Single, $10 - Multiple
HAYWARD FLAT - 106 Sites, Beach, Fee: $8 - Single, $12 - Multiple
ALPINE VIEW - 66 Sites, Fee: $8
RIDGEVILLE - 21 Boat-In Sites
RIDGEVILLE ISLAND - 4 Boat-In Sites
MARINER'S ROOST - 7 Boat-In Sites
CLARK SPRINGS - 15 Sites, Fee $5 (Next to Clark Springs Day Area)

MAIN ARM:

JACKASS SPRINGS - 21 Sites, Dirt Access and Interior Road, No Fee
CAPTAIN'S POINT - 3 Boat-In Sites

Boat-In Sites Offer Vault Toilets, No Water, No Fee

GROUP CAMPGROUNDS - Reservations Through Weaverville Ranger Station
STONEY CREEK - 50 People Maximum, Fee: $30
FAWN - 3 Loops, 100 People Per Loop, Fee: $40 Per Loop
BUSHY TAIL - 150 People Maximum, Fee: $40

U.S.F.S. DAY USE AREAS
CLARK SPRINGS - Picnic Area, Swim Beach, Bath House, Boat Ramp, Flush Toilets
STONEY CREEK - Swim Beach, Bath House, Flush Toilets

. . . Continued . . .

INFORMATION: Weaverville Ranger Station, Box 1190, Weaverville 96093, Ph: 916-623-2131

CAMPING	BOATING	RECREATION	OTHER
U. S. F. S. 424 Dev. Tent/RV Sites No Hookups Fee: $5 to $12 35 Boat-In Sites No Fee 3 Group Campgrounds to 300 People See Following Pages for Private Facilities	Open to All Boating 4 Full Service Marinas 7 Public Launch Ramps Rentals - Houseboats, Fishing, Pontoon & Ski Boats	Fishing - Large & Smallmouth Bass, Bluegill, Catfish Kokanee, Brown & Rainbow Trout Swim Beaches Picnic Areas Hiking & Riding Trails Back & Horse Packing Hunting: Deer, Bear	Complete Destination Facilities at Some Resorts and Trinity Center Airports - Trinity Center, Weaverville

TRINITY LAKE

PRIVATE MARINAS

TRINITY ALPS MARINA - FAIRVIEW - P.O. Box 670 Lewiston 96052-0670, 916-286-2282, Houseboat Rentals, Grocery Store, Gas Dock, Deli, Propane.

ESTRELLITA MARINA - P.O. Box 1163, Weaverville 96093, 916-286-2215, Grocery & Liquor Store, Paved Ramp, Mooring, Gas Dock, Repairs, Propane, Houseboat, Jet Skis, Fishing and Ski Boat Rentals.

CEDAR STOCK RESORT - Star Rt., Box 510, Lewiston 96052, 916-286-2225, Restaurant & Lounge, Cabins, Full Service Marina, Fuel Dock, Mooring, Dry Storage, Houseboats, Canoe, Paddle, Ski and Fishing Boat Rentals, Grocery Store.

RECREATION PLUS MARINA - P.O. Box 156, Trinity Center 96091, 916-266-3432, Launch Ramp, Store, Fuel Dock, Slips, Houseboat Rentals.

PRIVATE RESORTS

TRINITY ALPS RESORT - Star Rt., Box 490, Lewiston 96052, 916-286-2205, Housekeeping Cabins, Restaurant, Store, Horse Rides, Tennis Courts, River Swim Beach, Square Dancing.

PINEWOOD COVE RESORT - HC Rt. 1 Box 500, Lewiston 96052, 916-286-2201, 84 Tent/R.V. Sites, 43 Full Hookups, Dump Station, Grocery Store, Ramp, Dock, Slips, Fishing Boat Rentals, Game Room, Recreation Hall, Cabin and Trailer Rentals.

AIRPORTER INN - P.O. Box 59, Trinity Center 96091, 916-266-3223, Motel, Housekeeping Units, Restaurant, Lounge, Bicycle Rentals, Near Airport.

WYNTOON RESORT - P.O. Box 70, Trinity Center 96091, 916-266-3337, Complete 90 Acre Destination Resort, 136 R.V. Sites, Full Hookups, 80 Tent Sites, Cabins, Grocery Store, Gas Station, Propane, Snack Bar, Rental Boats, Private Dock, Laundromat.

ENRIGHT GULCH CABINS - 3500 Highway 3, P.O. Box 244, Trinity Center 96091, 916-266-3600, 6 Housekeeping Units, Quiet Private Road Surrounded by National Forest, Hiking Trails, Full Facilities Within 5 Miles.

This is only a partial list of the private facilities. For further information contact:

Trinity Chamber of Commerce
P.O. Box 517
Weaverville, CA 96093
Telephone: 916-623-6101

LEWISTON LAKE

Lewiston Lake is at an elevation of 1,902 feet in the Shasta Trinity National Forest. This beautiful Lake is 9 miles long and has a surface area of 750 acres. It is open to all boating but subject to a 10 MPH speed limit. The cold, constantly moving water flows into Lewiston Lake from the bottom waters of Trinity Lake providing an ideal habitat for large trout. Just below Lewiston Dam, the Trinity River, Rush Creek and other streams offer prize salmon and steelhead as well as trout. The Lewiston Fish Hatchery is the world's most automated salmon and steelhead hatchery.

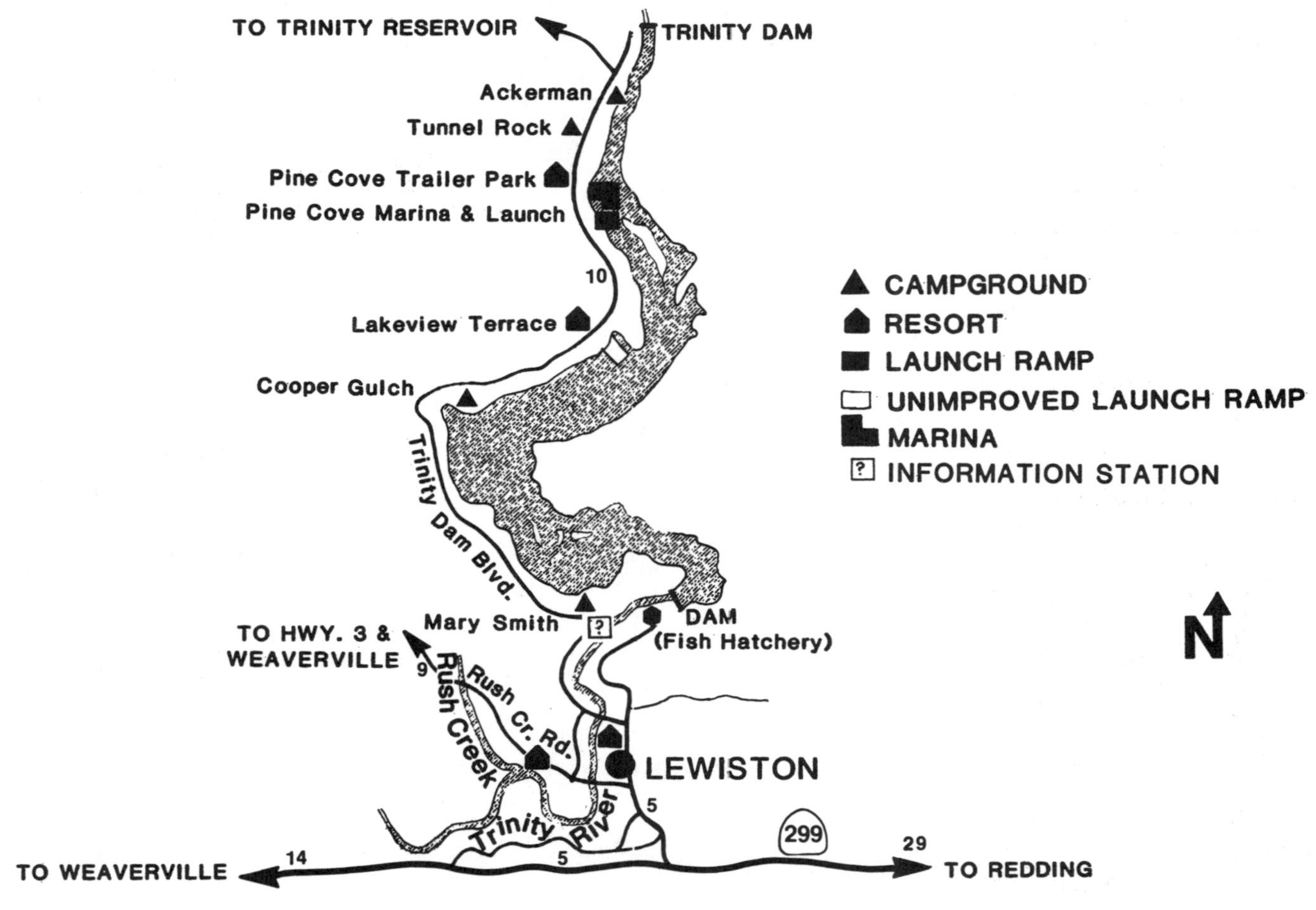

INFORMATION: Weaverville Ranger Station, Box 1190, Weaverville 96093, Ph: 916-623-2131

CAMPING	BOATING	RECREATION	OTHER
24 Dev. Sites for Tents Only 77 Dev. Sites for Tents & R.V.s Fee: $0 - $6 Disposal Station at Ackerman Camp Additional Campsites At Private Resorts	Power, Row, Canoe, Sail & Inflatable Speed Limit - 10 MPH Launch Ramps Rentals: Fishing Boats Docks, Gas, Dry Storage	Fishing: Rainbow & Brown Trout, Kokanee Salmon Picnicking Hunting: Deer, Bear, Fowl & Squirrel	Resorts: Contact - Trinity County Chamber of Commerce Box 517 Weaverville 96093 Ph: 916-623-6101 Snack Bars Restaurants Grocery Stores Bait & Tackle

WHISKEYTOWN LAKE AND KESWICK RESERVOIR

Whiskeytown, at an elevation of 1,209 feet, has 36 miles of coniferous shoreline. Tree shaded islands, numerous coves, and 3,220 surface acres of clear blue water invite the watersport enthusiast. The boater will find complete marina facilities and over 5 square miles of open water. Waterskiing and sailing are excellent. Fishing is good from bank or shore for trout, Kokanee salmon, bass and pan fish. The National Park Service maintains the facilities which include picnic areas and campgrounds. Keswick Reservoir is at an elevation of 587 feet and has a surface area of 630 acres. Fed by cold water released from Shasta Dam, Keswick provides the angler with large Rainbows. Keswick is open to all boating and the launch ramp and picnic area are operated by Shasta County.

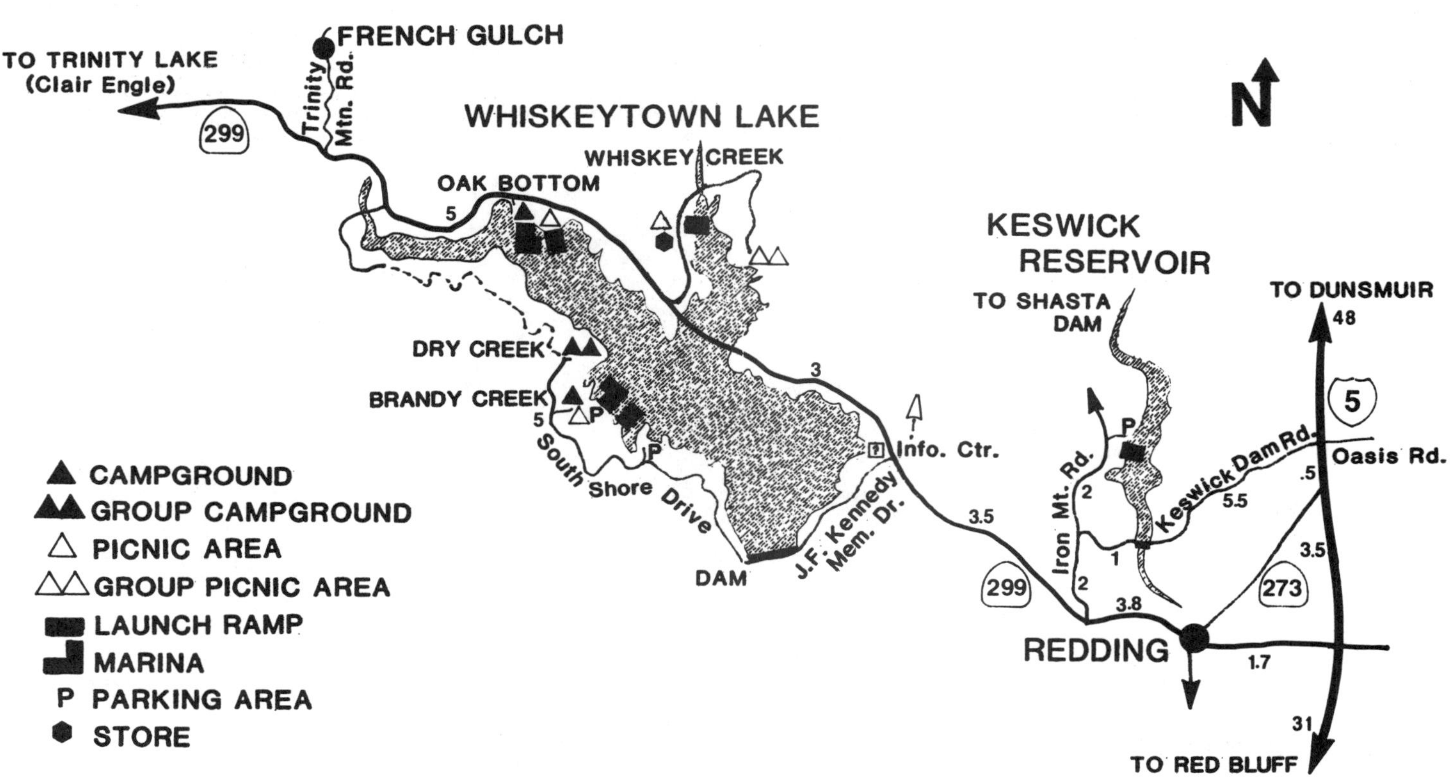

INFORMATION: Superintendent, P.O. Box 188, Whiskeytown 96095, Ph: 916-241-6584			
CAMPING	BOATING	RECREATION	OTHER
Brandy Creek: 37 Self-Contained R.V. Sites Disposal Station Oak Bottom: 100 Dev. Tent Sites & 50 R.V. Sites Disposal Station Dry Creek: Group Camp to 200 People-Reserve	Whiskeytown: Open to All Boats Full Service Marina Rentals: Fishing, Ski, Sail, Canoe & Pontoon Boats Sailing Regattas Keswick: Open to All Boats Paved Launch Ramp	Fishing: Kokanee Salmon, Brown, & Rainbow Trout, Spotted, Large & Smallmouth Bass, Bluegill, Crappie & Catfish Swimming Picnicking - Groups Hiking & Riding Trails	Campground Programs Scuba Diving Hunting: Deer & Waterfowl Grocery Store Snack Bar Bait & Tackle Keswick Reservoir: Bureau of Reclamation Shasta Dam Redding 96003 Ph: 916-275-1554

SHASTA LAKE

Shasta Lake is one of California's prime recreation lakes. It is located on the northern tip of the Sacramento Valley just off Interstate 5 at an elevation of 1,067 feet. The four main arms of this huge lake of 29,500 surface acres converge at the junction of the Cascade and Klamath Mountain Ranges and are fed by the Sacramento, McCloud and Pits Rivers and Squaw Creek. There are 370 miles of wooded and sometimes steep shoreline around the lake. This is more shoreline by a third than San Francisco Bay. Long favored by water sports enthusiasts, Shasta has been called "California's Water Wonderland." Not only is it the State's largest man-made lake, it is also one of its most popular. Boaters will find an abundance and variety of opportunities from quiet sheltered coves for houseboaters to warm open water for water-skiers. In addition to the many private marinas, there are 6 conveniently located public launch ramps. The angler will find over 16 species of fish from several varieties of bass to trout or sturgeon. If the salmon are not biting, try for a channel catfish. Shasta is operated under the jurisdiction of the U. S. Forest Service which provides many developed and boat-in campsites. In addition, shoreline camping is permitted.

...Continued...

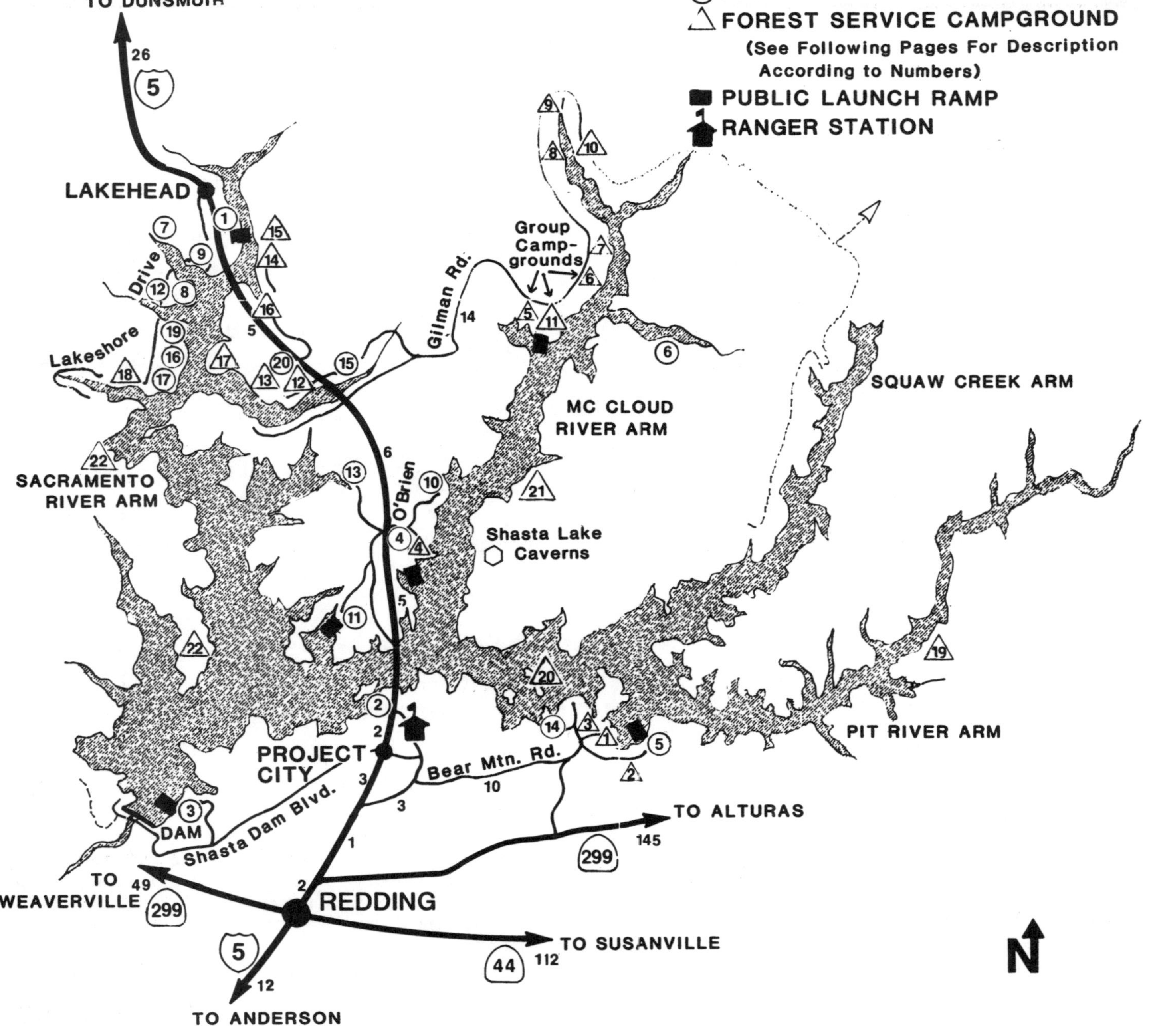

SHASTA LAKE

U. S. F. S. CAMPING FACILITIES WITH WATER AND TOILETS:

Fire Permits are required on shoreline or on boats touching shoreline, but they are not required in developed campgrounds. They are not required for stoves, ranges or lighting devices built into the vessel.

ALL FEES VARY WITH SEASON.

PIT RIVER ARM

From Interstate 5	See Map #	
11 Miles NE	1 (△)	Rocky Ridge - Reservation Group Campground, Capacity: 70 Fee: $35/Night, Reservation Fee: $10
11 Miles NE	2	Upper Jones Valley - 27 Tent/R.V. Sites, Boat Access, Fee: $6/Vehicle
11 Miles NE	3	Jones Inlet - Primitive Camp Sites, No Fee, Campfire Permit Required.

MC CLOUD RIVER ARM

At O'Brien:		
1 Mile E	4 (△)	Bailey Cove - 16 Tents/R.V. Sites, Launch Ramp, Fee: $6/Vehicle
At Gilman Rd.:		
9 Miles E	5	Hirz Bay - 38 Single - 38 Double Tent/R.V. Sites, Fee: $8/Single, $12/Double, Launch Ramp
10 Miles E	6	Dekkas Rock Group Camp North - Max. Capacity - 30 People, Fee: $25 South - Max. Capacity - 30 People, Fee: $25 Reservation Fee: $10
11 Miles E	7	Moore Creek - 13 Tent/R.V. Sites, Fee: $7
15 Miles E	8	Ellery Creek - 19 Tent/R.V. Sites, Fee: $10
16 Miles E	9	Pine Point - 13 Tent/R.V. Sites, Fee: $7
17 Miles E	10	McCloud Bridge - 21 Tent/R.V. Sites, Fee: $6
9 Miles E	11	Hirz Bay Group Camp - Camp #1 - Max. Capacity - 120 People, Fee: $60 Camp #2 - Max. Capacity - 80 People, Fee: $40 Reservation Fee: $10

. . . Continued . . .

INFORMATION: Shasta Lake Information Center, 6547 Holiday Rd., Redding 96003 Ph: 916-275-1589

CAMPING	BOATING	RECREATION	OTHER
U. S. F. S. 16 Walk-In Sites Fee: $5 299 Dev. Sites for Tents & R.V.s Fee: $5 - $10 65 Boat-In Sites No Fee 5 Group Camps See Following Pages	Power, Row, Canoe, Sail, Waterski, Jet Ski, Windsurf & Inflatable Full Service Marinas Launch Ramps Rentals: Houseboats, Fishing & Ski Boats Docks, Berths, Gas, Moorings, Storage Overnight in Boat Permitted Anywhere	Fishing: Trout, Bass, Catfish, Bluegill, Perch, Crappie & Kokanee Salmon Swimming-Lake & Pools Picnicking Hiking Backpacking Shasta Caverns Hunting: Deer, Elk, Bear, Turkey	Motels & Cabins Snack Bars Restaurants Grocery Stores Bait & Tackle Laundromats Gas Stations Trailer Parks Disposal Stations Floating Toilets on Lake

SHASTA LAKE

SACRAMENTO RIVER ARM

At Salt Creek:			
	.5 Mile W	12	Nelson Point - 8 Tent & R.V. Sites, Fee: $6
	1 Mile W	13	Oak Grove - 43 Tent & R.V. Sites, Fee: $6/Site, 13 Walk-In Sites
	3 Miles NE	14	Gregory Creek - 5 Tent Sites, 13 R.V. Sites. Fee: $6
		15	Gregory Beach - Primitive Camp Site, No Fee
At Lakehead:			
	1.7 Miles S	16	Antlers - 41 Single - 18 Double Tent/R.V. Sites, Launch Ramp, Adjacent to Resort with Full Facilities, Fee: $8/Single, $12/Double
	2.5 Miles S	17	Lakeshore East - 9 Walk-in Sites, 14 Tent/R.V. Sites, Adjacent to Resort with Full Facilities, Fee: $5 - $7
	4.6 Miles S	18	Bee Hive - Primitive Camp Sites, No Fee

BOAT ACCESS ONLY CAMPING WITH TOILETS, NO FEE, FIRE PERMITS REQUIRED:

19	Arbuckle Flat - 11 Sites
20	Between McCloud River and Squaw Creek: Ski Island - 29 Sites Water
21	McCloud River Arm: Green Creek - 11 Sites
22	Gooseneck Cove - 10 Sites

PUBLIC CAMPING:

Free shoreline camping is permitted providing fire and sanitation rules are observed. Fire permits are required. Since there is no garbage pickup at undeveloped sites, all litter and garbage must be removed.

For permits and further information, contact Shasta Lake Information Center.

SOME PRIVATE FACILITIES: See Map for Number Symbols

(1) **ANTLER'S R.V. & CAMPGROUND RESORT** - P.O. Box 127, Lakehead 96051, 916-238-2322, Campsites, Hookups, Showers, Laundry, Store, Snack Bar, Bait & Tackle, Pool.

1 **ANTLER MARINA RESORT** - P.O. Box 140, Lakehead 96051, 916-238-2553, Full Service Marina Ramp, Houseboat Rentals, Cabins, General Store, Bait & Tackle, Snack Bar, Gas, Competition Ski Boats

2 **BRIDGE BAY RESORT** - 10300 Bridge Bay Road, Redding 96003, 916-275-3021, Full Service Marina, Ramp, Boat & Jet Ski Rentals, Motel, Restaurant, Lounge, General Store, Bait & Tackle, Swimming Pool, Reservations: 800-752-9669.

3 **DIGGER BAY MARINA** - P.O. Box 1516, Central Valley 96019, 916-275-3072 or 800-752-6996, Full Service Marina, Ramp, General Store, Sports Equipment, Bait & Tackle, Gas, Marine Supplies.

4 **HOLIDAY HARBOR RESORT** - P.O. Box 112, O'Brien 96070, 916-238-2383 Full Service Marina, Ramp, Restaurant, Campsites, Hookups, Showers, General Store, Gas, All Types of Boat Rentals Including Jet Skis and Sea Sleds, Reservations: 800-258-BOAT in California, or 800-251-BOAT From Out of State.

5 **JONES VALLEY RESORT** - 8800 Bear Mtn. Rd., Redding 96003, 916-275-1204, Full Service Marina, General Store, Bait & Tackle, Boat Rentals, Gas, Opens April 1.

6 **KAMPLOOPS CAMP** - Via Boat from Hirz Bay, P. O. Box 113, Redding 96099, 916-357-2951, Campsites, Showers, Flush Toilets, Group Camps Available with "Cook Shack" Equipment Included, Docks, Seasonal.

7 **LAKEHEAD CAMPGROUND** - P.O. Box 647, Lakehead 96051, 916-238-2671, Campsites, Hookups, Laundry, Dump Station, Showers, General Store, Swimming Pool.

8 **LAKESHORE RESORT & MARINA** - Star Rt., Box 706, Lakehead 96051, 916-238-2301, Full Service Marina, Cabins, Restaurant & Lounge, Campsites, Hookups, Showers, General Store, Bait & Tackle, Swimming Pool, Gas, Camp Supplies, Houseboat, Patio, Fishing & Ski Boat Rentals, Jet Skis.

. . . Continued . . .

SHASTA LAKE

(9) **LAKE SHORE VILLA R. V. PARK** - Star Rt., Box 749-M, Lakehead 96051, 916-238-8688, R.V. Sites, Full Hookups, 15 Pull Throughs over 70 Feet Plus, Laundry, Dump Station, Showers, Docks, Satellite T.V.

10 **LAKEVIEW MARINA RESORT** - P.O. Box 2272, Redding 96099, 916-223-3003, Full Service Marina, Boat Ramp, Cabins, Snack Bar, General Store, Ice, Bait & Tackle, Sports Equipment.

11 **PACKER'S BAY MARINA** - P.O. Box 336B, Redding 96099, 916-221-5666, Boat Rentals, Boat Gas, Bait & Tackle.

12 **SHASTA LAKE TRAILER RESORT** - Star Rt., Box 800, Lakehead 96051, 916-238-2370, Moorage, Campsites, Hookups, Trailer Rentals, Laundry, Showers, General Store, Bait & Tackle, Gas, Swimming Pool.

13 **SHASTA MARINA** - P.O. Box E, O'Brien 96070, 916-238-2284, Full Service Marina, Boat Ramp, Campsites, Hookups, Showers, General Store, Bait & Tackle, House, Patio, Ski & Fishing Boat Rentals.

14 **SILVERTHORN RESORT** - P.O. Box 419, Redding 96099, 916-275-1571, Full Service Marina, Boat Ramp, Cabins, Restaurant & Lounge, General Store, Bait & Tackle, Houseboat & Jet Ski Rentals.

15 **SOLUS CAMPGROUND** - P.O. Box 377, Lakehead 96051, 916-238-2451, Campsites, Hookups, Laundry, Dump Station, Showers, General Store, Bait & Tackle, Swimming Pool.

16 **SUGARLOAF COTTAGES** - Star Rt., Box 845, Lakehead 96051, 916-238-2448, Cabins, Restaurant & Lounge, Pool, General Store, Bait & Tackle.

17 **SUGARLOAF MARINA & RESORT** - P.O. Box 599, Redding 96099, 916-243-4353, Full Service Marina, Snackbar, Campsites, Hookups, Dump Station, Showers, Pool, General Store, Bait & Tackle, Houseboat, Ski, Jet Skis and Fishing Boat Rentals.

18 **TRAIL INN** - Star Rt., Box 801, Lakehead 96051, 916-238-8533, Pull Through Campsites, Hookups, Pool, Laundry, Showers, Mini-Market.

19 **TSASDI RESORT** - Star Rt., Box 801, Lakehead 96051, 916-238-2575, Cabins, General Store, Bait & Tackle, Swimming Pool, Dock.

*Full Service Marina = Boat Rentals, Moorage, & Boat Gas

For Further Information on Private Facilities Contact:

Shasta Dam Area Chamber of Commerce
P.O. Box 1368R
Central Valley 96019
Telephone: 916-275-8862

MANZANITA, BUTTE, SUMMIT AND JUNIPER, MC CUMBER RESERVOIR, GRACE, NORA, DIAMOND AND PEAR LAKES

Manzanita, Butte, Summit and Juniper are within the 106,000 acres expanse of the beautiful Lassen Volcanic National Park. Boating is restricted to non-powered craft. The angler will find planted and native trout in lake and stream. There are over 150 miles of trails including a part of the Pacific Crest Trail for the hiker, backpacker and equestrian. Pets and vehicles are not allowed on trails. Pack and saddle stock must overnight in corrals by prior reservation. Grazing is not permittted so you must pack in feed. The lakes listed outside the Park boundaries are good fishing spots. McCumber Reservoir, Grace and Nora are P.G. & E. lakes off Highway 44 while Diamond and Pear Lakes are reached by primitive roads south of Mineral.

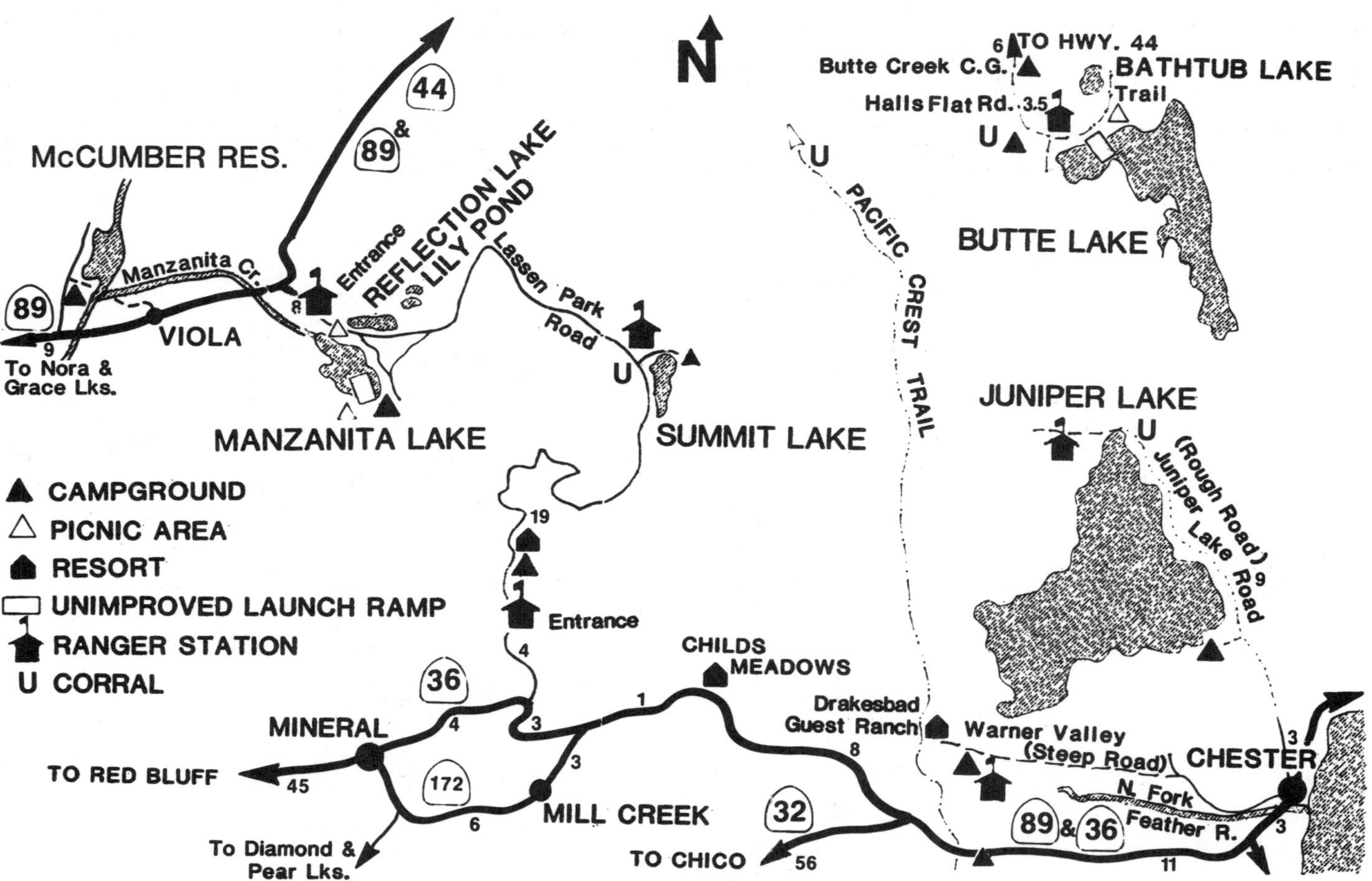

INFORMATION: Lassen Volcanic Nat. Park, P.O. Box 100, Mineral 96063, Ph: 916-595-4444			
CAMPING	**BOATING**	**RECREATION**	**OTHER**
Manzanita: 179 Sites Tents & R.V.s: $7 Butte: 98 Sites Tents & R.V.s: $7 Group Camp - 25 People Maximum Summit: 94 Sites Tents & R.V.s: $5-$7 Juniper: 18 Sites Tents Only-No Fee No Water Groups	No Power Motors Row, Sail, Windsurf & Inflatables Only Launch Ramps at Manzanita & Butte Only	Fishing: Rainbow, Brook & Brown Trout No Fish at Juniper Only Barbless Hooks at Manzanita Lake Swimming - Picnicking Hiking Backpacking-Parking Horseback Riding Trails & Corrals Campfire Programs No ORV's	For Lodging Facilities in This Area, Contact the Lassen Volcanic National Park P.G. & E. McCumber Reservoir 7 Tent Sites 5 Walk-In Sites Fee: $8-$9

CRATER, CARIBOU AND SILVER LAKES

In the Lassen National Forest, these Lakes provide a bounty of natural recreational opportunities. Crater Lake, at 6,000 feet elevation, has a surface area of 27 acres. This volcanic crater offers excellent fishing for Eastern Brook trout. The Lakes near Silver Lake border the Caribou Wilderness, a gentle, rolling, forested plateau which can easily be explored by the hiker, backpacker or horseman. Silver Lake and its neighbor, Caribou Lake, provide a quiet remote area for the small boater, camper and fisherman. The roads are dirt and rough, especially into Crater Lake so large trailers are not advised.

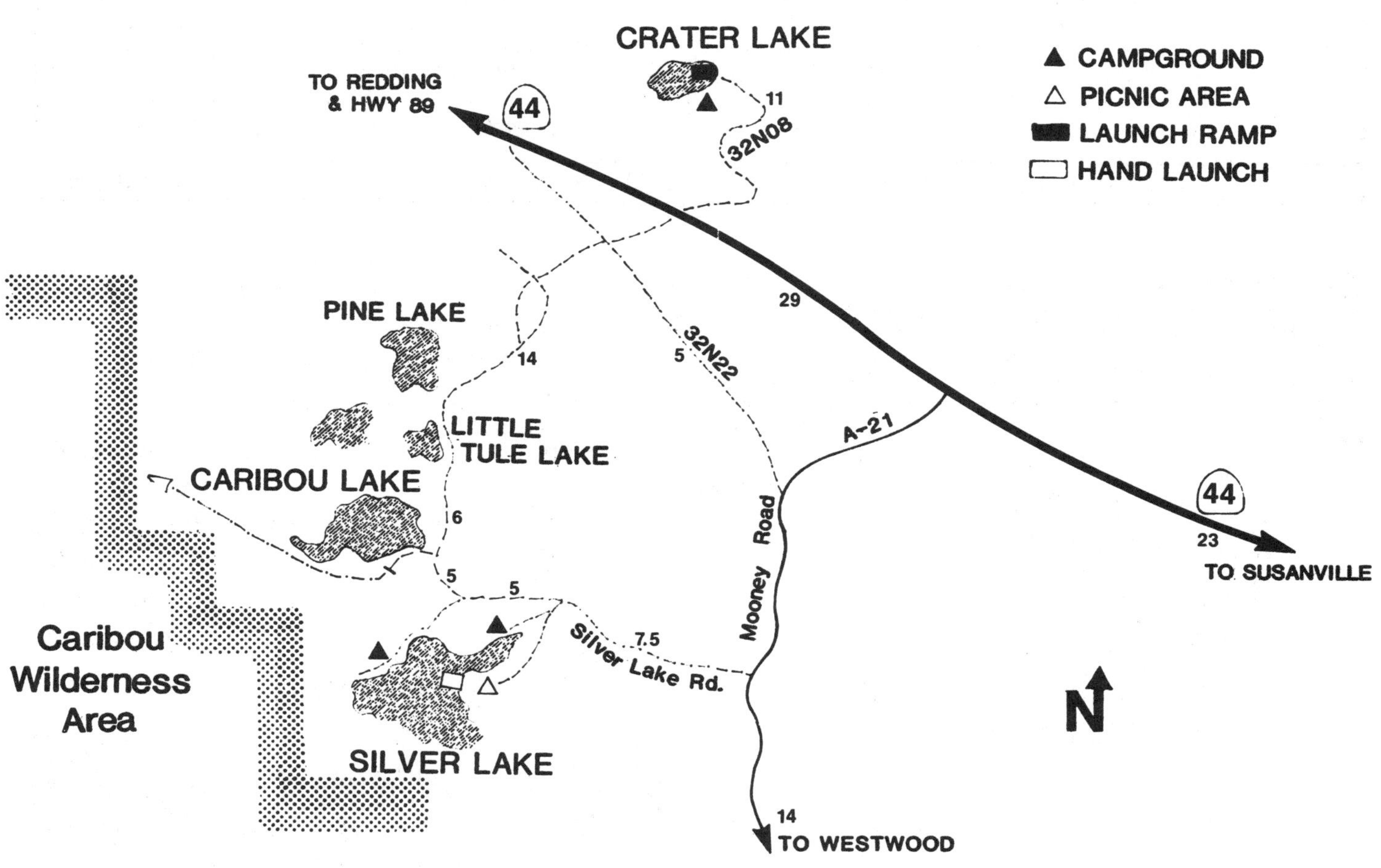

INFORMATION: Almanor Ranger District, Box 767, Chester 96020, Ph: 916-258-2141			
CAMPING	BOATING	RECREATION	OTHER
Silver Lake: Rocky Knoll: 7 Tent Sites 11 Tent or R.V. Sites Fee:$6 Silver Bowl: 18 Tent or R.V. Sites Fee: $6 Crater Lake: 17 Tent/RV Sites Fee: $6 R.V.'s Not Over 15 Feet Long	Silver & Caribou Lakes: Cartop Boats Hand Launch Only Crater Lake: No Motors Allowed Launch Ramp	Fishing: Rainbow & Eastern Brook Trout Picnicking Swimming Hiking & Riding Trails Backpacking Hunting: Antelope, Deer, Rabbit, Quail & Grouse	Crater Lake Campground: Eagle Lake Ranger District 55 S. Sacramento St. Susanville 96130 Ph: 916-257-2151 17 Dev. Sites Trailers Not Recommended

EAGLE LAKE

Eagle Lake is at an elevation of 5,100 feet in the Lassen National Forest. With a surface area of 27,000 acres and over 100 miles of timbered shoreline, it is the second largest natural lake in California. The slightly alkaline water is the natural habitat for the famous Eagle Lake trout, a favorite for the fisherman for its size of 3 pounds or better. Eagle Lake is ideal for water sports because there are no snags or underwater obstructions. The water is warm and clear, and the size of the lake offers plenty of room. There are 4 Forest Service campgrounds and 2 group campgrounds amid tall pines. Full hook-ups for R.V.s are located at Eagle Lake Park. McCoy Flat is a small reservoir for the fisherman with brown and rainbow trout.

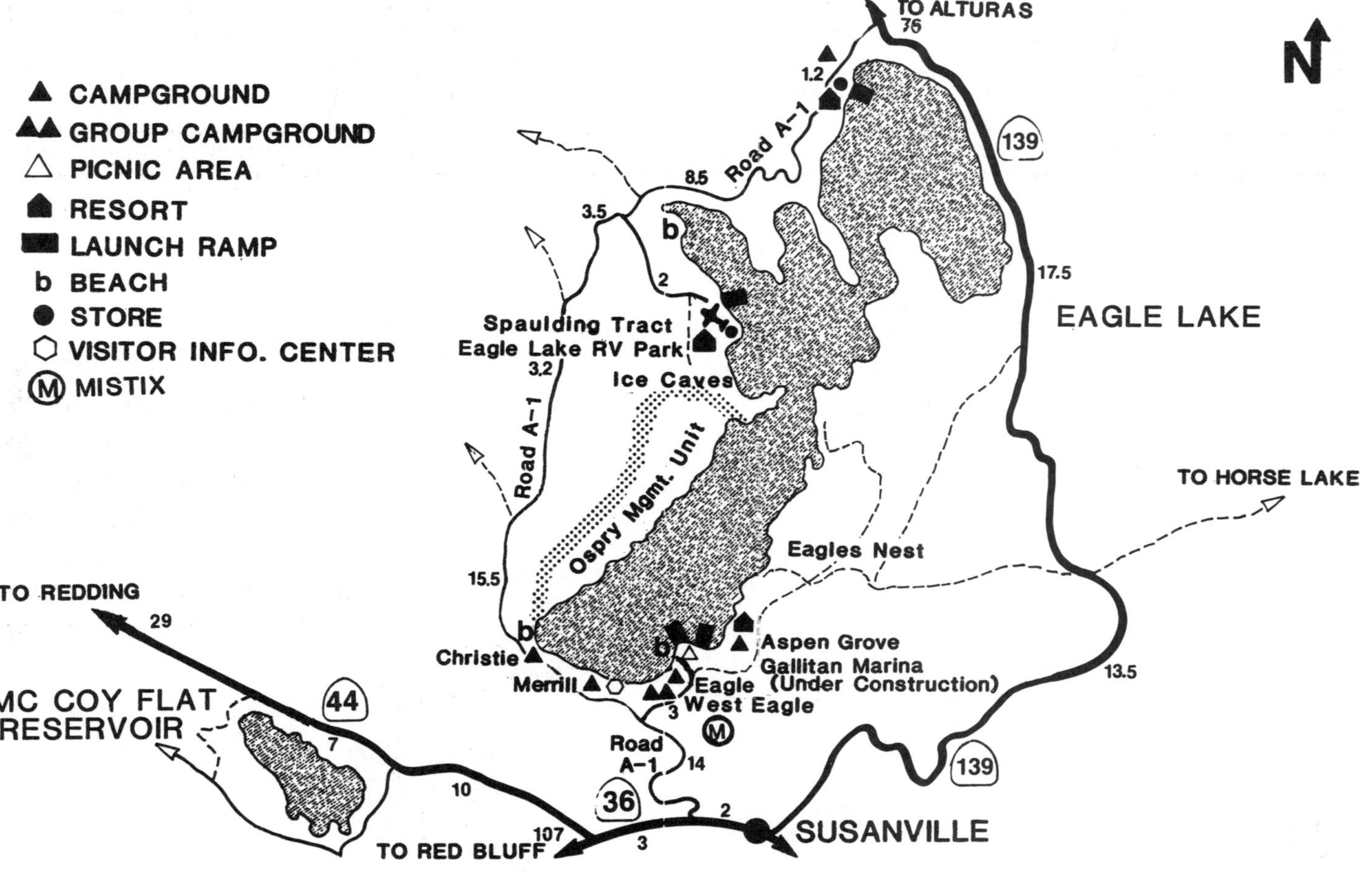

INFORMATION: U. S. F. S., 55 S. Sacramento St., Susanville 96130, Ph: 916-257-2151			
CAMPING	BOATING	RECREATION	OTHER
300 Dev. Sites for Tents & R.V.s 11 Multiple Vehicle Sites 25 Dev. Sites for Tents @ Aspen Grove 2 Group Camps #1 - 100 People #2 - 75 People Reserve: MISTIX Bureau of Land Management: 17 Dev. Sites	Power, Row, Canoe, Sail, Waterski, Jet Skis, Windsurfing, Inflatables Full Service Marinas Launch Ramps Rentals: Fishing Boats & Motors Docks, Moorings, Berths	Fishing: Eagle Lake, Rainbow & Brown Trout Swimming Picnicking Hiking Nature Walks Campfire Programs Hunting: Deer & Waterfowl Birdwatching: Bald Eagles, Osprey, Grebes, Pelicans and many Ducks	Eagle Lake R.V. Park 18 Palmetto Way Rt. 3 Susanville 96130 Ph: 916-825-3133 46 Full Hook-ups Motel & Cabin Rental Snack Bar-Restaurants Grocery Store Laundromat-Showers Disposal Station Gas Station & Propane Airstrip

RUTH LAKE

Ruth Lake is half way between Eureka and Red Bluff on Highway 36. This is quite a drive on a narrow road at times, but well worth the trip if you plan to stay awhile in this beautiful country. The Lake rests at an elevation of 2,654 feet and has a surface area of 1,200 acres. It was formed by damming the Mad River in 1962, and it is now a popular recreation facility offering boating of all kinds, fishing and camping. The Flying "AA" Ranch has its own airport, motel, horses, swimming pool, tennis courts and an excellent restaurant featuring a weekend open-pit barbecue.

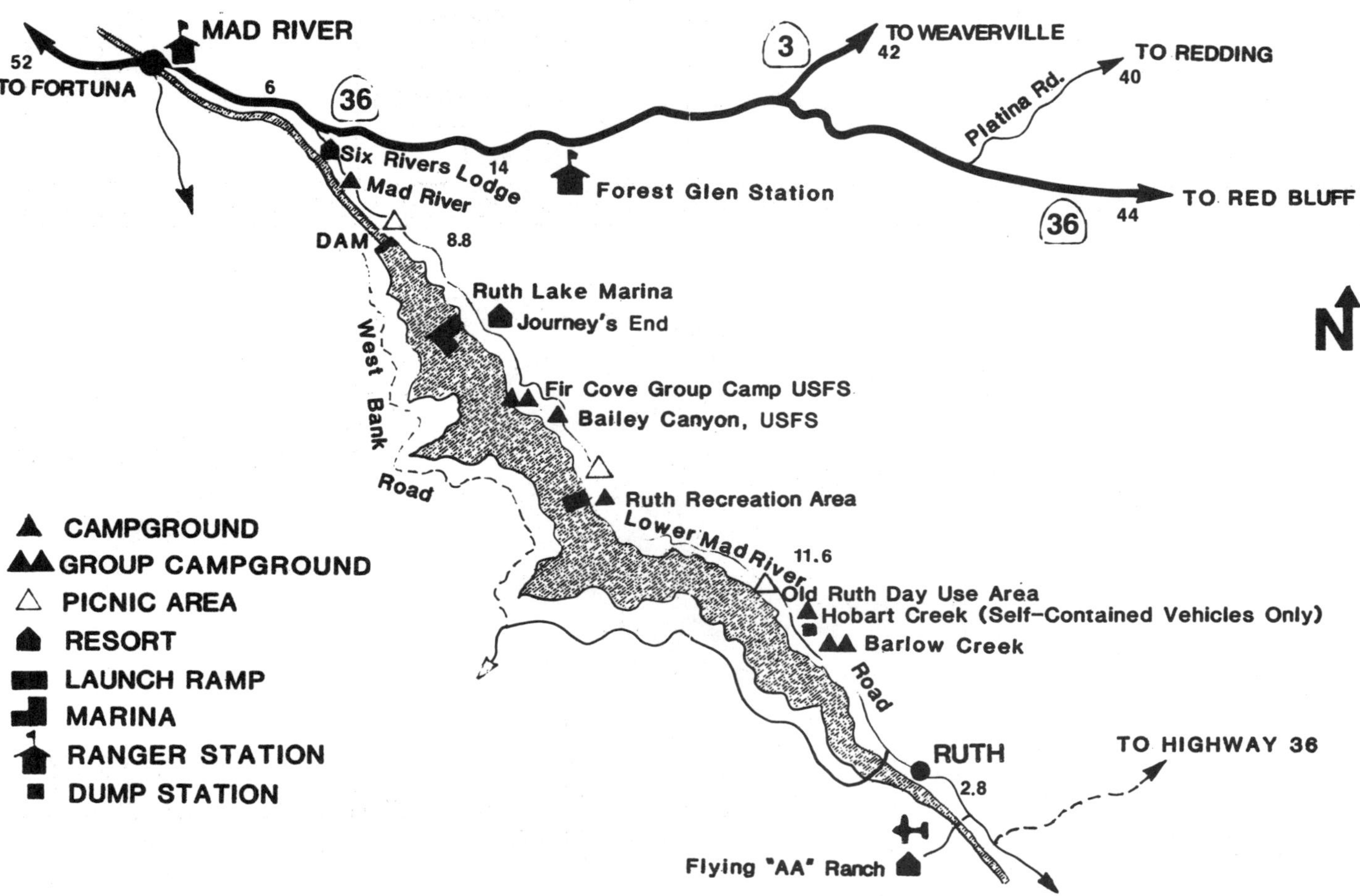

INFORMATION: Ruth Lake Comm. Serv., P.O. Box 31, Mad River 95552, Ph: 707-574-6332

CAMPING	BOATING	RECREATION	OTHER
U. S. F. S. 81 Dev. Sites for Tents & R.V.s Fee: $5 1 Group Site-Reserve Ph: 707-574-6233 Ruth Lake Community 100 Dev. Sites for Tents & R.V.s Fee: $5 Barlow Group Camp & Picnic Area Reserve: Ph: 707-574-6332	Power, Row, Canoe, Sail, Waterski, Jet Ski, Windsurf & Inflatables Full Service Marina Launch Ramps Rentals: Fishing Boats & Motors, Waterski, Pontoon Docks	Fishing: Rainbow Trout, Kokanee Salmon, Large & Smallmouth Bass, Catfish Waterplay Picnicking Hiking Horseback Riding -Trails & Rentals Hunting: Deer, Boar, Bear Quail, Grouse, Wild Turkey	Flying "AA" Ranch Ruth Star Rt. P.O. Box 700 Bridgeville 95526 Ph: 707-574-6227 Cabins, Restaurant Tennis, Swimming Pool, Airport, Car Rentals, Full Vacation Facilities Snack Bar-Restaurant Disposal Station

ROUND VALLEY RESERVOIR

Round Valley Reservoir is at an elevation of 4,600 feet in the Plumas National Forest. Located 2 miles south of Greenville, this small secluded lake is the water supply for Greenville so water sports are limited to fishing and boating. Swimming or body contact with the water is not permitted. Famous for black bass, Round Valley is an excellent warm water lake. The area offers nice hiking and nature study trails. Campsites are available at the Resort and also at the Greenville County Campground.

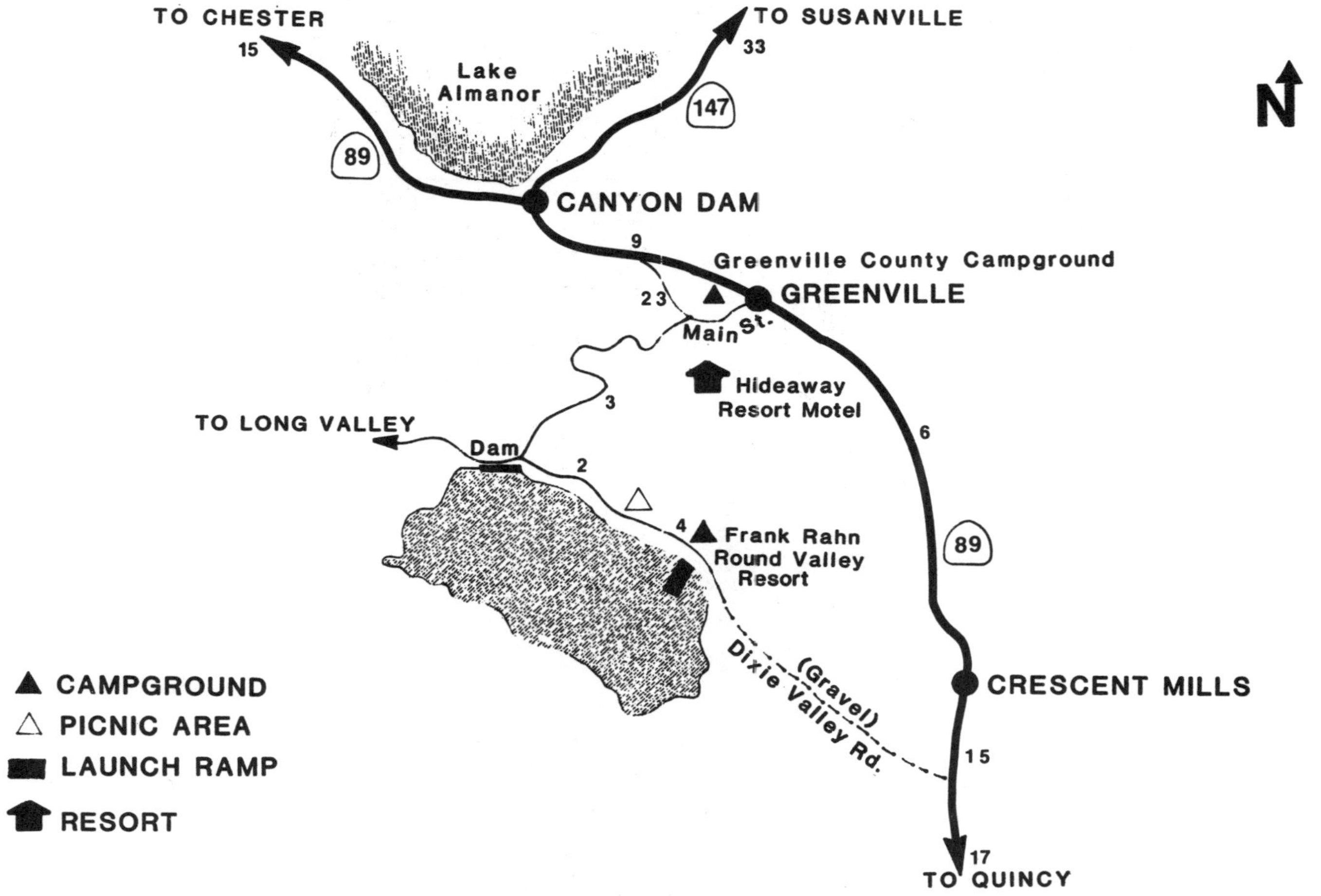

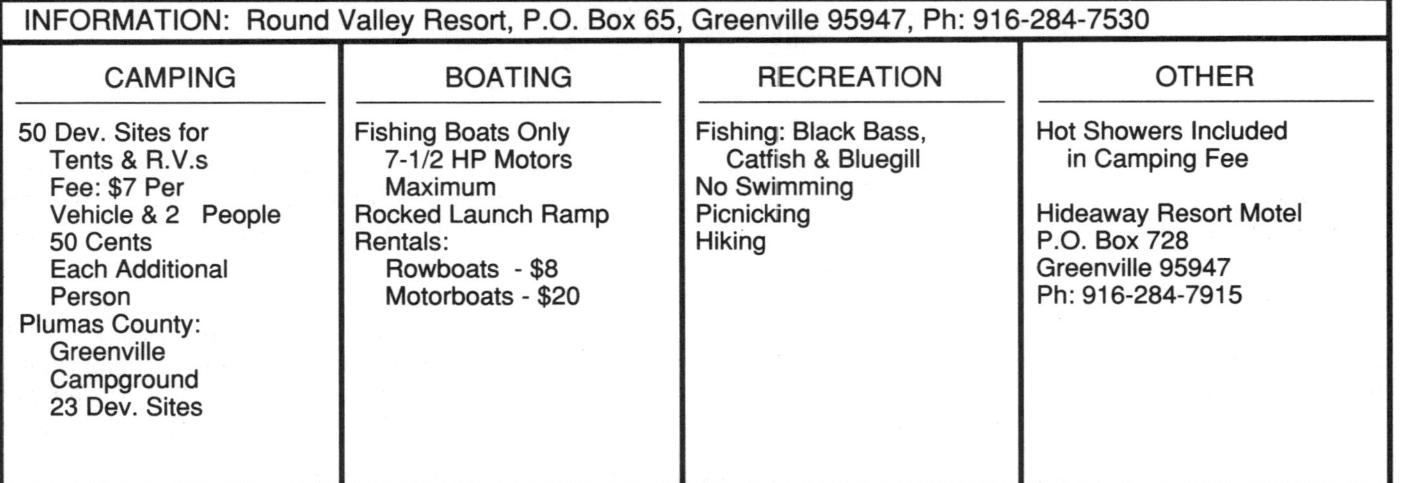

INFORMATION: Round Valley Resort, P.O. Box 65, Greenville 95947, Ph: 916-284-7530

CAMPING	BOATING	RECREATION	OTHER
50 Dev. Sites for Tents & R.V.s Fee: $7 Per Vehicle & 2 People 50 Cents Each Additional Person Plumas County: Greenville Campground 23 Dev. Sites	Fishing Boats Only 7-1/2 HP Motors Maximum Rocked Launch Ramp Rentals: Rowboats - $8 Motorboats - $20	Fishing: Black Bass, Catfish & Bluegill No Swimming Picnicking Hiking	Hot Showers Included in Camping Fee Hideaway Resort Motel P.O. Box 728 Greenville 95947 Ph: 916-284-7915

DO NOT DRINK UNTREATED NATURAL WATER

Is the water safe? Unless it is piped, it usually is not. A microscopic organism, Giardia Lambia, is polluting most of our lakes and streams. By drinking this contaminated water, a severe intestinal disease is passed on to you. Giardiasis can cause extreme discomfort and must be treated by a doctor.

Where drinking water is not available, it is best to bring your own. There are also several alternative methods. Although water purification tablets kill bacteria, they are not reliable when it comes to Giardiasis. Portable filtration systems are fast and effective. A sure protection is to boil your water for two minutes or at higher altitues, for five minutes.

Giardia is easily transmitted between animals and humans. All feces, human and animal, must be buried at least eight inches deep and one hundred feet away from natural water. Protect those who follow you by keeping our lakes, rivers and streams free of contamination.

LAKE ALMANOR

Lake Almanor rests at an elevation of 4,500 feet in the Lassen National Forest. There is an abundance of pine-sheltered campgrounds operated by P. G. & E., the Forest Service and private resorts. The lake is 13 miles long and 6 miles wide with a surface area of 28,000 acres. It is one of the largest man-made lakes in California. Almanor's clear, blue waters offer complete boating facilities. Caution is advised because small islands are exposed during low water levels. Gusty winds can also make boating hazardous. Fishing can be excellent for a variety of species in the lake and the many nearby streams are often productive. Mountain Meadow Reservoir is a small fishing lake in a scenic area near Westwood. There are no facilities but it is surrounded by numerous hiking and equestrian trails.

. . . Continued . . .

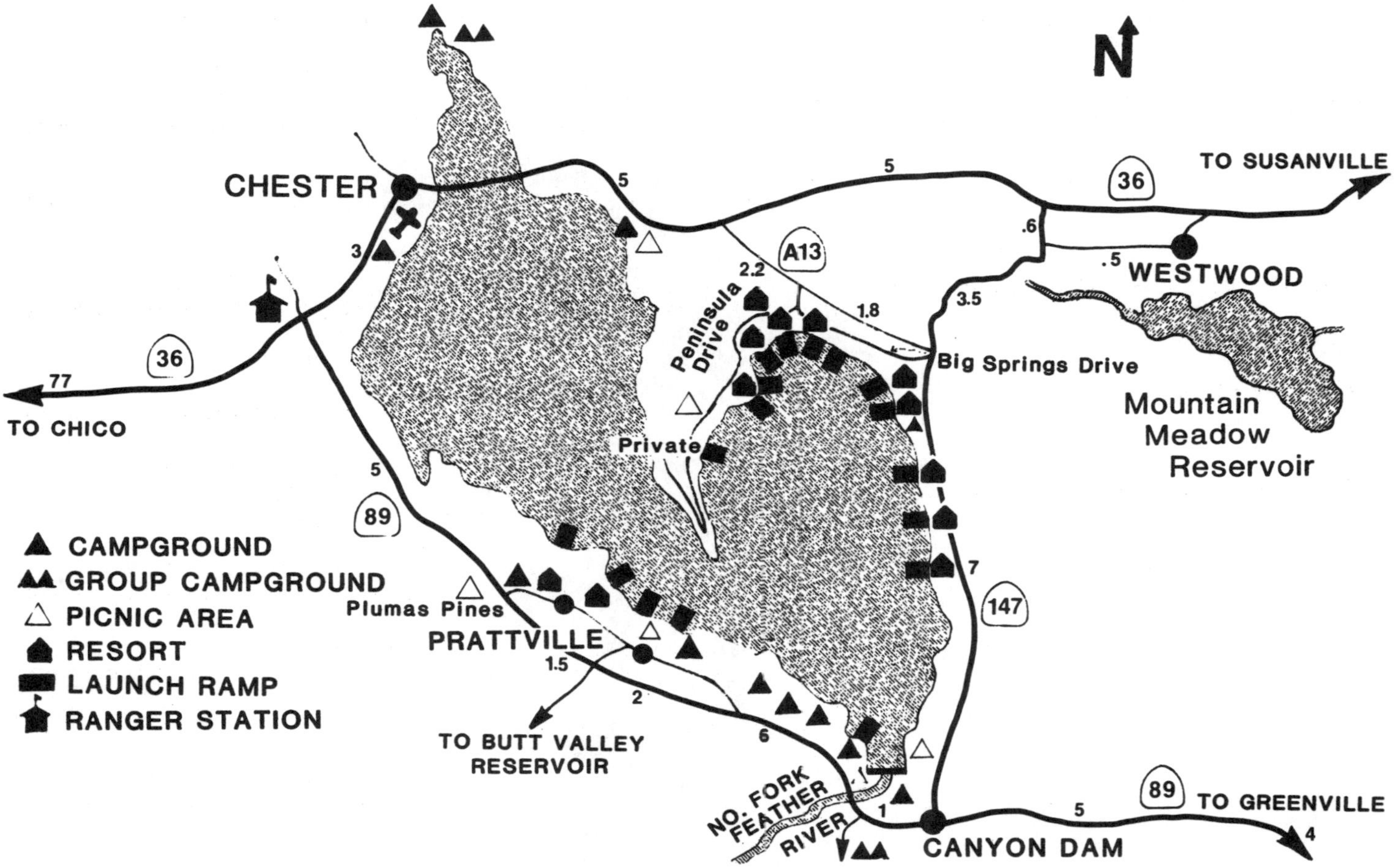

INFORMATION: P. G. & E. Regional Land Dept., P.O. Box 340, Red Bluff, 96080, Ph: 916-527-5880			
CAMPING	BOATING	RECREATION	OTHER
P. G. & E.: 125 Dev. Sites for Tents & R.V.s - Fee: $8 Group Camp to 50 People Maximum U. S. F. S.: 101 Dev. Sites for Tents & R.V.s - Fee: $7 Private Campgrounds Fees: $8 - $14	Power, Row, Canoe, Sail, Waterski, Inflatables Full Service Marinas Launch Ramps Rentals: Fishing, Canoe, Patio & Ski Docks, Berths, Gas	Fishing: Rainbow & Brown Trout, Large & Smallmouth Bass, Bluegill, Catfish, Perch, Kokanee & Coho Salmon Swimming Picnicking Hiking Hunting: Deer, Waterfowl Horseback Riding	Cabins & Motels Snack Bars Restaurant Grocery Stores Bait & Tackle Laundromats Disposal Stations Gas Stations Golf Course

LAKE ALMANOR

P. G. & E. CAMPING FACILITIES

Nearby Areas - Ph: 1-800-624-8087

Lake Almanor Campground - Off Highway 89 Westshore.
125 Tent/R.V. Sites, Handicapped Facilities

Camp Conery Group Camp - Off Highway 89 East of Dam.
50 People Maximum, Multi-purpose Utility Building with Cook area, Grill, Refrigeration, Showers and 5 Bunk Houses, Swimming Beach and Picnic Area - Reservations Only.

Last Chance Creek Campground - 4 miles northeast of Chester on Juniper Lake Road.
13 Tent/R.V. Group Sites - 3 Site Minimum by Reservation, 12 Tent/R.V. Individual Sites, Horse Camping.

U. S. FOREST SERVICE - ALMANOR RANGER DISTRICT

Ph: 916-258-2141

Almanor Campground - Off Highway 89 West Shore.
15 Tent Only Sites, 86 Tent/R.V. Sites to 22 Feet, Handicapped Facilities.

Almanor Group Camp - Off Highway 89 West Shore.
Groups to 100 People by Reservation Only.

SOME PRIVATE RESORTS

Martin's R.V. Park - P.O. Box 1099, Chester 96020, 916-258-3000
15 R.V. Sites, Full Hookups, Dump Station, Propane, Hot Showers, T.V. Hookups.

Northshore Campground - P.O. Box 455, Chester 96020, 916-258-3376
40 Tent Sites, 80 R.V. Sites, Full Hookups, Dump Station, Hot Showers, Flush Toilets, Boat Rentals.

Lake Almanor Resort - 2706 Big Springs Rd., Lake Almanor 96137, 916-596-3337
15 R.V. Sites, Full Hookups, 5 Cabins, Lodge with 9 Housekeeping Units, Showers, Flush Toilets, Launch Ramp, Fuel Dock, Slips, Rental Boats, General Store, Bait & Tackle, Grass Lawns.

Lake Cove Resort and Marina - P.O. Box 1, Canyondam 95923, 916-284-7697
55 R.V. Sites, Full & Partial Hookups, Dump Station, Showers, Flush Toilets, Laundry, Ramp, Rental Boats, Fuel Dock, General Store, Bait & Tackle.

Lassen View Resort - 7457 Hwy. 147, Lake Almanor 96137, 916-596-3437
60 R.V. Sites, 50 tent Sites, Full Hookups, Dump Station, Showers, Flush Toilets, Ramp, Slips, Fuel Dock, Cabins, Snack Bar, General Store.

Little Norway Resort - 432 Peninsula Dr., Lake Almanor 96137, 916-596-3225
Cabins, Full Service Marina, Fishing, Ski and Sailboat Rentals, Mini Groceries, Swim Dock.

Wilson's Camp Prattville - 2913 Lake Almanor Dr. West, Canyondam 95923, 916-259-2464
40 R.V. Sites, 3 Tent Sites, Showers, Flush Toilets, Housekeeping Units, Marina, Ramp, Docks, Restaurant, General Store, Bait & Tackle.

The above are a random selection of the many facilities around the Lake. For additional information contact:

Chester - Lake Almanor Chamber of Commerce
P.O. Box 1198
Chester, CA 96020
Ph: 916-258-2426

BUTT VALLEY RESERVOIR

Butt Valley Reservoir rests at an elevation of 4,150 feet in the Lassen National Forest. This picturesque mountain Lake is five miles long and three-quarters of a mile at its widest point. It is connected to Lake Almanor by a tunnel, and it is the second level of P. G. & E.'s "stairway of power" which flows down the Feather River into Lake Oroville. This is a nice boating Lake although marina facilities are limited to a launch ramp. There is a good fishery for both planted Rainbows, native Brown and Rainbow trout. The well-kept campground and picnic areas are under the jurisdiction of P. G. & E.

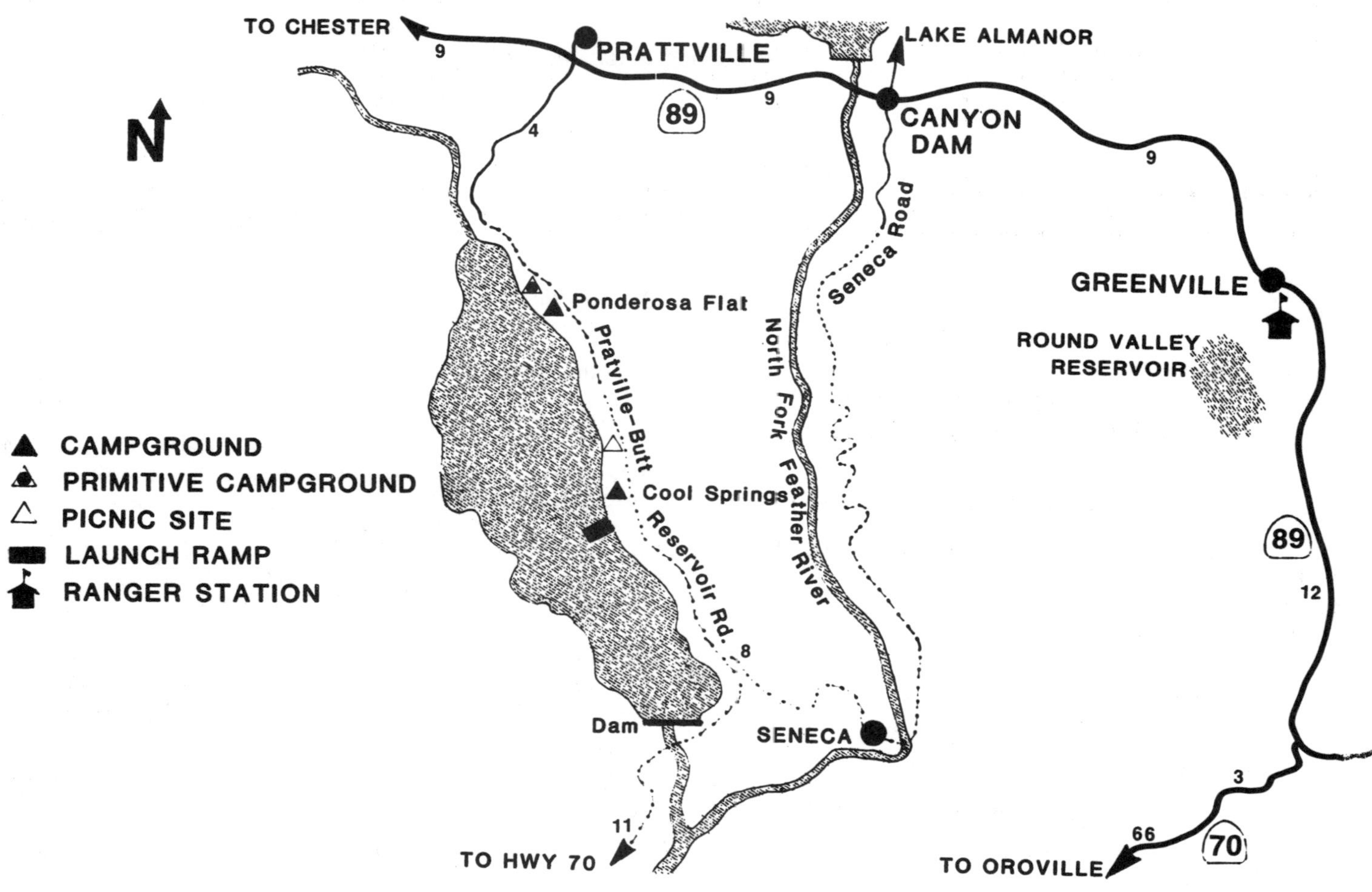

INFORMATION: P. G. & E. Regional Land Dept., Box 340, Red Bluff 96080, Ph: 916-527-5880

CAMPING	BOATING	RECREATION	OTHER
Cool Springs: 22 Sites for Tents & R.V.s Fee: $8 Ponderosa Flat: 45 Sites for Tents & R.V.s Fee: $8 Butt Overflow: 20 Sites Fee: $7	Open to All Boating Launch Ramp No Waterskiing	Fishing: Rainbow, Brown Trout, Catfish Picnicking Swimming Hiking Nature Study Hunting: Waterfowl & Deer Horseback Riding	Full Facilities in Chester 9 Miles

ANTELOPE LAKE

The Antelope Lake Recreation Area rests at an elevation of 5,000 feet in the Plumas National Forest. The Lake has 15 miles of timbered shoreline and a surface area of 930 acres. The sheltered coves and islands make this beautiful Lake a pleasant boating haven. The well maintained Forest Service campgrounds provide the camper with nice sites amid pine and fir trees. Good sized Rainbow and Eagle Lake trout await the fisherman. Indian Creek, below the dam, has some large German Brown trout as well as Rainbow for the stream fisherman.

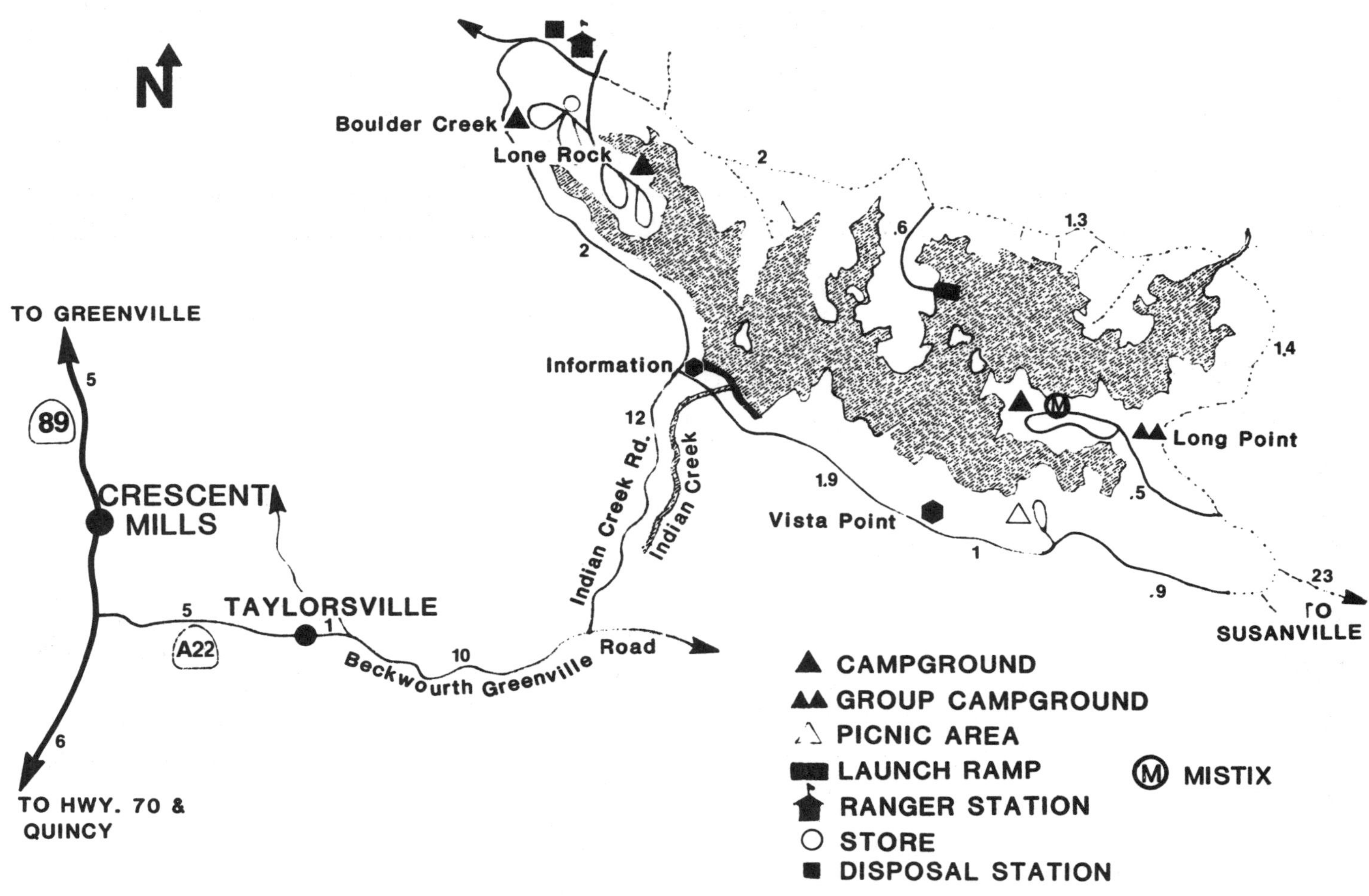

INFORMATION: Greenville Ranger District, P.O. Box 329, Greenville 95947, Ph: 916-284-7126

CAMPING	BOATING	RECREATION	OTHER
211 Dev. Sites for Tents & R.V.s Fee: $8 15 Dev. Sites - Can be used for Groups at Long Point Campground	Power, Row, Canoe, Sail, Waterski, Windsurfing & Inflatables Launch Ramp	Fishing: Rainbow & German Brown Trout, Catfish & Largemouth Bass Swimming Hiking (No Trails) Nature Trail Campfire Programs Hunting: Deer	Grocery Store Bait & Tackle Disposal Station Full Facilities - 26 Miles at Taylorsville

BENBOW LAKE

Benbow Lake State Recreation Area is at an elevation of 364 feet off Highway 101 in the Redwood Empire. This 230 acre lake is created every summer by damming the South Fork of the Eel River. Boating is limited to small non-powered craft so this is a nice lake for sailing and rowing. The California Department of Parks and Recreation maintains a park with picnic areas, campground and a swimming beach. The Benbow Inn, adjacent to the lake, is a lovely old hotel and restaurant. The Benbow Valley R.V. Resort offers 112 pull-through campsites with full hook-ups, cable T.V., swimming pool, jacuzzi and playgrounds.

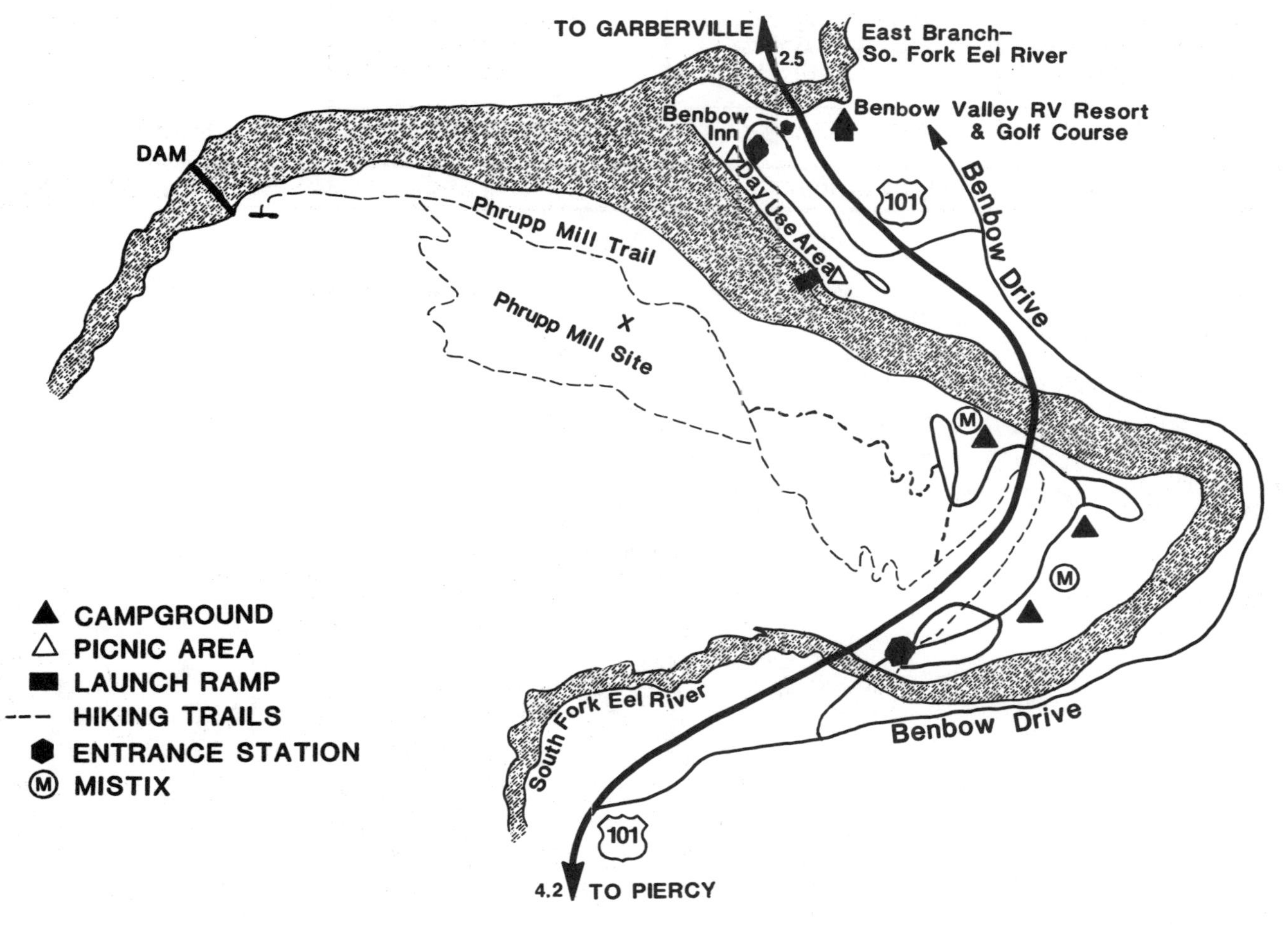

INFORMATION: Benbow Lake S.R.A., P.O. Box 100, Weott 95571, Ph: 707-946-2311

CAMPING	BOATING	RECREATION	OTHER
State Park 75 Dev. Sites for Tents & Self- Contained Units No Hook-ups Cold Showers Disposal Station Fee: $10 Reserve: MISTIX Ph: 800-444-7275 Day Use Fee: $3	Row, Sail, Canoe, Windsurfing & Inflatables No Motors Rentals: Canoes, Yak Boards Launch Ramp - Summer Only	Fishing: Not Recommended in Summer due to Young Steelhead & Salmon Swimming Picnicking Hiking Nature Study Campfire Programs	Benbow Valley R.V. Resort & Golf Course 7000 Benbow Dr. Garberville 95440 Ph: 707-923-2777 112 R.V. Sites Full Hook-ups Fee: $21 Benbow Inn and Restaurant Full Facilities in Garberville

LAKE CLEONE

Lake Cleone is at elevation of 20 feet within the MacKerricher State Park. This nice park along the scenic Mendocino Coast provides a variety of natural habitats from forest and wetlands to sand dunes and a 6-mile beach. Although swimming is not advised due to cold, turbulent seas, the 500-yard black sandy beach is a popular attraction. Lake Cleone, 40 surface acres, is open to shallow draft non-powered boating. The angler may fish for trout and an occasional bass at the Lake, steelhead and salmon in nearby rivers, and surf fish, rock fish and Ling cod in the ocean. Skin divers find abalone in several of the nearby coves. Hikers, riders and naturalists will find inviting trails around the Lake and along the beach.

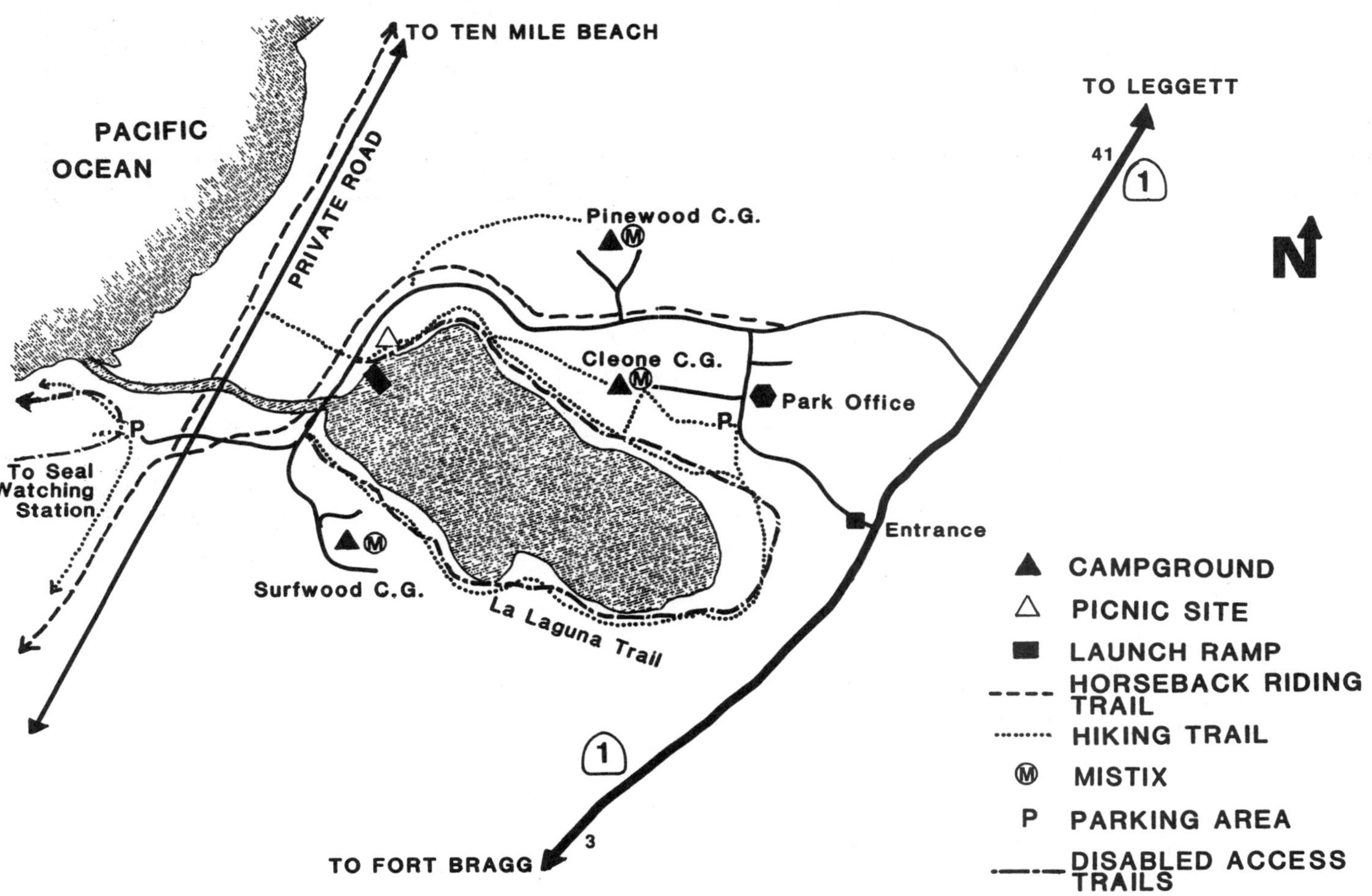

INFORMATION: MacKerricher State Park, P.O. Box 440, Mendocino 95460, Ph: 707-937-5804			
CAMPING	**BOATING**	**RECREATION**	**OTHER**
142 Dev. Sites for Tents & R.V.s Hot Showers Flush Toilets Disposal Station Reservations by Mistix 1-800-444-7275 11 Walk-In Camps	Open to Small, Shallow Draft Non-Powered Boats Paved Launch Ramp	Fishing: Trout Picnicking Hiking & Nature Study Trails Disabled Access Trails Horseback Riding Trails Campfire Programs Birding Beach Combing Skin Diving Seal Watching Station	Grocery Store Near Park Entrance Full Facilities at Fort Bragg

SNAG, PHILBROOK, DE SABLA AND PARADISE LAKES

These Lakes range in elevation from 3,000 feet at Paradise Lake to 5,000 feet at Philbrook Lake. Snag Lake is barren of game fish. Philbrook is a good fishing Lake, but trailers are not advised on the road. These two Lakes are part of the Lassen National Forest. P. G. & E. maintains a resort for its employees at De Sabla Reservoir, but the public may fish for Rainbow and some Browns on the south and east sides of the Lake nearest Skyway Boulevard. Paradise is a popular day use fishing Lake where the angler will find planted Rainbows, some Brown trout, bass, and Channel catfish.

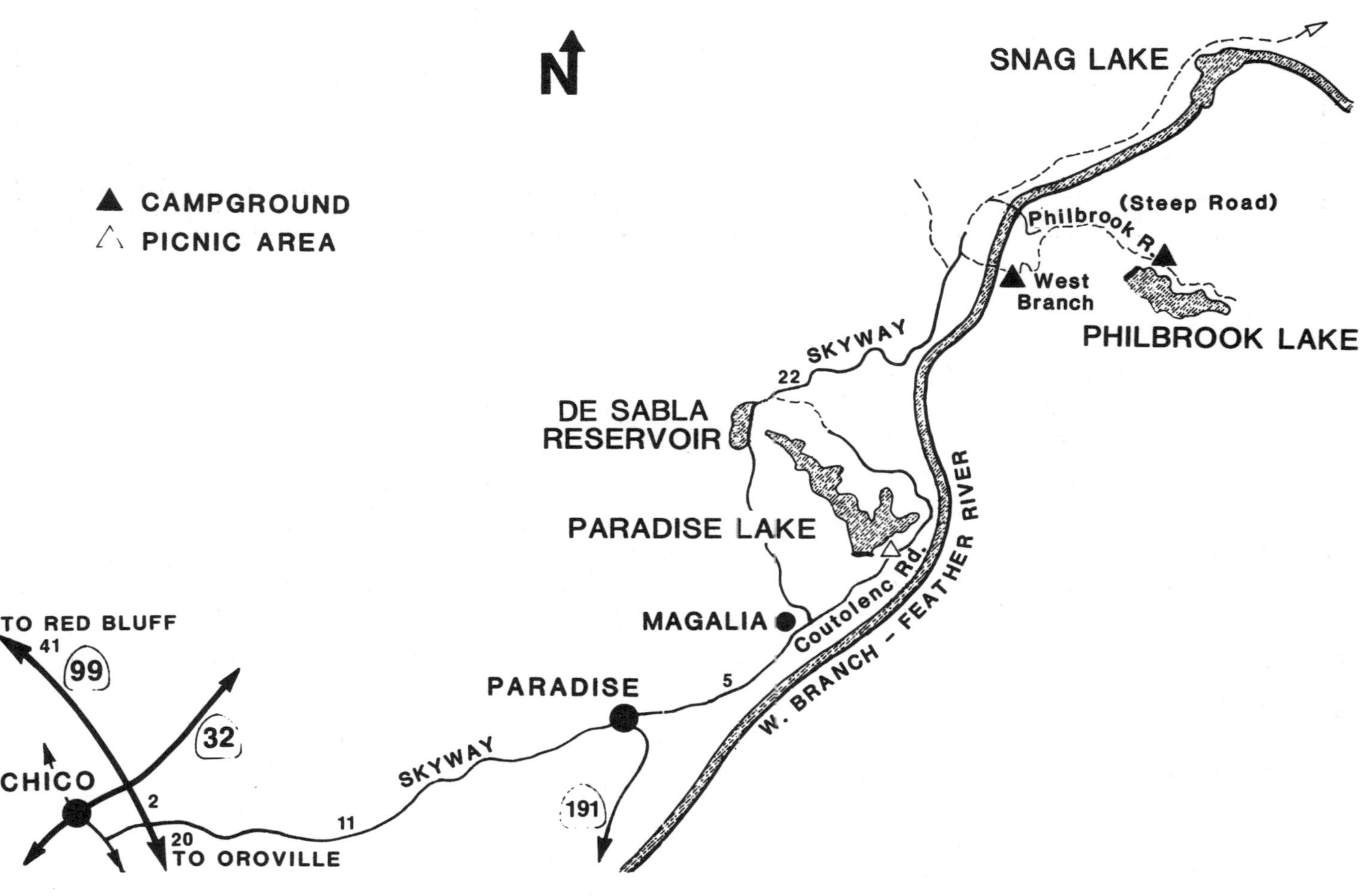

INFORMATION: Almanor Ranger District, P.O. Box 767, Chester 96020, Ph: 916-258-2141			
CAMPING	BOATING	RECREATION	OTHER
U. S. F. S. West Branch 15 Campsites Fee: $6 P. G. & E.: Philbrook Lake 20 Campsites Fee: $8	Philbrook - Open to All Boating Minimal Facilities Paradise Lake - Rowboats, Canoes & Electric Motors Minimal Facilities	Fishing: Rainbow, Brown & Eastern Brook Trout, Small & Largemouth Bass and Channel Catfish Picnicking Hiking Backpacking Swimming - Philbrook Lake Only	Recreation Permits and Fees are Required at Paradise Lake

BUCKS, SILVER AND SNAKE LAKES

The Bucks Lake Recreation Area in the Plumas National Forest is rich in wildlife and offers an abundance of outdoor recreation. Bucks Lake, at 5,153 feet elevation, has a surface area of 1,827 acres. There are facilities for all types of boating. Silver Lake, at 5,800 feet, offers excellent trout fishing. There is also good stream fishing. The newly created Bucks Lake Wilderness Area of 21,000 acres and the Pacific Crest Trail invite the hiker, horseback rider and backpacker to this area of gently rolling terrain, glaciated granite, forested meadows and perennial streams. Snake Lake is normally closed to boating and fishing during summer months due to a plant called Water Shield which covers the Lake.

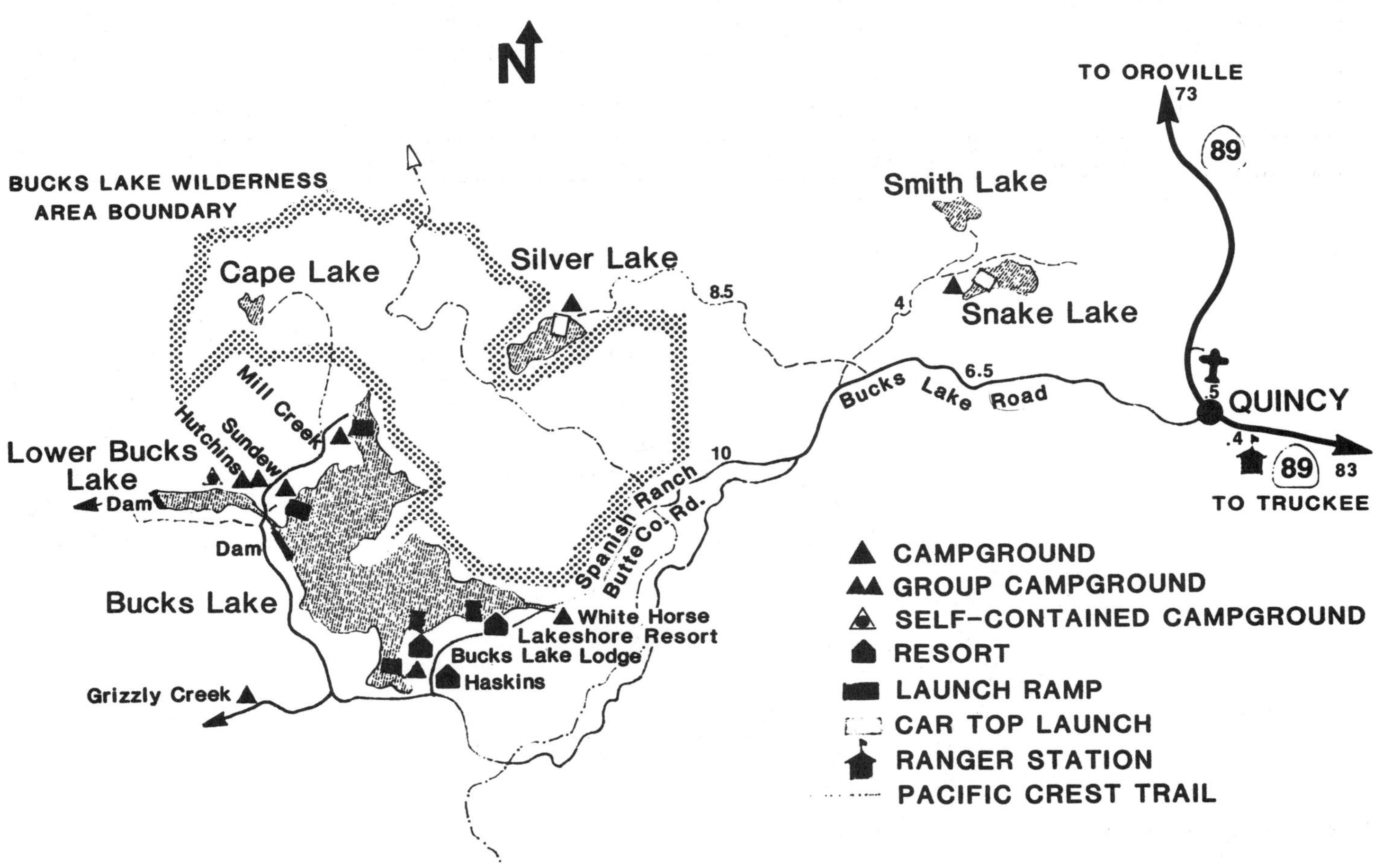

INFORMATION: Plumas National Forest, 875 Mitchell, Oroville 95965, Ph: 916-534-6500

CAMPING	BOATING	RECREATION	OTHER
U. S. F. S. 62 Dev. Sites for Tents & R.V.s to 22 feet - Fee: $5 P. G. & E. 65 Dev. Sites for Tents & R.V.s Group Camp to 25 People Maximum Reservations: Ph: 916-534-6500	Bucks Lake: Open to All Boats Full Service Marina Rental Fishing Boats Snake & Silver Lakes: Rowboats & Canoes Only No Motors Hand Launch	Fishing: Rainbow, German Brown & Brook Trout, Kokanee Salmon Swimming & Ski Beaches Hiking & Picnicking Backpacking-Parking Horseback Riding Trails & Rentals Hunting: Deer, Bear, Rabbits, Waterfowl	Lakeshore Resort P.O. Box 266 Quincy 95971 Ph: 916-283-2333 Bucks Lake Lodge P.O. Box 236 Quincy 95971 Ph: 916-283-2262 Cabins, General Stores, Restaurants Bars, Bait & Tackle Gas Stations

LAKE DAVIS

The Lake Davis Recreation Area is located in the Plumas National Forest. The Lake is at an elevation of 5,775 feet and has a total surface area of 4,026 acres. The Forest Service maintains three nice campgrounds on the eastern shore of the lake as well as launch ramps around the 32 miles of tree-covered shoreline. Steady winds make this an ideal lake for sailing although these winds can be a hazzard for small craft. Lake Davis is open to all types of boating, but water skiing is not permitted. There is a good warm water fishery along with an abundant population of both native and stocked trout. Relics of Basque sheepherders can be found in this area.

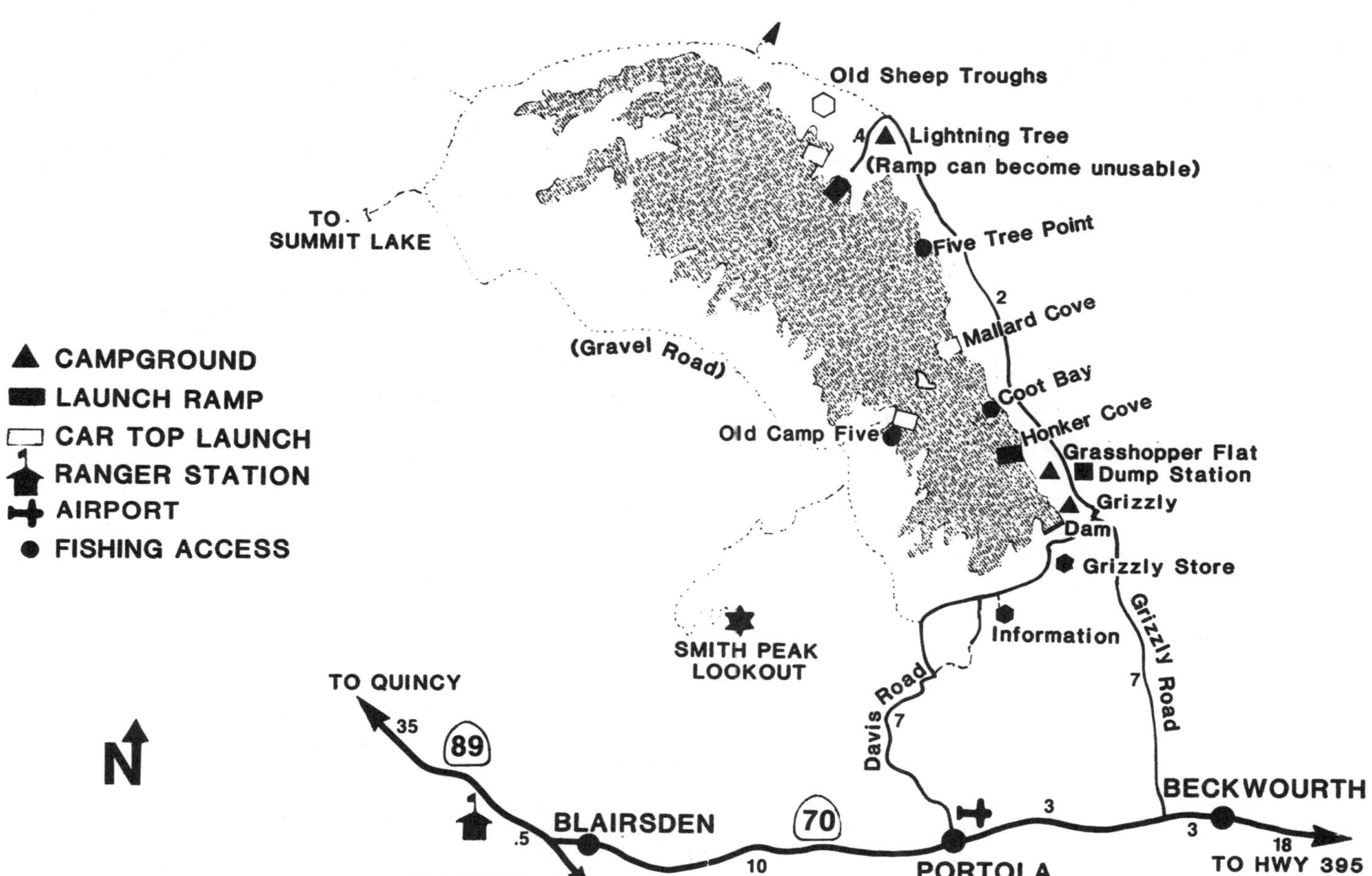

INFORMATION: Beckwourth Ranger Dist., Box 7, Blairsden 96103, Ph: 916-836-2575			
CAMPING	BOATING	RECREATION	OTHER
125 Dev. Sites for Tents & R.V.s Fee: $8 56 Sites for Self-Contained R.V.s Only No Fee Disposal Station Fee: $2	Power, Row, Canoe, Sail, Windsurf & Inflatable No Waterskiing Launch Ramps Cartop Boat Launch Areas Rentals: Fishing Boats at Grizzly Store	Fishing: Rainbow, Brown, Eagle Lake & Kamloop Trout, Bass & Catfish Swimming Picnicking Hiking Backpacking-Parking Hunting: Deer, Waterfowl, Upland Game Birds	Grizzly Store & Camp P.O. Box 203 Portola 96122 Ph: 916-832-0270 26 Dev. Sites for Tents & R.V.s Grocery Store Bait & Tackle Boat Rentals Airport & Full Facilities at Portola

FRENCHMAN LAKE

The Frenchman Reservoir Recreation Area offers a variety of recreational opportunities from waterskiing to ice fishing in the winter. Frenchman Lake, at an elevation of 5,888 feet, is within the Plumas National Forest. The 1,580 surface acres are surrounded by 21 miles of open sage and pine dotted shoreline. There are five campgrounds managed by concession permit from the Forest Service. Two handicapped sites are offered at the Big Cove Campground. There are also 24 picnic sites and six fishing access points around the lake. All types of boating are permitted as well as a water ski area. Fishing is often productive for a variety of trout including the large Eagle Lake Trout. This is a prime hunting area for the Rocky Mountain Mule Deer, but it must be done beyond the boundaries of the Recreation Area and the the Game Refuge.

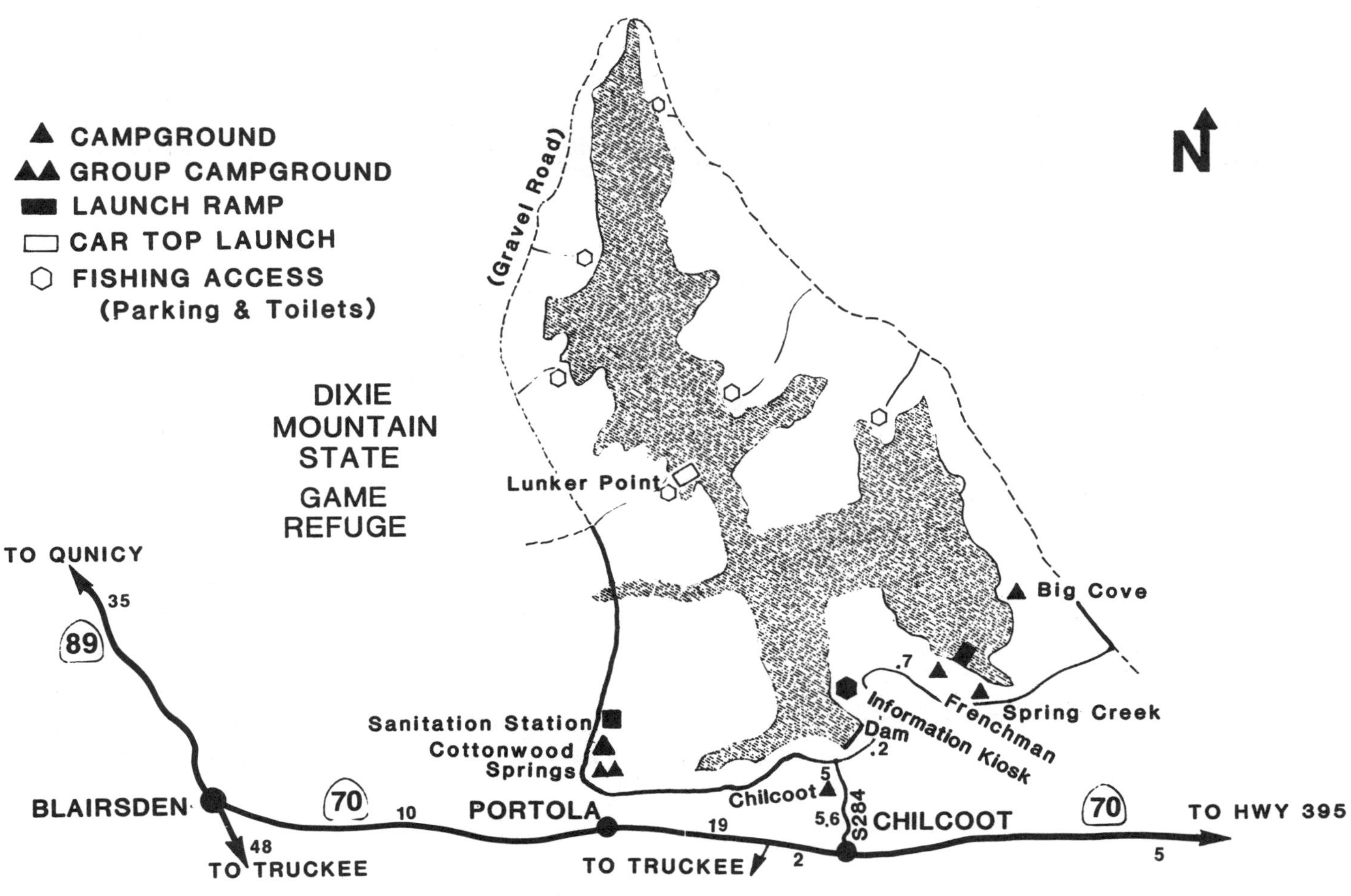

INFORMATION: Laufman Ranger Station, Milford 96121, Ph: 916:253-2223			
CAMPING	**BOATING**	**RECREATION**	**OTHER**
185 Dev. Sites for Tents & R.V.s up to 35 feet Fee: $8 24 Picnic Sites Group Campgrounds By Reservation Call MISTIX: 1-800-283-CAMP 1-25 People: $50 26-35 People: $70 36-50 People: $100	Power, Row, Canoe, Sail, Waterski, Jet Skis, Windsurf, Inflatables Launch Ramp	Fishing: Brown, Eastern Brook & Eagle Lake Trout, Channel Catfish Swimming Picnicking Hiking Backpacking-Parking Hunting: Deer, Waterfowl, Upland Game. No hunting on west side of Lake in Game Refuge	Full Facilities - 8 Miles at Chilcoot Off Road Vehicle Travel is Prohibited in Recreation Area

PLASKETT LAKE, LETTS LAKE AND EAST PARK RESERVOIR

Plaskett Lake at an elevation of 6,000 feet, and Letts Lake at 4,500 feet, are in contrast to the more primitive East Park Reservoir. East Park is a low, warm water fishery known for good bass fishing. It is open to all types of boating with limited facilities. Plaskett and Letts are remote trout Lakes with boating restricted to no motors. The Forest Service maintains good facilities in a mixed coniferous environment. Hikers and backpackers have found Letts Lake a popular attraction with Snow Mountain Wilderness and Summit Springs Trailhead nearby. Trailers over 16 feet are not advised at Plaskett and Letts Lakes due to poor access roads.

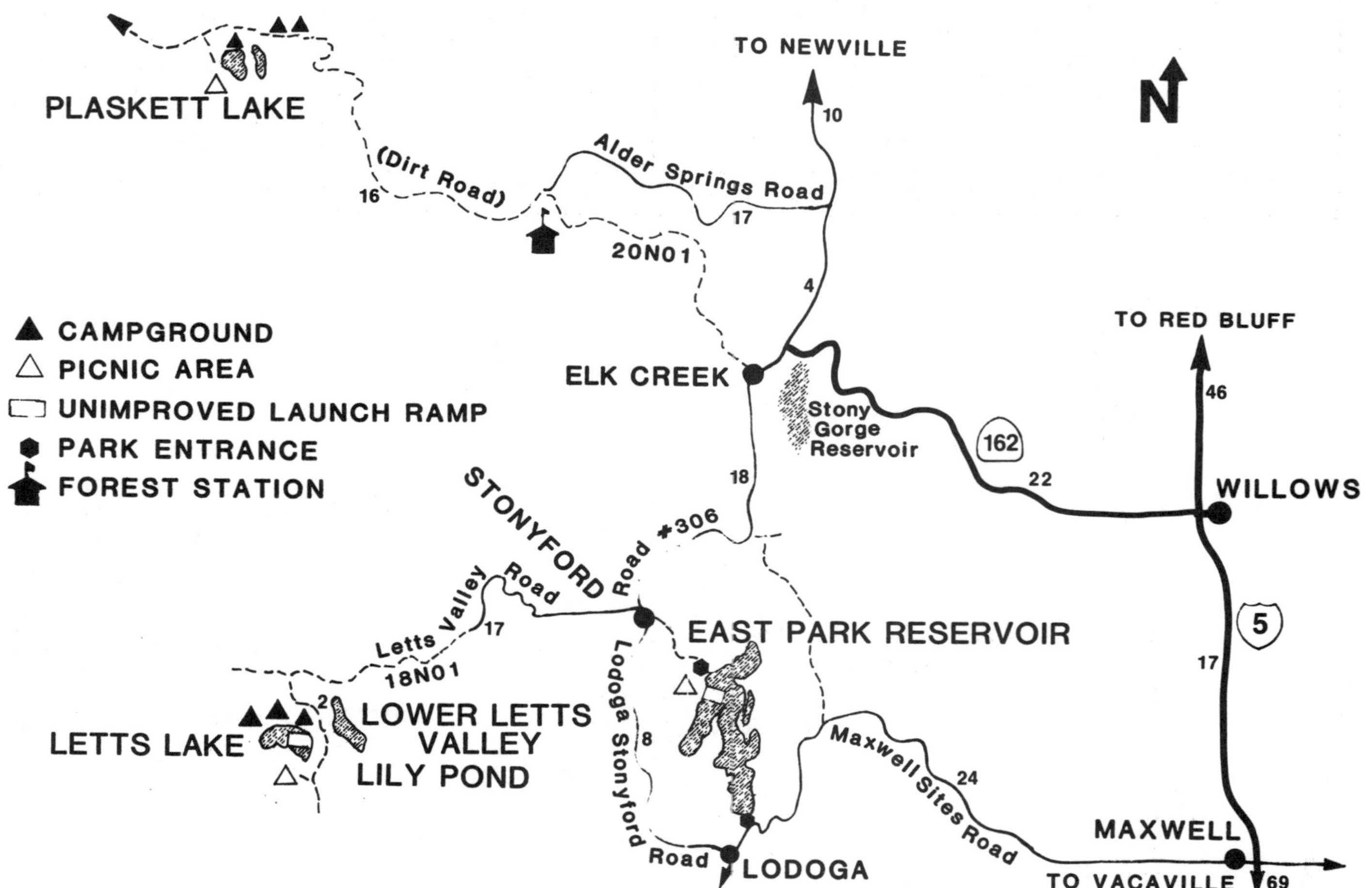

INFORMATION: Stonyford Ranger District, Star Rt., Box 12, Stonyford 95979, Ph: 916-963-3128			
CAMPING	BOATING	RECREATION	OTHER
Letts Lake: 40 Sites, Fee: $5 Plaskett Meadows Camp - 32 Sites Fee: $4 Masterson - 20 Sites Fee: $5 Group Site by Reservation - $15 East Park: Open Primitive Camping Around Most of Lake	Letts & Plaskett: No Motors - Gas or Electric East Park Reservoir: Open to All Boats Subject to Low Water Hazards Unimproved Ramp Boating Laws Strictly Enforced Ordinance Against Parasailing at East Park	Fishing: Plaskett: Trout Letts: Trout, Bass, Catfish East Park: Black & Spotted Bass, Bluegill, Crappie, Catfish, Perch Swimming Hiking/Nature Trails Letts & Plaskett: Hunting - Deer, Bear, Squirrel	Facilities Limited to Nearby Towns East Park: No Hunting No Firearms No ORV's

BLACK BUTTE LAKE

Black Butte is surrounded by rolling hills with basalt buttes and open grassland spotted with oak trees. It rests at an elevation of 470 feet. This 4,500 surface-acre Lake has a shoreline of 40 miles. The U. S. Army Corps of Engineers administers the well-maintained campgrounds and facilities at the Lake. Water level can change rapidly, and boaters are cautioned of possible hazards, such as sand bars, exposed during low water. This is a good warm water fishery especially in the the spring when the crappie are hungry. There is abundant wildlife, and the bird watcher will find a wide variety of avian life.

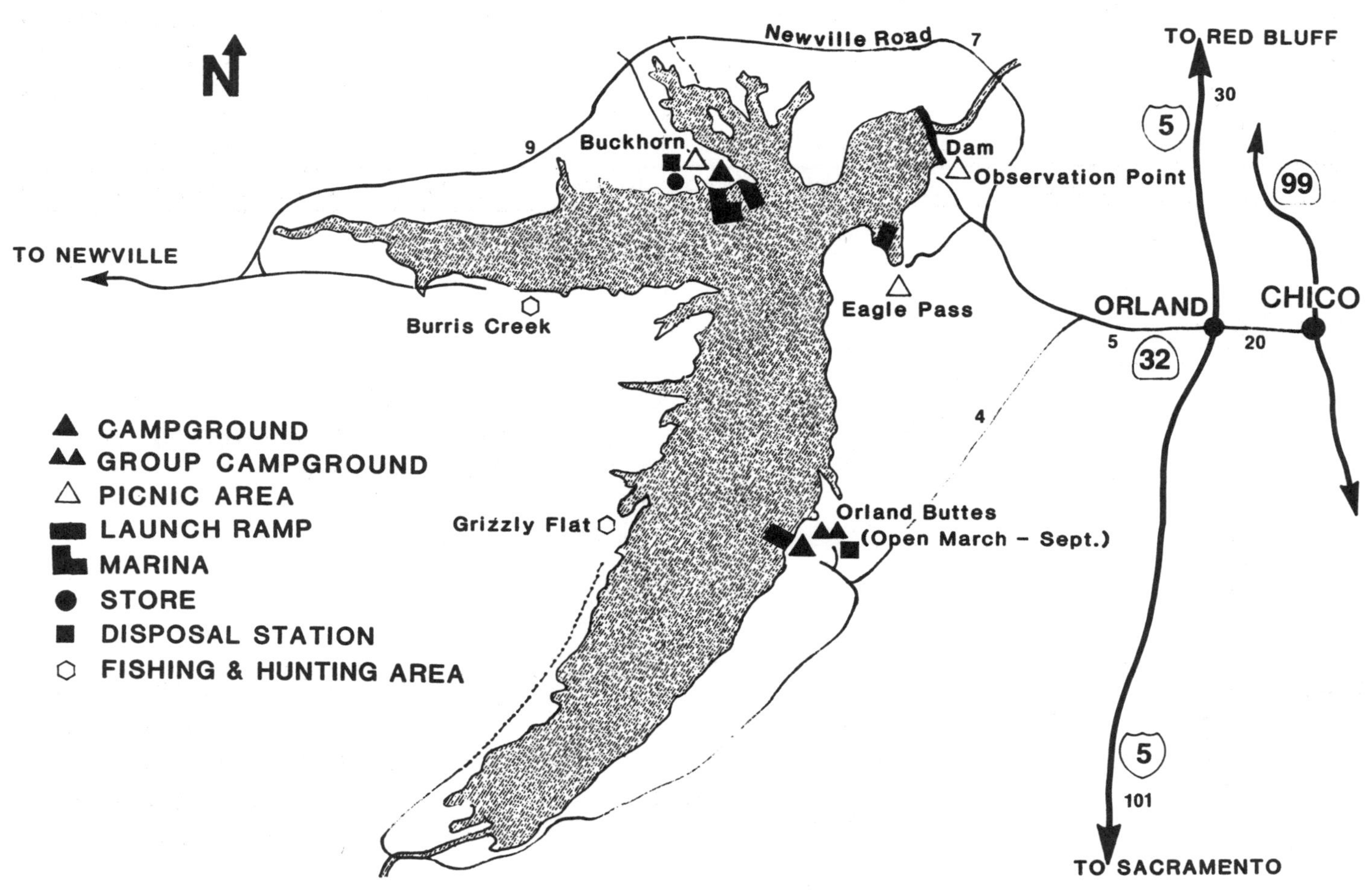

INFORMATION: Park Manager, Star Route, Box 30, Orland 95963, Ph: 916-865-4781

CAMPING	BOATING	RECREATION	OTHER
Buckhorn: 65 Dev. Sites for Tents & R.V.s - Fee: $8 20 Undeveloped Sites - Free Orland Buttes: 35 Dev. Sites for Tents & R.V.s - Fee: $8 Group Camp to 150 People - Fee: $35 Reserve for Groups Only. Open March through September. 14 Day Camping Limit	Power, Row, Canoe, Sail, Waterski, Jet Skis, Windsurf, Inflatables Full Service Marina Ph: 916-865-2665 Launch Ramps Rentals: Fishing Boats & Paddle Boats Docks, Berths, Storage, Gas Black Butte Marina Star Rt. Box 31 Orland 95963	Fishing: Large & Smallmouth Bass, Striped Bass, Channel Catfish, Crappie, Bluegill & Green Sunfish Swimming & Hiking Picnicking & Playground Campfire Programs Hunting: Deer, Dove, Quail, Pheasant, Waterfowl (Shotgun & Archery Only)	Snack Bar Grocery Store Bait & Tackle Hot Showers Disposal Station 100-Acre Motorcycle Park - Open June through February Full Facilities - 8 Miles at Orland

STONY GORGE RESERVOIR

Stony Gorge Reservoir is at an elevation of 800 feet in the foothills west of Willows in the upper Sacramento Valley. The Lake has a surface area of 1,275 acres and is under the administration of the U. S. Forest Service. The rolling hills surrounding the 25 miles of shoreline are dotted with oak, digger pine and brush. Although there are a number of campsites, they are relatively primitive. Boating facilities are limited to a paved launch ramp which is unusable during late summer and fall. The fishing is good for warm water species in this pretty Lake, and for those who enjoy a natural setting, Stony Gorge will prove a pleasant retreat.

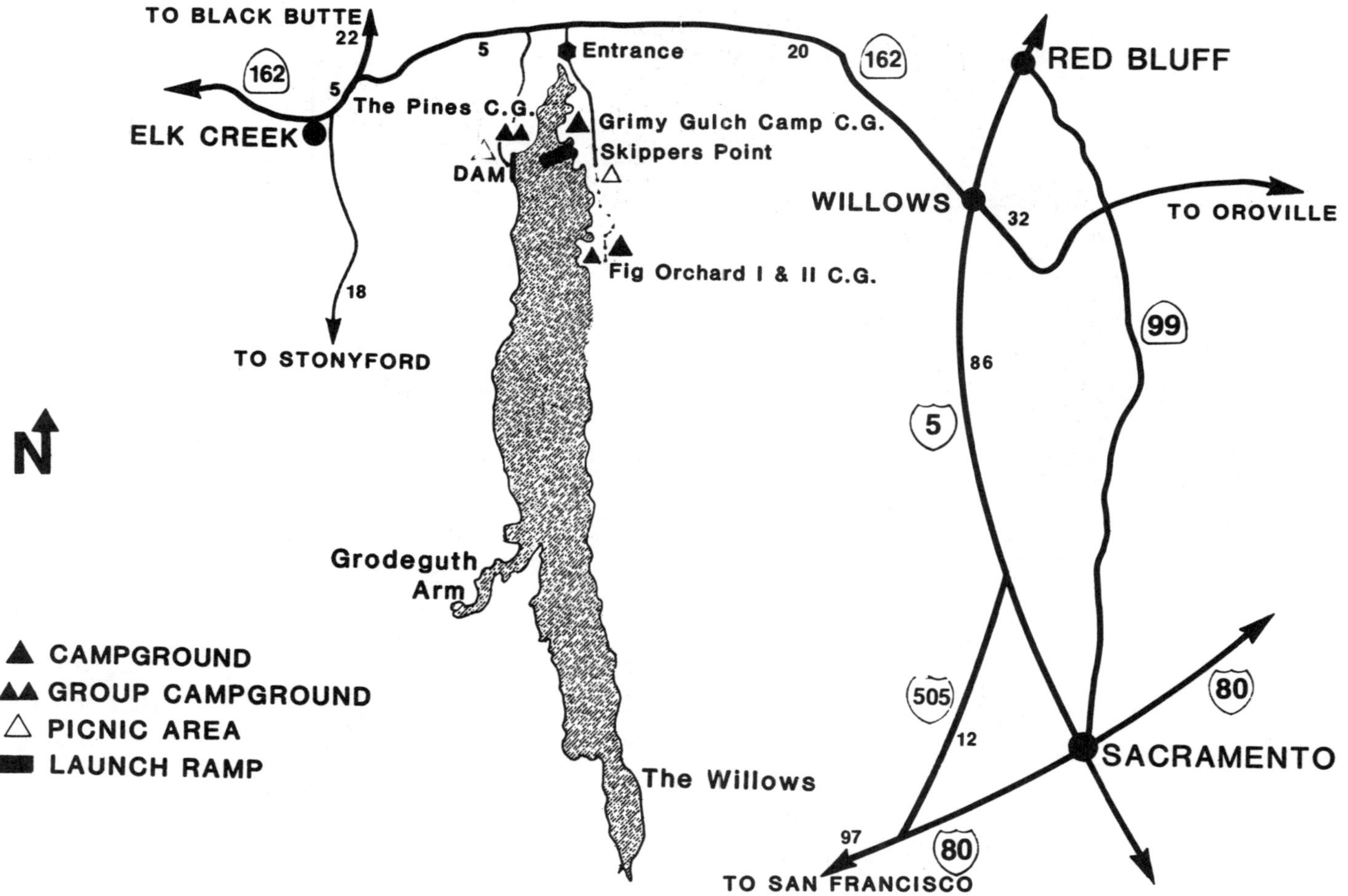

INFORMATION: Stonyford Ranger District, Star Rt., Box 12, Stonyford 95979, Ph: 916-963-3128			
CAMPING	BOATING	RECREATION	OTHER
150 Primitive Sites for Tents & R.V.s Group Camp or Day Use - 200 People Maximum Reservations Only Ph: 916-963-3128 No Fees No Drinking Water	Power, Row, Canoe, Sail, Waterski, Windsurf & Inflatables No Houseboats Permitted Launch Ramp Underwater Hazards Due to Fluctuation in Lake Level	Fishing: Catfish, Bluegill, Crappie, Bass & Perch Swimming Picnicking - 200 People Group site No ORV's and No Hunting	Country Store Gas Station Full Facilities in Elk Creek or Willows

BOATING

Boating is a popular activity at our California Lakes. Many of these lakes permit boating of all types from sailboats to jet skis. All are subject to specific rules and regulations which vary from lake to lake.

The type of boating permitted varies at each lake. Although RECREATION LAKES OF CALIFORNIA lists what type of boats are allowed, it is always wise to check for regulations by calling the information number to confirm your particular boat can be launched. Don't be disappointed by arriving at your destination only to find you cannot enjoy your boat.

Before launching a boat, check the local laws. The speed limit is specific at each lake. There are also speed limits in certain areas such as near swimmers, docks or congested areas. There are often restricted areas or specific areas for waterskiing, sailing or fishing. The local ranger or manager will usually give you a copy of the rules and regulations.

For California State Boating Regulations, see the Department of Motor Vehicle's booklet, "ABC's of California Boating Laws." This booklet may be obtained at your DMV Office.

LAKE OROVILLE

Oroville Dam is the highest dam in the United States towering 770 feet above the City of Oroville. Lake Oroville, at 900 feet elevation, has 15,500 surface acres with a shoreline of 167 miles. Although water levels drop late in the summer, the Lake offers unlimited recreation the year around. This is an excellent boating Lake with good marina facilities. There are numerous boat-in campsites and houseboat moorings for those who wish to spend the night on the Lake. The angler will find an extensive variety of game fish from Smallmouth bass to King salmon. Thermalito Forebay has 300 surface acres for boating, fishing and swimming.

. . . Continued . . .

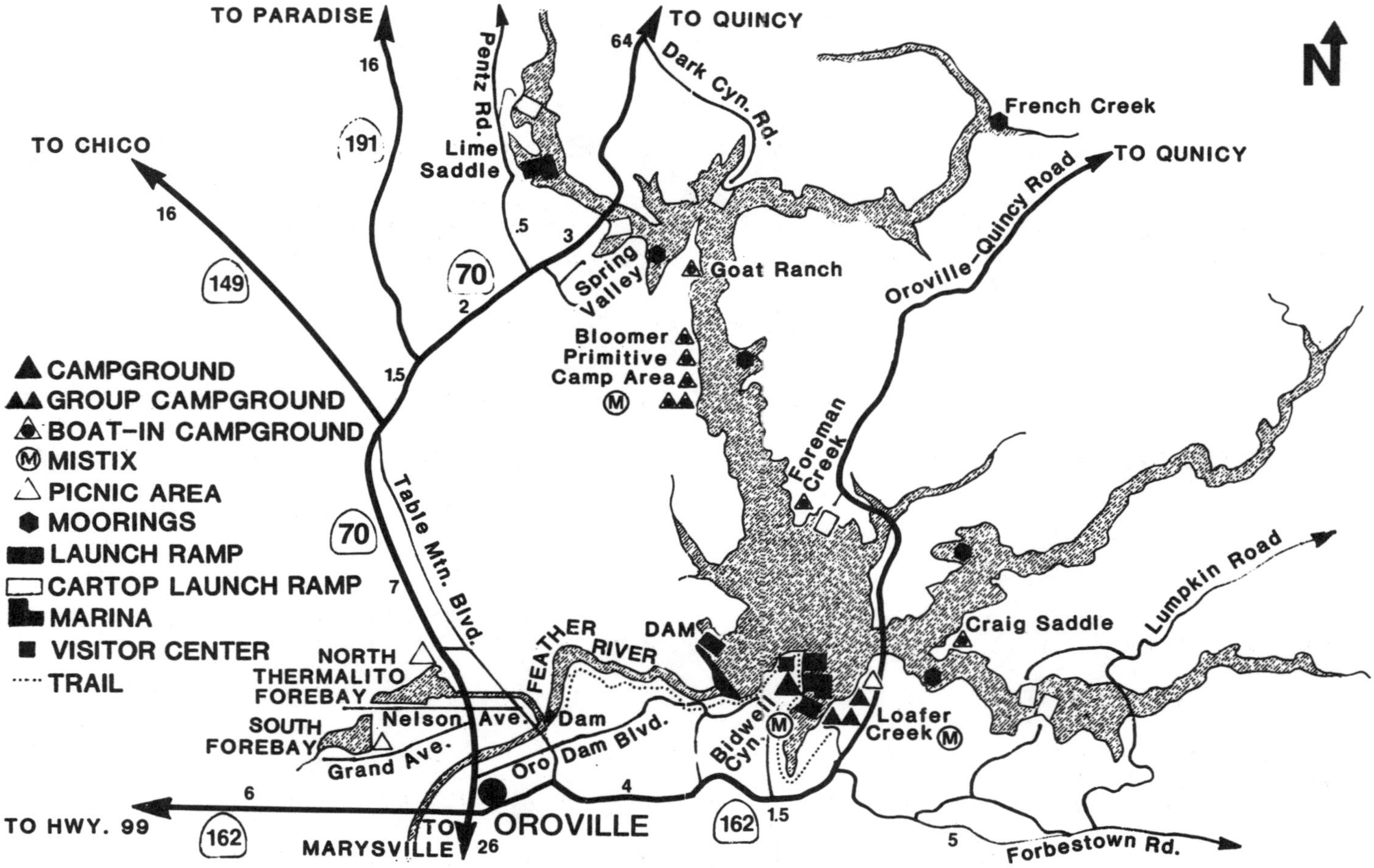

TO PARADISE
16
Pentz Rd.
TO QUINCY
64
Dark Cyn. Rd.
N
French Creek
TO CHICO
191
Lime Saddle
TO QUNICY
Oroville-Quincy Road
16
.5
3
70
Spring Valley
Goat Ranch
149
2
Bloomer
Primitive
Camp Area
1.5
CAMPGROUND
GROUP CAMPGROUND
BOAT-IN CAMPGROUND
MISTIX
PICNIC AREA
MOORINGS
LAUNCH RAMP
CARTOP LAUNCH RAMP
MARINA
VISITOR CENTER
TRAIL
Table Mtn. Blvd.
70
Foreman Creek
Lumpkin Road
7
FEATHER RIVER
DAM
Craig Saddle
NORTH THERMALITO FOREBAY
SOUTH FOREBAY
Nelson Ave.
Dam
Grand Ave.
Oro Dam Blvd.
Bidwell Cyn.
Loafer Creek
6
4
TO HWY. 99
162
TO MARYSVILLE
26
OROVILLE
162
1.5
5
Forbestown Rd.

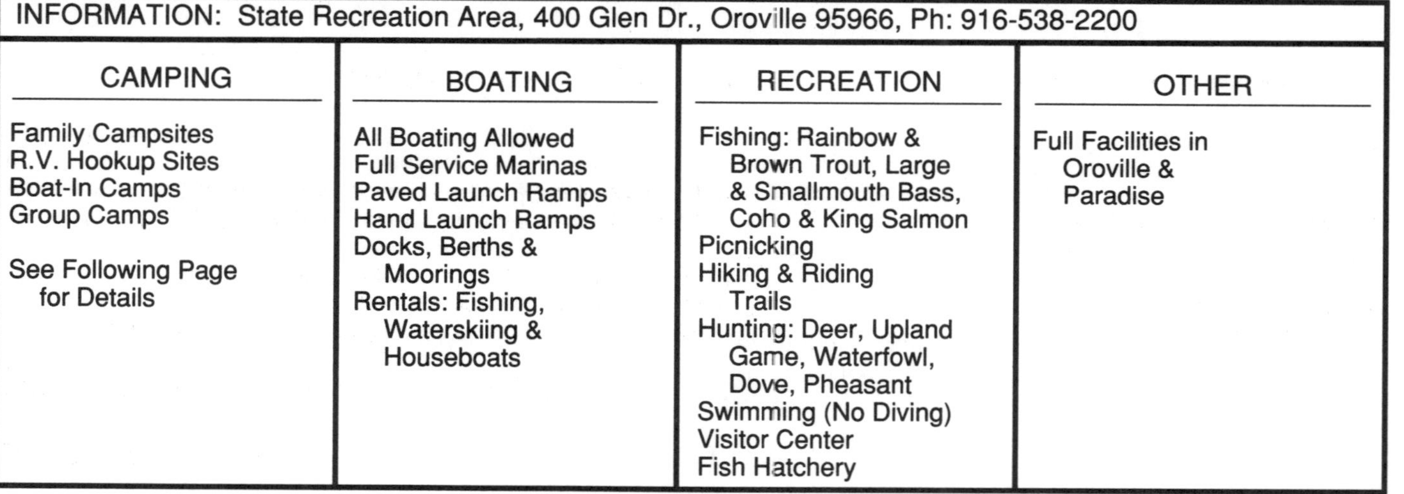

INFORMATION: State Recreation Area, 400 Glen Dr., Oroville 95966, Ph: 916-538-2200			
CAMPING	BOATING	RECREATION	OTHER
Family Campsites R.V. Hookup Sites Boat-In Camps Group Camps See Following Page for Details	All Boating Allowed Full Service Marinas Paved Launch Ramps Hand Launch Ramps Docks, Berths & Moorings Rentals: Fishing, Waterskiing & Houseboats	Fishing: Rainbow & Brown Trout, Large & Smallmouth Bass, Coho & King Salmon Picnicking Hiking & Riding Trails Hunting: Deer, Upland Game, Waterfowl, Dove, Pheasant Swimming (No Diving) Visitor Center Fish Hatchery	Full Facilities in Oroville & Paradise

LAKE OROVILLE

CAMPING FACILITIES: Reservations Through Mistix - California State Parks - Ph: 800-444-7275

LOAFER CREEK: 137 Sites for Tents & R.V.s to 31 feet. Fee: $10. Water, Flush Toilets, Showers, Laundry Tubs, Disposal Station, 100 Picnic Sites, Swim Beach, Launch Ramp.Group Camps: 6 Well-Developed Group Camps Each Accommodating 25 People. Fee: $37.50.

BIDWELL CANYON: 75 R.V. Sites with Full Hookups, Fee: $16 Launch Ramp, Full Service Marina, Boat Rentals, Grocery Store, Laundry Tubs, Snack Bar, Disposal Station. Ph: 916-589-3165

BOAT-IN CAMPS:

109 sites at: Craig Saddle, Sycamore Creek, Foreman Point, Goat Ranch, Primitive Area - North Point, Knoll, South Cove, Bloomer. Fee: $6

Group Camp for 75 People Located at South Bloomer - Tables, Toilets, No Drinking Water. Reservations Accepted for Group Site Through Park Headquarters.

LIME SADDLE MARINA, P.O. Box 1088, Paradise 95969, Ph: 916-877-2414

Full Service Marina, 5-Lane Launch Ramp, Gas, Boat Shop, OMC-Johnson Sales/Serv. Rentals: Houseboats, Ski Boats, Fishing & Pontoon Boats, Patio Boats Overnight Moorings, Docks, Covered & Open Slips, Water Ski Sales and Rentals, Marine Supplies, Grocery Store, Delicatessen, Bait & Tackle, Propane.

BIDWELL CANYON MARINA, 801 Bidwell Canyon Road, Oroville 95965, Ph: 916-589-3165 or 916-589-3152
Full Service Marina, Seven-Lane Launch Ramp, Gas
Rentals: Fishing, Patio, Houseboats, Water Ski Sales, Overnight Moorings, Docks, Covered & Open Slips, Dry Storage, Gift Shop, Grocery Store, Bait & Tackle Shop, Pumpout Station and Ice

PAVED LAUNCH RAMPS ALSO LOCATED AT:

SPILLWAY: 13-Lane Launch Ramp, Parking, Chemical Toilets, Overnight Camping for Self-Contained R.V.s

ENTERPRISE: Free Paved 2-Lane Launch Ramp, Cartop Launch During Low Water.

THERMALITO FOREBAY

The North End of the Forebay is for Day Use. There are 300 Surface Acres. Facilities include a 2-lane launch ramp, sandy swim beach, picnic tables, shade ramadas, potable water and many lovely trees. This area is for sailboats and other non-power boats only. The group area is by reservation at Park Headquarters.

The South End of the Forebay has a 4-lane launch ramp and is for power boats and fishing boats only. There is no shade or potable water.

LITTLE GRASS VALLEY LAKE, SLY CREEK AND LOST CREEK RESERVOIRS

Little Grass Valley, at 5,040 feet elevation, and Sly Creek, at 3,560 feet elevation, are pretty lakes in the Plumas National Forest. Little Grass Valley which has a surface area of 1,615 acres is a good boating lake. There is an abundance of developed campsites in this forested area. Sly Creek Reservoir has 562 surface acres with facilities for boating and camping. Its neighbor, Lost Creek Reservoir, is surrounded by private land except for a small portion of Forest Service land on the north side which is relatively unusable due to the steep slopes.

INFORMATION: Challenge Ranger Station, Drawer 369, Challenge 95925, Ph: 916-675-2462			
CAMPING	**BOATING**	**RECREATION**	**OTHER**
Little Grass Valley: 290 Dev. Sites 40 Ft. Max. Length Reservations for Red Feather Through Mistix 1-800-283-CAMP 2 Disposal Stations Sly Creek: 33 Dev. Sites for Tents Tents & R.V.s	Little Grass Valley: Open to Small Boats 3 Paved Launch Ramps Sly Creek: Open to Small Boats 1 Paved Launch Ramp 1 Cartop Launch Ramp	Fishing: Rainbow, Brook & Brown Trout Swimming Picnicking Hiking & Riding Backpacking Nature Study Goldpanning Hunting: Waterfowl Upland Game & Deer	Facilities: 3-1/2 Miles at La Porte Abandoned Mining Towns Nearby Access to: Pacific Crest Trail Feather Falls Trail One of the Highest Falls in the U.S. Middle Fork of the Feather River - A Wild & Scenic River

GOLD LAKE AND THE LAKES BASIN RECREATION AREA

More than 30 natural lakes bless this area of scenic abundance. Gold Lake is the largest of these lakes which range in elevation from 5,000 to 6,000 feet. While several of the lakes can be reached by car, many can only be reached by trail. The angler will find good trout fishing in both lake and stream. This is a popular fly fishing area especially along the Middle Fork of the Feather River which has been designated a natural Wild and Scenic River. The Lakes Basin is in both the Plumas and Tahoe National Forests. The hiker and packer will find numerous trails leading to the Pacific Crest Trail. Although this area remains relatively unspoiled, there are a number of resorts and facilities that complement the natural setting of this beautiful country.

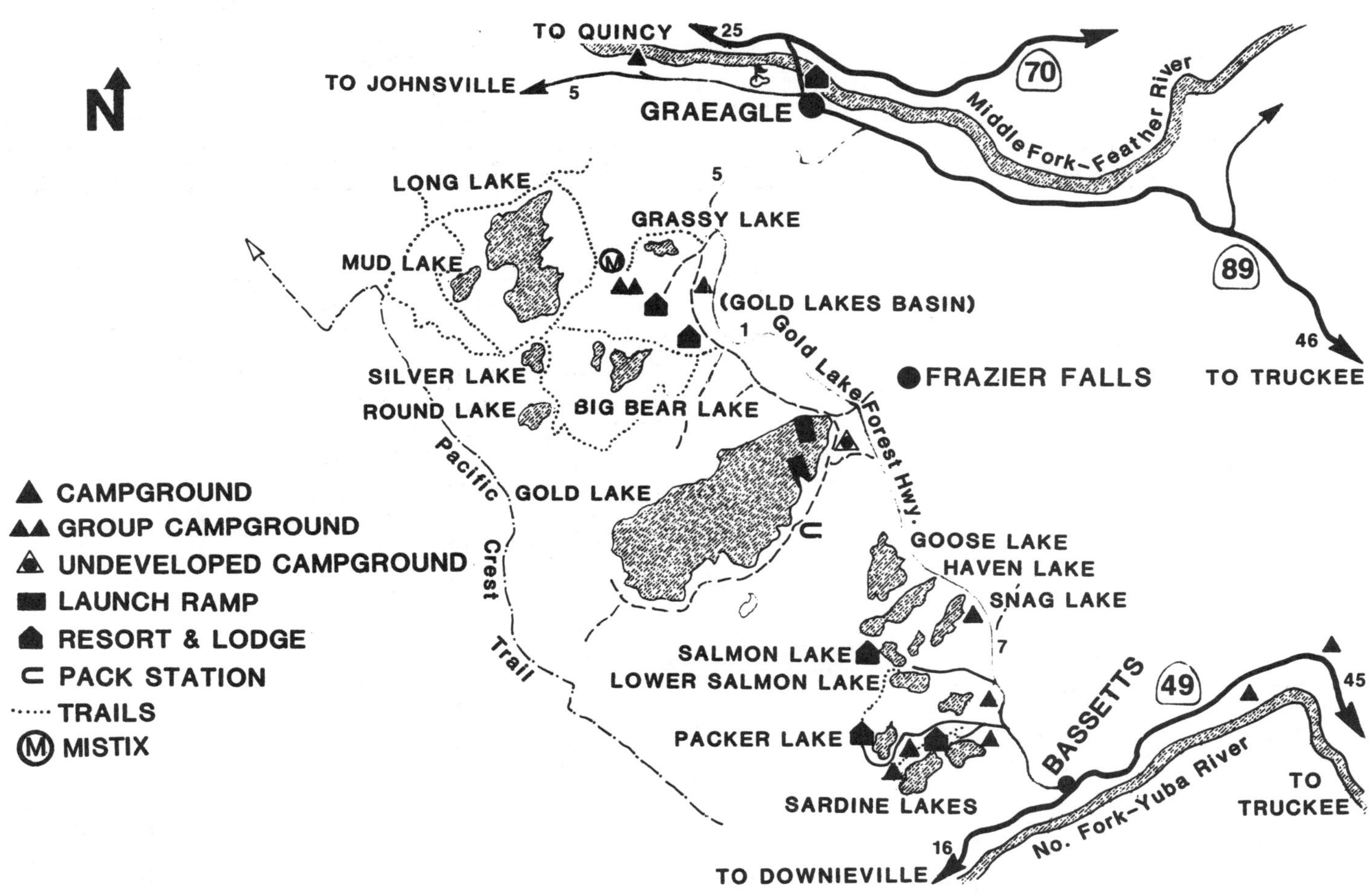

INFORMATION: Mohawk Ranger Station, P.O. Box 7, Blairsden 96103, Ph: 916-836-2575

CAMPING	BOATING	RECREATION	OTHER
Many Forest Service Campgrounds in Area Fee: $6 Lakes in North Area: Mohawk Ranger Station See Information Above Lakes in South Area: Downieville Ranger Dist. Ph: 916-288-3231 Group Camp to 25 People by Reservation Fee: $25 MISTIX Ph: 1-800-283-CAMP	Power, Row, Sail, Windsurfing & Waterskiing (Gold Lake) Launch Ramp at Gold Lake	Fishing: Rainbow, Brown & Brook Trout Mackinaw at Gold Lake Picnicking Hiking & Riding Trails Backpacking Horse Rentals & Pack Station Swimming Hunting: Deer Golf	Numerous Facilities & Resorts in this Area Contact: Plumas County Chamber of Commerce P.O. Box 11018 Quincy 95971 Ph: 916-283-6345

BULLARDS BAR RESERVOIR

Bullards Bar Reservoir is at an elevation of 2,000 feet in the Tahoe and Plumas National Forests surrounded by rugged countryside. This beautiful large lake of 4,700 surface acres has 56 shoreline miles. The area is heavily wooded so all campsites are shaded by trees. All boating is allowed including waterskiing. Fishing is open year around for both warm and cold water fish. This is a prime lake for kokanee salmon. The Emerald Cove Marina is a full service facility offering houseboat and fishing boat rentals, private houseboat moorings, boat access camps, lakeside camping and an unimproved area for R.V.s. Recent improvements by the Emerald Cove Resort & Marina make Bullards Bar Reservoir a good place to visit for a variety of outdoor recreation.

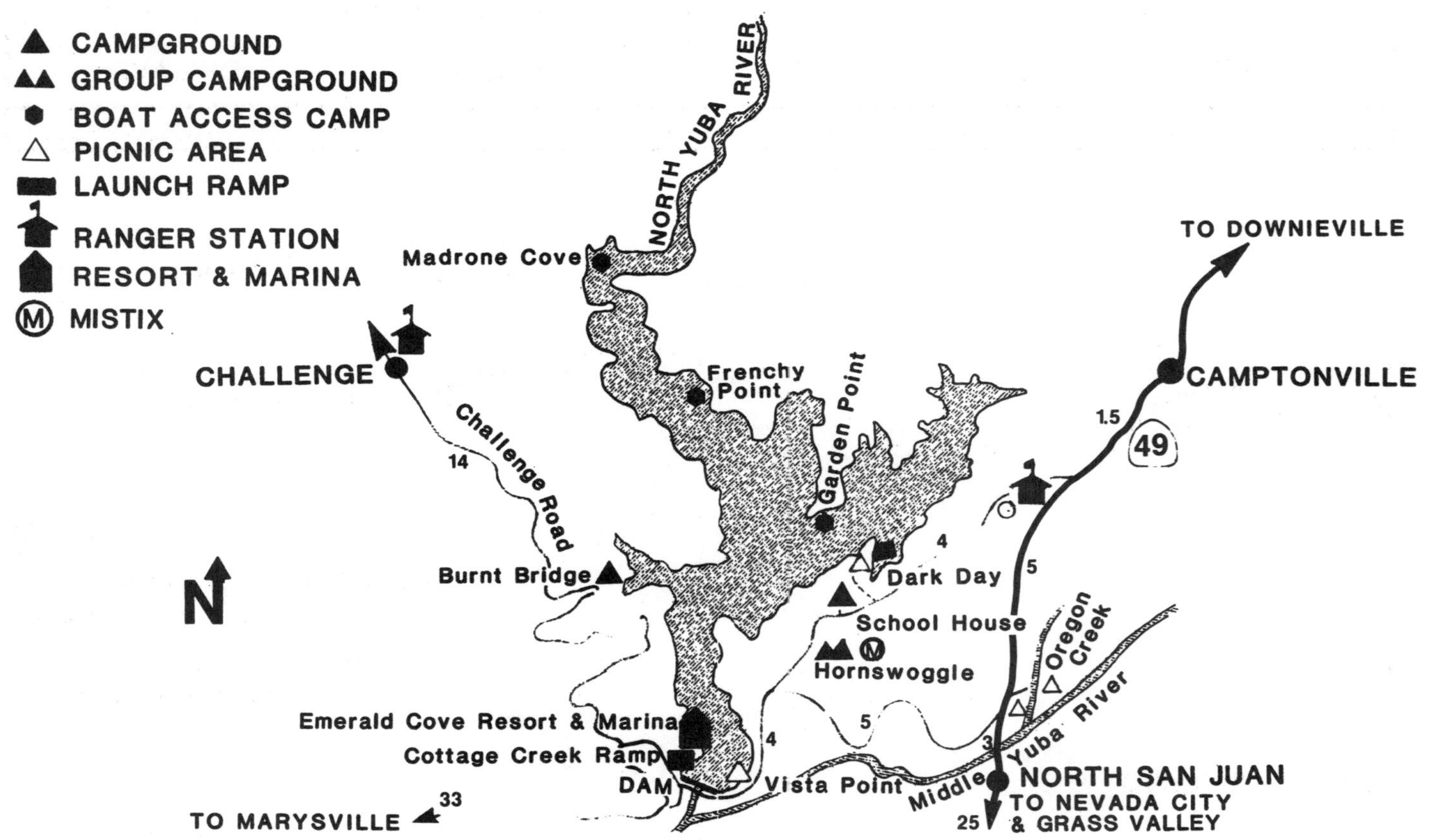

INFORMATION: Emerald Cove Resort & Marina, P.O. Box 180, Dobbins 95935, Ph: 916-692-2166			
CAMPING	BOATING	RECREATION	OTHER
Emerald Cove Resort: 39 Boat Access Camps Lakeside Camping Unimproved R.V. Sites Reservations Accepted U.S.F.S. N. Yuba Ranger Station Ph: 916-288-3231 School House: 67 Tent/R.V. Sites Fee: $6 Hornswoggle: Groups to 150 People Reservations	Open to All Boating Waterskiing Launch Ramps - No Fee Boat Access Camps Full Service Marina Gas and Propane Rentals: Fishing & Houseboats Private Houseboat Moorings	Fishing: Rainbow & Brown Trout, Bluegill, Catfish, Crappie, Large & Smallmouth Bass, Kokanee Salmon Swimming Picnicking Hiking Trails	Snack Bar Groceries Beer, Wine, Ice Bait & Tackle Floatel for Overnight Accommodations $49 a Day

BOWMAN LAKE

Bowman Lake is the largest of several small Lakes in the scenic Bowman Road Area of the Tahoe National Forest. Bowman is 6 miles south of Jackson Meadows Reservoir and 16 miles north of Highway 20. These are often steep and rocky roads; 4-wheel drive vehicles are advised. The Lakes range in altitude from 5,600 feet to 7,000 feet in this beautiful high Sierra country. The Forest Service maintains a number of campsites in this area, but be sure to bring your own drinking water as only Grouse Ridge has potable water. Stream and Lake fishing can be excellent in this rugged and remote but scenic environment.

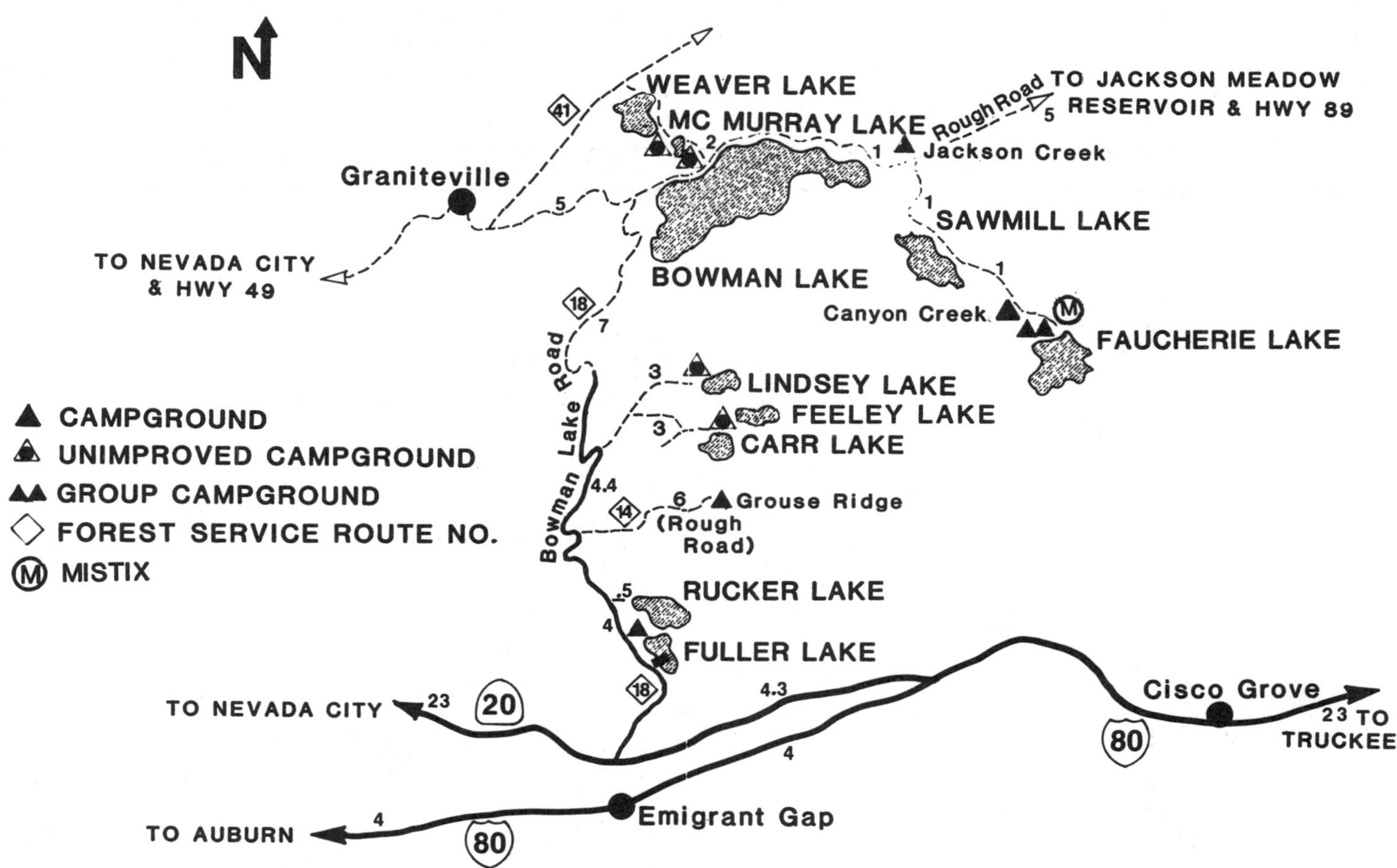

INFORMATION: USFS., Nevada City Ranger Dist., Hwy 49 & Coyote St., Nevada City 95959, Ph: 916-265-4531			
CAMPING	BOATING	RECREATION	OTHER
Primitive Camping No Fee Group Camp - 25 People Maximum Fee: $25 Reservations Required	Small Boats Only 10 MPH Speed Limit No Motors Allowed on Rucker Lake Cartop Launching	Fishing: Rainbow, Brook & Brown Trout Swimming Picnicking Hiking Backpacking Horseback Riding Nature Study Hunting: Deer	Full Facilities in Truckee or Along Highway 80 Rough Roads Not Recommended for Cars, Trailers or R.V.s

EAGLE, FORDYCE, STERLING, KIDD, CASCADE, LONG AND SERENE LAKES

These Lakes, off Interstate Highway 80 near Soda Springs, rest at elevations of about 7,000 feet in the Tahoe National Forest. This beautiful high Sierra country offers a variety of recreational opportunities. Boating is limited to non-powered craft with limited facilities, but you will find rentals at Serene Lakes. The serious angler will find trout and catfish. The numerous trails invite the hiker, backpacker and equestrian to get away from it all in this natural paradise. The roads into Eagle, Fordyce, and Sterling are not advised for any vehicles but 4-wheelers.

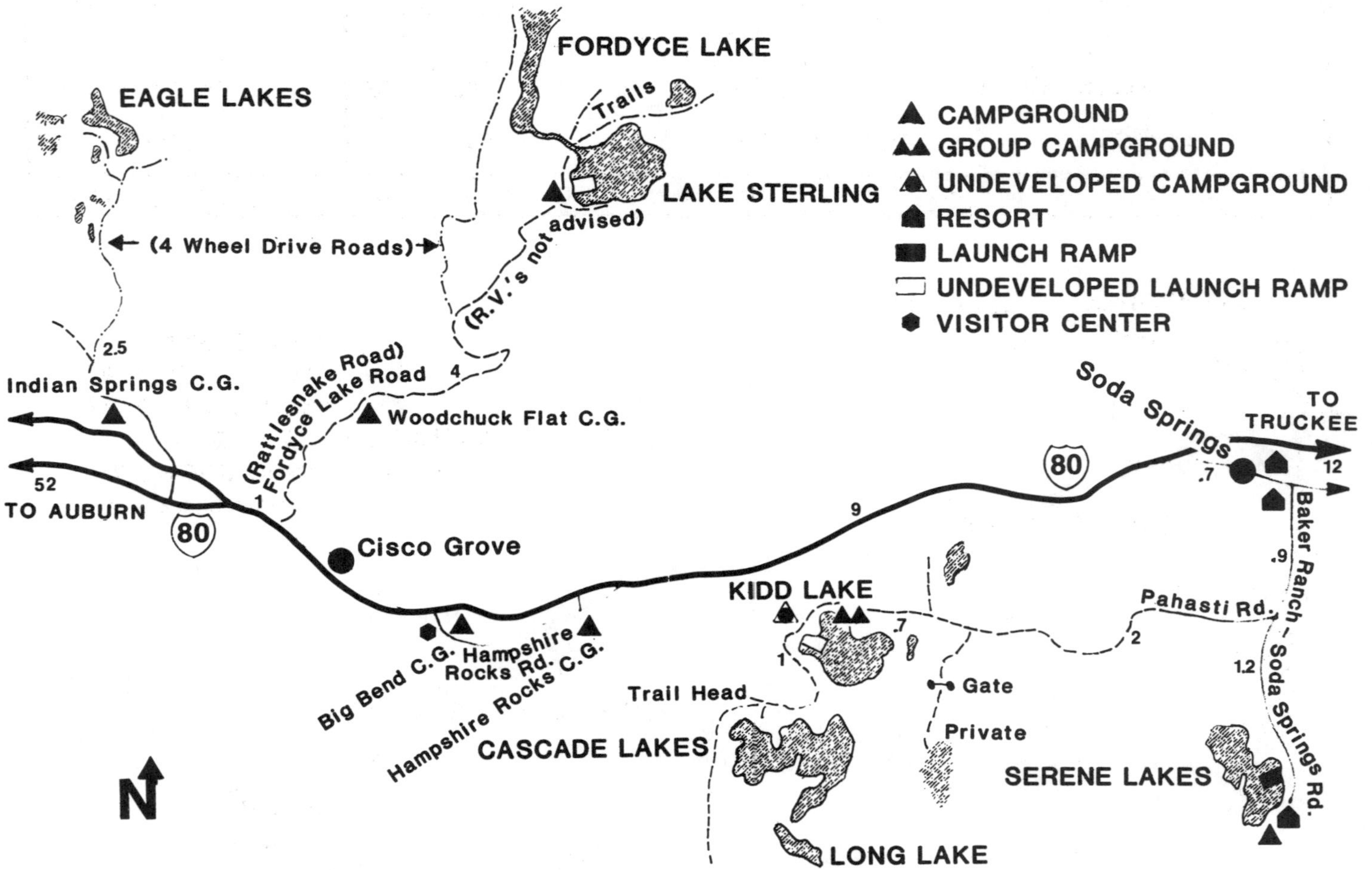

INFORMATION: Chamber of Commerce, P.O. Box 2757, Truckee 95734, Ph: 916-587-2757			
CAMPING	BOATING	RECREATION	OTHER
U. S. F. S. - Nevada City Ranger District Sites for Tents & R.V.s - Fee: $6 For Info: Ph: 916-265-4531 Kidd Lake: Groups to 100 -Reserve: P. G. & E. P.O. Box 340 Red Bluff 96080 Ph: 916-527-5880	Electric Motors Allowed at Sterling Lake No Motors at Other Lakes Rentals at Serene Lakes	Fishing: Trout & Catfish Swimming Picnicking Numerous Hiking & Riding Trails Horse Rentals Backpacking Nature Study Photography	Serene Lakes Campground: R.V. Hookups Fee: $7.50 Ph: 916-426-9001 Monthly Rentals Motel/Lodge Restaurant & Cocktail Lounge Bait & Tackle Gas Station

JACKSON MEADOW RECREATION AREA

The Jackson Meadow Recreation Area is at an elevation of 6,200 feet in the Tahoe National Forest. This area of forested slopes, alpine meadows, lakes and streams provides an abundance of recreational opportunities. Jackson Meadows Reservoir is the hub of this area with well maintained camping and recreational facilities dotting its 11 miles of shoreline. Nearby Milton Lake and the Middle Fork of the Yuba River between Jackson Meadow and Milton are subject to specific artificial lure, species and size limitations. Refer to the California Sport Fishing Regulations for details. The hiker, backpacker and equestrian will find a trailhead to the Pacific Crest Trail at Pass Creek Bridge.

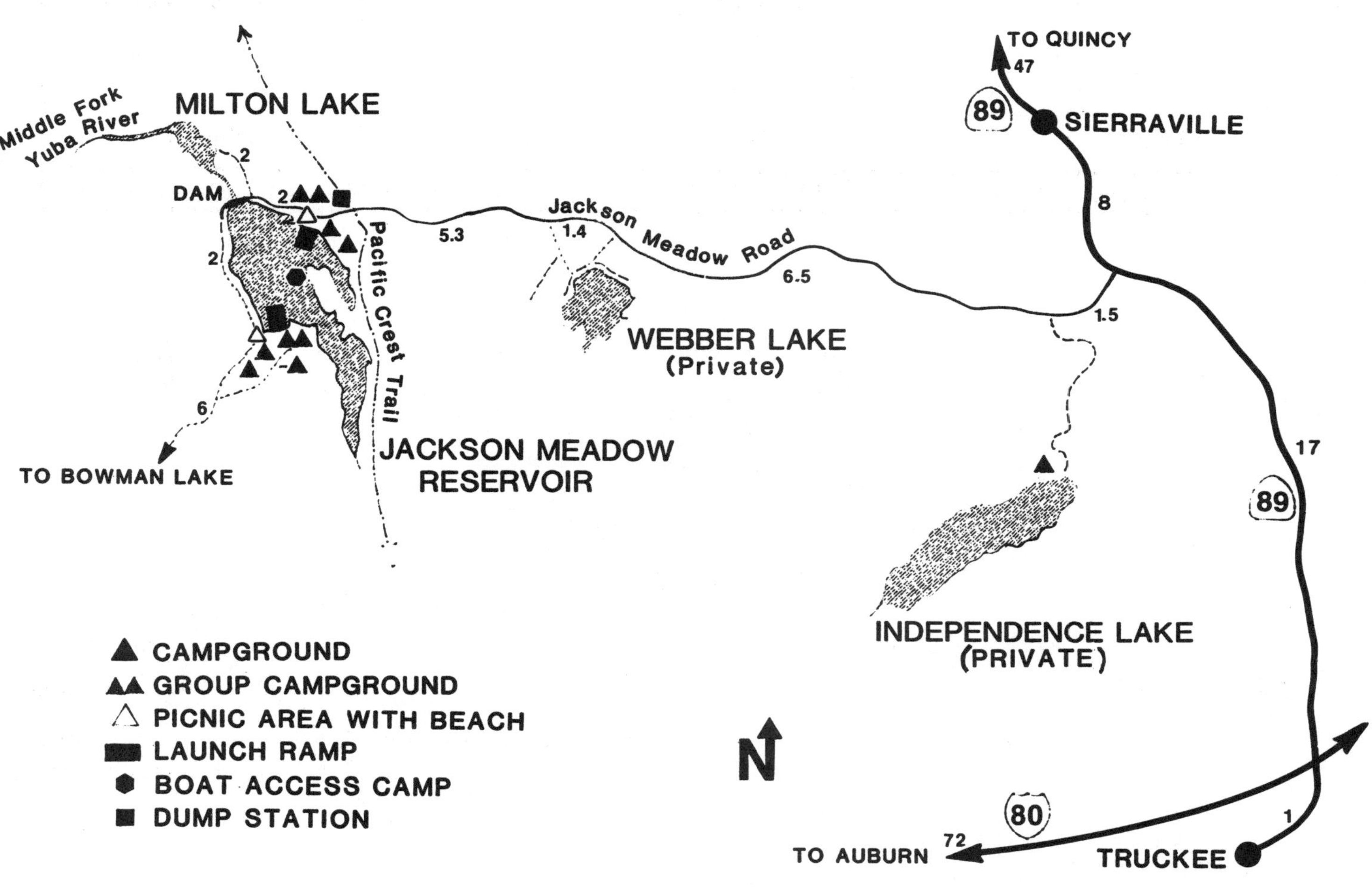

INFORMATION: Sierraville R.S., P.O. Box 95, Sierraville 96216, Ph: 916-994-3401

CAMPING	BOATING	RECREATION	OTHER
139 Dev. Sites for Tents & R.V.s Fee: $7 10 Boat Access Only Sites 5 Group Camps 4 Camps-25 People Maximum 1 Camp-50 People Maximum	Power, Row, Canoe, Sail, Waterski, Jet Ski, Windsurf & Inflatables Noise Level Laws Enforced 2 Launch Ramps	Fishing: Rainbow & Brown Trout 2 Swimming Beaches With Dressing Rooms Picnicking Backpacking-Parking Hiking, Horseback Riding & Nature Trails Hunting: Deer - Outside Recreation Area	Disposal Station Fee: $5 Full Facilities - 28 Miles at Sierraville or 31 Miles at Truckee

STAMPEDE RESERVOIR

Stampede Reservoir is at an elevation of 5,949 feet in the Tahoe National Forest northeast of Truckee. Stampede has a surface area of 3,440 acres with 25 miles of sage and coniferous covered shoreline. This large open Lake offers westerly winds for the sailor, and its vast open waters invite the waterskier. The angler will find Rainbow and Brown trout. While the campground at Davis Creek has limited facilities, the Forest Service maintains nicely developed campsites near the Lake. Unfortunately, the Lake is drained at the end of the season into Pyramid Lake in Nevada via the Truckee River to support a rare species of fish which are near extinction.

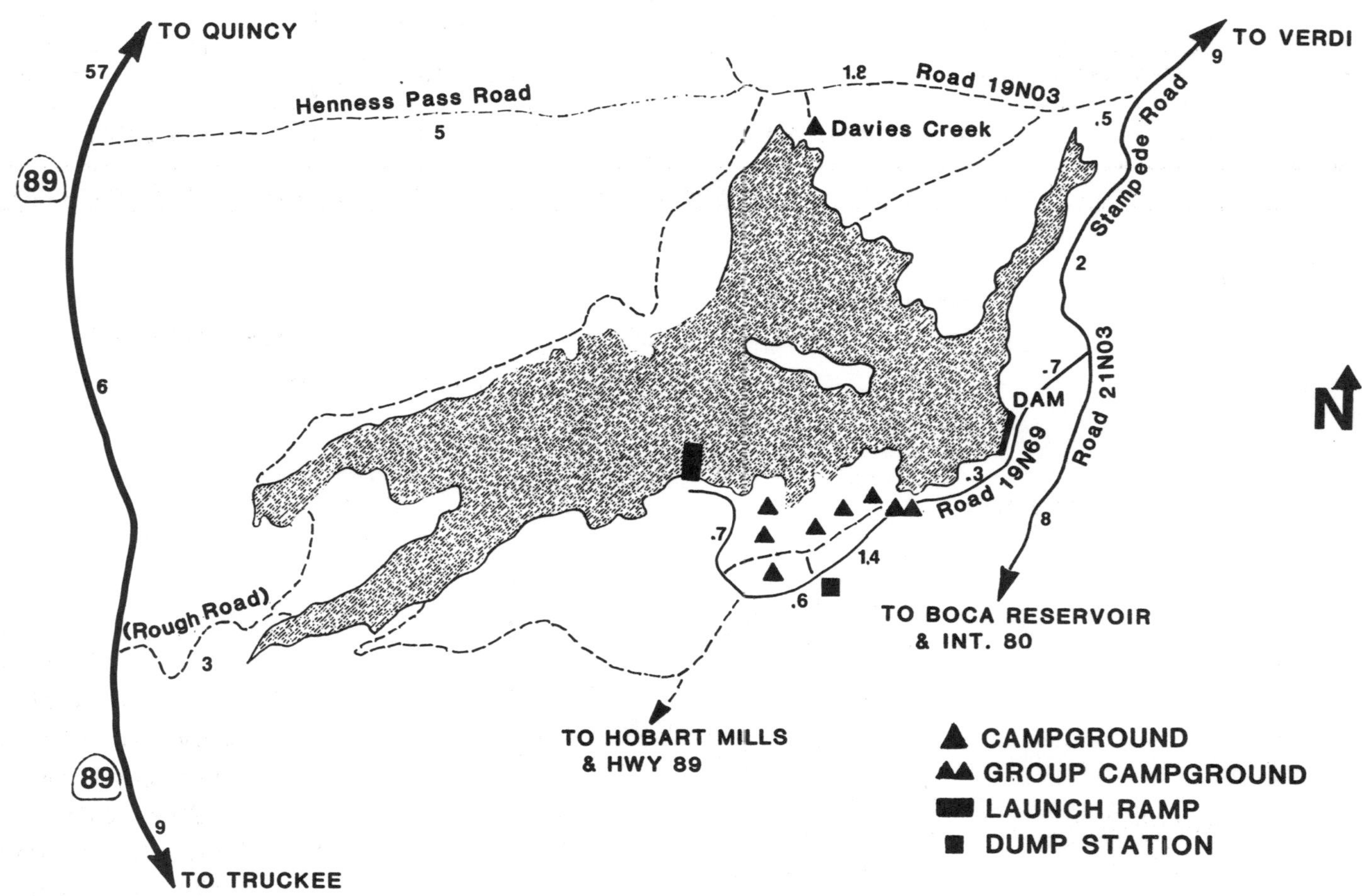

INFORMATION: Truckee Ranger District, P.O. Box 909, Truckee 95734, Ph: 916-587-3558			
CAMPING	BOATING	RECREATION	OTHER
252 Dev. Sites for Tents & R.V.s Fee: $7 `10 Primitive Sites on Davies Creek No Facilities No Water - No Fee Horses Allowed Group Camp - 150 People Maximum For Reservations Ph: 800-283-CAMP	Power, Row, Canoe, Sail, Waterski, Jet Ski, Windsurf & Inflatables Water Very Low In Fall Launch Ramp Extended for Low Water Launching	Fishing: Rainbow & Brown Trout Swimming Picnicking Hiking Hunting: Deer	Full Facilities - 14 Miles at Truckee

PROSSER CREEK RESERVOIR

Prosser Creek Reservoir is at an elevation of 5,711 feet located in the scenic Tahoe National Forest. This 740 surface acre lake rests in an open canyon surrounded by 11 miles of sage and coniferous-covered hills. The Donner Camp picnic area was the site of the Donner Party tragedy of the winter of 1846-47. Boating is limited to 10 MPH so waterskiing, power boating and jet skiing are eliminated from this facility. Launching is hampered in the fall by low water conditions. There are trout for the fisherman in this serene reservoir.

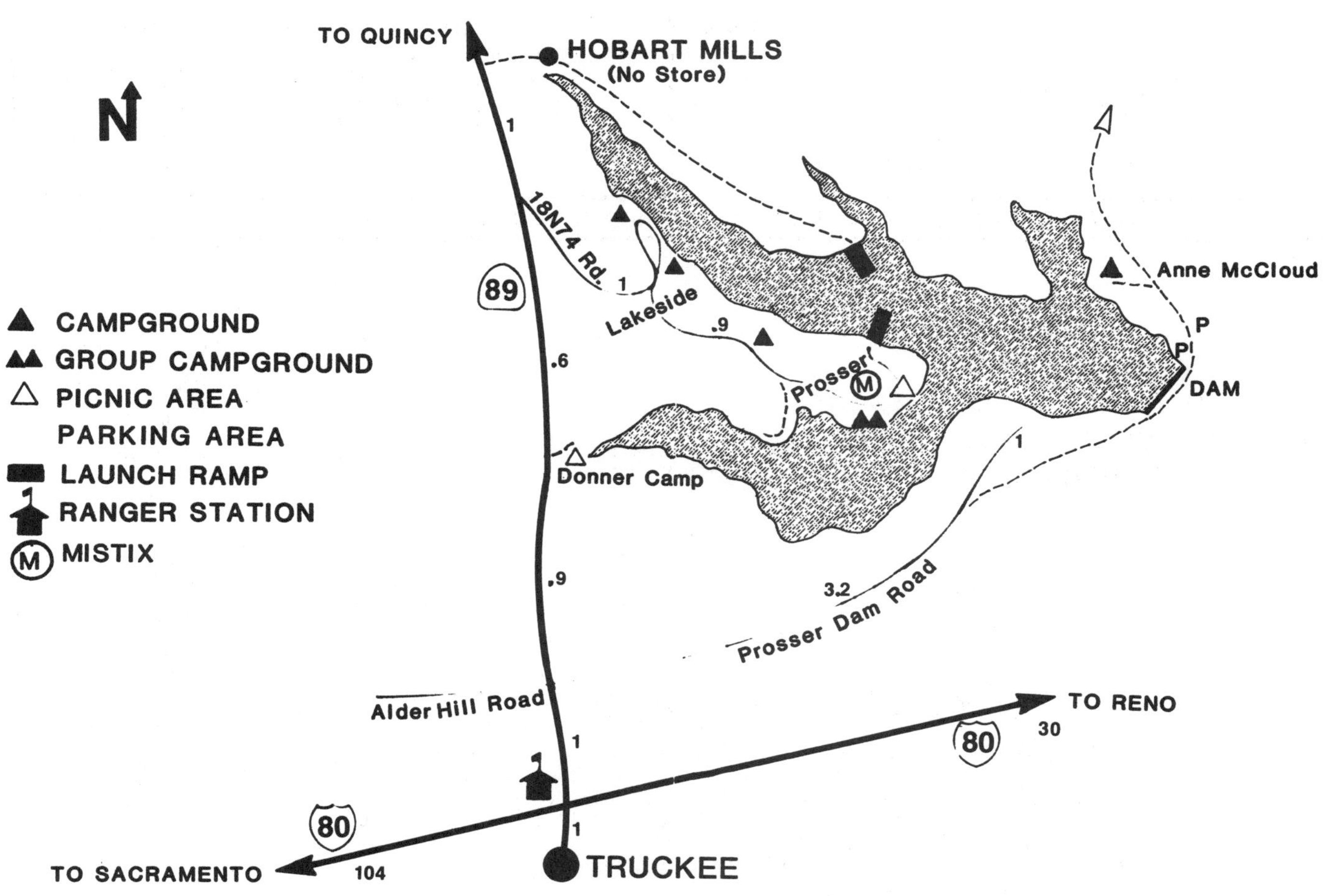

INFORMATION: Truckee Ranger District, P.O. Box 909, Truckee 95734, Ph: 916-587-3558			
CAMPING	BOATING	RECREATION	OTHER
Prosser: 29 Dev. Sites for Tents & R.V.s Max. Length-24 Ft. Fee: $6 Lakeside: 100 Primitive Sites for Tents & R.V.s Toilets, No Water Annie McCloud: 10 Sites Toilets, No Water Rough Roads	Power, Row, Canoe, Sail, Windsurf, & Inflatables Speed Limit - 10 MPH Launch Ramps	Fishing: Rainbow & Brown Trout Swimming Picnicking at Donner Camp Hiking Hunting: Deer Group Picnic Sites At Group Camp By Reservations	Full Facilities - 5 Miles at Truckee Group Camp 50 People Maximum Ph: 916-587-3558 for Reservations

BOCA RESERVOIR

Boca Reservoir is in the Tahoe National Forest at an elevation of 5,700 feet. The Lake has a surface area of 980 acres and 14 miles of shoreline which is a lovely combination of steep bluffs and low grassy areas amid tall pine trees. The many inlets and prevailing winds create an excellent atmosphere for sailing and boating. The water level is relatively constant as it is fed by Stampede Reservoir, 5 miles above, but there is a drop in late fall.

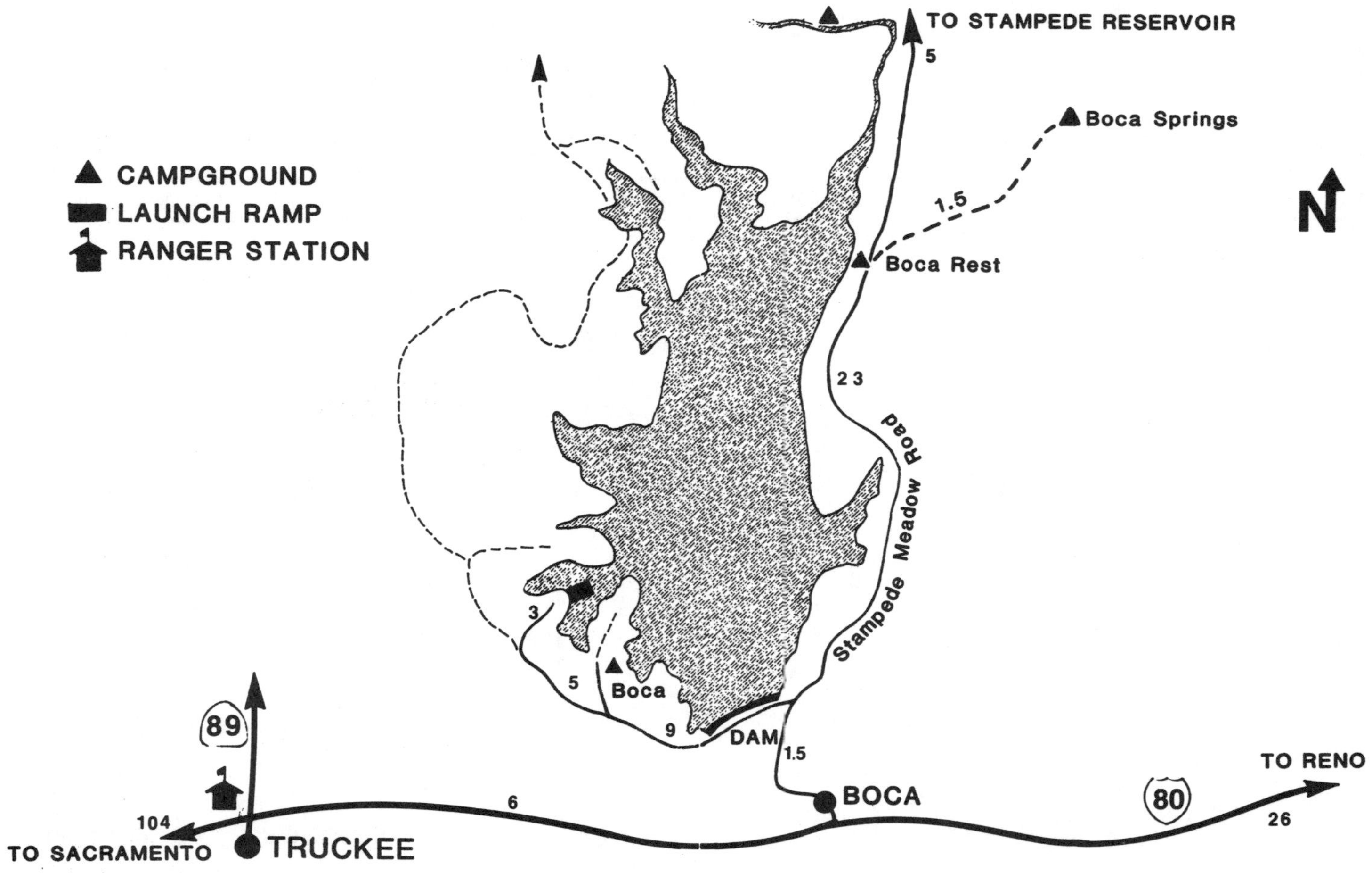

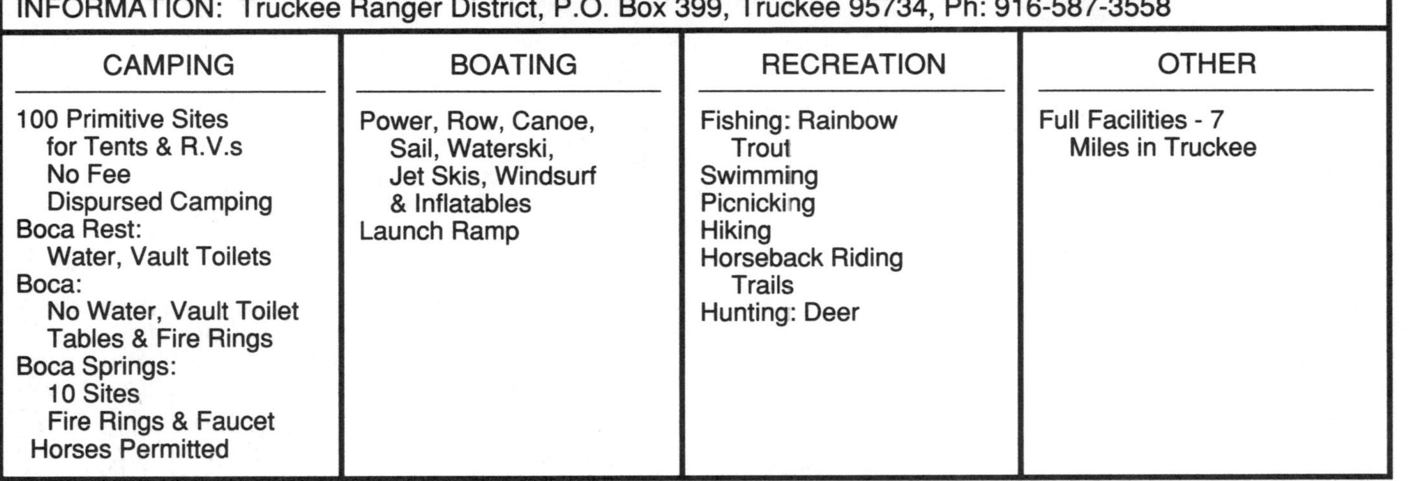

INFORMATION: Truckee Ranger District, P.O. Box 399, Truckee 95734, Ph: 916-587-3558

CAMPING	BOATING	RECREATION	OTHER
100 Primitive Sites for Tents & R.V.s No Fee Dispursed Camping Boca Rest: Water, Vault Toilets Boca: No Water, Vault Toilet Tables & Fire Rings Boca Springs: 10 Sites Fire Rings & Faucet Horses Permitted	Power, Row, Canoe, Sail, Waterski, Jet Skis, Windsurf & Inflatables Launch Ramp	Fishing: Rainbow Trout Swimming Picnicking Hiking Horseback Riding Trails Hunting: Deer	Full Facilities - 7 Miles in Truckee

LAKE SPAULDING

Lake Spaulding rests at an elevation of 5,014 feet in a glacier carved bowl of granite. The Lake has a surface area of 698 acres surrounded by giant rocks and a conifer forest. Now a part of Pacific Gas and Electric Company's Drum-Spaulding Project, the dam was originally built in 1912 for hydraulic mining. P. G. & E. now operates the facilities at this pretty lake which includes a campground and launch ramp. The lake is open to all types of boating although launching large boats can be difficult. Fishing from the bank or boat is often rewarding. This is a fine lake for a family outing with a spectacular setting of granite boulders reaching into the clear, blue waters.

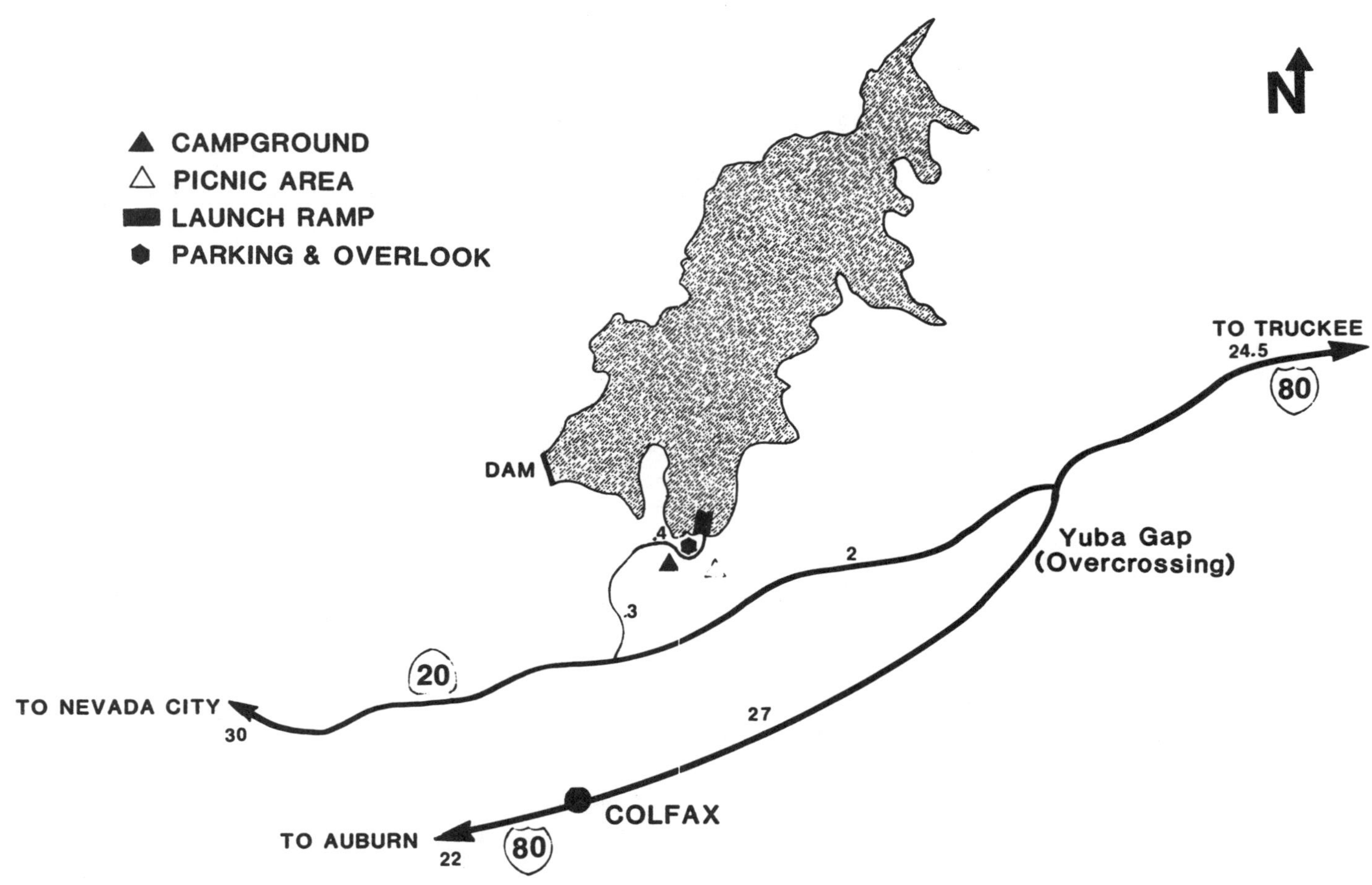

INFORMATION: P. G. & E. Regional Land Dept., P.O. Box 340, Red Bluff 96080, Ph: 916-527-0354			
CAMPING	**BOATING**	**RECREATION**	**OTHER**
25 Dev. Sites for Tents & R.V.s Fee: $8	Power, Row, Canoe, Sail, Waterski, Jet Ski, Windsurf & Inflatables Launch Ramp Fee: $3 Summer Use Only Hazardous Rocks In Late Summer As Water Level Drops	Fishing: Rainbow & Brown Trout Swimming - Beaches Picnicking Hiking Backpacking-Parking Hunting: Deer	Full Facilities at Colfax

DONNER LAKE

Donner Lake is at an elevation of 5,963 feet in the Tahoe National Forest next to Interstate 80 west of Truckee. The Lake is 3 miles long and 3/4 mile wide with a shoreline of 7-1/2 miles of high alpine woods. The Donner State Memorial Park was named after the tragic Donner Party whose fate in the winter of 1846 attests to the hardships encountered by California's early settlers. This well-maintained park has 154 developed campsites with campfire programs and nature trails. The Emigrant Trail Museum is open daily from 10:00 a.m. to Noon and from 1:00 p.m. to 4:00 p.m. The water in the Lake is clear and cold. A popular sailing Lake, Donner has its own local Sailing Club, but beware of periodic afternoon winds that can be hazardous.

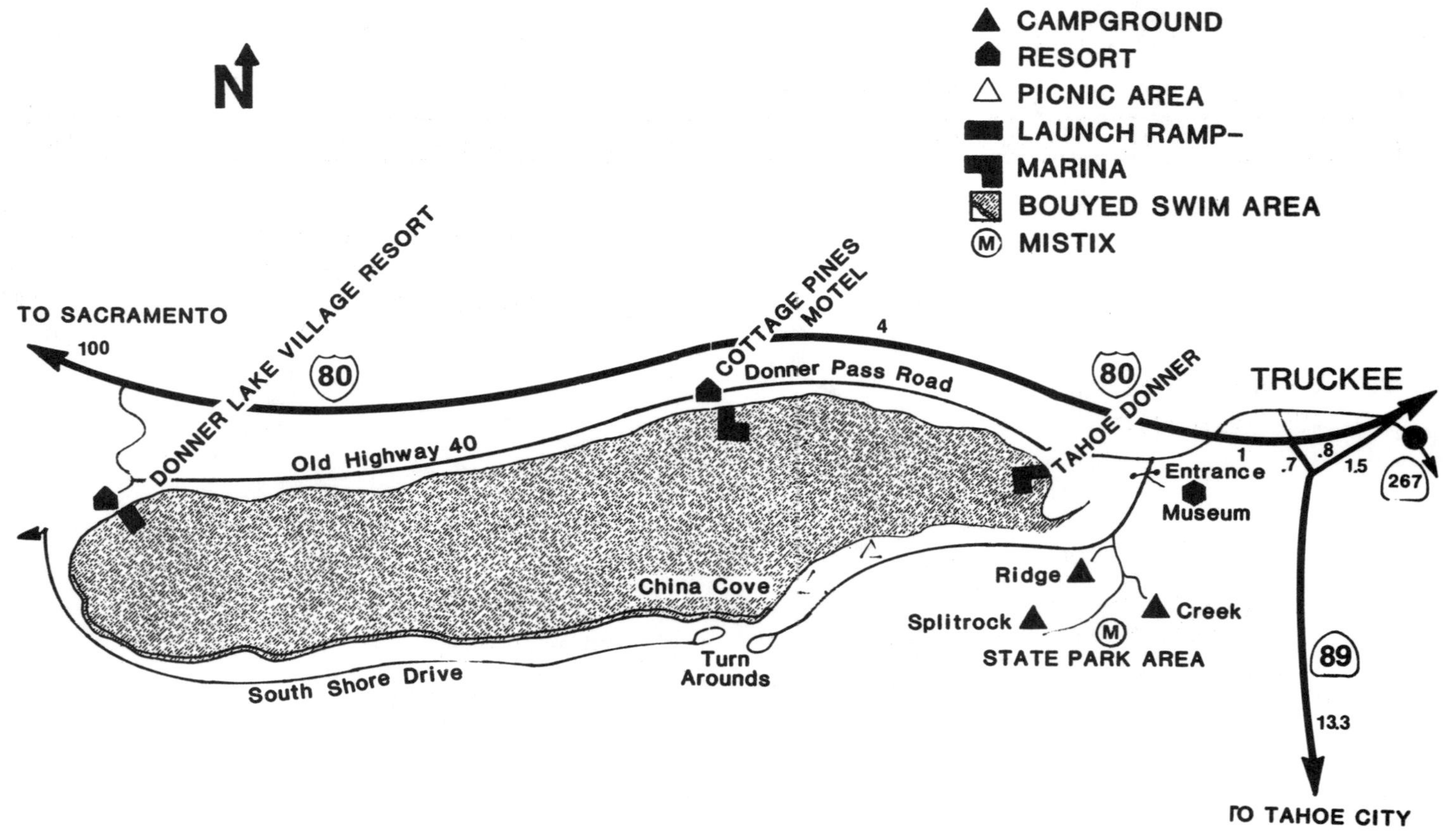

INFORMATION: Chamber of Commerce, P.O. Box 2757, Truckee 95734, Ph: 916-587-2757			
CAMPING	BOATING	RECREATION	OTHER
Donner Memorial State Park 154 Dev. Sites for Tents & R.V.s Fee: Camping - $10 Day Use - $3 Museum - $1 Adult .50 Youth Ph: 916-587-3841 or Reserve MISTIX Ph: 1-800-283-CAMP	Power, Row, Canoe, Sail, Waterski, Jet Skis, Windsurf & Inflatables No Launching From State Park Public Launch Ramp At West End Rentals: Fishing, Sail, Pontoon & Paddleboats	Fishing: Rainbow Trout, Mackinaw, Kokanee Salmon Swimming - Beaches Picnicking Hiking Bicycle Trails Horseback Riding Trails & Rentals Campfire Programs Nature Study Playgrounds River Rafting Nearby	Motels, Cabins Snack Bar Restaurant Cocktail Lounge Grocery Store Bait & Tackle Laundromat Gas Station Airport With Auto Rentals - 2 Miles Tennis, Golf, Movies

MARTIS CREEK LAKE

Martis Creek Lake was California's first "Wild Trout Lake" and probably one of its most unique. Originally built in 1972 by the U. S. Army Corps of Engineers for flood control and a water supply for Reno, this 70 acre minimum pool lake was selected by the California Department of Fish and Game as an exclusive naturally producing trophy trout fishery for the endangered Lahontan Cutthroat Trout. It was opened in 1979 under a special catch and release program, and for several years the Cutthroats thrived where catches up to 4 pounds were common and fish of 16 inches to 18 inches were average. But that is past history for a voracious population of native German Browns destroyed the Cutthroats. Now Martis Creek is a trophy German Brown fishery at this catch and release lake. The facilities and nearby 1,000 acre wildlife area are administered by the Corps of Engineers.

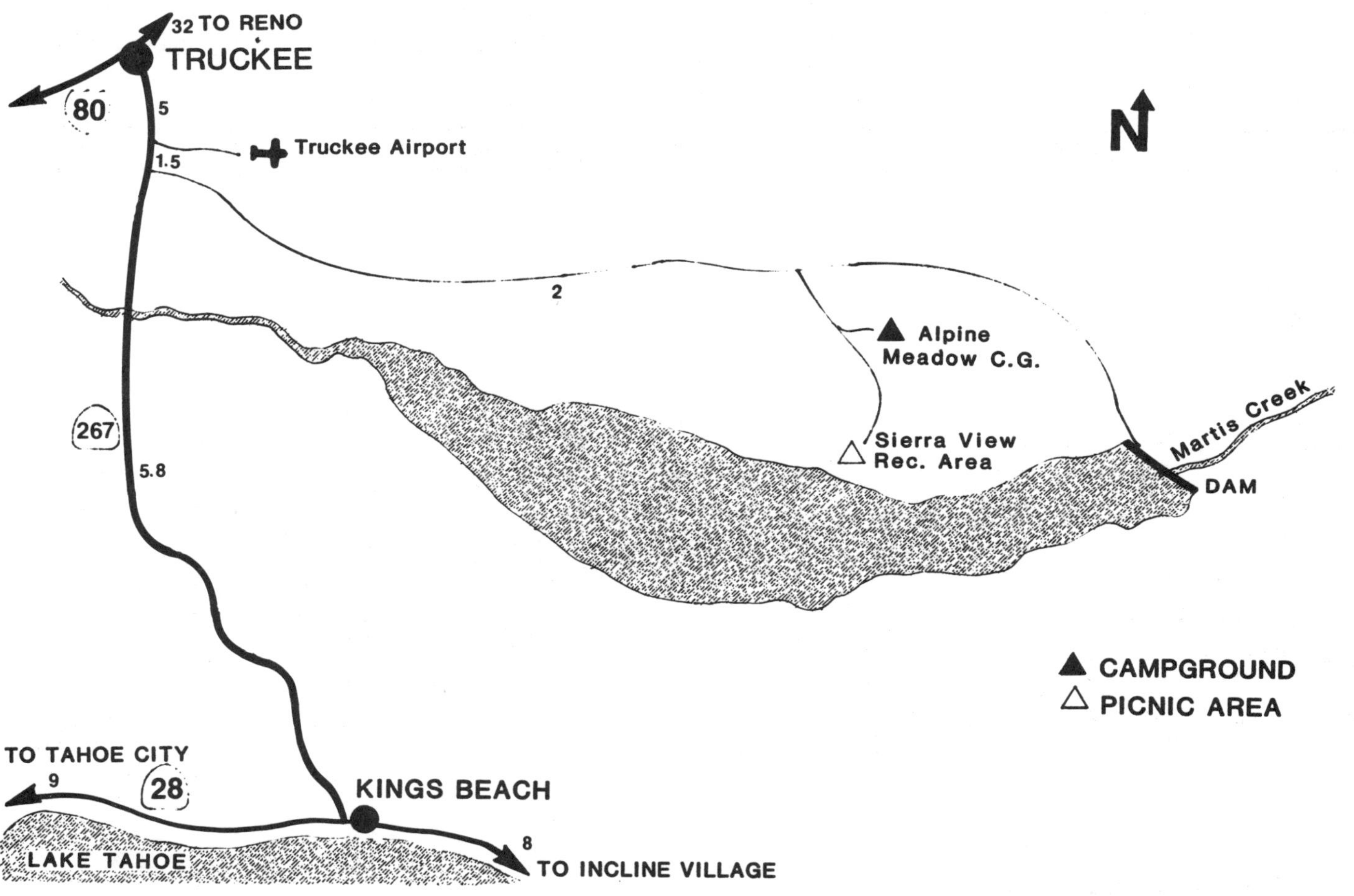

INFORMATION: Park Manager, P.O. Box 6, Smartville 95977, Ph: 916-639-2342

CAMPING	BOATING	RECREATION	OTHER
6 Dev. Sites for Tents 19 Dev. Sites for R.V.s No Fees 2 Handicap Sites May Be Reserved Campground Closed in Winter	No Power Boats Sail, Row, Canoe, Inflatables & Windsurf Only Hand Launch Only	Fishing: Brown & Rainbow Trout Artificial Lures and Flies Only Barbless Hooks Zero Limit Swimming Picnicking Hiking Backpacking Nature Trails Campfire Programs	Full Facilities - 7 Miles at Truckee Airport Within 5 Miles

COLLINS LAKE

The Collins Lake Recreation Area is at an elevation of 1,200 feet in the delightful Mother Lode Country. The Lake has a surface area of over 1,000 acres with 12-1/2 miles of shoreline. The modern campground and R.V. Park provide well-separated sites under oak and pine trees. There is a broad, sandy beach and many family and group picnic sites. All boating is allowed, but waterskiing is permitted only from May 15 through September 15 of each year. One of the finest fishing Lakes in California, it is famous for Trophy trout along with a variety of warm water species. There are zones for the exclusive use of fishermen throughout the year.

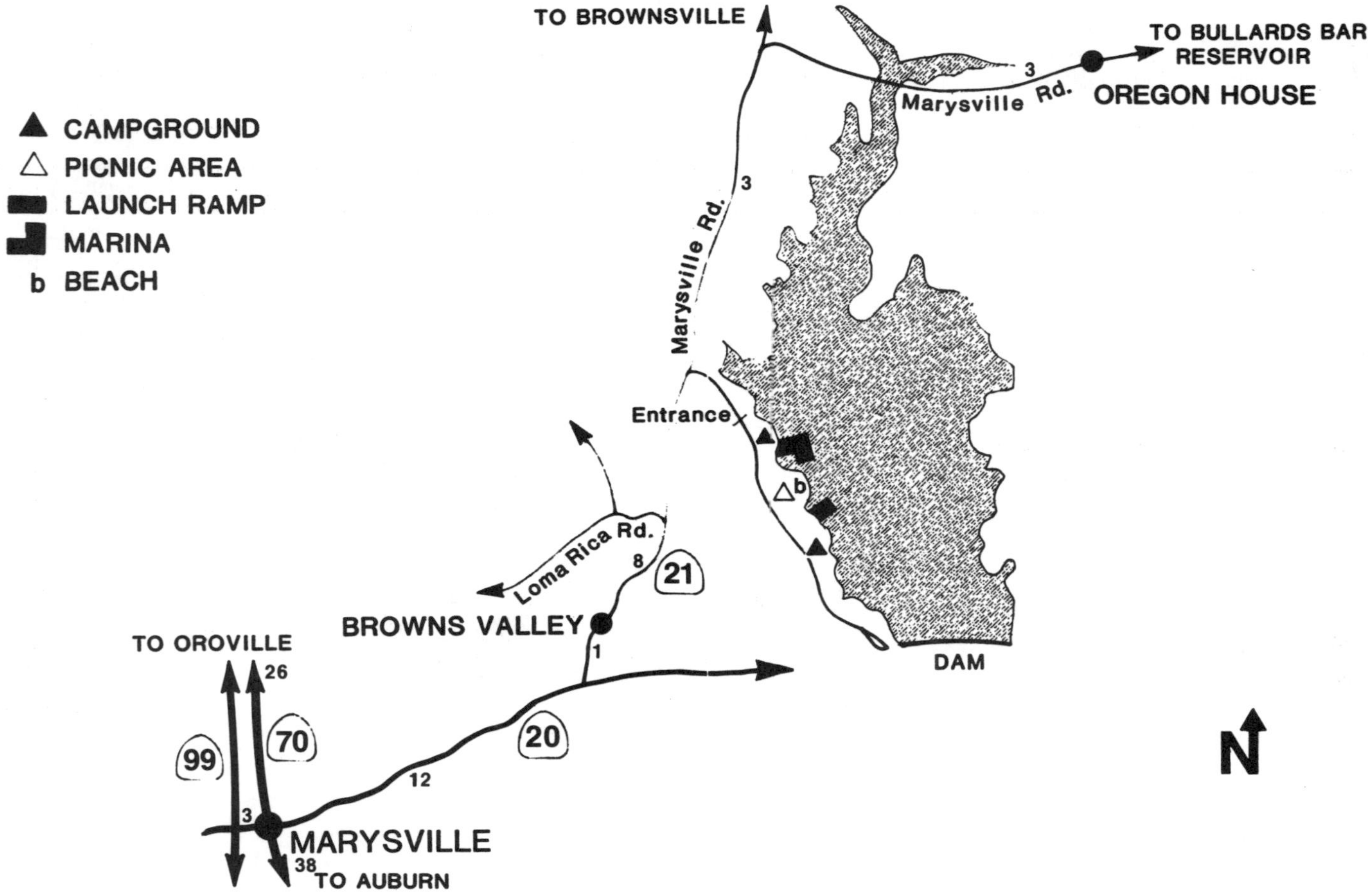

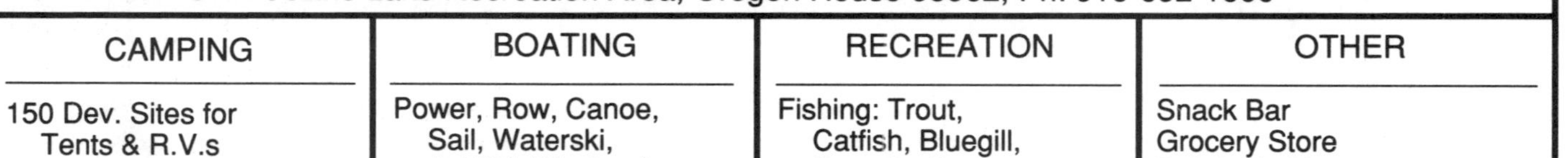

INFORMATION: Collins Lake Recreation Area, Oregon House 95962, Ph: 916-692-1600

CAMPING	BOATING	RECREATION	OTHER
150 Dev. Sites for Tents & R.V.s Fee: $11.75-$16.75 Electric, Water, & Sewer Hookups Available Reservations Accepted Open Camp Areas Along Shoreline Fee: $9.75 Discount on Weeknights	Power, Row, Canoe, Sail, Waterski, Jet Ski, Windsurf & Inflatables Launch Ramp - $4 Rentals: Outboard Fishing, Row, Paddle & Patio Boats Docks, Berths Moorings, Dry Storage	Fishing: Trout, Catfish, Bluegill, Crappie, Bass Swimming - Sand Beach, Diving Raft Picnicking - Families & Groups	Snack Bar Grocery Store Bait & Tackle Hot Showers Disposal Station Gas Station Propane Group or Club Discounts Full Facilities at Oregon House

ENGLEBRIGHT RESERVOIR

Englebright Reservoir is at an elevation of 527 feet northeast of Marysville. The Lake has a surface area of 815 acres with a shoreline of 24 miles that reaches 9 miles above the dam. Englebright is a boat camper's bonanza. Boats can be launched at Headquarters or at Joe Miller. They can also be rented at Skippers Cove. You can then proceed up the Lake to a campsite. The shoreline is steep and rocky except at the campgrounds where there are some sandy beaches with pine and oak trees above the high water line. The water level remains full all year at this reservoir. Fishing is good in the quiet, narrow coves. Waterskiing is not allowed above Upper Boston.

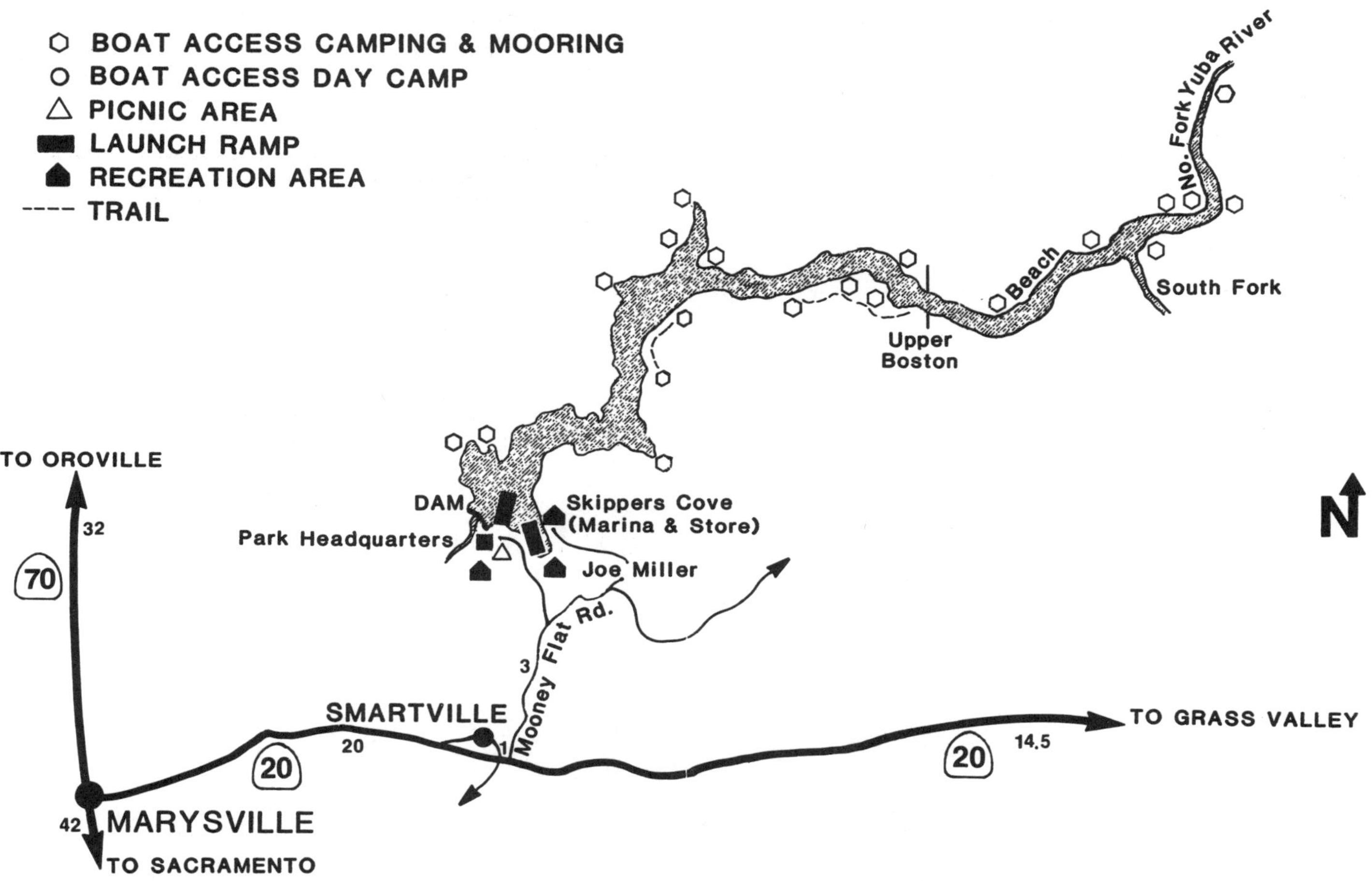

INFORMATION: U. S. Army Corps of Eng., P. O. Box 6, Smartville 95977, Ph: 916-639-2342			
CAMPING	BOATING	RECREATION	OTHER
100 Developed Boat-In Sites No Fees	Power, Row, Canoe, Sail, Waterski, Jet Ski, Windsurf & Inflatables Full Service Marina Launch Ramps Rentals: Fishing, Canoe & Waterski Boats, Houseboats & Patio Boats Docks, Berths, Moorings, Gas	Fishing: Trout, Catfish, Bluegill & Bass Swimming Picnicking Hiking Campfire Programs	Skippers Cove Marina P.O. Box 5 Smartville 95977 Ph: 916-639-2272 Grocery Store Hot Sandwiches Beer & Wine Gas - Propane Bait & Tackle

SCOTTS FLAT LAKE

Scotts Flat Lake is at an elevation of 3,100 feet at the gateway to the Tahoe National Forest. The Lake has a surface area of 850 acres with 7-1/2 miles of coniferous shoreline. This is a nice boating Lake with two launch ramps and marina facilities. Fishing is good for trout and warm water fish. The Scotts Flat Campground is family oriented with modern campsites, a picnic area, sandy beaches and a store. This is a quiet, relaxing facility where nature provides a beautifully forested environment. Don't forget a camera.

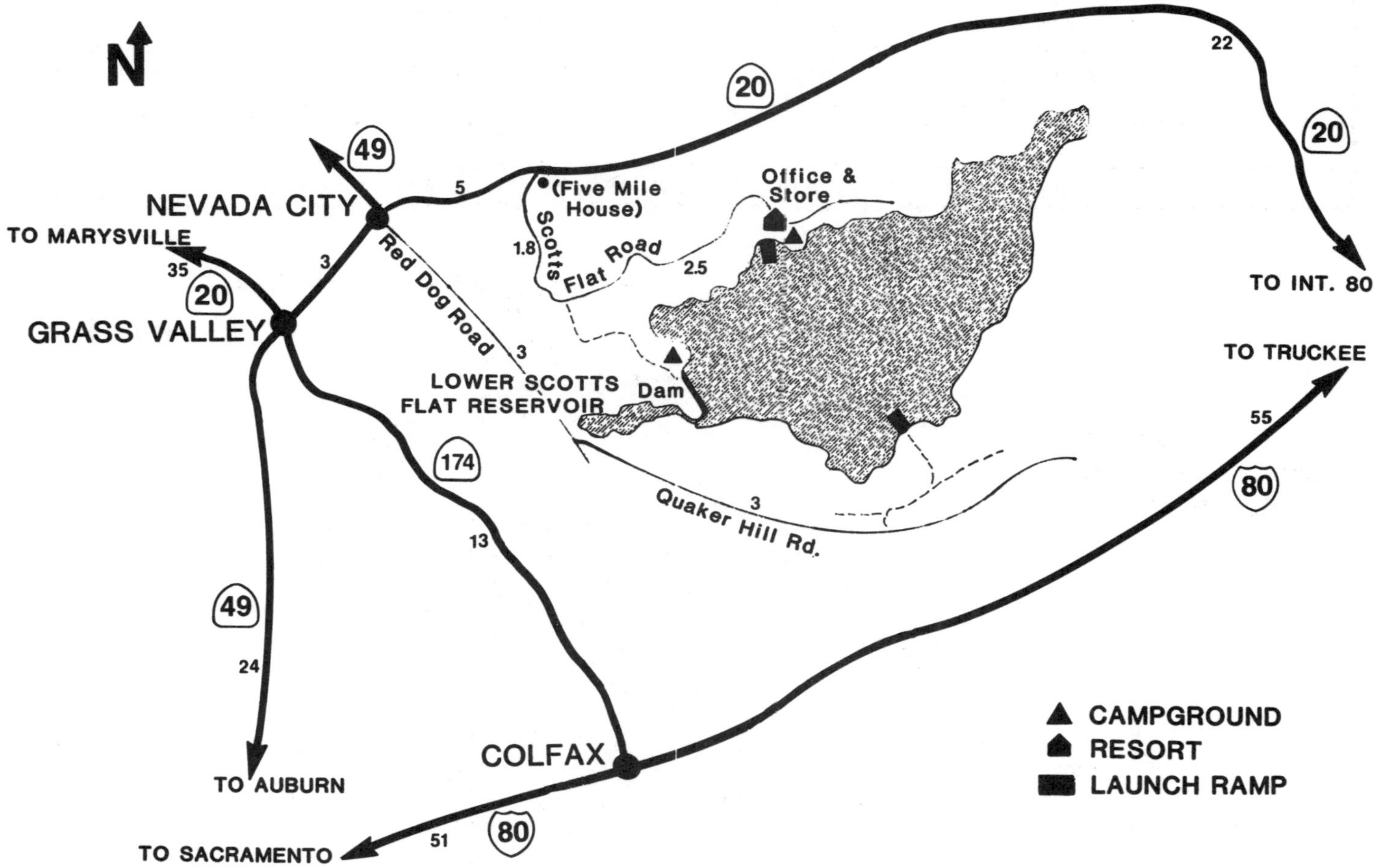

INFORMATION: Scotts Flat, 18848 State Hwy. 20, Nevada City 95959, Ph: 916-265-5302

CAMPING	BOATING	RECREATION	OTHER
20 Dev. Sites for Tents 165 Dev. Sites for R.V.s Fee: $10 Reservations Accepted	Power, Row, Canoe, Sail, Waterski & Inflatables Full Service Marina Launch Ramps Rentals: Fishing & Pedal Boats Moorings & Dry Storage	Fishing: Rainbow & German Brown Trout, Large & Smallmouth Bass, Kokanee Swimming Picnicking Hiking Volleyball Goldpanning Horseshoes	Coffee Shop Grocery Store Bait & Tackle Hot Showers Disposal Station Children's Playground No Motorbikes, Motorcyles or Horses

ROLLINS LAKE

Rollins Lake is at an elevation of 2,100 feet in the Gold Country of the Western Sierra near Colfax. The Lake has a surface area of 900 acres with 26 miles of shoreline. The Rollins Lake Corporation maintains four nicely kept campgrounds around the oak and pine covered shoreline. Each campground has its own personality. Orchard Springs is for group camping. Greenhorn is popular for day use and offers campsites for individuals and large groups. Peninsula is the most remote, and Long Ravine is the most accessible. This is a good Lake for sailing and waterskiing with many coves and long stretches of open water. Fishing is good from both boat and shore for a wide variety of trout and warm water species.

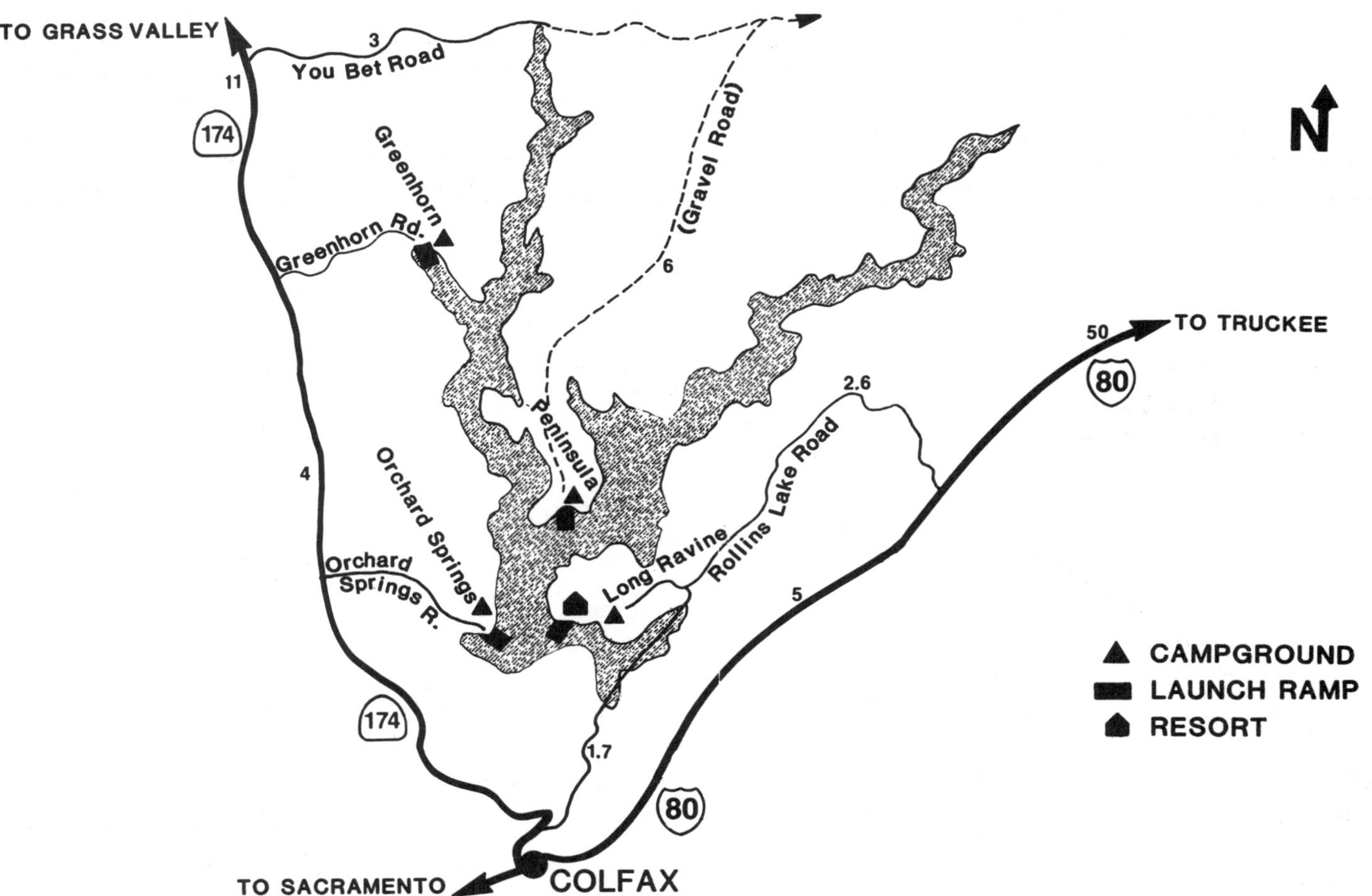

INFORMATION: Rollins Lake, P.O. Box 60, Colfax 95713, Ph: 916-346-6166			
CAMPING	BOATING	RECREATION	OTHER
250 Dev. Sites for Tents & R.V.s Fee: $10 - $14 Plus $2 for Pets Full Hookups R.V. & Trailer Storage Disposal Station Flush Toilets Hot Showers	Power, Row, Canoe, Sail, Waterski, Jet Ski, Windsurf Full Service Marina Floating Gas Docks 4 Launch Ramps Houseboat Mooring Rentals: Fishing Boats with Motors, Canoes & Paddle Boats	Fishing: Rainbow & Brown Trout, Sunfish, Crappie, Small & Largemouth Bass Picnicking Swimming Hiking & Riding Trails Riding Stables	Snack Bar & Grill Mini-Mart Bait & Tackle Family Style Bar with Saturday Night Dances Greenhorn Campground: Ph: 916-272-6100 Orchard Springs Campground Ph: 916-346-2212

LAKE VALLEY RESERVOIR
KELLY LAKE

Lake Valley Reservoir is at 5,800 feet elevation. The shoreline is surrounded by tall trees and granite boulders with clear, cold water. The campsites are very pretty, situated under the trees near the Lake. Waterskiing is not allowed. The steep shoreline combined with the steady west wind allows for good sailing. Coming out from Lake Valley to Highway 80, the second right turn goes into Kelly Lake. This is a small, lovely Lake well worth a day's outing, with 5 picnic sites, tables, firepits and toilets. Trout fishing can be excellent at both these High Sierra Lakes.

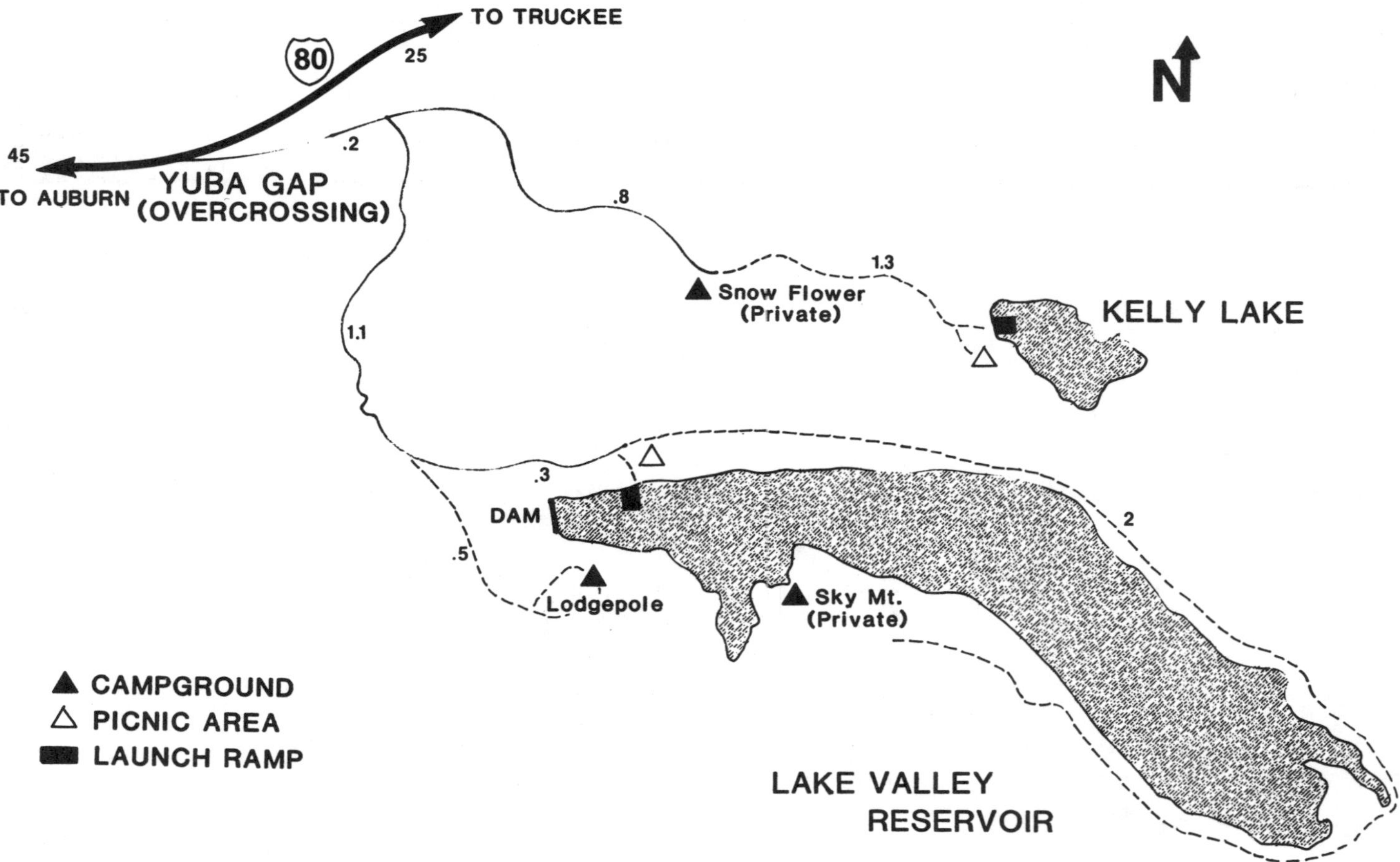

INFORMATION: P. G. & E. Regional Land Dept., P.O. Box 340, Red Bluff 96080, Ph: 916-527-0354

CAMPING	BOATING	RECREATION	OTHER
Lake Valley: 18 Dev. Sites for Tents & R.V.s to 40 feet Fee: $8 Kelly Lake: Day Use Only	Lake Valley: Fishing, Row, Canoe, Sail & Inflatables No Waterskiing Launch Ramp Kelly Lake: No Motors	Fishing: Rainbow & Brown Trout Swimming Picnicking Hiking	Full Facilities at Truckee

LAKE PILLSBURY

The Lake Pillsbury Recreation Area provides a wide range of outdoor opportunities. Located in a mountainous setting at an elevation of 1,818 feet in the Mendocino National Forest, this 2,003 maximum surface acre lake has 65 miles of varied shoreline. It is open to all types of boating including boat camping in designated areas. There is a trout, bass and "Pogie" (sunfish) fishery in the Lake. The more adventurous angler will find trout, salmon, and steelhead in the nearby Eel River and its tributaries. The Bloody Rock Area is popular with equestrians. Hang gliding at Hull Mountain (elevation 6,873 feet) offers spectacular views of the surrounding country. For further information contact Lake County Visitor Information Center, 875 Lakeport Blvd., Lakeport 95453, Ph: 1-800-LAKESIDE.

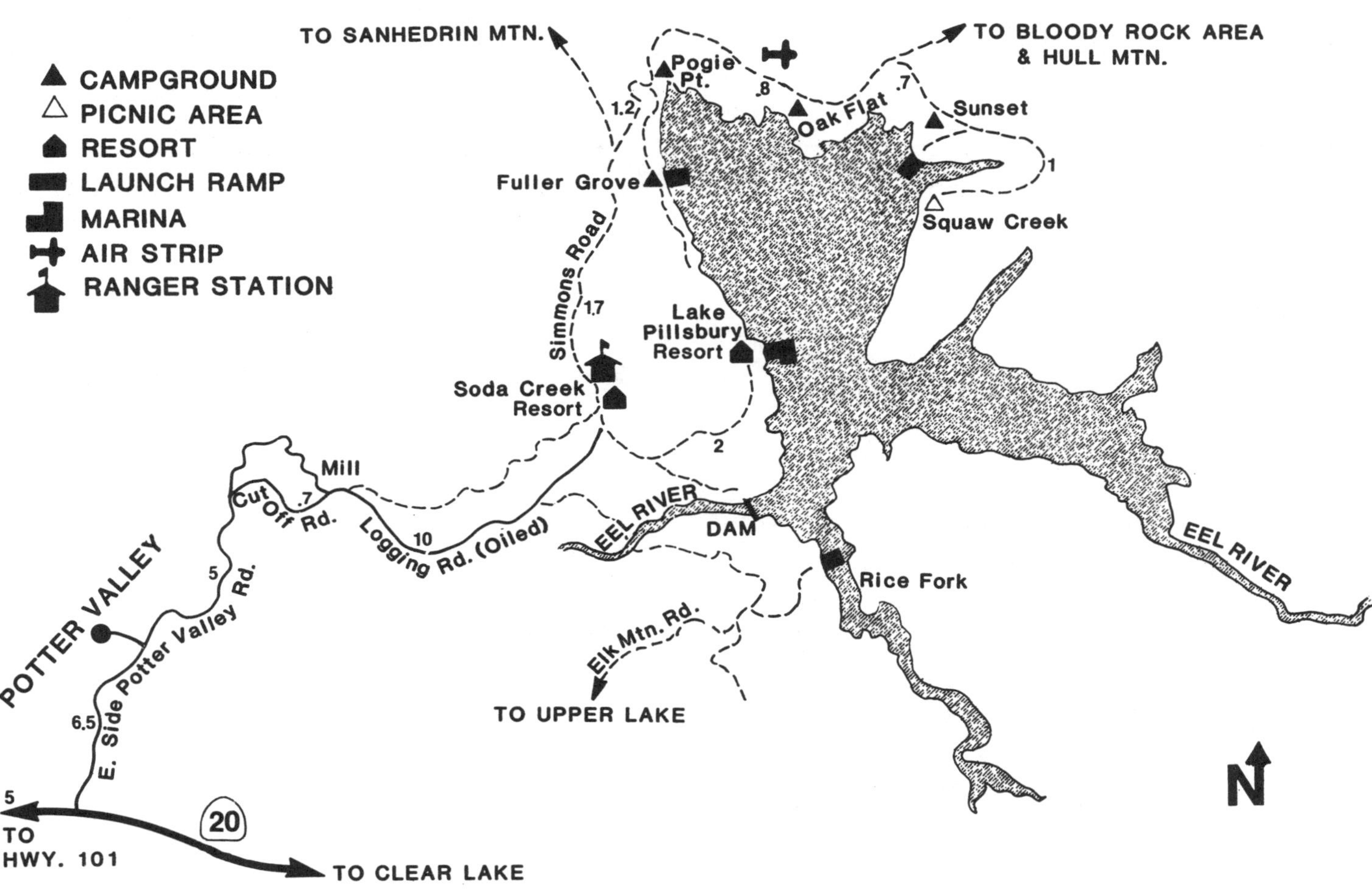

INFORMATION: U. S. F. S., P.O. Box 96, Upper Lake 95485, Ph: 707-275-2361

CAMPING	BOATING	RECREATION	OTHER
U. S. F. S.: 141 Tent/RV Sites Fee: $6 Lake Pillsbury Resort: Livery Service to & from Airport 30 Tent Sites Flush Toilets Showers	Open to All Boating Overnight in Designated Areas Launch Ramps Rentals: Fishing Boats & Canoes Marina: Fuel, Slips & Deck Supplies	Fishing: Black Bass, Rainbow & Brown Trout, Sunfish, Salmon & Steelhead Swimming Picnicking Hiking & Riding Trails Backpacking Hang Gliding	Lake Pillsbury Resort P.O. Box 37 Potter Valley 95469 Ph: 707-743-1581 Soda Creek Resort Lake Pillsbury Potter Valley 95469 Ph: 707-743-1593 Snack Bars, Groceries Restaurant-Cocktails Bait & Tackle Gas Station

LAKE MENDOCINO

Lake Mendocino is at an elevation of 748 feet above Coyote Dam on the East Fork of the Russian River. This is wine country with many small valleys of vineyards and pear trees. The Lake has a surface area of 1,740 acres with 15 miles of oak-wooded shoreline. The U. S. Army Corps of Engineers maintain the quality facilities which include numerous campsites, picnic sites and 7 group picnic shelters each with a massive stone barbecue pit. There is a large protected swim beach and a 5-kilometer hiking trail. Equestrians will find a staging area and riding trails. Several smaller interpretive trails, and an Interpretive Cultural Center are also available. The fishing is good with Channel catfish going to 30 pounds and Stripers to 40 pounds.

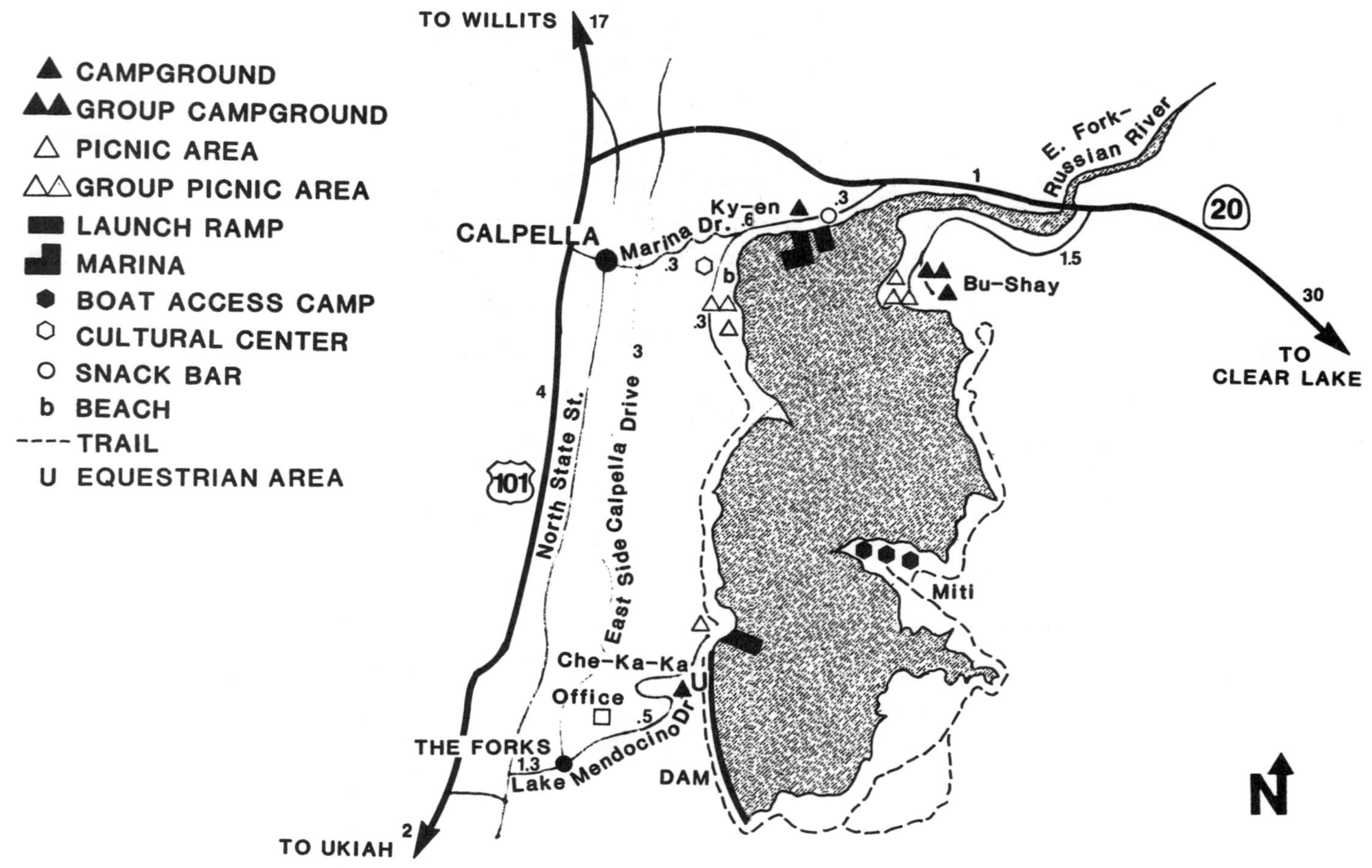

INFORMATION: Park Manager, 1160 Lake Mendocino Dr., Ukiah 95482, Ph: 707-462-7581			
CAMPING	**BOATING**	**RECREATION**	**OTHER**
319 Dev. Sites for Tents & R.V.s Fee: $8 No Reservations 3 Group Camps By Reservation 165 People Maximum 18 Boat Access Only Sites	Power, Row, Canoe, Sail, Waterski & Inflatables Jet Ski, Wind Surfers Full Service Marina Launch Ramps Rentals: Fishing, Power, Canoe, Waterski & Pontoon Docks, Berths Dry Storage, Gas	Fishing: Catfish, Bluegill, Crappie Large, Smallmouth & Striped Bass Swimming Picnicking Hiking Junior Ranger & Interpretive Programs Hunting: Waterfowl Special Seasonal Turkey Hunts	Lake Mendocino Marina P.O. Box 13 Calpella 95418 Ph: 707-485-8644 (Off Highway 20 at North End) Snack Bar Mini-Market Beer, Wine, Ice Boat & Slip Rentals Gasoline for Boats

Keep This Checklist Handy For Camping

Here is a list of frequently used camping gear. This is a good basic start, but your own personal needs will largely influence your equipment selection. The available space in your vehicle should also be a factor in your preparation, adds The Coleman Company.

- ☐ Air Mattress
- ☐ Batteries
- ☐ Blankets
- ☐ Camera and film
- ☐ Radiant heater (in cold weather)
- ☐ Coffee Pot
- ☐ Compass
- ☐ Cooking Utensils
- ☐ Cooler
- ☐ Dishpan and Pot Scrubbers
- ☐ Eating Utensils
- ☐ First Aid Kit
- ☐ Flares/Mirror-other emerg. device
- ☐ Flashlights
- ☐ Folding chairs or camp stools
- ☐ Fuel
- ☐ Ground Cloth
- ☐ Hammer
- ☐ Hand Ax
- ☐ Ice or Ice substitutes
- ☐ Insect Repellent
- ☐ Jug of water
- ☐ Knife
- ☐ Lantern
- ☐ Lighter-Disposable Butane
- ☐ Mantles
- ☐ Maps
- ☐ Matches & Waterproof container
- ☐ Pad, pen or pencil
- ☐ Prescription medicine
- ☐ Rope or cord
- ☐ Shovel-small folding type
- ☐ Sleeping bags
- ☐ Snakebite kit
- ☐ Soap-biodegradable
- ☐ Stakes
- ☐ Stove
- ☐ Sunglasses
- ☐ Suntan oil or lotion
- ☐ Tablecloth
- ☐ Tent, poles
- ☐ Toilet paper
- ☐ Toiletries
- ☐ Towels-Paper & Bath
- ☐ Trash bags
- ☐ Water container/purification tablets

You may want to keep track of those pieces of equipment which you had and didn't need or needed and didn't have. This would help you on your future trips. Happy Camping!

Courtesy of The Coleman Company

BLUE LAKES - LAKE COUNTY

The Blue Lakes are at an elevation of 1,400 feet off Highway 20 between Clear Lake and Lake Mendocino. Located just 5 miles north of the town of Upper Lake (Clear Lake), these popular Lakes are nestled in a beautiful setting of dense groves of madrones, oak, and evergreen. These two small spring fed Lakes have been in existence for over 10,000 years. Their clear blue waters make this a delightful retreat for fishing, swimming, boating, or just plain relaxing. The Lakes are limited to a 12 MPH boating speed, so sailors, paddlers, or trollers often have the Lake to themselves. The private resorts surrounding the Lakes provide complete vacation facilities including shaded campsites, cabins, restaurants, boat rentals, swim beaches, and picnic areas.

. . . Continued. . .

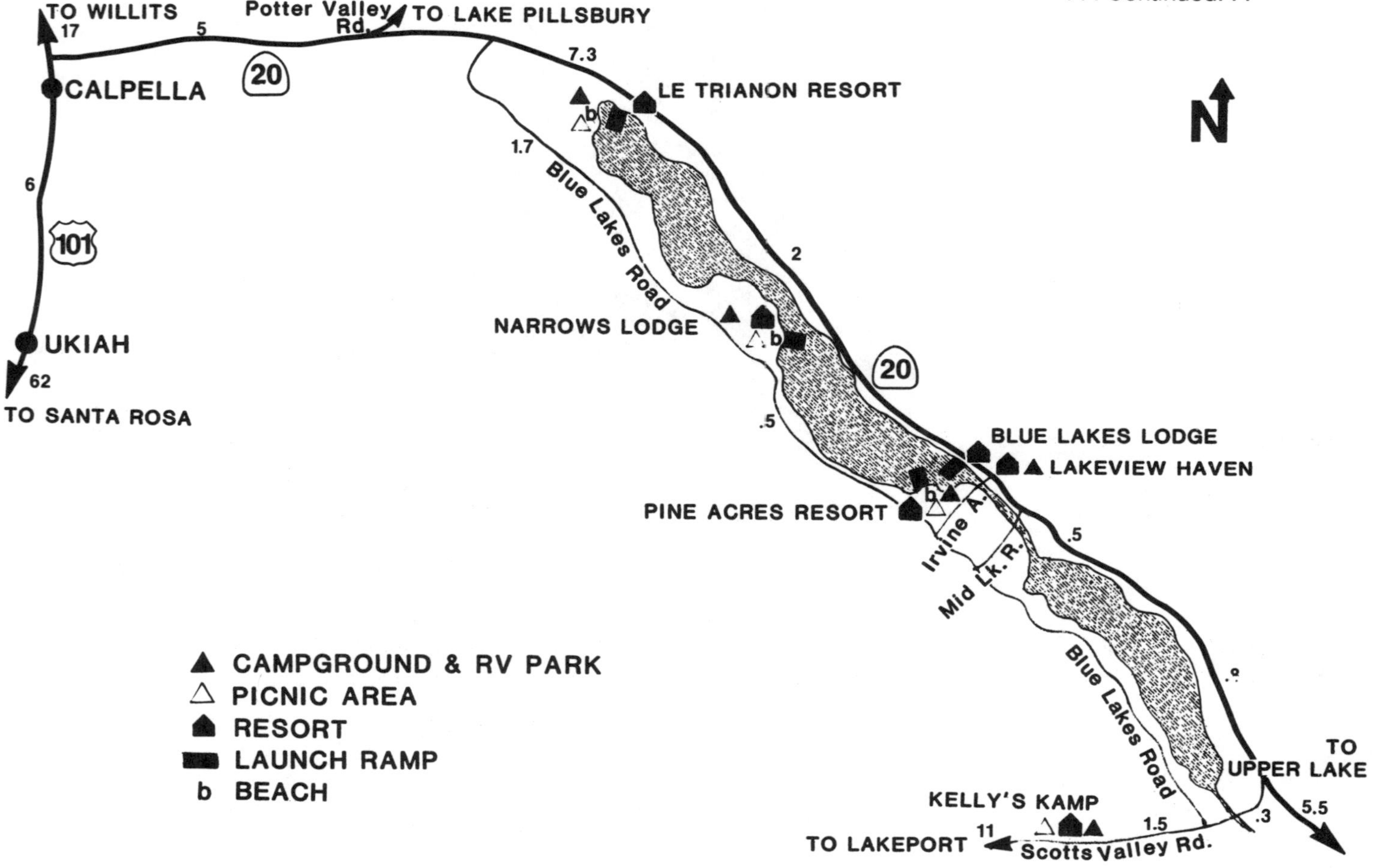

TO WILLITS
17
5
Potter Valley Rd.
TO LAKE PILLSBURY
20
CALPELLA
7.3
LE TRIANON RESORT
N
1.7
Blue Lakes Road
6
101
2
NARROWS LODGE
UKIAH
62
TO SANTA ROSA
20
.5
BLUE LAKES LODGE
LAKEVIEW HAVEN
PINE ACRES RESORT
Irvine A.
.5
Mid Lk. R.
Blue Lakes Road
.9
TO UPPER LAKE
KELLY'S KAMP
1.5
.3
5.5
11
TO LAKEPORT
Scotts Valley Rd.

▲ CAMPGROUND & RV PARK
△ PICNIC AREA
RESORT
LAUNCH RAMP
b BEACH

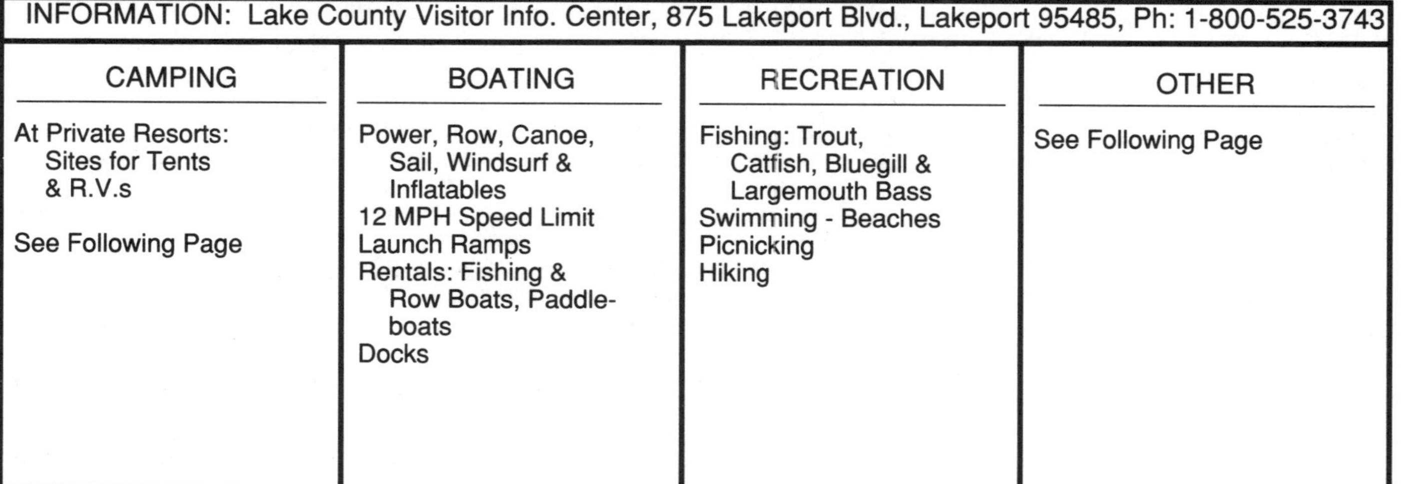

INFORMATION: Lake County Visitor Info. Center, 875 Lakeport Blvd., Lakeport 95485, Ph: 1-800-525-3743

CAMPING	BOATING	RECREATION	OTHER
At Private Resorts: Sites for Tents & R.V.s See Following Page	Power, Row, Canoe, Sail, Windsurf & Inflatables 12 MPH Speed Limit Launch Ramps Rentals: Fishing & Row Boats, Paddle- boats Docks	Fishing: Trout, Catfish, Bluegill & Largemouth Bass Swimming - Beaches Picnicking Hiking	See Following Page

BLUE LAKES - LAKE COUNTY

LE TRIANON RESORT: 5845 E. Hwy. 20, Ukiah 95482, Ph: 707-275-2262

Le Trianon Resort offers housekeeping cabins as well as 300 sites for tent camping, R.V.s or trailers and group sites. There are 400 picnic tables, electricity, water, dump station, laundry, toilets and showers. Also available are a launch ramp, dock, swim area and boat rentals along with R.V. storage.

NARROWS LODGE: 5690 Blue Lakes Road, Upper Lake 95485, Ph: 707-275-2718

The Narrows Lodge Resort provides all the comforts of modern conveniences in a lovely tree-studded setting. There are fully equipped housekeeping cabins and motel units. The R.V. Park has 20 sites with complete hookups. 10 sites have water and electric hookups. Tent sites are also available. The Resort has a launch ramp, fishing dock and swim area. Rowboats and paddleboats can be rented. The Dinner House serves excellent meals and cocktails with piano bar entertainment on Saturday nights. Open year round.

PINE ACRES RESORT: 5328 Blue Lakes Road (off Irvine Ave.), Upper Lake 95485, Ph: 707-275-2811

Pine Acres Resort offers a motel and fully equipped cabins with daily maid service. 32 R.V. sites are available, 23 with water and electric hookups and 4 with full hookups, including cable T.V. throughout. There are shaded lawns, BBQs, picnic tables, horseshoe court, campfire area, swimming beach with float, fishing pier, launch ramp, boat rentals, bait and tackle shop, and dump station. A gazebo has been built for pot lucks, square dancing, conferences and other uses.

BLUE LAKES LODGE: 5315 W. Highway 20, Upper Lake 95485, Ph: 707-275-2178

This Resort has a motel with housekeeping units with T.V.s and air conditioning as well as a restaurant and cocktail bar open year round. Live entertainment and dancing is available on weekends. There is a launch ramp, fishing dock, swim area and boat rentals also. A swimming pool and jacuzzi complete this full facility Resort.

KELLY'S KAMP: 8220 Scotts Valley Road, Upper Lake 95485, Ph: 707-263-5754

Kelly's Kamp offers quiet family camping on spacious sites with frontage on Scotts Creek. There are 30 tent sites and 48 R.V. sites with water and electric hookups. Also offered are Kamp Store, modern restrooms, laundromat, disposal station, hot showers, firewood, picnic tables and BBQ grills. Recreational facilities include swimming, 2-acre Lake with floats, fishing, volleyball, badminton, croquet, horseshoes, and hiking. R.V. storage is available, and a pavilion area with a built-in barbecue for large groups.

LAKEVIEW HAVEN RESORT: 5135 West Highway 20, Upper Lake 95485, Ph: 707-275-2178

Lakeview Haven offers a motel and a 46 site R.V. park with full hookups. There is a restaurant, coctail lounge and game room. Also available are a launch ramp, canoe and rowboat rentals, bait and tackle and a swimming pool.

CLEAR LAKE

Clear Lake, at an elevation of 1,320 feet, is the largest natural Lake in California. It has a surface area of 43,000 acres. The Lake's shoreline of 100 miles has been the same for thousands of years. The water level remains constant. This was once the home of the Pomo and Lile'ek tribes who were drawn here by the abundant fish and game. Often called "~The Bass Capital of the West," Clear Lake provides the angler with a productive warm water fishery. Miles of open water, many coves and inlets entice the boater, waterskiier and sailor. Numerous launch ramps, marinas, beaches, campgrounds and resorts dot the shoreline. Clear Lake State Park has a nice campground, swim beach, hiking trails and a naturalist program. Nearby Highland Springs Reservoir offers a warm water fishing and non-powered boating. The County Park has picnic facilities.

. . . Continued . . .

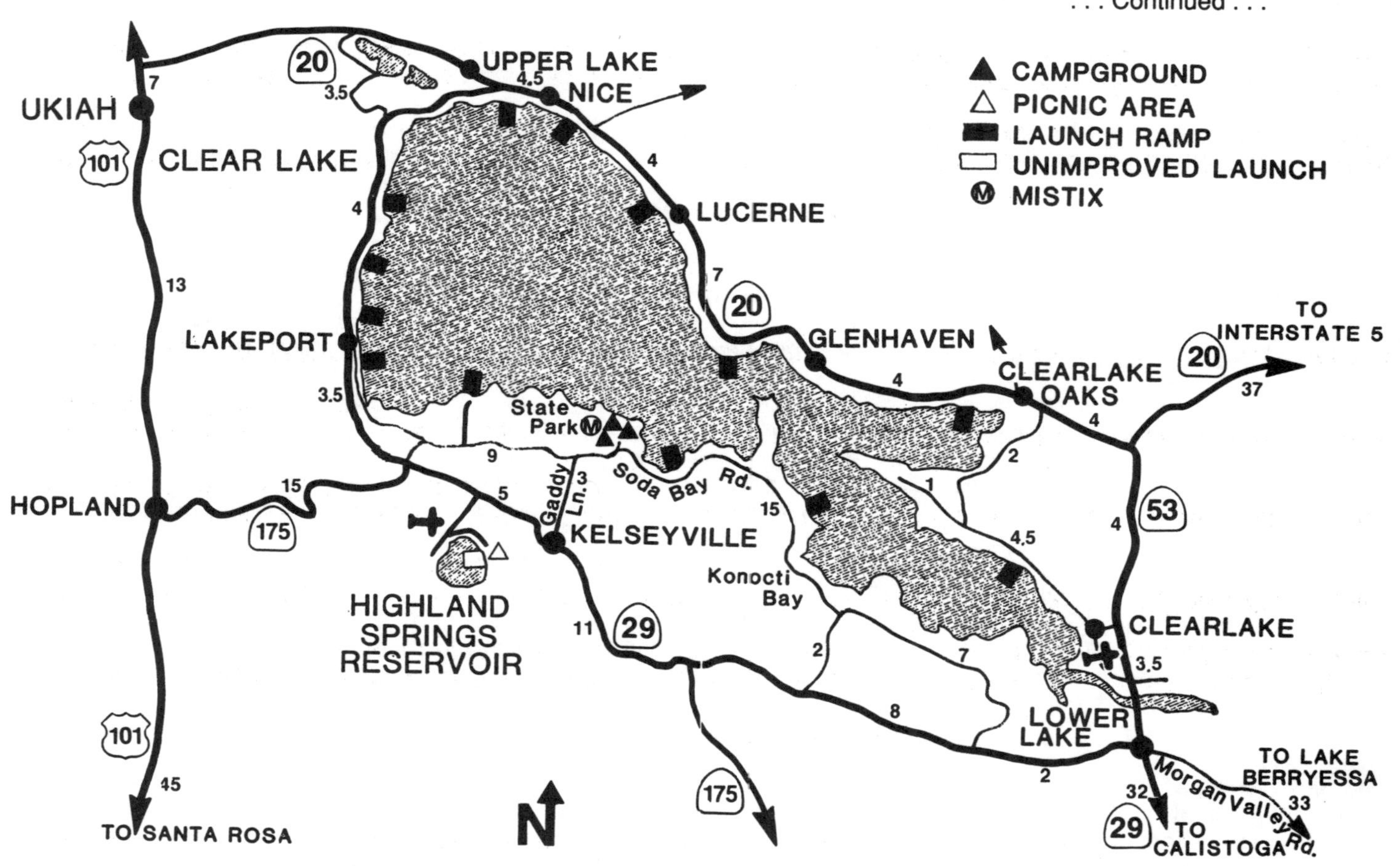

INFORMATION: Visitor Information Center, 875 Lakeport Blvd., Lakeport 95453, Ph: 707-263-9544

CAMPING	BOATING	RECREATION	OTHER
Clear Lake State Park 5300 Soda Bay Rd. Kelseyville 95451 Ph: 707-279-4293 Reservations-Mistix 1-800-444-PARK 147 Dev. Tent/RV Sites Fee: $10 For Additional Resorts & Campgrounds, See Following Pages	Open to All Boating Full Service Marinas 11 Public Launch Ramps Boat Rentals - Fishing, Sail, & Ski Para Sailing	Fishing: Florida & Northern Bass, Yellow & Blue Channel Catfish, Crappie & Bluegill Swimming - Beaches & Pools Nature Trails Hiking Rock Hounding Hunting Nearby: Deer, Dove, Quail, & Waterfowl	Winery Tours Golf Courses Complete Facilities in Nearby Towns Anderson Marsh State Historical Park - Archeological Sites of Indian Villages and Sanctuary for Water Birds and Fish

CLEAR LAKE

There are over 100 private campgrounds and resorts around Clear Lake. The following are randomly selected facilities with launch ramps:

NORTHSHORE - NICE, LUCERNE

HOLIDAY HARBOR - P.O. Box 26, 3605 Lakeshore Blvd., Nice 95464, 707-274-1136, 33 Sites, Hookups, Dump Station, Flush Toilets, Showers, Laundry, Ramp, Fuel, Slips, Rental Boats.

NORTHSHORE RESORT & MARINA - P.O. Box 493, 2345 Lakeshore Blvd., Nice 95464, 707-274-7771, 31 Sites, Hookups, Flush Toilets, Showers, Laundry, Ramp, Fuel, Dock, Pier, Repairs, Boat Rentals, Snacks & Sundries, Bait & Tackle.

ARROW TRAILER PARK - P.O. Box 407-6720, E. Hwy. 20, Lucerne 95458, 707-274-7715, 24 Sites, Hookups, Dump Station, Flush Toilets, Showers, Ramp, Pier, Mooring, Storage, Fuel, Bait & Tackle, Groceries, Snack Bar.

TALLEY'S FAMILY RESORT - P.O. Box 538, 3827 Hwy. 20, Nice 95464, 707-274-1177, 10 Cottages with T.V., 7 R.V. Sites, Hookups, Showers, Laundry, Fish Room, Snack Bar, BBQ, Beach, Pier, Mooring/Launch, Boat Rentals.

GLENHAVEN - CLEARLAKE OAKS

GLENHAVEN BEACH CAMPGROUND & MARINA - P.O. Box 406, 9625 E. Hwy. 20, Glenhaven 95423, 707-998-3406, 44 RV Sites, Hookups, Flush Toilets, Hot Showers, Laundry, Paved Ramp, Mooring, Slips, Fuel Dock, Rental Boats, Groceries.

M & M CAMPGROUND - P.O. Box 654, 13050 Island Dr., Clearlake Oaks 95423, 707-998-9943, 38 Sites, Flush Toilets, Showers, Ramp.

DARNELL'S NORTHWOOD PARK - P.O. Box 451, 10090 E. Hwy. 20, Clearlake Oaks 95423, 707-998-3389, 20 Sites, Hookups, Flush Toilets, Showers, Dock, Pier & Slips.

ISLAND PARK - P.O. Box 126, 12840 Island Dr., Clearlake Oaks 95423, 707-998-3940, 19 R.V. Sites, Hookups, Showers, Laundry, Boat Launch, Docks.

LAKE HAVEN MOTEL - P.O. Box 232, 100 Short St., Clearlake Oaks 95423, 707-998-3908, 32 Units, T.V., Boat Launching, Pier, Docks, Pool.

CLEARLAKE - SOUTH SHORE

AUSTIN'S CAMPGROUND & MARINA - P.O. Box 2617, 14067 Lakeshore Dr., Clearlake 95422, 707-994-7623, 40 Sites, Hookups, Dump Station, Flush Toilets, Showers, RV Storage, Laundry, Groceries, Ramp, Slips, Fuel Dock, Bait & Tackle.

GARNER'S RESORT - P.O. Box 509, 6235 Old Hwy. 53, Clearlake 95422, 707-994-6267, 92 Tent/RV Sites, Hookups, Dump Station, RV Storage, Flush Toilets, Showers, Laundry, Groceries, Swimming Pool, Ramp, Rental Boats, Fuel Dock, Slips.

TROMBETTA'S BEACH RESORT - P.O. Box 728, 5865 Old Hwy. 53, Clearlake 95422, 707-944-2417, 21 Sites, Hookups, Cottages, Flush Toilets, Showers, Laundry, Swimming Pool, Ramp, Dock, Moorings, Boat Rentals, Fishing Pier.

. . . Continued . . .

CLEAR LAKE

KELSEYVILLE - SODA BAY - KONOCTI BAY

EDGEWATER RESORT - 6420 Soda Bay Rd., Soda Bay, Kelseyville 95451, 707-279-0208, 30 Tent Sites, 40 R/V Sites, Hookups, Flush Toilets, Showers, Laundry, Cabins, Ramp, Pier, Rental Boats, Restaurant.

KONOCTI HARBOR INN - 8727 Soda Bay Rd., Kelseyville 95451, 707-279-4281, 250 Rooms, Laundry, Cable T.V., Restaurant & Lounge, 4 Swimming Pools, Tennis Courts, Ramps, Piers, Slips, Boat Rentals, Snack Bar, Full Service Marina.

RICHMOND PARK - 9435 Konocti Bay Rd., Kelseyville 95451, 707-277-7535, 10 Tent Sites, 8 RV Sites, Hookups, Flush Toilets, Showers, Laundry, Ramp, Rental Boats, Snack Bar, Lounge.

FERNDALE RESORT - 6190 Soda Bay Rd., Soda Bay, Kelseyville 95451, 707-279-4866, 14 Rooms, 2 Cottages, TV, Paved Ramp, Slips, Pier, Large Rental Fleet, Snack Bar.

LAKEPORT

ANCHORAGE INN - 950 N. Main St., Lakeport 95453, 707-263-5417, 34 Units, TV, Laundry, Pool, Sauna, Jacuzzi, Ramp, Berthing, Dock.

CLEAR LAKE INN - 1010 N. Main St., Lakeport 95453, 707-263-3551 - 40 Units, TV, Pool, Dock, Fishing Pier.

WILL-O-POINT RESORT - One First St., Lakeport 95453, 707-263-5407, 158 Tent/RV Sites, 10 Sites With Hookups, Dump Station, Flush Toilets, Showers, Laundry, Groceries, Swim Beach, Ramp, Fuel Dock, Rental Boats.

SKYLARK MOTEL - 1120 N. Main St., Lakeport 95453, 707-263-6151, 45 Units, T.V., Pool, Dock, Playground.

In addition to the above and other resorts not mentioned, there are 11 public launch ramps as shown on our map. The State Park is shown on the graph. For information on additional resorts and other attractions, contact the following Information Centers:

1. Lake County Visitor Information Center - 875 Lakeport Blvd., Lakeport 95453, 707-263-9544, (Toll-Free in California) 800-LAKESIDE

2. Lake County Chamber of Commerce - #1 First St., Lakeport 95453, 707-263-6131

3. Lakeport Chamber of Commerce - P.O. Box 295 (290 S. Main St.), Lakeport 95453, 707-263-5092

4. Clear Lake Chamber of Commerce - Austin Park - P.O. Box 629, Clearlake 95422, 707-994-3600

INDIAN VALLEY RESERVOIR

Indian Valley Reservoir is under the jurisdiction of the Yolo County Flood Control District. Resting at an elevation of 1,476 feet, this remote 3,800 acre Lake has 39 shoreline miles. The Lake is an excellent Rainbow trout fishery and a developing warm water fishery. Since there is a 10 MPH speed limit, this is a delightfully quiet place for sailing, canoeing and fishing. The crystal clear warm water makes for pleasant swimming. The concession at Indian Valley Store operates a newly developed campground. The area surrounding the Reservoir is an important wintering area for both bald and golden eagles and waterfowl. There is a public launch ramp and unimproved camping on the North Shore.

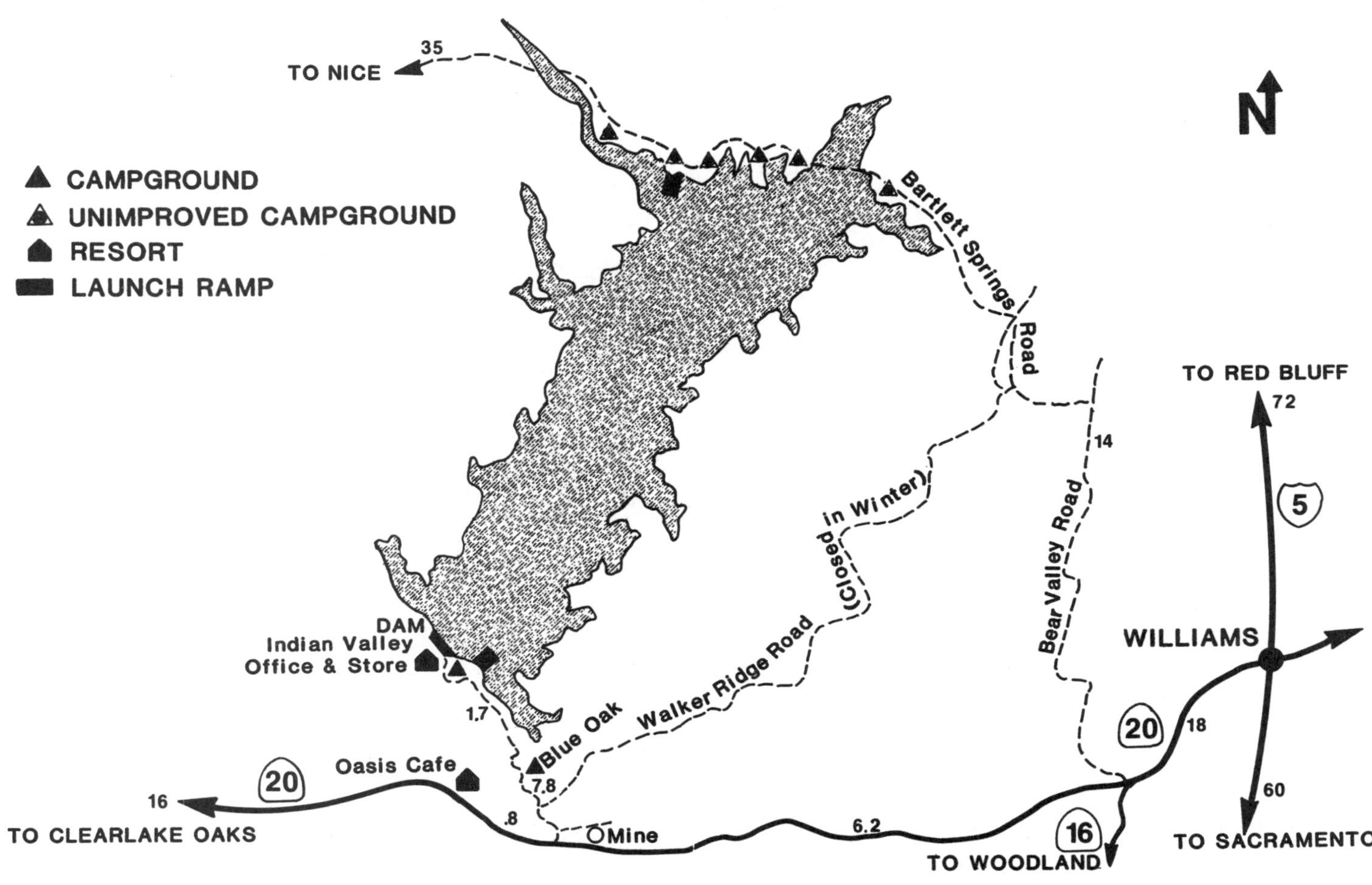

INFORMATION: Indian Valley Store, P.O. Box 4939, Clear Lake 95422, Ph: 916-662-0607			
CAMPING	BOATING	RECREATION	OTHER
20 Dev. Sites for Tents 50 Dev. Sites for R.V.s Fee: $5 Disposal Station Hot Showers Trailer Rentals Day Use Fee: $2	Open to All Boating 10 MPH Speed Limit Paved Launch Ramp Rentals: Fishing Boats and Motors	Fishing: Rainbow Trout, Large & Smallmouth Bass, Catfish & Redear Perch Picnicking & Swimming Hiking Birding Nature Study Hunting: Waterfowl, Quail, Dove, Turkey, Pigs & Bear	Grocery Store Bait & Tackle Propane, Gas Oasis Cafe: Restaurant For Further Info: Lake County Visitor Information Center 875 Lakeport Blvd., Lakeport 95453 In California 1-800-LAKESIDE

CENTRAL SECTION

LAKES 59 — 148

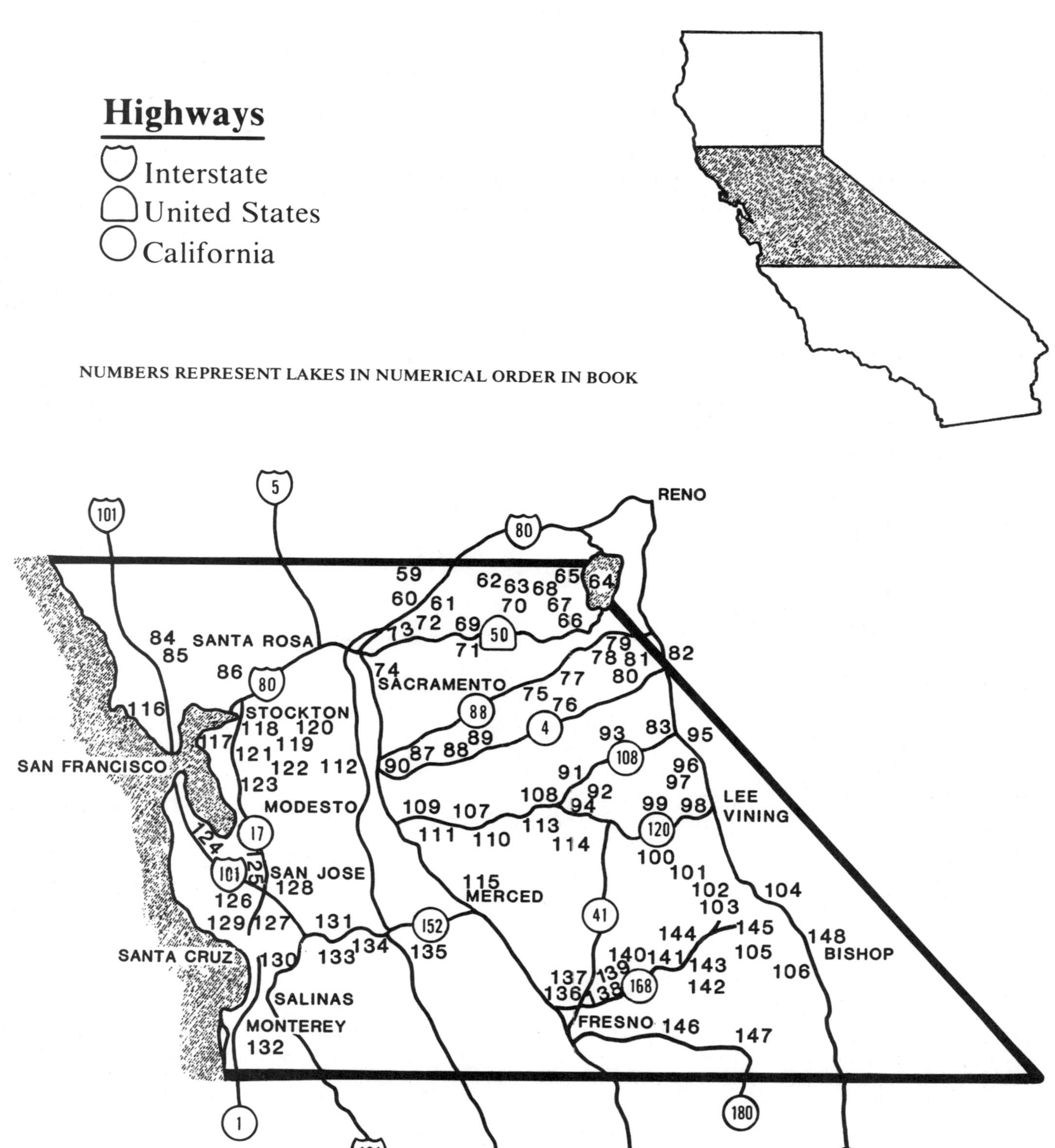

SUGAR PINE AND BIG RESERVOIRS
LAKE CLEMENTINE

Sugar Pine Reservoir, at an elevation of 3,618 feet, is a 160 surface acre reservoir in the Tahoe National Forest. The modern recreation complex offers handicapped facilities and will accommodate R.V.s and trailers up to 40 feet. Its neighbor, Big or sometimes called Morning Star Lake, rests at 4,092 feet in a heavily forested area. The facilities at this 70 acre lake are under concession to Morning Star Resort. Down the road in the foothill canyons of the American River, Lake Clementine is a part of the Auburn State Recreation Area. The lake is a 3-1/2 mile long stretch of the North Fork of the American River. The facilities are primitive although there is a launch ramp and the lake is open to all boating.

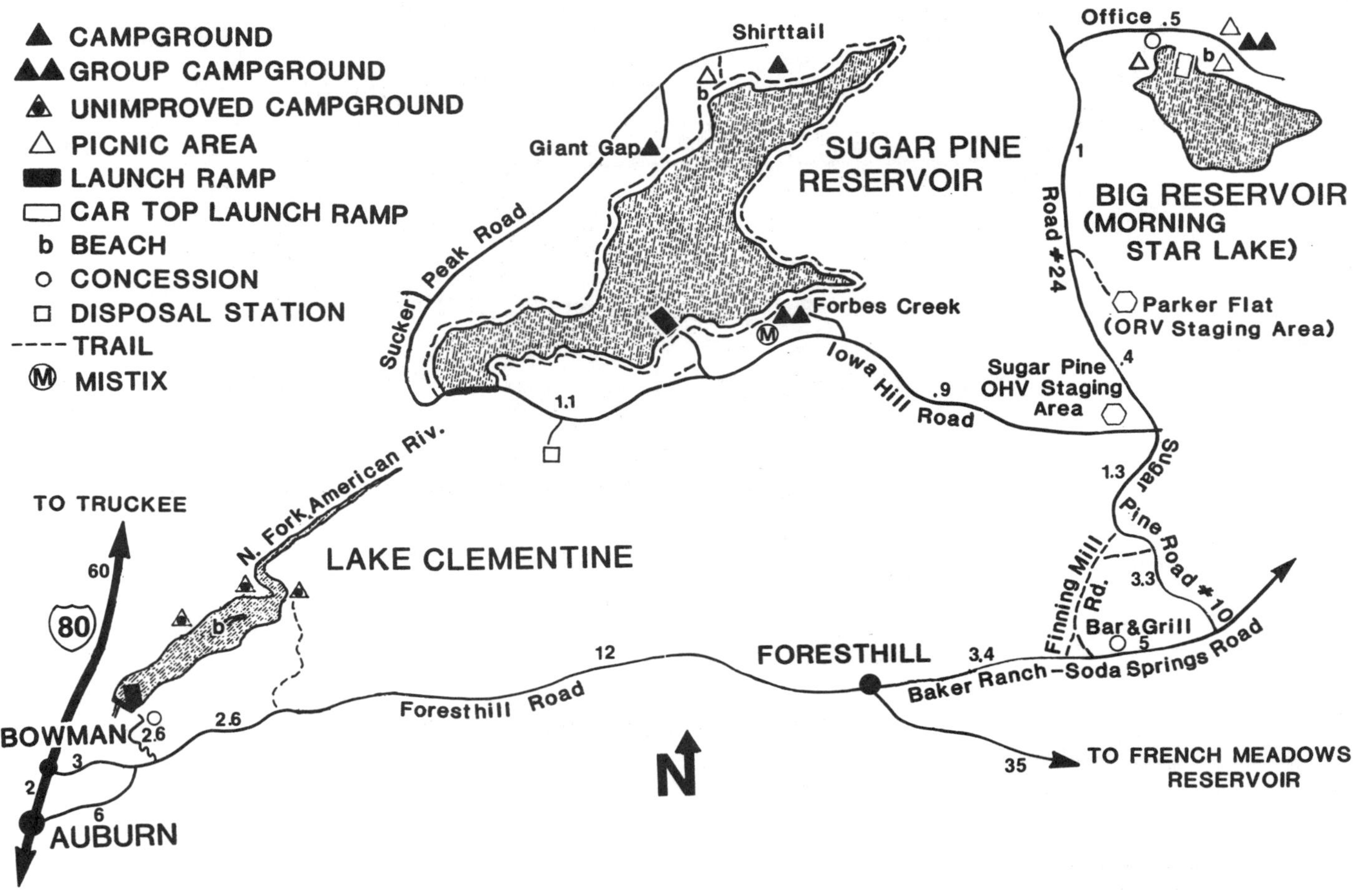

INFORMATION: Tahoe Nat. Forest, Foresthill Ranger Station, Foresthill 95631, Ph: 916-367-2224

CAMPING	BOATING	RECREATION	OTHER
Sugar Pine: 60 Dev. Sites for Tents & R.V.s Fee: $6 2 Group Sites Disposal Station Reservations: MISTIX Ph: 1-800-283-CAMP Big Reservoir: 120 Dev. Sites for Tents & R.V.s: $8 2 Group Sites Lake Clementine: Unimproved Campground	Sugar Pine: Open to All Boating 10 MPH Speed Limit Launch Ramp No Motor Size Limit Big Reservoir: Open to Non-Powered Boating Electric Motors Permitted Car Top Launch	Fishing: Rainbow & Brown Trout, Black Bass, Bluegill & Perch Picnicking Paved & Unpaved Trails Swimming Hiking & Backpacking ORV Trails Nearby Hunting: Deer & Bear	Facilities at Foresthill Morning Star Lake Resort P.O. Box 119 Foresthill 95631 Ph: 916-367-2129 Lake Clementine Auburn State Rec. Area P.O. Box 3266 Auburn 95604 Ph: 916-885-4527

CAMP FAR WEST LAKE

Camp Far West Lake is at an elevation of 320 feet in the Sierra foothills northeast of Roseville. The lake has a surface area of 2,000 acres with a shoreline of 29 miles. The water temperature rises up to 85 degrees in the summer when the climate can be quite hot although there are many oak trees providing ample shade. The lake is open year around, but the north entrance is closed at the end of summer. This is a good lake for all types of boating and waterskiing, but the boater should be aware of the rocky area as noted on the map. The water level normally is low in late summer. There is a warm water fishery especially for landlocked Stripers, smallmouth and black bass at the Bear River and Rock Creek Arms.

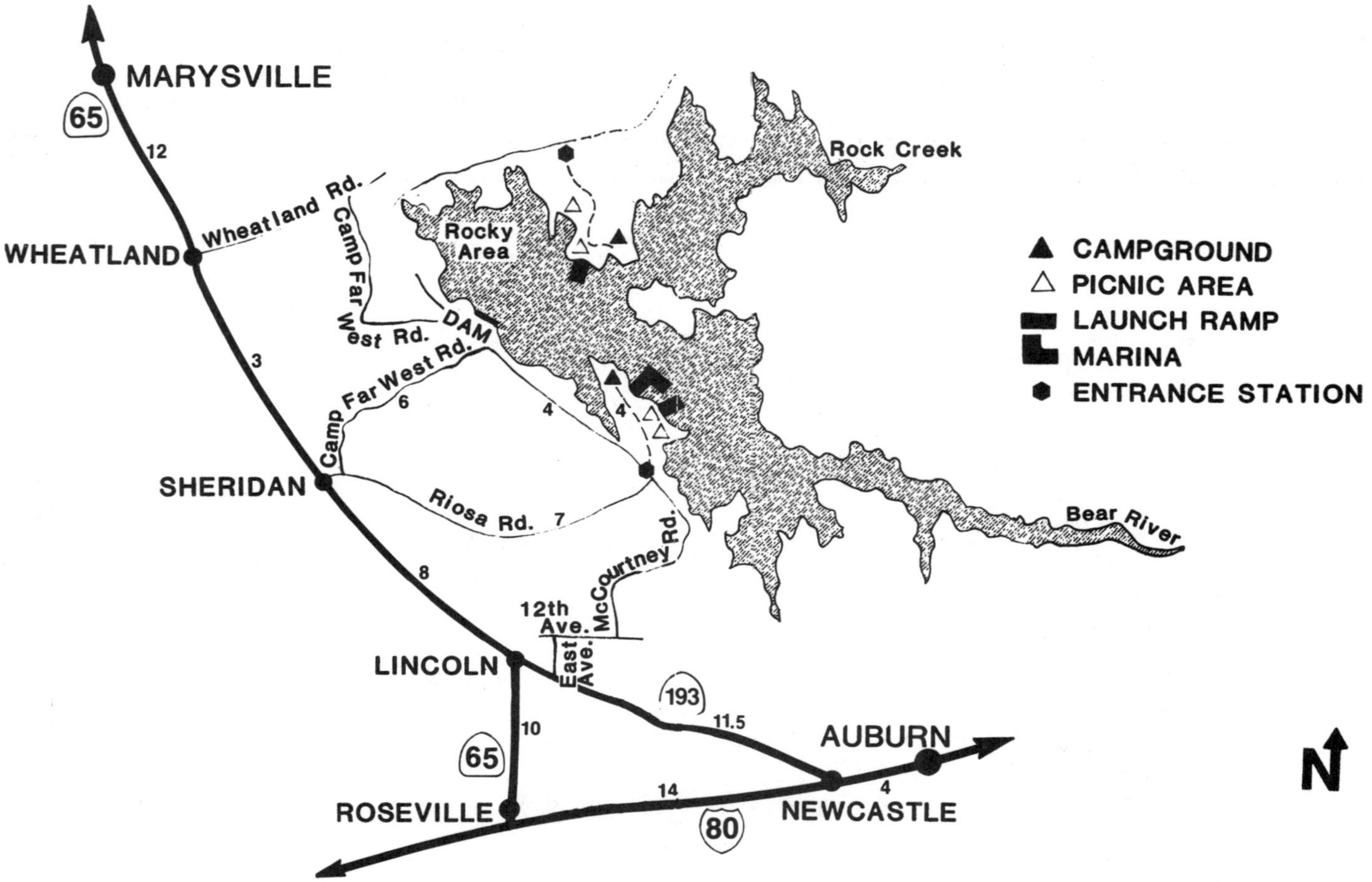

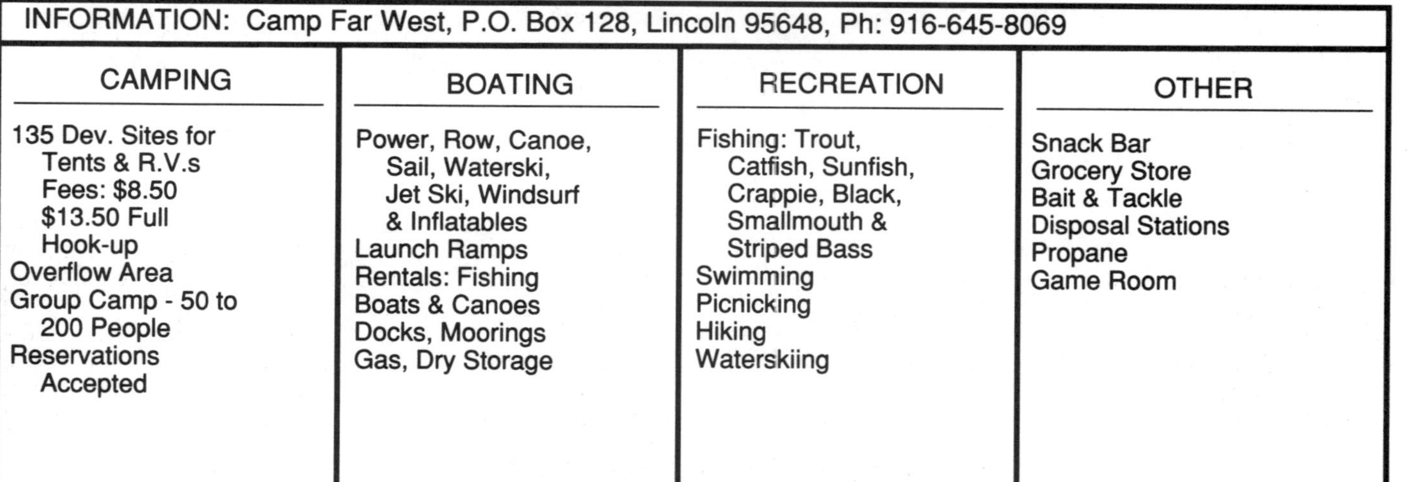

INFORMATION: Camp Far West, P.O. Box 128, Lincoln 95648, Ph: 916-645-8069

CAMPING	BOATING	RECREATION	OTHER
135 Dev. Sites for Tents & R.V.s Fees: $8.50 $13.50 Full Hook-up Overflow Area Group Camp - 50 to 200 People Reservations Accepted	Power, Row, Canoe, Sail, Waterski, Jet Ski, Windsurf & Inflatables Launch Ramps Rentals: Fishing Boats & Canoes Docks, Moorings Gas, Dry Storage	Fishing: Trout, Catfish, Sunfish, Crappie, Black, Smallmouth & Striped Bass Swimming Picnicking Hiking Waterskiing	Snack Bar Grocery Store Bait & Tackle Disposal Stations Propane Game Room

FRENCH MEADOWS RESERVOIR

French Meadows Reservoir rests at an elevation of 5,200 feet on the western slope of the Sierra Nevada. This man-made reservoir of 1,920 surface acres is often subject to low water levels late in the season. Although open to all types of boating, these low water conditions along with underwater hazards make waterskiing and speed boating extremely dangerous. If the angler can suffer through the loss of tackle from these hazards, you are sometimes rewarded with a beautiful German brown or rainbow trout up to 7 pounds. The U.S. Forest Service maintains numerous campsites around the lake along with picnic areas and two launch ramps. There are several natural swimming beaches. Hiking the Western States Trail can be rewarding. This is a nice family camping area though remote so plan on staying awhile.

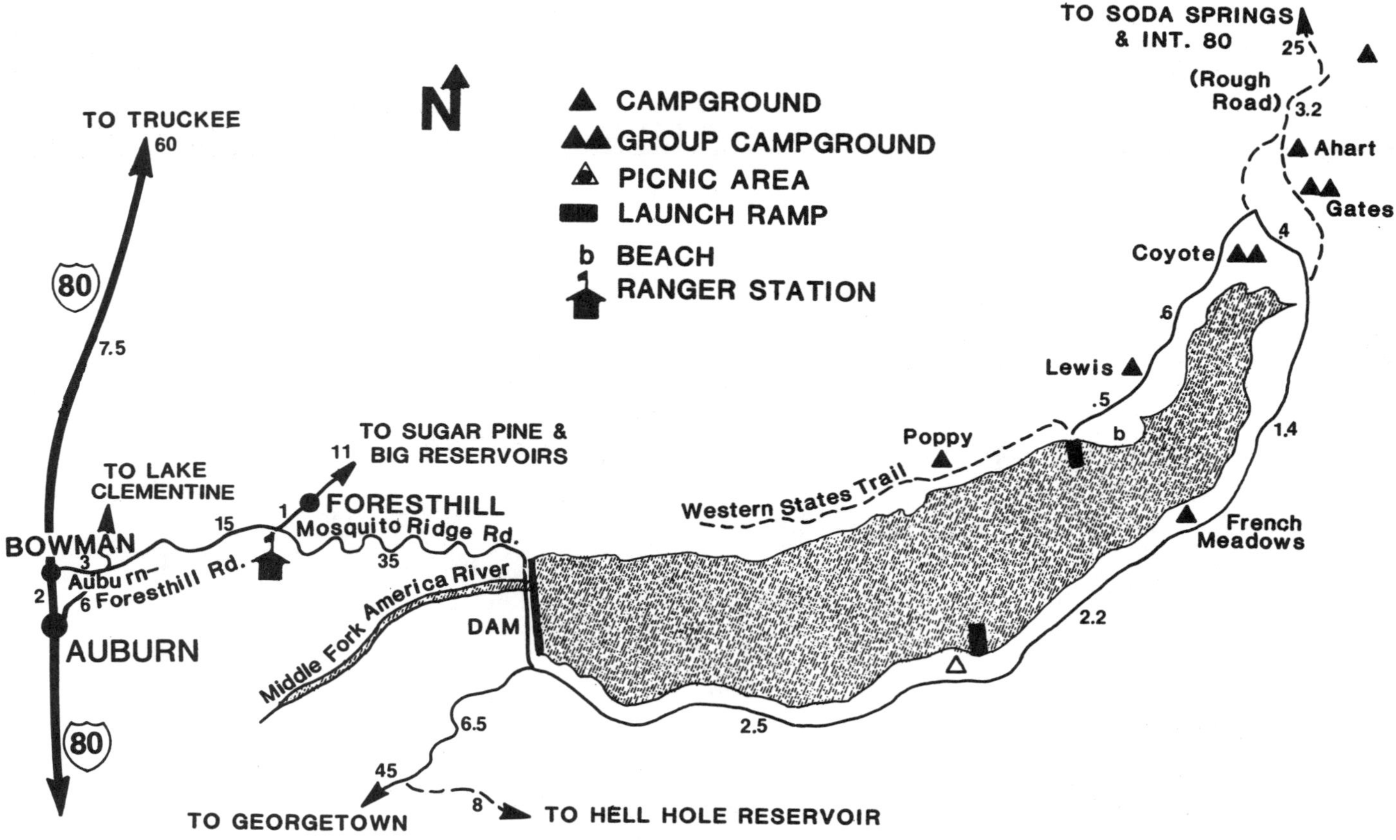

INFORMATION: Tahoe National Forest, 22830 Foresthill Rd., Foresthill 95631, Ph: 916-367-2224			
CAMPING	BOATING	RECREATION	OTHER
French Meadows: 115 Dev. Sites Fee: $8 12 Boat or Walk-In Sites 7 Group Sites Reservations: MISTIX Ph: 800-283-CAMP	French Meadows: Open to All Boats Speed Boats & Waterskiing Not Advised Due to Submerged Hazards	Fishing: Rainbow & Brown Trout Picnicking Swimming Hiking Backpacking-Parking	Nearest Supplies and Facilities 39 Miles in Foresthill

HELL HOLE RESERVOIR AND RALSTON AFTERBAY

Hell Hole Reservoir is in the Eldorado National Forest at an elevation of 4,700 feet. The facilities are operated and maintained by the U. S. Forest Service. Hell Hole is 15 miles south of French Meadows Reservoir in a rugged, rocky area on the Rubicon River. The Lake of 1,300 surface acres is in a deep gorge surrounded by granite boulders with cold, clear water, creating an awesome setting. It is especially scenic where the water leaves the power house and drops into the Lake so be sure to bring a camera. There are no facilities other than the launch ramp and campgrounds so come well supplied. Ralston Afterbay is on the Middle Fork of the American River with a nice picnic area and gravel launch ramps.

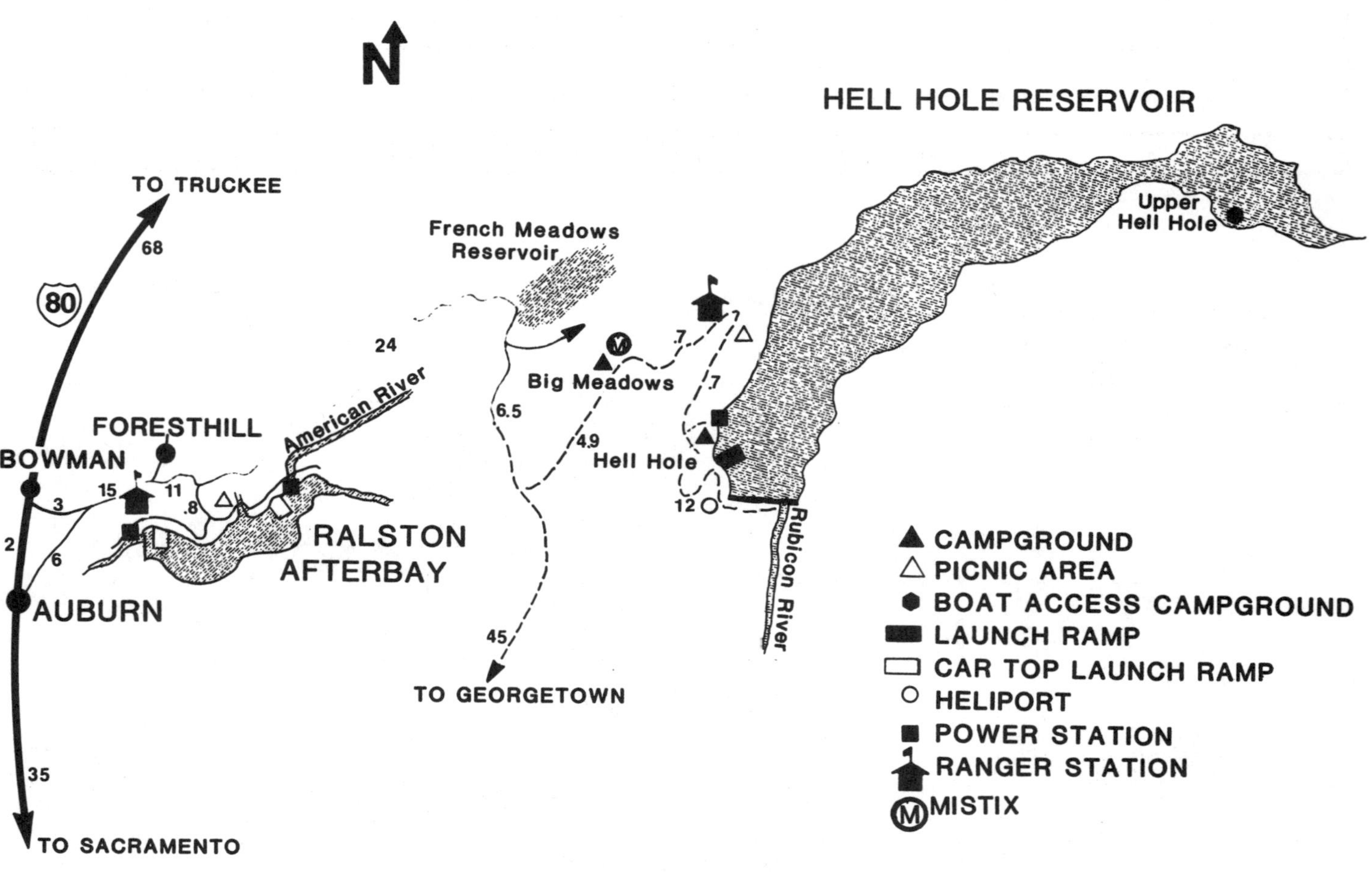

INFORMATION: Georgetown Ranger District, Georgetown 95634, Ph: 916-333-4312

CAMPING	BOATING	RECREATION	OTHER
Hell Hole: 10 Tent Sites No Fee No Reservations Big Meadows: 55 Tent/RV Sites Upper Hell Hole: 15 Boat Access Sites - No Fee No Water Ralston Afterbay: No Campgrounds	Hell Hole: Power, Row, Canoe, Sail, Waterski & Inflatable Launch Ramp Caution - Afternoon Winds Can Be Hazardous Ralston Afterbay: Small Craft Only Hand Launch	Fishing: Rainbow, Brown, Cutthroat & Kamloop Trout Picnicking Hiking Backpacking Horseback Riding Trails Hunting: Deer, Bear	Nearest Facilities From Hell Hole Reservoir - 55 Miles at Georgetown

STUMPY MEADOWS RESERVOIR AND FINNON LAKE

Stumpy Meadows is at an elevation of 4,260 feet in the Eldorado National Forest. This pretty lake of 320 acres is surrounded by conifers and the water is clear and cold. Boating is restricted to 5 MPH so waterskiing is not allowed. The angler will find German Brown and Rainbow trout.

Finnon Lake, at 2,420 feet, is a small lake administered by Eldorado County. Boating is limited to rowboats. Fishing, swimming, hiking and horseback riding are the primary activities. Small trailers only are advised at both of these lakes.

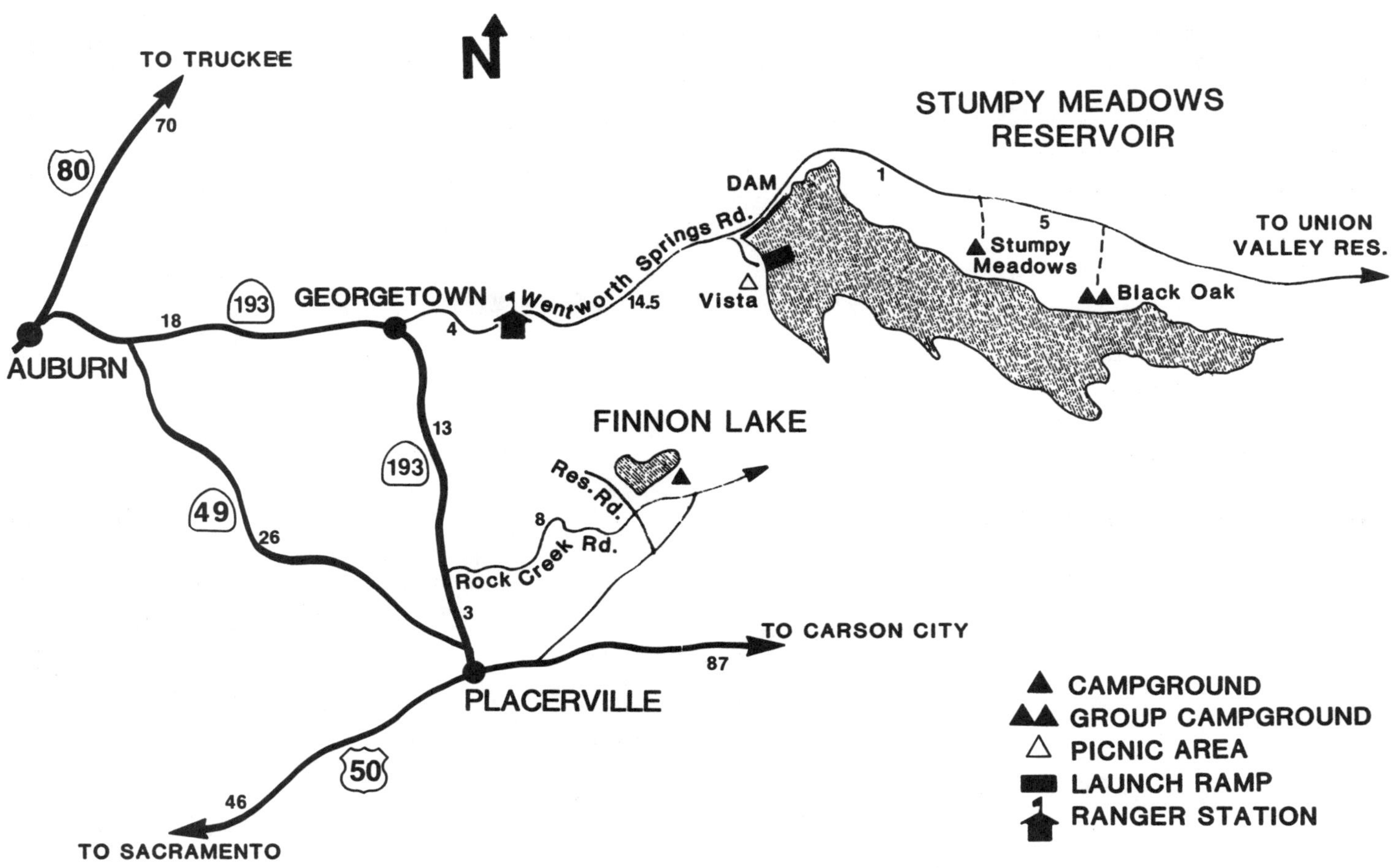

INFORMATION: Georgetown Ranger District, Georgetown 95634, Ph: 916-333-4312

CAMPING	BOATING	RECREATION	OTHER
Stumpy Meadows: 40 Dev. Sites for Tents & R.V.s 4 Group Sites to 225 People by Reservation Max. Trailer Length 22 feet Finnon Lake: 28 Dev. Sites Small Trailers	Stumpy Meadows: Open to All Boats 5 MPH Speed Limit 10 HP Motors Max. Improved Launch Ramp Finnon Lake: Rowboats Only	Fishing: Rainbow & Brown Trout Picnicking Swimming at Finnon Lake Only Hiking & Riding Trails	Finnon Lake Resort: 9100 Rock Creek Rd. Placerville 95667 Ph: 916-622-9314 Finnon Lake: Store Snack Bar Restaurant

LAKE TAHOE

Lake Tahoe was named "The Lake of the Sky" by Mark Twain for its sky blue waters. At 6,229 feet, Tahoe is one of America's largest and most beautiful mountain Lakes. It is 22 miles long, 12 miles wide and 71 miles around. Tahoe is a prime recreation lake with a variety of opportunities and abundant support facilities. Boaters, skiers and sailors find its vast expanse of clear open water an exciting challenge.

The varied trout fishery ranges from planted Rainbows to the huge Lake trout or Mackinaw. Hikers, backpackers and equestrians enjoy the numerous trails within the surrounding mountains and the nearby Desolation Wilderness. Add to these outdoor activities, the excitement and luxury of Nevada's casinos, the "Lake" has it all.

...Continued...

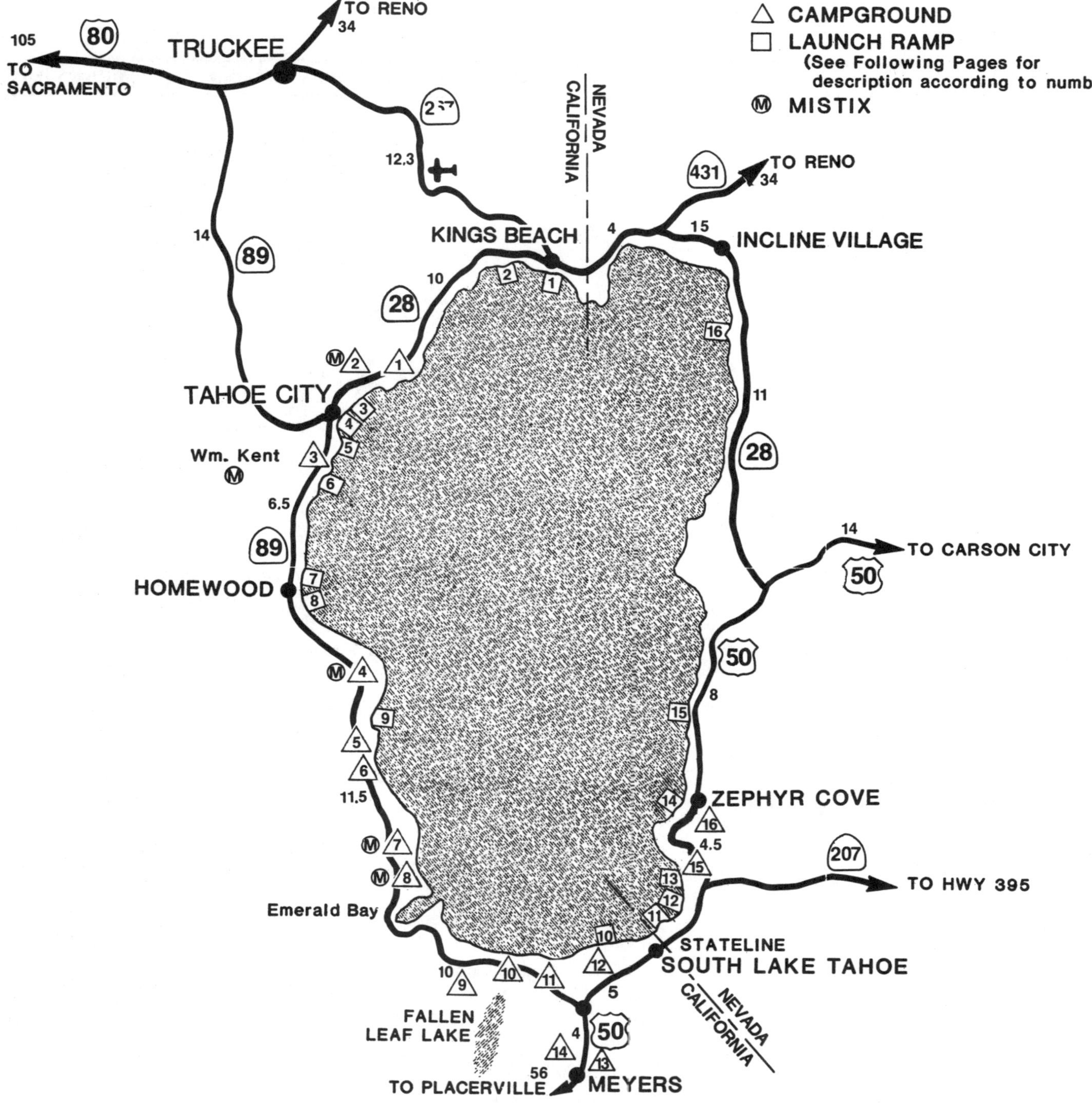

LAKE TAHOE

LAUNCH RAMPS AND MARINE FACILITIES AS PER NUMBER IN SQUARE ON MAP

1 **KINGS BEACH BOAT LAUNCHING FACILITY** - North Lake Tahoe Parks and Recreation, P.O. Box 39, Tahoe Vista 95732, 916-546-7248, Paved Ramp, Power & Sail Boat Rentals, Full Facilities Nearby.

2 **NORTH TAHOE MARINA** - P.O. Box 348, 7360 N. Lake Blvd., Tahoe Vista 95732, 916-546-8248, Paved Ramp, Full Service Marina, Fuel and Repairs, Boat and Accessory Sales, Power Boat & Ski Equipment Rentals.

3 **SIERRA BOAT CO.** - 5146 North Lake Blvd., Carnelian Bay 95711, 916-546-2552, Hoist (No Ramp), Buoys, Fuel and Repairs, Full Facilities Nearby.

4 **TAHOE BOAT COMPANY** - 700 No. Lake Blvd., Box 1314, Tahoe City 95730, 916-583-5567, Hoist (No Ramp), Full Service Marina, Fuel, Repairs, Marine Accessories, Ski Boat Rentals, Winter Storage, Boat Sales.

5 **LAKE TAHOE PUBLIC ACCESS FACILITY** - 2 Miles North of Tahoe City, off SR-28, 916-583-5544, Paved Ramp, Limited Facilities, Picnic Areas, Trailer Parking, $5 a Day, No Overnights.

6 **SUNNYSIDE RESORT** - P.O. Box 5969, Tahoe City 95730, 916-583-7200, Hoist, Slips, Buoys, Pump Station, Fuel, Repairs, Restaurant, Ski & Sail Boat Rentals & Sales, Ski School, Store & Supplies.

7 **HOMEWOOD MARINE** - HIGH & DRY, 5180 Hwy. 89, Homewood 95718, 916-525-5966, Hoist (No Ramp), Fuel, Power Boat Rentals, Complete Sailboat Line & Hardware.

8 **OBEXERS**, 5355 West Lake Blvd., Homewood 95718, 916-525-7962, Paved Ramp and Travel Lift, Power Boat Rentals, Fuel, Marine Accessories, Boat Sales & Service, Groceries, Snack Bar, Bait & Tackle.

9 **MEEKS BAY RESORT AND MARINA** - One Resort Drive, Meeks Bay 95730, 916-525-7242, Paved Ramp, Slips, Fuel, Row, Power & Sail Boat Rentals, Groceries, Bait & Tackle, Snack Bar, Motel, RV Park

. . . Continued . . .

INFORMATION: See Above and Following Pages			
CAMPING	**BOATING**	**RECREATION**	**OTHER**
See Following Page for Public & Private Campgrounds	Open to All Boating Full Service Marinas & Support Facilities Around the Lake See Above for Details	Fishing: Rainbow, Brook & Brown Trout, Lake Trout (Mackinaw), & Kokanee Salmon Swimming Picnicking Nature Trails Hiking Backpacking Horseback Riding & Rentals Winter Sports	Casinos Live Entertainment Complete Destination Facilities See Following Pages for Further Information

LAKE TAHOE

LAUNCH RAMPS AND MARINA FACILITIES AS PER NUMBER IN SQUARE ON MAP...Continued...

10 **TAHOE KEYS MARINA** - 2435 Venice Dr. East, South Lake Tahoe 95731, 916-541-2155, Paved Ramp, Full Service Marina, Sail and Power Boat Rentals, Fuel, Repairs, 360 Slips, Largest Marina on Lake, Overnight Parking, Restaurant.

11 **EL DORADO PUBLIC BOAT RAMP** - US 50 & Lakeview Ave., South Lake Tahoe 95731, 916-541-4611, Free Public Use Facility, Paved Ramp, Swim Beach, Picnic Area, Campground.

12 **TIMBER COVE MARINA** - 3411 Lake Tahoe Blvd., South Lake Tahoe 95731, 916-544-8092, Unpaved Ramp, Hoist, Mooring, Fuel, Repairs, Power & Sail Boat Rentals, Snack Bar.

13 **SKI RUN MARINA** - P.O. Box 14272, South Lake Tahoe 95731, 916-544-0200, Paved Ramp, Mooring, Slips, Power & Sail Boat Rentals, Fuel, Repairs, Snack Bar.

14 **ZEPHYR COVE MARINA** - 760 US 50, Zephyr Cove, NV 89448, 702-588-3833, Paved Ramp, Mooring, Fuel, Power & Sail Boat Rentals, Full Resort Facilities, Picnic Area, Motel, Cabins, Campground, Restaurant, M.S. Dixie Cruises.

15 **CAVE ROCK PUBLIC LAUNCH FACILITY** - Off Hwy. 50, North of Zephyr Cove, Paved Ramp, No Fee, Restrooms, Parking.

16 **LAKE TAHOE NEVADA STATE PARK** - 4 Miles South of Incline Village at Sand Harbor - Paved Launch Ramp, Slips, Swim Beach, Picnic Areas, Restrooms.

CAMPGROUNDS AS PER NUMBER IN TRIANGLE ON MAP

U.S.F.S. CAMPGROUNDS - First-Come, First-Serve

3 **WILLIAM KENT** - 2 Miles south of Tahoe City on Hwy. 89, 94 Tent/RV Sites to 24 Feet, Disposal Station, Flush Toilets, Piped Water, Swim Beach, Fee: $7, Information: 916-583-3642.

6 **MEEKS BAY** - 2 Miles South of Tahoma on Hwy. 89, 40 Tent/RV Sites to 24 Feet, Flush Toilets, Piped Water, Swim Beach, Marina Nearby, Fee: $7, Information: 916-573-2600.

15 **NEVADA BEACH** - 2 Miles North of Stateline, NV off Hwy. 50, 54 Tent/RV Sites to 24 Feet, Flush Toilets, Piped Water, Boat-In Picnic Area, Group Picnic Area to 100 People, Fee: $8 for Single Site, Information: 916-573-2600.

CALIFORNIA STATE PARK CAMPGROUNDS - Reservations Through MISTIX 1-800-446-7275

7 **D. L. BLISS STATE PARK** - 3 Miles North of Emerald Bay, off Hwy. 89, 168 Tent/RV Sites to 21 Feet, Group Camp, Flush Toilets, Showers, Information: 916-525-7277.

8 **EMERALD BAY STATE PARK** - 8 Miles North of South Lake Tahoe off Hwy. 89, 100 Tent/RV Sites to 24 Feet, Flush Toilets, Showers, Information: 916-525-7277.

...Continued...

LAKE TAHOE

CALIFORNIA STATE PARK CAMPGROUNDS...Continued...

SUGAR PINE POINT STATE PARK - 1 Mile South of Tahoma off SR 89, 205 Tent/RV Sites to 30 Feet, Disposal Station, Flush Toilets, Showers, 916-525-7982.

2 **TAHOE STATE RECREATION AREA** - 1/4 Mile East of Tahoe City, 15 Tent Sites (Hillside Area), 22 Tent/RV Sites (Lakeside Area) to 21 Feet, Flush Toilets, Showers, Groceries, Laundromat, 916-525-7232.

CITY OF SOUTH LAKE TAHOE - P.O. Box 1210, South Lake Tahoe 95705, 916-573-2059

EL DORADO RECREATION AREA - 1 Mile South of Stateline on Hwy. 50 & Rufus Allen Blvd., 170 Tent/RV Sites, Disposal Station, Flush Toilets, Showers, Laundromat, Groceries & Supplies, Swimming Pool, Launch Ramp, 3 Weeks Advance Mail Reservation Required, 2 Nights Plus $1 Deposit ($29.50), Fee: $14.25, 916-573-2059.

TAHOE CITY PARKS AND RECREATION - 380 North Lake Blvd., Tahoe City 95730

LAKE FOREST CAMPGROUND - 2 Miles East of Tahoe City, 20 Tent/RV Sites, Flush Toilets, Fee: $10, 916-583-5544 or (Seasonal - 916-581-4017.)

PRIVATELY OPERATED CAMPGROUNDS

CAMP RICHARDSON RESORT - 3 Miles West of the "Y", 193 Tent/RV Sites to 35 Feet, Some Hookups, Flush Toilets, Showers, Disposal Station, Laundromat, Groceries, Propane, Supplies, Fee: $8, 916-541-1801.

9 **CAMP SHELLY** - 1-1/2 Miles West of Camp Richardson off Hwy. 89, 28 Tent/RV Sites to 22 Feet, Flush Toilets, Showers, No Piped Water, Laundromat, Groceries, Propane, Fee: $7.50, 916-541-6985.

13 **KOA CAMPGROUND** - Off Hwy. 50 West of Meyers, 16 Tent Sites, 52 RV Sites to 30 Feet, Full Hookups, Disposal Station, Flush Toilets, Showers, Laundry, Groceries, Propane, Swimming Pool, Recreation Room, Fee: $13.55, 916-577-3693, Reservations: P.O. Box 11552, Tahoe Paradise 95708.

5 **MEEKS BAY RESORT** - 10 Miles South of Tahoe City, RV Park, Full Hookups, Disposal Station, Flush Toilets, Motel, Launch Ramp, Full Service Marina, 702-323-2110.

14 **TAHOE PINES CAMPGROUND AND RV PARK** - Off Hwy. 50, West of Meyers, 80 Tent Sites, 31 RV Sites with Hookups to 35 Feet, Disposal Station, Flush Toilets, Showers, Laundromat, Groceries, Propane, Fee: $13.75, 916-544-1279

11 **TAHOE VALLEY RECREATION AREA -** 1/4 Miles West of the "Y" at South Lake Tahoe, 110 Tent Sites, 290 RV Sites with Full Hookups, Disposal Station, Flush Toilets, Showers, Playground, Laundromat, Groceries, Propane, Recreation Room, 916-541-2222.

16 **ZEPHYR COVE RESORT** - 1-1/2 Miles North of Zephyr Cove, 50 Tent Sites, 106 RV Sites to 35 Feet, Full Hookups, Flush Toilets, Showers, Cabins, Lodge, Marina, Groceries, Propane, Restaurant, 702-588-6644.

...Continued...

LAKE TAHOE

GENERAL INFORMATION

Lodging and accommodations are extensive throughout the Lake Tahoe Basin. The casinos offer luxurious hotel rooms with complete facilities. Condominiums, cabins and houses are available for rent. In addition to the enormous variety of lodging available, there is an abundance of recreational and service facilities.

For Full Information and Reservations Contact:

Lake Tahoe Visitors Authority
P.O. Box 16299
South Lake Tahoe 95706
Toll Free: 1-800-AT-TAHOE

Tahoe North Visitors and Convention Bureau
P.O. Box 5578
Tahoe City 95730
Toll Free: 1-800-824-6348

Chambers of Commerce:

South Lake Tahoe
3066 Highway 50
South Lake Tahoe 95702
Ph: 916-541-5255

North Lake Tahoe
P.O. Box 884
Tahoe City 95730
Ph: 916-583-2371

WATER SKIER HAND SIGNALS

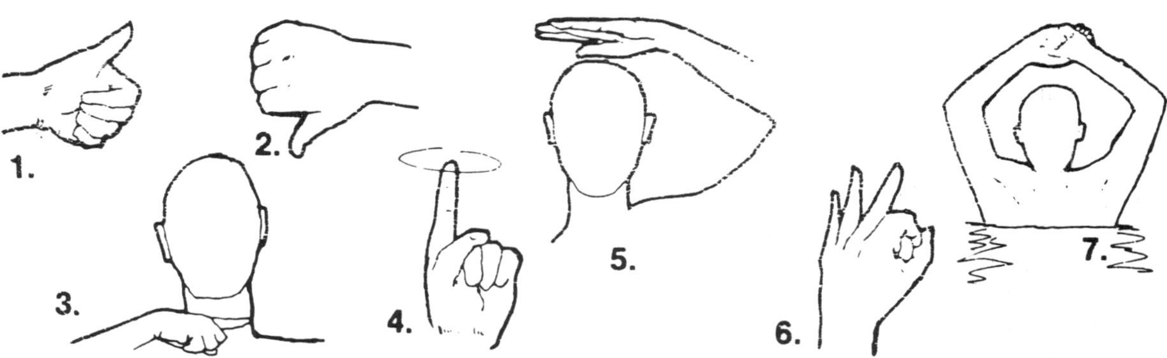

1. Thumb Up: Speed up the boat.
2. Thumb Down: Slow down the boat.
3. Cut Motor/Stop: Immediately stop boat. Slashing motion over neck (also used by driver or observer).
4. Turn: Turn the boat (also used by driver). Circle motion — arms overhead. Then point in desired direction.
5. Return to Dock: Pat on the head.
6. OK: Speed and boat path OK. Or, signals understood.
7. I'm OK: Skier OK after falling.

Courtesy of The American Water Ski Association

SAFETY FIRST WHEN WATER SKIING

Water skiing is remarkably safe considering the number of participants (more than 15 million annually) and the nature of the action. The answer comes in the observance of a few commonsense rules of safety by participants who learn them.

In addition to establishing proper communication with the boat driver, the skier should:

- Always wear a Coast Guard-approved Type III flotation jacket no matter how well he can swim.
- Stay clear of solid objects such as water markers, docks, bridge abutments, other boats and the like.
- Keep a reasonable distance from swimmers, fishermen and other skiers.
- Be thoroughly familiar with the water in which you are skiing to avoid stumps, shoals and other impediments that may be unseen just beneath the surface.
- Know the driver and his ability, and agree in advance on the signals you will use.

- Never water ski at night.
- Always come in parallel to the shore when landing. Speed over the water is deceptive, and the risk of injury is greater when a skier comes directly onto the beach after he has "whipped away" from the towboat.
- Never ski doubles with different rope lengths. If the skier on the long rope falls, the line can entangle the skier on the short rope.
- Never use alcoholic beverages when skiing or boating. Alcohol impairs the skier's and the boat driver's ability, creating a hazard for themselves and others.

For a free booklet, "Guide to Safe Water Skiing," and a list of other water ski booklets, send a stamped, self-addressed envelope to: American Water Ski Association, P.O. Box 191, Winter Haven, FL 33882.

FALLEN LEAF LAKE

Fallen Leaf Lake is at an elevation of 6,400 feet just south of Lake Tahoe in the Lake Tahoe Basin Management Unit. The lovely property around this Lake is partially private and partially National Forest land. The shoreline is heavily forested with pine trees to the water's edge. This is a nice family recreation Lake with boating facilities and fishing. It is within easy access to the Desolation Wilderness and near the numerous attractions at South Lake Tahoe and the casinos at Stateline. The Forest Service maintains a campground on the north end of the Lake; there are no overnight facilities at Fallen Leaf Lodge, just a marina and store.

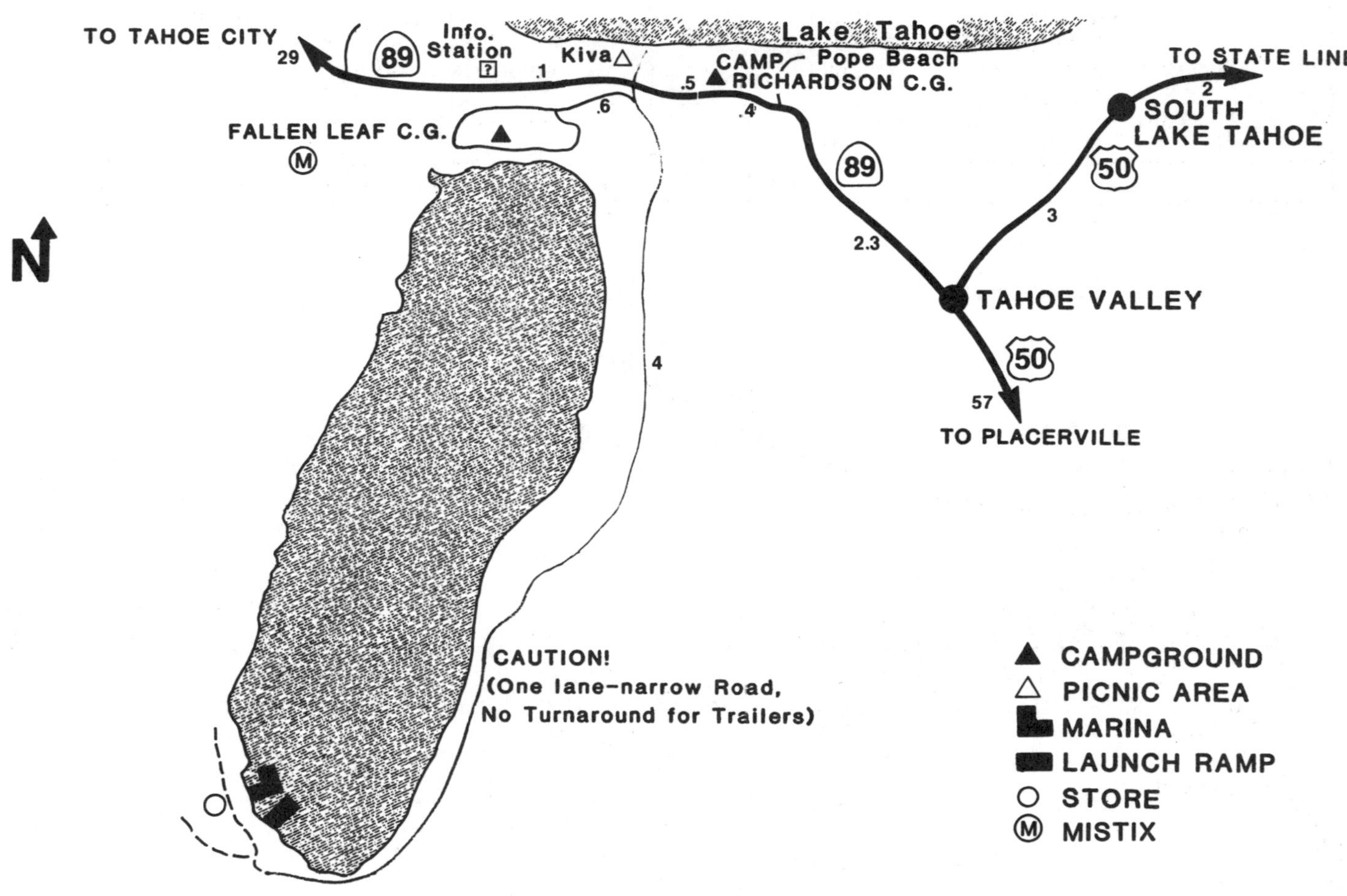

INFORMATION: Lake Tahoe Basin, Box 731002, S. Lake Tahoe 95731, Ph: 916-573-2600

CAMPING	BOATING	RECREATION	OTHER
U. S. F. S. 206 Dev. Sites for Tents & R.V.s Fee: $10 Reservations Through Mistix	Power, Row, Canoe, Sail Launch Ramp Rentals: Row, Sail, Fishing Boats with Motors, Canoes, Kayaks & Ski Boats	Fishing: Rainbow, German Brown & Mackinaw Trout Swimming Picnicking Hiking Backpacking Horseback Riding Trails Nature Study	Fallen Leaf Lodge Fallen Leaf 95716 Marina 916-544-0787 Store 916-541-4671 Memorial Day to Labor Day Grocery Store Bait & Tackle

ECHO LAKE

Echo Lake is nestled at 7,414 feet in between high mountains near Echo Summit off Highway 50. This is one of the most beautiful natural Lakes to be found in the High Sierra. All types of boating are allowed, but waterskiing is not permitted on Upper Echo Lake. The bordering Desolation Wilderness has 63,475 acres of trails, Lakes, and streams easily accessible for the backpacker or horseman. Echo Chalet, the only facility on the Lake, provides a taxi service to the Upper Lake which shortens the hike into the Wilderness Area by 3-1/2 miles. The Rubicon and American Rivers along with over 50 Lakes and streams welcome expectant anglers to the uncrowded waters of this area.

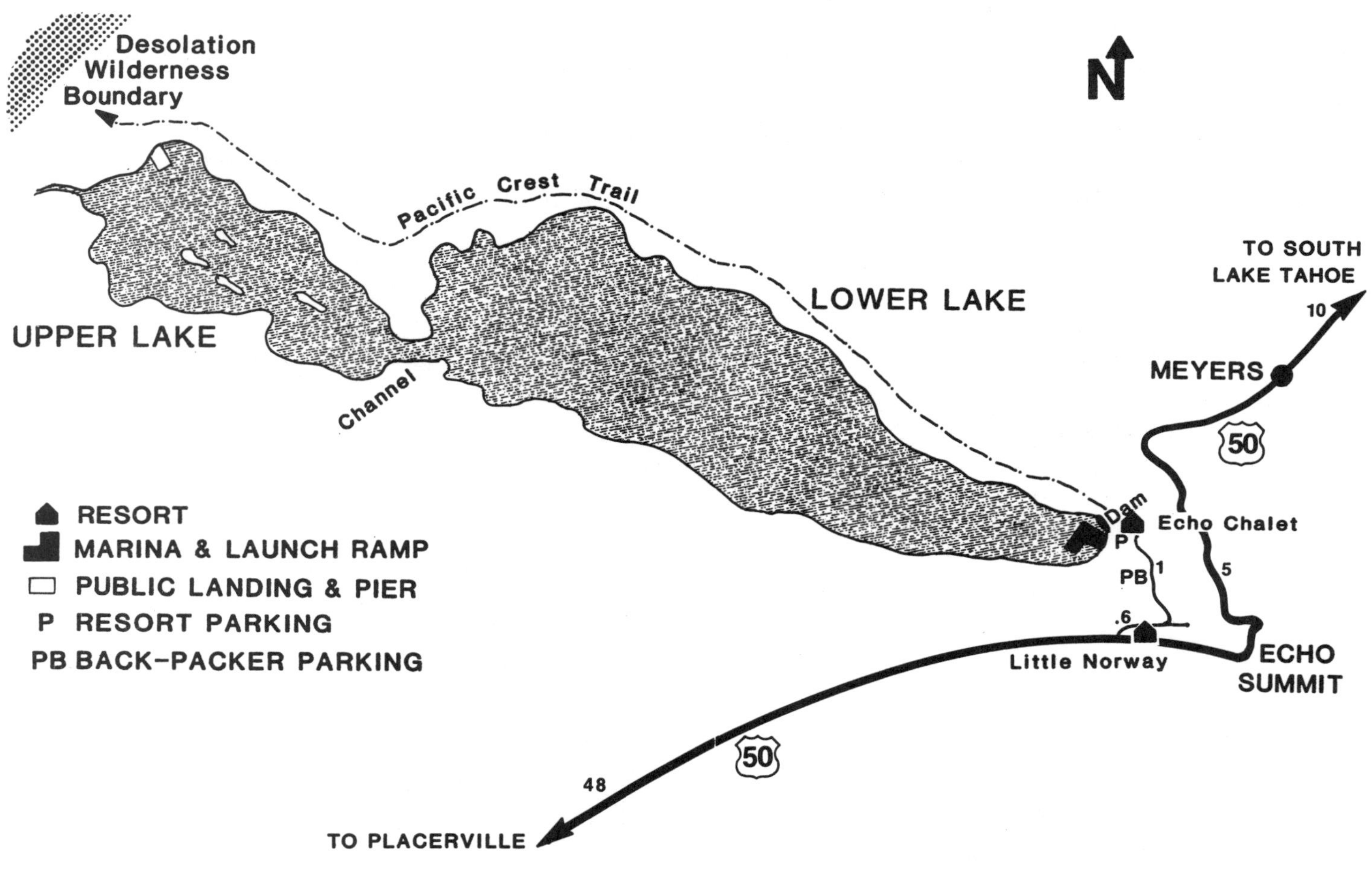

INFORMATION: Echo Chalet, Echo Lake 95721, Ph: 916-659-7207

CAMPING	BOATING	RECREATION	OTHER
No Overnight Camping or Trailers Allowed in Echo Lake Basin Camping Allowed in Desolation Wilderness Area with Permit from U. S. F. S. (Obtain at South Lake Tahoe or Placerville)	Power, Row, Canoe, Sail, Waterski, Windsurf & Inflatable Full Service Marina Launch Ramp - $9 Cartops/ Inflatables - $4 Rentals: Fishing Boats & Canoes Docks, Berths, Gas, Storage	Fishing: Rainbow, Brook & Cutthroat Trout; Kokanee Salmon Swimming Picnicking Hiking Backpacking-Parking Horseback Riding Trails Hunting: Deer, Quail	Housekeeping Cabins Snack Bar Grocery Store Hardware & Sporting Goods Bait & Tackle Fishing Licenses Gas Station Day Hike Permits to Wilderness Area

WRIGHTS LAKE

Wrights Lake has a surface area of 65 acres. It is at an elevation of 7,000 feet in the Eldorado National Forest, one of many Lakes in this area. The high Sierra setting provides a unique retreat for the outdoorsman. The Trailheads for Rockbound Pass and Desolation Wilderness Areas border the Lake, making it popular for the equestrian, hiker and backpacker. Wrights Lake offers good fishing, and the other Lakes and streams in this vicinity are equally inviting to the angler. Boating is restricted to hand launching, and motors are not allowed. Wilderness permits are required for entry into the Desolation Wilderness Area. They are available at the U. S. F. S. Information Center on Highway 50.

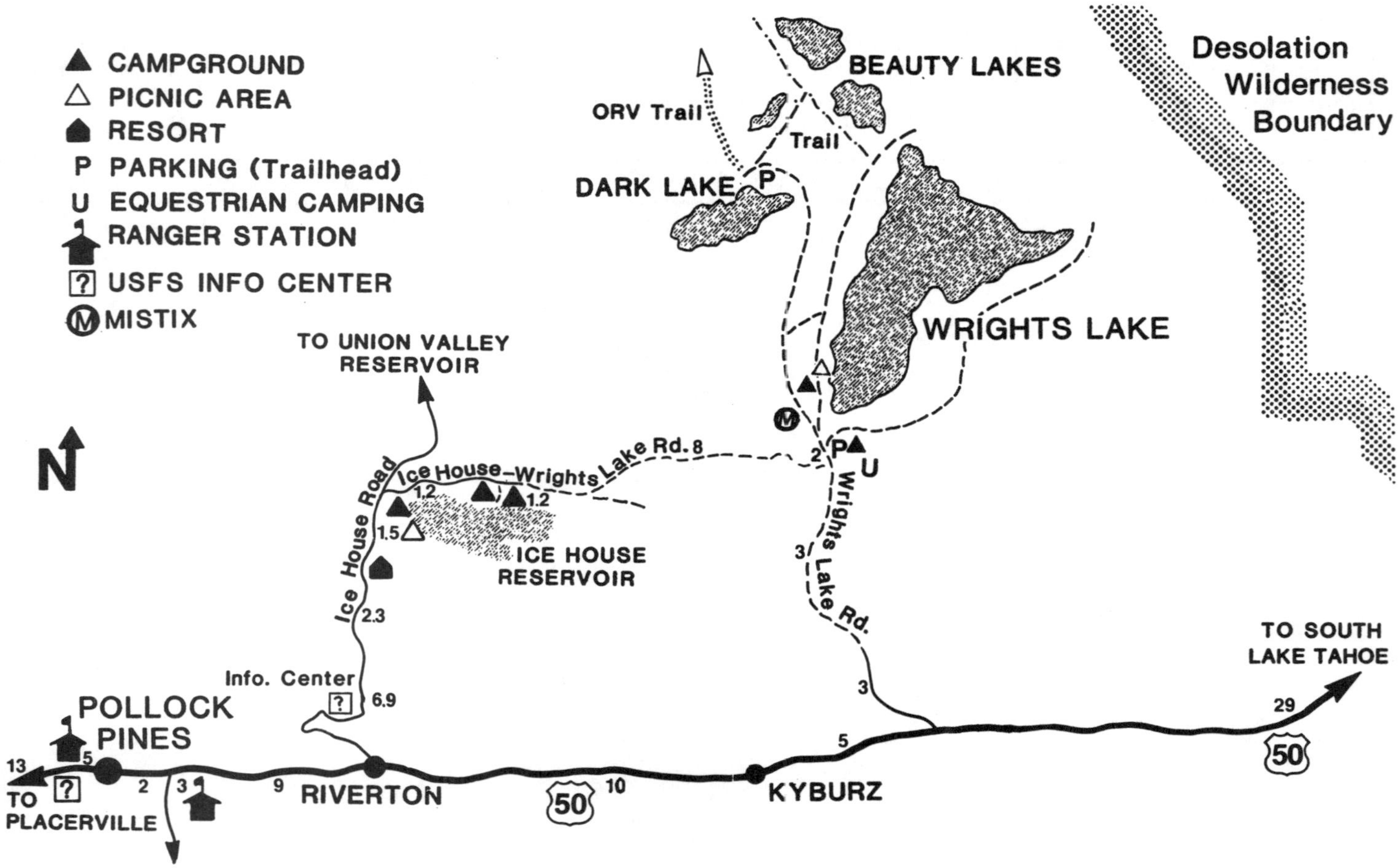

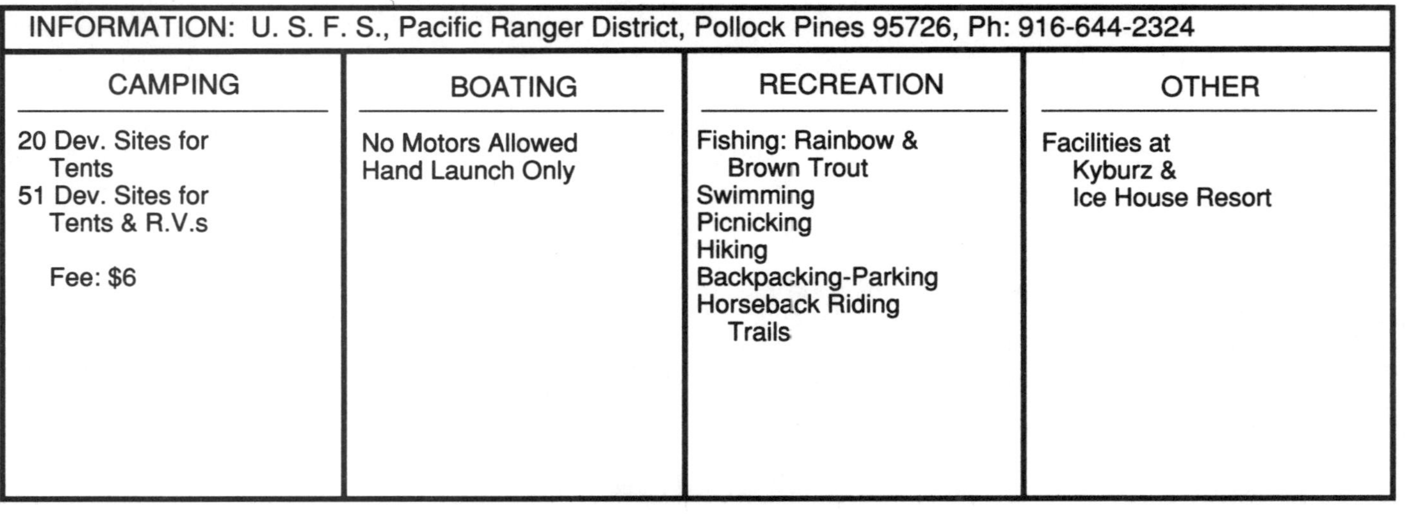

INFORMATION: U. S. F. S., Pacific Ranger District, Pollock Pines 95726, Ph: 916-644-2324			
CAMPING	BOATING	RECREATION	OTHER
20 Dev. Sites for Tents 51 Dev. Sites for Tents & R.V.s Fee: $6	No Motors Allowed Hand Launch Only	Fishing: Rainbow & Brown Trout Swimming Picnicking Hiking Backpacking-Parking Horseback Riding Trails	Facilities at Kyburz & Ice House Resort

LOON LAKE AND GERLE CREEK RESERVOIR

Loon Lake is at an elevation of 6,500 feet in the Crystal Basin Recreation Area of the Eldorado National Forest. The Forest Service maintains the campground, picnic area, paved launch ramp, and a walk-in or boat-in campground. This is a good Lake for sailing and boating in general, but waterskiing is not advised due to extremely cold water. Fishing can be excellent for Rainbow and German Brown trout. There is trailhead parking for the Desolation Wilderness, and trail conditions are good for hikers and horses. Gerle Creek Reservoir has a 50-site campground and picnic area with a handicap fishing pier. Boats with motors are not allowed at this facility.

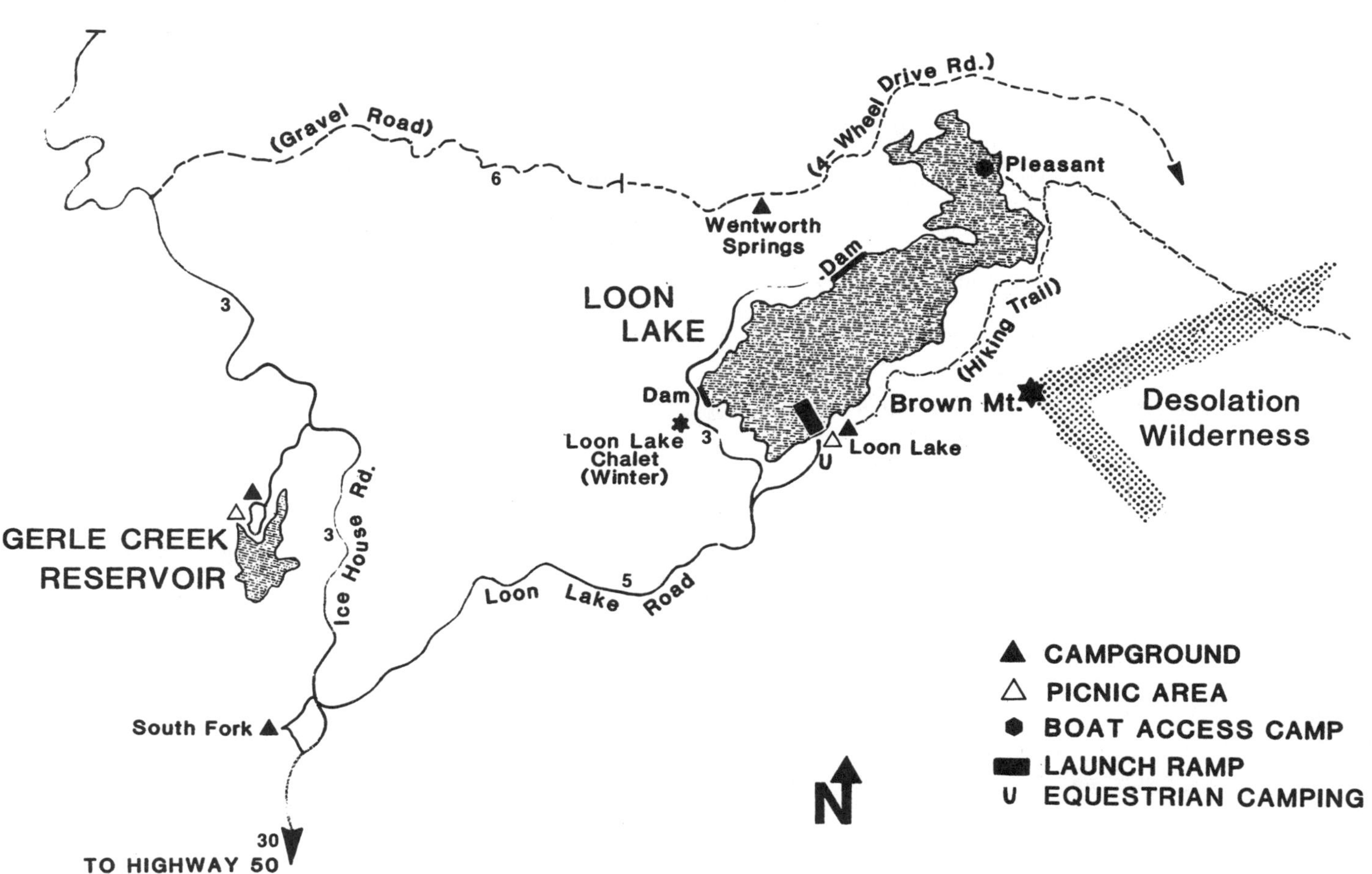

INFORMATION: U. S. Forest Service, Pollock Pines 95726, Ph: 916-644-2324

CAMPING	BOATING	RECREATION	OTHER
34 Dev. Sites for Tents & R.V.s Fees Charged 6 Unit Equestrian Campground Fees Charged 11 Sites at Wentworth Springs Not Recommended For Trailers or RV's Gerle Creek Reservoir 50 Dev. Sites for Tents & R.V.s Fees Charged	Power, Row, Canoe & Sail Waterskiing is Not Recommended Launch Ramp Gerle Creek Reservoir: No Motors	Fishing: Rainbow & German Brown Trout Picnicking Hiking Backpacking-Parking Entrance to Desolation Wilderness Horseback Riding Trails ORV Trails	Handicap Toilet & Fishing Pier at Gerle Creek Reservoir Full Facilities - 23 Miles at Ice House Resort

ICE HOUSE RESERVOIR

Ice House Reservoir is at an elevation of 5,500 feet in the Crystal Basin Recreation Area of the Eldorado National Forest. The surface area of the lake is 678 acres of clear, cold water. The surrounding shoreline is covered with conifers at this high Sierra lake. In addition to the popular campground, the Forest Service maintains a launch ramp and picnic facilities on the lake. There are nice swimming areas. The roads are paved and well maintained, but beware of logging trucks. This is an excellent boating lake especially for sailing. The angler will find good fishing for trout and Kokanee.

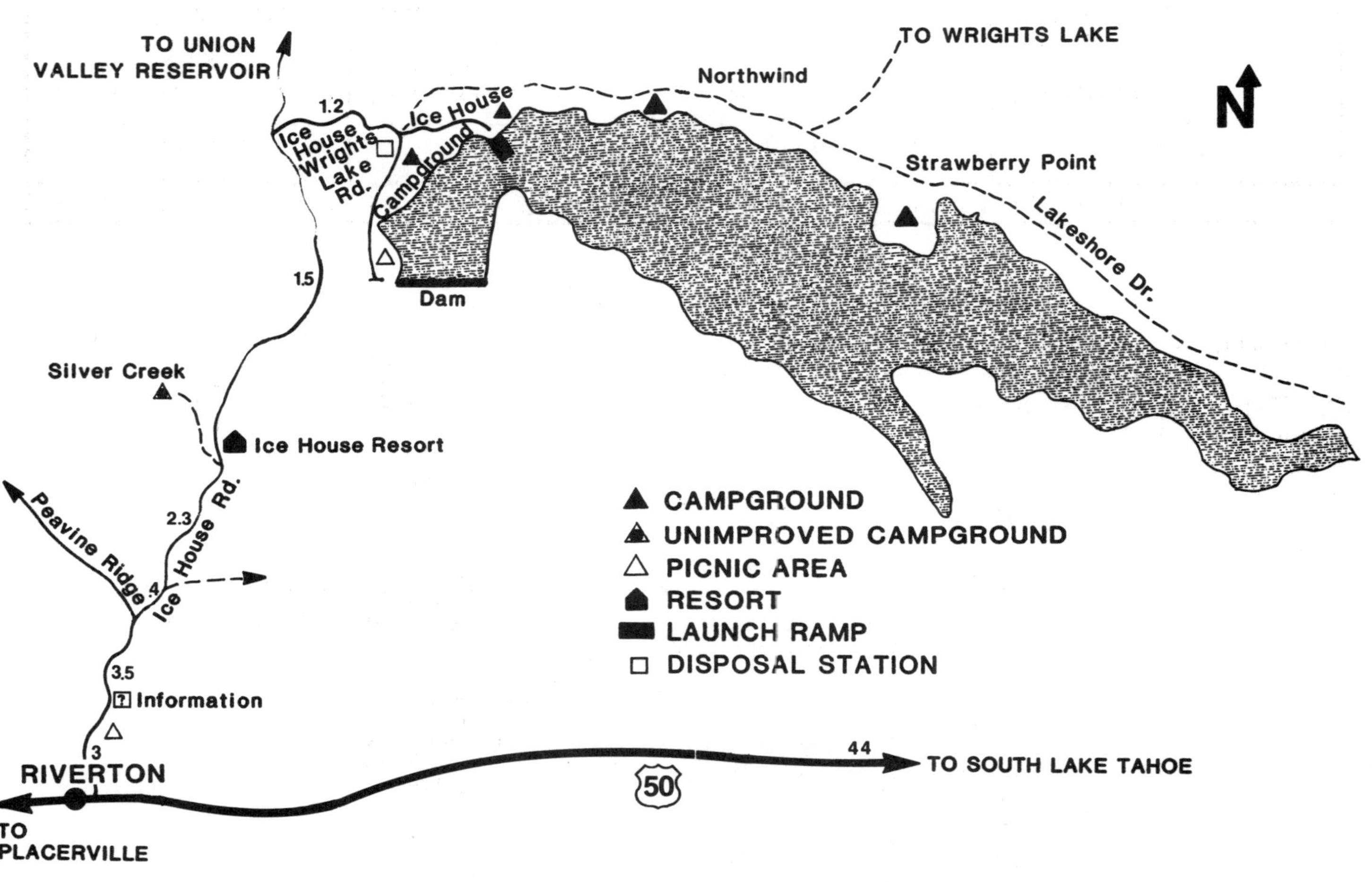

INFORMATION: U. S. Forest Service, 100 Forni Rd., Placerville 95667, Ph: 916-622-5061

CAMPING	BOATING	RECREATION	OTHER
Ice House: 83 Dev. Sites for Tents & R.V.s Fees Charged 3 Handicap Sites Northwind & Strawberry Point Campgrounds: 10 Dev. Sites Each for Tents & R.V.s - No Fees Silver Creek: 11 Primitive Sites for Tents Only No Fees	Power, Row, Canoe, Sail, Windsurf & Inflatables Launch Ramp	Fishing: Rainbow & Brown Trout, Kokanee Salmon Swimming Picnicking Hiking	Ice House Resort: Motel Restaurant Grocery Store Gas Station

UNION VALLEY RESERVOIR

Union Valley Reservoir is located at an elevation of 4,900 feet in the Crystal Basin Recreation Area of the Eldorado National Forest. This area is in the pine and fir forests of the western Sierra and is dominated by the high granite peaks of the Crystal Range. The Reservoir has a surface area of 2,860 acres. The Forest Service maintains 2 launch ramps on the Lake, 1 picnic area, 3 campgrounds and 1 group campground. Union Valley is an excellent Lake for sailing, and many sailing clubs use this facility during the summer. Fishing is popular by boat or along the shoreline of this lovely Lake.

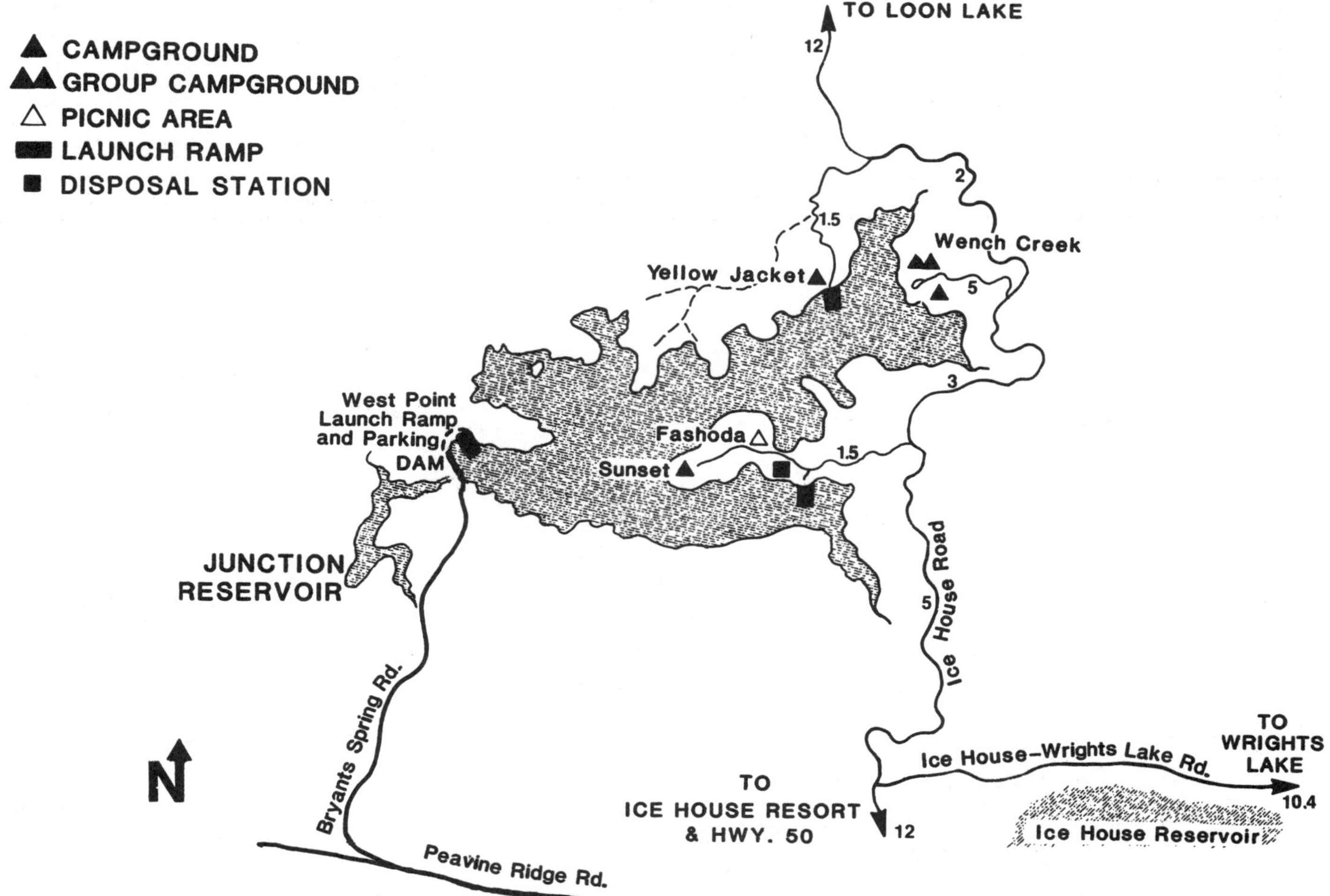

INFORMATION: U. S. Forest Service, 100 Forni Rd., Placerville 95667, Ph: 916-622-5061

CAMPING	BOATING	RECREATION	OTHER
271 Dev. Sites for Tents & R.V.s Fees Charged 2 Group Campgrounds 50 People Maximum Each	Power, Row, Canoe, Sail, Windsurf & Inflatables Launch Ramps	Fishing: Rainbow & Brown Trout Swimming Picnicking Hiking	Disposal Station Facilities - 7 Miles at Ice House Resort

JENKINSON LAKE SLY PARK RECREATION AREA

Jenkinson Lake is at an elevation of 3,478 feet in the Sly Park Recreation Area south of Pollock Pines. The Lake has a surface area of 640 acres with 8 miles of coniferous-covered shoreline. The Eldorado Irrigation District has jurisdiction over the modern facilities at this pretty Lake. Facilities include a paved 3-lane launch ramp with floats, a nice small marina and a boat storage area. There are a variety of individual, first come-first served and group campsites offering equestrian, handicapped and youth facilities. The water is clear, and fishing can be good along the coves. Winds are usually favorable for sailing. Waterskiing is in a counter-clockwise direction in the central section of the Lake. A 5 MPH speed limit is enforced in the northeast area.

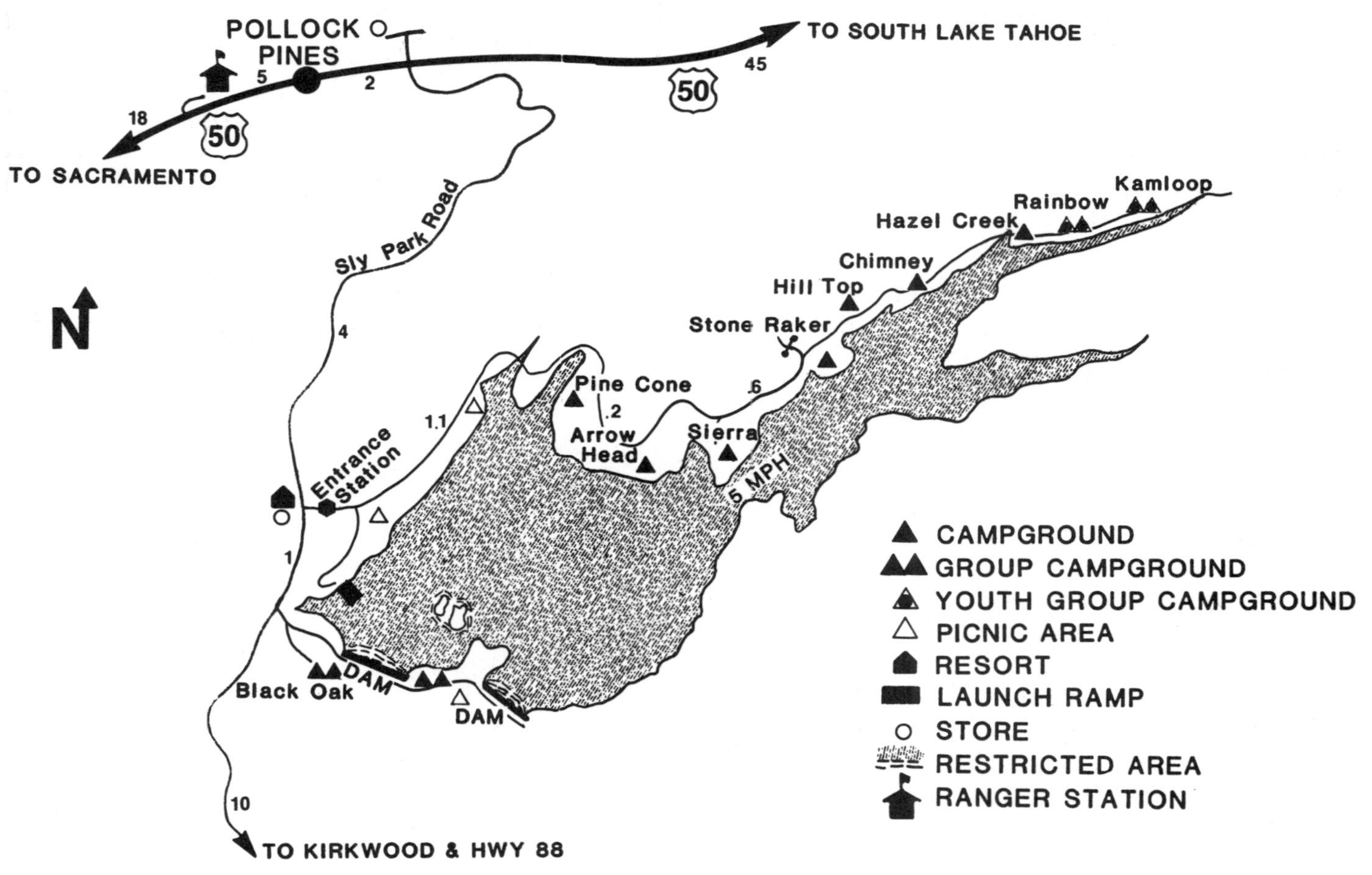

INFORMATION: Sly Park Recreation Area, P.O. Box 577, Pollock Pines 95726, Ph: 916-644-2545

CAMPING	BOATING	RECREATION	OTHER
182 Dev. Sites for Tents & R.V.s Fee: $8.50 Handicapped & Equestrian Facilities First Come Basis Group & Youth Camp Areas - 100 People Maximum - Reserve: Ph: 916-644-2792	Power, Row, Canoe, Sail, Waterski, Windsurf & Inflatables Launch Ramp Docks, Dry Storage	Fishing: Rainbow, Brown & Mackinaw Trout, Bass & Bluegill Swimming Picnicking Hiking Equestrian Trails	Sly Park Store 4782 Sly Park Road Pollock Pines 95726 Ph: 916-644-1113 Bar & Grill Grocery Store Bait & Tackle Gas Station

FOLSOM LAKE

The Folsom Lake State Recreation Area is one of the most complete recreation parks in California. This 18,000 acre Recreation Area offers an abundance of campsites, picnic areas, swimming beaches, and marina facilities. Folsom Lake has 11,930 surface acres with 75 shoreline miles. Fishing is popular and often productive for a wide range of game fish. The lake offers a variety of boating experiences from waterskiing to windsurfing or canoeing. You can camp aboard your self-contained boat after registering at the Marina or Granite Bay. This is a popular equestrian area with 80 miles of hiking and riding trails around the lake. There is a bicycle trail that links Beals Point via the American River Bike Trail to downtown Sacramento.

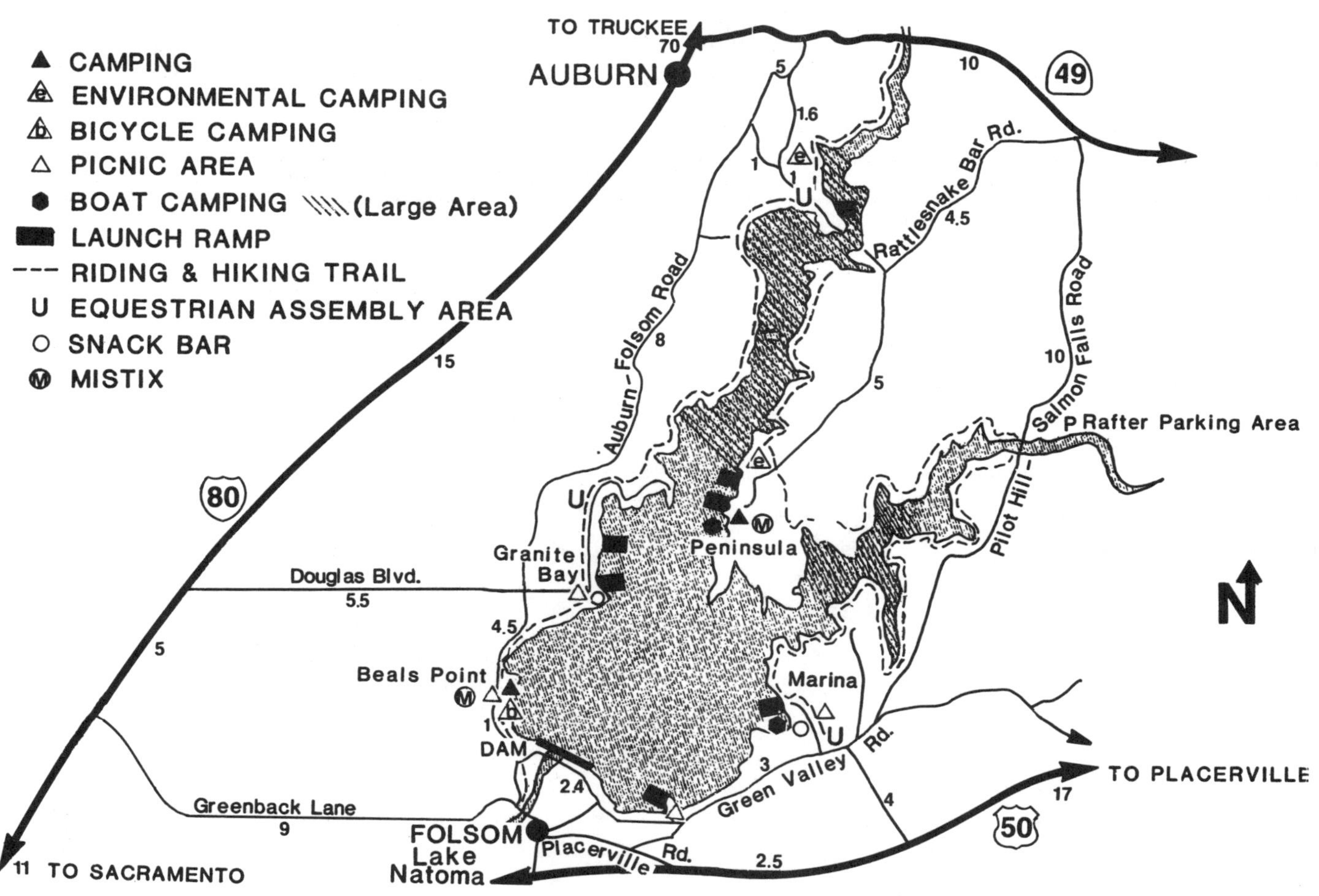

INFORMATION: Folsom Lake, 7806 Folsom-Auburn Rd., Folsom 95630, Ph: 916-988-0205			
CAMPING	**BOATING**	**RECREATION**	**OTHER**
149 Dev. Sites for Tents & R.V.s Fee: $10 2 Environmental Camps Reached by Foot, Boat or Bicycle Equestrian Assembly Area Accommodates up to 50 Riders & Horses Contact Park Hdqtr. Boat Camping	Open to All Boating Full Service Marina Launch Ramps - $2 Rentals: Fishing, Canoe, Sail & Windsurfing Docks, Berths, Dry Storage & Gas Windsurfing Lessons Low Water Hazards	Fishing: Rainbow Trout, Coho Salmon, Catfish, Bluegill, Crappie, Bass, Perch & Sturgeon Picnicking Swimming Beaches Bicycle, Hiking & Riding Trails Horse Rentals	Campfire Programs Snack Bar Bait & Tackle Day Use Fee: $4 Full Facilities in Folsom

LAKE NATOMA

Lake Natoma is a part of the Folsom Lake Recreation Area. Resting at an elevation of 126 feet just below Folsom Dam, Natoma is the regulating Reservoir for Folsom Lake. Water levels can fluctuate 3 or 4 feet in a day. This small Lake of 500 surface acres flows over dredging pilings. While the pilings can create a good fish habitat, they are a boating hazard. There is a 5 MPH boating speed limit. Jet or waterskiing are not permitted, but this is a nice canoeing or sailing Lake. Fishing can be difficult, but for those who know the Lake it can be rewarding. There are shade structures with picnic tables, swimming beaches and a campground above Negro Bar. Good trails are available for the equestrian, bicyclist, and hiker.

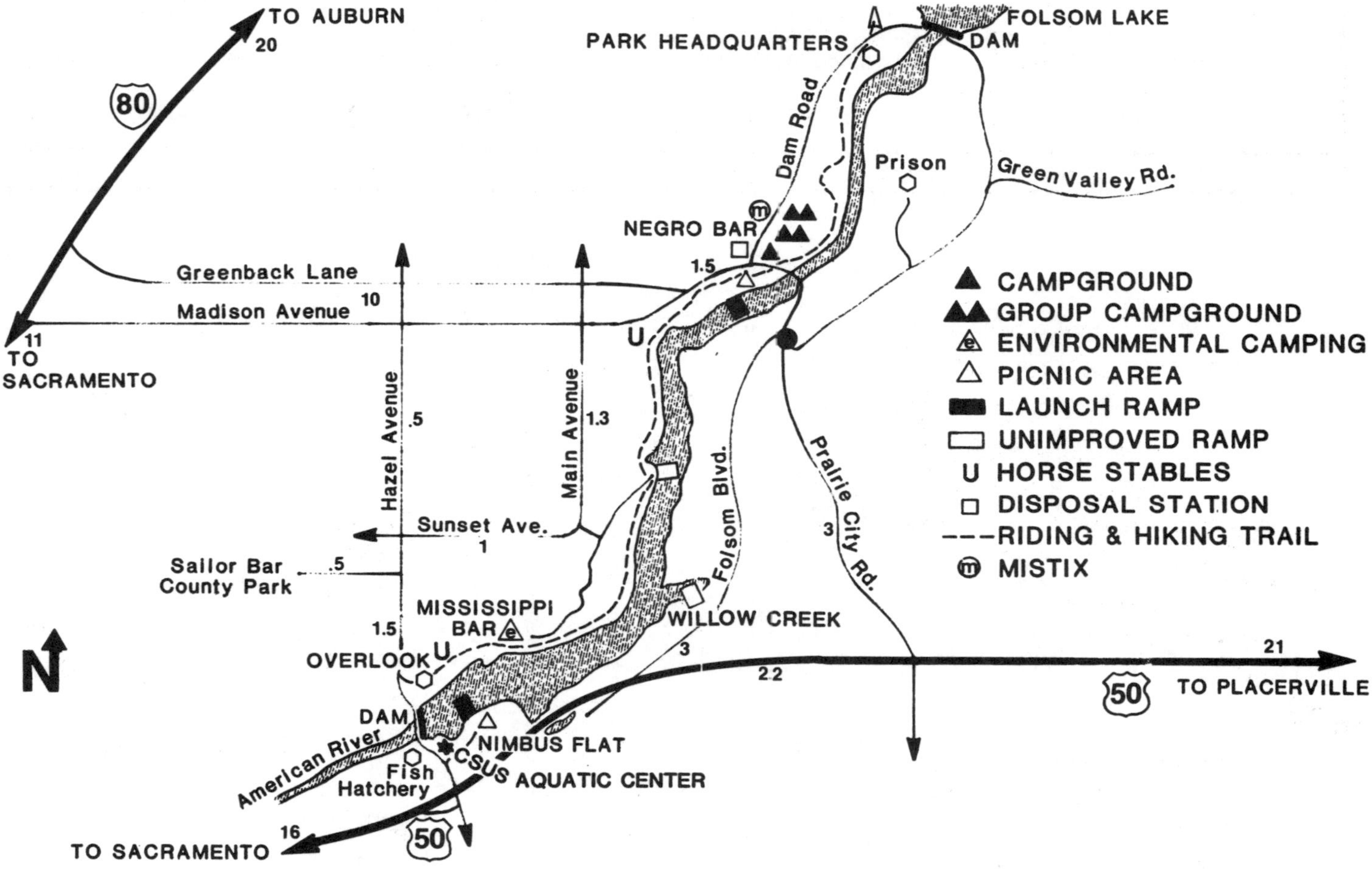

INFORMATION: Folsom Lake, 7806 Folsom-Auburn Rd., Folsom 95630, Ph: 916-988-0205

CAMPING	BOATING	RECREATION	OTHER
20 Dev. Sites for Tents & R.V.s Fee: $10 2 Group Camps	Power, Row, Canoe, Sail, Windsurf & Inflatables Speed Limit-5 MPH Launch Ramps - $2 CSUS Aquatic Center Rowing, Waterski, Sail & Windsurfing Lessons Students & Members Only	Fishing: Rainbow Trout, Bluegill, Catfish, Crappie, Large & Smallmouth Bass Swimming - Beaches Picnicking Hiking Horseback Riding Bicycle Trails Home of the Pacific Coast Rowing Championships	Day Use Fee: $4 Full Facilities - 1 Mile at Folsom

RANCHO SECO, GIBSON RANCH, AND ELK GROVE PARKS

All of these Sacramento County Parks provide the angler with a warm water fishery. Rainbow trout are planted during the fall and winter months. Rancho Seco Park is the most water oriented facility with its 160 surface acre Lake which is open to sail and non-powered boating. There are launch ramps, docks, fishing piers, and a sandy swimming beach. Elk Grove Park has a small 3 acre Lake, and within this 125 acre park are numerous picnic areas, a children's playground, amphitheater, 12 ball fields, a swimming pool, and a multi-purpose lighted equestrian arena. Gibson Ranch has a true ranch character with farm animals, an 8 acre fishing pond, swimming hole and extensive equestrian facilities and a new Ranch Camp.

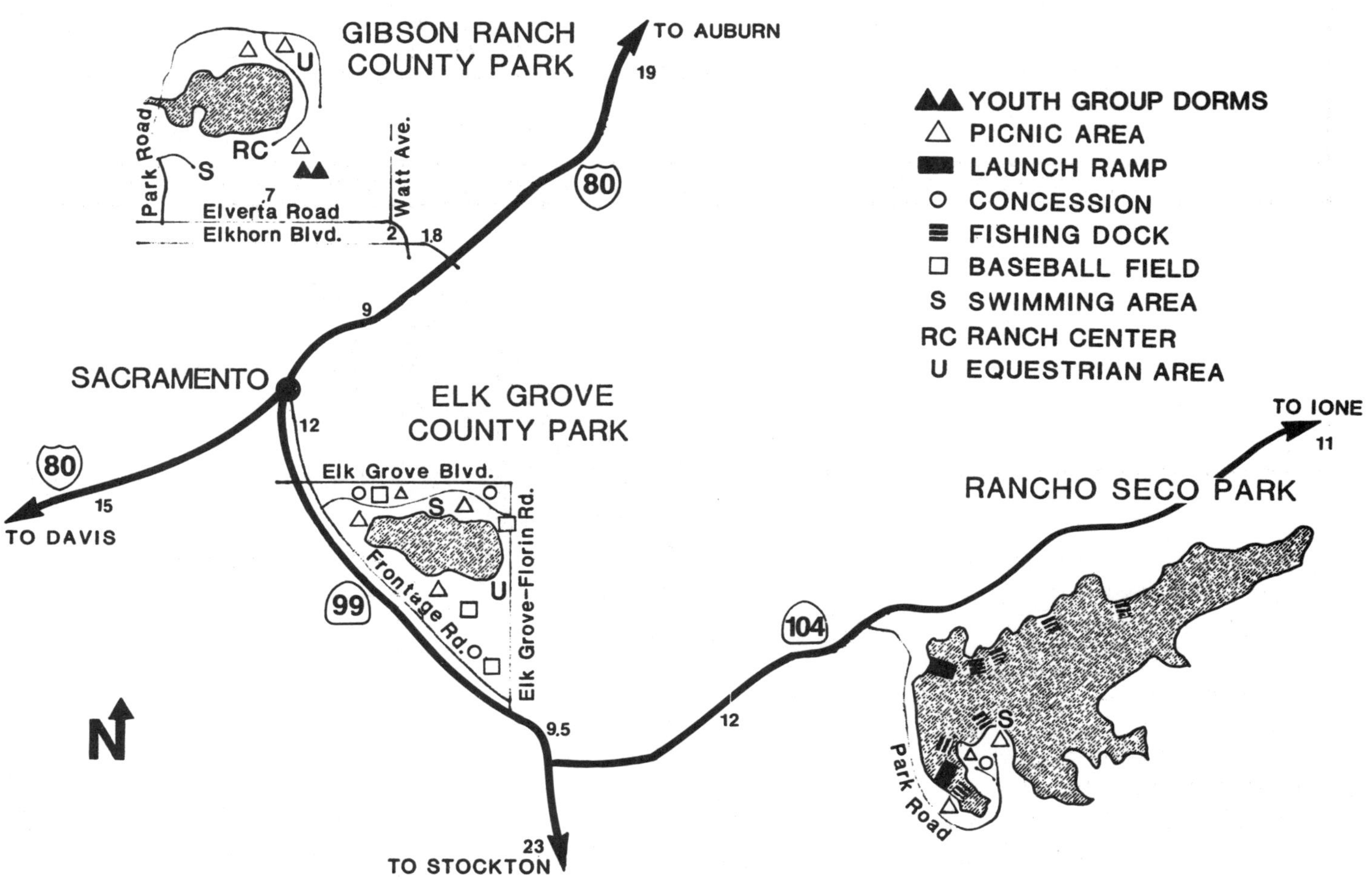

INFORMATION: Sacramento County Parks & Rec., 3711 Branch Center Rd., Sacramento 95827			
CAMPING	BOATING	RECREATION	OTHER
Group Camping at Rancho Seco & Gibson Ranch Sacramento Co. Parks & Rec. Phone: 916-366-2061	Rancho Seco: Open to Sail & Row Boats Launch Ramps Docks Club Seco: Sailboard Rentals & Lessons-Thurs. thru Sunday, May-October Ph: 209-748-5559 Gibson Ranch & Elk Grove Park: No Boating	Fishing: Rainbow Trout, Florida Bass Bluegill, Red Ear Sunfish & Catfish Family & Group Picnic Areas Swimming Areas & Pool Hiking, Riding & Cycling Equestrian Center Nature Study	Complete Facilities Nearby

SALT SPRINGS RESERVOIR

Salt Springs Reservoir rests at an elevation of 3,900 feet in the spectacular Mokelumne River Canyon of the Eldorado National Forest. This P. G. & E. Reservoir has a surface area of 961 acres. The lake is open to boating but it is restricted to hand-launched craft. Hazardous afternoon winds can create problems for small boats. Fishing is often productive in both the lake and the Mokelumne River as well as other nearby streams. The Forest Service maintains three campgrounds along the river just below the dam. A trailhead into the beautiful 102,00 acre Mokelumne Wilderness is located just above the dam.

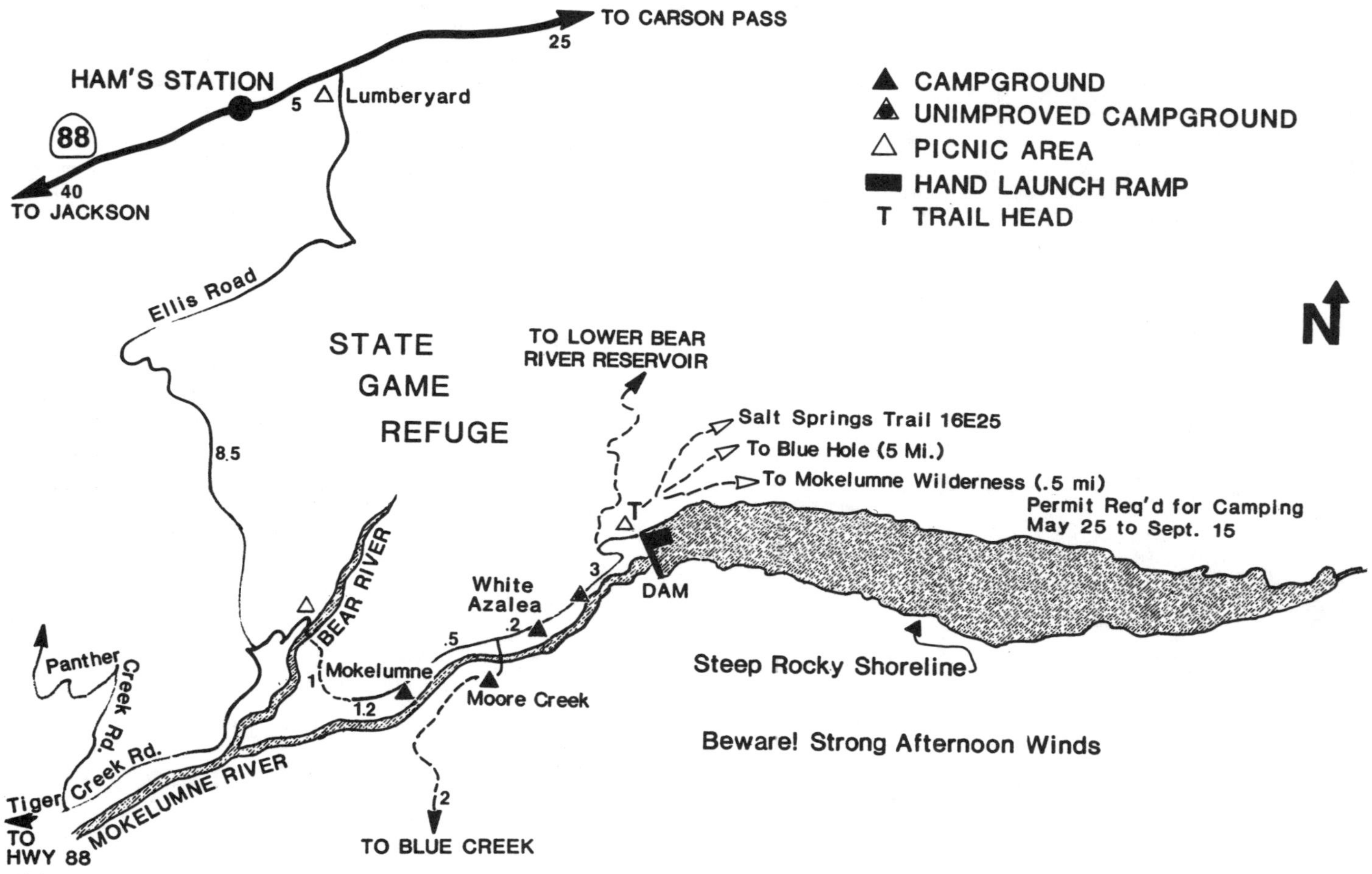

TO CARSON PASS
25
HAM'S STATION
5
Lumberyard
88
40
TO JACKSON
Ellis Road
STATE
GAME
REFUGE
8.5
TO LOWER BEAR
RIVER RESERVOIR
Salt Springs Trail 16E25
To Blue Hole (5 Mi.)
To Mokelumne Wilderness (.5 mi)
Permit Req'd for Camping
May 25 to Sept. 15
T
DAM
3
White
Azalea
.2
.5
BEAR RIVER
Mokelumne
1
1.2
Moore Creek
Steep Rocky Shoreline
Beware! Strong Afternoon Winds
Panther
Creek Rd.
Tiger Creek Rd.
TO
HWY 88
MOKELUMNE RIVER
2
TO BLUE CREEK
CAMPGROUND
UNIMPROVED CAMPGROUND
PICNIC AREA
HAND LAUNCH RAMP
T TRAIL HEAD
N

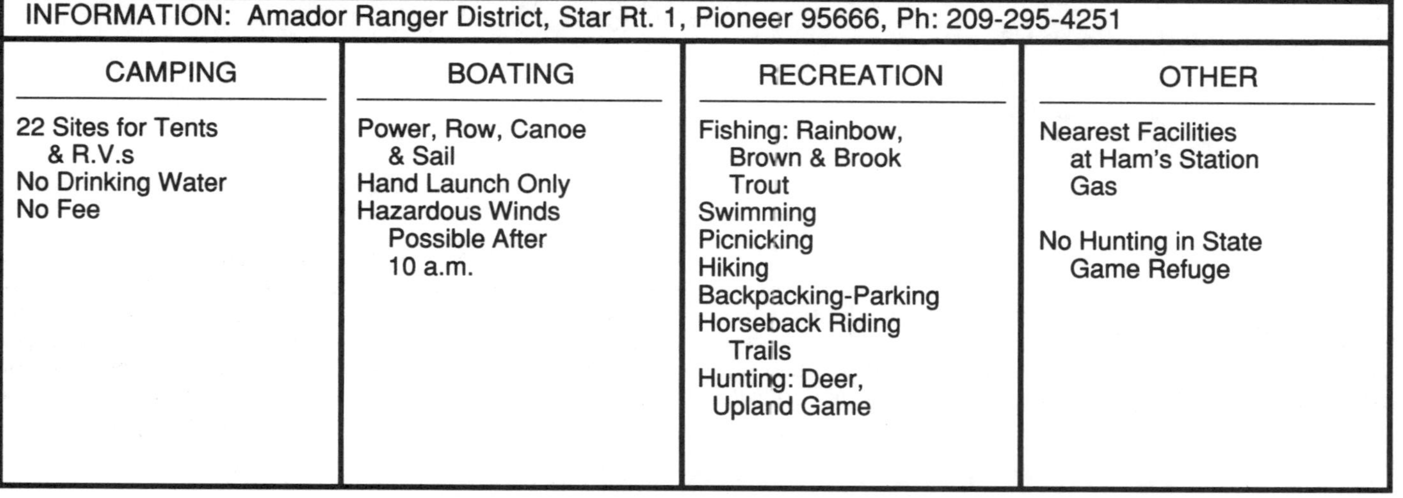

INFORMATION: Amador Ranger District, Star Rt. 1, Pioneer 95666, Ph: 209-295-4251

CAMPING	BOATING	RECREATION	OTHER
22 Sites for Tents & R.V.s No Drinking Water No Fee	Power, Row, Canoe & Sail Hand Launch Only Hazardous Winds Possible After 10 a.m.	Fishing: Rainbow, Brown & Brook Trout Swimming Picnicking Hiking Backpacking-Parking Horseback Riding Trails Hunting: Deer, Upland Game	Nearest Facilities at Ham's Station Gas No Hunting in State Game Refuge

LOWER BEAR RIVER RESERVOIR

Lower Bear River Reservoir rests at an elevation of 5,800 feet in the Eldorado National Forest. This pretty Lake of 727 acres is surrounded by a coniferous forest reaching to water's edge. There are good boating facilities at the resort. Afternoon breezes make sailing a delight. The Lake is regularly stocked, and fishing is usually productive. The Forest Service campgrounds at South Shore and Bear River are operated by Sierra Recreation Managers, P.O. Box 278, Pioneer 95666. The Bear River Resort has complete camping and marina facilities with hot showers, flush toilets, groceries, bait and tackle, snack bar, trailer rentals and storage. The hiker and backpacker will find parking and trails leading into the Mokelumne Wilderness.

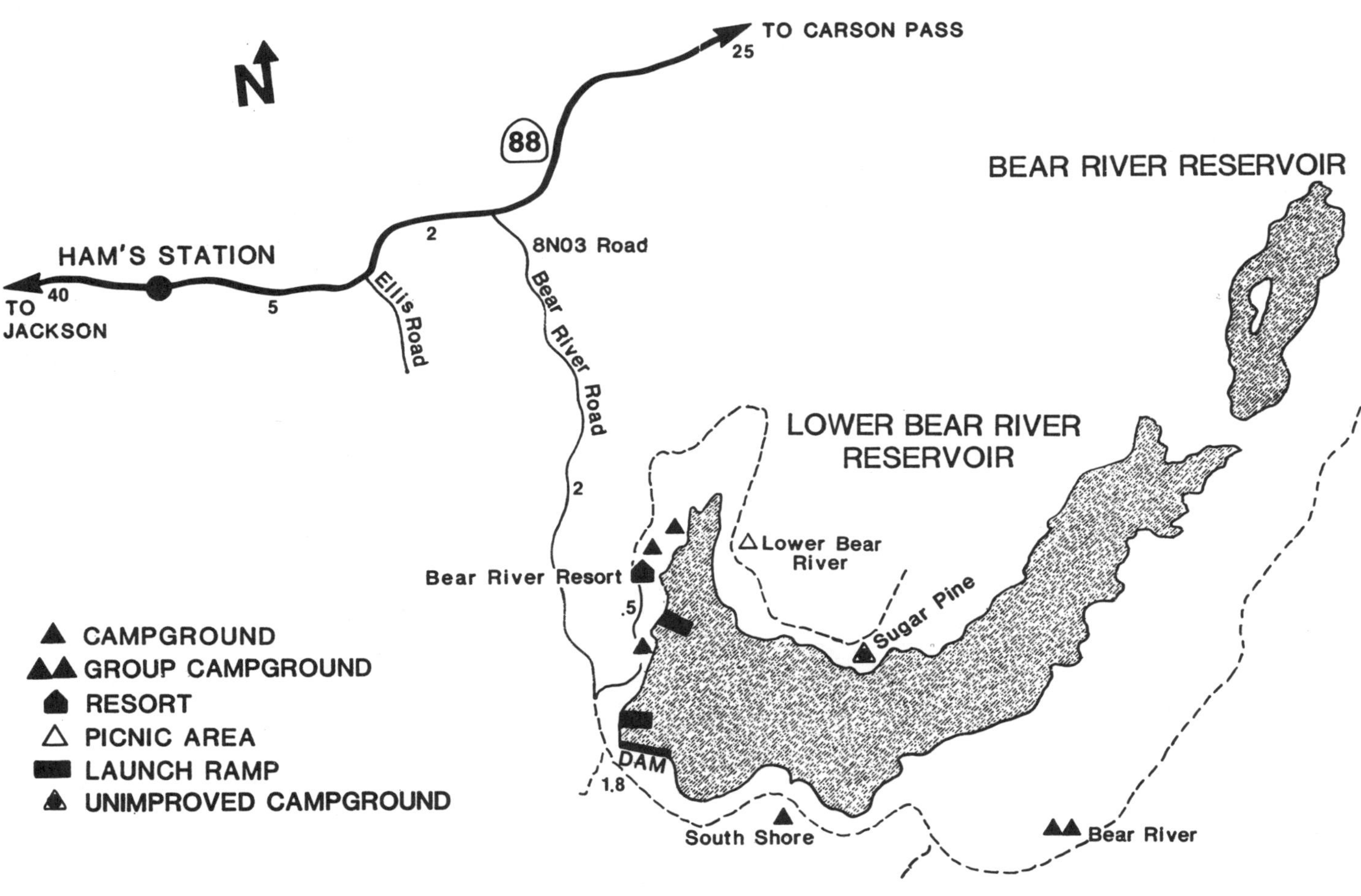

INFORMATION: Amador Ranger Station, Pioneer 95666, Ph: 209-295-4251

CAMPING	BOATING	RECREATION	OTHER
U. S. F. S.: 22 Dev. Sites for Tents & R.V.s Fee: $8 5 Double Sites-$16 2 Group Sites - 25 People - $30 1 Group Site - 50 People-$60 Group Reservations: Ph: 209-295-4512	Open to All Boating Full Service Marina Paved Launch Ramp Rentals: Fishing Boats Low Water Hazards Late in Season	Fishing: Rainbow & Brown Trout Picnicking Swimming Hiking - Backpacking Hunting: Deer	Lower Bear River Resort 40800 Hwy. 88 Pioneer 95666 Ph: 209-295-4868 125 Dev. Sites with Hookups Fee: $14-$16 Group Camp to 60 People Disposal Station Storage

SILVER LAKE

Silver Lake rests at an elevation of 7,200 feet in a big granite basin just west of the Sierra Summit in the Eldorado National Forest. This exceptionally beautiful Lake was once a resting place on the Emigrant Trail cut by Kit Carson. You can still see the trail markers carved in trees. The descendants of Raymond Peter Plasse, who established a trading post in 1853, operate a resort at the Lake. A popular recreation area for over a century, Silver Lake offers a variety of natural resources and facilities for the camper, angler, boater, hiker and equestrian.

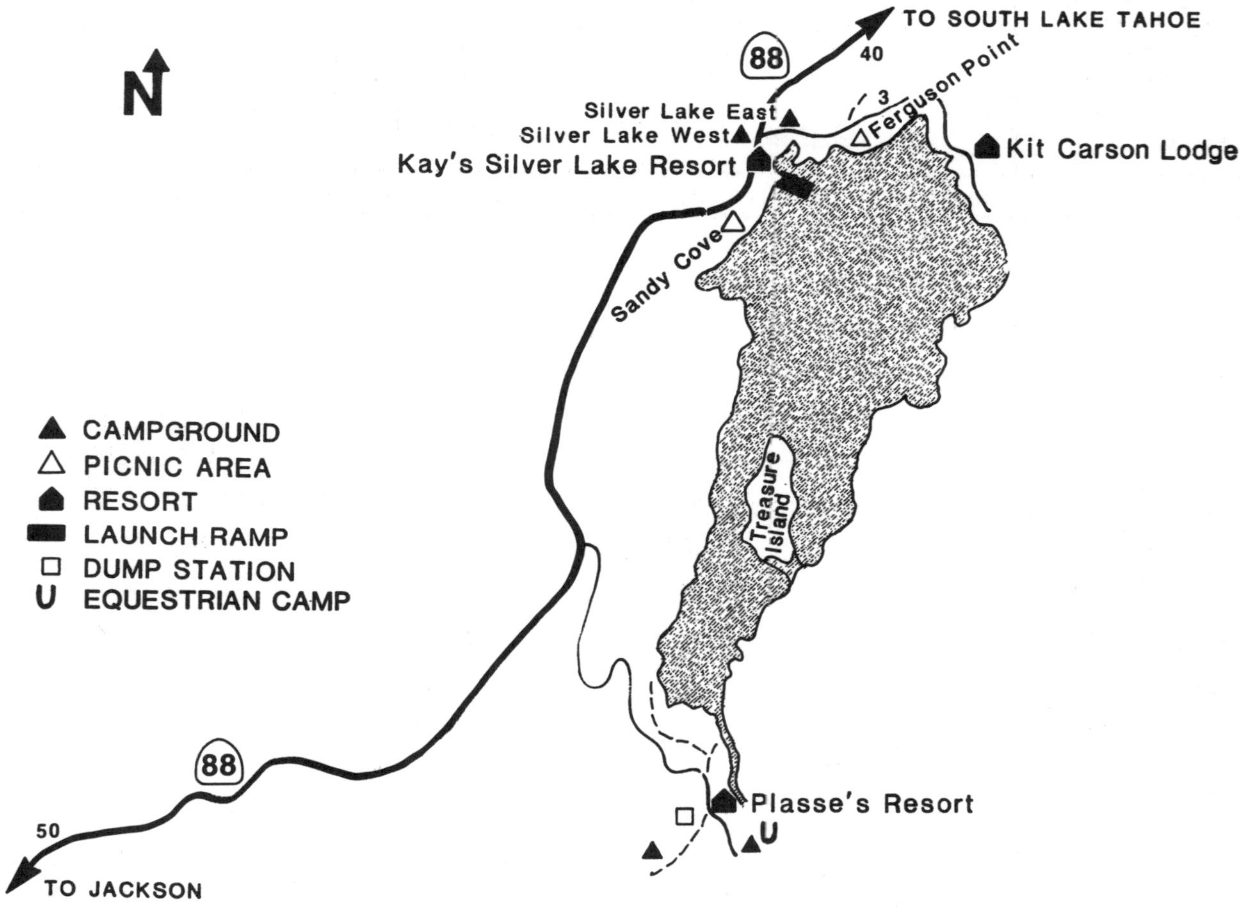

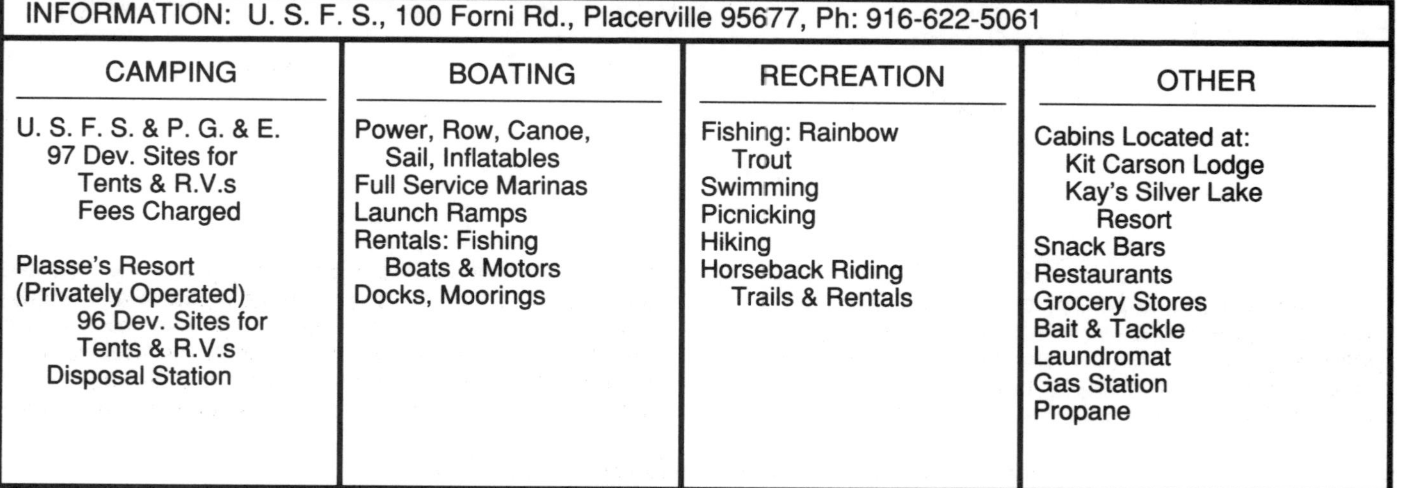

INFORMATION: U. S. F. S., 100 Forni Rd., Placerville 95677, Ph: 916-622-5061

CAMPING	BOATING	RECREATION	OTHER
U. S. F. S. & P. G. & E. 97 Dev. Sites for Tents & R.V.s Fees Charged Plasse's Resort (Privately Operated) 96 Dev. Sites for Tents & R.V.s Disposal Station	Power, Row, Canoe, Sail, Inflatables Full Service Marinas Launch Ramps Rentals: Fishing Boats & Motors Docks, Moorings	Fishing: Rainbow Trout Swimming Picnicking Hiking Horseback Riding Trails & Rentals	Cabins Located at: Kit Carson Lodge Kay's Silver Lake Resort Snack Bars Restaurants Grocery Stores Bait & Tackle Laundromat Gas Station Propane

CAPLES AND KIRKWOOD LAKES

Caples Lake is at an elevation of 7,950 feet in the Eldorado National Forest near the summit of Carson Pass. The nights and mornings are cool, and the water is cold in this 600 surface acre Lake. Kirkwood Lake is 3 miles to the west of Caples Lake at an elevation of 7,600 feet, and the road is not suitable for larger R.V.s or trailers. Motor boats are not allowed on Kirkwood, but you may use a motor up to 5 MPH on Caples. Fishing is good for a variety of trout in these Lakes as well as other nearby lakes and streams. Trails lead into the Mokelumne Wilderness to entice the hiker or backpacker. This entire area is a photographer's delight.

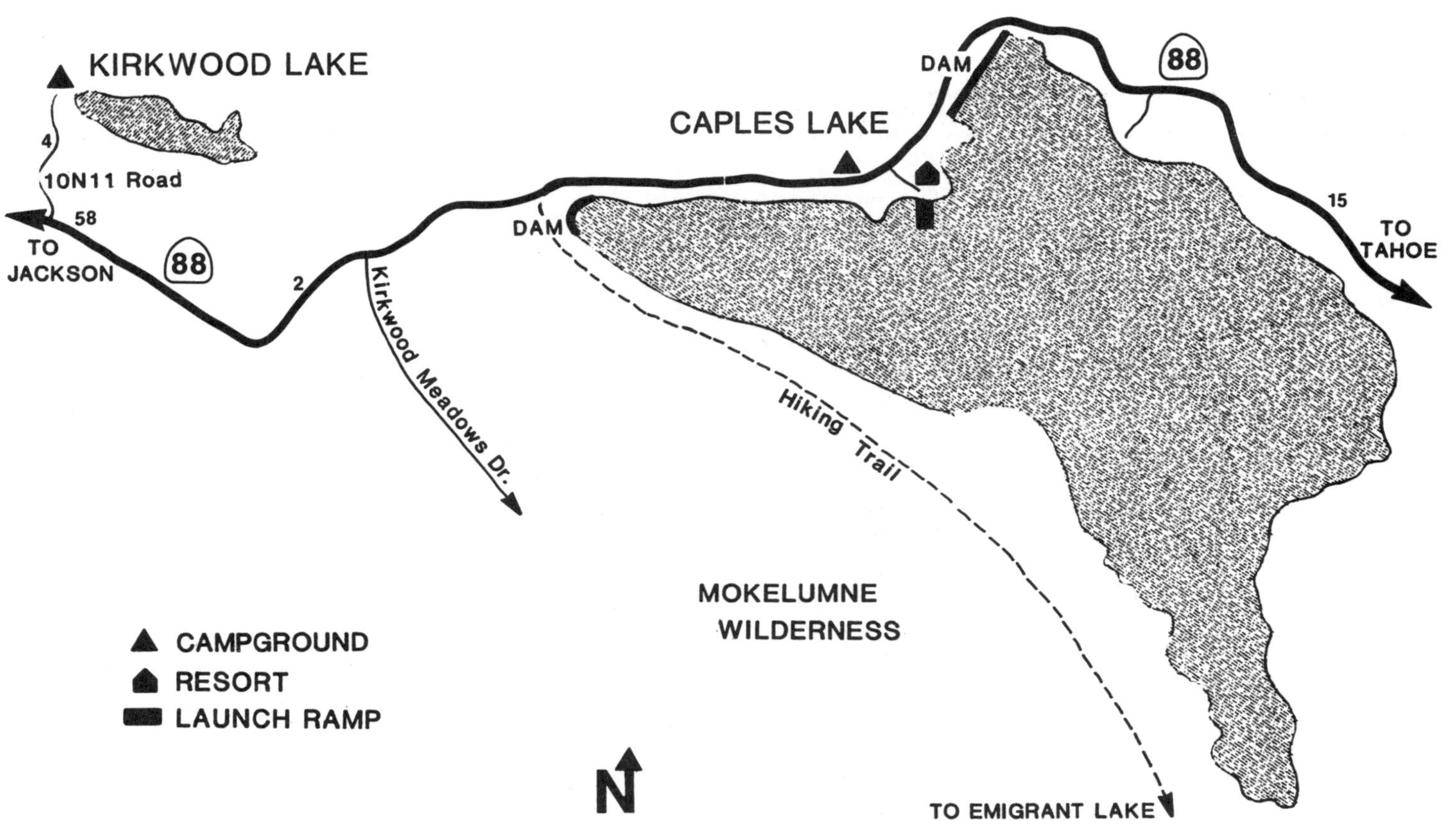

INFORMATION: Ranger Station, 26820 Silver Dr., Pioneer 95666, Ph: 209-295-4251

CAMPING	BOATING	RECREATION	OTHER
Caples Lake: 35 Dev. Sites for Tents & R.V.s Fee: $7 Kirkwood Lake: 12 Dev. Sites for Tents & R.V.s Fee: $6	Power, Row, Canoe, Sail & Inflatables 5 MPH Speed Limit on Caples Lake Launch Ramp Rentals: Fishing Boats Water Taxi No Motors on Kirkwood	Fishing: Rainbow, Brown, Brook & Cutthroat Trout Swimming Picnicking Hiking Backpacking Hunting: Deer	Caples Lake Resort P.O. Box 8 Kirkwood 95646 Ph: 209-258-8888 Lodge & Restaurant Housekeeping Cabins Grocery Store Bait & Tackle Gas Station

WOODS AND RED LAKES

Woods Lake is at an elevation of 8,200 feet southwest of the Carson Pass in the Eldorado National Forest. This lovely hidden retreat just 2 miles south of Highway 88 offers a variety of recreational opportunities. In addition to the campground, the Forest Service provides a nice picnic area at the water's edge with facilities for the handicapped. Fishing can be good from boat or along the bank as well as in the streams throughout the area. Motorboats are not permitted on the Lake. Trails lead to Winnemucca and Round Top Lakes and into the Mokelumne Wilderness. The Pacific Crest Trail runs to the east of Woods Lake. Most of Red Lake is private land with restricted access and limited facilities.

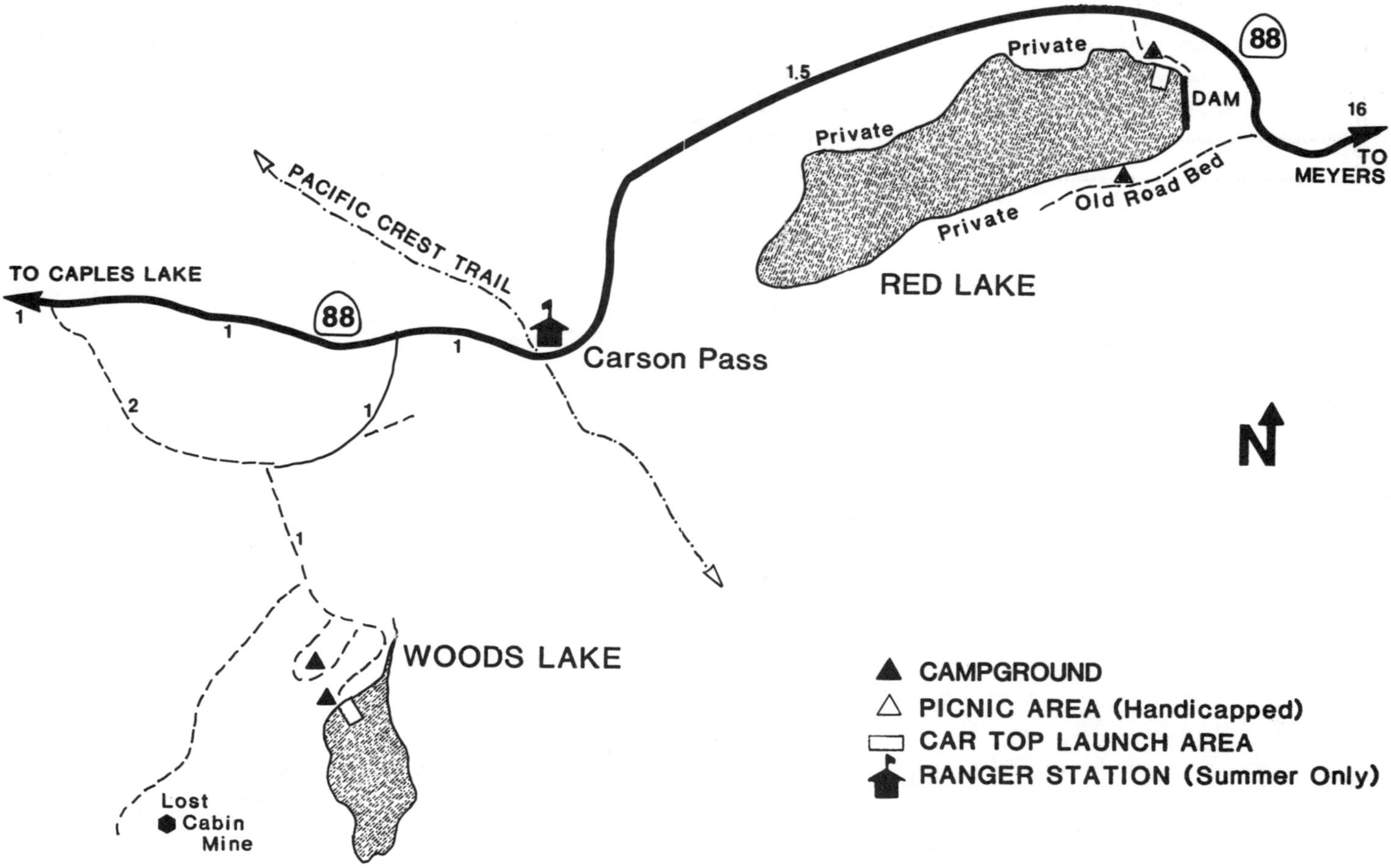

TO CAPLES LAKE
PACIFIC CREST TRAIL
Carson Pass
RED LAKE
Private
Old Road Bed
DAM
TO MEYERS
WOODS LAKE
Lost Cabin Mine

▲ CAMPGROUND
△ PICNIC AREA (Handicapped)
▭ CAR TOP LAUNCH AREA
RANGER STATION (Summer Only)

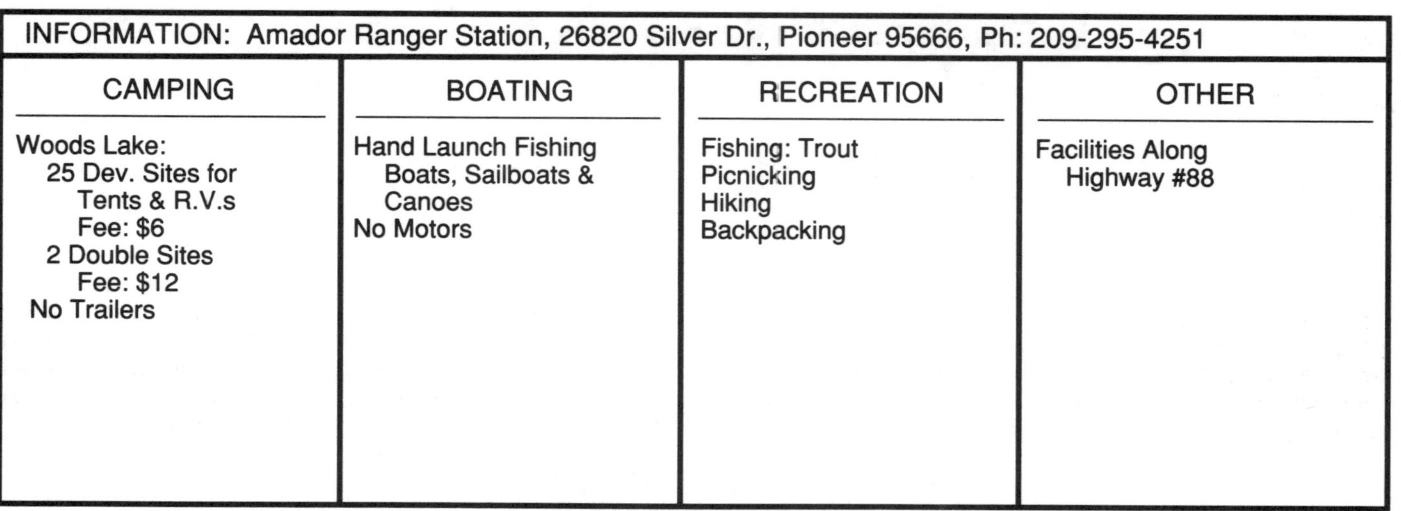

INFORMATION: Amador Ranger Station, 26820 Silver Dr., Pioneer 95666, Ph: 209-295-4251

CAMPING	BOATING	RECREATION	OTHER
Woods Lake: 25 Dev. Sites for Tents & R.V.s Fee: $6 2 Double Sites Fee: $12 No Trailers	Hand Launch Fishing Boats, Sailboats & Canoes No Motors	Fishing: Trout Picnicking Hiking Backpacking	Facilities Along Highway #88

BLUE LAKES ALPINE COUNTY

The Blue Lakes are at an elevation of 8,000 feet in this remote country of the Eldorado National Forest. The evenings and mornings are cool and the water is clear and cold. Boating is limited to small craft and fishing can be good. There are numerous hiking trails, some leading into the Mokelumne Wilderness. The campgrounds are maintained by P. G. & E. except for Hope Valley which is operated by the U. S. Forest Service, Carson Ranger District, Toiyabe National Forest. Facilities are limited, so come well prepared. Only the first 7 miles of road are paved from Highway 88.

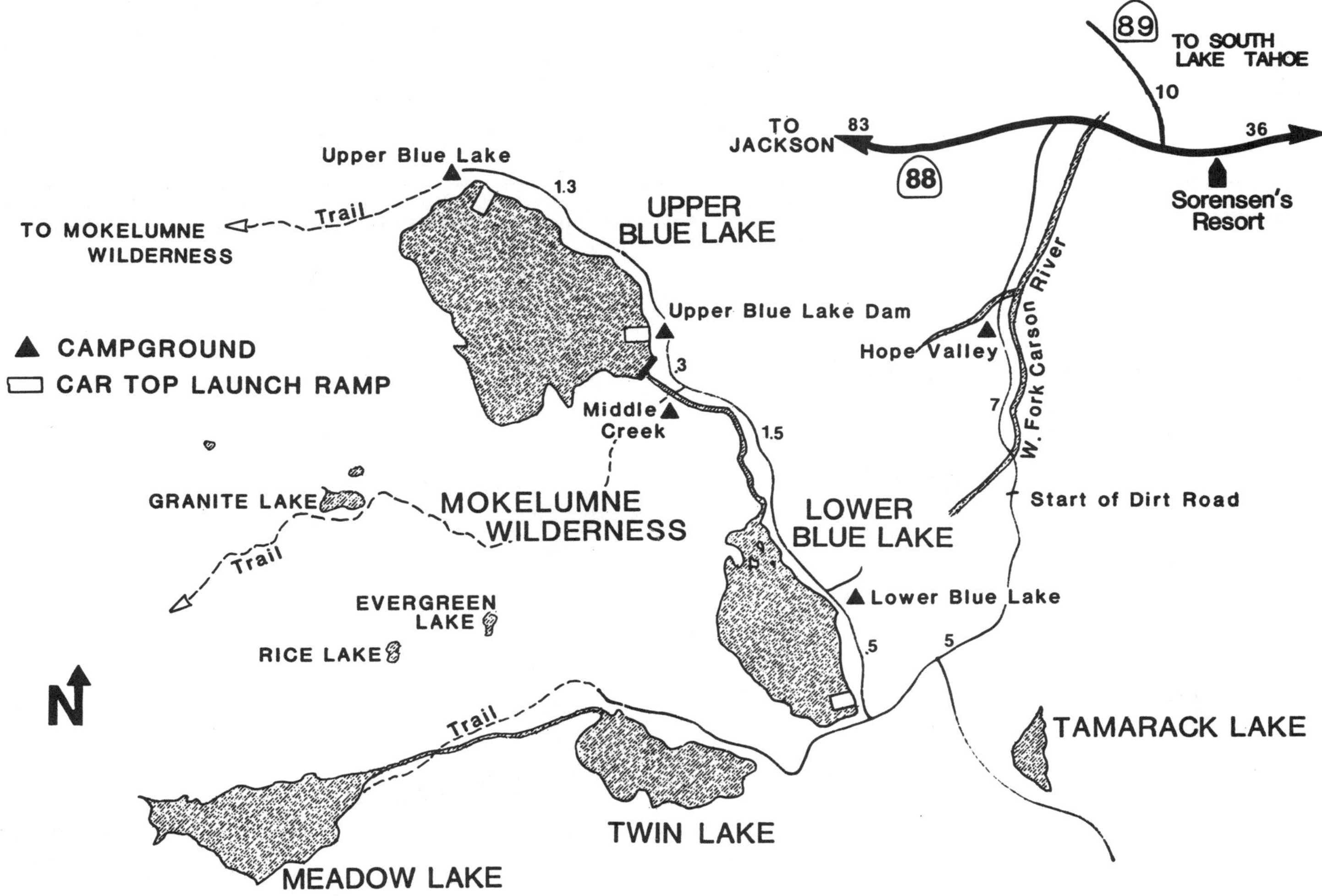

<table>
<tr><td colspan="4">INFORMATION: P. G. & E. Recreation Supervisor, 1401 Fulton, Fresno 93760</td></tr>
<tr><th>CAMPING</th><th>BOATING</th><th>RECREATION</th><th>OTHER</th></tr>
<tr><td>78 Dev. Sites for Tents & R.V.s
P. G. & E.
Fee: $8

26 Dev. Sites for Tents & R.V.s
U. S. F. S.
Fee: $4</td><td>Small Boats Only
Undeveloped Launch Ramps</td><td>Fishing: Rainbow Trout
Swimming
Picnicking
Hiking
Backpacking-Parking</td><td>Sorensen's Resort
Hope Valley 96120
Ph: 916-694-2203
25 Cabins
Restaurant
Fly Fishing & Tying Lessons
Fishing Supplies
Licenses</td></tr>
</table>

INDIAN CREEK RESERVOIR AND HEENAN LAKE

Indian Creek Reservoir is at an elevation of 5,600 feet on the eastern slope of the Sierra. The Bureau of Land Management maintains more than 7,000 acres in this beautiful area of Jeffrey and Pinon Pines. This 160 acre Lake of recycled water offers good fishing and small craft boating. Nearby Heenan Lake, 129 acres, provides a good catch and release fishery. After 21 years of being off limits, this operating hatchery now provides for zero limit fishing by artificial lures and barbless hooks. Contact the California Department of Fish and Game at 916-355-7090 for specific regulations. A popular attraction in this area is Grover Hot Springs State Park where you can enjoy a hot mineral bath. Camping reservations are advised.

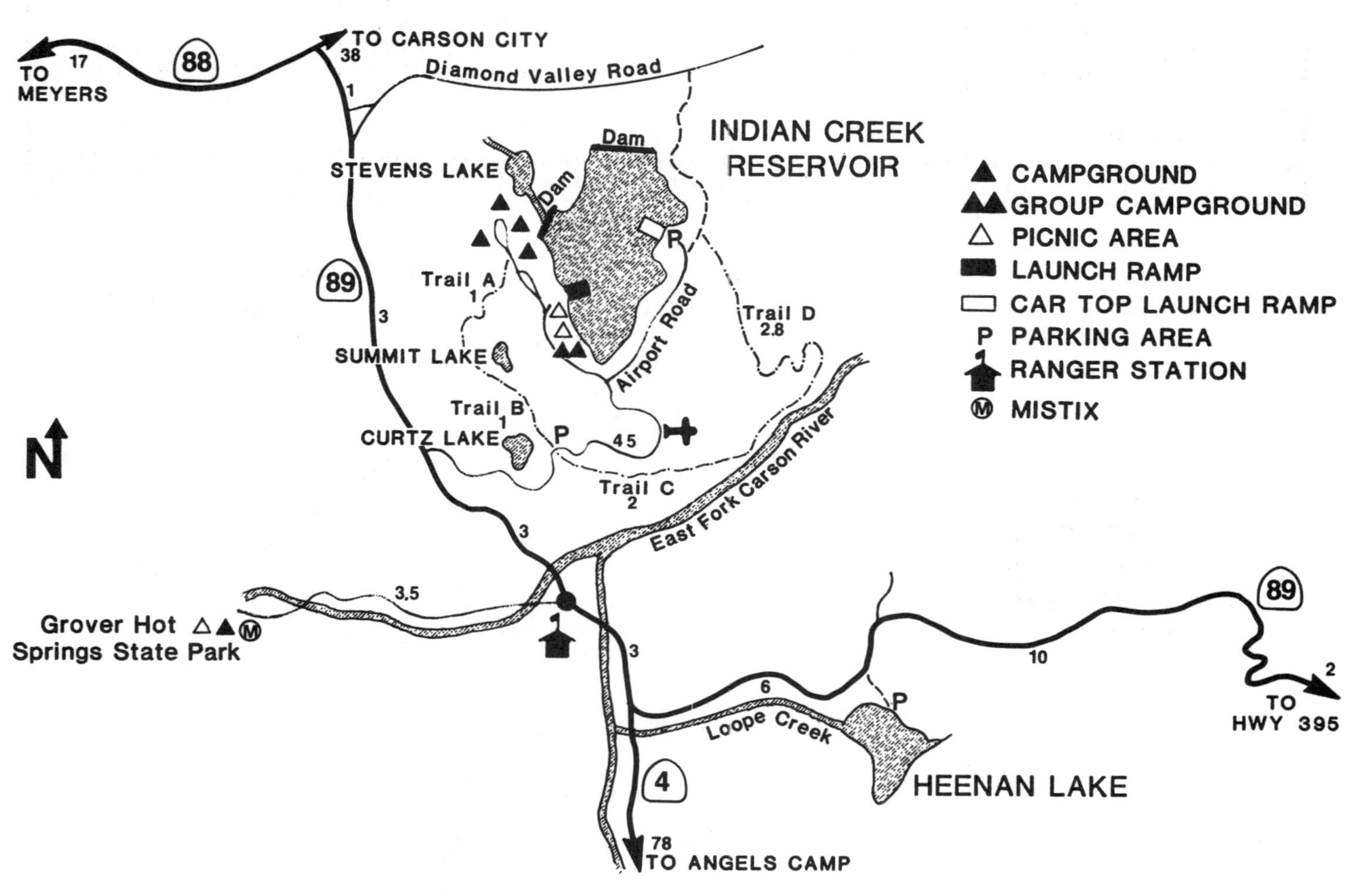

INFORMATION: B. L. M., 1535 Hot Springs Rd. Ste. 300, Carson City, NV 89706, Ph: 702-882-1631

CAMPING	BOATING	RECREATION	OTHER
Indian Creek: 29 Dev. Tent & R.V. Sites-Fee: $4-$6 Group Camp to 60 People-Fee: $10 Reservations Grover Hot Springs: 76 Dev. Sites Fee: $10 Reserve Mistix Ph: 1-800-444-7275	Indian Creek: Open to All Small Boats Launch Ramp Heenan Lake: Small Hand Launch Boats No Gas Motors Electric Motors Allowed	Fishing: Indian Creek - Rainbow & Brown Trout Heenan - Lahontan Cutthroat Trout - Zero Limit Picnicking Hiking & Nature Trails Backpacking Rockhounding Hot Springs	Grover Hot Springs State Park P.O. Box 188 Markleville 96120 Ph: 916-694-2248 Over 18: $3 Under 18: $2 For Additional Facilities Contact: Alpine Chamber of Commerce Ph: 916-694-2475

TOPAZ LAKE

Topaz Lake rests on the California-Nevada State Line at an elevation of 5,000 feet. This 1,800 acre Reservoir is nestled amid sage covered mountains with a sandy shoreline of 25 miles. The Lake is open to all types of boating including overnight but beware of potential heavy afternoon winds. Both California and Nevada stock the Lake which is closed to fishing for three months beginning October 1. As a result, trophy sized trout up to 8 pounds are no surprise. Since half of Topaz Lake is in Nevada, the nearby casinos offer games of chance for those so inclined.

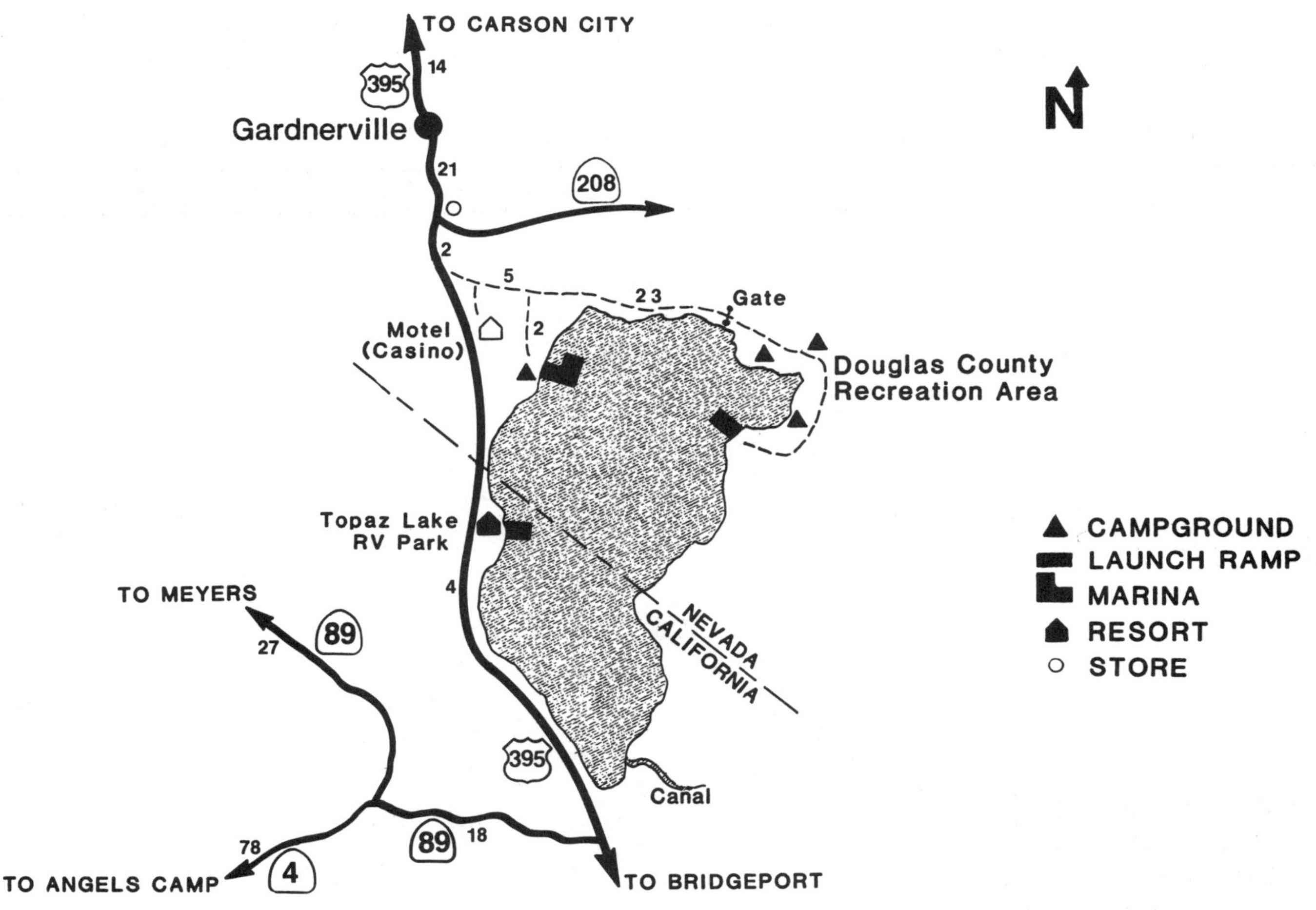

INFORMATION: Douglas County, 3700 Topaz Park Rd., Gardnerville, NV 89410, Ph: 702-266-3343			
CAMPING	BOATING	RECREATION	OTHER
Douglas County Park 28 R.V. Sites Hookups - $7.50 39 Campsites Fee: $5 Topaz Lake RV Park 50 R.V. Sites Full Hookups Topaz Marina 28 Dev. Sites for Tents & R.V.s, Some Hookups Fee: $3 - $6	Power, Row, Canoe, Sail, Waterski, Jet Ski, Windsurf, & Inflatables Full Service Marina County Launch Ramp - $2 Rentals: Fishing Boats Docks, Berths, Dry Storage, Moorings & Gas Overnight Boating	Fishing: Rainbow, Brown & Cutthroat Trout Swimming - Beaches Picnicking Hiking Playgrounds	Douglas County Park Ph: 702-266-3343 Topaz Lake R.V. Park Ph: 916-495-2357 Topaz Marina Ph: 702-266-3236 Motel Restaurant & Lounge Casinos Bait & Tackle at Topaz Marina Disposal Station

LAKE ALPINE

Lake Alpine is at an elevation of 7,320 feet in the Stanislaus National Forest. The Lake has a surface area of 180 acres and is regularly stocked with Rainbow trout. All boating is allowed within a 10 MPH speed limit, and the steady breezes make this a good sailing Lake. Trails leading to the new Carson-Iceberg Wilderness to the south of Lake Alpine and the Mokelumne Wilderness a few miles to the north, are accessible to the hiker, backpacker and horseman. The Forest Service maintains 4 campgrounds near the Lake plus a special area set aside for backpackers. The historic Lake Alpine Lodge overlooks this beautiful Lake in its heavily timbered mountain setting.

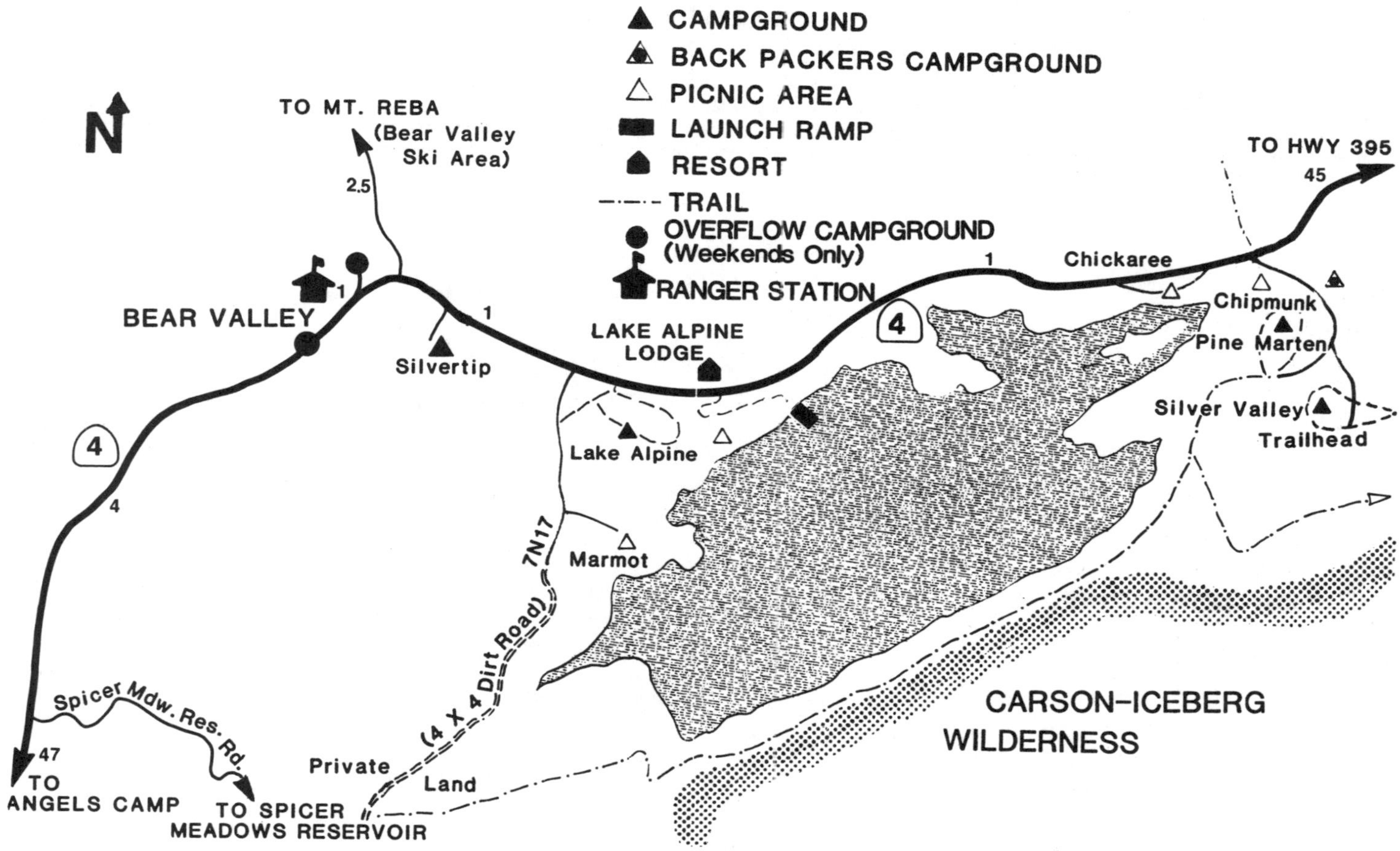

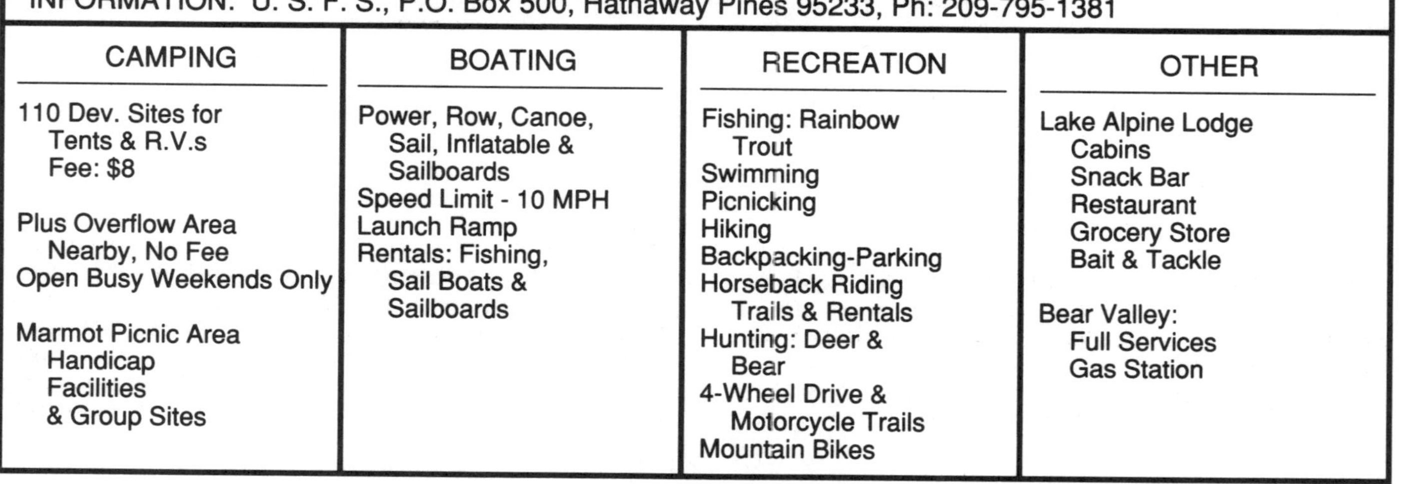

INFORMATION: U. S. F. S., P.O. Box 500, Hathaway Pines 95233, Ph: 209-795-1381

CAMPING	BOATING	RECREATION	OTHER
110 Dev. Sites for Tents & R.V.s Fee: $8 Plus Overflow Area Nearby, No Fee Open Busy Weekends Only Marmot Picnic Area Handicap Facilities & Group Sites	Power, Row, Canoe, Sail, Inflatable & Sailboards Speed Limit - 10 MPH Launch Ramp Rentals: Fishing, Sail Boats & Sailboards	Fishing: Rainbow Trout Swimming Picnicking Hiking Backpacking-Parking Horseback Riding Trails & Rentals Hunting: Deer & Bear 4-Wheel Drive & Motorcycle Trails Mountain Bikes	Lake Alpine Lodge Cabins Snack Bar Restaurant Grocery Store Bait & Tackle Bear Valley: Full Services Gas Station

LAKE SONOMA

Lake Sonoma is nestled amid the rolling foothills of Northern California's coastal range at an elevation of 451 feet. Located in the "wine country" just west of Healdsburg, this scenic lake offers 3,600 surface acres of prime recreational waters. There are many secluded coves for the quiet boater, sailor or angler. Water and jet skiers are allowed only in designated areas. The U. S. Army Corps of Engineers have developed and are developing a variety of enhancing facilities. The 53 miles of oak shaded hilly shoreline have almost 40 miles of lake access trails for the hiker or equestrian. There are 15 primitive walk or boat-in campsites. The new Liberty Glen Campground offers 110 oak shaded modern campsites. There is a 5-lane public launch ramp at Stewarts Point. The privately operated marina has complete support facilities.

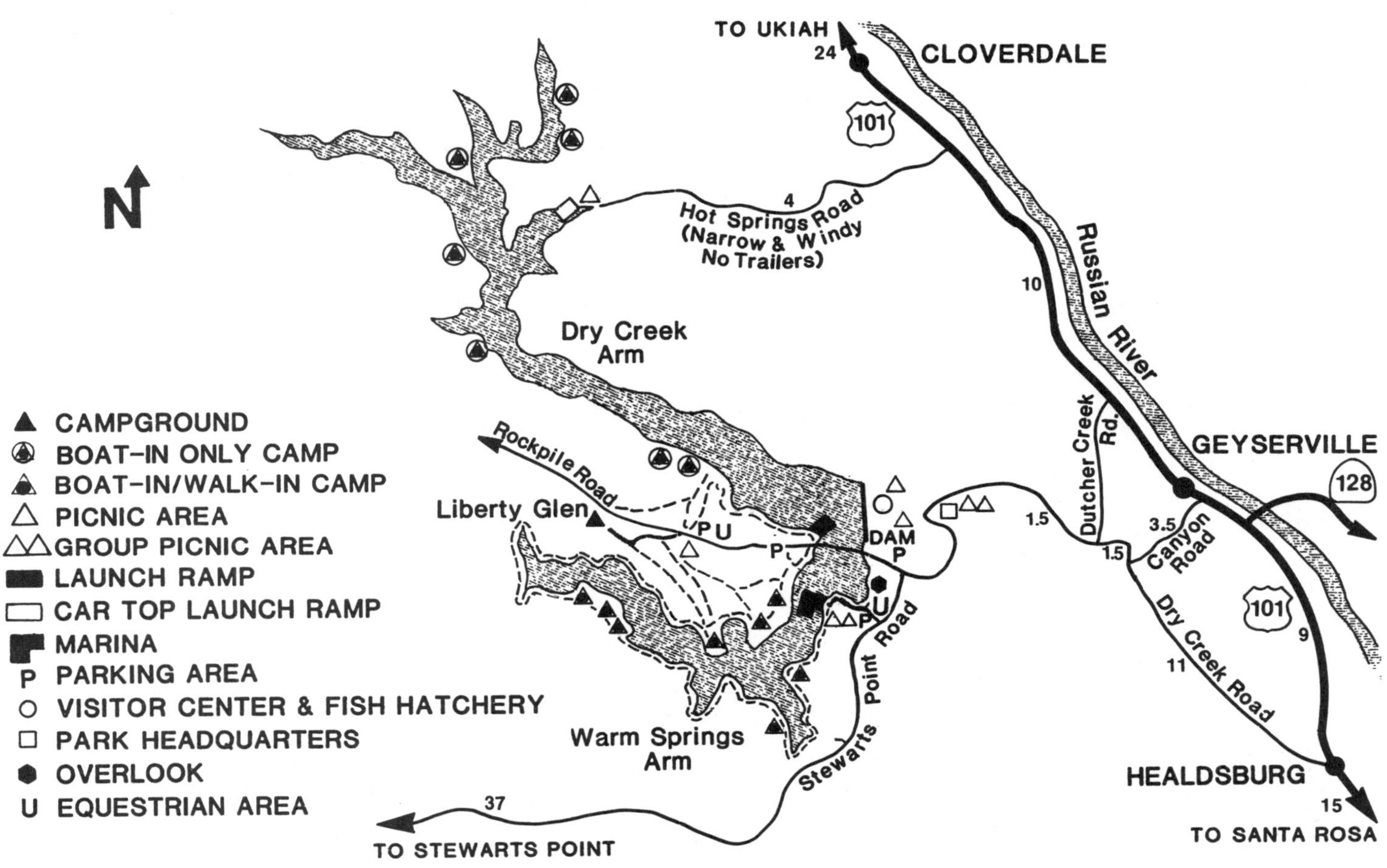

INFORMATION: Lake Sonoma Rec. Area, 3333 Skaggs Springs Rd., Geyserville 95441, 707-433-9483			
CAMPING	**BOATING**	**RECREATION**	**OTHER**
Liberty Glen 113 Tent/RV Sites Disposal Station Flush Toilets 15 Boat/Walk-in Primitive Camping Areas Chemical Toilets No Water Permits Required	Open to All Boating, Jet Skiing & No Wake Areas Paved Public Launch Ramp - Free Full Service Marina Gas & Slip Rentals Boat Storage Boat Rentals Jet Ski Rentals Water Ski School Launch Ramp: $8 Hand Launch at Hot Springs Road	Fishing: Large & Smallmouth Bass, Sacramento Perch, Channel Catfish & Redear Sunfish Picnic Areas Group Picnic Area Swim Beach Hiking & Equestrian Trails 2 Equestrian Staging Areas Visitor Center Fish Hatchery	Lake Sonoma Resort P.O. Box 1345 Healdsburg 95448 707-433-2200 Snack Bar, General Store, Restrooms, Beer & Wine Gardens Bait & Tackle Day Use Fee: $3

SPRING LAKE AND LAKE RALPHINE

Spring Lake is under the jurisdiction of the Sonoma County Regional Parks Department. This nice 320 acre Park has picnic areas, a campground, swim lagoon and well maintained trails. This is a popular equestrian area. The 75 acre Lake is open to non-powered boating. Lake Ralphine is within the City of Santa Rosa's Howarth Park. This day use facility has an abundance of children's attractions. Lake Ralphine also allows non-powered boating with sailing being a special attraction. There is a warm water fishery in addition to planted trout at both Lakes. A bicycle path connects these parks.

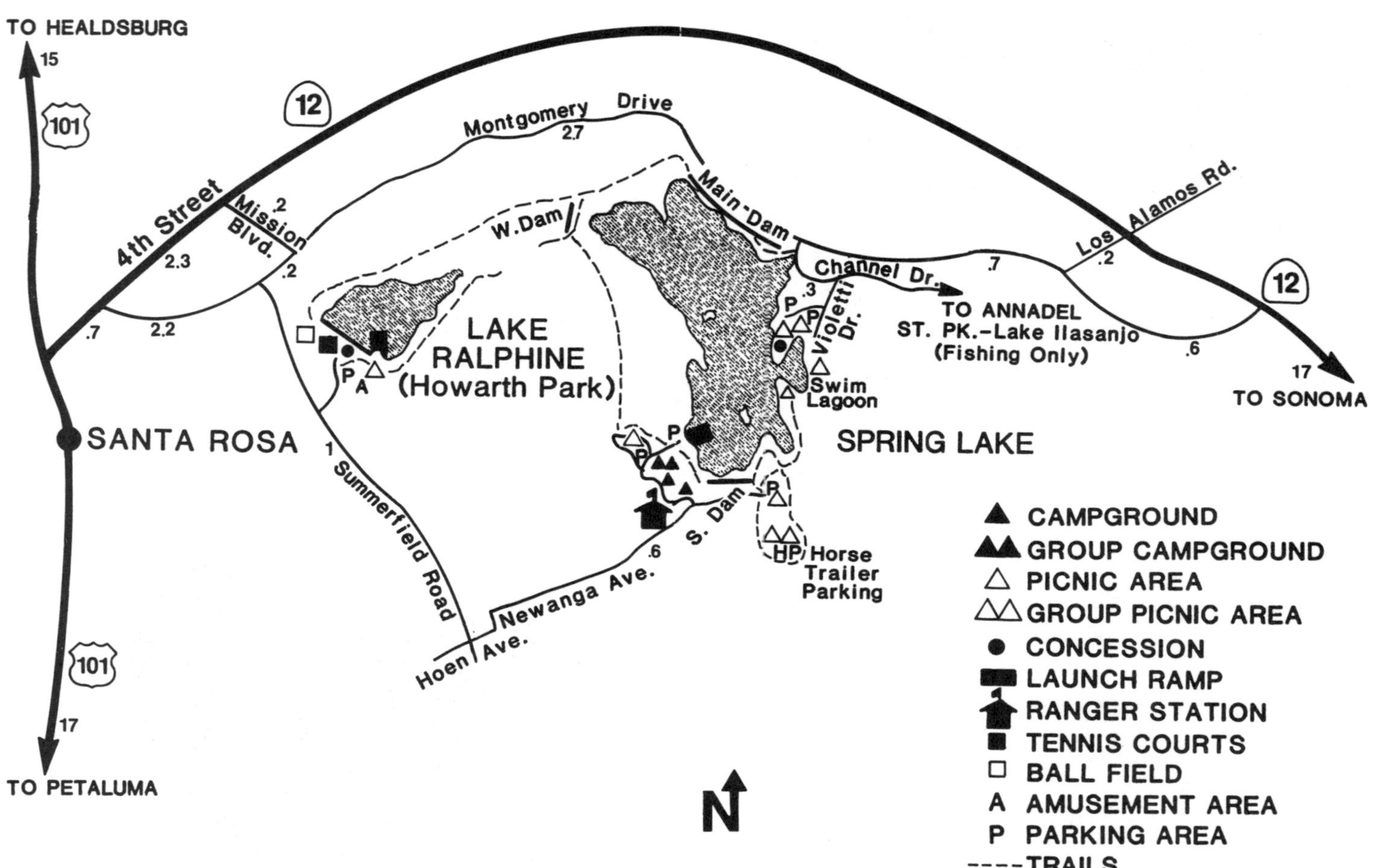

INFORMATION: Spring Lake, 5390 Montgomery Dr., Santa Rosa 95405, Ph: 707-539-8092

CAMPING	BOATING	RECREATION	OTHER
31 Dev. Sites for Tents & R.V.s No Hookups Hot Showers Fee: $11 Group Camp to 100 People - Reservations Req'd. Disposal Station Campground Open Weekends & Holidays Only From Sept. 15 to May 15	Spring Lake: Row, Sail, Canoe & Inflatables (2 Chambers) Electric Motors Rentals: Row, Canoe & Sailboats (Summer Only) Life Jackets Required Lake Ralphine: Private Boats Under 20 ft. - No Motors Rentals: As Above	Fishing: Trout, Bluegill, Redear Sunfish & Bass Swim Lagoon Picnic Areas: Group Reservations Available at Spring Lake Hiking, Riding & Bicycle Trails Tennis Courts No Swimming in Lake Ralphine	Howarth Park: Santa Rosa Rec. & Parks Dept. Ph: 707-528-5116 Miniature Steam Train, Pony Rides Merry-Go-Round, Pony Rides & Animal Farm, For Info: Ph: 707-576-5116

PETS

Pets are welcome at most recreation facilities. A nominal fee is charged and there are some specific requirements. The pet must have a valid license and proof of a current rabies vaccination. There is usually a leash rule where the pet must be restrained by a leash no longer than ten feet. Pets must not be allowed to contaminate the water. As a rule, they are not permitted in public areas such as beaches and hiking trails. They are permitted in Wilderness Areas only when they are under your direct control. Always be certain your pet does not disturb others by picking up after it and keeping it next to you at all times.

LAKE BERRYESSA AND LAKE SOLANO

Lake Berryessa is one of Northern California's most popular recreation Lakes. One of the State's largest man-made lakes, its 13,000 surface acres and 165 miles of hilly oak and madrone covered shoreline provide quality recreational opportunities. Known for its excellent year-round fishing, the angler will find trophy trout, three species of bass and a good warm water fishery. The average water temperature of 78 degrees lures the skier and swimmer while the light and variable winds lure the sailor. Complete resort, camping and marine facilities complement this low elevation lake's natural atttractions. To the west of Berryessa off Highway 128 is Lake Hennessy. Under the jurisdiction of the City of Napa, this small Lake offers limited facilities and recreational opportunities. In contrast, Lake Solano, southeast of Berryessa, provides numerous recreational opportunities, such as swim lagoons, picnic sites, boat rentals and a 50-site campground. Solano offers non-powered boating and trout fishing.

...Continued...

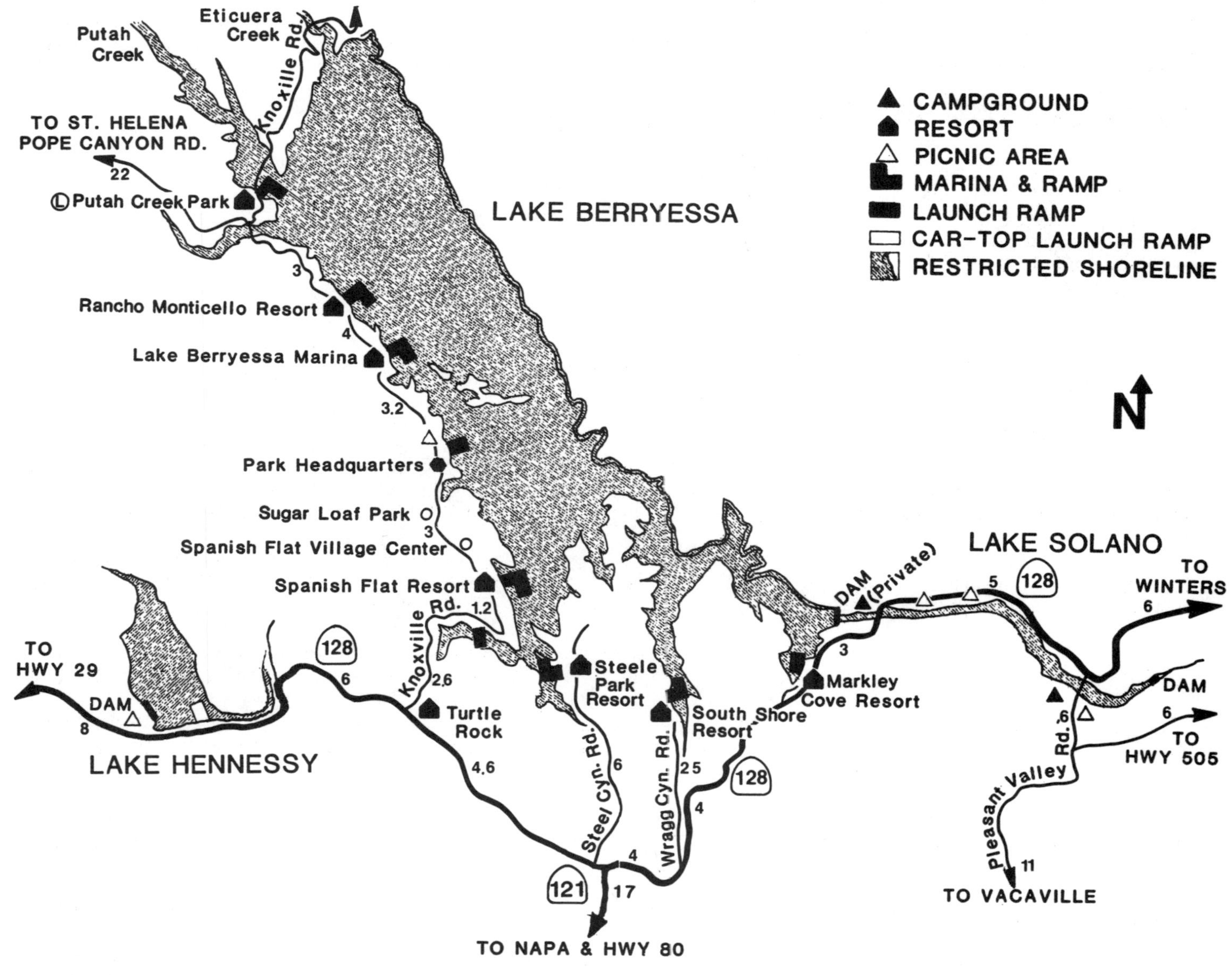

LAKE BERRYESSA ACCOMMODATIONS

LAKE BERRYESSA MARINA RESORT - 5800 Knoxville Rd., Napa 94558, 707-966-2161, Tent/RV Park, Full Hookups, Dump Station, Courtesy Pumpout in Mornings, Hot Showers, Flush Toilets, Picnic Area, Grocery Store, Laundromat, Restaurant & Lounge, Swim Beach, Full Service Marina, Fishing, Patio & Ski Boat Rentals, Fuel Dock & Ramp, Courtesy Dock.

MARKLEY COVE RESORT - P.O. Box 987, Winters 95694, 707-966-2134, Fishing, Patio & Houseboat Rentals, Paved Ramp, Berths, Restaurant & Lounge.

PUTAH CREEK PARK - 7600 Knoxville Rd., Napa, 707-966-2116, Tent/RV Park, Partial and Full Hookups, 2 Dump Stations, Hot Showers, Flush Toilets, Picnic Area, Motel, Full Service Marina, Ski Boat Rentals, Storage, Bait & Tackle, Store, Restaurant & Lounge, Snack Bar.

RANCHO MONTICELLO RESORT - 6590 Knoxville Rd., Napa 94558, 707-966-2188, Tent/RV Sites, Full Hookups, 2 Dump Stations, Hot Showers, Flush Toilets, Picnic Areas, Store, Snack Bar, Launch Ramp, Fishing Boat Rentals.

SOUTH SHORE REOSRT - 6100 Hwy. 128, Napa 94558, 707-966-2172, Tent/RV Sites, Full Hookups, Dump Station, Hot Showers, Flush Toilets, Fuel Dock, Slips, Storage, Grocery Store, Restaurant & Lounge.

SPANISH FLAT RESORT - 4310 Knoxville Rd., Napa 94558, 707-966-2101, Tent/RV Sites, Hot Showers, Flush Toilets, Dump Station, Electric and Water Hookups, Full Service Marina, Berthing, Fishing, Patio, Ski and Jet Ski Boat Rentals, Grocery Store, Snack Bar, Picnic Sites, Barbercues, Swim Beach.

STEELE PARK RESORT - 1605 Steel Canyon Rd., Napa 94558, 707-966-2123, Largest Resort on Lake, RV Sites, Full Hookups, Dump Station, Hot Showers, Flush Toilets, Motel, Housekeeping Cottages, Full Service Marina, Paved Ramp, Covered Berths, Dry Storage, Fuel Dock, Ski School, Swim Beach, Pool, Tennis Courts.

For further information on facilities contact:

LAKE BERRYESSA CHAMBER OF COMMERCE
P.O. Box 9164
Spanish Flat Station, Napa 94558
Ph: 707-966-2116

INFORMATION: See Lake Berryessa Chamber of Commerce			
CAMPING	BOATING	RECREATION	OTHER
Lake Berryessa 650 Tent/RV Sites at Resorts See Above for Details Lake Solano 50 Tent/RV Sites Lake Hennessy No Camping	Lake Berryessa Open to All Boating Full Service Marina House, Ski, Fishing & Patio Boat Rentals Lake Solano Non-power Boating Only Lake Hennessy 10 HP Max. Limit No Kayaks or Windsurfers	Fishing: Rainbow & Brown Trout, Large & Smallmouth Bass, Catfish, Bluegill, Crappie & Silver Salmon Swimming-Lake & Pools Picnic Areas Hiking & Riding Trails Wine Country Excursions	Complete Destination Facilities at Resorts on Lake Berryessa Lake Solano County of Solano Parks 603 Texas Street Fairfield 94533 Ph: 916-795-2990

LAKE AMADOR

Lake Amador is at an elevation of 485 feet in the Sierra Foothills, one mile east of historic Buena Vista. The surface area of the lake is 425 acres. The shoreline of 13-1/2 miles is surrounded by black oak covered hills. The brush along the water's edge provides a thriving warm water fishery. A Northern California record limit of 80 pounds for Florida bass was set in 1981, and in 1986 the individual lake record was set for 17 pounds, 1-1/4 ounces. This is a nice boating lake with good winds for sailing. The lake is open to boating and fishing 24 hours a day. The visitor will find a 1 acre swim pond with sandy beaches and playgrounds for the children making Amador a good family recreation area.

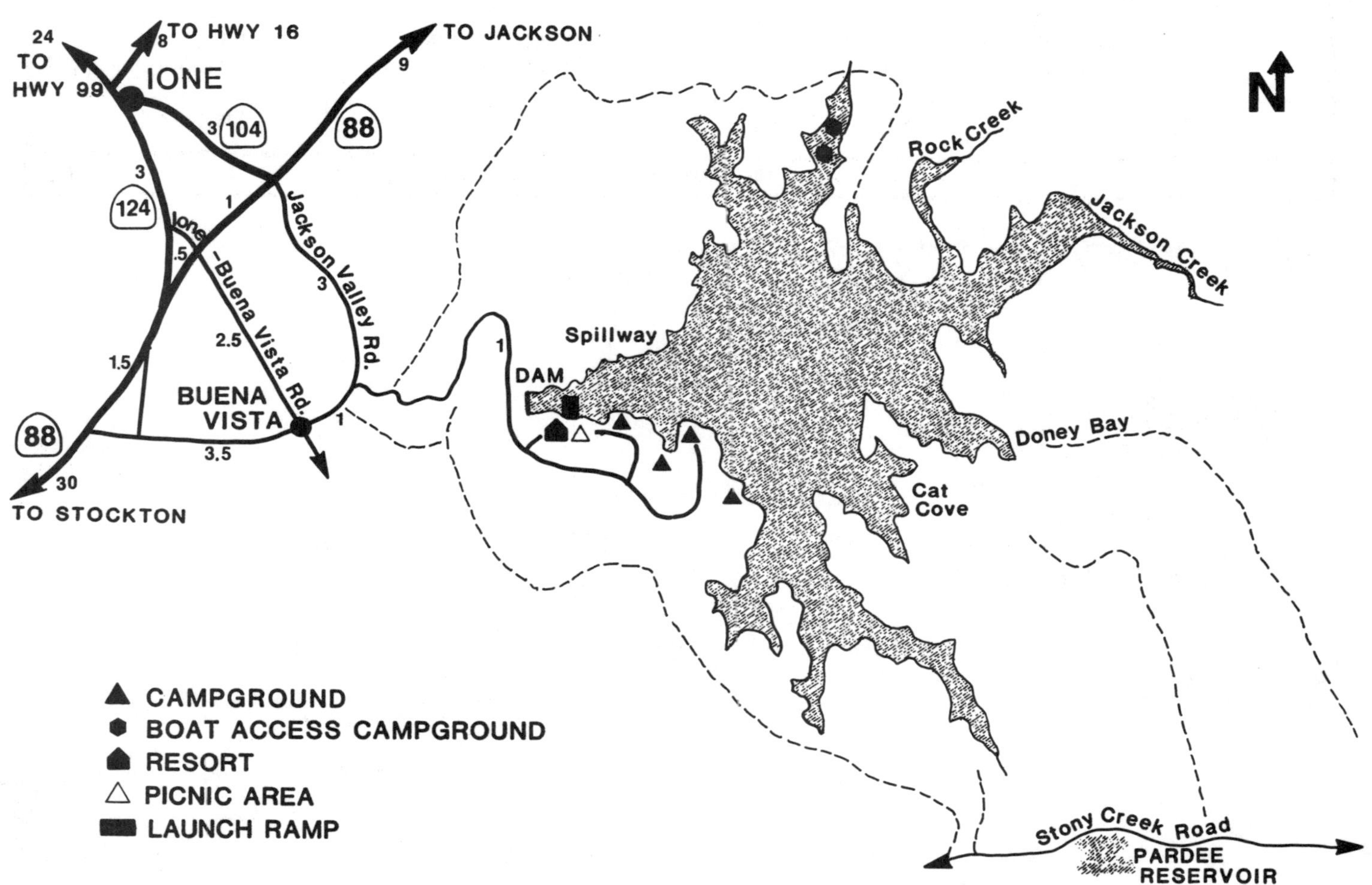

INFORMATION: Lake Amador Resort, 7500 Amador Dr., Ione 95640, Ph: 209-274-4739			
CAMPING	**BOATING**	**RECREATION**	**OTHER**
150 Dev. Sites for Tents, Fee: $10 73 Full Hookups for RV & Trailers Fee: $15 - $18 12 Boat-In or Walk-In Sites Group Camp to 50 Vehicles Reservations for All Sites Suggested	Power, Row, Canoe, Sail, Windsurf & Inflatables No Waterskiing or Jetskis Launch Ramp - $3.50 Rentals: Fishing Boats Docks, Storage Fishing Floats Around Shoreline	Fishing: Trout, Largemouth Bass, Catfish, Bluegill, Crappie & Perch Swimming - Pond Free Waterslide Picnicking Hiking Mountain Biking	Snack Bar Restaurant Grocery Store Bait & Tackle Hot Showers Disposal Station Gas Station & Propane Club House & Recreation Room

PARDEE LAKE

Pardee Lake rests at an elevation of 568 feet in the heart of the "Mother Lode Country" and its historic gold towns. Under the jurisdiction of the East Bay Municipal Water District, this popular fishing lake in the Sierra foothills has a surface area of 2,200 acres surrounded by 43 miles of rolling woodland. Trout and Kokanee are the primary gamefish. The dedicated angler will find a good smallmouth fishery as well as its big brother, the largemouth bass. Pan and catfish are also abundant. Boating is generally related to fishing since waterskiing and jet skiers are prohibited. There are marine support facilities. This is a nice family area with a large campground, a swimming pool (no lake swimming), picnic area, playground and store.

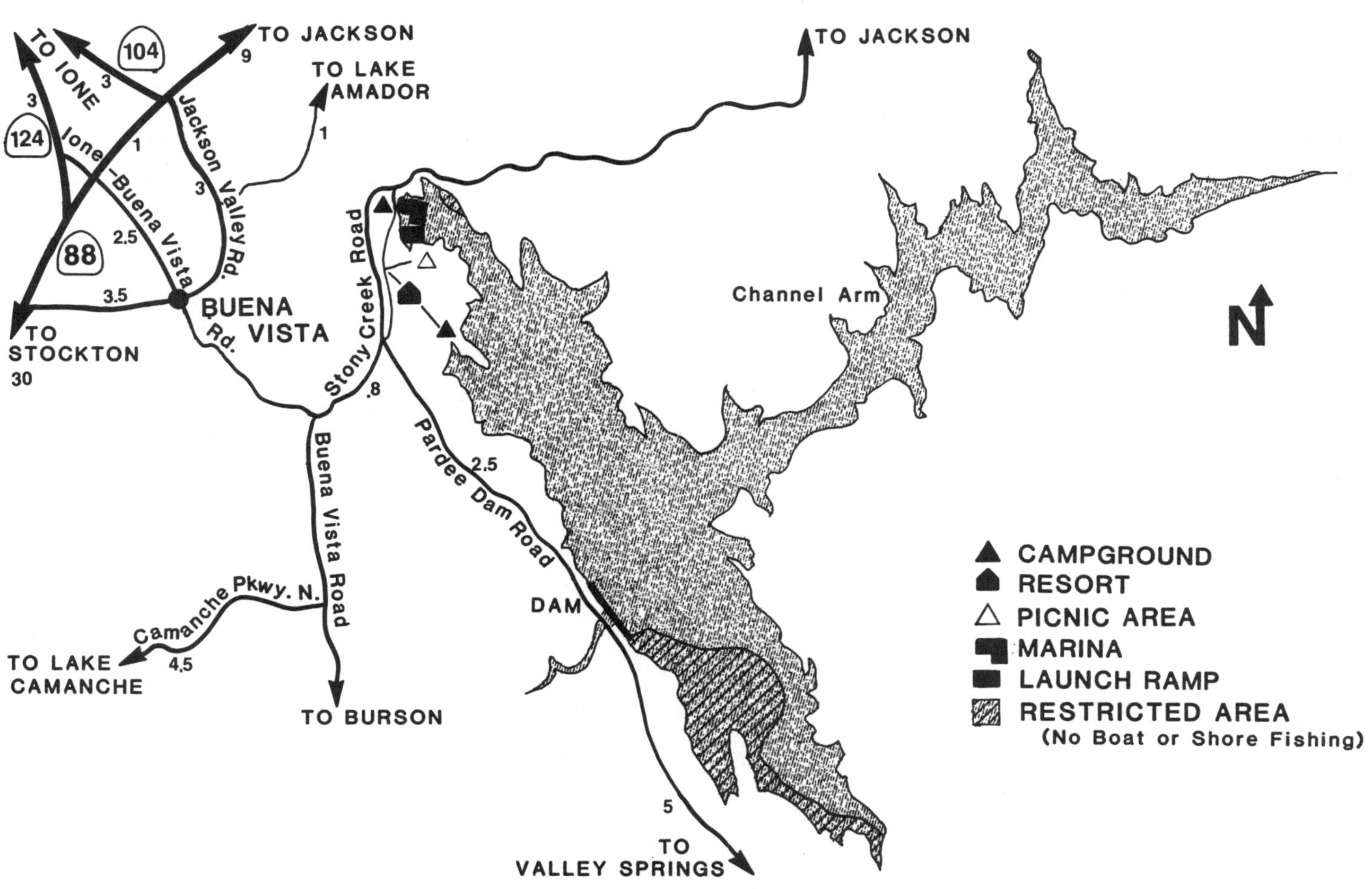

INFORMATION: Pardee Lake Resort, 4900 Stony Creek Rd., Ione 95640, Ph: 209-772-1472

CAMPING	BOATING	RECREATION	OTHER
100 Dev. Tent Sites Fee: $8 90 Dev. R.V. Sites With Full Hookups Fee: $13 Groups to 100 People Reservations Taken at R.V. Sites Only	Power, Row, Canoe, Sail & Inflatables No Body Contact With the Water Full Service Marina Launch Ramp Rentals: Fishing Boats & Pontoons Docks, Berths, Moorings, Gas Dry Storage	Fishing: Rainbow & Brown Trout, Kokanee Salmon, Catfish, Bluegill, Crappie, Small & Largemouth Bass Swimming in Pool Picnicking Bicycle Trails Playground	Snack Bar Restaurant Grocery Store Laundromat Disposal Station Gas & Propane

LAKE CAMANCHE

Lake Camanche is at an elevation of 235 feet in the foothills of the Sierra Nevada. This East Bay Municipal Utility District Reservoir has 7,700 surface acres and a shoreline of 53 miles. Located in the famous "Mother Lode Country," panning for gold is still popular in the spring when streams are high. Indian grave sites are visible along the shoreline. The water is warm and clear making watersports a delight.

Fishing for a variety of species can be excellent. The Resorts at Camanche Northshore and South Camanche Shore offer modern, complete camping, marine and recreation facilities. There are over 15,000 acres of park lands for the hiker and equestrian. Camanche is one of the most complete facility Lakes within easy distance of the San Francisco Bay Area.

. . . Continued . . .

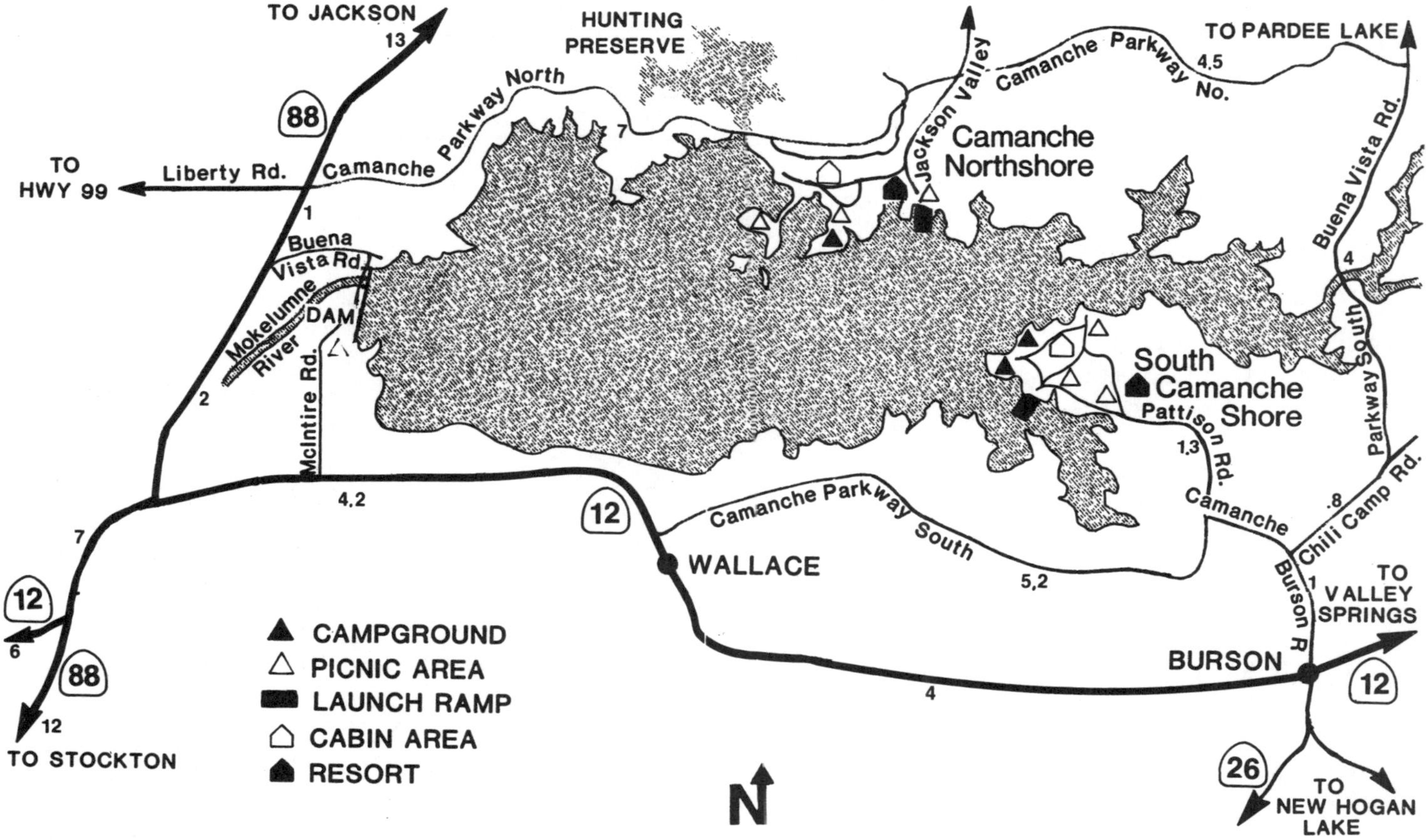

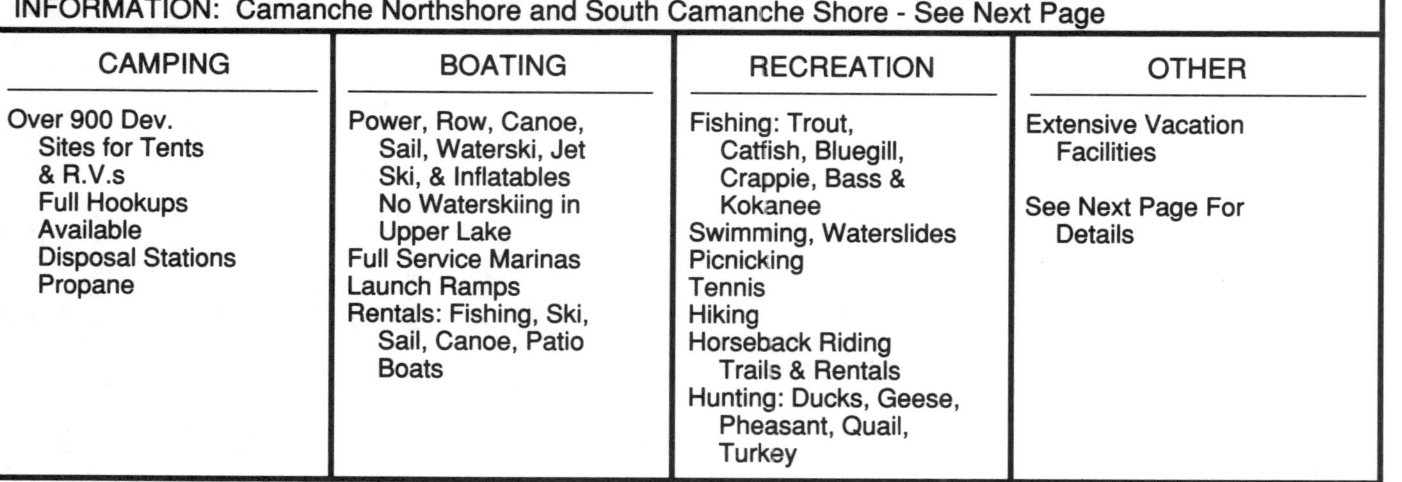

INFORMATION: Camanche Northshore and South Camanche Shore - See Next Page			
CAMPING	BOATING	RECREATION	OTHER
Over 900 Dev. Sites for Tents & R.V.s Full Hookups Available Disposal Stations Propane	Power, Row, Canoe, Sail, Waterski, Jet Ski, & Inflatables No Waterskiing in Upper Lake Full Service Marinas Launch Ramps Rentals: Fishing, Ski, Sail, Canoe, Patio Boats	Fishing: Trout, Catfish, Bluegill, Crappie, Bass & Kokanee Swimming, Waterslides Picnicking Tennis Hiking Horseback Riding Trails & Rentals Hunting: Ducks, Geese, Pheasant, Quail, Turkey	Extensive Vacation Facilities See Next Page For Details

LAKE CAMANCHE

CAMANCHE NORTHSHORE RESORT
2000 Jackson Valley - Camanche Rd.
Ione, CA 95640
Ph: 209-763-5121

200 Campsites for Tents & R.V.s - Water, Toilets, Showers, Disposal Station, Trailer Storage, Laundromat, Playgrounds, Store, Coffee Shop. Fee: $12

Full Service Marina - 10-Lane Launch Ramp, Fee: $6, Boat Rentals: Sail, Fishing, Canoes, Patio Boats, Storage, Berths, Moorings, Fishing & Waterskiing Equipment Rentals, Sailing School, Bike Rentals, Canoe River Trips, Patio Boat Tours, For Information Phone: 209-763-5511. General Store and Coffee Shop: Phone 209-763-5166.

Riding Stables - Breakfast Rides, Cross Country, Sunset Rides, Barbecue Dinners and Campfires, Haywagon Rides, Pony Rides, Lessons, Training, Boarding. For Information Phone: 209-763-5295.

Cottages - Rentals of Deluxe Housekeeping Cottages for 2 to 12 People, Motel Rooms, Tennis Courts.

Conference and Seminar Facilities - Groups up to 100 People, Bird Hunting Preserve and Club, Golf Nearby, Special Events.

Other Facilities - Restaurant, Amphitheater with Movies and Entertainment. Pavilion for Dancing and Concerts. Two Mobile Home Parks with Sales Division.

SOUTH CAMANCHE SHORE
P.O. Box 92
Wallace, California 95254
Ph: 209-763-5178

Over 678 Campsites for Tents & R.V.s - Water, Toilets, Showers, Full Hookups, Disposal Station, Laundromat, Store & Snack Bars. Fees: Dry - $12, Full Hookups - $16.

Full Service Marina - 7-lane Launch Ramp, Boat Rentals: Fishing & Pontoon Boats, Fuel Dock, Storage, Berths, Moorings.

Other Facilities - Housekeeping Cottages, Tennis Courts, Amphitheater with Movies and Entertainment, Group Reservations for Camping or Picnicking, Mobile Home Park and Sales, Recreation Hall.

NEW HOGAN LAKE

New Hogan Lake is at an elevation of 713 feet in the foothills east of Stockton. The U. S. Army Corps of Engineers holds jurisdiction over the lake and maintains the modern marine and camping facilities. The surface area of the lake is 4,400 acres with 50 miles of shoreline covered with oak, digger pine and brushlands of chamise and manzanita. In spring a variety of wild flowers provide a colorful display. Wildlife is abundant with over 153 species of birds. New Hogan is ideal for water-oriented recreation and especially for its varied gamefish. The Florida strain of largemouth bass is a prime target. Waterskiing is allowed in the central lake although many coves and the swimming beaches are restricted.

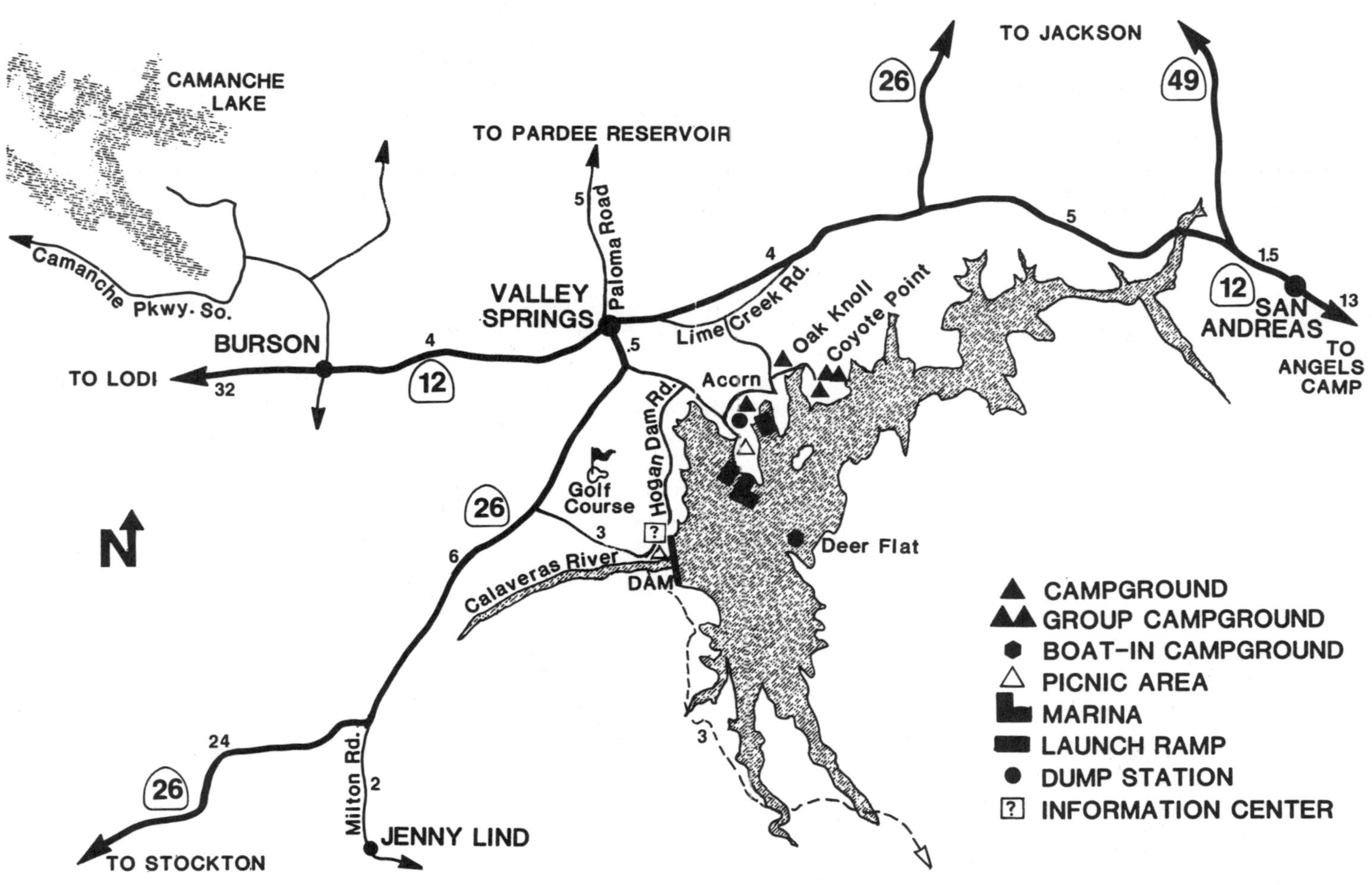

INFORMATION: New Hogan Lake, P.O. Box 128, Valley Springs 95252, Ph: 209-772-1343

CAMPING	BOATING	RECREATION	OTHER
Acorn: 122 Dev. Sites for Tents & R.V.s Fee: $8 Oak Knoll: 58 Undev. Sites Fee: $4 10 Free Sites 30 Boat Access Camps - No Fee & No Water No Reservations	Power, Row, Canoe, Sail, Waterski, Jet Ski, Windsurf & Inflatable On Board Boat Camping in Designated Areas - Must Have Sealed Waste Holding Tank Night Boating: 15 MPH Full Service Marina Launch Ramps Rentals: Fishing Boats & Motors	Fishing: Catfish, Bluegill, Crappie, Large, Smallmouth & Striped Bass Swimming Picnicking Hiking, Nature & Equestrian Trails Campfire Program Bird Watching Hunting: Quail, Dove	Dam Tours Grocery Store Bait & Tackle Hot Showers Disposal Station Gas Station Docks, Moorings, Dry Storage La Contenta Golf Course Nearby Full Facilities: Valley Springs

HIGHLAND AND MOSQUITO LAKES-UTICA, UNION AND SPICER MEADOW

These relatively remote and undeveloped lakes in the Stanislaus National Forest are often passed by people visiting the more popular and developed Lake Alpine. For those who enjoy a rustic and quiet environment, these lakes are worth a visit. The elevation is high, ranging from 6,500 feet at Big Meadow Campground to 8,730 feet at Ebbetts Pass. Highland Lakes offers the only developed facilities with a 35 site campground, pumped water and a gravel launch ramp. Spicer Meadows, Union and Utica Reservoirs are undeveloped although there is a primitive campground off Spicer Meadows Road on the Stanislaus River. Mosquito Lakes have several undeveloped campgrounds nearby. There is often good fishing at the lakes, river and streams. This is a popular area for deer and bear hunting in season.

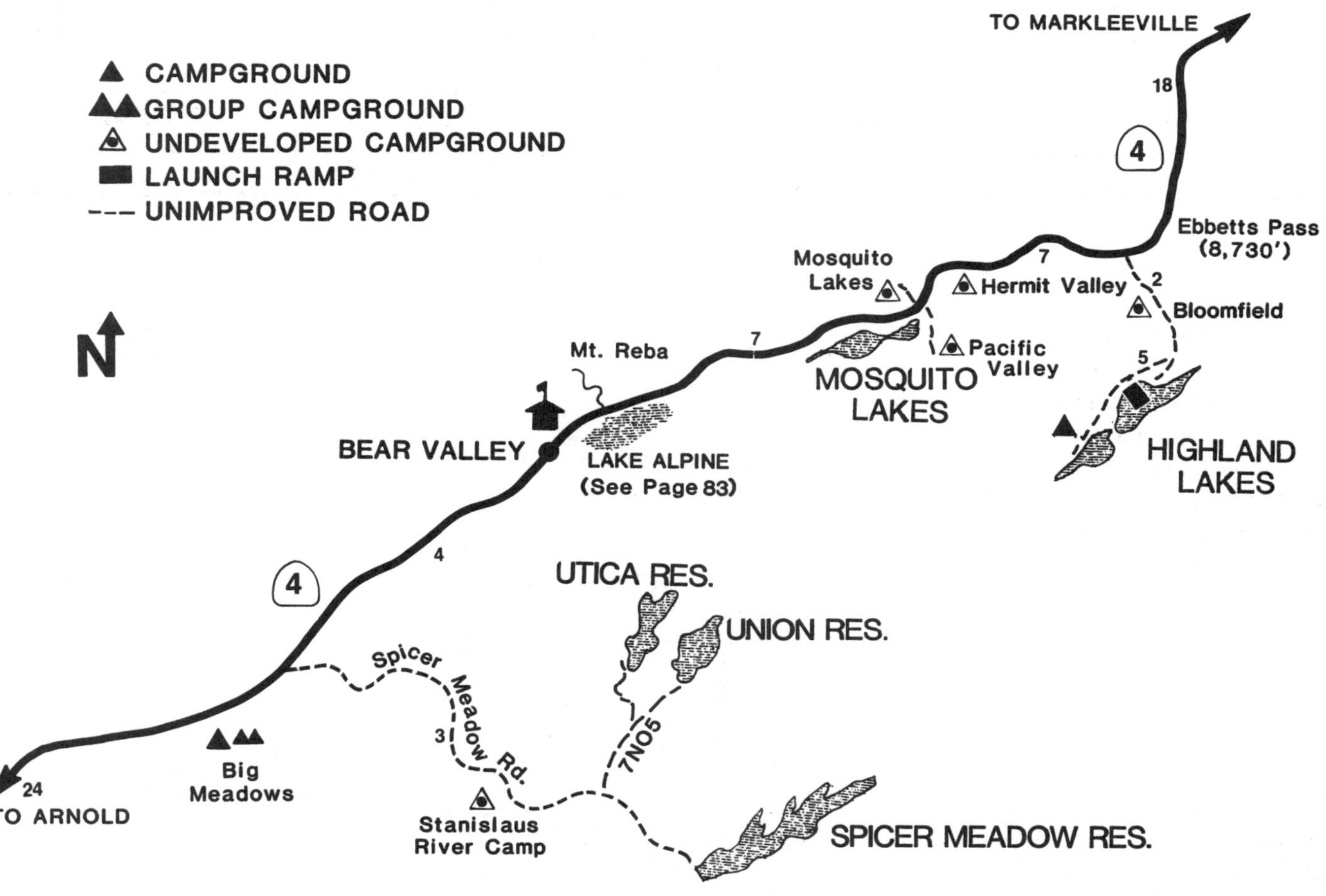

INFORMATION: Calaveras Ranger District, P.O. Box 500, Hathaway Pines 95233, Ph: 209-795-1381			
CAMPING	**BOATING**	**RECREATION**	**OTHER**
Highland Lakes: 35 Dev. Sites - Fee: $4 Mosquito Lakes: Undev. Sites No Water - No Fee Big Meadows: 68 Tent/R.V. Sites Fee: $7 Group Campground 10 Tent/R.V. Sites Fee: $30 Stanislaus River: 8 Tent/R.V. Sites No Water - Fee: $4	Highland Lakes: Open to All Boats Within a 15 MPH Speed Limit Mosquito, Spicer Meadows Union & Utica: Small Hand Launch Only	Fishing: Rainbow, Eastern Brook & German Brown Trout, Black Bass & Channel Catfish Picnicking Hiking Backpacking-Parking No Swimming	Limited Facilities

PINECREST LAKE

Pinecrest Lake is at an elevation of 5,600 feet in Stanislaus National Forest. At times called Strawberry Reservoir, Pinecrest has a surface area of 300 acres with 3.6 miles of mountainous, tree-covered shoreline. The Forest Service, under concession, maintains 300 campsites, a group camp, picnic sites next to the beach and a paved launch ramp. In addition, they provide nature trails and tours plus campfire programs. Pinecrest Lake Resort is a complete modern destination facility with extensive accommodations. Trout are planted weekly in season at Pinecrest Lake, and there are a number of other lakes and streams within easy walking distance to entice the angler. Boating is limited to 20 MPH, and waterskiing is not permitted. There is a large swim beach adjacent to the picnic area.

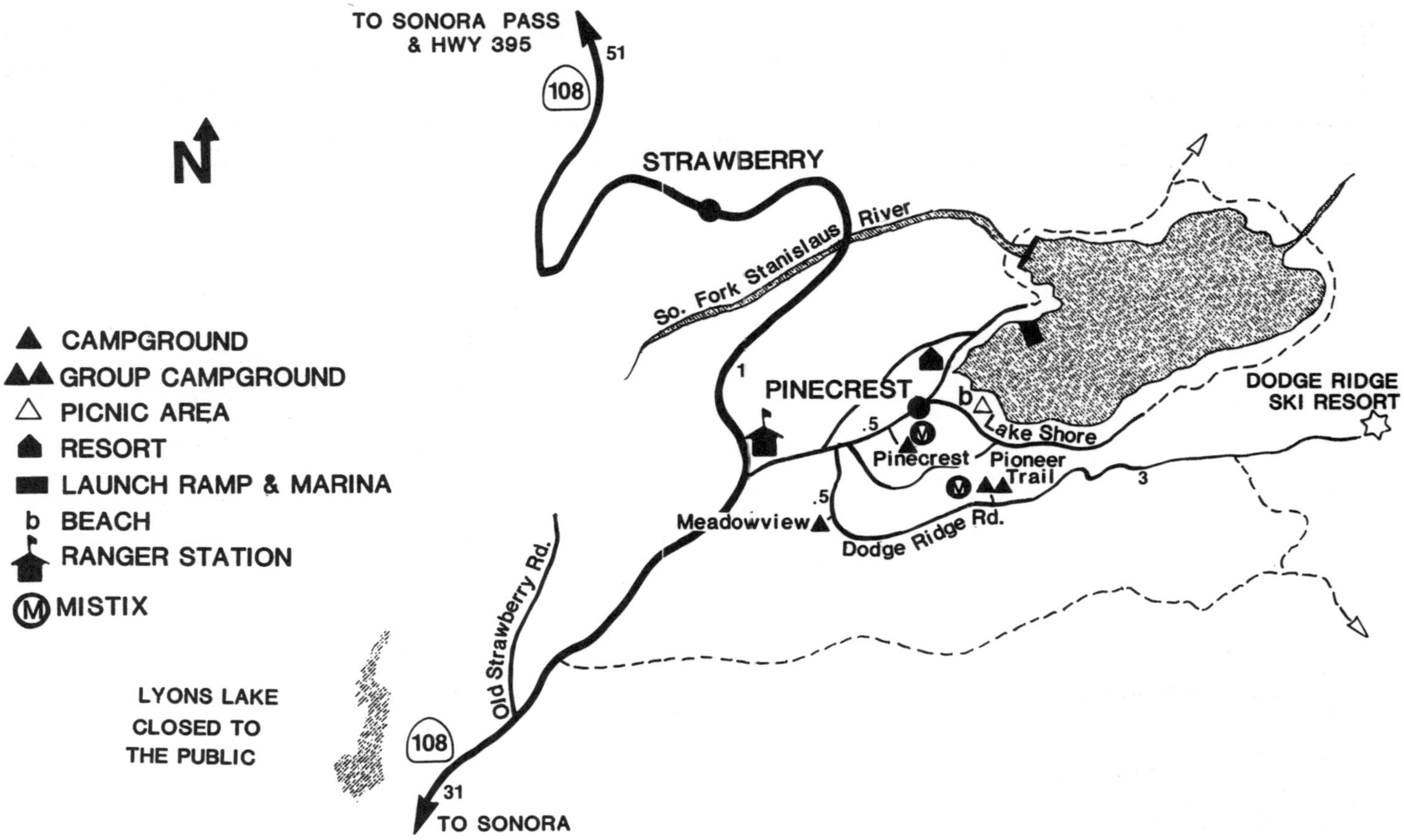

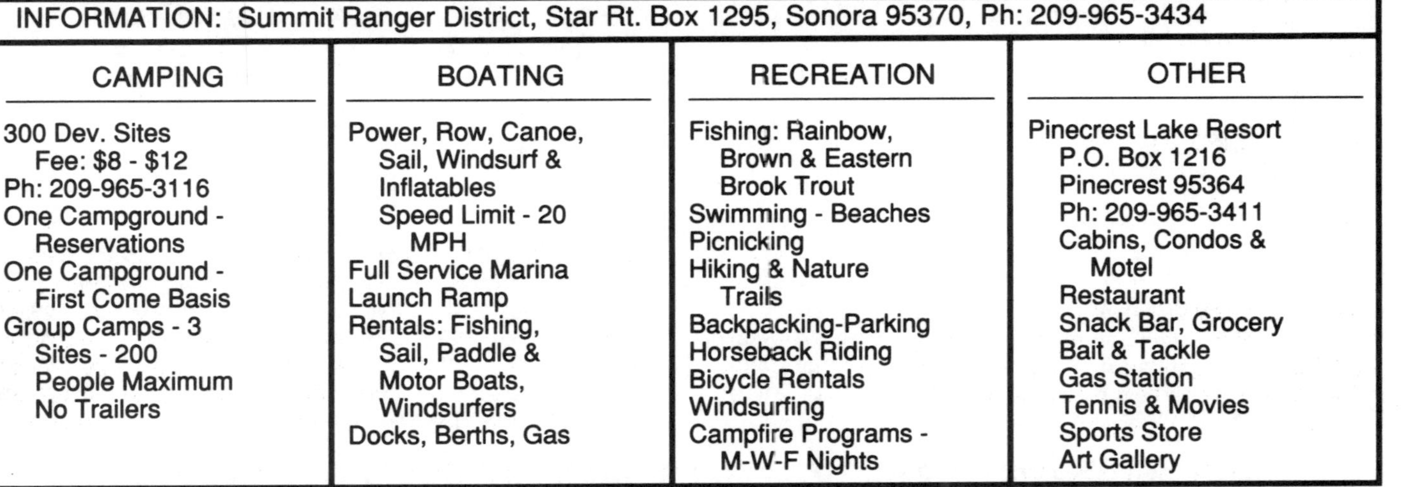

INFORMATION: Summit Ranger District, Star Rt. Box 1295, Sonora 95370, Ph: 209-965-3434

CAMPING	BOATING	RECREATION	OTHER
300 Dev. Sites Fee: $8 - $12 Ph: 209-965-3116 One Campground - Reservations One Campground - First Come Basis Group Camps - 3 Sites - 200 People Maximum No Trailers	Power, Row, Canoe, Sail, Windsurf & Inflatables Speed Limit - 20 MPH Full Service Marina Launch Ramp Rentals: Fishing, Sail, Paddle & Motor Boats, Windsurfers Docks, Berths, Gas	Fishing: Rainbow, Brown & Eastern Brook Trout Swimming - Beaches Picnicking Hiking & Nature Trails Backpacking-Parking Horseback Riding Bicycle Rentals Windsurfing Campfire Programs - M-W-F Nights	Pinecrest Lake Resort P.O. Box 1216 Pinecrest 95364 Ph: 209-965-3411 Cabins, Condos & Motel Restaurant Snack Bar, Grocery Bait & Tackle Gas Station Tennis & Movies Sports Store Art Gallery

HARTLEY (BEARDSLEY), DONNELLS, LEAVITT AND KIRMAN LAKES

Ascending the western slopes of the Sierra Nevada above Sonora, these lakes along Highway 108 provide a relatively remote experience. Often overlooked by those visitng Pinecrest Lake, these lakes range in elevation from 3,400 at Hartley to 7,000 feet at Leavitt Lake. The fishing is often good although it is sometimes a bit difficult to reach. Donnells and Leavitt are undeveloped with no facilities. Hartley has picnic sites and a launch ramp. Kirman Lake is a designated Wild Trout Lake where barbless hooks are required and there is a two trout limit. Numerous trails throughout the area invite the equestrian, hiker and backpacker to this beautiful high Sierrra area within the Stanislaus and Toiyabe National Forests.

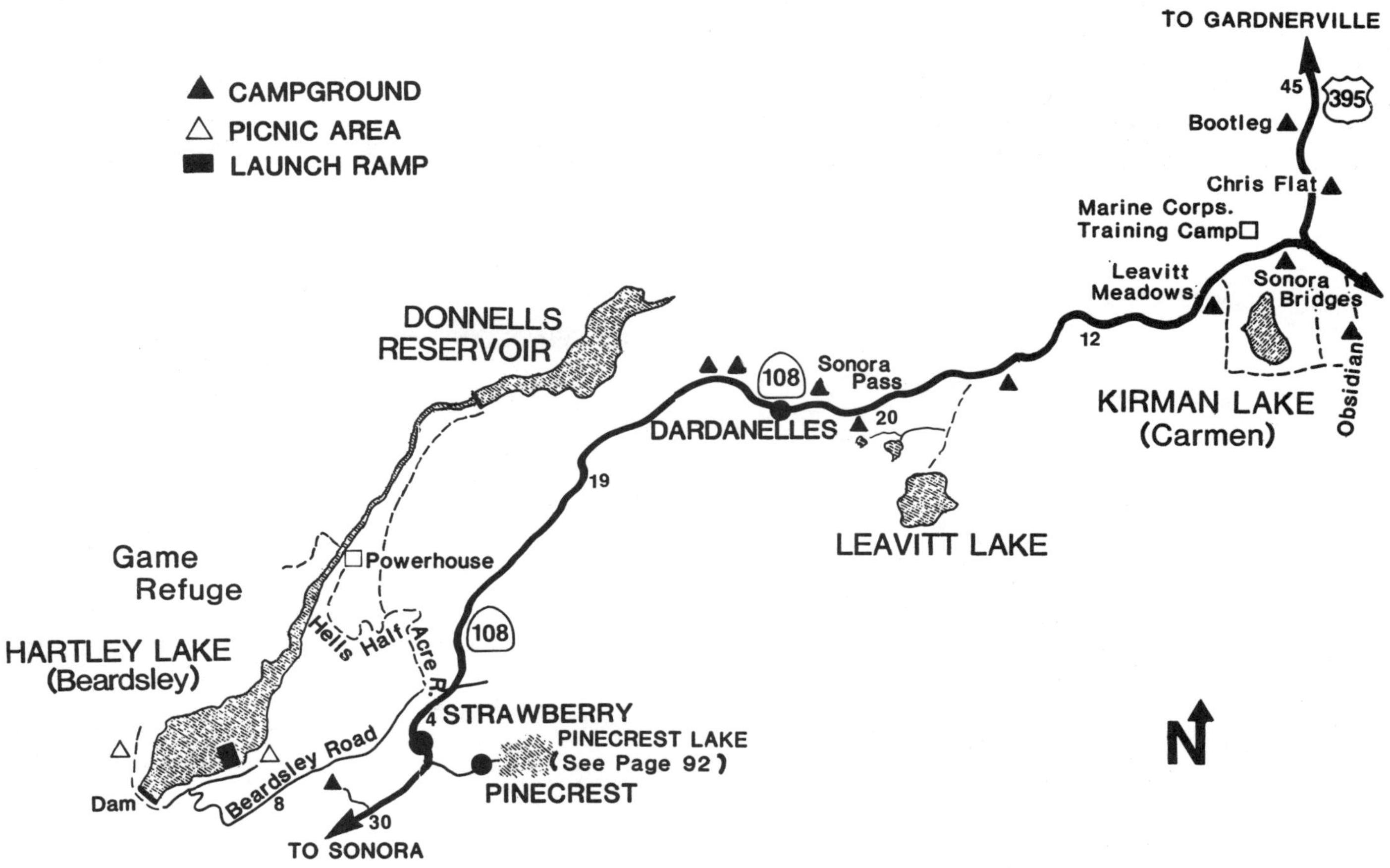

INFORMATION: Summit Ranger District, Highway 108, P.O. Box 1295, Sonora 95370, Ph: 209-965-3434			
CAMPING	BOATING	RECREATION	OTHER
Numerous U.S.F.S. Campgrounds Along Highway 108 - Contact Summit Ranger District Toiyabe National Forest Bridgeport Ranger Dist. Ph: 619-932-7070 Leavitt Meadows: 20 Tent/R.V. Sites Fe: $5 Sonora Bridge: 23 Tent/R.V. Sites Fee: $5	Hartley Lake: Open o All Boats 2-Lane Paved Launch Ramp Leavitt: Small Hand-Launch Donnells: Not Advised	Fishing: Rainbow, German Brown & Brook Trout Picnicking Swimming Hiking & Riding Trails Backpacking Hunting: Deer, Bear No Hunting in Game Refuge Near Hartley	Limited Facilities

CHERRY LAKE

Cherry Lake, sometimes mistakenly called Cherry Valley Reservoir, is at an elevation of 4,700 feet in the beautiful rugged back country of the Stanislaus National Forest. This remote mountain lake offers a good trout fishery. Boating is only limited by an unimproved launch ramp which is subject to low water levels. This is truly a place to get away from it all with a nice campground and limited facilities. There are numerous small lakes and streams within hiking distance. The Cherry Valley Pack Station has rental horses, mules, and guides for day trips or extended trips into the nearby Yosemite National Park and Emigrant Wilderness. The roads into Cherry Lake are winding and long.

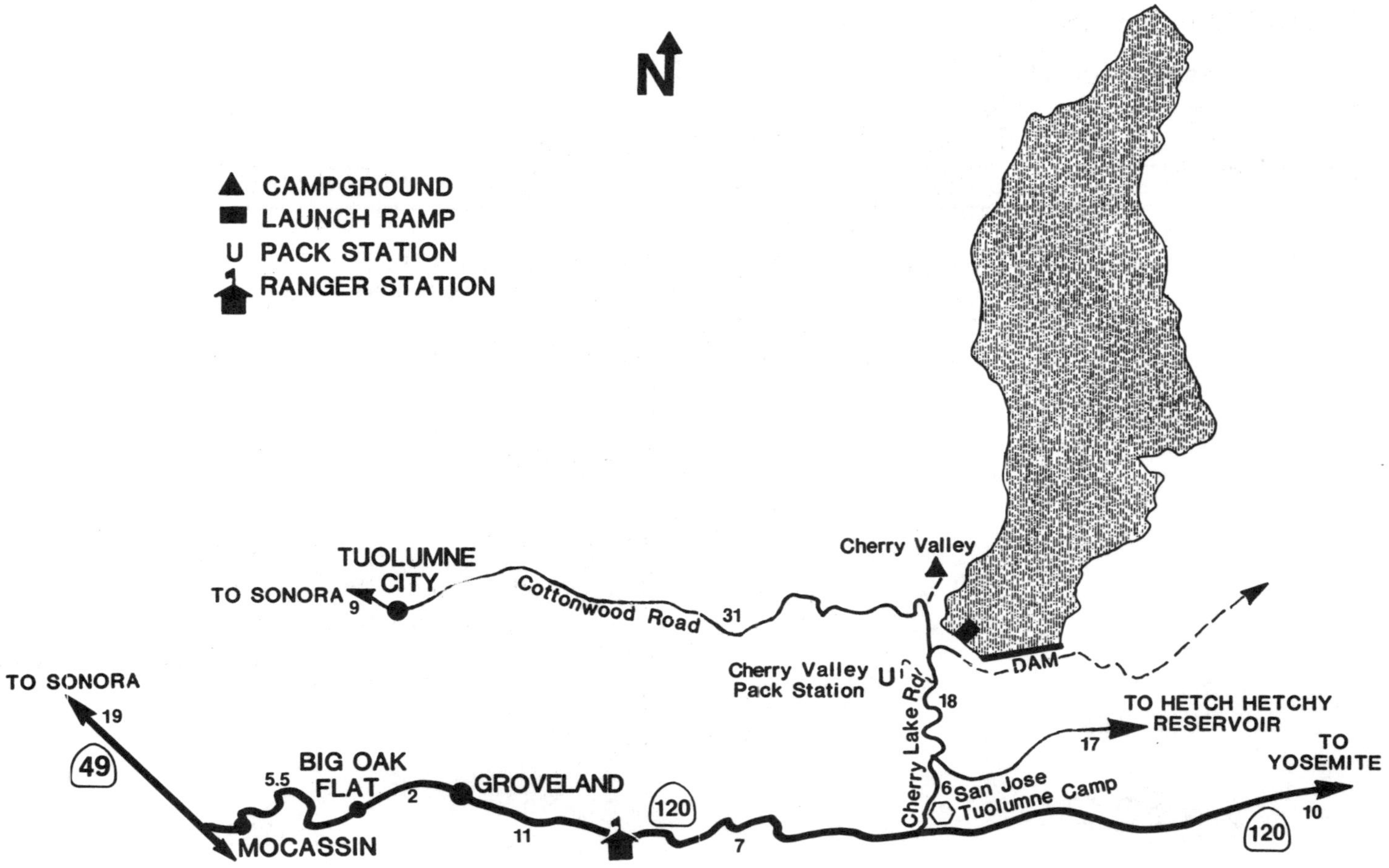

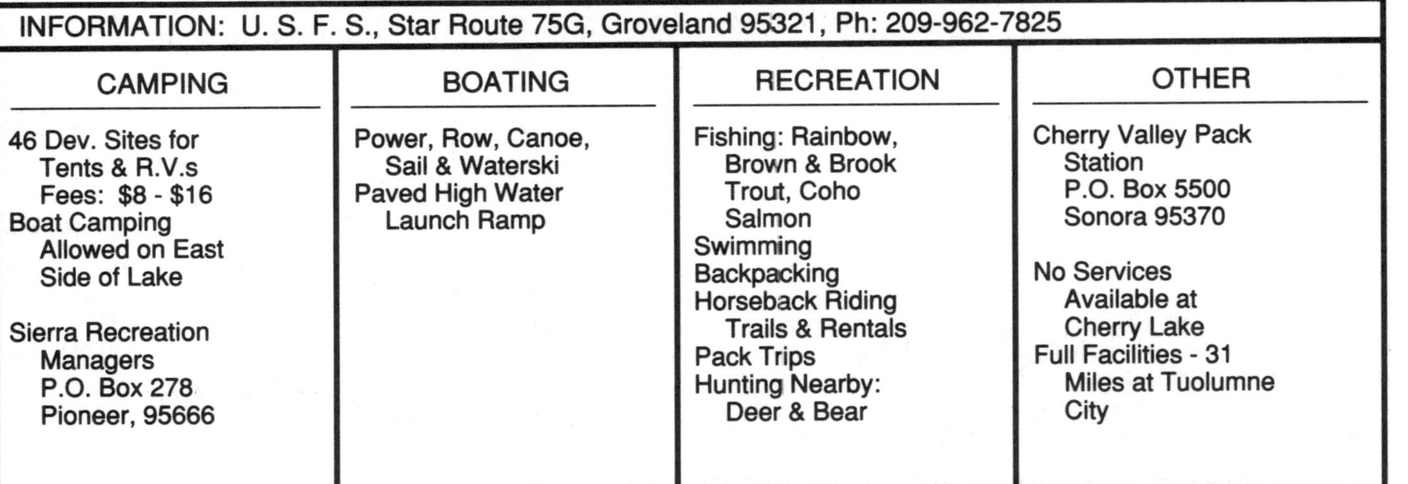

INFORMATION: U. S. F. S., Star Route 75G, Groveland 95321, Ph: 209-962-7825

CAMPING	BOATING	RECREATION	OTHER
46 Dev. Sites for Tents & R.V.s Fees: $8 - $16 Boat Camping Allowed on East Side of Lake Sierra Recreation Managers P.O. Box 278 Pioneer, 95666	Power, Row, Canoe, Sail & Waterski Paved High Water Launch Ramp	Fishing: Rainbow, Brown & Brook Trout, Coho Salmon Swimming Backpacking Horseback Riding Trails & Rentals Pack Trips Hunting Nearby: Deer & Bear	Cherry Valley Pack Station P.O. Box 5500 Sonora 95370 No Services Available at Cherry Lake Full Facilities - 31 Miles at Tuolumne City

Lakes on Hwy. 395 From Bridgeport to Bishop

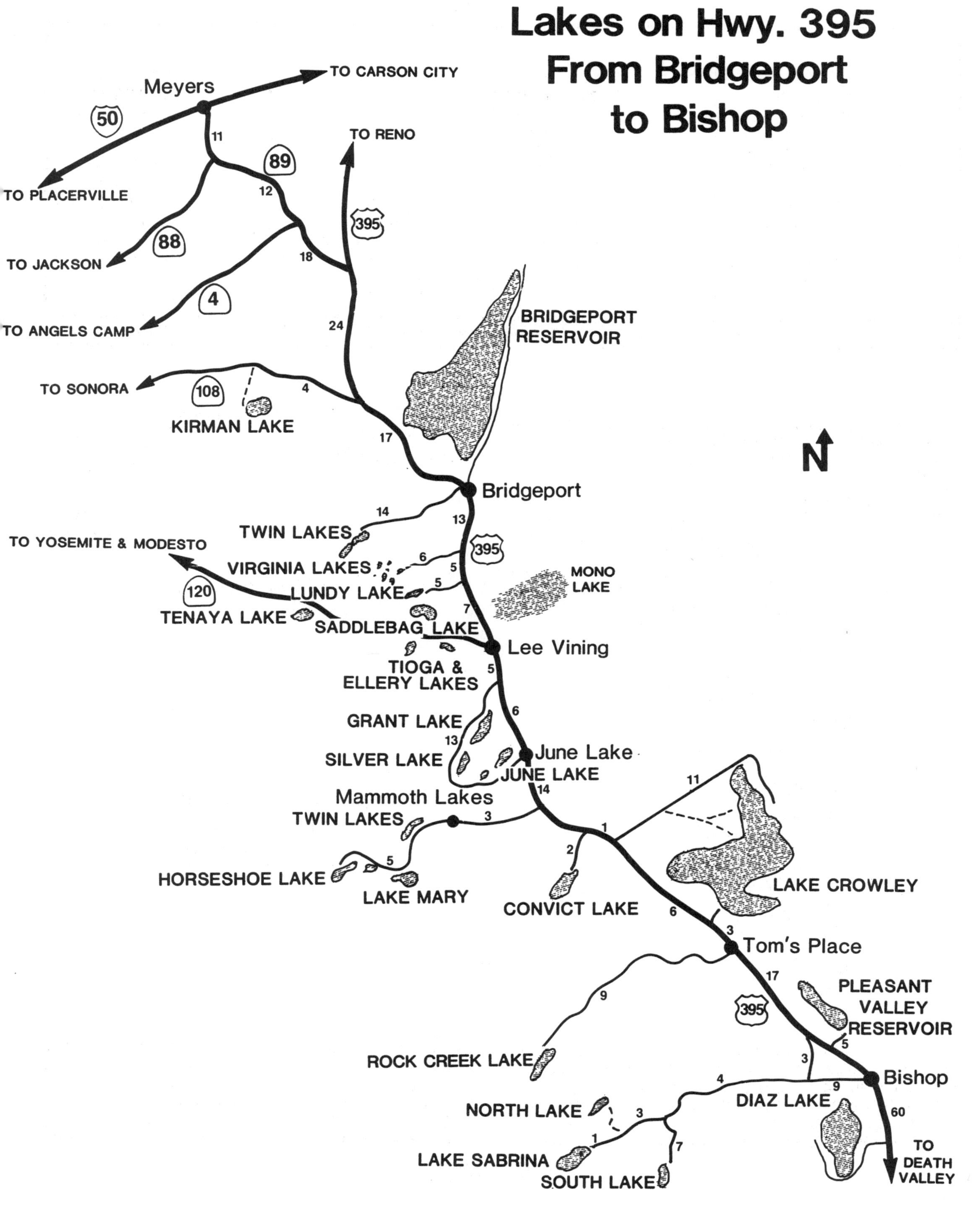

BRIDGEPORT RESERVOIR

Bridgeport Reservoir rests at an elevation of 6,500 feet in a large mountain meadow. This 4,400 surface acre lake is famous for big trout, especially when trolling early in the season. In addition to the excellent fishing at Bridgeport, the angler will find 35 lakes and streams within 15 miles. The East Walker River, designated as a Wild Trout Stream, is considered prime waters for large German Browns. Artificial lures or flies are required and there is an 18-inch minimum with a 2-fish limit. The lake is open to all boating. In addition to the facilities shown on the map, the U. S. Forest Service operates many campgrounds in this area. (See the Twin Lakes page.)

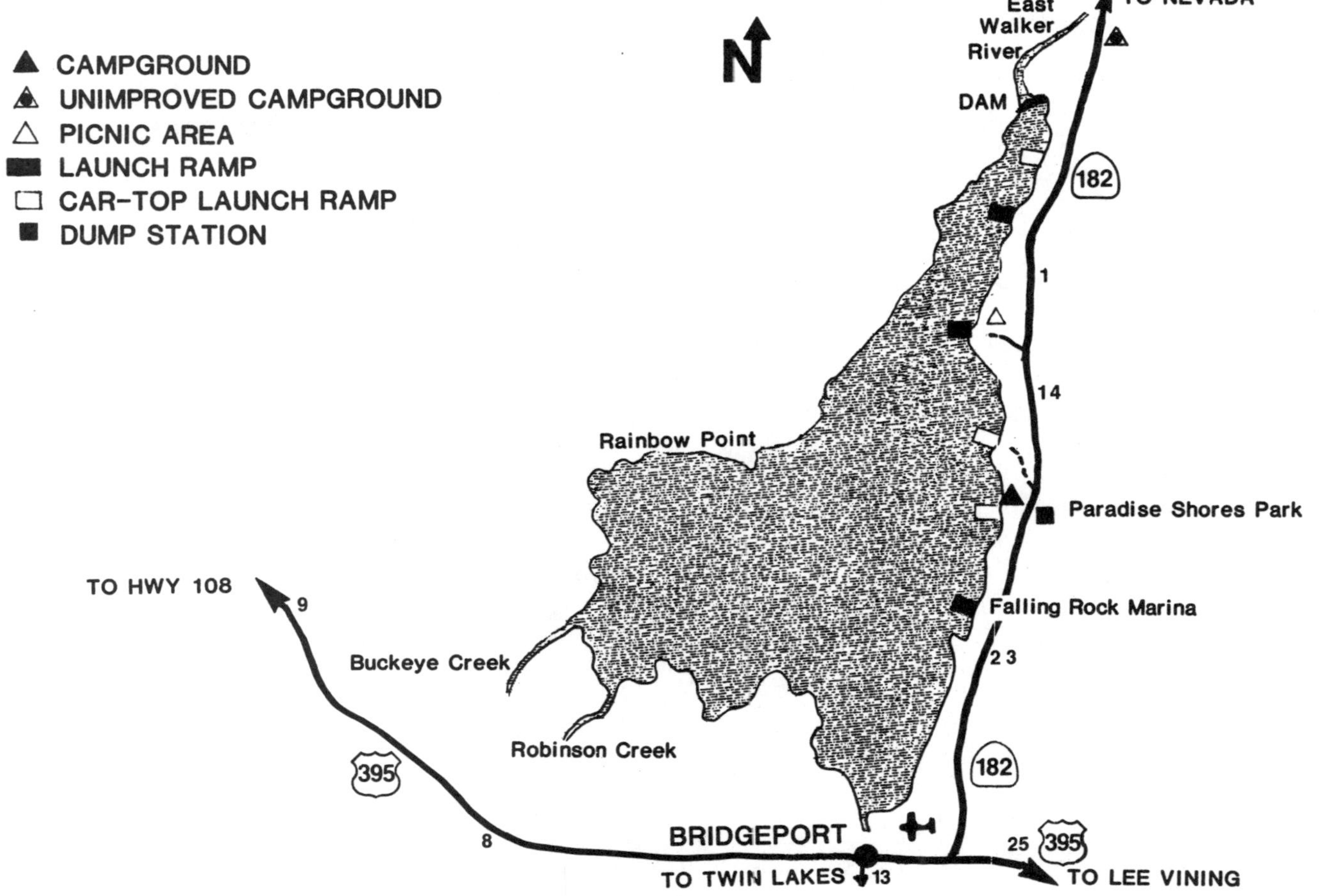

INFORMATION: Falling Rock Marina or Paradise Shore Park, Bridgeport 93517			
CAMPING	BOATING	RECREATION	OTHER
Falling Rock Marina Ph: 619-932-7001 23 Dev. Tents Sites 19 R.V. Sites with Full Hookups Fees: $8 - $12 Paradise Shores Park Ph: 619-932-7735 35 R.V. Sites with Full Hookups Plus 10 with No Hookups	Power, Row, Canoe, Sail & Inflatables Full Service Marina 3 Improved Ramps 3 Unimproved Ramps Rentals: Fishing Boats & Motors Docks, Berths, Moorings, Storage Overnight in Boat Permitted Anywhere	Fishing: Rainbow, German Brown & Brook Trout Swimming Backpacking-Parking Bicycle Trails Rockhounding Hunting: Deer & Waterfowl	Snack Bar Restaurant Bait & Tackle Laundromat Trailer Rentals Gas Station Airport Full Facilities at Bridgeport

TWIN LAKES

Twin Lakes are 12 miles southwest of Bridgeport in the Eastern Sierra at an elevation of 7,000 feet. The private campgrounds at the lake are in a pine forest. Complete resort and marine facilities are available. There are 5 Forest Service Campgrounds along Robinson Creek. These lakes provide excellent fishing for large rainbow and brown trout. Upper Twin Lake has taken away from Lower Twin Lake the State record for German Brown with a 26 lb. 8 oz. master caught in May of 1987. Doc and Al's Resort is a pleasant fisherman's retreat. The Hunewill Guest Ranch is a working cattle ranch offering excellent accommodations, food and excursions on horseback into this beautiful country. The nearby Hoover Wilderness invites the adventurous packer into its many scenic trails, Lakes and streams.

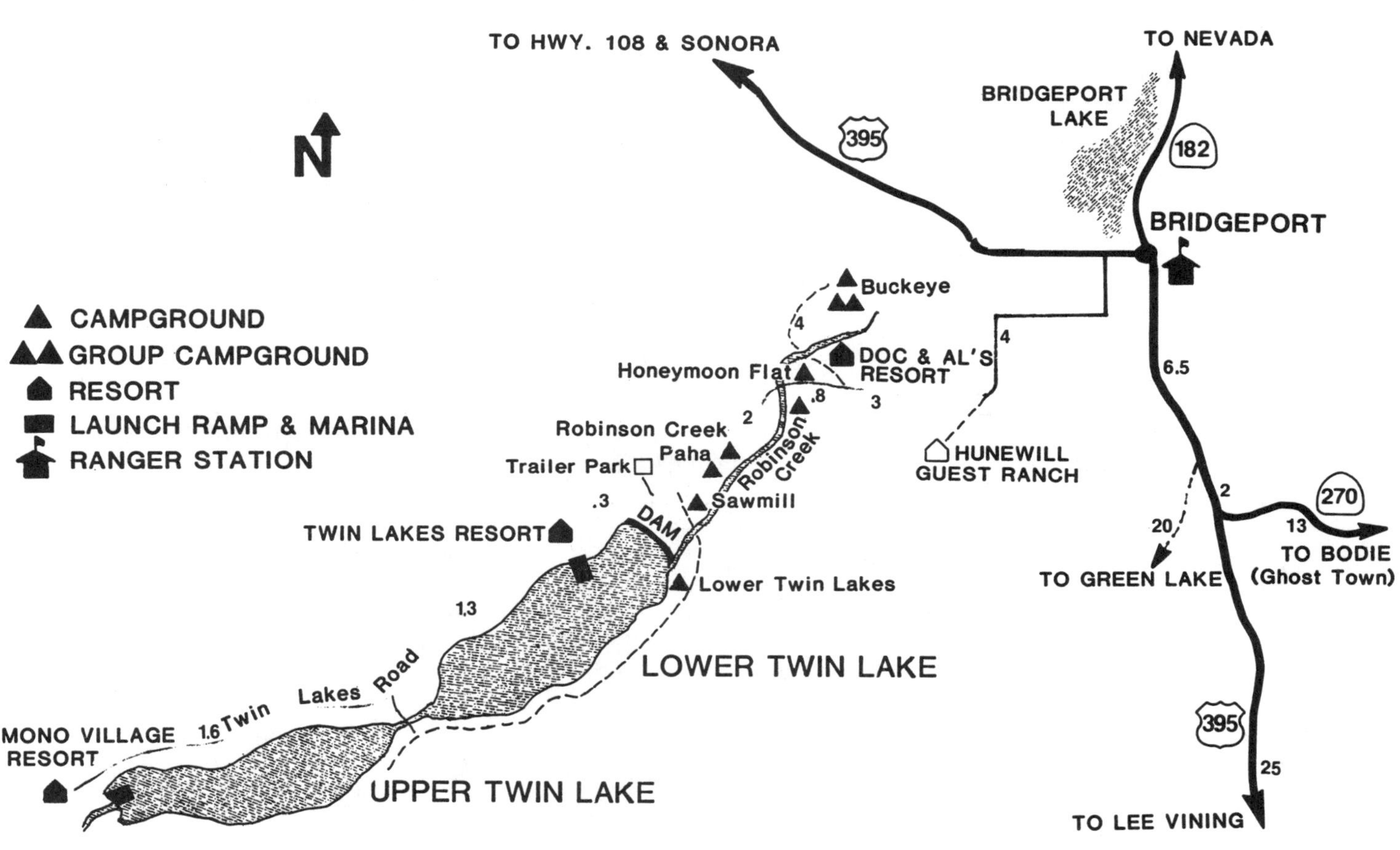

INFORMATION: Bridgeport Ranger District, Bridgeport 93517, Ph: 619-932-7070			
CAMPING	**BOATING**	**RECREATION**	**OTHER**
U. S. F. S. 400 Dev. Sites for Tents & R.V.s Fee: $5 - $8 Group Unit: $25 30 People Reservations: MISTIX Ph: 800-283-CAMP Privately Owned Campsites: Mono Village Ph: 619-932-7071 Twin Lakes Resort Ph: 619-932-7751	Twin Lakes: Power, Row, Canoe, Sail & Inflatables Waterskiing at Upper Lake Only Full Service Marina Launch Ramps Boat Rentals Docks	Twin Lakes-Fishing: Rainbow, German Brown, Eastern Brook & Kamloop Trout Picnicking Backpacking-Parking Hoover Wilderness Horseback Riding Hunting: Deer & Waterfowl	Doc & Al's Resort Ph: 619-932-7051 Hunewill Guest Ranch Ph: 619-932-7710 Reservations Only Cabins Restaurant Grocery Store Bait & Tackle Disposal Station Full Facilities at Bridgeport

VIRGINIA LAKES

The Virginia Lakes are 10 small lakes at 9,700 feet elevation located 6.3 miles west of Highway 395. No swimming is allowed in the lakes. Virginia Lake Resort has cabins, a grocery store, fishing supplies and restaurant. The U. S. Forest Service operates campsites by Trumbull Lake. There is a Pack Station with horses available for lovely scenic rides or trips into the Hoover Wilderness. The interesting Ghost Town of Bodie is nearby. This is truly a fisherman's paradise as the 10 lakes and miles of streams are within 1-1/2 miles of the Lodge.

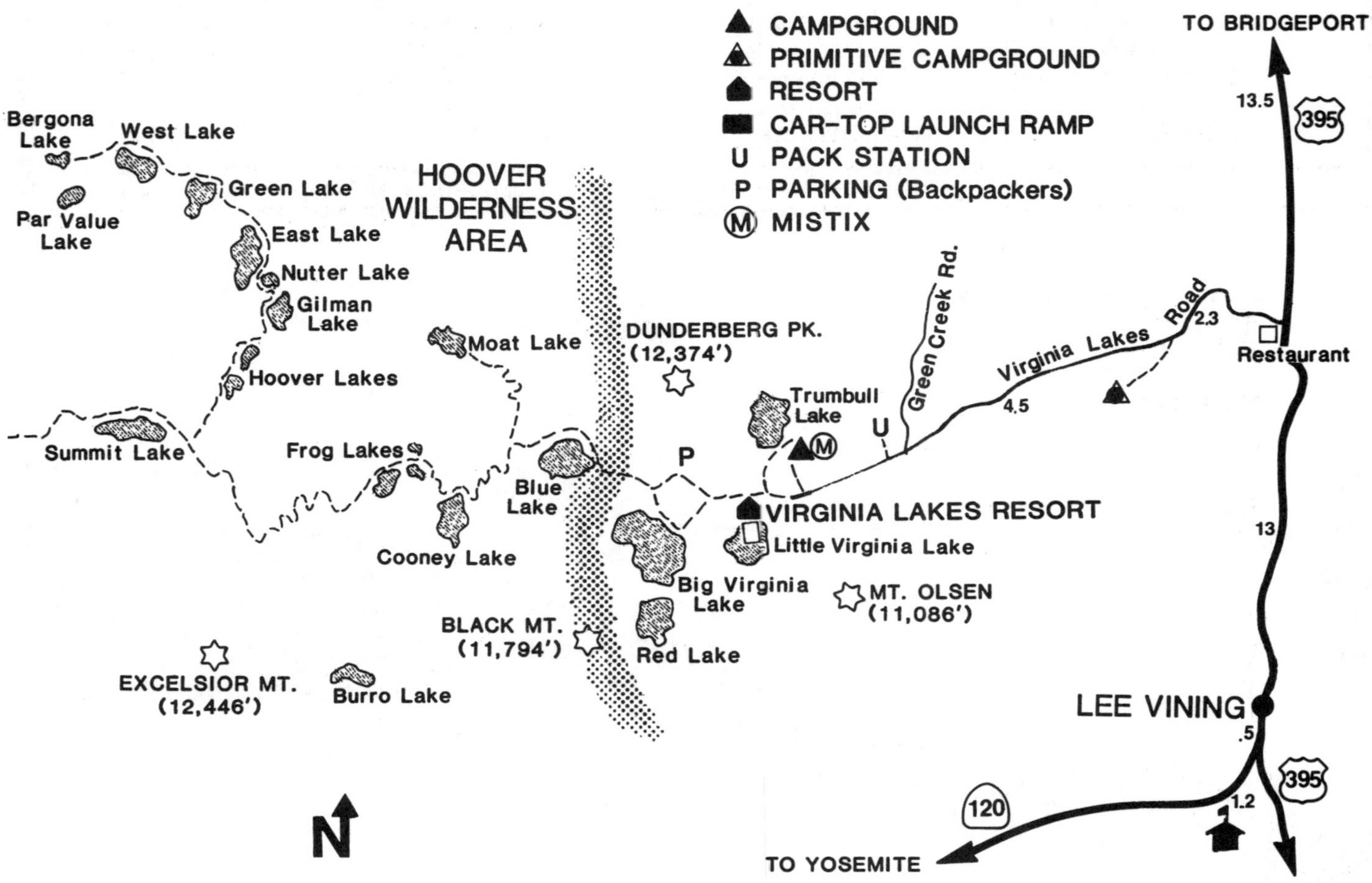

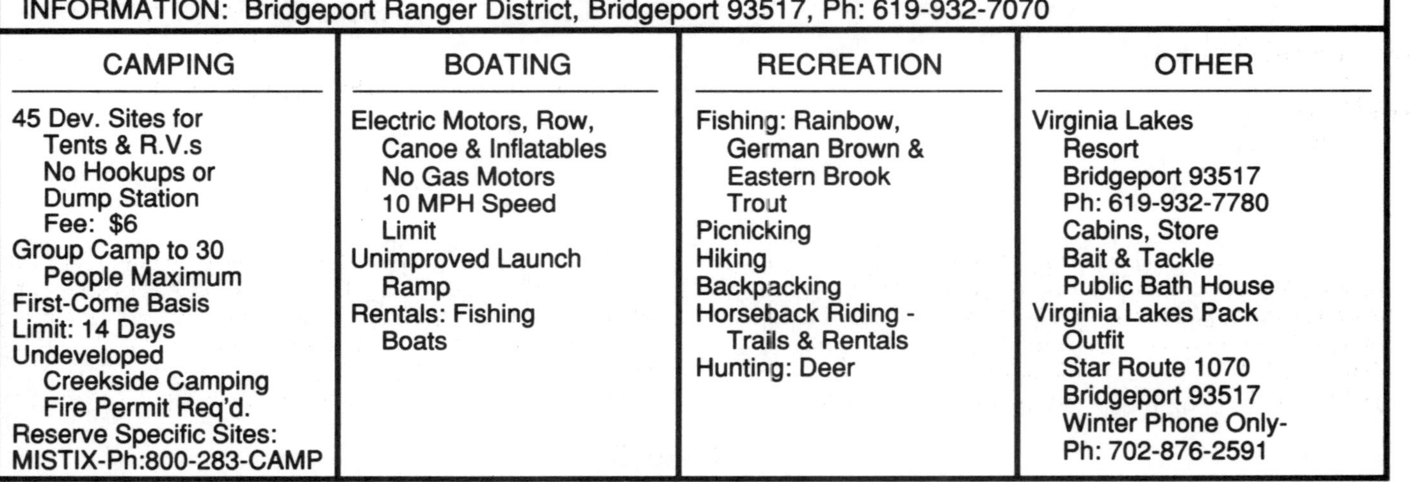

INFORMATION: Bridgeport Ranger District, Bridgeport 93517, Ph: 619-932-7070

CAMPING	BOATING	RECREATION	OTHER
45 Dev. Sites for Tents & R.V.s No Hookups or Dump Station Fee: $6 Group Camp to 30 People Maximum First-Come Basis Limit: 14 Days Undeveloped Creekside Camping Fire Permit Req'd. Reserve Specific Sites: MISTIX-Ph:800-283-CAMP	Electric Motors, Row, Canoe & Inflatables No Gas Motors 10 MPH Speed Limit Unimproved Launch Ramp Rentals: Fishing Boats	Fishing: Rainbow, German Brown & Eastern Brook Trout Picnicking Hiking Backpacking Horseback Riding - Trails & Rentals Hunting: Deer	Virginia Lakes Resort Bridgeport 93517 Ph: 619-932-7780 Cabins, Store Bait & Tackle Public Bath House Virginia Lakes Pack Outfit Star Route 1070 Bridgeport 93517 Winter Phone Only- Ph: 702-876-2591

LUNDY LAKE

Nestled in a valley at an elevation of 7,800 feet, Lundy Lake is the Trailhead to the 20 Lakes Basin. High, majestic mountains and a rocky, aspen and pine covered shoreline provide for spectacular scenery. The lake is 1 mile long and 1/2 mile wide, and the water is clear and cold. This is a popular fishing lake where fishermen stay for the summer at Mill Creek Campground. Fishing is good at the lake, in the streams and beaver ponds as well as many other lakes above Lundy reached by trail. The atmosphere is relaxed and rustic with good facilities at the Resort. Mono Lake rests just off Highway 395. This huge, barren salt water lake is the nesting site for 95 percent of California's gulls.

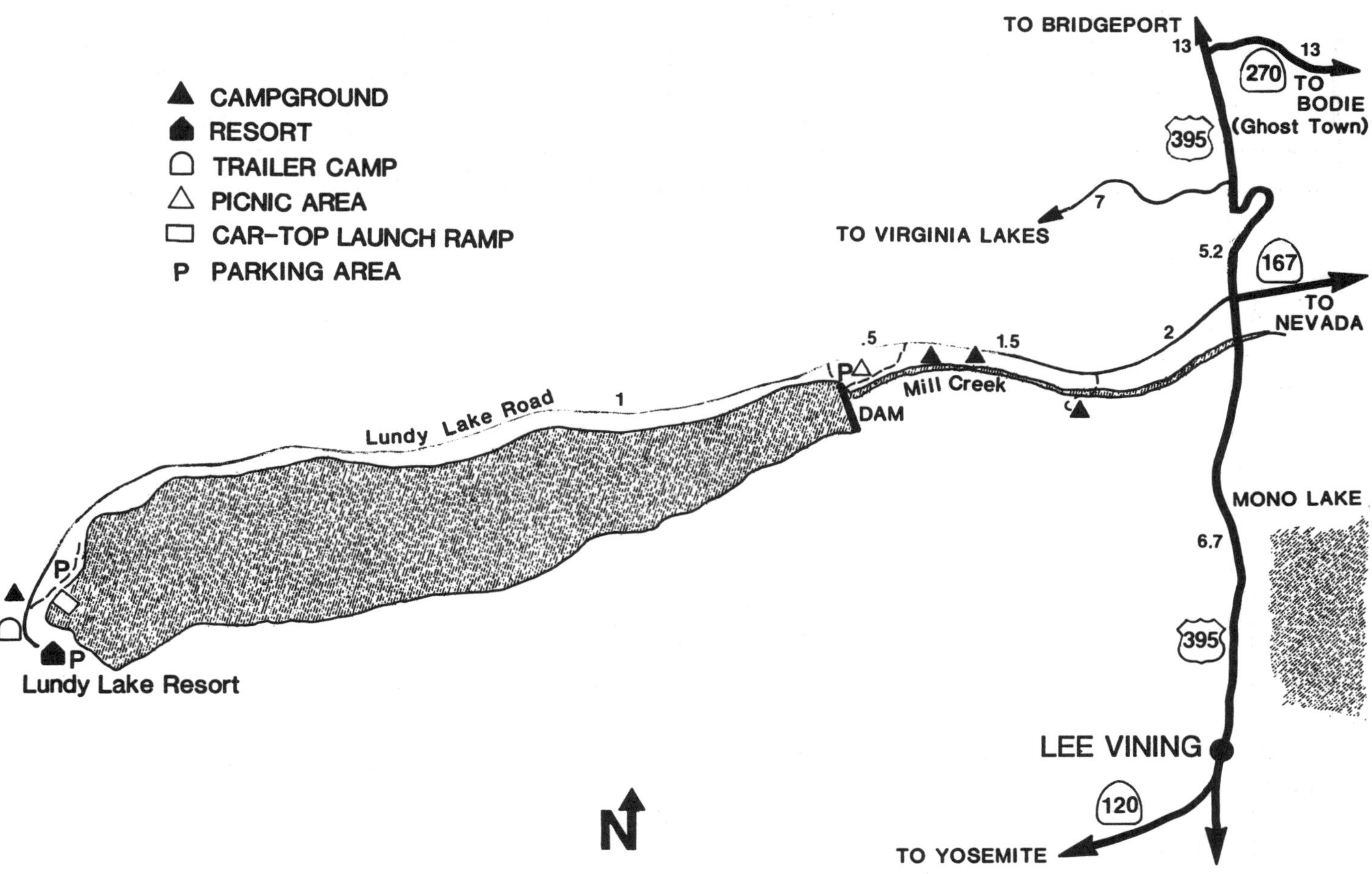

INFORMATION: Lundy Lake Resort, P.O. Box 265, Lee Vining 93541			
CAMPING	**BOATING**	**RECREATION**	**OTHER**
Lundy Lake Resort 27 Tent Sites 3 Camp Huts 8 R.V. Sites with Full Hookups Mill Creek Campground 54 Sites Mono County Parks P.O. Box 655 Bridgeport 93517 Ph: 619-932-7911	Fishing Boats, Canoes & Inflatables Speed Limit-10 MPH Hand Launch Only Rentals: Fishing Boats & Motors	Fishing: Rainbow, German Brown & Eastern Brook Trout Picnicking Hiking Backpacking Bird Watching Hunting: Deer	Housekeeping Cabins Grocery Store Bait & Tackle Hot Showers Laundromat Camping Supplies

SADDLEBAG LAKE

Saddlebag Lake, at an elevation of 10,087 feet, is the highest lake in California reached by public road. The 2-1/2 mile unpaved road off Highway 120 is steep so large R.V.s and trailers over 22 feet are not advised. For those who enjoy a spectacular alpine setting surrounded by rugged mountain peaks, Saddlebag is a must. Fishing from boat, bank or stream can be excellent. Located near the trailhead into the Hoover Wilderness Area, an hour or less of easy hiking from Saddlebag can bring you to any of the lakes and streams of the twenty-lake basin of the Hoover Wilderness. This Wilderness area is a popular destination for many hikers and backpackers who may overnight in the area, but open fires are prohibited so bring your own stove and be sure to get a permit. Mt. Conness Glacier is popular with experienced climbers.

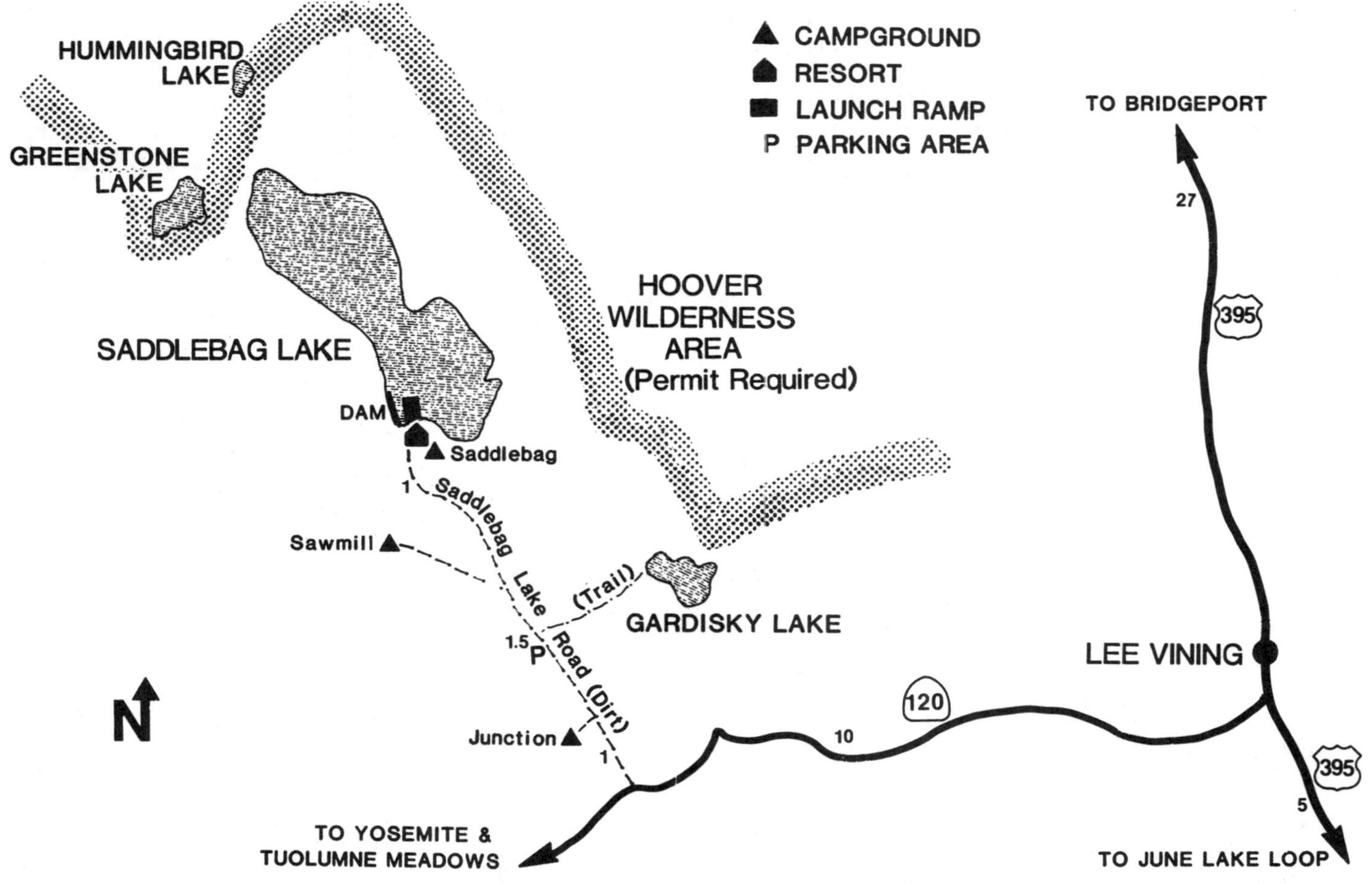

INFORMATION: Mono Lake Ranger District, Box 429, Lee Vining 93541, Ph: 619-647-6525			
CAMPING	BOATING	RECREATION	OTHER
Saddlebag Campground 21 Sites for Tents & Small R.V.s Fee: $7 Sawmill Campground 5 Walk-In Sites No Fee	Fishing & Sail Boats, Canoes & Inflatables Unimproved Launch Ramp for Boats to 16 Feet - $2 Rentals: Fishing Boats & Motors Water Taxi	Fishing: Rainbow, Cutthroat, Brook, Golden & Kamploop Trout Hiking Backpacking- Parking Mountain Climbing Nature Study	Saddlebag Lake Resort P.O. Box 440 Lee Vining 93541 (Winter Address: 27591 Villa Ave. Highland, 92346) Snack Bar Grocery Store Bait & Tackle Wilderness Permits

ELLERY, TIOGA AND TENAYA

These lovely lakes are in the spectacular Eastern Sierra along Highway 120 west of Tioga Pass. Ellery and Tioga Lakes are 2 miles outside the eastern entrance to Yosemite National Park. Tenaya is 15 miles inside the Park. An abundance of natural attractions are offered the outdoorsman. An interesting sidetrip into the Ghost Town of Bennetville is a 20 minute hike from the Tioga Pass Resort. The water in these lakes is clear and cold providing the fisherman with some excellent opportunities. There are also numerous streams and other small lakes in this area.

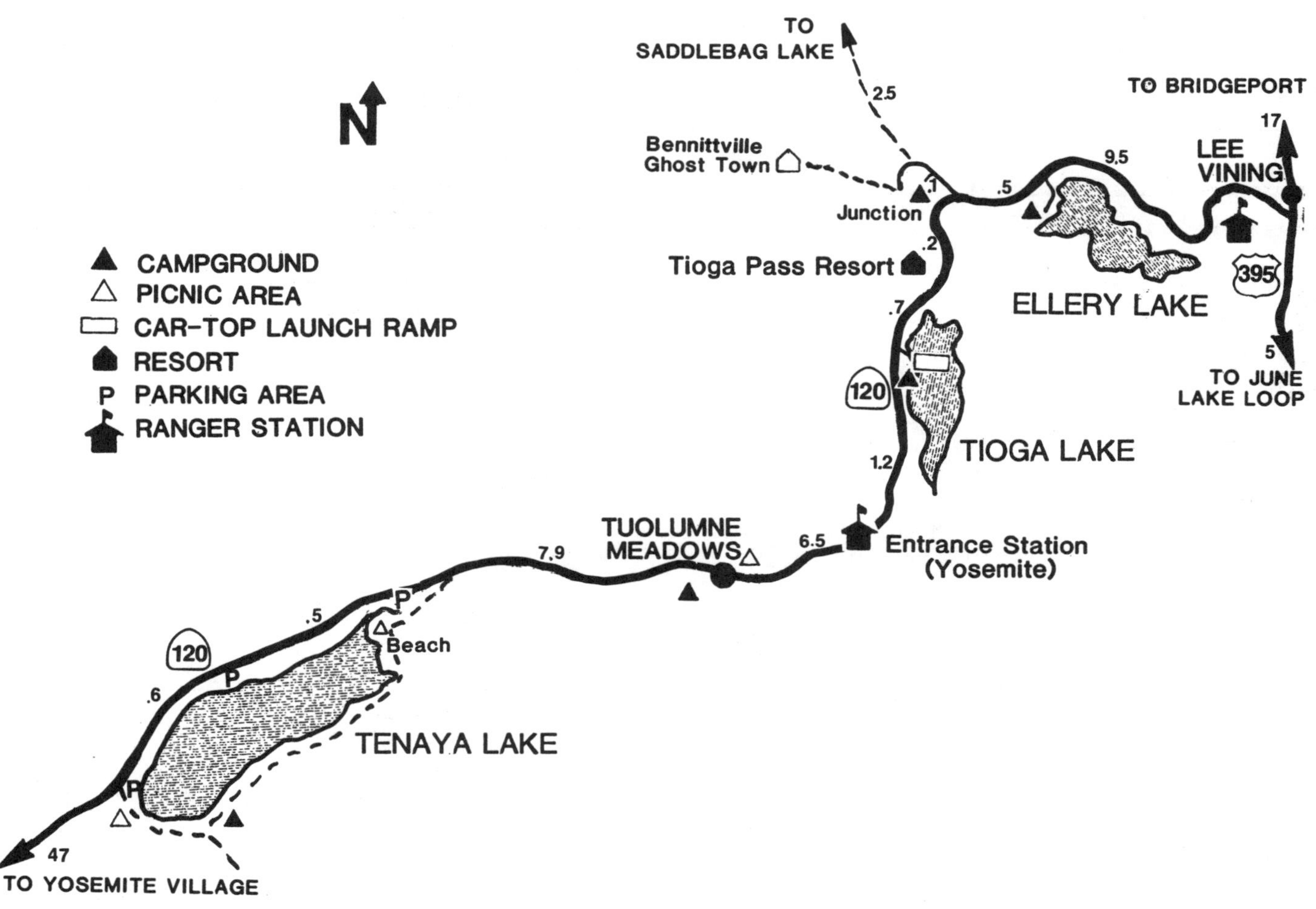

INFORMATION: Mono Lake Ranger District, Box 10, Lee Vining 93541, Ph: 619-647-6525IN

CAMPING	BOATING	RECREATION	OTHER
U. S. F. S. Ellery Lake: 12 Dev. Sites Fee: $7 Tioga Lake: 13 Dev. Tent Sites Fee: $7 Junction Camp: 14 Dev. Sites Yosemite Nat. Park Tenaya Lake: 50 Walk-In Sites Tuolumne Meadows: 371 Dev. Sites	Ellery & Tioga Lakes: Motors Permitted Hand Launch at Ellery Small Trailered Boats at Tioga Tenaya Lake: No Motors Hand Launch Only	Fishing: Rainbow, Brook, Brown & Golden Trout Picnicking Hiking & Rock Climbing Nature Trails Campfire Programs Horseback Riding Hunting Outside Park Limits: Deer, Upland Game	Yosemite Nat. Park Box 577 Yosemite 95389 Ph: 209-372-0265 Tioga Pass Resort Box 7 Lee Vining 93541 Cabins, Lodge, Gas Cafe: 7 am - 9 pm Groceries, Tackle, Sporting Goods & Gas

JUNE LAKE LOOP

The June Lake Loop presents 4 scenic mountain lakes off the eastern slope of the high Sierra. Resting at an elevation of 7,600 feet in the Inyo National Forest, these popular lakes provide outstanding recreational opportunities, especially fishing. Grant is the largest lake on the Loop with 1,000 surface acres; Silver has 80 acres; Gull, the smallest, has 64 acres; and June has 160 acres. Each of these lakes is interconnected by stream or creek and all are prime trout waters whether your interest be lunker browns or stocked rainbows. Hikers, equestrians and packers are lured into the nearby Ansel Adams Wilderness Area by its spectacular scenery and numerous small lakes and streams. This area is enhanced by numerous Forest Service campsites and private support facilities.

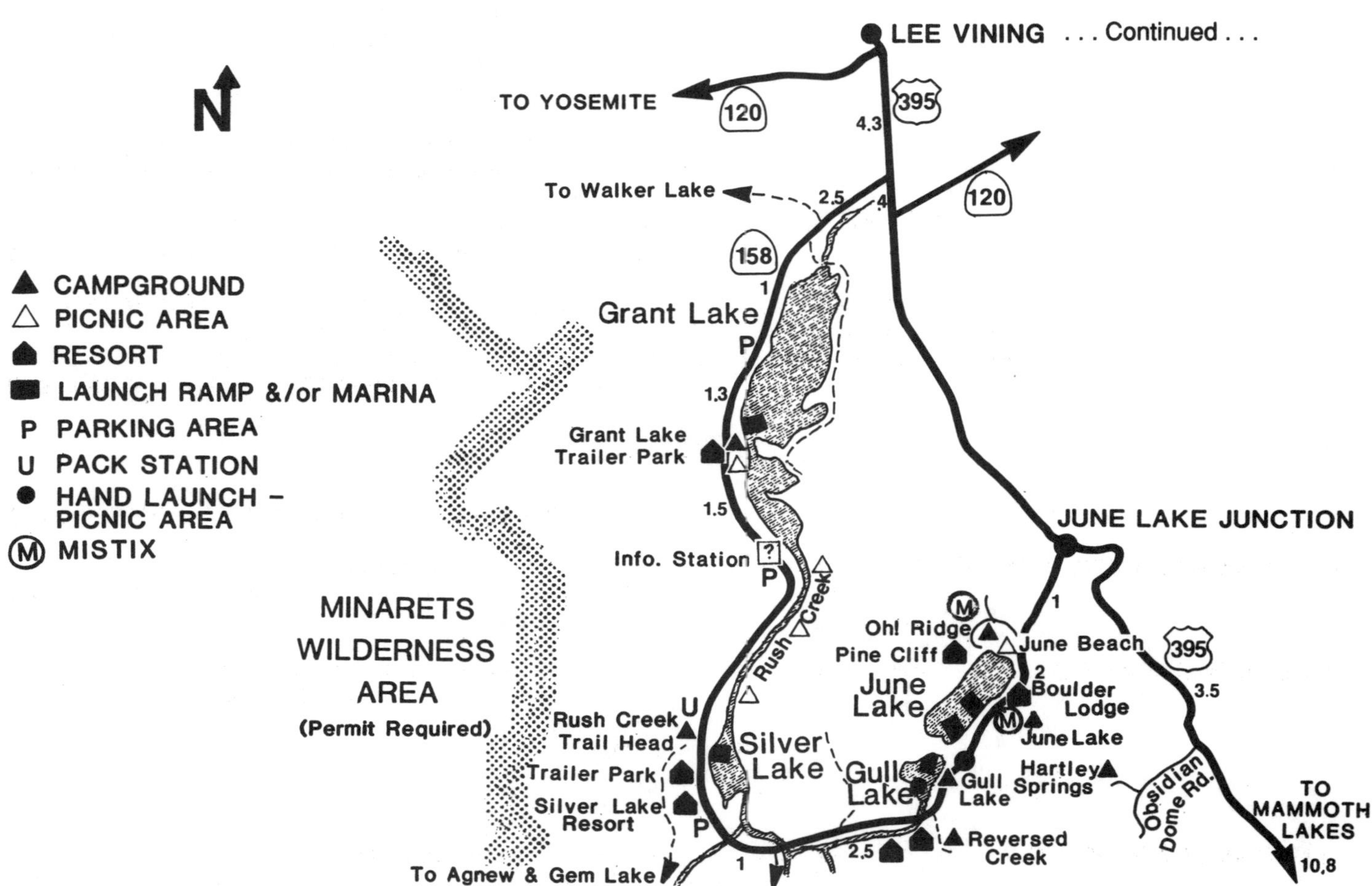

INFORMATION: Mono Lake Ranger District, P.O. Box 10, Lee Vining 93541, Ph: 619-647-6525

CAMPING	BOATING	RECREATION	OTHER
U. S. Forest Service 300 Plus Campsites for Tents & R.V.s Fee: $8 See Following Page for Details	Power, Row, Canoe, Sail, Windsurf & Inflatables Waterskiing at Grant Lake Only Other Lakes: 10 MPH Speed Limit Launch Ramps Rentals: Fishing Boats & Motors, Paddleboats Docks, Gas, Repairs	Fishing: Rainbow, Brown & Brook Trout Swimming - June Lake Backpacking-Parking Horseback Riding Trails & Pack Station Hunting: Deer, Dove Geese, Duck, Quail & Pheasant	Housekeeping Cabins Snack Bars Restaurants Grocery Stores Bait & Tackle Laundromats Further Info: June Lake Chamber of Commerce P.O. Box 2 June Lake 93529 Ph: 619-648-7584

GRANT LAKE

Grant Lake Marina, Star Route 3, Box 19, June Lake 93529, Ph: 619-648-7964
70 Developed Sites for Tents & R.V.s (Hookups). Fee: $10. Water, Toilets, Fire Pits, Hot Showers, Disposal Station, Restaurant, Store, Bait & Tackle, Propane, Boat Rentals & Dock Rental, Trailer Rentals. Waterskiing Approximately April - October.

SILVER LAKE

U. S. Forest Service Campground
65 Developed Sites for Tents & R.V.s. Fee: $8. Water, Toilets & Barbecues

Silver Lake Resort, P.O. Box 116, June Lake 93529, Ph: 619-648-7525
Full Housekeeping Cabins, Store, Bait & Tackle, Restaurant, Gas Station, Disposal Station, Launch Ramp, Rental Boats. 75-Unit Trailer Park with Full Hookups. 5 MPH Speed Limit on Lake.

Frontier Pack Train, Route 3, Box 18, June Lake 93529, Ph: 619-648-7701
Various Horseback and Pack Trips into the Minaret Wilderness with Remote Lakes and Streams Nearly 2 Miles High.

GULL LAKE

U. S. Forest Service Campgrounds
Gull Lake Campground - 11 Sites. Fee: $8. Public Ramp. Reversed Creek Campground - 17 R.V. Sites. Fee: $8. Public Ramp.

Gull Lake Boat Landing, P.O. Box 65, June Lake 93529, Ph: 619-648-7539
Full Service Marina, 30 Rental Boats & Motors, Paddleboats, Docks, Launch Ramps, Bait & Tackle, Beer & Wine, Ice

Gull Meadows Cartop Launch Ramp and Picnic Area

JUNE LAKE

U. S. Forest Service Campgrounds (Concessionaire Operated)
Oh Ridge - 148 Developed Sites for Tents & R.V.s. Fee: $8. Reservations through Mistix.
June Lake - 22 Developed Sites for Tents & R.V.s. Fee: $8. Reservations through Mistix.
Hartley Springs - South on Highway 395 - 20 Sites for Tents & R.V.s - No Fee.

June Lake Marina, P.O. Box 26, June Lake 93529, Ph: 619-648-7726
Full Service Marina, Boat Rentals, Docks, Bait & Tackle, Launch Ramp, Gas.

For Other Resorts and Reservations Contact:
June Lake - June Mountain Reservation Service
P.O. Box 216
June Lake 93529
619-648-7794
Vacation Planning & Accommodations
Rainbow Ridge Realty and Reservations
P.O. Box C
June Lake 93529
800-462-5589
619-648-7811

MAMMOTH LAKES BASIN

The Mammoth Lakes Basin rests at the doorway to magnificent high Sierra scenery. These small glacial-formed lakes range in elevation from 8,540 feet to 9,250 feet. They are easily accessible by road or pine-shaded trails. Fishing in lake or stream is often excellent. This is an ideal area for the hiker, backpacker or horsepacker as trails lead into the John Muir and Ansel Adams Wildernesses. Numerous resorts and campgrounds are available and complete facilities are located in the community of Mammoth Lakes. While Sotcher and Starkweather Lakes are outside the Lakes Basin, they share a similar scenic and recreational abundance.

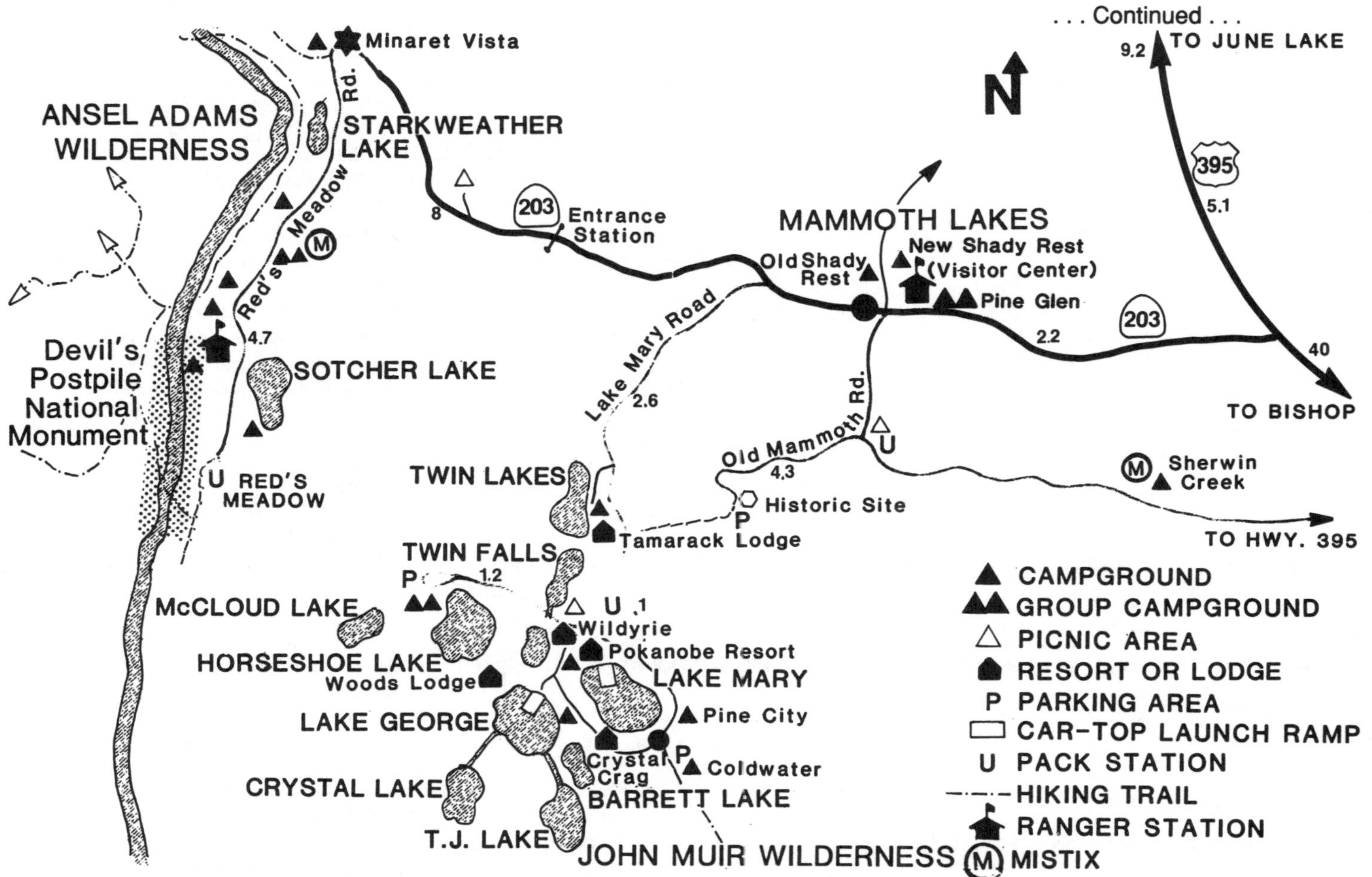

INFORMATION: Mammoth Lakes Visitors Center, Box 148, Mammoth Lakes 93546, Ph: 619-934-2505			
CAMPING	BOATING	RECREATION	OTHER
Dev. Tent/R.V. and Group Sites - USFS Resorts Wilderness Permits Required for Over-night in Ansel Adams and John Muir Wilderness Areas See Following Page	Power, Row, Canoe & Sail 10 MPH Speed Limit Rentals: Fishing Boats and Motors Starkweather Lake & Sotcher Lake: Rowboats & Canoes Only	Fishing: Rainbow, Brown & Brook Trout Swimming at Horseshoe Lake Only Hiking & Riding Trails Nature Study Backpacking Picnicking Hunting: Deer Pack Stations & Horse Rentals	Numerous Resorts & Full Facilities In Town of Mammoth Lakes Nature Guided Activities Provided by Mammoth Visitor Center Mandatory Day Use of Shuttle into Red's Meadow & Devil's Postpile Areas

U.S. FOREST SERVICE DEVELOPED CAMPGROUNDS:

For Information and Group-Handicapped Reservations Contact:

Mammoth Lakes Visitors Center*
P.O. Box 148
Mammoth Lakes 93546
Ph: 619-934-2505

TWIN LAKES CAMPGROUND
98 Tent/RV Sites, 7 Day Limit, Fee: $7

HORSESHORE LAKE CAMPGROUND
6 Group Tent/RV Sites, Maximum Persons per Site varies from 15 to 50, Fee: $20 - $45
Reservations: Ph: 1-800-283-CAMP (MISTIX)

LAKE GEORGE CAMPGROUND
16 Tent/RV Sites, 7 Day Limit, Fee: $7, Boat Ramp and Rentals Nearby

LAKE MARY CAMPGROUND
48 Tent/RV Sites, 14 Day Limit, Fee: $7

COLDWATER CAMPGROUND
78 Tent/RV Sites, 14 Day Limit, Fee: $7, Trailhead into the John Muir Wilderness

PINE CITY CAMPGROUND
12 Tent/RV Sites, 14 Day Limit, Fee: $7

NEW SHADY REST CAMPGROUND
97 Tent/RV Sites, Disposal Station, 14 Day Limit, Fee: $7

OLD SHADY REST CAMPGROUND
51 Tent/RV Sites, 14 Day Limit, Fee: $7

SHERWIN CREEK CAMPGROUND
Concessionaire Operated, 87 Tent/RV Sites, 21 Day Limit, Fee: $6
Reservations: Ph: 1-800-283-CAMP (MISTIX)

PINE GLEN CAMPGROUND
11 Tent/RV Family Sites for Handicapped use or as overflow during holiday weekends only. Fee: $7.
Campers must obtain permission before using these Sites.

6 Group Tent/RV Sites, Maximum Persons per Site varies from 15 to 30.
Reservations For Group Sites, Ph: 1-800-283-CAMP (MISTIX)

*Overnight visitors into the Sotcher Lake/Red's Meadow/Devil's Postpile Areas must obtain a road permit at the Minaret Vista Entrance Station during the hours of 7:30 a.m. to 5:30 p.m. There is a mandatory shuttle bus system for day users from 7:30 a.m. to 5:30 p.m. during the summer months. Inquire at the Visitors Center for further details. The Visitors Center also provides a number of guided nature activities.
*Wilderness Permits are required year round for any overnight or longer trips into the John Muir or Ansel Adams Wildernesses. Obtain Permits from the Visitor Center.

. . . Continued . . .

MAMMOTH LAKES BASIN

SOME PRIVATE FACILITIES NEAR THE LAKES:

TWIN LAKES:

TAMARACK LODGE - P.O. Box 69, Mammoth Lakes 93546, Ph: 619-934-2442
Housekeeping Cabins, Restaurant, Grovery Store, Lanuch Ramp, Rental Boats.

LAKE MAMIE:

WILDYRIE LODGE - P.O. Box 684, Mammoth Lakes 93546, Ph: 619-934-2444
Housekeeping Cabins, Grocery Store, Boat Rentals.

LAKE GEORGE:

WOODS LODGE - P.O. Box 105, Mammoth Lakes 93546, Summer Ph: 619-934-2261, Winter Ph: 619-934-2342, Housekeeping Cabins, Bait & Tackle, Unimproved Ramp, Dock, Rental Boats & Motors.

LAKE MARY:

CRYSTAL CRAG LODGE - P.O. Box 88, Mammoth Lakes 93546, Ph: 619-934-2436
Housekeeping Cabins, Boat & Motor Rentals.

POKONOBE RESORT - P.O. Box 72, Mammoth Lakes 93546, Ph: 619-934-2437
Camp Sites, Grocery Store, Boat Rentals, Ramp & Dock.

LAKE MARY STORE - P.O. Box 4087, Mammoth Lakes 93546, Ph: 619-934-5353
Grocery Store, Boat Rentals.

MAMMOTH MOUNTAIN RV PARK: P.O. Box 288, Mammoth Lakes 93546, Ph: 619-934-3822
130 RV Sites, Electric & Water Hookups, Hot Showers, Flush Toilets, Disposal Station, Spa, & Cable TV Hookups, Swimming Pool.

Mammoth Lakes is a complete destination resort city. There are major grocery chain stores, as well as small retail outlets, to fill your every need. Gourmet restaurants in addition to McDonalds, many resorts, motels, and condominiums offering lodging are all too numerous to mention. We are listing below a few of the reservation services in this area which will help you find a place to fit your needs:

Visitor Information Center
P.O. Box 48, Mammoth Lakes 93546
800-367-6572 or 619-934-2712
Provides Complete Visitors Service

Resort Reservations
P.O. Box 8527, Mammoth Lakes 93546
800-MAM-MOTH or 619-934-4541
Lodge and Condominium Reservations

Mammoth Realty and Reservation Bureau
P.O. Box 8, Mammoth Lakes 93546
619-934-7260
800-462-5571 (Southern California Only)
Condiminium Reservations & Sublet

CONVICT LAKE

Convict Lake is one of the most beautiful lakes in California. Its crystal clear waters are surrounded by steep, rugged granite peaks. Resting at an elevation of 7,583 feet, this small mountain lake is 1 mile long and 1/2 mile wide; its 3 miles of shoreline is shaded by pine trees. Boating is popular with a 10 MPH speed limit. The fishing can be excellent in both lake and stream. The energetic hiker, backpacker, and horseman will find a trail leading through a rock-walled canyon to 8 lakes in the nearby John Muir Wilderness. This is a part of the Inyo National Forest which maintains a developed 88 site campground off Convict Creek. There are rustic housekeeping cabins and other resort facilities including a nice dinner house. Pack trips into the wilderness are offered.

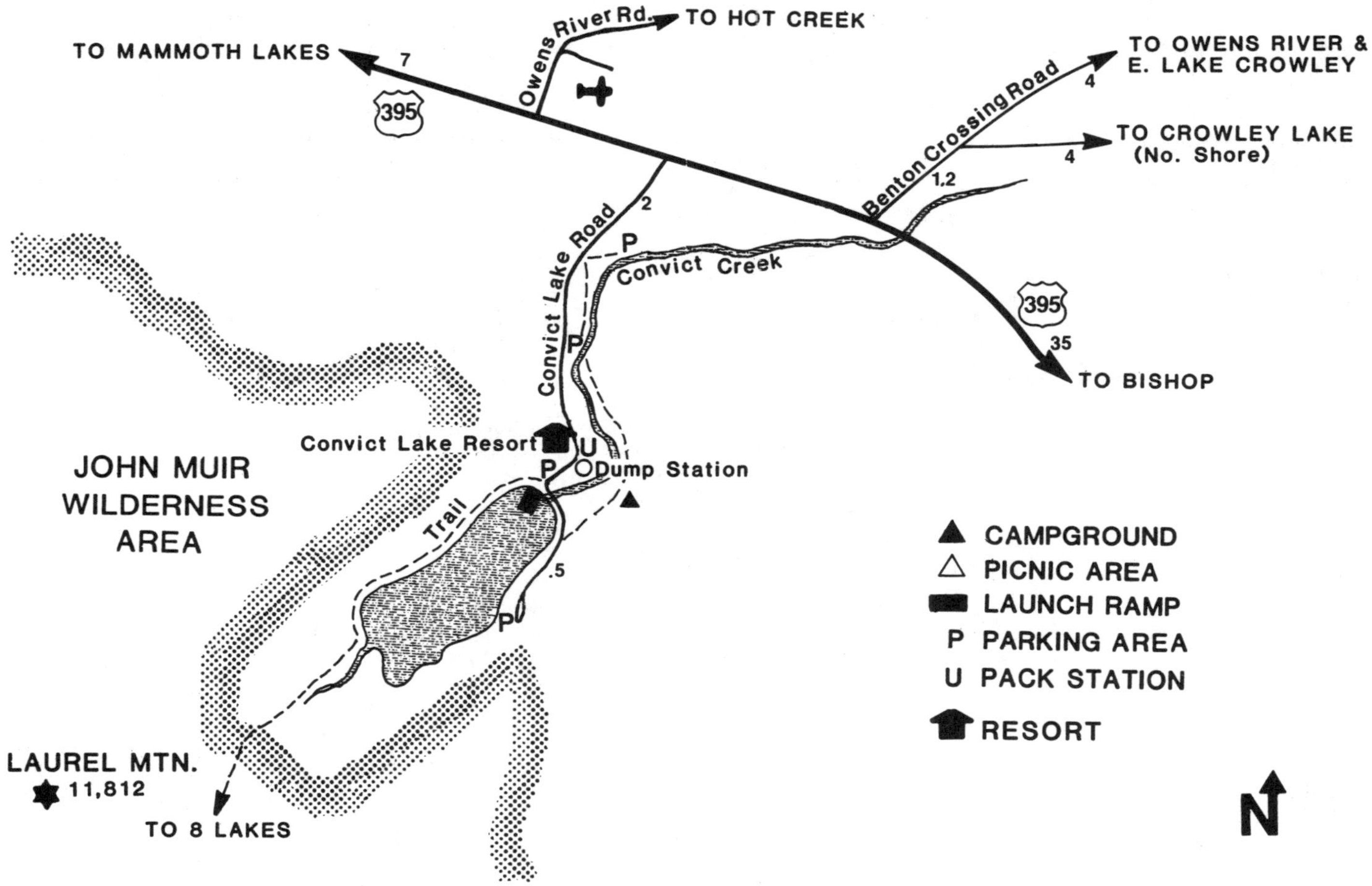

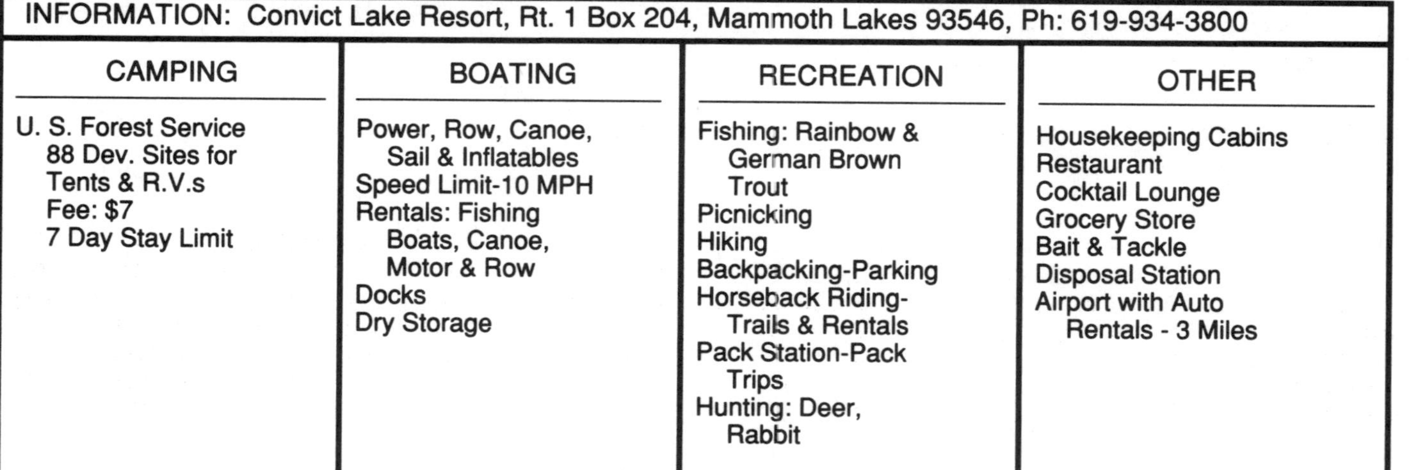

INFORMATION: Convict Lake Resort, Rt. 1 Box 204, Mammoth Lakes 93546, Ph: 619-934-3800

CAMPING	BOATING	RECREATION	OTHER
U. S. Forest Service 88 Dev. Sites for Tents & R.V.s Fee: $7 7 Day Stay Limit	Power, Row, Canoe, Sail & Inflatables Speed Limit-10 MPH Rentals: Fishing Boats, Canoe, Motor & Row Docks Dry Storage	Fishing: Rainbow & German Brown Trout Picnicking Hiking Backpacking-Parking Horseback Riding- Trails & Rentals Pack Station-Pack Trips Hunting: Deer, Rabbit	Housekeeping Cabins Restaurant Cocktail Lounge Grocery Store Bait & Tackle Disposal Station Airport with Auto Rentals - 3 Miles

CROWLEY LAKE

Crowley Lake is one of California's most productive and popular fishing lakes. Resting at an elevation of 6,720 feet on the eastern side of the high Sierra, near Mammoth, anglers jam its shores and waters on opening weekends. This 650 acre lake once held the German Brown State record of 25 pounds, 11 ounces. In addition to the season listed below, there is a special trout and perch season from August 1 to October 31 where single hook artificial lures are required; there is a minimum trout size of 18 inches and a 2-fish limit. There is a good sailing program supported by the City of Los Angeles which has jurisdiction over the lake. Boating and waterskiing are also popular. Numerous resorts and other recreational opportunities are nearby.

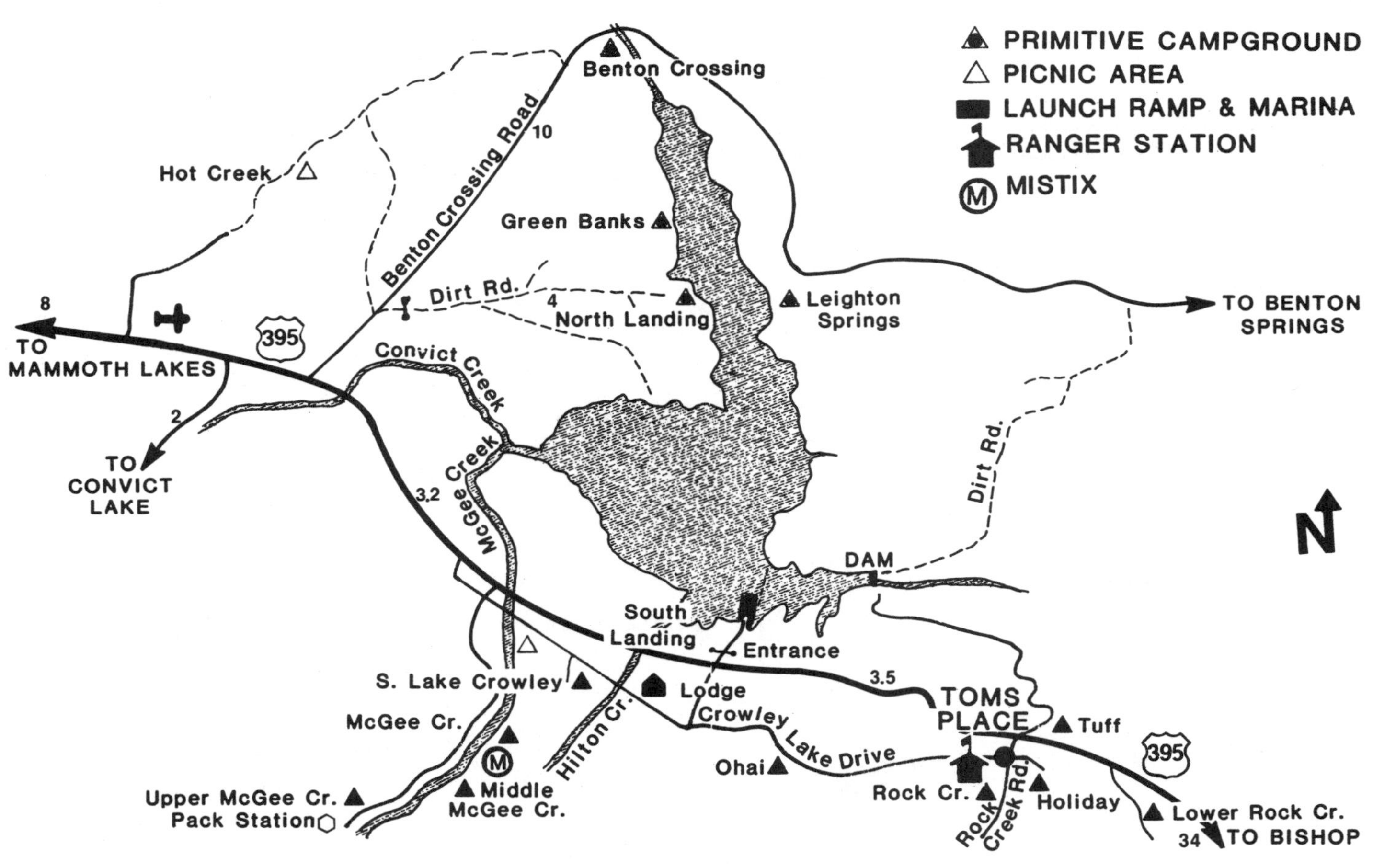

INFORMATION: City of Los Angeles-Camping, 200 N. Main St., Los Angeles 90012, Ph: 213-485-4853

CAMPING	BOATING	RECREATION	OTHER
North Landing: Unlimited Camping- Tents & R.V.s Fee: Starting at $5 South Landing: Tents & R.V.s Opening Weekend Only Fee: $15 Per Car Per Weekend Other Campgrounds - See Map	Power, Waterskiing, Windsurf, Inflatable & Sail (Memorial to Labor Day) 12 Ft. & 5HP Minimum & Safety Equipped Permit Fee Required All Craft Must Register Launch Ramps Full Service Marina Rentals: Boat & Motor	Fishing: Rainbow, Brown, & Kamloop Trout, Sacramento Perch Season: Last Sat. in April to July 31 Check Regulations Waterskiing: Season: July 4 to Labor Day Picnicking Hiking & Backpacking	Grocery Store Bait & Tackle Pack Trips Full Facilities at Mammoth Lakes

ROCK CREEK LAKE

Rock Creek Lake, at an elevation of 9,682 feet, is one of the highest lakes in California. Located in the Rock Creek Canyon of Inyo National Forest, this eastern Sierra area has over 60 lakes and streams for the adventuresome equestrian, backpacker and angler. Snow fed streams flow into Rock Creek, a natural lake of 63 surface acres. Rainbow and German Brown trout are planted throughout the season while native Eastern Brook and Golden trout are found in the waters of the John Muir Wilderness. There are several Forest Service campgrounds along Rock Creek. Boating is limited to a 5 MPH speed limit. Rock Creek Pack Station offers rental horses for a day or extended trips.

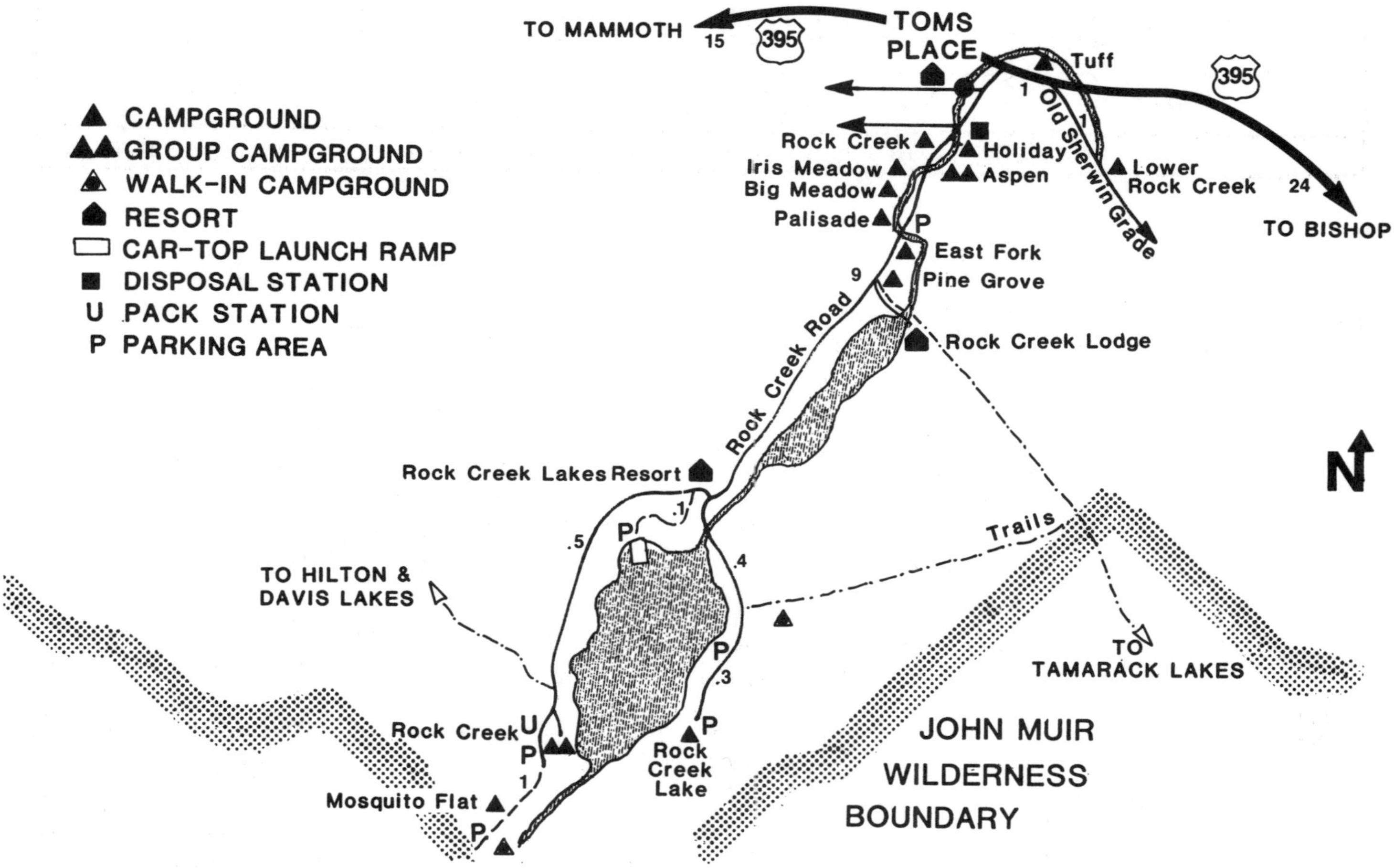

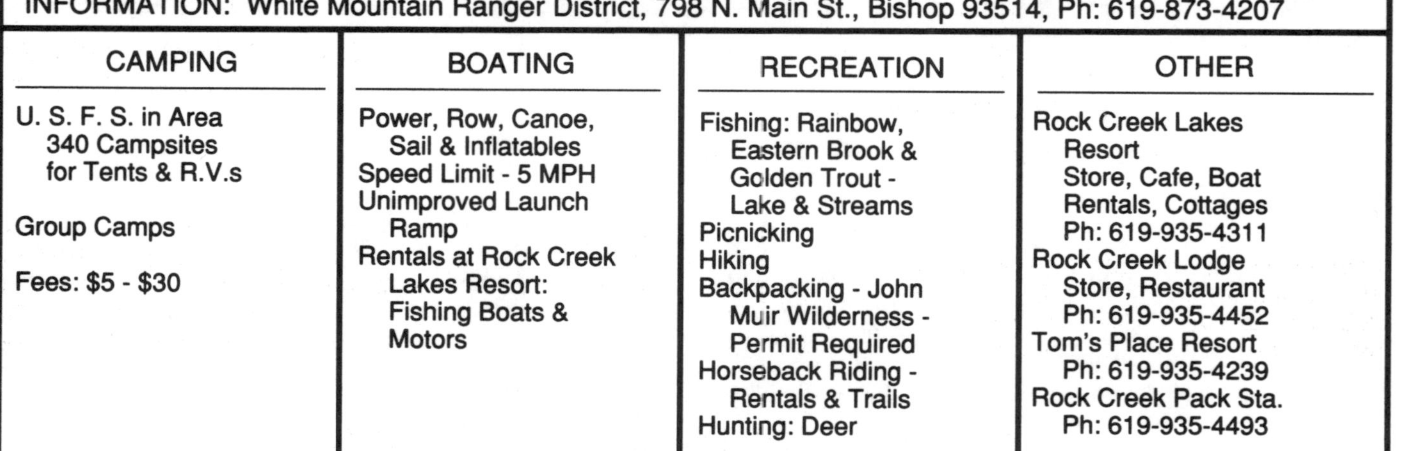

INFORMATION: White Mountain Ranger District, 798 N. Main St., Bishop 93514, Ph: 619-873-4207

CAMPING	BOATING	RECREATION	OTHER
U. S. F. S. in Area 340 Campsites for Tents & R.V.s Group Camps Fees: $5 - $30	Power, Row, Canoe, Sail & Inflatables Speed Limit - 5 MPH Unimproved Launch Ramp Rentals at Rock Creek Lakes Resort: Fishing Boats & Motors	Fishing: Rainbow, Eastern Brook & Golden Trout - Lake & Streams Picnicking Hiking Backpacking - John Muir Wilderness - Permit Required Horseback Riding - Rentals & Trails Hunting: Deer	Rock Creek Lakes Resort Store, Cafe, Boat Rentals, Cottages Ph: 619-935-4311 Rock Creek Lodge Store, Restaurant Ph: 619-935-4452 Tom's Place Resort Ph: 619-935-4239 Rock Creek Pack Sta. Ph: 619-935-4493

NORTH LAKE, LAKE SABRINA, SOUTH LAKE
BISHOP CREEK CANYON

Bishop Creek Canyon is on the eastern slope of the Sierra Nevada at elevations ranging from 7,500 feet to 9,500 feet. This area is popular with backpackers by both foot and horseback into the nearby John Muir Wilderness. Lake Sabrina has a surface area of 150 acres. South Lake has 180 acres, and North Lake is much smaller. These lakes, along with Bishop Creek, are planted weekly with trout during the summer. The U. S. Forest Service offers numerous campsites, and there are private resorts with full vacation facilities.

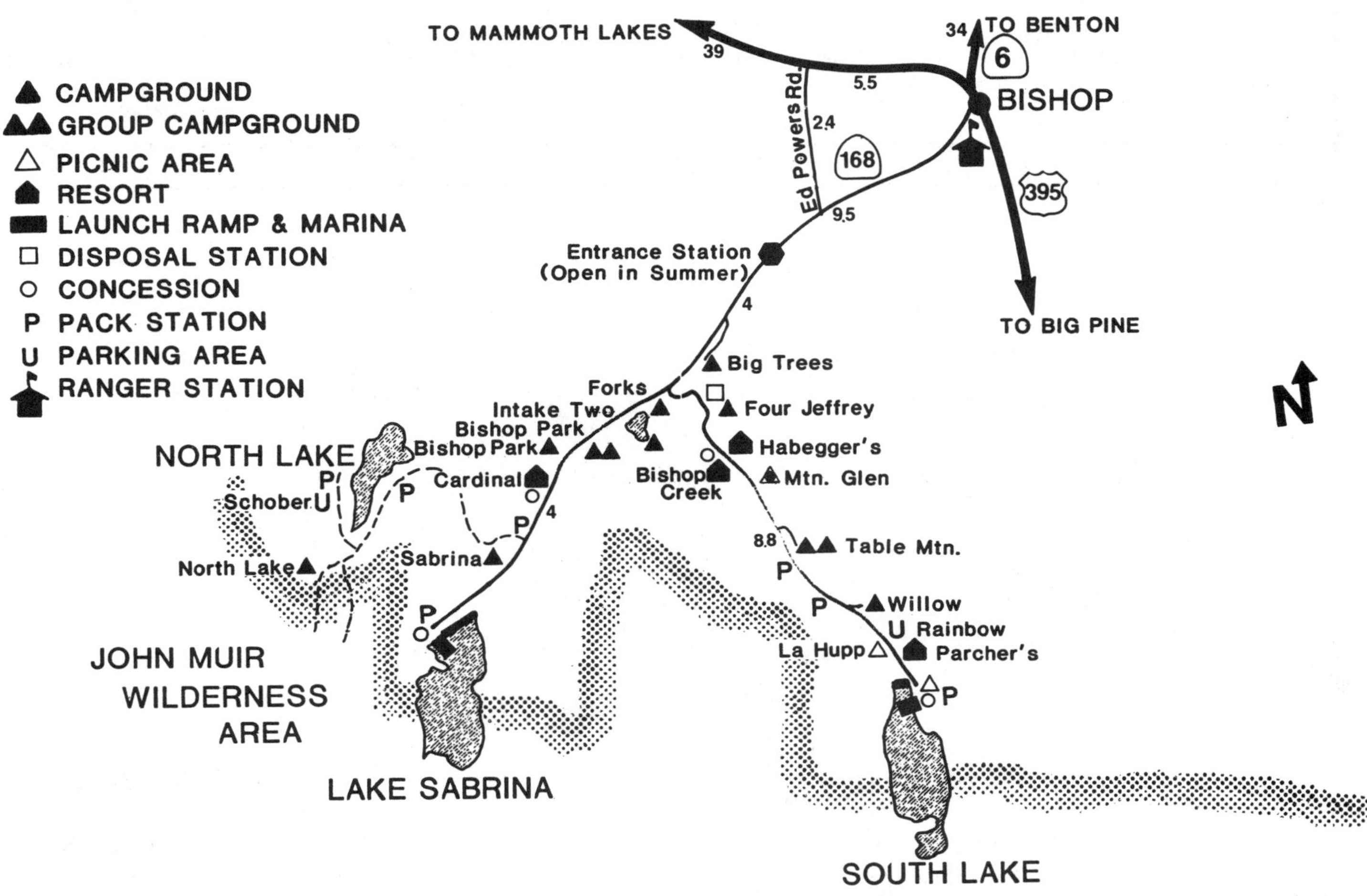

INFORMATION: U. S. F. S., 798 N. Main St., Bishop 93514, Ph: 619-873-4207			
CAMPING	**BOATING**	**RECREATION**	**OTHER**
205 Tent/R.V. Sites Group Camps Fees: $5 to $30 Disposal Station	Power, Row, Canoe, Sail & Inflatables 5 MPH Speed Limit Unimproved Launch Ramps at South Lake and Sabrina Rentals: Fishing and Motorboats Boat Gas Only	Fishing: Rainbow & German Brown Trout Picnicking & Hiking Backpacking - Permit Required Horseback Riding Trails & Rentals Rainbow Packers: Ph: 619-873-8877	Resorts: Bishop Creek Lodge Cardinal Lodge Habegger's Resort Parcher's Rainbow Village Cabins Restaurants Grocery Stores Campfire Programs

NEW MELONES LAKE

New Melones rests at an elevation of 1,085 feet in the "Mother Lode Gold Country" of Central California. Its dam, completed in 1979, is the second largest earth and rock filled dam in the United States. This damming of the Stanislaus River has created the largest lake in the area with 12,500 surface acres and over 100 miles of tree covered shoreline. This is one of California's prime recreation lakes. Extensive recreation facilities have recently been developed under the management of the U. S. Bureau of Reclamation. There are 2 large campgrounds at Glory Hole and Tuttletown as well as several day use areas. The boater will find launching areas and a new marina. Fishing for a variety of species is considered good.

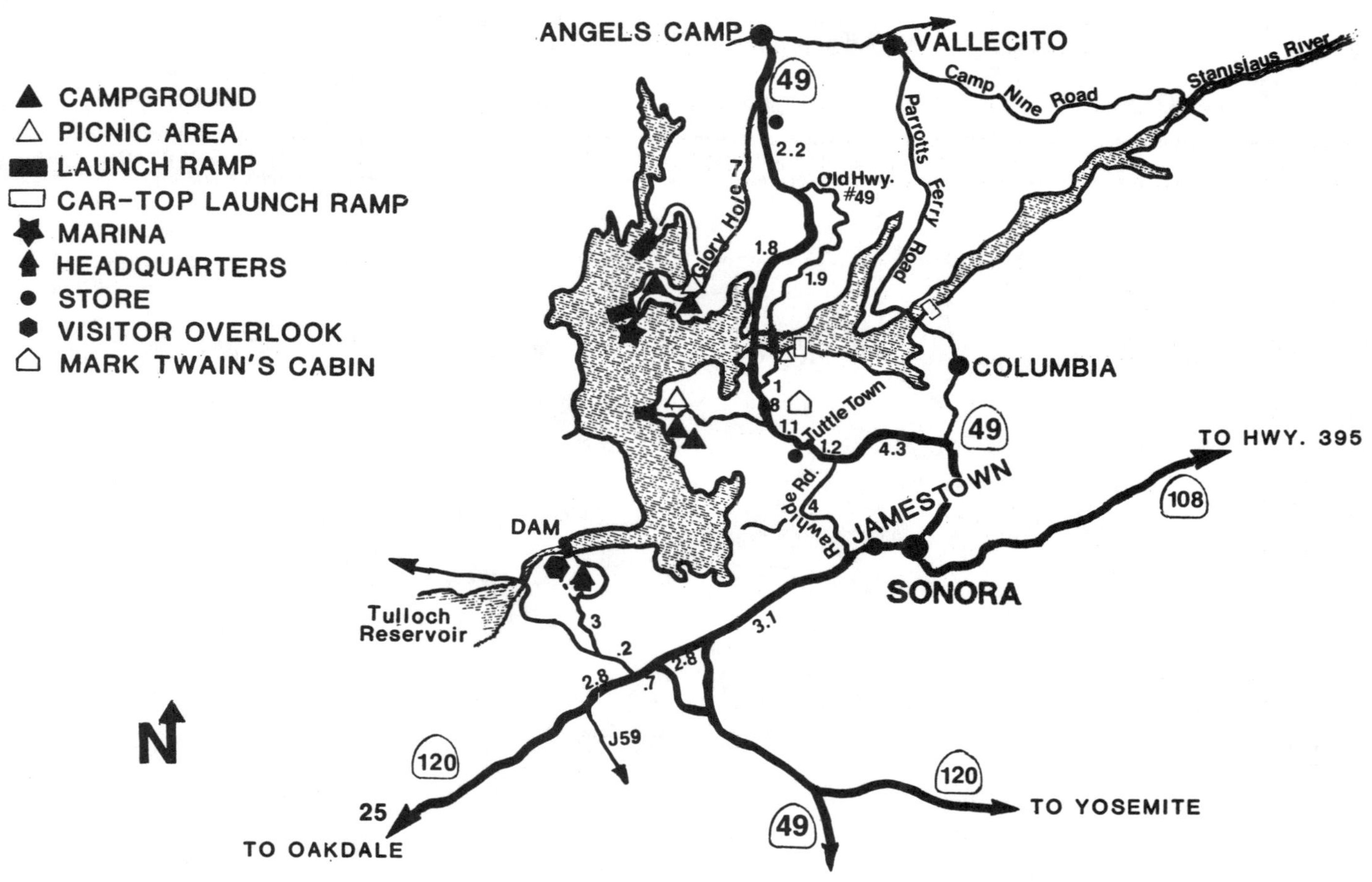

INFORMATION: Park Manager, 16805 Peoria Flat Road, Jamestown 95327, Ph: 209-984-5248			
CAMPING	**BOATING**	**RECREATION**	**OTHER**
Glory Hole: 144 Dev. Sites for Tents & R.V.s Tuttletown: 95 Dev. Sites for Tents & R.V.s Fee: $7 2 Cars, 8 People Maximum 2nd Car: $4 Camping Only at Designated Sites	Open to All Boating, Sailing & Waterskiing 1 Unimproved Launch Area 3 Improved Launch Ramps with 3 Floats Full Service Marina Fuel Dock, Pumpout Covered & Uncovered Slips, Houseboat Mooring Rentals - Fishing, Pontoon, Houseboats	Fishing: Rainbow & Brown Trout, Large & Smallmouth Bass, Bluegill, Catfish & Crappie Picnicking Hiking Gold Panning No Off Road Vehicles Mark Twain's Cabin	Full Facilities in Nearby Towns New Melones Lake Marina (Canteen Corp.) P.O. Box 1389 Angels Camp, 95222 Ph: 209-785-3300 Store

LAKE TULLOCH

Lake Tulloch, at an elevation of 510 feet, is on the western slope of the Sierras just east of Modesto. Its 55 miles of shoreline encompass two submerged valleys surrounded by oak-studded rolling hills. This "Gold Country" lake is open to all types of boating and offers good marine support facilities. Fishing for trout and warm water species is popular especially since Tulloch is known as one of California's prime smallmouth bass waters. The South Shore offers developed and open camping. Lake Tulloch Marina provides a launch ramp, gas dock, snack bar, groceries and a campground. Poker Flat has a luxury motel on the water with gas docks, launch ramp, swimming pool and beach, restaurant and bar. Copper Cove provides an R.V. campground with a restaurant and bar overlooking the water. A gas dock, moorings and launch ramp are nearby.

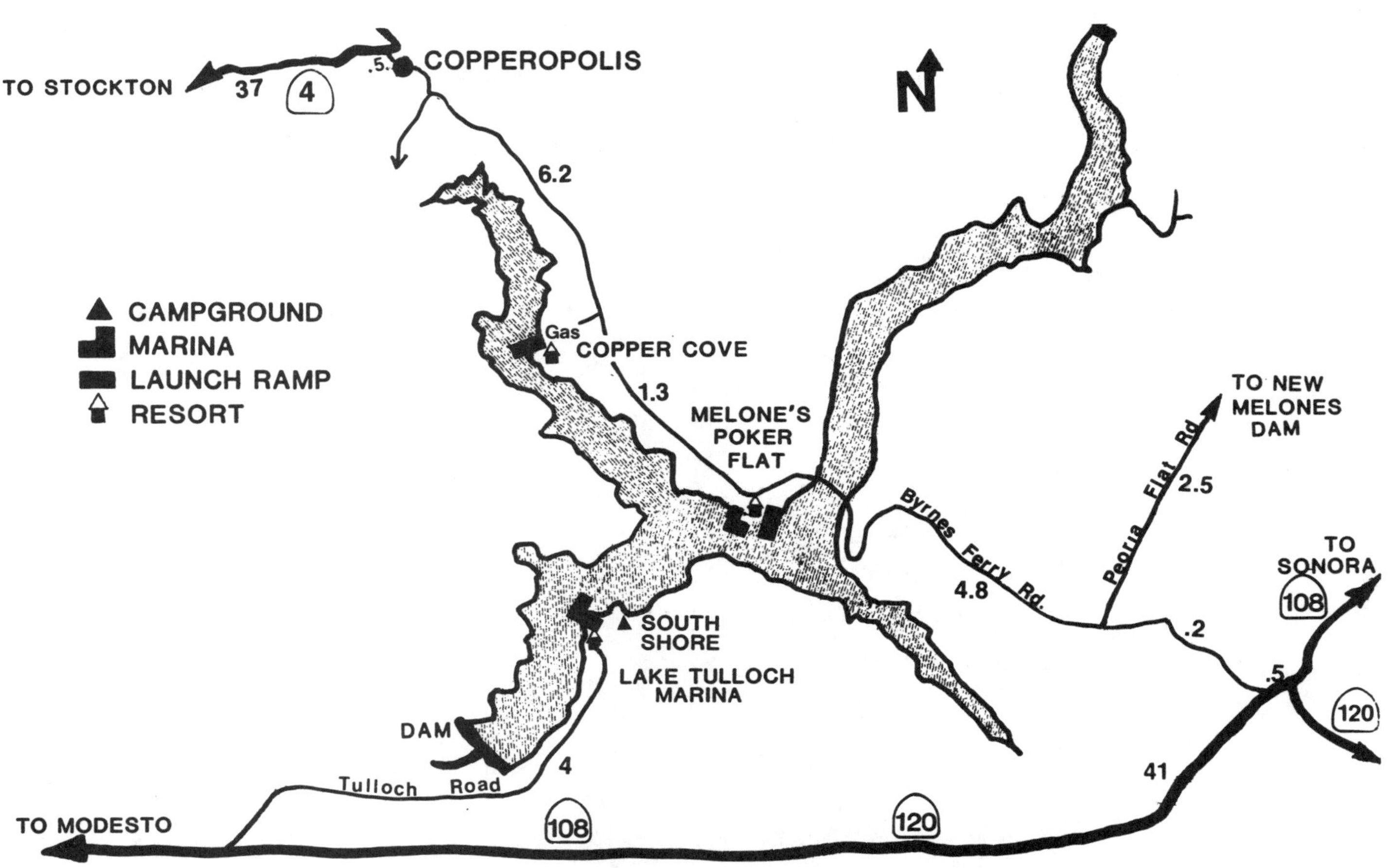

INFORMATION: Copper Cove, Melone's Poker Flat and Lake Tulloch Marina - See Below

CAMPING	BOATING	RECREATION	OTHER
Copper Cove Marina 6603 Lake Tulloch Dr. Copperopolis 95228 Ph: 209-785-2240 11 R.V. Sites Full Hookups, Fee: $20 Lake Tulloch Marina 14578 Tulloch Dam Rd. Jamestown 95327 Ph: 209-881-3335 40 Dev. Sites for Tents & R.V.s on Lake No Hookups, Fee	Power, Row, Canoe, Sail, Waterski, Jet Ski, Windsurf & Inflatables Marinas Gas Docks Launch Ramps Rentals: Fishing & Waterski Boats Overnight Boating Allowed Lakeshore Camping at Campground	Fishing: Rainbow Trout, Small & Largemouth Bass, Bluegill, Catfish, Crappie Picnicking Swimming - Beaches Hiking & Riding Trails Gold Panning Hunting: Quail, Dove, Pheasant, Waterfowl & Deer	Melone's Poker Flat Resort Star Rt. Box 31 Copperopolis 95228 Ph: 209-785-2286 Bait & Tackle Snack Bars Grocery Store Gas Station Ken's Boat Works Ph: 209-785-2438

WOODWARD RESERVOIR

Woodward Reservoir is at an elevation of 210 feet in the low, rolling, grassy foothills 6 miles north of Oakdale. This 2,900 surface acre irrigation reservoir is under the jurisdiction of Stanislaus County. The 23 miles of shallow shoreline has many quiet coves and inlets for the boater and fisherman. The lake is divided by speed limit restrictions with a few "No Boat" areas. There is ample space for all boaters to enjoy their sport. There is a good warm water fishery. The County maintains a nice tree-covered campground on the edge of the lake and a large overflow primitive camping area with limited facilities. This is a popular family area for Valley residents.

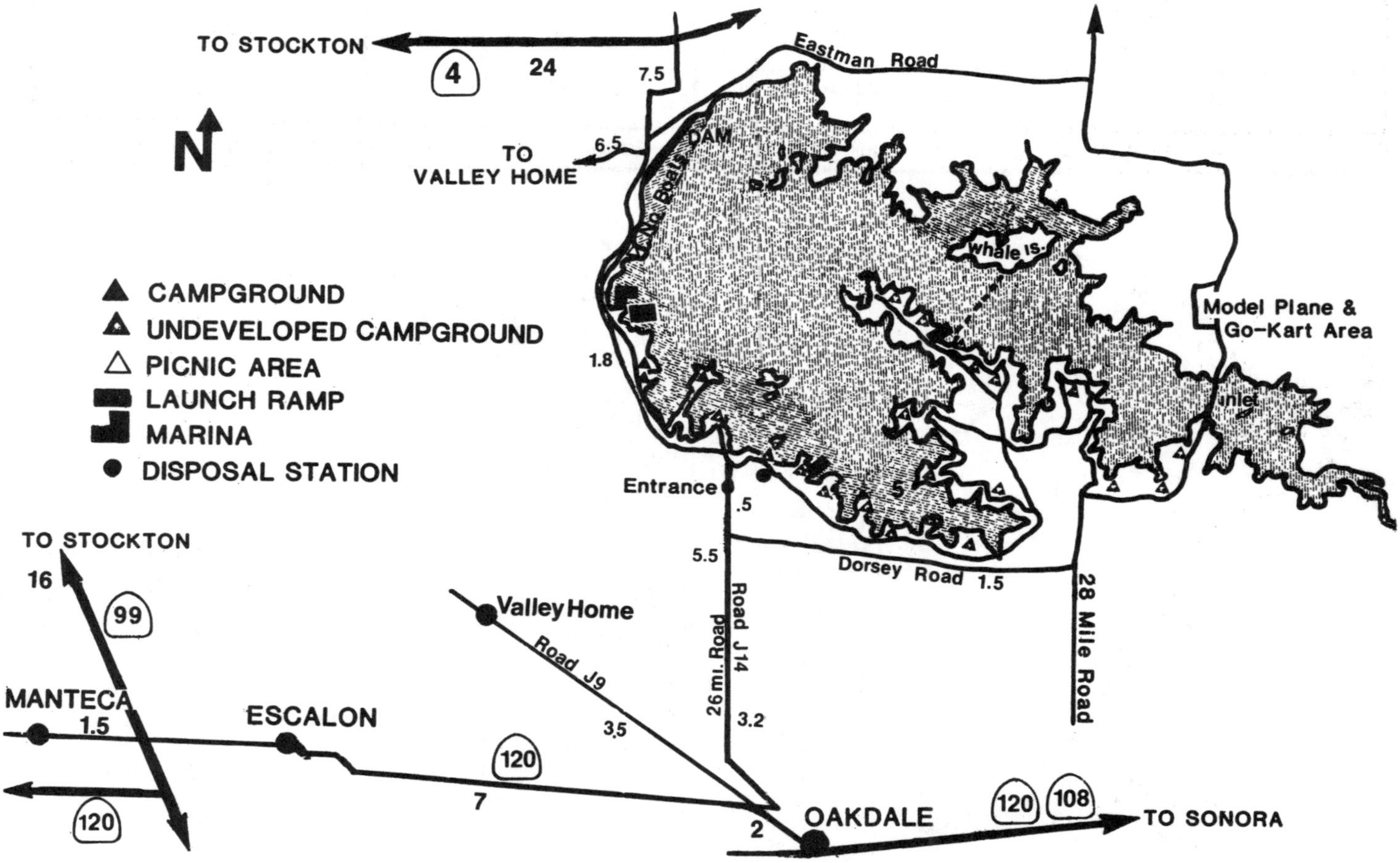

INFORMATION: Woodward Reservoir, 14528-26 Mile Rd., Oakdale 95361, Ph: 209-847-3304			
CAMPING	**BOATING**	**RECREATION**	**OTHER**
82 Dev. Sites for Tents & R.V.s Fee: $12 1,200 Acres for Primitive Camping Fee: $9	Power, Row, Canoe, Sail, Waterski, Jet Ski, Windsurf, Inflatables Restricted Speed Limit Areas Launch Ramps - $4 Full Service Marina Rentals: Fishing & Canoe	Fishing: Catfish, Perch, Bluegill, Crappie, Large-mouth Bass Swimming Picnicking: Large Shelter to Reserve Hunting: Waterfowl With Permit Volleyball Court Horseshoe Pits	Snack Bar Grocery Store Bait & Tackle Disposal Station Hot Showers Full Facilities - 6 Miles at Oakdale

DON PEDRO LAKE

Don Pedro Lake rests at an elevation of 800 feet in the Sierra foothills of the southern Mother Lode. This huge lake has a surface area of 12,960 acres with a pine and oak dotted shoreline of 160 miles. There is an abundance of camping, marine and recreation facilities under the jurisdiction of the Don Pedro Recreation Agency. The vast size and irregular shoreline provides a multitude of boating opportunities from boat-in camping to waterskiing. The angler, from the novice to those on the Pro Bass Tour, will find the varied fishery satisfying. Emerging rocks and islands due to the fluctuating lake levels can be a problem late in the season.

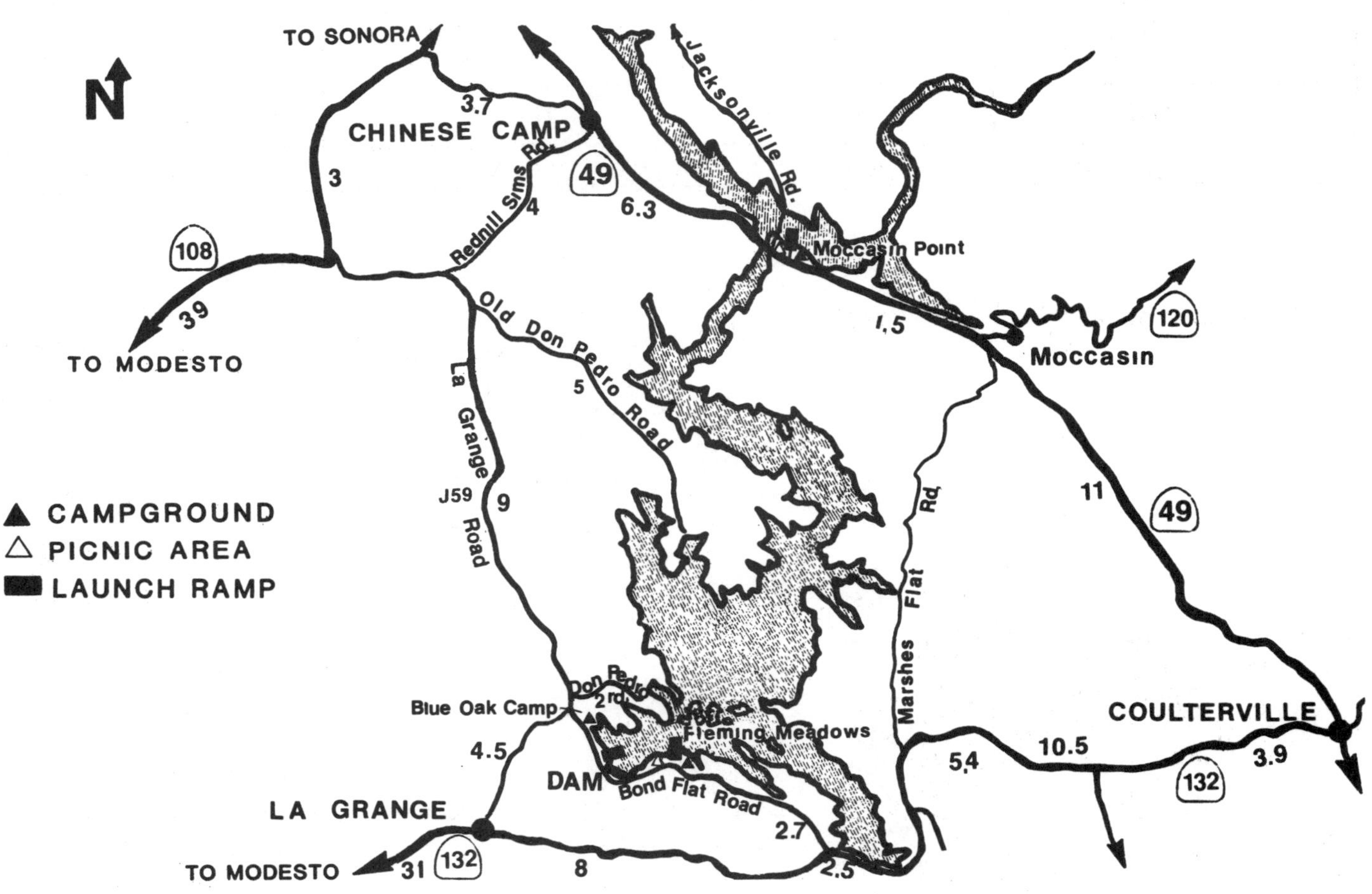

INFORMATION: Don Pedro Recreation Agency, Box 160, La Grange 95329, Ph: 209-852-2396

CAMPING	BOATING	RECREATION	OTHER
540 Dev. Sites for Tents & R.V.s Fees: Tents - $12 Full Hookups - $16 Boat-In & Walk-In Sites Reservations Accepted Overnight on Boat in Designated Areas Dogs Prohibited	Power, Row, Canoe, Sail, Waterski, Jet Ski, Windsurf & Inflatable Full Service Marinas Launch Ramps - $5 Rentals: Fishing, Houseboats & Pontoons Docks, Berths, Moorings, Dry Storage & Gas	Fishing: Trout, Catfish, Bluegill, Crappie, Perch, Silver Salmon, Florida Black Bass Swimming Lagoon - Handicap Access Picnicking Hiking Private Houseboats Subject to Permit	Snack Bars Restaurant Grocery Store Bait & Tackle Hot Showers Laundromat Disposal Station Gas Station Propane Sailing Slalom Course

MODESTO RESERVOIR

Modesto Reservoir is at an elevation of 210 feet in the low hills, orchards and pastureland northeast of Modesto. The lake has a surface area of 2,700 acres with 31 miles of shoreline. This is a good boating lake with many pretty coves for unlimited boat camping, westerly breezes for sailing and vast open water for the skier. Boaters should be advised that there is a 5 MPH speed limit on the southern area of the lake and around the populated areas. There are also several no boating zones; refer to rules or ask a Ranger for specific areas. Submerged trees along with the many coves provide a good warm water fishery. The facilities are under the jurisdiction of the Stanislaus County Parks Department.

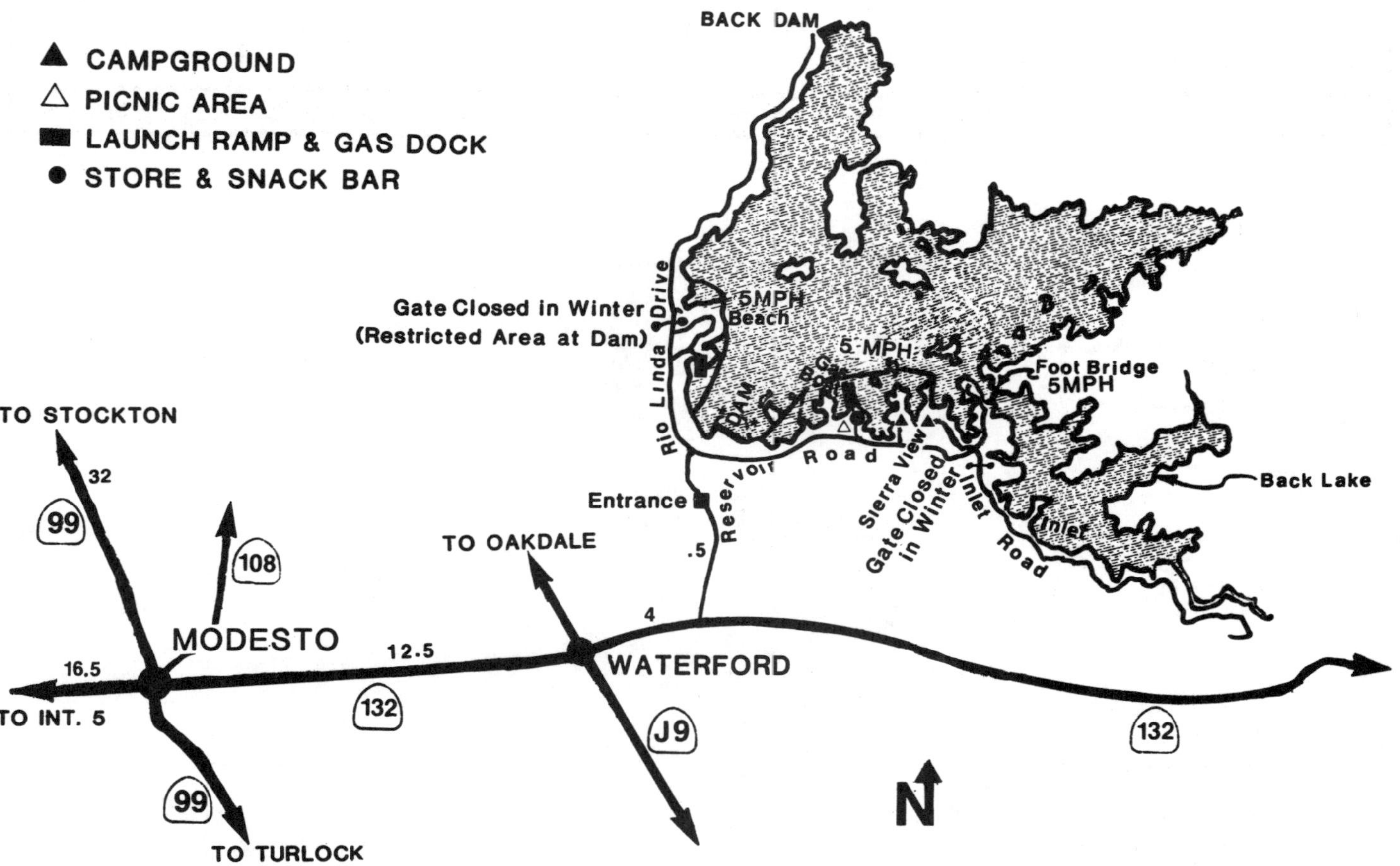

INFORMATION: Modesto Reservoir, 1716 Morgan Rd., Modesto 95351, Ph: 209-874-9540

CAMPING	BOATING	RECREATION	OTHER
90 Dev. Sites for Tents & R.V.s Fee: $12 Unlimited Primitive Sites Fee: $9 Entrance Fees Cars: $4 Boats: $4 Dogs MUST be Licensed and Leashed at All Times	Power, Row, Canoe, Sail, Waterski, Jet Ski, Windsurf & Inflatable Launch Ramps Full Service Marina Rentals: Paddleboats Docks, Moorings, Gas Overnight in Boat Permitted Anywhere	Fishing: Catfish, Bluegill, Crappie, Large & Smallmouth Bass Swimming - Beaches Picnicking Hiking Backpacking-Parking Duck Hunting By Permit Only	Snack Bar Grocery Store Bait & Tackle Hot Showers Disposal Station Gas Station Full Facilities at Modesto

OAKWOOD LAKE

Bordering the San Joaquin River just off the junction of Interstate 5 and Highway 120, Oakwood Lake is one of the most unique and largest RV campgrounds and water "fun" parks in the West. There are 20 water slides; 2 are free to children. Arcades, roller skating, thrill and rapids rides, and playgrounds are a part of the fun. There is a large swimming lagoon. Boating is restricted to paddle boats, canoe, inflatables, sailboards and sailboats. There are 400 campsites with full hookups located on shady lawns. For those who enjoy power boating and a broader fishery, there is the San Joaquin River. This is a family park for those who enjoy a multitude of activities.

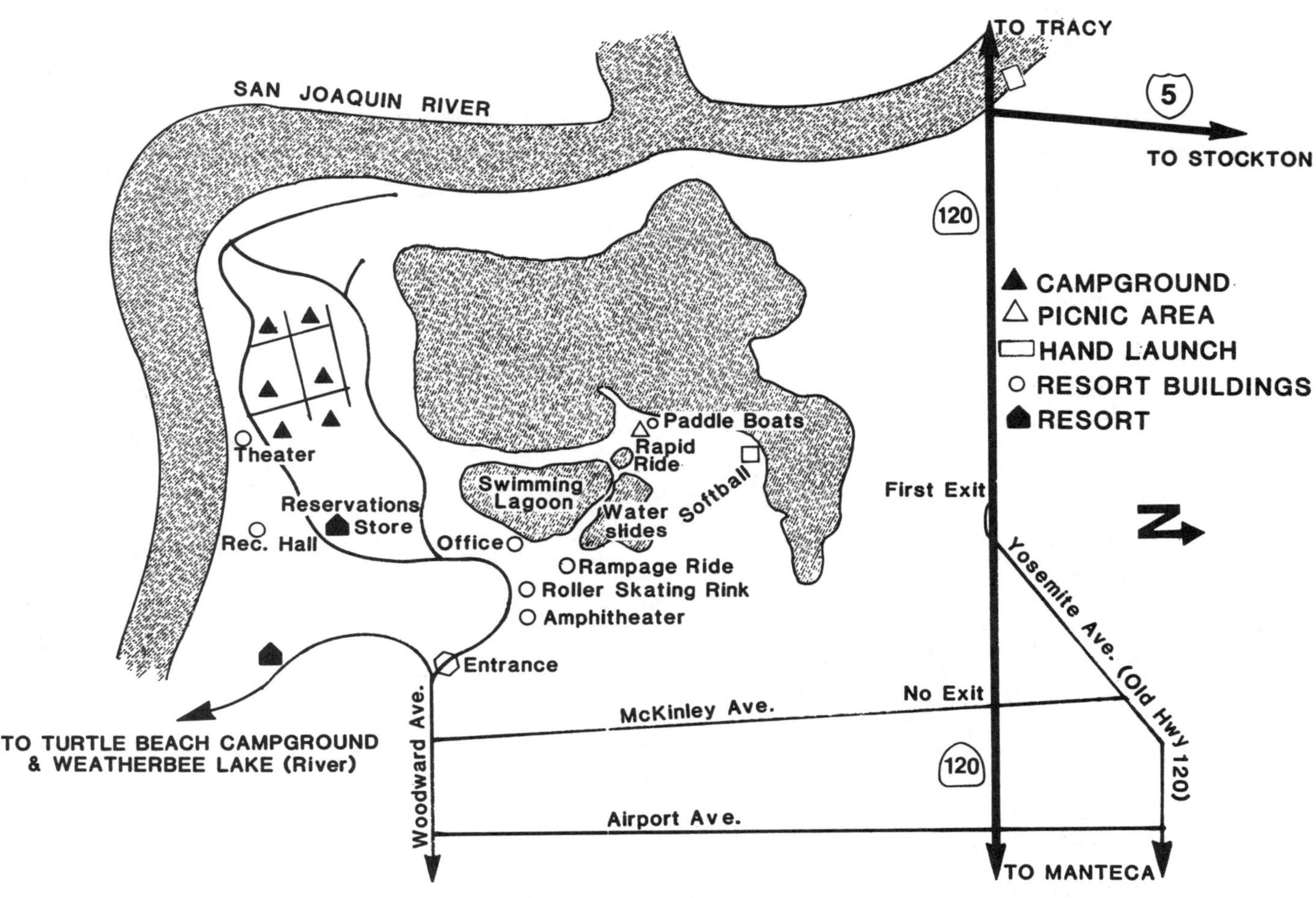

INFORMATION: Oakwood Lake, 874 E. Woodward, Manteca 95336, Ph: 209-239-2500

CAMPING	BOATING	RECREATION	OTHER
400 Dev. Sites for R.V.s with Full Hookups Tent Camping Fees Start @ $18 Group Sites Discount Rates for R.V. Clubs and Groups Reservations Only: Ph: 209-239-9566	Row, Sail, Canoe & Inflatables No Motors on Park Lake HandLaunch Only Sailboards San Joaquin River: Power Boats and Waterskiing-Launch Ramp off Hwy. 120	Fishing: Catfish & Bass - Guests Only Swimming Lagoon Picnicking 2 Large Day-Use Areas Waterslides The Turbo Tube The Rampage Rapids Ride Softball Complex Movies & Bingo Paddleboats Group Rates	Snack Bar Grocery Store Bait & Tackle Hot Showers Laundromat Playground Arcades R.V. Storage LP Gas Disposal Station

TURLOCK LAKE

Turlock Lake, at an elevation of 250 feet, is nestled in the foothills 21 miles east of Modesto. As a part of the Turlock State Recreation Area, Turlock Lake is included in the California State Park System. It offers a surface area of 3,500 acres of open water which is surrounded by 26 shoreline miles of rolling grasslands. Open year around, this popular recreation area offers varied and abundant recreation. The lake is open to all types of boating although in late season, low water can be a hazard. There is a good warm water fishery and trout are planted on a regular basis in season. Swimming is popular at several beaches. The campground is away from the beach on the Tuloumne River. There are nice shaded level campsites overlooking the river. Reservations are advised. Phone 1-800-444-7275.

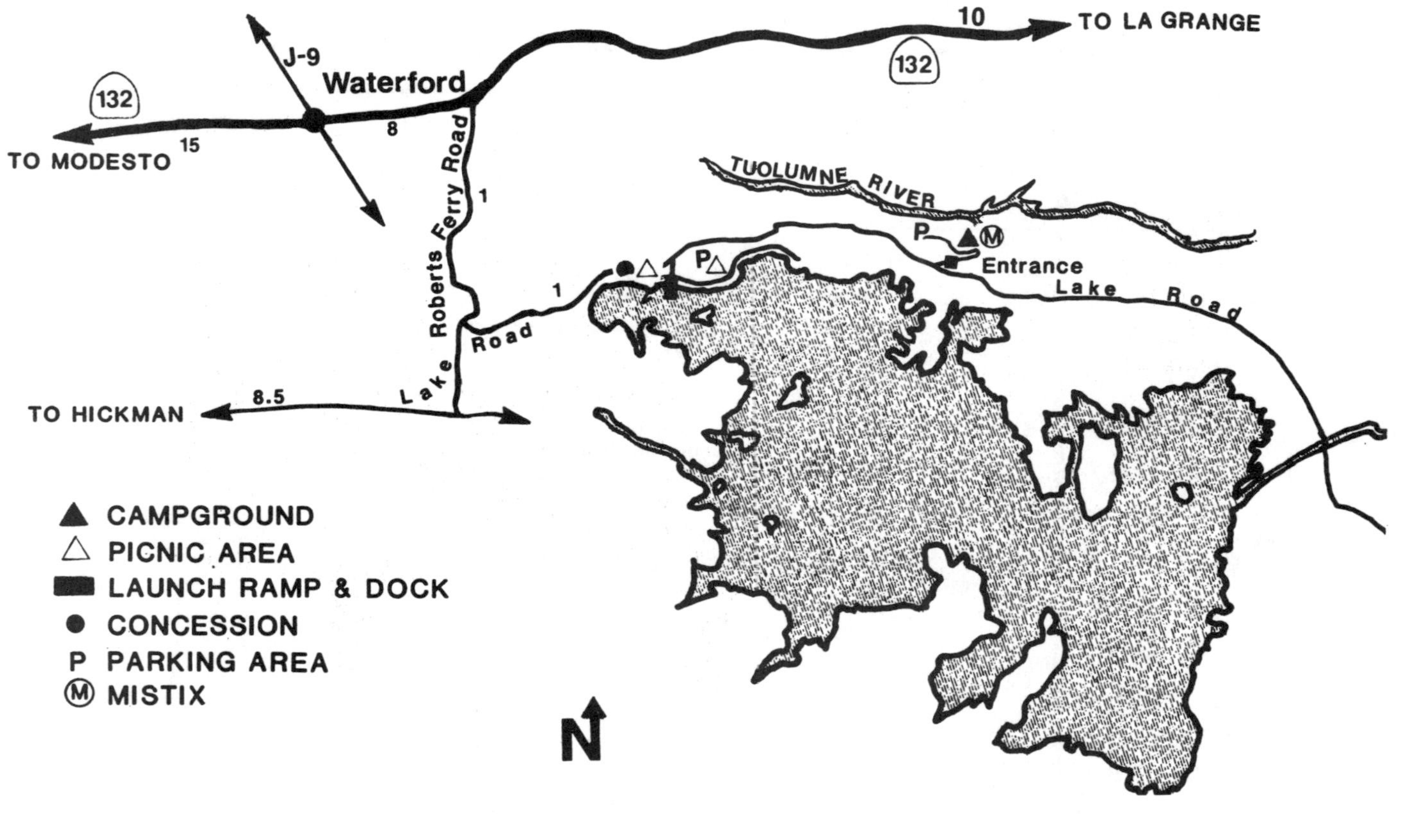

INFORMATION: Turlock State Recreation Area, 22600 Lake Rd., La Grange 95329, Ph: 209-874-2008			
CAMPING	BOATING	RECREATION	OTHER
State Park 67 Dev. Sites for Tents & R.V.s Fee: $10 Hot Showers Flush Toilets Campfire & Junior Ranger Program Day Use Fee: $4	Power, Row, Canoe, Sail, Waterski, Jet Ski, Windsurf & Inflatable Launch Ramp - $2 Low Water Late in Season	Fishing: Trout, Catfish, Bluegill, Crappie, Large & Smallmouth Bass Swimming - Beaches Picnicking Hiking No Alcohol on Beaches or Day Use Area	Snack Bar Full Facilities at Waterford

SWIMMING

Swimming in our California Lakes is a popular and rewarding experience but there are potential hazards that can be minimized by using common sense and following some basic rules. Never swim alone; always have a partner. Never venture beyond your swimming and physical ability. Always swim in designated areas and obey the local regulations. Know the water conditions and environment prior to taking unnecessary risks, such as diving. When in trouble, call or wave for help. But most of all have fun and "swim with care."

LAKE MC CLURE AND LAKE MC SWAIN

At an elevation of 867 feet, these lakes are in the Mother Lode Country of the Sierra foothills. Lake McClure has a surface area of 7,100 acres with 82 miles of pine and oak covered shoreline. The fine recreation areas around the lake have modern campgrounds, marinas and recreation facilities. Many coves are popular for houseboats, and the waterskier will find 26 miles of open water. Lake McSwain is actually the forebay of Lake McClure. The cold flowing water from McClure has created a good fishery. Boating is popular, but waterskiing and houseboats are not allowed at McSwain.

. . . Continued . . .

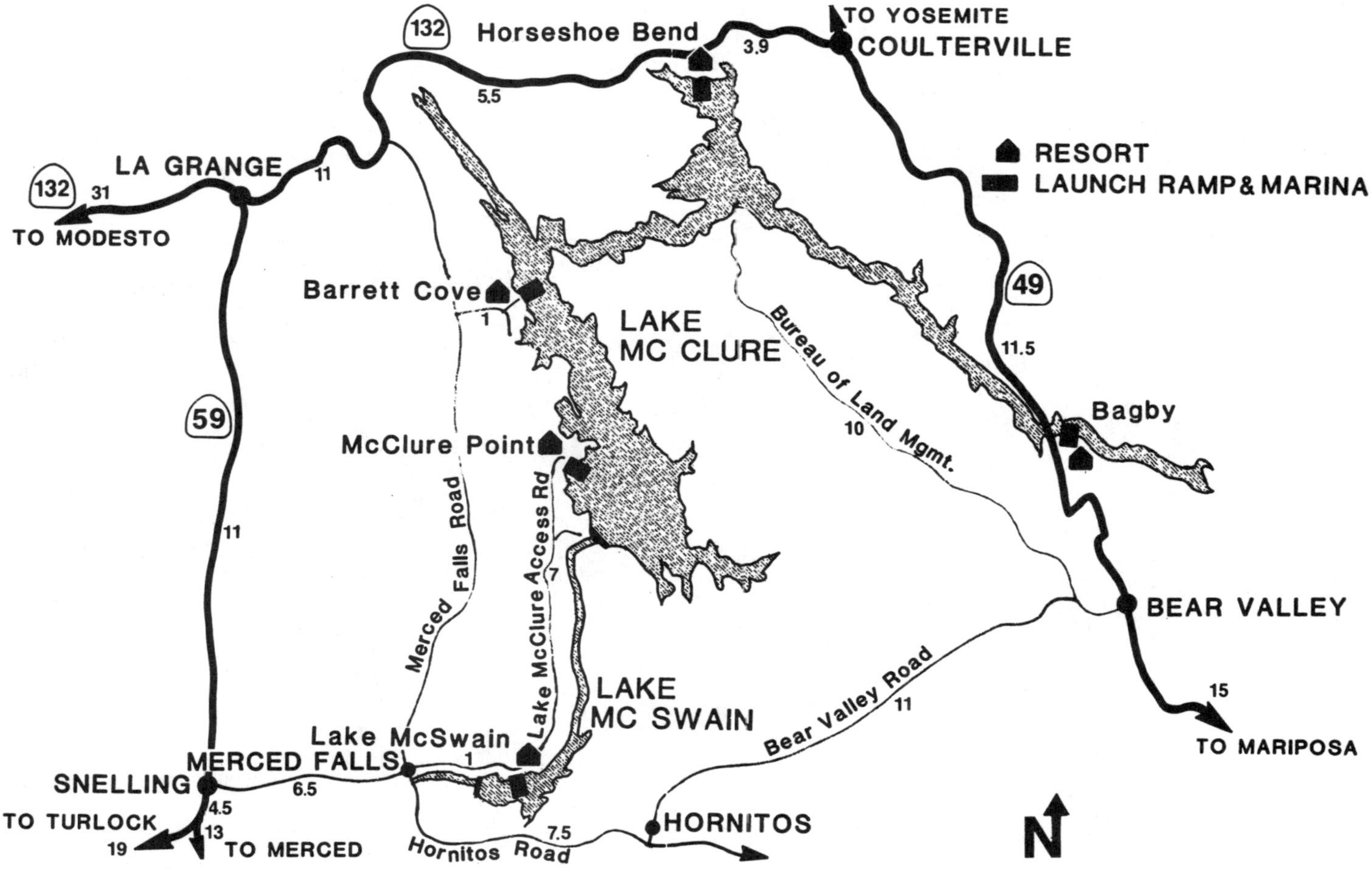

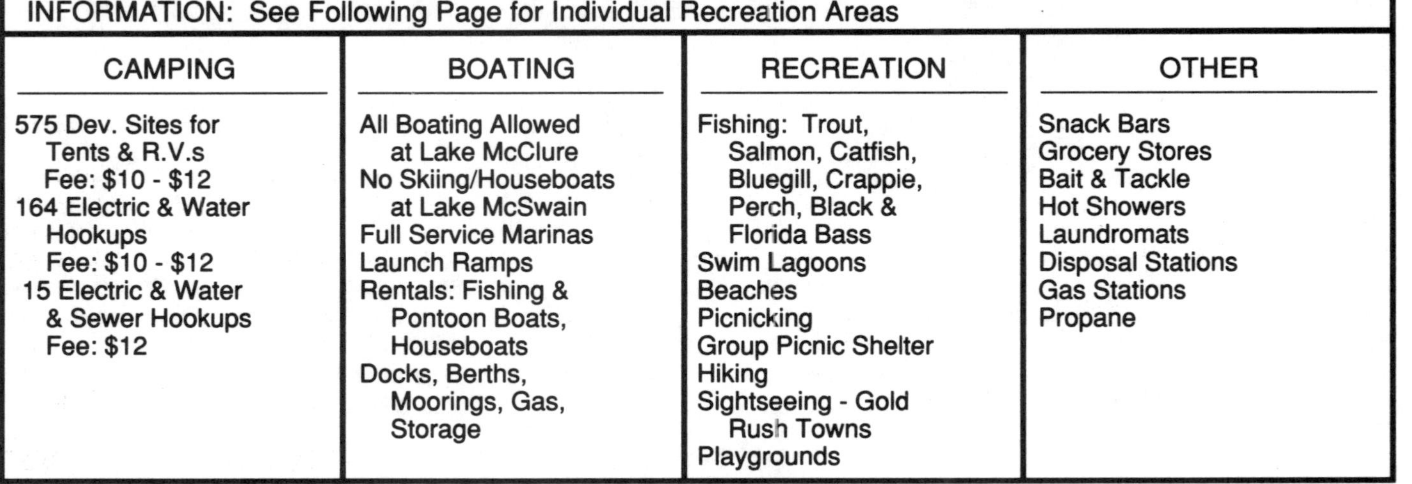

INFORMATION: See Following Page for Individual Recreation Areas

CAMPING	BOATING	RECREATION	OTHER
575 Dev. Sites for Tents & R.V.s Fee: $10 - $12 164 Electric & Water Hookups Fee: $10 - $12 15 Electric & Water & Sewer Hookups Fee: $12	All Boating Allowed at Lake McClure No Skiing/Houseboats at Lake McSwain Full Service Marinas Launch Ramps Rentals: Fishing & Pontoon Boats, Houseboats Docks, Berths, Moorings, Gas, Storage	Fishing: Trout, Salmon, Catfish, Bluegill, Crappie, Perch, Black & Florida Bass Swim Lagoons Beaches Picnicking Group Picnic Shelter Hiking Sightseeing - Gold Rush Towns Playgrounds	Snack Bars Grocery Stores Bait & Tackle Hot Showers Laundromats Disposal Stations Gas Stations Propane

LAKE MC CLURE AND LAKE MC SWAIN

MC CLURE POINT:

M I D Parks Department
9090 Lake McClure Rd.
Snelling 95369
Ph: 209-378-2521

McClure Point Marina
Call for Information
at Barrett Cove Marina
Ph: 209-378-2441

100 Developed Campsites for Tents & R.V.s, 41 Water & Electric Hookups. Fees: $10 - $12. Group Camp to 30 People Maximum. 64 Picnic Units. Full Service Marina with Gas for Boats & Cars, 5-Lane Launch Ramp, Boat Rentals: Fishing, Houseboats, Pontoons, Docks, Berths, Moorings, Storage. Swim Lagoon, Snack Bar, Grocery Store, Laundromat, Showers. Reservations through Parks Department Office at 1-800-468-8889. Reservation Fee: $3.

BARRETT COVE:

M I D Parks Department
Barrett Cove Rec. Area
Star Route
La Grange 95329
Ph: 209-378-2711

Barrett Cove Marina
Star Route
La Grange 95329
Ph: 209-378-2441

275 Developed Campsites for Tents & R.V.s, 33 Full Hookups, 35 Water and Electric Hookups. Fees: $10 - $12. Group Camp to 100 People Maximum. 100 Picnic Units. Full Service Marina with Gas for Boats & Cars, 4-lane Launch Ramp, Boat Rentals: Fishing, Houseboats, Pontoons, Jet Skis, Moorings, Storage. Swim Lagoon, Playground, Snack Bar, Grocery Store, Laundromat, Showers. Reservations through Parks Department Office at 1-800-468-8889. Reservation Fee: $3.

HORSESHOE BEND:

M I D Parks Department
Horseshoe Bend Rec. Area
4244 Highway 132
Coulterville 95311
Ph: 209-878-3452

Horseshoe Bend Marina
Call for Information
at Barrett Cove Marina
Ph: 209-378-2441

90 Developed Campsites for Tents & R.V.s, 15 Water & Electric Hookups. Fees: $10 - $12. 32 Picnic Units. Full Service Marina, 2-lane Launch Ramp, Boat Rentals: Houseboats, Moorings, Storage, Gas for Boats & Cars, Playground Area, Docks, Berths, Swim Lagoon, Snack Bar, Grocery Store, Laundromat, Showers. Reservations through Parks Department Office at 1-800-468-8889. Reservation Fee: $3.

BAGBY:

USONA Corporation (Concessionaire)
Bagby Recreation Area
8324 Highway 49 North
Mariposa 95338

25 Developed Campsites for Tents & R.V.s. 25 Picnic Units. Full Service Marina, Launch Ramp, Boat Rentals, Moorings, Snack Bar, Grocery Store.

LAKE MC SWAIN:

M I D Parks Department
9090 Lake McClure Rd.
Snelling 95369
Ph: 209-378-2521

Lake McSwain Marina
8044 Lake McClure Road
Snelling 95369
Ph: 209-378-2534

90 Developed Campsites for Tents & R.V.s, 30 Water & Electric Hookups. Fees: $10 - $12. Group Picnic Facility up to 200 People Maximum. Picnic Area. Full Service Marina with Gas for Boats & Cars, 2-lane Launch Ramp, Rentals: Fishing Boats, Moorings. Snack Bar, Grocery Store, Laundromat, Showers, Playground Area. Reservations through Parks Department Office at 1-800-468-8889. Reservation Fee: $3.

LAKE YOSEMITE

Lake Yosemite is nestled in the rolling foothills of the Sierra Nevada, east of Merced. This 387 surface acre lake is under the jurisdiction of the County of Merced. The County maintains a nice day use park with shaded picnic areas for families and groups to 200 people. Group reservations are required. There are swimming beaches and excellent marine facilities. All types of boating are allowed with designated areas for waterskiing, sailing and rowing. Fishing can be productive at this pleasant park in the San Joaquin Valley just east of Merced.

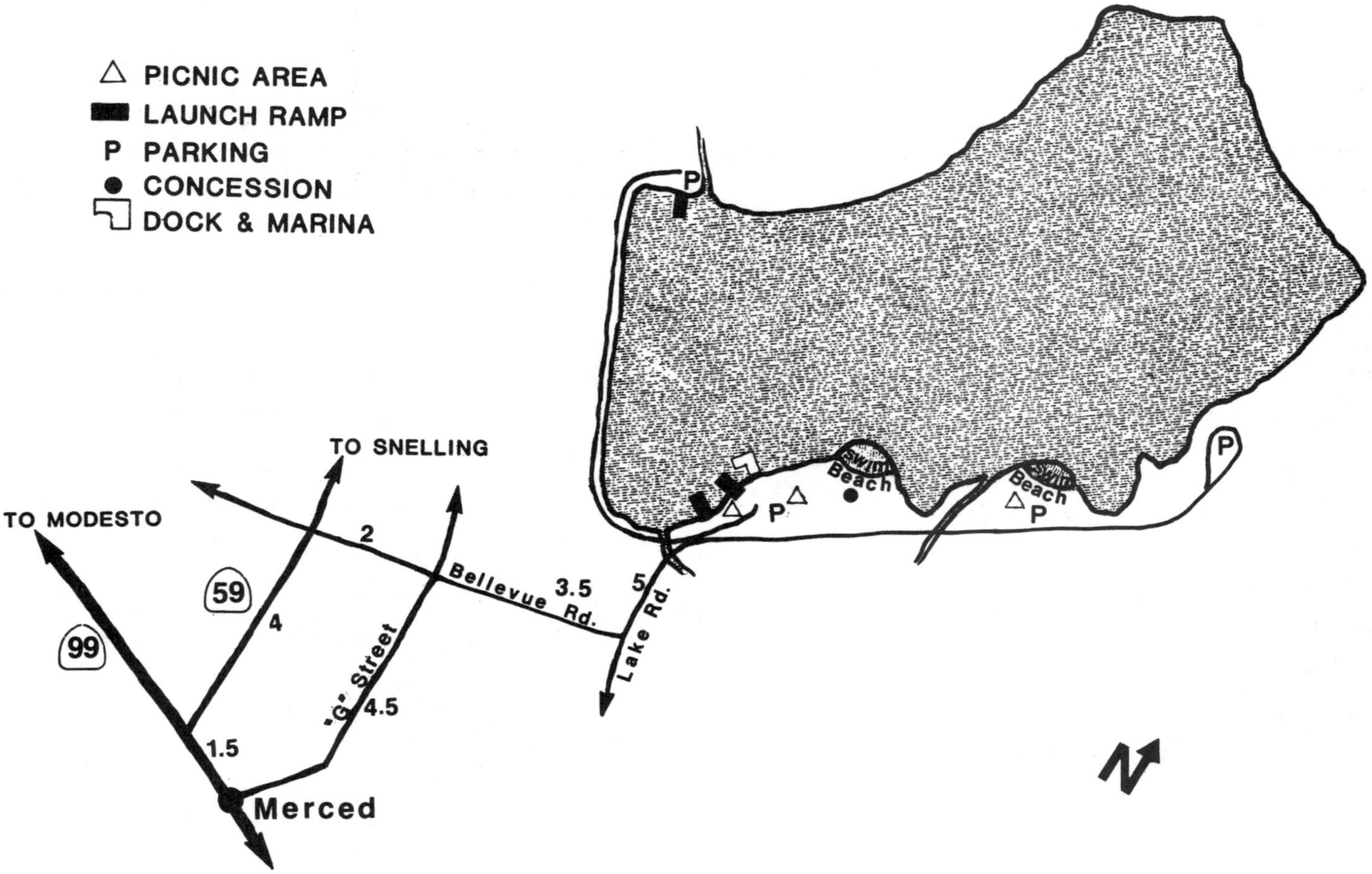

△ PICNIC AREA
▬ LAUNCH RAMP
P PARKING
● CONCESSION
DOCK & MARINA

TO MODESTO
TO SNELLING
99
59
4
2
Bellevue Rd.
3.5
5
Lake Rd.
"G" Street
4.5
1.5
Merced
Swim Beach
Swim Beach
N

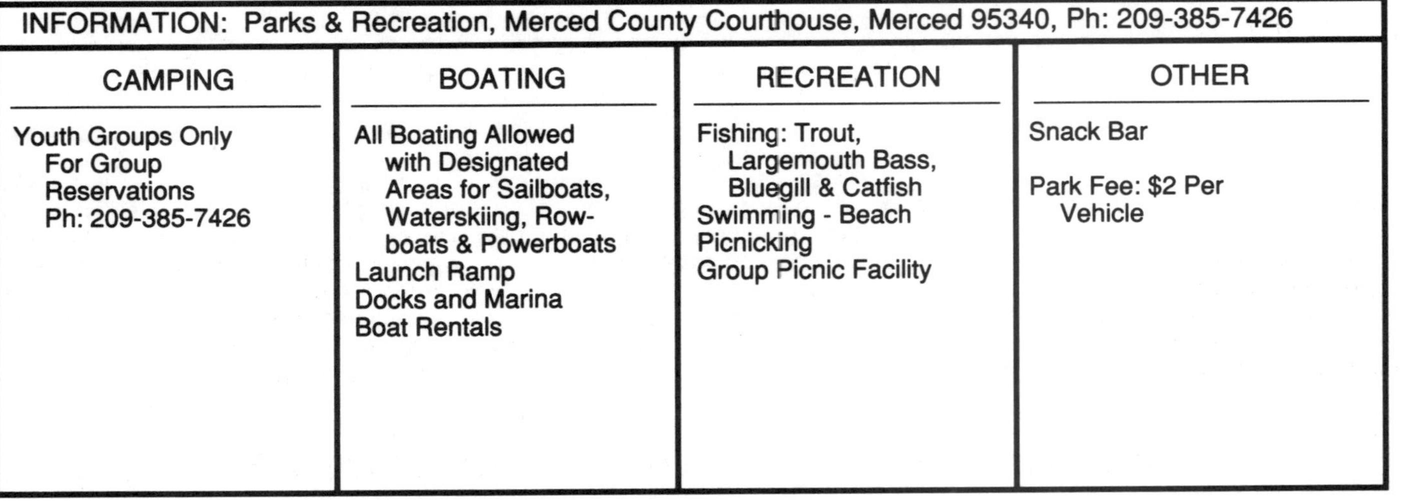

INFORMATION: Parks & Recreation, Merced County Courthouse, Merced 95340, Ph: 209-385-7426			
CAMPING	BOATING	RECREATION	OTHER
Youth Groups Only For Group Reservations Ph: 209-385-7426	All Boating Allowed with Designated Areas for Sailboats, Waterskiing, Rowboats & Powerboats Launch Ramp Docks and Marina Boat Rentals	Fishing: Trout, Largemouth Bass, Bluegill & Catfish Swimming - Beach Picnicking Group Picnic Facility	Snack Bar Park Fee: $2 Per Vehicle

SOULAJULE, STAFFORD, NICASIO, PHOENIX, LAGUNITAS, BON TEMPE, ALPINE AND KENT LAKES

All of these lakes are nestled on the slopes of Mt. Tamalpais are under the jurisdiction of the Marin Municipal Water District except for Stafford Lake which is a part of the North Marin Water District. There are picnic facilities near each lake. Beautiful redwood shaded hiking and equestrian trails abound. Boating, swimming and wading are not permitted.

In all the lakes except Lagunitas, there is a planted trout fishery. Nicasio Reservoir also has warm water angling. Lagunitas Lake is being developed as a natural trout lake where only artificial lures with single barbless hooks may be used; there will be a limit where only 2 fish between 10-16 inches total length may be retained.

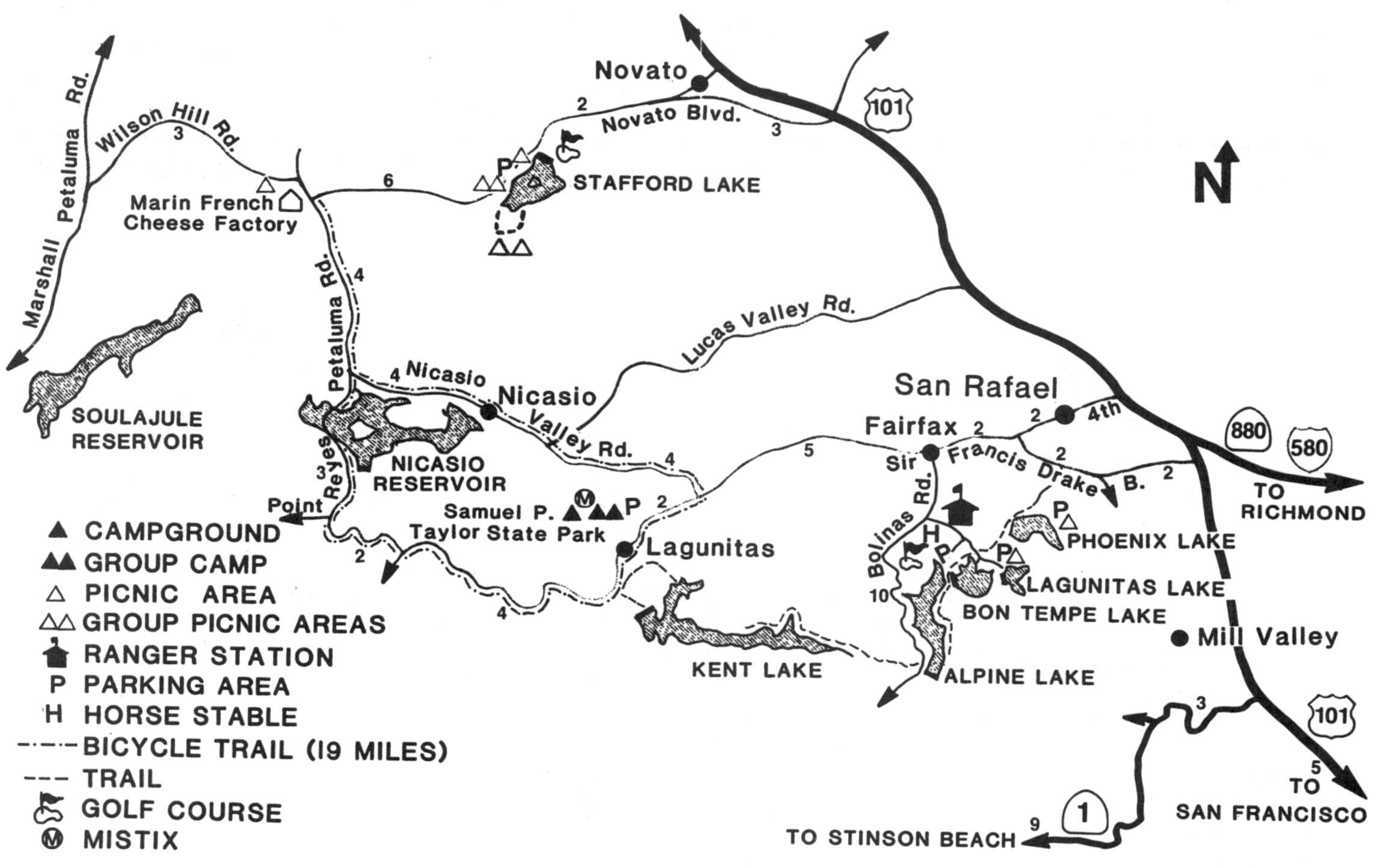

INFORMATION: Marin Municipal Water District, 200 Nellen Ave., Corte Madera, Ph: 415-924-4600			
CAMPING	BOATING	RECREATION	OTHER
Samuel P. Taylor Park P.O. Box 251 Lagunitas 94938 Ph: 415-488-9897 Fee: $10 Reserve Mistix Lakes: Day Use Only Vehicle Fees: $3 Open: 8 a.m. to Sunset Campsites Being Renovated - Call for Current Status	No Boating	Fishing: Trout, Bass, Bluegill, Catfish & Crappie Hiking & Equestrian Trails Bicycle Loop Nature Study Picnicking No Swimming or Wading Pets To Be Leashed At All Times	Stafford Lake: North Marin Water District P.O. Box 146 Novato 94948 Ph: 415-897-4133 Cheese Factory: 4 Miles North of Nicasio Reservoir Full Facilities in Nearby Towns

ANZA, BERKELEY AQUATIC PARK, MERRITT AND TEMESCAL

Lake Anza is a small lake within the beautiful Charles Lee Tilden Regional Park. While Lake Anza offers minimal water recreation, Tilden Park is one of the most extensively developed day use facilities in the Bay Area. Temescal is a small 10 acre lake within the 48 acre Temescal Recreation Area. The City of Oakland administers the 160 acre saltwater Lake Merritt. The surrounding Lakeside Park provides expansive shaded lawns, picnic areas, children's playground and North America's oldest bird sanctuary. The Berkeley Aquatic Park is a popular rowing, sailing and windsurfing salt water lake. While there are private facilities for waterskiing, it is not open to the public for power boating.

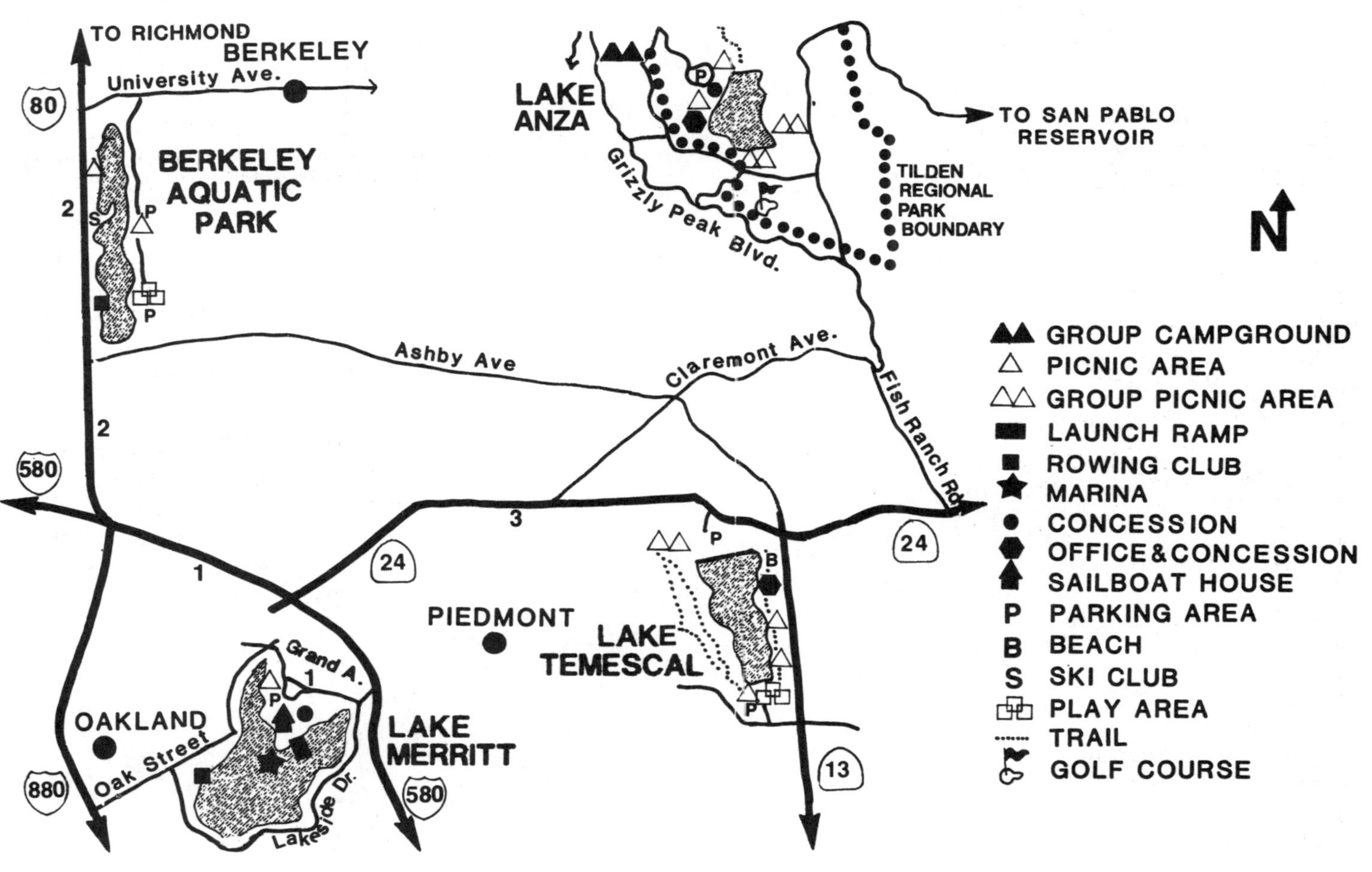

INFORMATION: East Bay Regional Park District, 11500 Skyline Blvd., Oakland 94619, Ph: 415-531-9300

CAMPING	BOATING	RECREATION	OTHER
No Camping At Tilden Regional Park Except for Youth Groups and Equestrian Groups 14 Day Advance Reservations Ph: 415-531-9043	Lake Anza: No Boating Berkeley Aquatic: Sail, Windsurf & Row Rental Sailboats Lake Merritt: Sail, Windsurf & Manually Powered Launch Ramp & Hoist Rental: Sail, Row Canoe & Pedal Sailing Instructions Indoor Boat Storage	Fishing: Trout, Bass, Catfish, Crappie & Perch Picnicking Hiking, Jogging & Riding Trails Playground Nature Study Bird Sanctuary Boat Tours at Merritt Swimming: Anza & Temescal Only	Lake Merritt Sailboat House Oakland Office of Parks & Recreation 1520 Lakeside Dr. Oakland 94612 Ph: 415-444-3807 Berkeley Aquatic Park

SAN PABLO RESERVOIR

San Pablo Reservoir rests at an elevation of 313 feet east of the Berkeley hills. This 860 acre lake is a drinking water reservoir under the jurisdiction of the East Bay Municipal Utility District. The winds make for good sailing. Although windsurfing, waterskiing and swimming are prohibited, this is a popular boating lake with good marine facilities. Extensive fisheries habitat along with a tremendous planting schedule (300,000 trout planted in 1988) make this one of the most productive lakes in the State. There are 142 picnic sites with barbecues overlooking the water in addition to a large children's play area. In addition, there are two large group picnic areas which can be reserved. Hiking and riding trails that are available by permit lead to Briones and Tilden Regional Park.

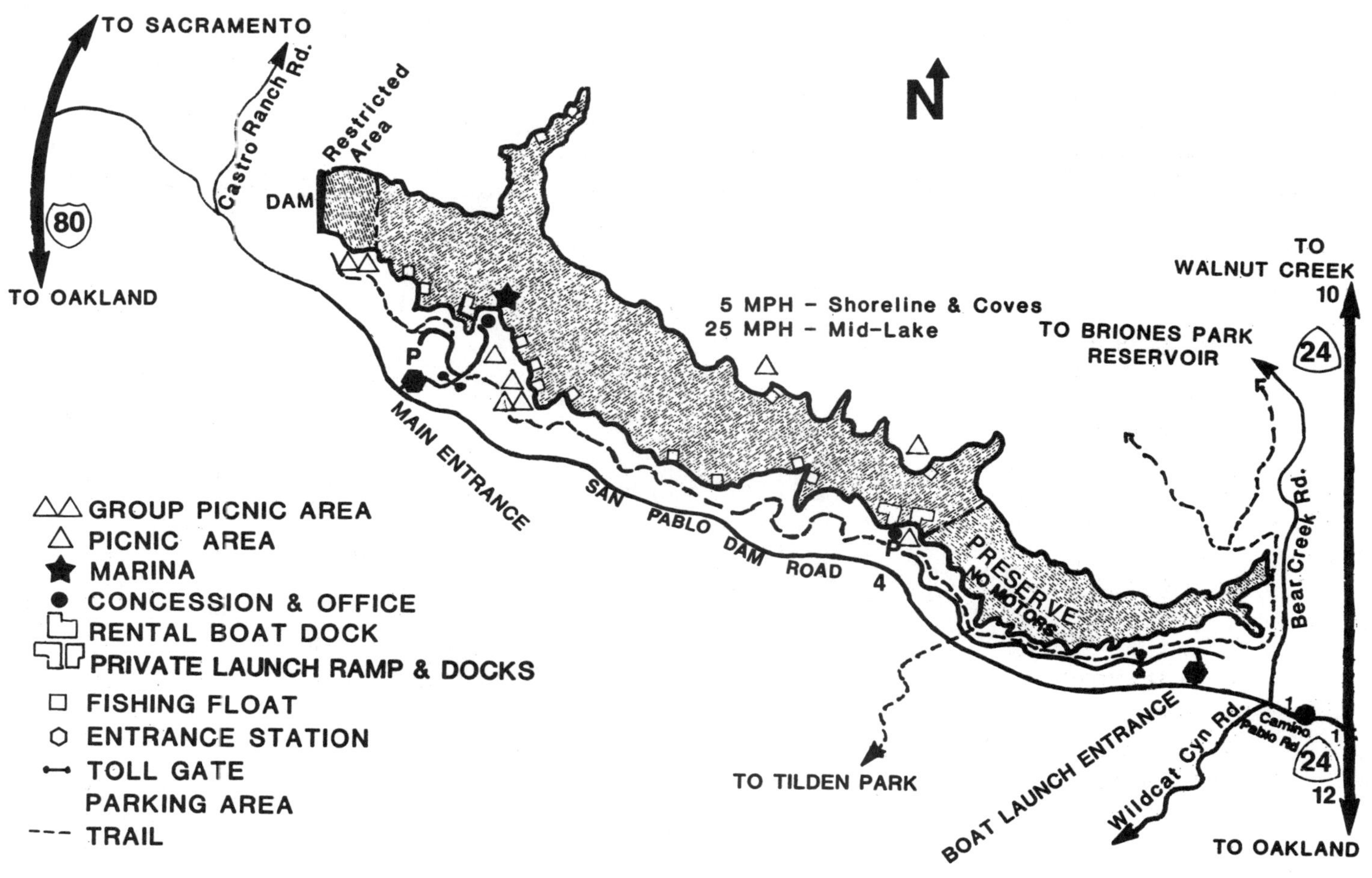

INFORMATION: San Pablo Reservoir, 7301 San Pablo Dam Rd., El Sobrante 94803, Ph: 415-223-1661			
CAMPING	**BOATING**	**RECREATION**	**OTHER**
Day Use Only 2 Group Picnic Areas for 100 & 250 People - By Reservation Only	All Boating Subject to Permit or Rental Waterskiing, Windsurf & Racing Boats Not Allowed Full Service Marina 8-Lane Launch Ramp Docks Rentals: Fishing - 7-1/2 HP Motors, Row Boats	Fishing: Trophy Trout, Large, Smallmouth & Spotted Bass, Sturgeon, Channel Catfish, Crappie & Bluegill Fishing Docks Fishing Access Trail Picnic Areas Hiking, Bicycle & Horse Riding Trails Children's Play Area No Swimming or Wading	Restaurant Bait & Tackle Sundries

LAFAYETTE RESERVOIR

Lafayette Reservoir provides a natural retreat from the urban demands that surround it. Nestled amid the rolling oak-covered hills of Contra Costa County and within the city limits of Lafayette, this 115 acre lake is popular among sailors, canoers and non-powered boaters. Electric motors are permitted. Although you must hand launch your boat, there is a boat house and sailing dock for the small boat owner. There are also rental boats. In addition to planted trout, the angler will find a viable warm water fishery. Most of the picnic sites surrounding the lake have barbecues. There are two reserved group picnic areas. A paved walking trail surrounds the lake. In the hills above, there is a hiking trail. The facilities are under the jurisdiction of the East Bay Municipal Utility District.

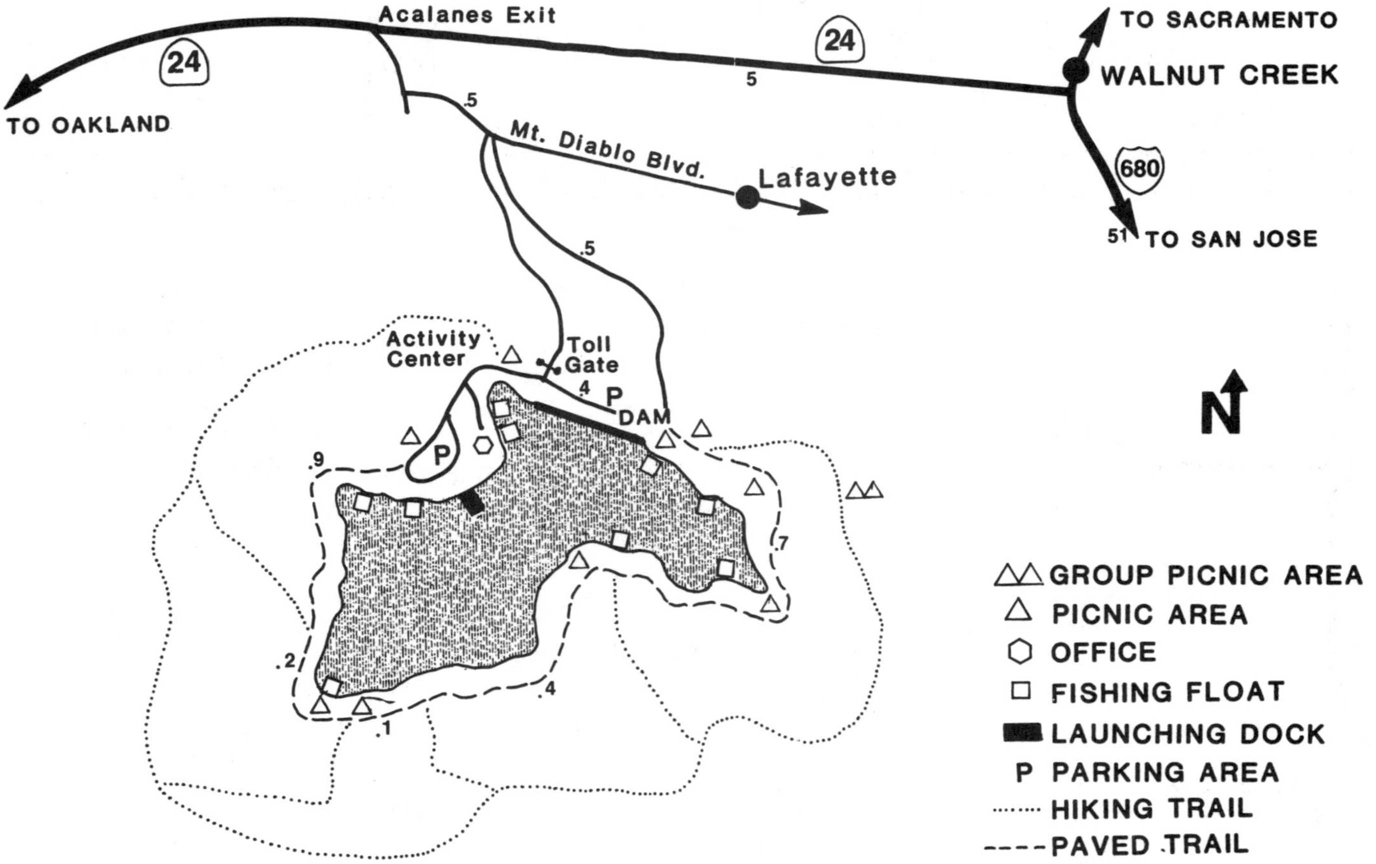

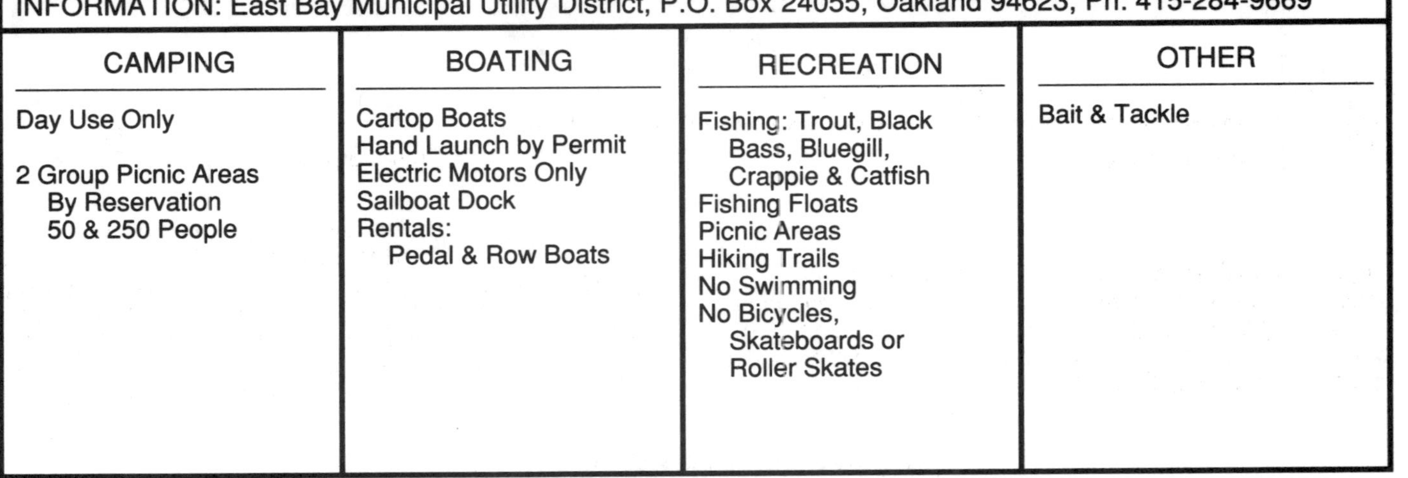

INFORMATION: East Bay Municipal Utility District, P.O. Box 24055, Oakland 94623, Ph: 415-284-9669

CAMPING	BOATING	RECREATION	OTHER
Day Use Only 2 Group Picnic Areas By Reservation 50 & 250 People	Cartop Boats Hand Launch by Permit Electric Motors Only Sailboat Dock Rentals: Pedal & Row Boats	Fishing: Trout, Black Bass, Bluegill, Crappie & Catfish Fishing Floats Picnic Areas Hiking Trails No Swimming No Bicycles, Skateboards or Roller Skates	Bait & Tackle

CONTRA LOMA RESERVOIR

Contra Loma Reservoir is located in the rolling hills of eastern Contra Costa County. This 71 acre reservoir is within the 772 acre Contra Loma Regional Park. Hiking and riding trails run through the open grasslands of the park into the adjoining Black Diamond Mines Regional Preserve. The concentration of greenery and facilities are near the water. Large shaded, turfed picnic areas and playgrounds await the visitor. There is a sandy swimming beach with a solar powered bathhouse. Wind, oar and electric powered boats are popular. The angler will find catfish, bluegill and large-mouth bass and a good striped bass population. This facility is under the jurisdiction of the East Bay Regional Park District.

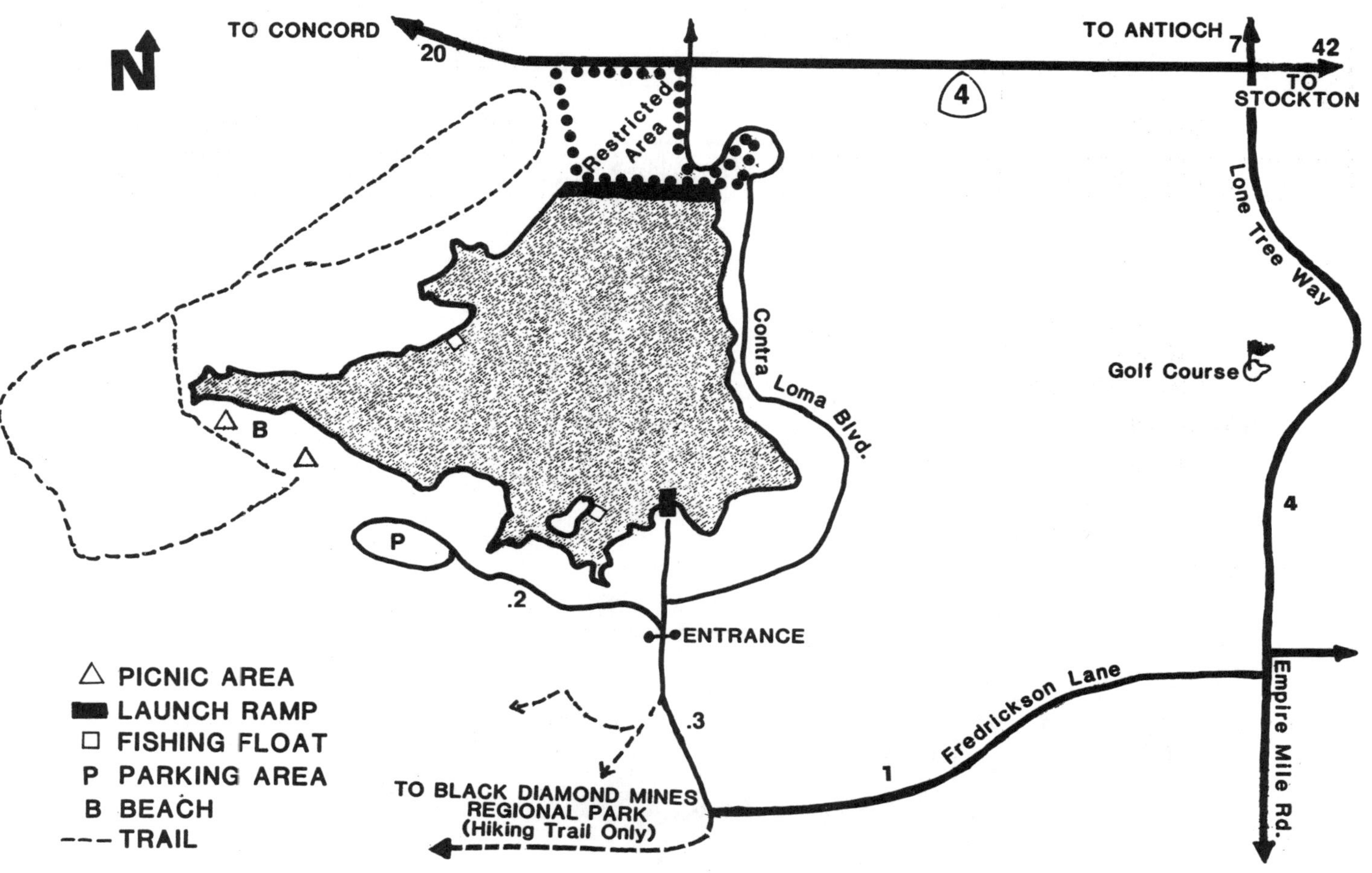

INFORMATION: East Bay Regional Parks, 11500 Skyline Blvd., Oakland 94619, Ph: 415-757-0404

CAMPING	BOATING	RECREATION	OTHER
Day Use Only	Open to Electric & Non-Powered Boats to 17 feet By Permit Launch Ramp Rentals Windsurfing Lessons	Fishing: Black Bass, Bluegill, Catfish, Crappie, Perch & Striped Bass Fishing Docks Picnic Area Hiking & Riding Trails Swimming Children's Play Area Golf Course Nearby	Snack Bar Bait & Tackle

CHABOT, CULL CANYON, DON CASTRO AND JORDAN POND

These four small lakes are within the East Bay Regional Park District. The angler will find a warm water fishery at all of these facilities and trout at Lake Chabot and Don Castro. Boating is limited to rentals at Lake Chabot. Each of these Regional Parks provide an abundance of natural attractions along with picnic facilities, hiking and riding trails. There are swimming lagoons at Cull Canyon and Don Castro. The 4,684 acre Anthony Chabot Regional Park provides an abundance of recreation facilities including an equestrian center. Cull Canyon has won the Governor's Design Award for Recreation Development. Jordan Pond is within the 1,316 acre Garin and Dry Creek Pioneer Regional Park. This scenic Park offers an interpretive center and programs conducted by park naturalists.

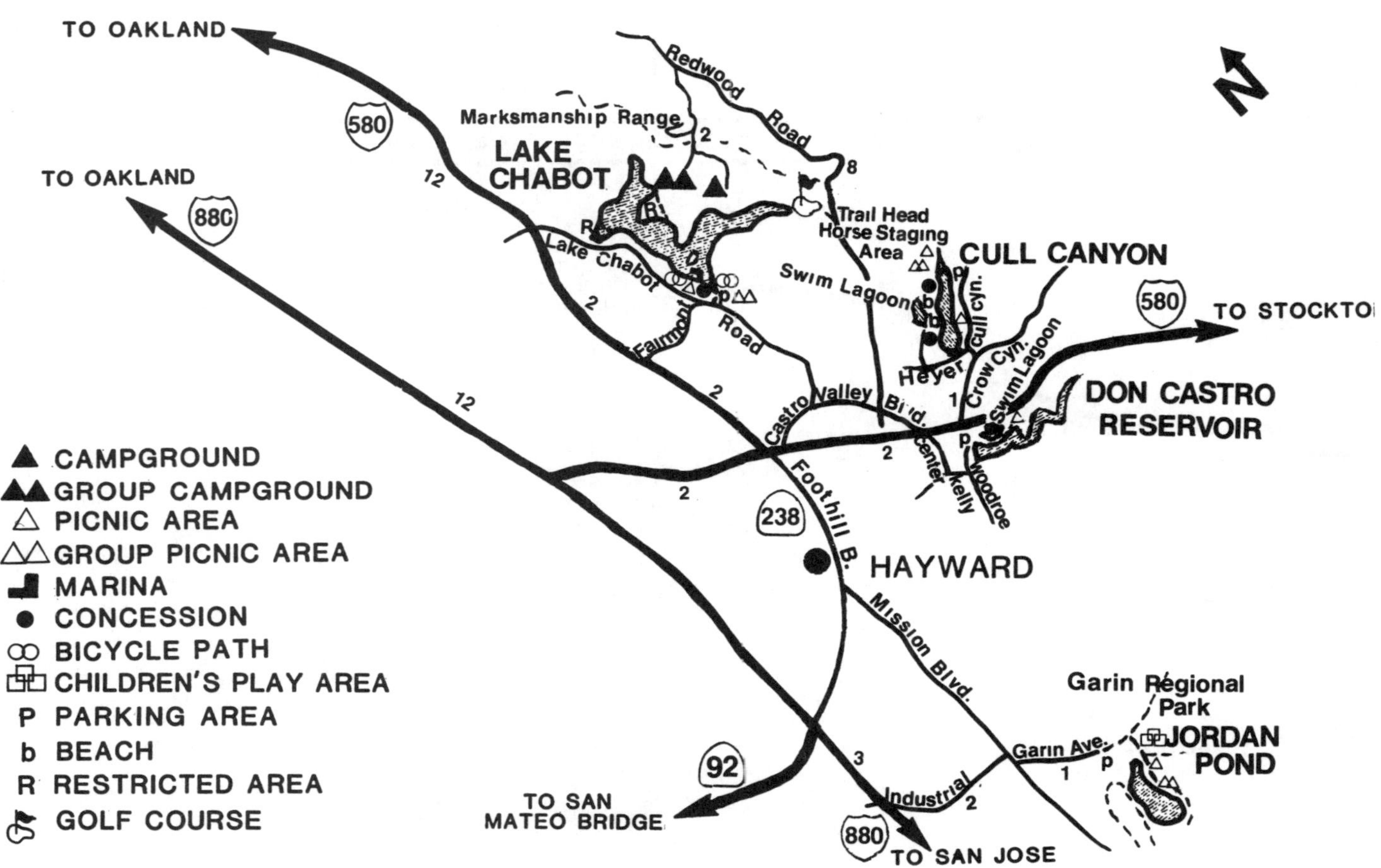

INFORMATION: East Bay Reg. Parks, 11500 Skyline Blvd., Oakland 94619, Ph: 415-531-9300

CAMPING	BOATING	RECREATION	OTHER
Lake Chabot: 73 Family Sites Youth Group Sites Phone for Current Status	Lake Chabot: No Private Boats Rentals: Electric, Row, Paddle & Canoe "Chabot Queen" Boat Tour No Boating at Other Lakes	Fishing: Trout, Black Bass, Bluegill, Catfish & Crappie Hiking, Jogging & Equestrian Trails Swimming: Don Castro & Cull Canyon Only Nature Study & Interpretive Center Playgrounds	Lake Chabot: Golf Course Equestrian Center Horse Rentals Off Skyline Blvd.

THE CALIFORNIA AQUEDUCT

The California Aqueduct provides the angler with 343 miles of open canals and 18 developed fishing access sites with parking and toilets. Striped bass, largemouth bass, catfish, crappie, green sunfish, bluegill and starry flounder are found in the San Joaquin Valley section. Striped bass, bluegill and catfish are found south of the Tehachapis where the Aqueduct splits into west and east branches.

In addition to fishing, the California Aqueduct Bikeway gives the adventurous cyclist an interesting challenge. While parking and rest stops are provided every ten miles, careful planning is advised since water, food and spare parts are not always available.

As of this publishing date, the Southern Section of the Bikeway will be closed for repairs. The 70-mile Northern Section remains open to cyclists.

Caution is advised. There are often strong currents. Although safety ladders are provided every 500 feet along the steep, slippery concrete sides of the Aqueduct, stay out of the water. It is dangerous. The 17 pumping stations are closed for 400 yards at each location.

FOR INFORMATION CONTACT:

The Department of Water Resources
P.O. Box 942836
Sacramento, CA 94236-0001

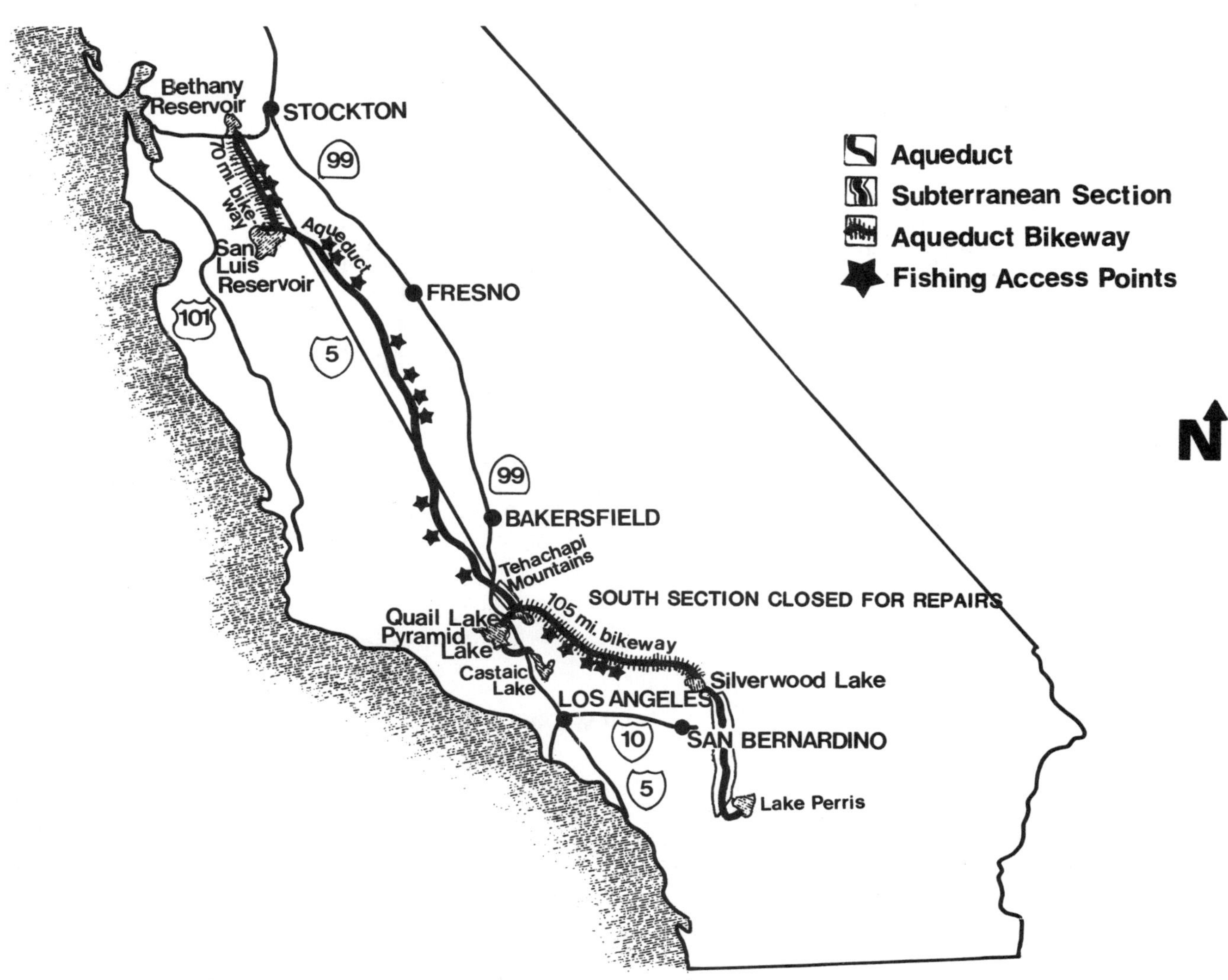

BETHANY RESERVOIR, SHADOW CLIFFS RESERVOIR, LAKE ISABEL, LAKE ELIZABETH

Within the greater Bay Area, these lakes provide an abundance of recreational opportunities. The bicycler will find a 70 mile challenge at Bethany Reservoir on the California Aqueduct Bikeway or a leisurely ride on the 2 mile bikeway around Lake Elizabeth. Boating, fishing or a day at the park can be found at these popular facilities.

. . . Continued . . .

INFORMATION: See Individual Lake for Information			
CAMPING	**BOATING**	**RECREATION**	**OTHER**
Day Use Facilities Only	Varies at Each Lake - See Following Page	Fishing: Trout, Largemouth & Striped Bass, Catfish, Bluegill & Crappie Picnicking Nature, Hiking & Jogging Trails Bicycle Trails Swimming Beaches & Lagoons	Children's Play Area Athletic Fields Waterslide Concessions at Shadow Cliffs, Isabel & Elizabeth Full Facilities Near Each Lake

BETHANY RESERVOIR, Department of Parks and Recreation, Diablo Area, 4180 Treat Blvd., Suite D, Concord 94521, Ph: 415-687-1800. Day Use Fee: $3.

Bethany Reservoir State Recreation Area rests in gently rolling, grass-covered hills overlooking the vast Delta of the Sacramento and San Joaquin Rivers. This 162 acre reservoir is open to all types of boating with a 5 MPH speed limit. Jet skis are not permitted at any time. Strong winds can be a hazard. This is a popular warm water fishery for striped bass and catfish. There is a parking lot for 120 cars, a 2-lane launch ramp and 4 picnic ramadas. Bethany is the northern terminus for the California Aqueduct Bikeway.

SHADOW CLIFFS RESERVOIR, East Bay Regional Park District, 11500 Skyline Blvd., Oakland 94619, Ph: 415-531-9300. Parking Fee.

This reservoir has been transformed from a bleak sand and gravel quarry to a complete 249 acre park. The 74 surface acre lake is open to all non-powered boating, and you may rent a fishing boat, canoe or paddle boat. Trout, largemouth bass, and channel and white catfish and Bluegill await the angler. There is a sandy beach and swimming. A waterslide is in a separate area of the park. The park has picnic areas, turfed areas, hiking and equestrian trails and a food concession. Handicap facilities are available.

LAKE ISABEL, 1421 Isabel Avenue, Livermore 94550, Ph: 415-462-1281. Day Use.
Fees: $9.00 Adults, $4.50 Children.

This 35 acre private lake was opened to the public in the fall of 1982. There are no facilities for private boats, but you may rent a fishing boat with electric motor. Rainbow trout range from 3/4 pounds to 10 pounds and are planted weekly in season. When the water is too warm for trout, channel catfish up to 10 pounds will be planted. There are plenty of bluegill, crappie and largemouth bass. The concession has tackle, bait, food and beer. Picnic areas and facilities for the handicapped are available.

LAKE ELIZABETH, The Boathouse, P.O. Box 5006, Fremont 94538, Ph: 415-791-4340. Day Use and Lake Use Fee.

This Lake is within the beautiful Fremont Central Park and has been expanded recently to 80 surface acres. There are complete facilities for non-powered boating including ramps, docks, storage and rental canoe and paddle boats. This is a good sailing lake with westerly winds which can become strong in the afternoons. Trout are planted except for the summer months when the water is too warm. There are also black bass, bluegill and catfish. The well maintained park has an abundance of recreational facilities with open turfed areas, snack bars, picnic areas, tennis courts, athletic fields, and a swim lagoon. The 1.96 mile pedway around the lake accommodates joggers, hikers and bikers at this complete city facility.

DEL VALLE RESERVOIR

Del Valle Reservoir is at an elevation of 700 feet in oak-covered rolling hills near Livermore. The Lake has a surface area of 750 acres with 16 miles of shoreline. The 4,249 acre Del Valle Park is under the jurisdiction of the East Bay Regional Park District. In addition to the large tree-shaded campgrounds, there are primitive group campsites, picnic areas and marina facilities. Ten miles of scenic trails await the hiker or equestrian. Boating is limited to 10 miles per hour. Two guarded swimming beaches are open from May through September. During the rest of the year, you can swim at your own risk. This is a very popular windsurfing lake.

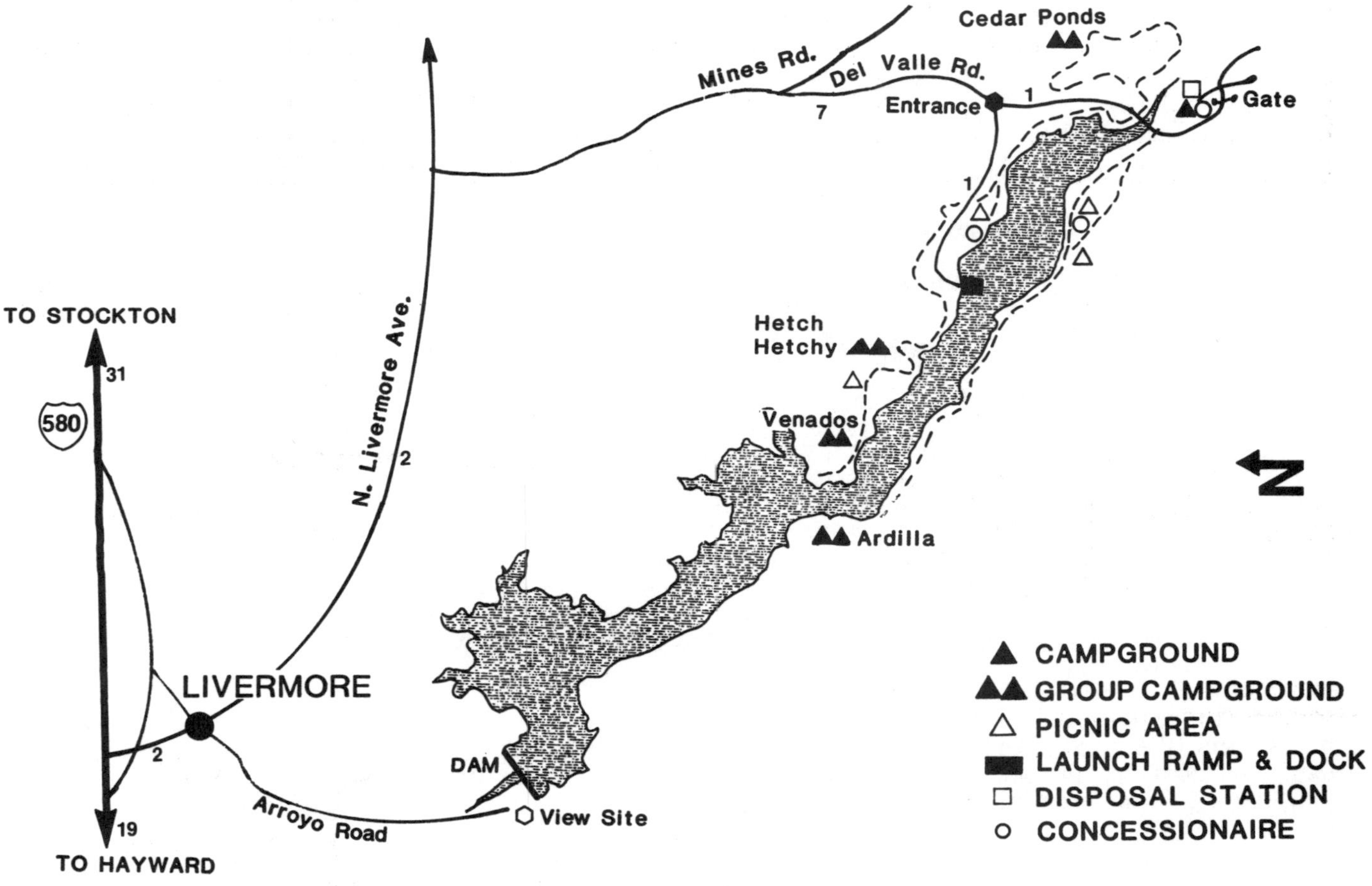

TO STOCKTON
31
580
TO HAYWARD
19
LIVERMORE
2
N. Livermore Ave.
Arroyo Road
DAM
View Site
Mines Rd.
Del Valle Rd.
7
Entrance
1
Cedar Ponds
Gate
Hetch Hetchy
Venados
Ardilla
N

CAMPGROUND
GROUP CAMPGROUND
PICNIC AREA
LAUNCH RAMP & DOCK
DISPOSAL STATION
CONCESSIONAIRE

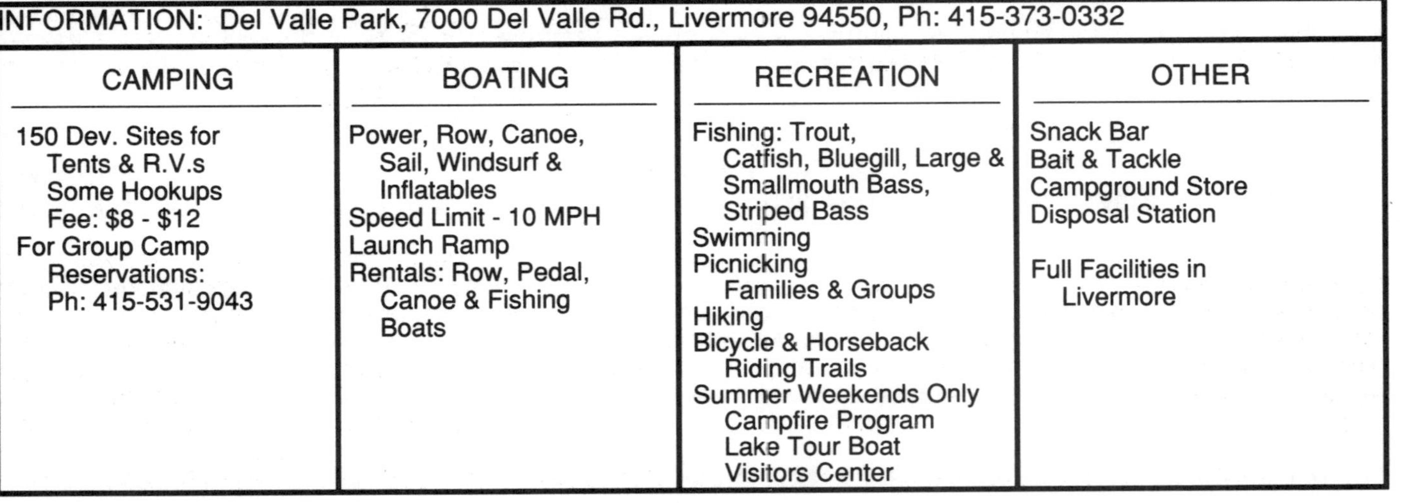

INFORMATION: Del Valle Park, 7000 Del Valle Rd., Livermore 94550, Ph: 415-373-0332

CAMPING	BOATING	RECREATION	OTHER
150 Dev. Sites for Tents & R.V.s Some Hookups Fee: $8 - $12 For Group Camp Reservations: Ph: 415-531-9043	Power, Row, Canoe, Sail, Windsurf & Inflatables Speed Limit - 10 MPH Launch Ramp Rentals: Row, Pedal, Canoe & Fishing Boats	Fishing: Trout, Catfish, Bluegill, Large & Smallmouth Bass, Striped Bass Swimming Picnicking Families & Groups Hiking Bicycle & Horseback Riding Trails Summer Weekends Only Campfire Program Lake Tour Boat Visitors Center	Snack Bar Bait & Tackle Campground Store Disposal Station Full Facilities in Livermore

LAKE MERCED, SHORELINE PARK AND STEVENS CREEK RESERVOIR

These three urban lakes provide a welcome variety of recreation opportunities. Lake Merced has a surface area of 396 acres. This is a popular sailing lake and one of the better fishing lakes where Rainbow and some Brook trout grow to Lunker size while feeding on fresh water shrimp. The relatively new Shoreline Lake provides the windsurfer and sailor with 50 acres of saltwater excitement. Shoreline Park is primarily open space with protected wildlife areas reached by paved trails. The prevailing north westerly winds make this a popular windsurfing lake. Stevens Creek Reservoir, 92 acres when full, provides the angler with a warm water fishery and small craft boating. There are nice oak-shaded trails for the hiker and equestrian. Family and group picnic sites are available.

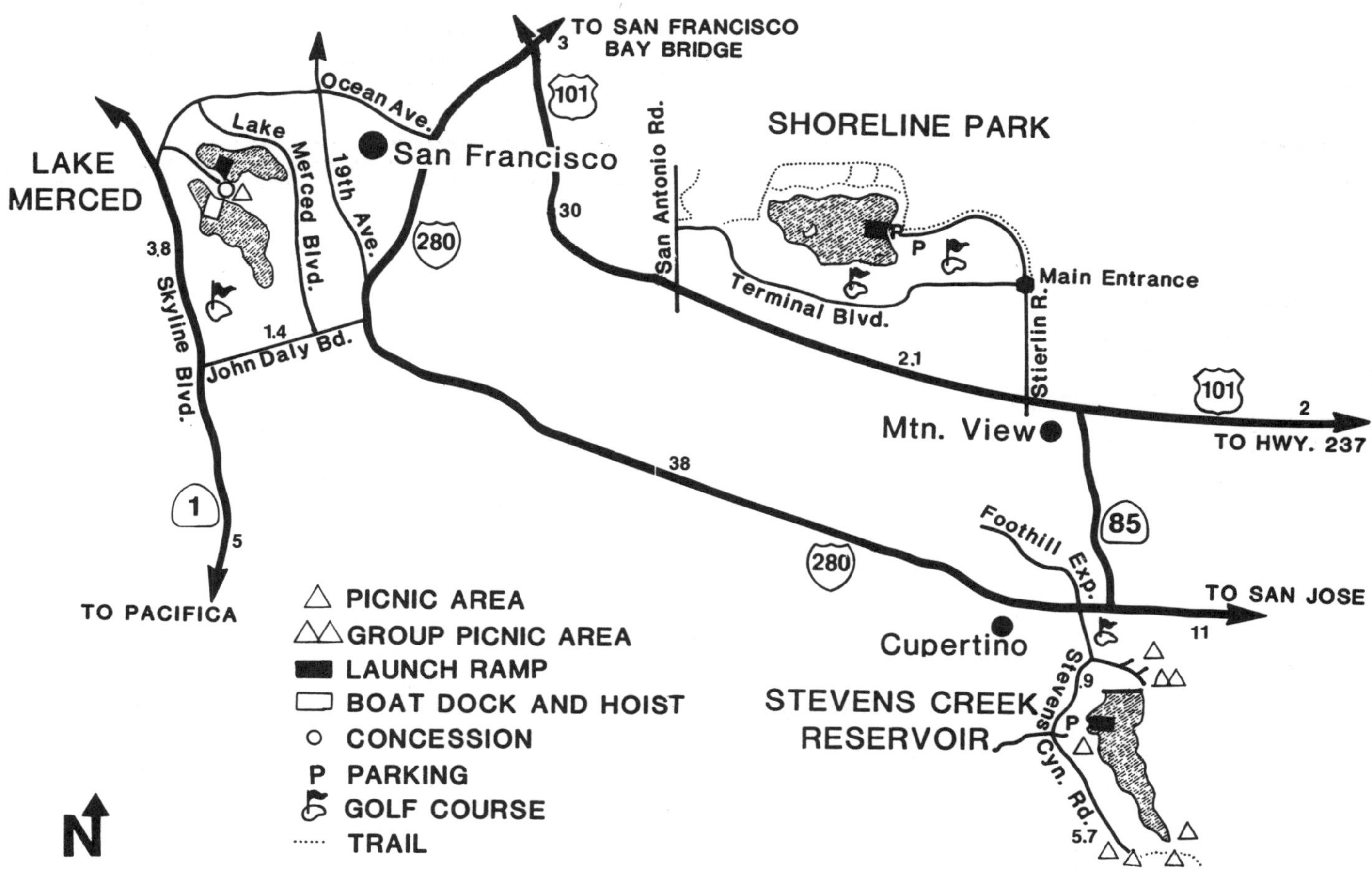

INFORMATION: Lake Merced Boat House, 1 Harding Way, San Francisco, Ph: 415-753-1101			
CAMPING	BOATING	RECREATION	OTHER
Day Use Only No Camping Stevens Creek Park: Group Picnic Area Reservations: Ph: 408-358-3751	**Lake Merced:** Sail & Row to 18 Feet Hoists & Floats Rentals: Fishing Boats, Electric Motors **Shoreline Park:** Row, Sail, Canoe & Windsurf to 14' Lessons Launch Ramp & Docks STEVENS CREEK: Sail & Row Boats No Power Boats 2-Lane Launch Ramp	Fishing: Rainbow & Brook Trout, Bass, Bluegill, Catfish & Crappie Picnicking Hiking, Bicycle & Riding Trails Nature Study Birdwatching	Spinnaker Sailing Shoreline Park Mountain View 94040 Ph: 415-965-7474 Stevens Creek Res. Santa Clara County Parks Dept. 298 Garden Hill Dr. Los Gatos 95030 Ph: 408-358-3741 Lake Merced Boathouse: Sports Bar, Restaurant, Night Club

VASONA, LEXINGTON AND LOS GATOS CREEK PARK

These three lakes are located off Highway 17 in the southwest corner of Santa Clara County. They are under the jurisdiction of the County's Parks and Recreation Department. Lexington is the largest of the three. While facilities are limited, rowers, windsurfers and anglers find its waters attractive. Vasona is a pretty 57 acre Lake surrounded by 94 acres of turfed activity areas, picnic sites and paved paths.

This popular family park offers good sailing and support facilities. Los Gatos Creek Park is commonly known as the "Campbell Perculation Ponds." Although boating is not allowed, seldom can you drive by on Highway 17 and not see the colorful sails of windsurfers. Fishing is popular and there are picnic facilities available as well as walking, exercise, and bicycle paths.

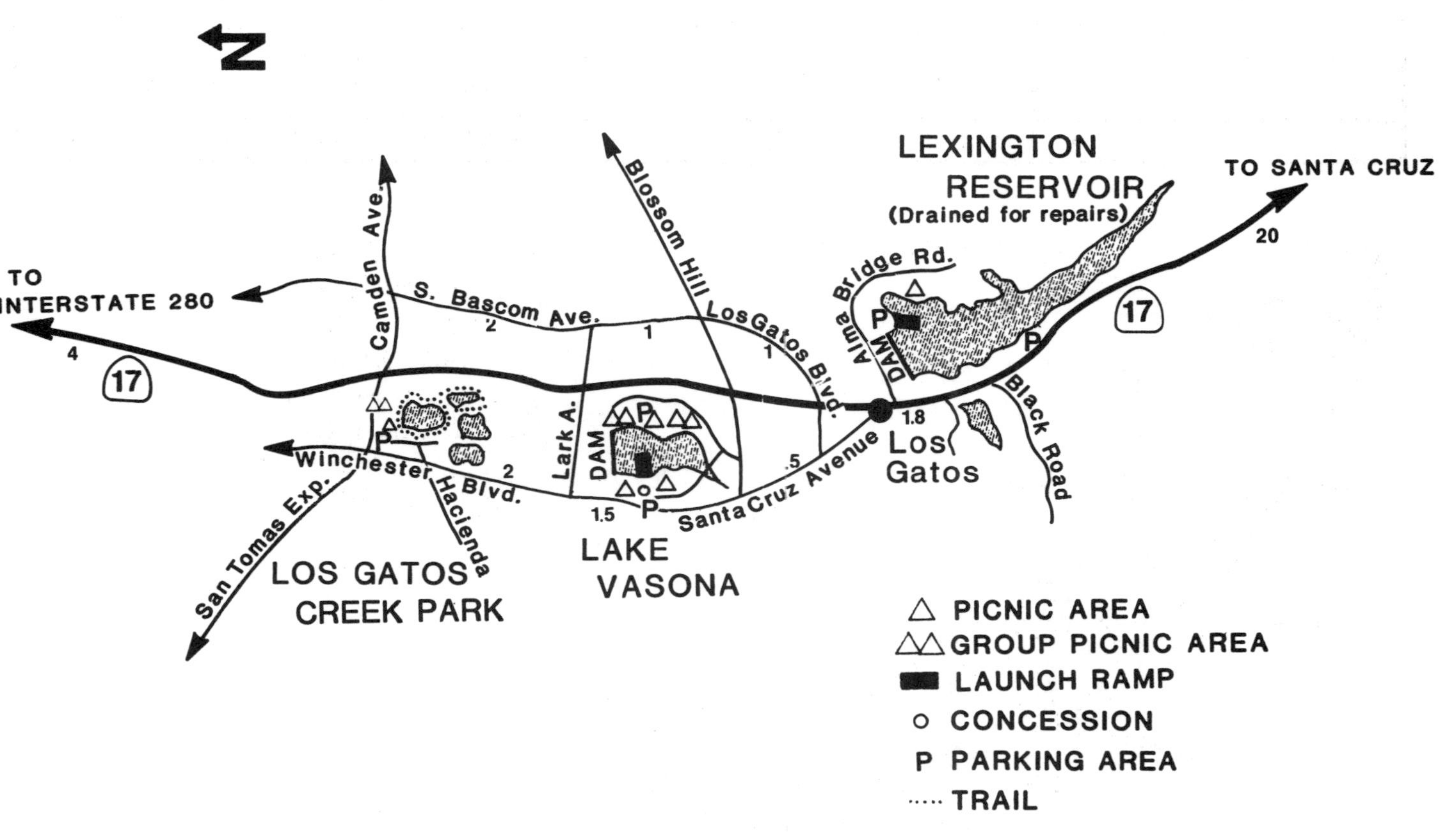

INFORMATION: County Parks & Rec., 298 Garden Hill Dr., Los Gatos 95030, Ph: 408-358-3741			
CAMPING	BOATING	RECREATION	OTHER
Day Use Only No Camping Reservations for Group Picnic Areas or Special Events: Ph: 408-358-3751	VASONA: Sail, Canoe Row, Windsurfer No Motors Launch Ramp - $2 Docks, Dry Storage LEXINGTON: Power Boats:& Even-numbered Days Sail & Under 10 HP Boats: Odd-numbered Days Launch Ramp - $2 Check for Current Conditions	Fishing: Trout, Bass, Bluegill, Catfish & Crappie Picnic Areas Hiking & Jogging Trails Playground at Oak Meadow Next to Vasona and Bill Jones Railroad	Full Facilities in Los Gatos & San Jose Water Level is Often Low in Late Summer and Fall

ALMADEN LAKE, GUADALUPE, CALERO, CHESBRO, UVAS, AND ALMADEN RESERVOIRS

Almaden Lake Regional Park is administered by the City of San Jose. There is a small 36 acre sailing and fishing lake, a swim beach and lagoon and picnic sites within this 36 acre park. The following lakes are under the jurisdiction of Santa Clara County: Guadalupe and Almaden Reservoirs, approximately 60 acres each, are open to non-powered boating and fishing. They are adjacent to Almaden Quicksilver Park which is a popular hiking and equestrian facility. Chesbro and Uvas, under the jurisdiction of Santa Clara Valley Water District, are primarily small fishing lakes with picnic sites. Calero Reservoir, 349 surface acres, is a popular power boating and waterskiing lake with a sandy beach and picnic facilities. At low water levels, from approximately October through January, the ramp may be closed.

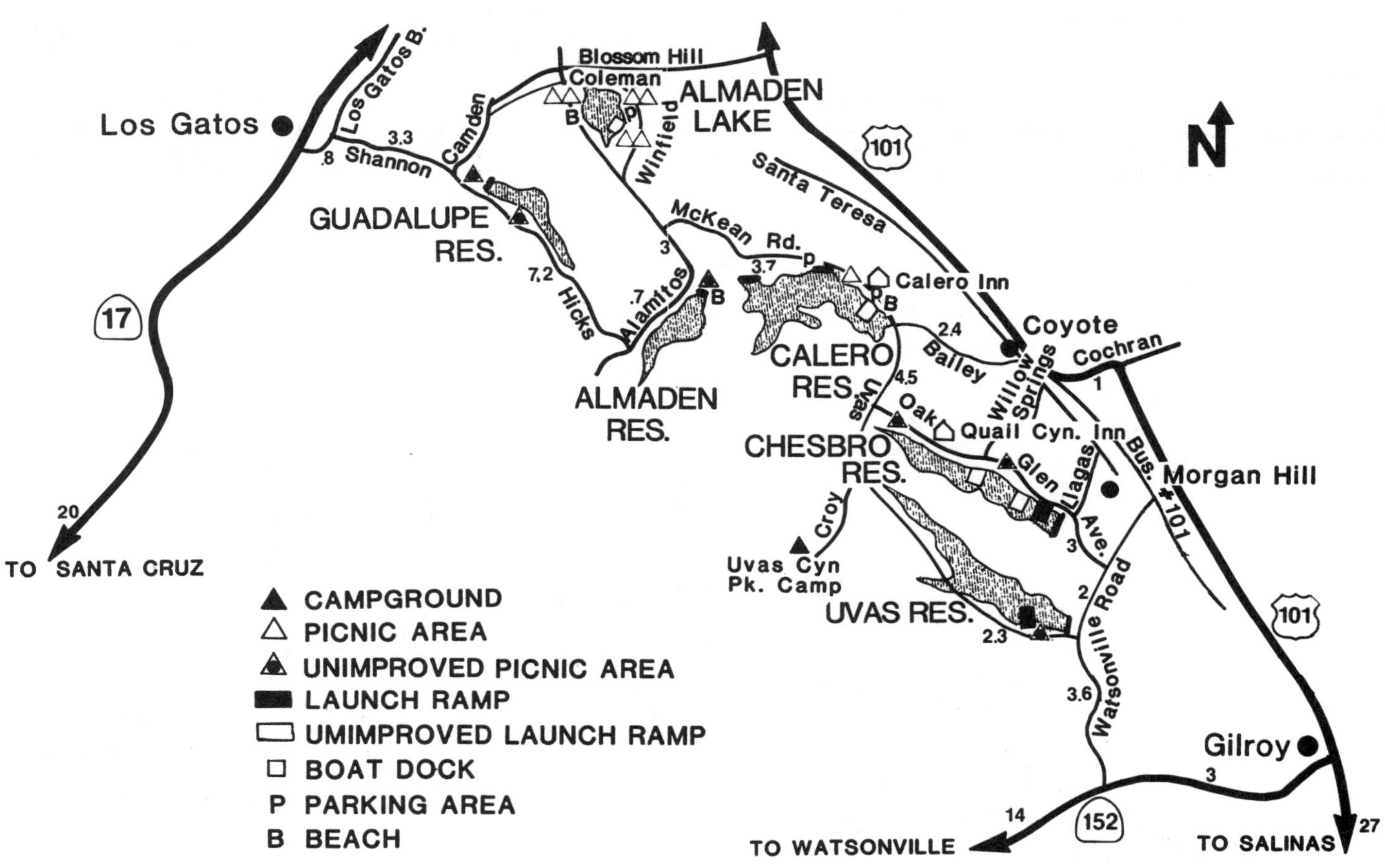

INFORMATION: County Parks, 298 Garden Hill Dr., Los Gatos 95030, Ph: 408-358-3741

CAMPING	BOATING	RECREATION	OTHER
Uvas Canyon Park: 30 Dev. Sites for Tents & R.V.s Fee: $8 No Reservations Youth Group Camping Ph: 408-358-3751 Almaden Lake - Open May - September	Almaden Lake: Sail & Non-Power Boating Launch Ramp - Fee: $2 Windsurf & Paddleboat Rentals Guadalupe & Almaden Rs: Non-Power Boating Chesbro & Uvas: Sail, Row & Electric Motors - Launch Ramp Calero: Power, Waterskiing, Jet Skis Launch Ramp	Fishing: Bass, Catfish, Bluegill & Crappie Swimming: Almaden Lake & Calero Picnicking Hiking Riding Trails Almaden Lake: Parking: $2 Walk-In: 50 cents	Almaden Lake: City of San Jose 151 W. Mission St. San Jose 95110 Ph: 408-277-4661 Santa Clara Water Dist. 5750 Almaden Express. San Jose 95118 Ph: 408-265-2600 Almaden Quicksilver Park: 3,598 Acres of Trails

LAKE CUNNINGHAM, ED. R. LEVIN, J. D. GRANT AND COYOTE-HELLYER PARKS

Lake Cunningham Regional Park is under the jurisdiction of the City of San Jose. This 200 acre park provides the visitor with numerous turfed picnic sites, walking and jogging paths and a 50 acre boating and fishing Lake. Its Raging Waters concession provides a variety of waterslides, activity pools, swimming lagoon, beach, river rides, and a myriad of other activities. The County of Santa Clara operates Ed R. Levin Park, Coyote-Hellyer Park and the mountainous J. D. Grant Park. Hellyer provides a velodrome and an 8-foot wide, 5.9 mile long bicycle trail. The rugged 9,422 acres of Grant Park offers the adventuresome angler, hiker, mountain biker and equestrian a more remote experience. There are horse rentals at Grant Stables, phone 408-274-9258.

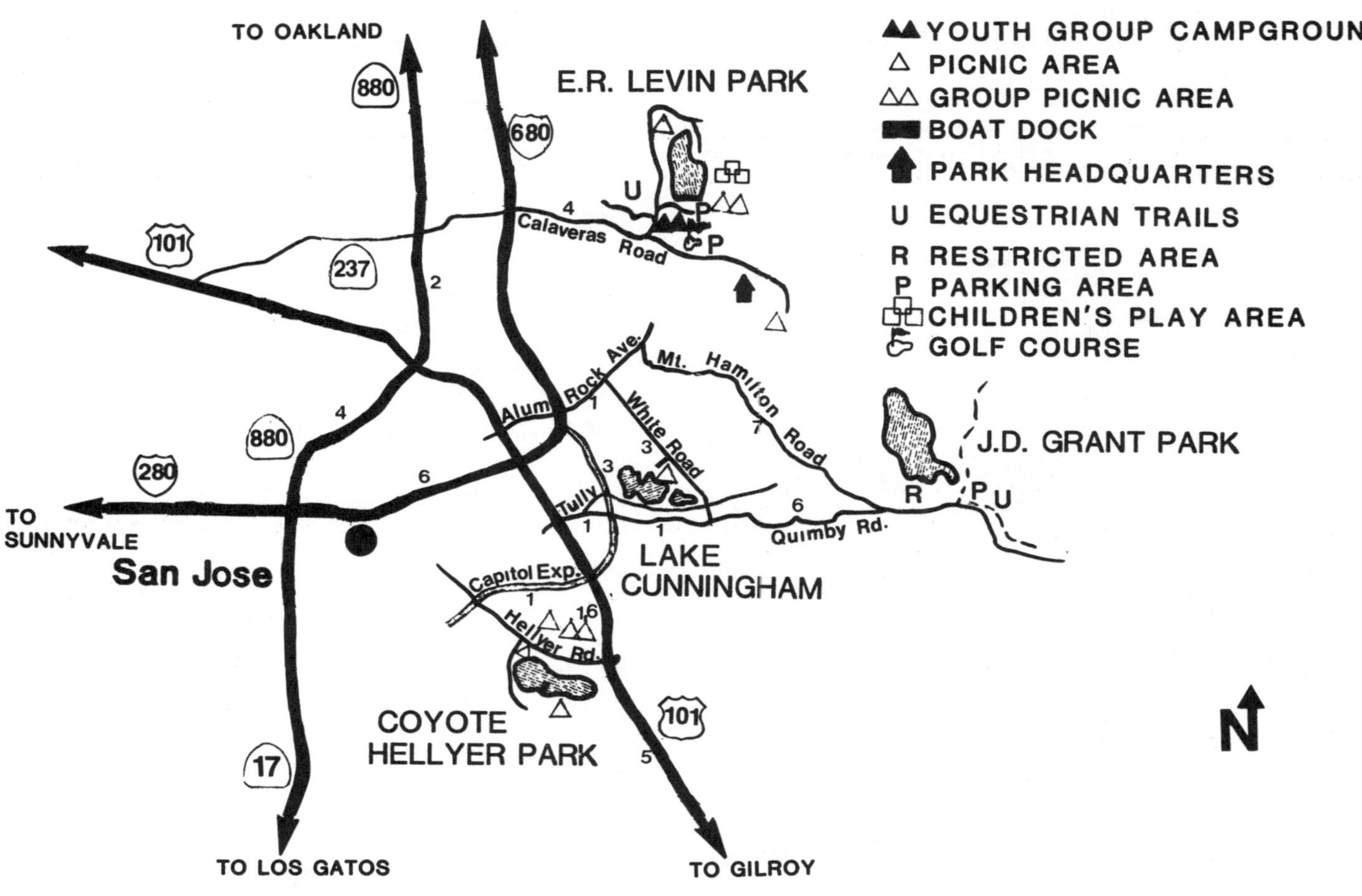

INFORMATION: Lake Cunningham - 151 W. Mission, Rm. 203, San Jose 95110, Ph: 408-277-4661			
CAMPING	**BOATING**	**RECREATION**	**OTHER**
Day Use Only Lake Cunningham Regional Park Parking Fee: $1 Levin, Grant & Hellyer: Youth Group Camping, Picnicking & Special Events Ph: 408-358-3751	Lake Cunningham: Non-Power Boats, Sail & Windsurf Launch Ramp Rentals: Row, Canoe Paddle, Sail & Windsurf Levin & Hellyer: Small Sail, Row & Electric Motor Boats Launch Ramp at Coyote-Hellyer	Fishing: Largemouth Bass, Bluegill, Crappie & Catfish Coyote-Hellyer: Trout Picnicking Walking & Jogging Cycle Races Hiking & Riding Trails Mountain Biking Bicycling, Golf Horse Rentals Near E. R. Levin Park	Levin, Grant & Hellyer Parks: Santa Clara Co. 298 Garden Hill Dr. Lost Gatos 95030 Ph: 408-358-3741 Raging Waters: 2333 S. White Rd. San Jose 95148 Ph: 408-238-9900 Fees: $12.50 Group Rates

ANDERSON AND PARKWAY LAKES

Anderson Lake is the largest body of fresh water in Santa Clara County. It is 7 miles long with a surface area of 1,244 acres. This is a popular boating and waterskiing lake. Afternoon winds make for good sailing and windsurfing. There are two launch ramps and the angler will find a warm water fishery. The County of Santa Clara has picnic sites near the dam as well as a boat-in picnic area on the northwestern shore. Parkway is a 35-acre privately operated fishing lake. Planted year around with large trout, channel catfish and Florida strain largemouth bass and sturgeon, the lake usually rewards the angler with a good catch.

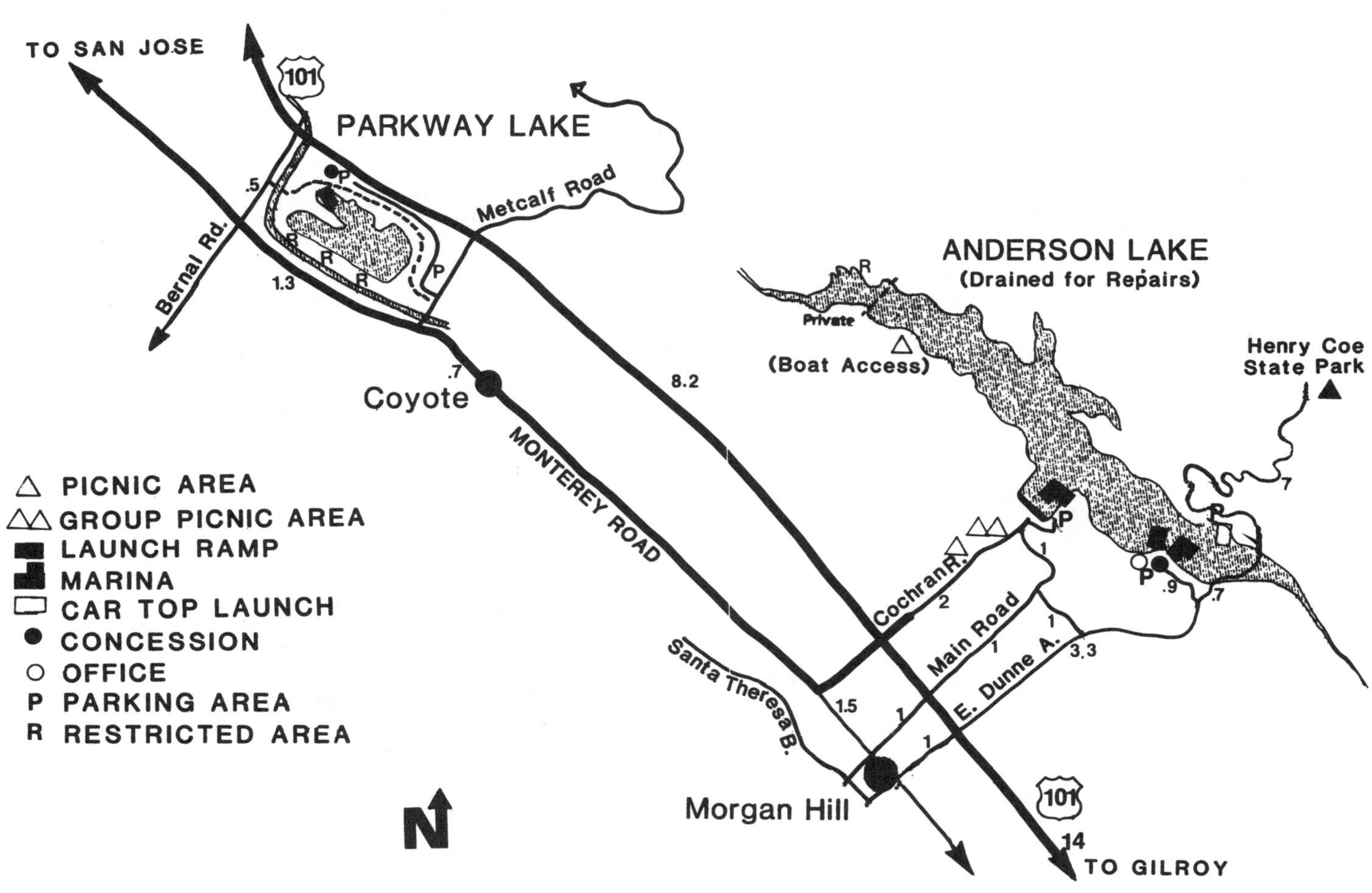

INFORMATION: Anderson Lake Co. Parks, 298 Garden Hill Dr., Los Gatos 95030, Ph: 408-358-3741			
CAMPING	**BOATING**	**RECREATION**	**OTHER**
Day Use Only Henry Coe State Park: 20 Tent & R.V. Primitive Sites P.O. Box 846 Morgan Hill Ph: 408-779-2728 Anderson: Group Picnic Areas For Reservations: Ph: 408-358-3751	ANDERSON: Open to All Boating - Check for Current Conditions Launch Ramps & Docks PARKWAY: No Private Boats Fishing Boat Rentals: $15	Fishing: Rainbow Trout, Largemouth Bass, Catfish, Crappie & Bluegill Sturgeon in Parkway Picnicking Hiking Riding Trails Parkway Fishing Fee: $10 - Adults $ 6 - Children $ 3 - Spectator	Parkway Lake: Metcalf Road Coyote 95013 Ph: 408-463-0383 Concession: Bait & Tackle Snacks

LOCH LOMOND

Loch Lomond rests at an elevation of 577 feet in the Santa Cruz Mountains. This scenic 3-1/2 mile long Reservoir is under the jurisdiction of the City of Santa Cruz. The Lake is open to quiet non-powered boating. Although there is a launch ramp, water level fluctuation can limit its use, so call for current status. Fishing is a prime attraction and often productive. An aeration system has been recently installed which should enhance the already good fishery. There are over 100 picnic sites around the shoreline. Several hiking trails are along the shore and into the coniferous forest of oak, madrone, pine and redwood trees. In addition to naturalist programs, there is a self-guided Big Trees Nature Trail.

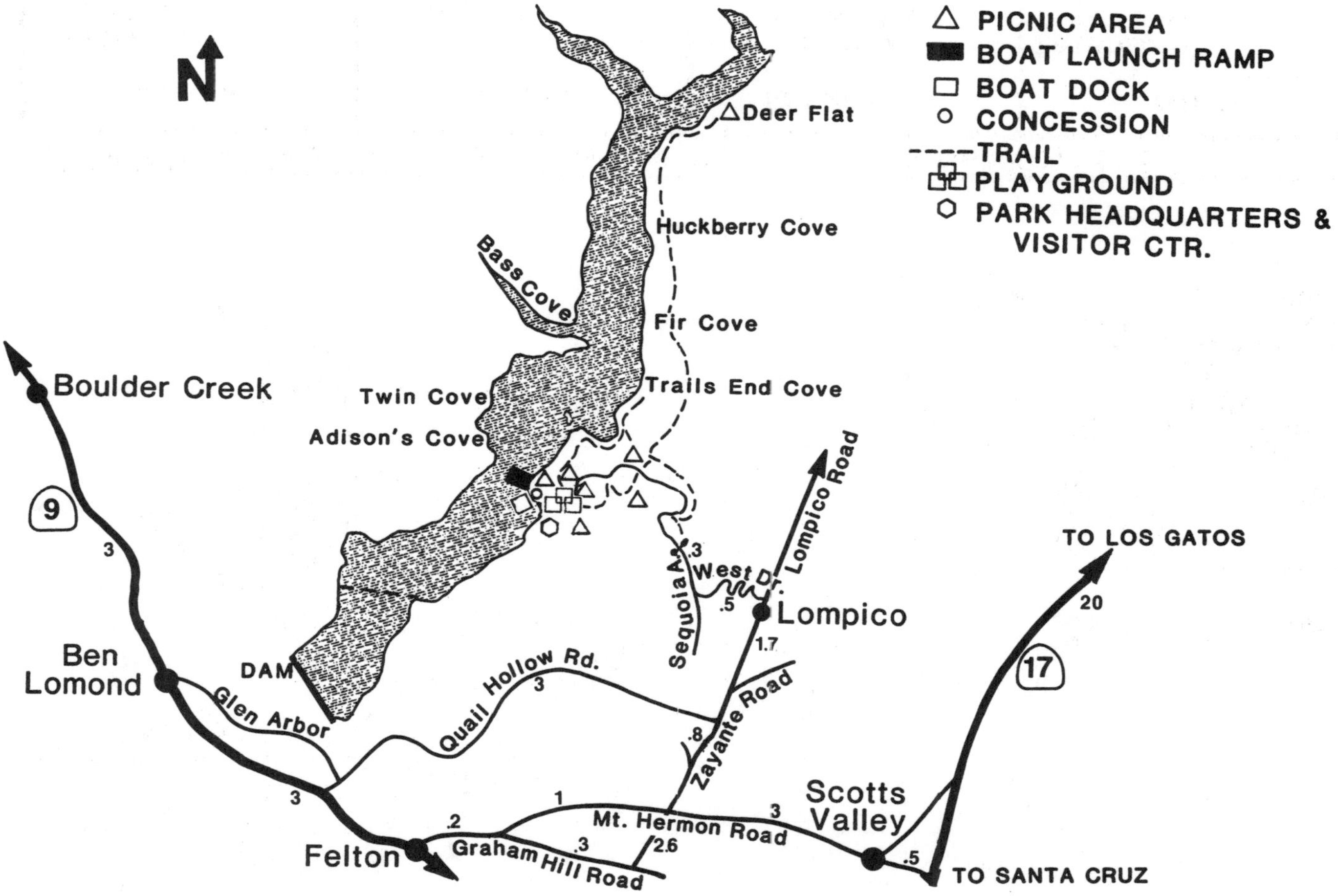

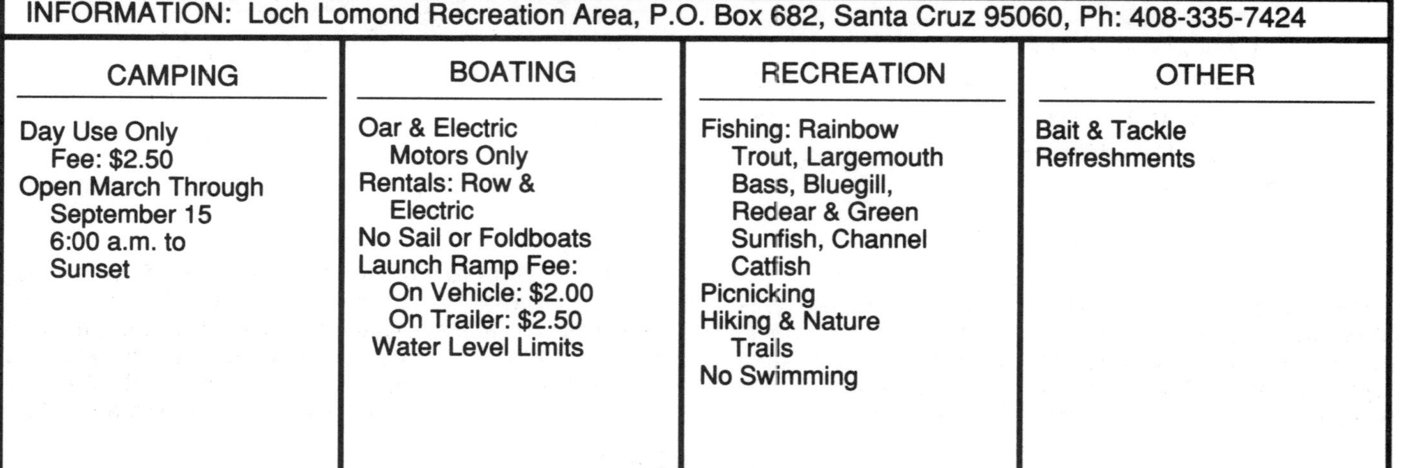

INFORMATION: Loch Lomond Recreation Area, P.O. Box 682, Santa Cruz 95060, Ph: 408-335-7424			
CAMPING	BOATING	RECREATION	OTHER
Day Use Only Fee: $2.50 Open March Through September 15 6:00 a.m. to Sunset	Oar & Electric Motors Only Rentals: Row & Electric No Sail or Foldboats Launch Ramp Fee: On Vehicle: $2.00 On Trailer: $2.50 Water Level Limits	Fishing: Rainbow Trout, Largemouth Bass, Bluegill, Redear & Green Sunfish, Channel Catfish Picnicking Hiking & Nature Trails No Swimming	Bait & Tackle Refreshments

PINTO LAKE

Pinto Lake is under the jurisdiction of the City of Watsonville. This nice facility provides the visitor with a picnic area, a group picnic site, large turfed areas and a baseball field. The 92 acre Lake is popular with sailors and windsurfers who enjoy incoming Pacific breezes. There is a warm water fishery along with planted trout. Marmo's is a privately owned campground on the south westerly shore of the Lake offering campsites, a launch ramp, boat rentals and cafe. Santa Cruz County maintains a 180 acre wildlife refuge and park on the north end of the Lake with over 130 species of birds, nature trails and group picnic facilities. For reservations, phone 408-425-2394.

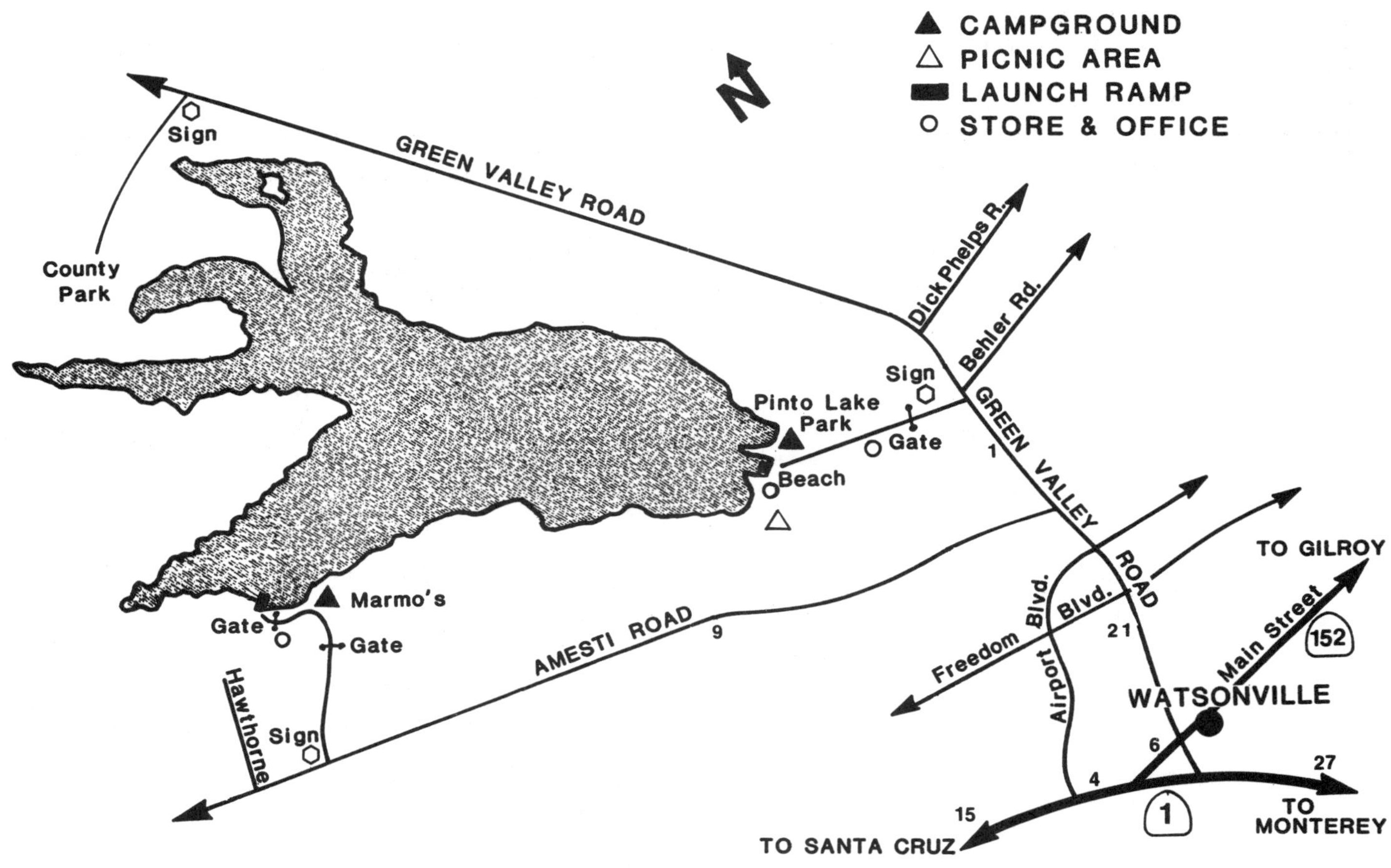

INFORMATION: Pinto Lake, 451 Green Valley Rd., Watsonville 95076, Ph: 408-722-8129			
CAMPING	BOATING	RECREATION	OTHER
Pinto Lake Park: 28 R.V. Sites Full Hookups Fee: $12 Marmo's Pinto Lake: 22 Tent & R.V. Sites Water & Electric Hookups Fee: $15	Power, Row, Canoe, Sail, Windsurf Speed Limit: 5 MPH Rentals: Fishing, Paddle, Canoe & Windsurfer Windsurfing Lessons	Fishing: Rainbow Trout, Largemouth Bass, Bluegill, Crappie & Catfish Picnicking Group Picnicking - Reservations Swimming - Designated Areas Hiking & Nature Trails Bird Watching	Snack Bar Bait & Tackle Marmo's Pinto Lake 324 Amesti Road Watsonville 95076 Ph: 408-722-4533

COYOTE RESERVOIR

Coyote Reservoir is at an elevation of 777 feet in the scenic, oak-covered hills near Gilroy. Santa Clara County provides facilities for lakeside camping, picnicking, hiking, fishing and all types of boating. This pretty lake is open at the northwest end, so the breezes come down the length of the Lake which makes for good sailing and windsurfing. The Reservoir is open year around from 8:00 a.m. to sunset for day users. Campers may fish from shore during the night, but there is no night boating permitted.

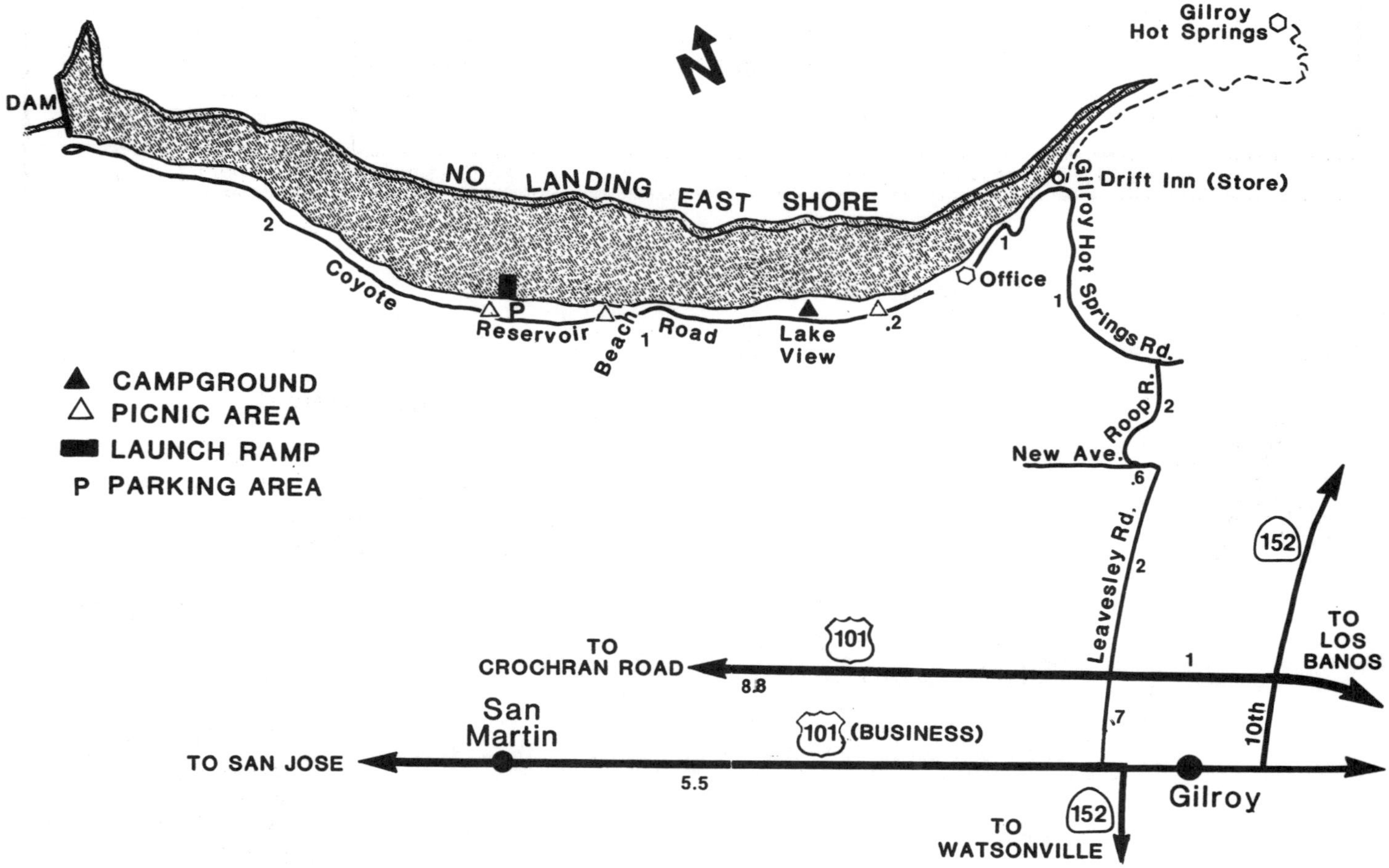

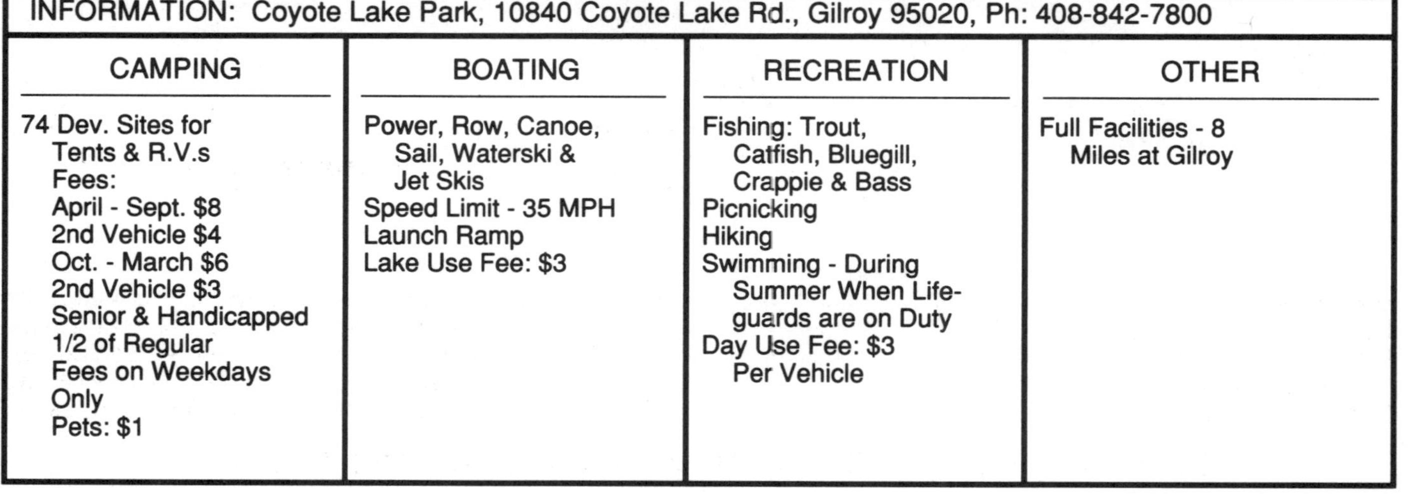

INFORMATION: Coyote Lake Park, 10840 Coyote Lake Rd., Gilroy 95020, Ph: 408-842-7800

CAMPING	BOATING	RECREATION	OTHER
74 Dev. Sites for Tents & R.V.s Fees: April - Sept. $8 2nd Vehicle $4 Oct. - March $6 2nd Vehicle $3 Senior & Handicapped 1/2 of Regular Fees on Weekdays Only Pets: $1	Power, Row, Canoe, Sail, Waterski & Jet Skis Speed Limit - 35 MPH Launch Ramp Lake Use Fee: $3	Fishing: Trout, Catfish, Bluegill, Crappie & Bass Picnicking Hiking Swimming - During Summer When Life-guards are on Duty Day Use Fee: $3 Per Vehicle	Full Facilities - 8 Miles at Gilroy

EL ESTERO, LAGUNA SECA, LOWER AND UPPER ABBOTT LAKES

These three Recreation Parks in Monterey County range from a nice day use City Park in Monterey to a Forest Service Campground at Arroyo Seco. The Laguna Seca Recreational Area is one of the most complete parks in the State with a modern campground and a small 10 acre Lake. El Estero is a pretty Lake in downtown Monterey with a children's play area, picnic facilities and athletic fields. The Abbott or Twin Lakes are in the Los Padres National Forest and offer family and group campgrounds and a warm water fishery. Trout fishing and swimming are popular in the Arroyo Seco River.

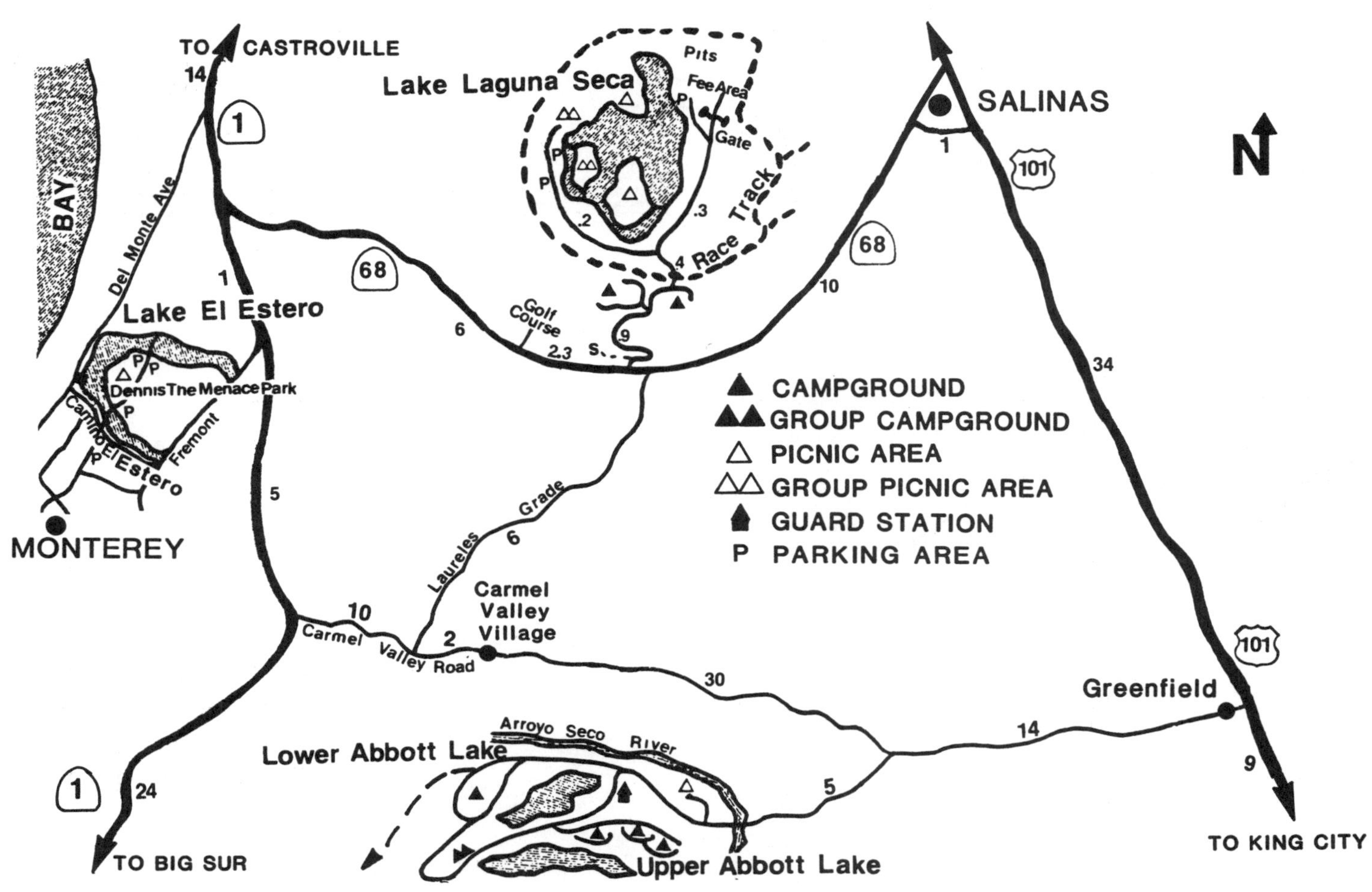

INFORMATION: Laguna Seca Recreation Area, P.O. Box 5279, Salinas 93915, Ph: 408-755-4899			
CAMPING	BOATING	RECREATION	OTHER
Laguna Seca: 77 Tents Sites 98 R.V. Sites with Electric & Water Ph: 408-755-4899 U. S. F. S. Arroyo Seco—Abbott Lakes: 46 Sites & Group Site King City Ranger Station Ph: 408-385-5434	El Estero: Paddle Boat Rental Abbott Lakes: Canoeing	Fishing: Trout, Bass & Catfish Picnicking Hiking Playgrounds Laguna Seca: Rifle & Pistol Range Motorcross Track Festivals Concerts Auto Races Race School	El Estero Lake: City of Monterey Recreation & Community Services Department 546 Dutra St. Monterey 93940 Ph: 408-646-3866 Full Facilities & Golf Courses in Monterey Monterey Jazz Festival Salinas Rodeo

SAN JUSTO RESERVOIR

San Justo Reservoir rests in the low rolling hills west of Hollister. First opened to the public in the fall of 1988, this is San Benito County's first and one of California's newest recreation lakes. This pretty 200 surface acre lake offers a varied recreational format. Boating is restricted to non-powered craft except for those with electric motors. The prevailing winds make this a good sailing and windsurfing environment.

A black bass and catfish population is being established which should be enhanced by anchored trees at the bottom of the lake for fish habitat. Facilities are limited to a launch ramp and sheltered picnic areas. The lake is open to the public on Saturday, Sunday and Monday from sunrise to sunset.

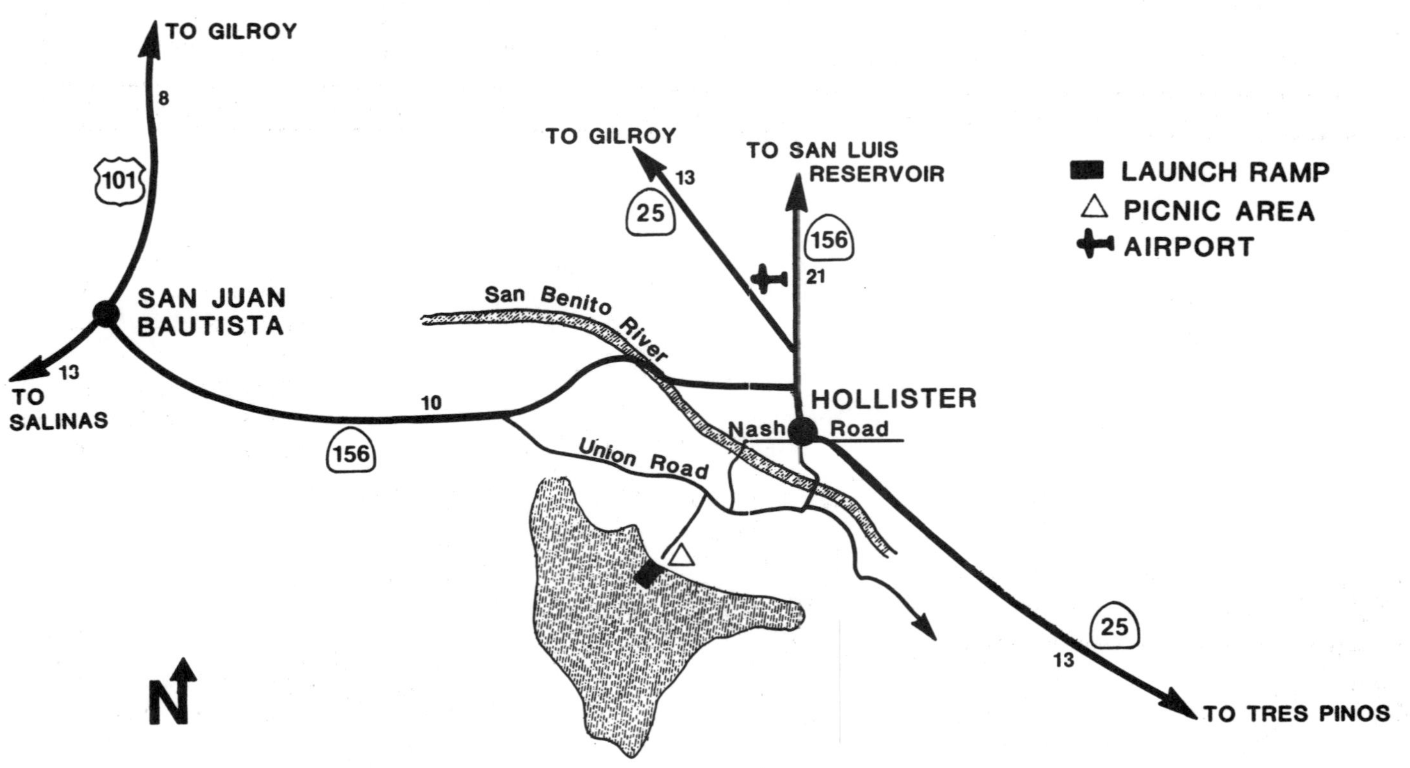

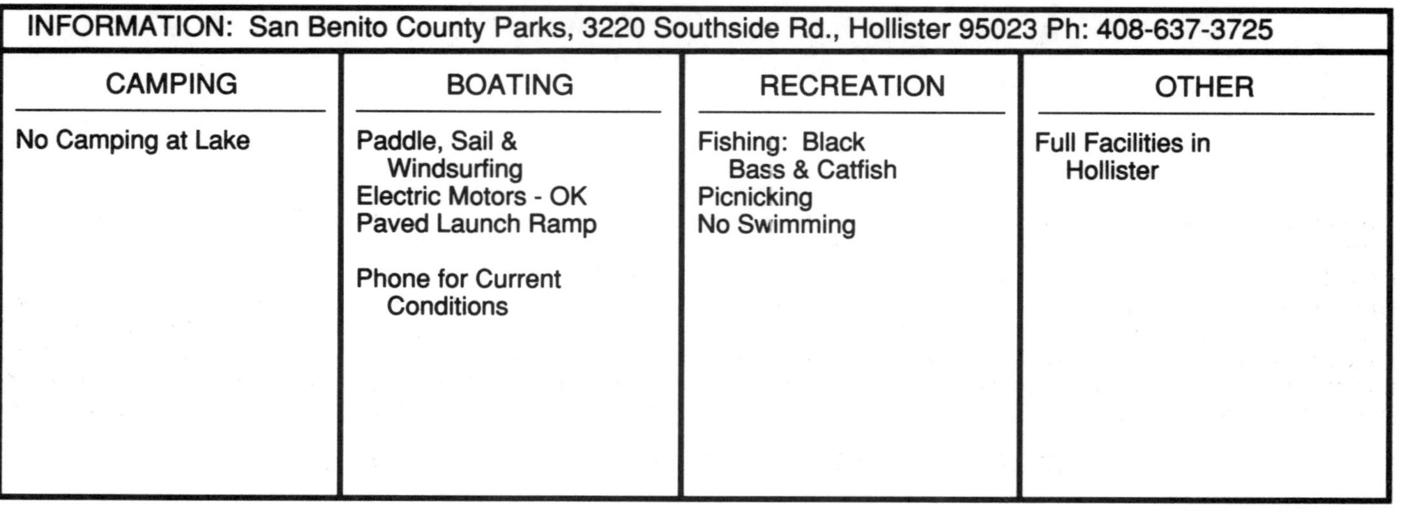

INFORMATION: San Benito County Parks, 3220 Southside Rd., Hollister 95023 Ph: 408-637-3725

CAMPING	BOATING	RECREATION	OTHER
No Camping at Lake	Paddle, Sail & Windsurfing Electric Motors - OK Paved Launch Ramp Phone for Current Conditions	Fishing: Black Bass & Catfish Picnicking No Swimming	Full Facilities in Hollister

SAN LUIS RESERVOIR AND O'NEILL FOREBAY

San Luis Reservoir State Recreation Area is at an elevation of 544 feet at high pool in the eastern foothills of the Diablo Mountain Range west of Los Banos. This huge reservoir has a surface area of 13,800 acres and 65 miles of grassy, oak-dotted shoreline. Although fish have never been planted, most species found in the Sacramento Delta are found at San Luis and the Forebay. In addition to good fishing, San Luis is popular for boating, swimming and waterskiing but sudden strong winds can be a hazard. Warning lights are located at the Romero Overlook and on Quien Sabe Point on the Reservoir and at San Luis Creek Area on the Forebay. The O'Neill Forebay below San Luis Reservoir has a surface area of 2,000 acres with 14 miles of shoreline. The 67 mile San Joaquin Section of the California Aqueduct Bikeway ends at the Forebay. Boating and fishing are popular. Waterfowl hunting is allowed on the lakes when in season

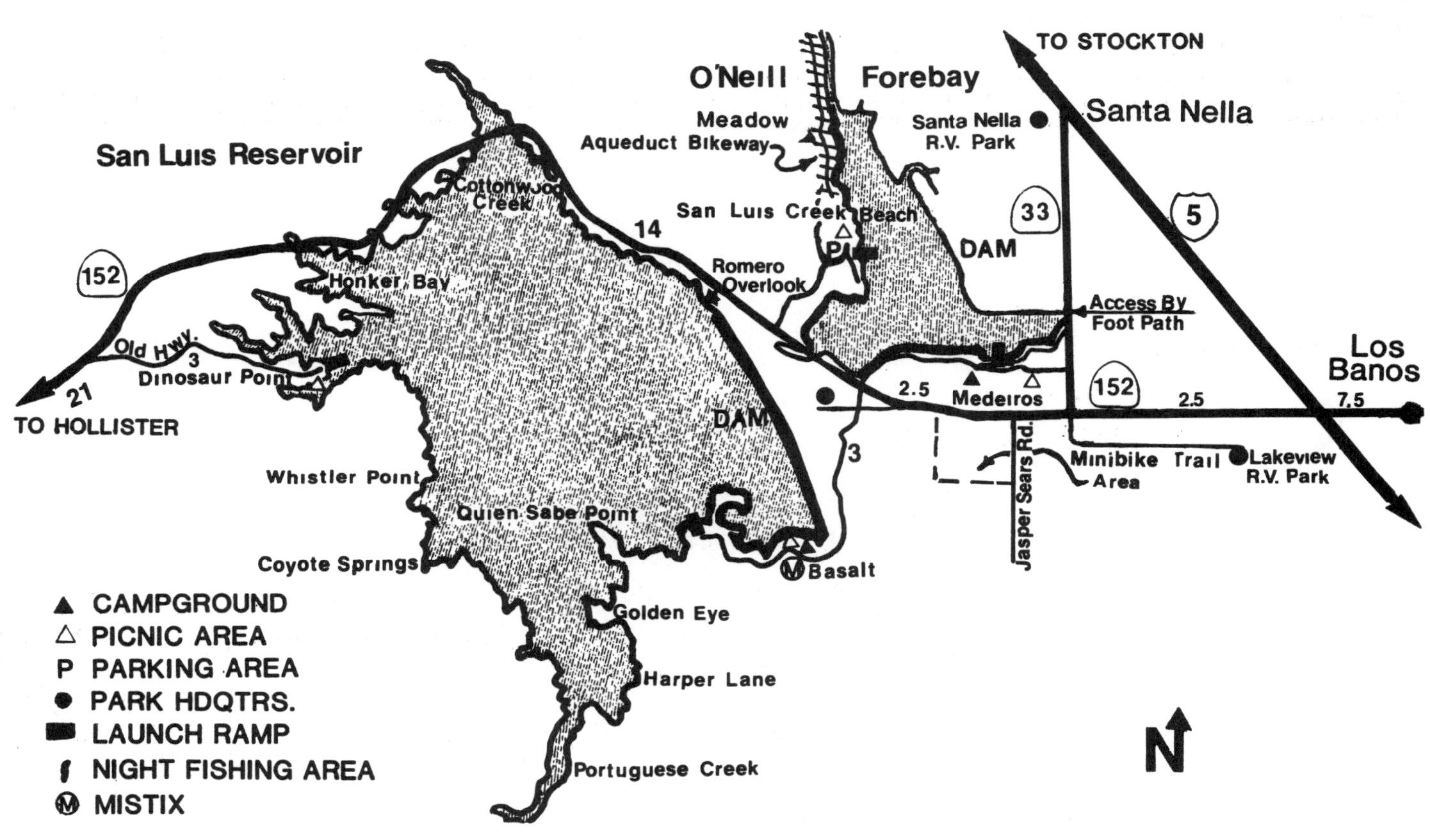

INFORMATION: Four Rivers District, 31426 W. Hwy. 152, Santa Nella 95322, Ph: 209-826-1196

CAMPING	BOATING	RECREATION	OTHER
Basalt Area: 79 Dev. Sites for Tents/R.V.s-$10 Medeiros: Undev. Sites for Tents/R.V.s-$6 Water & Porta Potties Plus Area for 400 R.V.s San Luis Creek Area: Meadow Campground 51 Undev. Sites for Tents/R.V.s-$6 Water & PortaPotties	Power, Row, Canoe, Sail, Waterski, Jet Ski, Windsurf & Inflatable Launch Ramps - $2 Life Jackets Required for Everyone Except Windsurfers Beware of Sudden Strong Winds	Fishing: Catfish, Bluegill, Crappie, Striped & Black Bass, Sturgeon, Shad Swimming - Beaches Picnicking Hunting: Waterfowl 157 Acre Minibike Trail Area - 250cc Engine Only	Santa Nella R.V. Park Full Hookups Ph: 209-826-3105 Lakeview R.V. Park Full Hookups Ph: 209-826-1196 Full Facilities in Los Banos and Santa Nella California Aqueduct Bikeway

LOS BANOS RESERVOIR

Los Banos Reservoir is at an elevation of 328 feet in the hilly grasslands west of Los Banos. The surface area of this small lake is 410 acres with 12 miles of shoreline. There are several planted trees around the campgrounds along with shade ramadas. Los Banos is under the jurisdiction of the Four Rivers District of the California Parks and Recreation Department. There is a small campground and a paved launch ramp. This facility is primarily used as a warm water fishery. Swimming is also popular as is waterfowl hunting when in season. There are usually good winds for sailing and windsurfing.

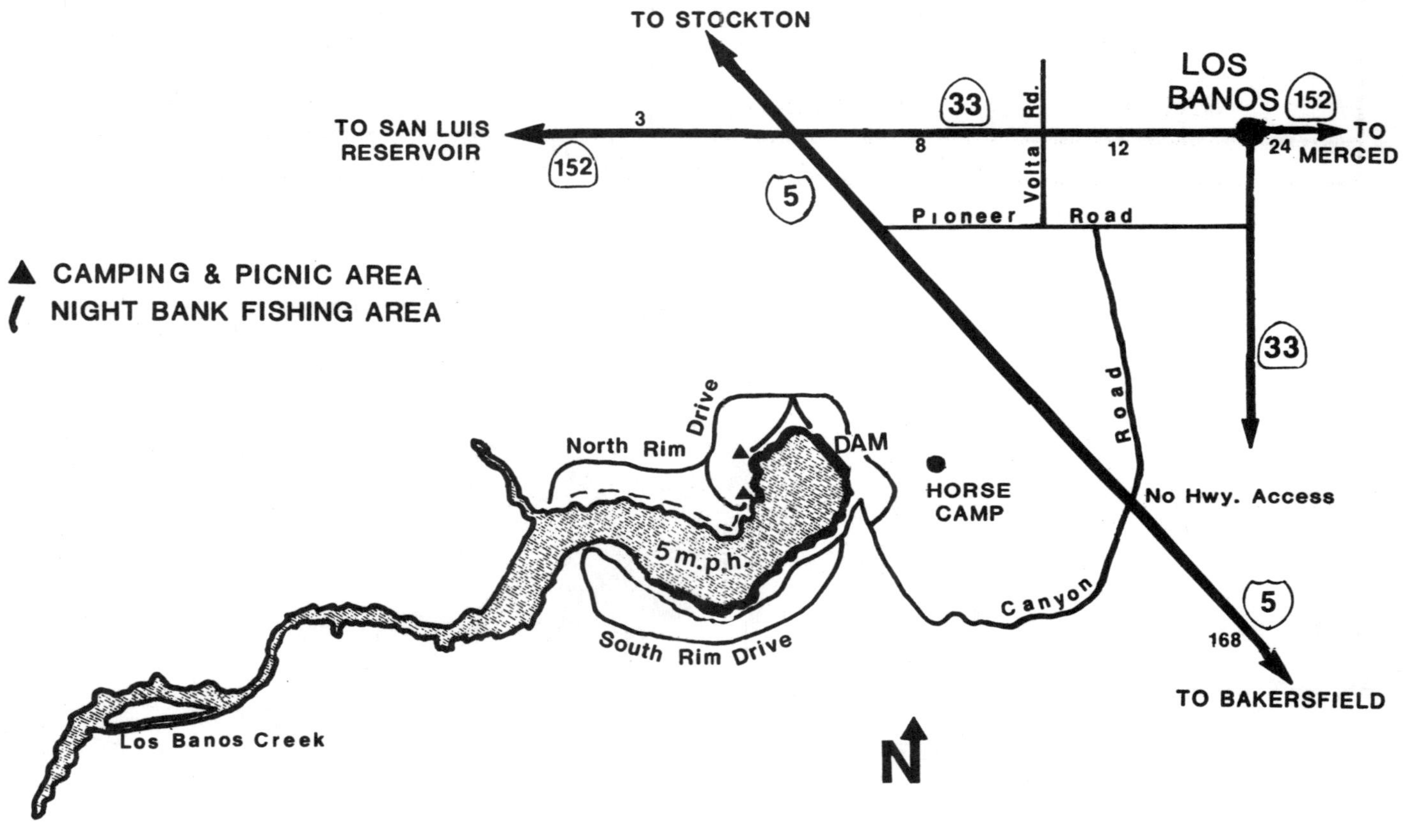

INFORMATION: Four Rivers Area, 31426 W. Hwy. 152, Santa Nella 95322, Ph: 209-826-1196			
CAMPING	BOATING	RECREATION	OTHER
20 Primitive Sites for Tents & R.V.s Fee: $6 (Hauled In Water) Day Use: $3	Power, Row, Canoe, Sail, Windsurf & Inflatables Speed Limit - 5 MPH Up To 10 HP Motors Only Paved Launch Ramp	Fishing: Trout, Catfish, Bluegill, Large & Smallmouth Bass Swimming Picnicking Hiking Horseback Riding Trails Hunting: Waterfowl in Season	Full Facilities at Los Banos

HENSLEY LAKE

Hensley Lake lies at an elevation of 540 feet in the gently rolling foothills northeast of Madera. The surrounding hills are covered with majestic oaks and granite outcroppings. The lake has a surface area of 1,570 acres with 24 miles of shoreline. The U. S. Army Corps of Engineers provides a campground, picnic areas and boating facilities. A large expanse of open water and many secluded quiet coves invites all types of boating. The fishing is good with an abundant warm water fishery. There are two swimming beaches. Hiking trails lead into the Wildlife Area where many birds, animals and native wildflowers may be observed.

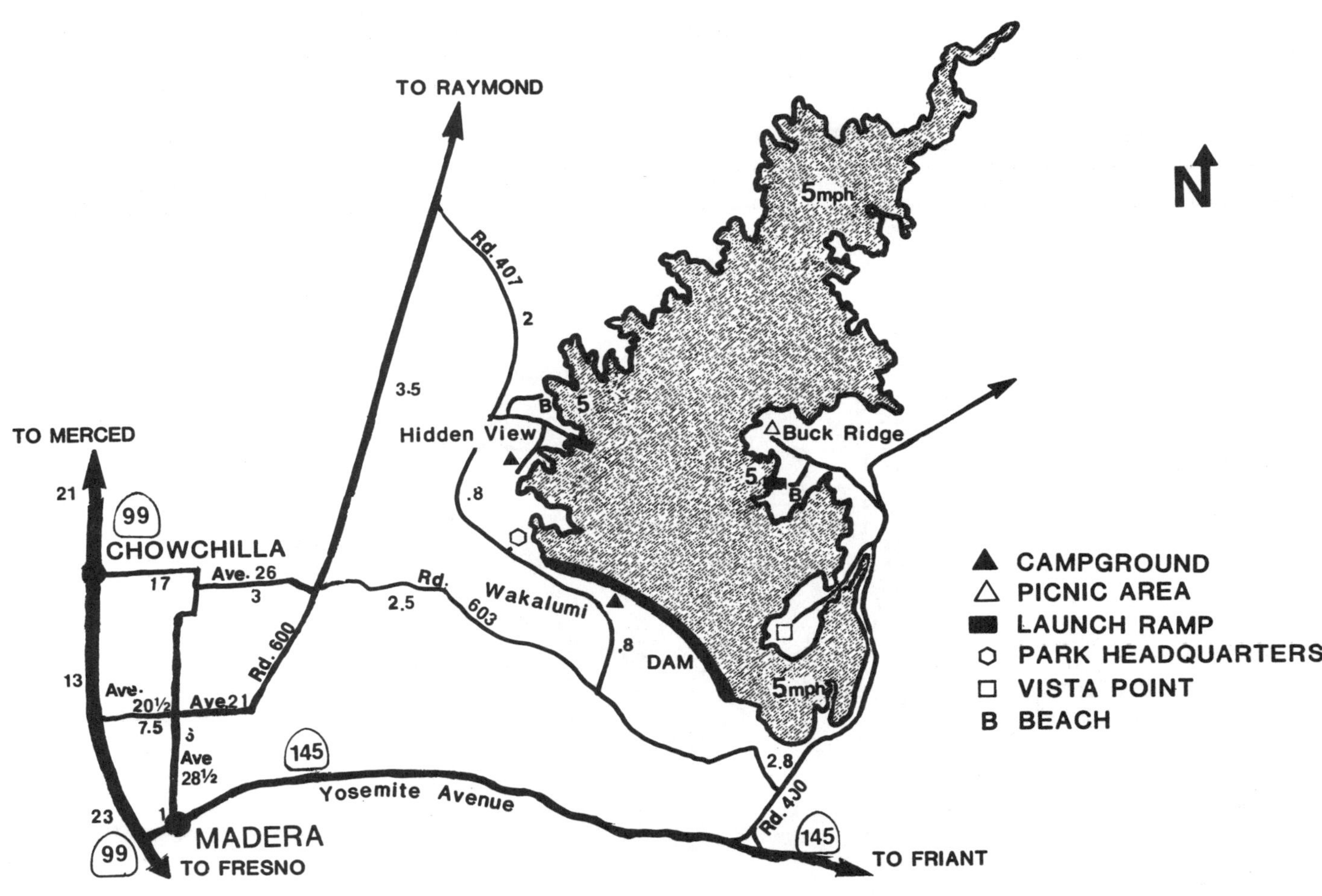

INFORMATION: Hensley Lake, P.O. Box 85, Raymond 93653, Ph: 209-673-5151

CAMPING	BOATING	RECREATION	OTHER
52 Dev. Sites for Tents & R.V.s Fee: $8 (No Fee Oct. 1 - April 1) 10 Primitive Sites Group Camp Area Disposal Station	Power, Row, Canoe, Sail, Waterski, Jet Ski, Windsurf & Inflatable 2 Paved Launch Ramps Submerged Hazards During Low Water	Fishing: Trout in Winter, Largemouth Bass, Bluegill, Catfish & Crappie Night Fishing Swimming - Beaches Picnicking: Family & Group Sites Hiking & Nature Trails	Full Facilities in Madera

EASTMAN LAKE

The U. S. Army Corps of Engineers completed Buchanan Dam in 1975, and the recreational facilities of Eastman Lake were opened to the public in 1978. Located in the oak-covered foothills 25 miles northeast of Chowchilla, this 1,780 acre Lake provides modern facilities for the outdoorsman. Brush shelters were provided for wildlife, and underwater fish shelters were also added. This is a good fishing Lake for warm water species. Boating and sailing are popular, and the well-maintained facilities are open year around. Berenda Reservoir to the west is a small day-use Lake with boating and fishing from shore during the summer only.

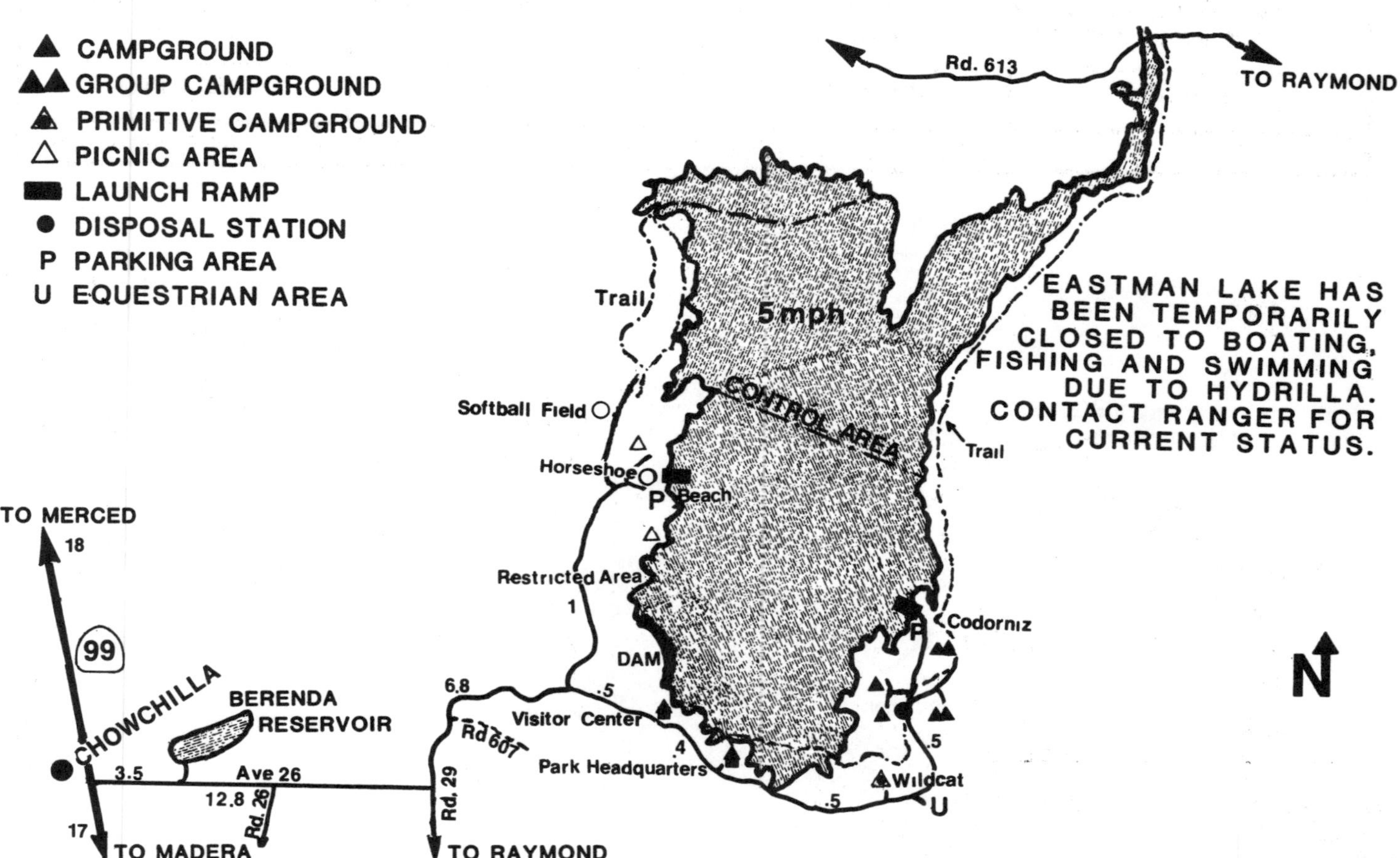

INFORMATION: Park Manager, Eastman Lake, Box 67, Raymond 93653, Ph: 209-689-3255			
CAMPING	BOATING	RECREATION	OTHER
62 Dev. Sites for Tents & R.V.s Fee: $8 March 1 to Sept. 30 No Hookups 19 Primitive Sites 2 Group Areas to 100 People Fee: $30 Per Night Reservation Only	Power, Row, Canoe, Sail, Windsurf & Inflatables Launch Ramps Berenda Reservoir: Summers Only Drag Boat Racing For Information: Chowchilla Parks & Recreation Ph: 209-665-4808	Fishing: Trout, Catfish, Bluegill, Crappie & Black Bass Swimming Picnicking Hiking Horseback Riding Trails Nature Study Horseshoes Softball	Disposal Station Full Facilities in Chowchilla or Madera

MILLERTON LAKE AND LOST LAKE PARK

The Millerton State Recreation Area is a part of the California State Park System which provides an abundance of modern picnic, camping and marine facilities. This popular 5,000 surface acre lake offers excellent boating and sailing opportunities for all types of craft. The angler will find a good warm water fishery. There are sandy swimming areas and picnic sites around the lake. The Lost Lake Recreation Area is a separate facility under the jurisdiction of Fresno County. This pretty 350 acre park on the San Joaquin River below Millerton offers a small 35 acre lake which is open to non-powered boating and fishing. There are family and group picnic areas, a campground and ball fields.

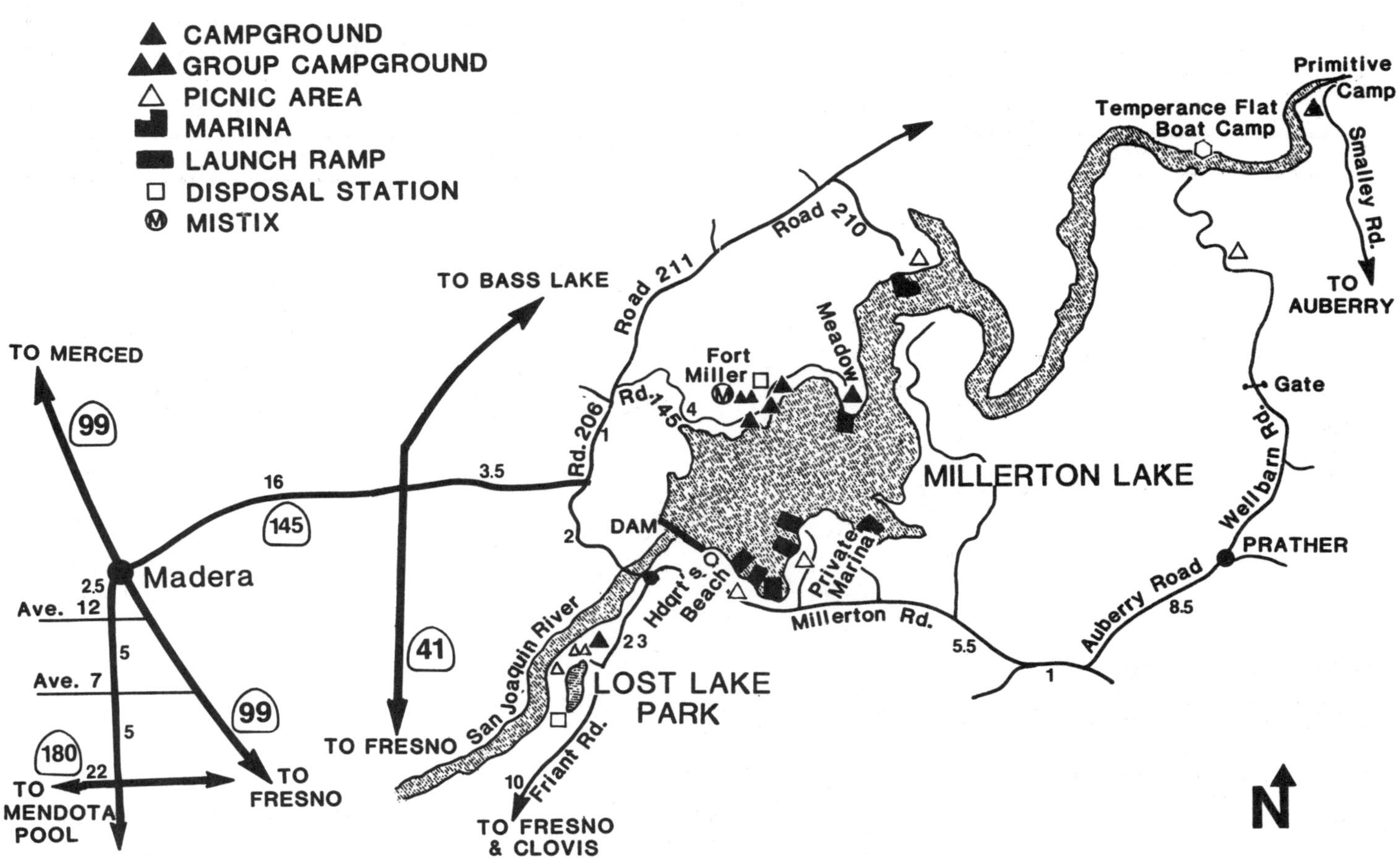

INFORMATION: Millerton Lake, P.O. Box 205, Friant 93626, Ph: 209-822-2332

CAMPING	BOATING	RECREATION	OTHER
MILLERTON LAKE: 137 Dev. Sites for Tents & R.V.s Fee: $10 15 Boat Camp Sites 25 Boat Access Sites Group Sites for 75 and 125 People Day Use Fee: $4 LOST LAKE: 42 R.V. Sites Fee: $9	MILLERTON: Open to All Boats Full Service Marina Launch Ramps: $2 Rentals: Fishing Boats & Motors LOST LAKE: No Gas-Powered Motors Hand Launch Only	Fishing: Alabama Spotted, Large & Smallmouth Bass, Catfish & Panfish Swimming - Millerton Only Picnicking Hiking & Horseback Riding Trails Birdwatching Nature Study Area Wildlife Refuge	Lost Lake Rec. Area Fresno County Parks 2220 Tulare St. Fresno 93721 Ph: 209-488-3004 Concessions Bait & Tackle Market Disposal Stations

BASS LAKE

Bass Lake, at an elevation of 3,400 feet, is within the Sierra National Forest. This beautiful forested recreation area provides an abundance of recreational opportunities. Boating and sailing on this 1,165 surface acre lake is extremely popular. Water levels are generally maintained through Labor Day. There are 16 different species of fish to challenge the angler. Facilities on the South Shore are administered by the U. S. Forest Service and managed by California Land Management. Resorts, cabins and R.V. parks are available at privately owned areas around the lake. For full information, contact the Bass Lake Chamber of Commerce.

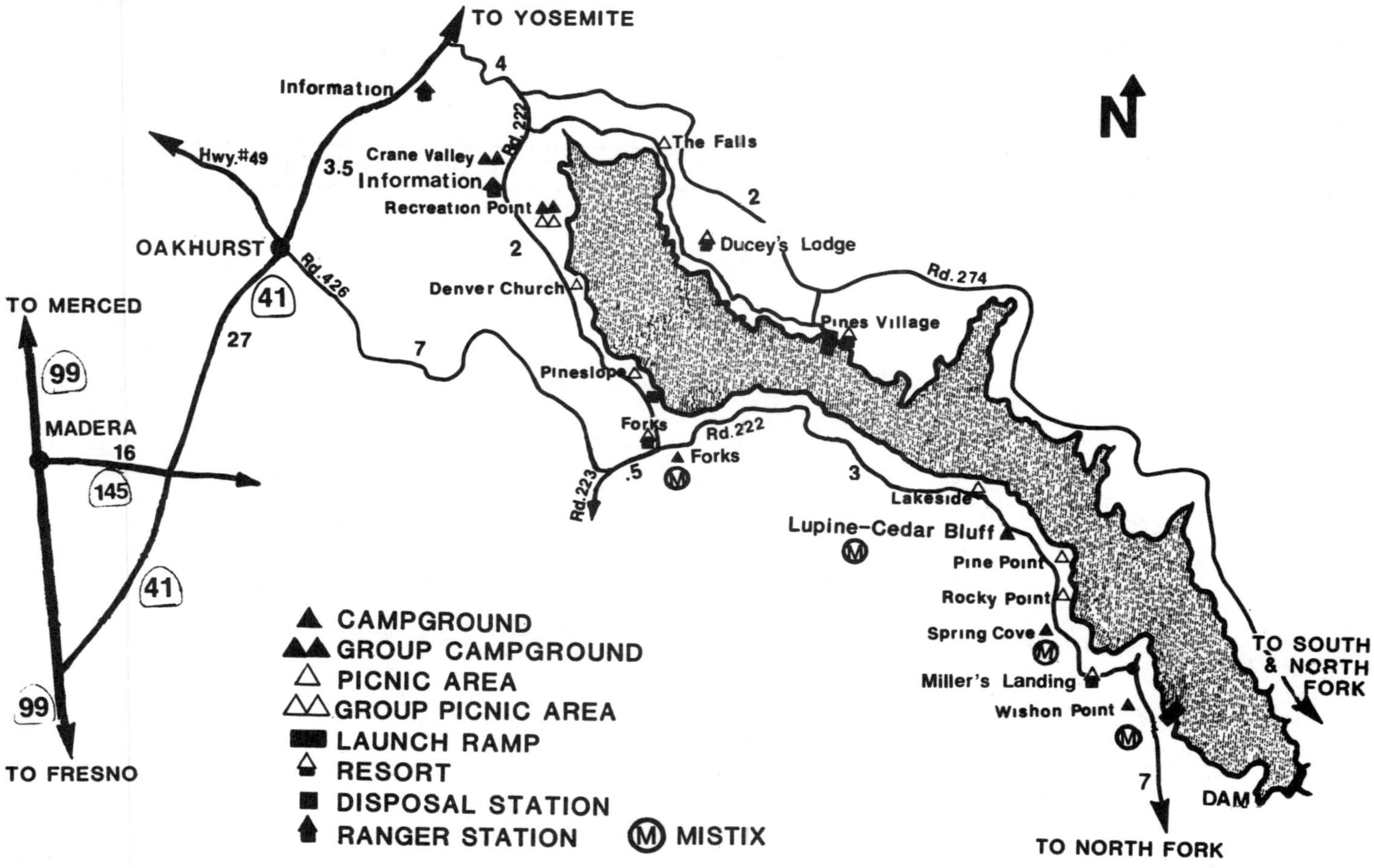

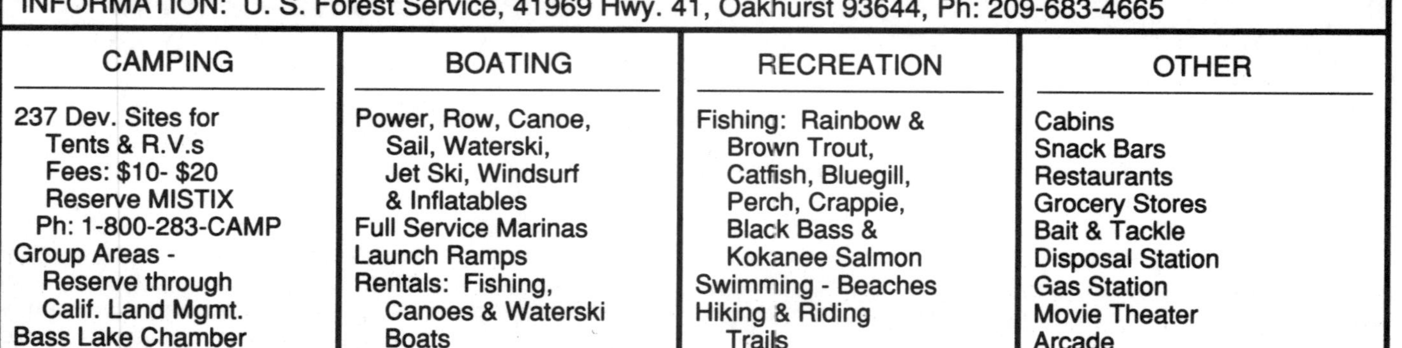

INFORMATION: U. S. Forest Service, 41969 Hwy. 41, Oakhurst 93644, Ph: 209-683-4665

CAMPING	BOATING	RECREATION	OTHER
237 Dev. Sites for Tents & R.V.s Fees: $10- $20 Reserve MISTIX Ph: 1-800-283-CAMP Group Areas - Reserve through Calif. Land Mgmt. Bass Lake Chamber of Commerce P.O. Box 126 Bass Lake 93604 Ph: 209-642-3676	Power, Row, Canoe, Sail, Waterski, Jet Ski, Windsurf & Inflatables Full Service Marinas Launch Ramps Rentals: Fishing, Canoes & Waterski Boats Moorings, Gas	Fishing: Rainbow & Brown Trout, Catfish, Bluegill, Perch, Crappie, Black Bass & Kokanee Salmon Swimming - Beaches Hiking & Riding Trails Visitor Programs Nature Study	Cabins Snack Bars Restaurants Grocery Stores Bait & Tackle Disposal Station Gas Station Movie Theater Arcade

REDINGER LAKE & KERCKHOFF RESERVOIR

Redinger Lake is at an elevation of 1,400 feet in a narrow valley with surrounding mountains rising 1,000 feet above the lake's surface. The lake is 3 miles long and 1/4 mile wide. The surrounding area of digger pine and chaparral is intermingled with live and valley oak. There is a variety of wildlife that can be observed. Redinger is primarily a boating lake as fishing is very limited. Kerckhoff Reservoir is located 6 miles to the west. Fishing for striped bass is the dominant activity and boating is limited to hand launch boats. Camping is available at both lakes but the sites are not developed. Redinger has numerous sandy beaches and is a pretty lake although remote.

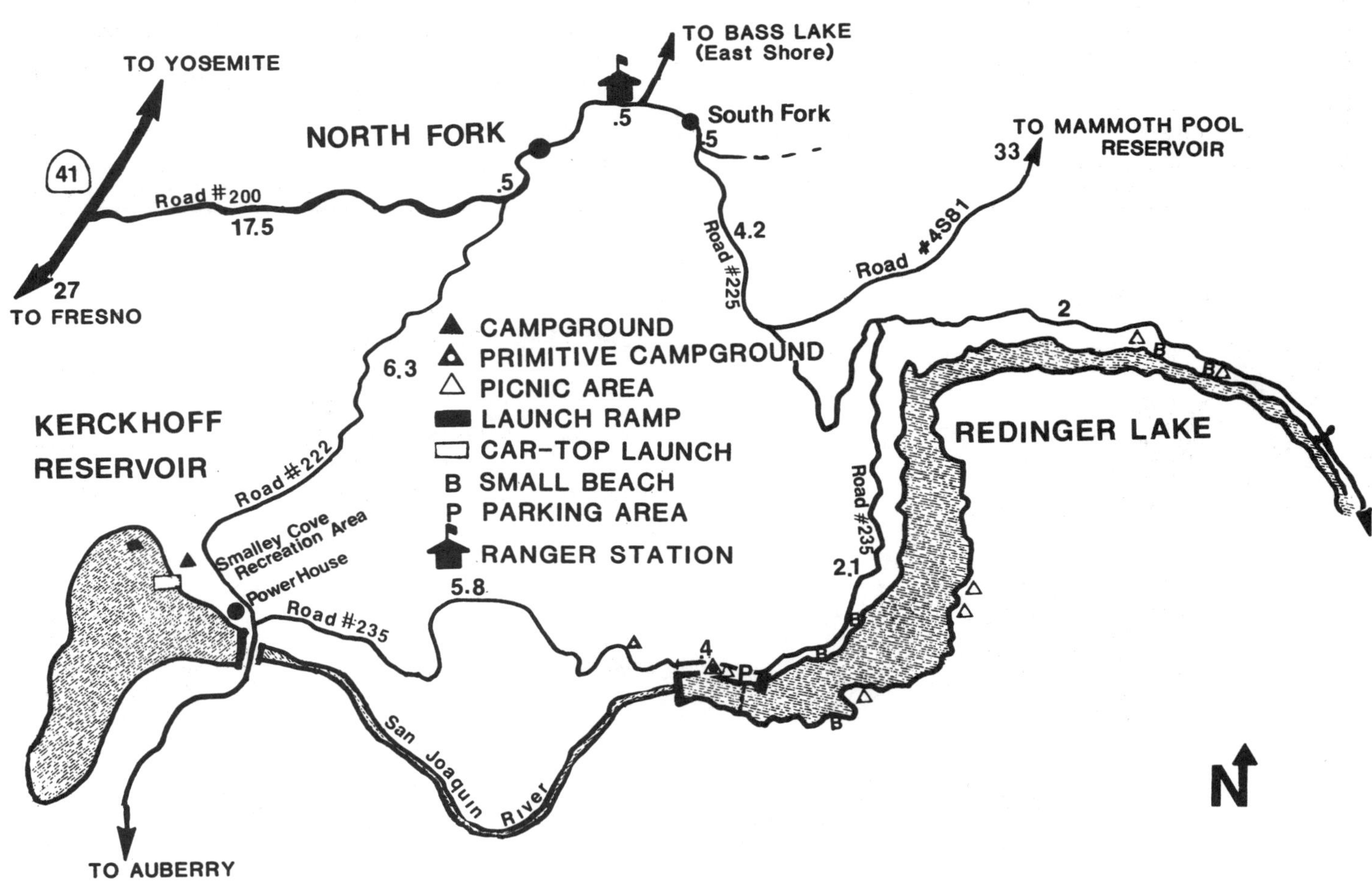

INFORMATION: Minarets Ranger District, North Fork 93643, Ph: 209-877-2218			
CAMPING	BOATING	RECREATION	OTHER
Redinger Lake: Primitive Camp Sites in Designated Areas Only Kerckhoff: Smalley Cove Rec. Area 5 Campsites (1 for Handicapped) 5 Picnic Sites Extreme Fire Danger No Campfires	Power, Row, Canoe, Sail & Inflatables Speed Limit - 35 MPH Launch Ramp at Redinger Lake Only Car Top Boats Only at Kerckhoff	Fishing: Striped Bass Swimming Picnicking Hiking Nature Study Hunting: Valley Quail, Rabbit & Deer	Nearest Facilities at North Fork

MAMMOTH POOL RESERVOIR

Mammoth Pool Reservoir is located on the San Joaquin River at an elevation of 3,330 feet. The dam was completed in 1959 by Southern California Edison Company to produce hydroelectric power. The lake is nestled in a narrow valley of ponderosa pine, incense cedar, black and live oak with mountains rising 2,000 feet above its shoreline. The surface area of Mammoth Pool is 1,107 acres when full although the water level drops 90 feet in the fall, closing the improved launch ramp. The access road climbs to 5,300 feet rendering it impassable when winter snow arrives. Mile High Vista Point offers a 180 degree view of magnificent mountains including Mount Ritter and Mammoth Mountain.

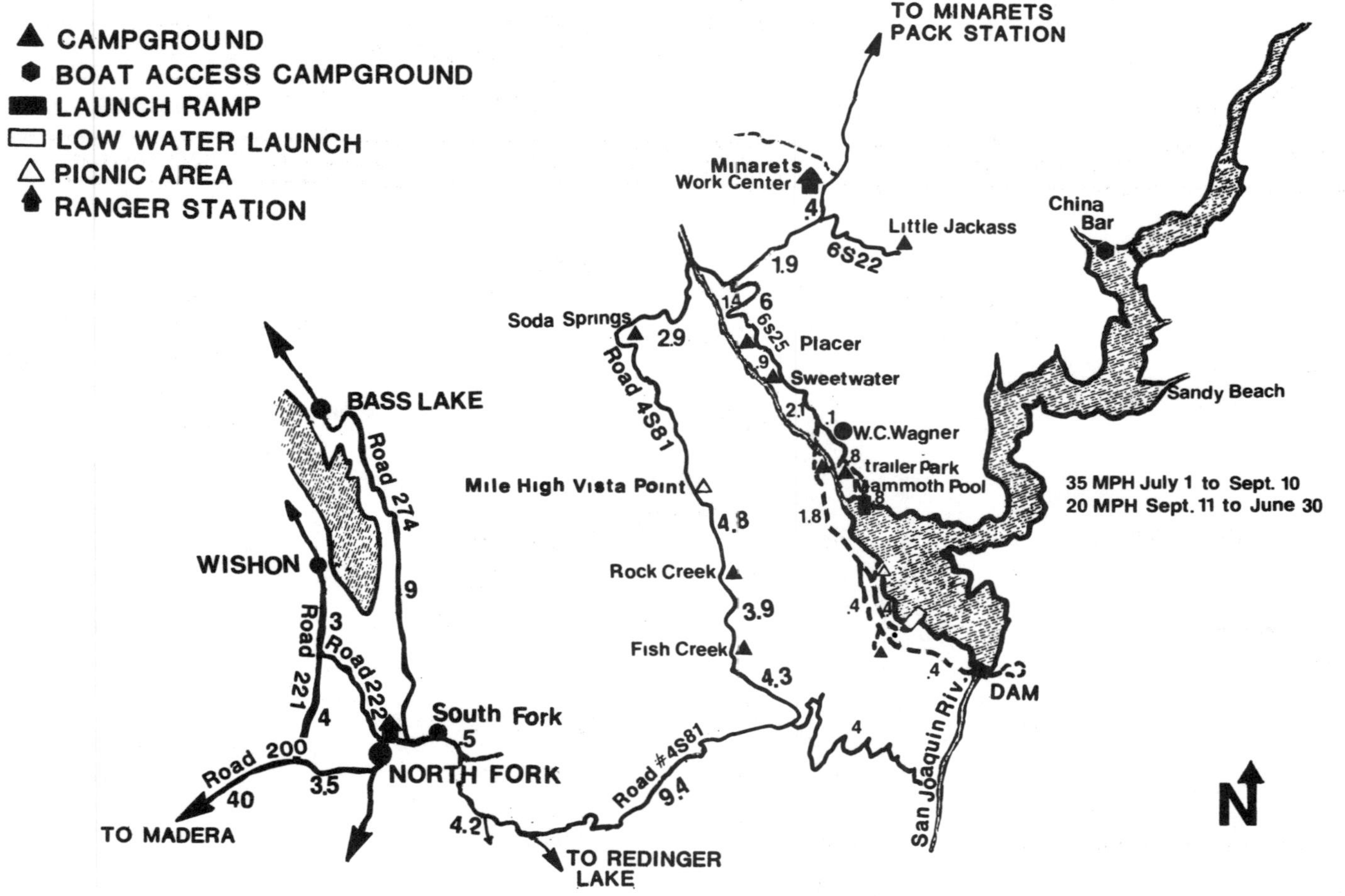

INFORMATION: Minarets Ranger District, North Fork 93643, Ph: 209-877-2218			
CAMPING	**BOATING**	**RECREATION**	**OTHER**
30 Dev. Sites for Tents 34 Dev. Sites for Tents & R.V.s Fee: Mammoth Pool Campground - $5 Fee: Placer Campground - $3 No Fee at Other Forest Service Campgrounds 6 Boat-In Sites	Power, Sail, Row, Canoe, Windsurf & Inflatables Waterskiing Subject to 35 MPH Speed Limit 7/1 to 9/10 Only Improved Launch Ramp & Gravel Launch Ramp	Fishing: Rainbow, Eastern Brook & German Brown Trout Lake Closed to Fishing & Boating May 1 to June 16 Swimming Picnicking Hiking-Nature Trail Pack Station Hunting: Deer	Wagner's Resort 21101 Rte. 209 Madera 93638 35 Dev. Sites for Tents & R.V.s Short Orders & Sandwiches Lunch Counter Grocery Store Bait & Tackle Gas Station Open: Memorial Day-End Deer Season

WISHON, COURTRIGHT AND BLACK ROCK RESERVOIRS

These lakes range in elevation from 8,200 feet at Courtright, 6,500 feet at Wishon to 4,200 feet at Black Rock. They are a part of the Kings River Drainage System. Located in the beautiful Sierra National Forest, these lakes offer good fishing for native trout. In addition, the angler will find numerous lakes and streams and the newly completed Upper King's River angler's access site. Wishon Village offers complete resort facilities in this relatively remote area. The Forest Service operates numerous campgrounds as shown on the map. Those seeking a wilderness adventure will find trailheads leading into the John Muir and Dinkey Lakes Wilderness Areas. The Helms Creek Hydroelectric Project affects water levels at Wishon, Courtright and Black Rock.

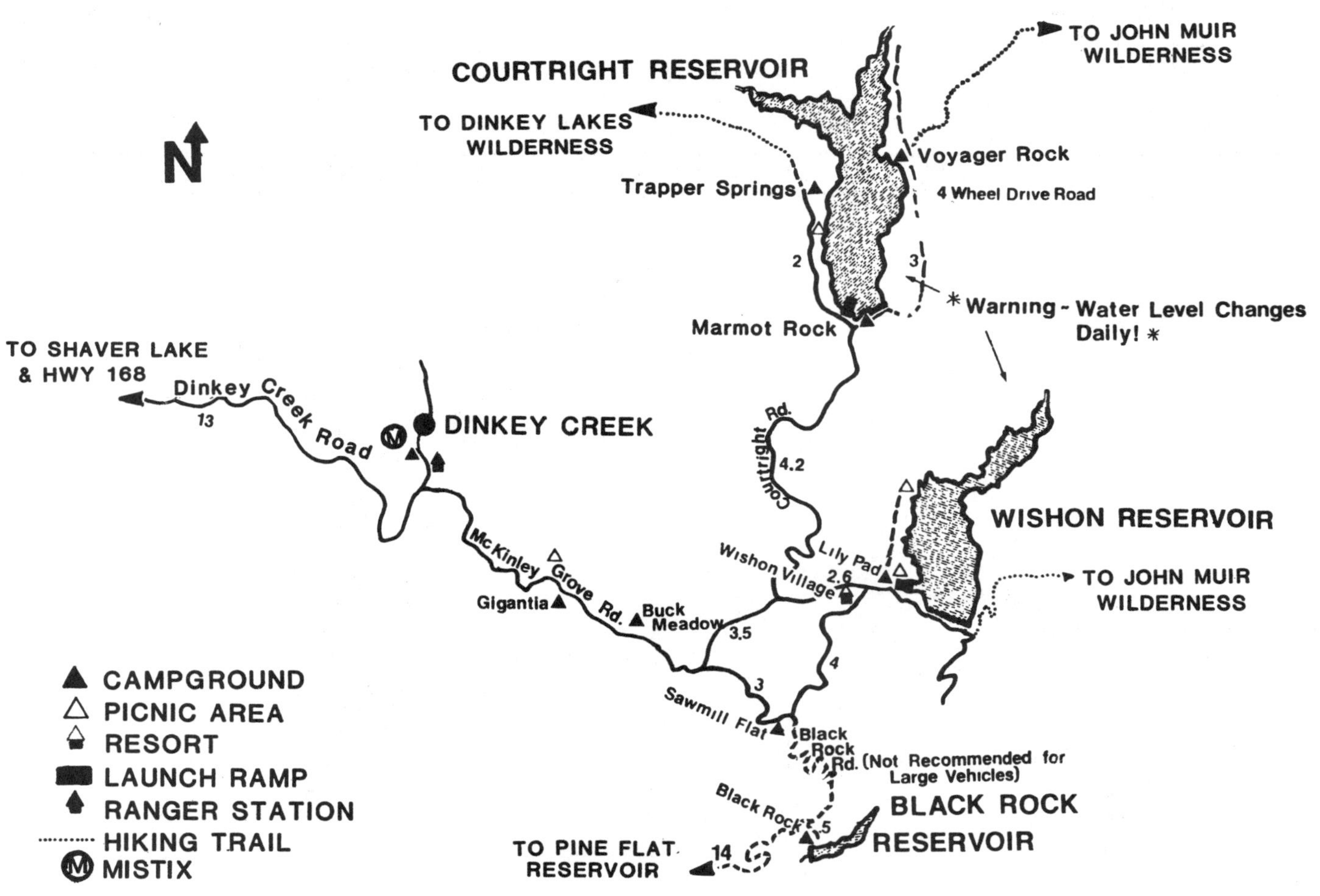

INFORMATION: U. S. Forest Service, 34849 Maxon Rd., Sanger 93657, Ph: 209-855-8321

CAMPING	BOATING	RECREATION	OTHER
Numerous U. S. F. S. Campgrounds in Area Dinkey Creek Ranger Station Ph: 209-841-3404 Wishon Village 54890 McKinley Grove Dinkey Creek 93664 Ph: 209-841-5361 25 Tent Sites & 97 R.V. Sites Full Hookups	Open to All Boating Except Waterskiing & Jet Skiing 15 MPH Speed Limit Rentals: Fishing Boats at Wishon	Fishing: Rainbow, Brown & Brook Trout Swimming Picnicking Hiking & Backpacking Horse Rentals & Pack Services Hunting: Deer, Mountain Quail ORV Roads	Wishon Village: Store, Gas Station, Laundromat, Propane Ice Bait & Tackle Full Facilities at Shaver Lake

SHAVER LAKE

Shaver Lake is at an elevation of 5,370 feet in the Sierra National Forest. The lake has a surface area of 2,000 acres with a shoreline of 13 miles. Tall pine trees blend with granite boulders to the water's edge. This is a popular boating lake with good marine facilities. In addition to excellent fishing at Shaver, there are numerous trout streams nearby awaiting the expectant angler. The John Muir and Dinkey Lakes Wilderness Areas lure the hiker and backpacker. Both the U. S. Forest Service and Southern California Edison offer well-maintained campgrounds in this beautiful setting. The Forest Service Campgrounds are operated by California Land Management under a Special Use Permit from the Forest Service.

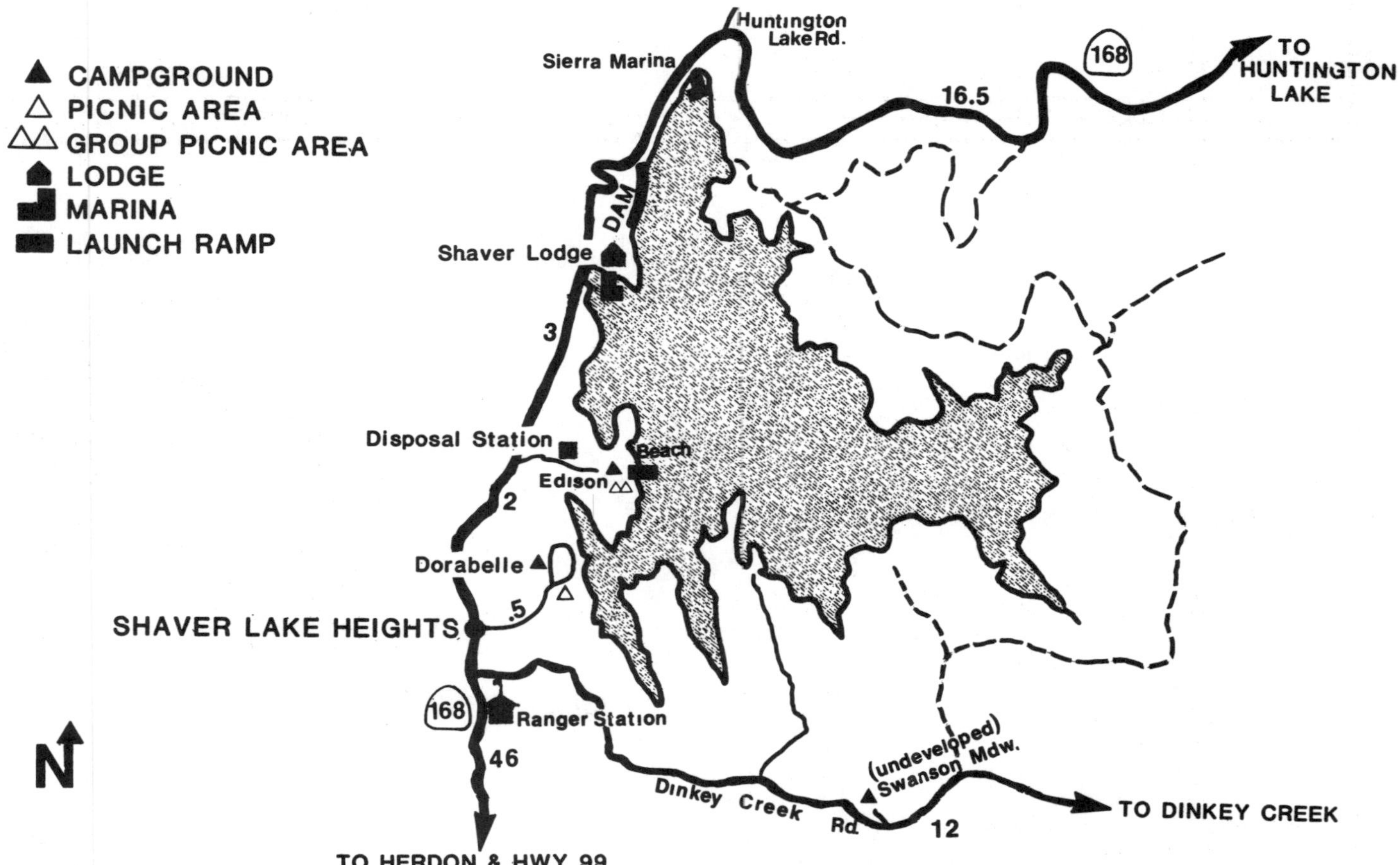

INFORMATION: U. S. F. S., Box 300 or Camp Edison, Box 6, Shaver Lake 93664			
CAMPING	BOATING	RECREATION	OTHER
U. S. F. S.: Ph: 209-841-3311 69 Dev. Sites for Tents & R.V.s, Fee: $8 9 Primitive Sites SO. CAL. EDISON: Ph: 209-841-3444 150 Dev. Sites for Tents & R.V.s, Fee: $12.50 Electric Hookups Disposal Station Each Additional Vehicle: $2	Power, Row, Canoe, Sail, Waterski, Jet Ski, Windsurf & Inflatable Full Service Marinas Rental: Fishing Boats & Motors, Pontoons Berths Gas	Fishing: Rainbow, Brown & Brook Trout, Large & Smallmouth Bass, Catfish & Redear Sunfish Picnicking Swimming - Beaches Hiking & Riding Trails	Motels & Cabins Restaurants Cocktail Lounges Grocery Stores Bait & Tackle Gas Station

HUNTINGTON LAKE

Huntington Lake is at an elevation of 7,000 feet in the Sierra National Forest. Resting in a forested natural basin, this man-made Lake is 6 miles long and 1/2 mile wide with 14 miles of shoreline. The Forest Service Campgrounds are operated by California Land Management under a Special Use Permit from the Forest Service. There are many private resorts under Special Use Permits. This is a good Lake for sailing and regattas are held in the summer to take advantage of the westerly winds. Hiking and horseback riding trails surround Huntington. The backpacker will find the nearby Kaiser Wilderness with its 22,750 timbered acres an exciting adventure. Permits are required. Fishing from shore or boat is usually productive and nearby Lakes and streams offer a variety of opportunities.

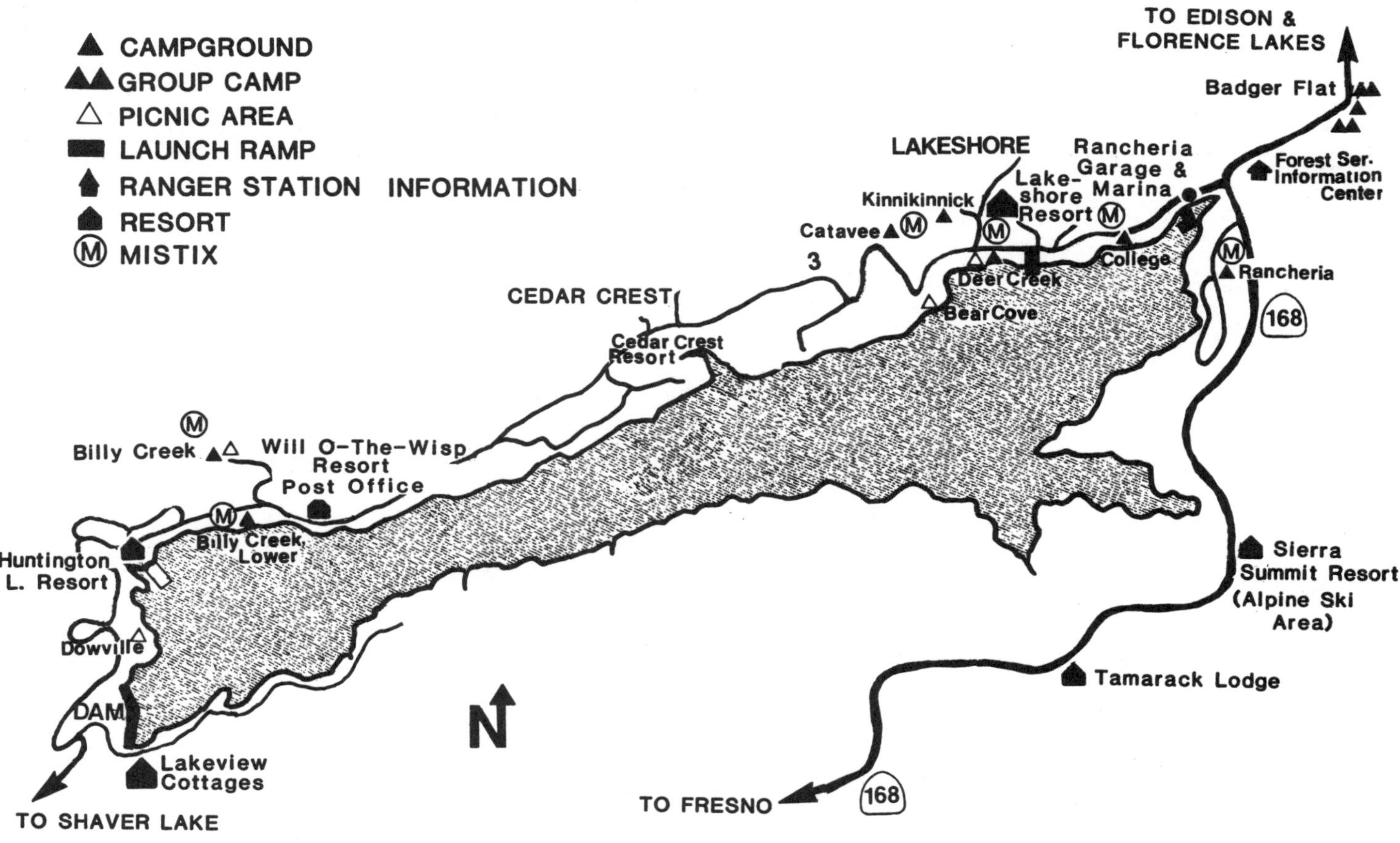

INFORMATION: Pineridge Ranger District, P.O. Box 300, Shaver Lake 93664, Ph: 209-841-3311			
CAMPING	BOATING	RECREATION	OTHER
297 Dev. Sites for Tents & R.V.s Single: $9, Double: $18 Add'l. Vehicle: $3 Reserve: MISTIX Group Campgrounds Reserve: Calif. Land Management for Midge Creek & Badger Flat Ph: 415-322-1181 or 209-893-2111 (Summer)	Power, Row, Canoe, Sail, Waterski, Windsurf & Inflatable Full Service Marinas Launch Ramp Rentals: Fishing & Sailboats, Canoes, Paddleboats, Jet Skis & Patio Boats	Fishing: Rainbow, Brown & Brook Trout, Kokanee Swimming Picnicking Hiking Backpacking-Parking Horseback Riding Trails & Rentals Nature Study	Motels & Cabins Restaurants Grocery Stores Bait & Tackle Gas Station Summer Ranger Station Eastwood Visitor Center Ph: 209-893-6611

EDISON AND FLORENCE LAKES

Edison Lake is at 7,700 feet and Florence Lake is at 7,400 feet elevation in the beautiful high Sierra bordering the John Muir and Ansel Adams Wilderness Areas. Granite boulders and sandy beaches around the timbered shorelines make a lovely setting. In addition to the Forest Service Campgrounds, Vermillion Valley Resort at Edison Lake offers cabins, restaurant, grocery store, boat rentals and launch facilities. Florence lake has a small store with limited supplies. A resort with store, cabins, restaurant and hot mineral baths is located at Mono Hot Springs. A ferry service for backpackers into the Wilderness Areas is available at both Lakes. Fishing in both lakes and streams is excellent in this truly delightful high mountain retreat. Forest Service Campgrounds are operated by California Land Management under a Special Use Permit from the Forest Service.

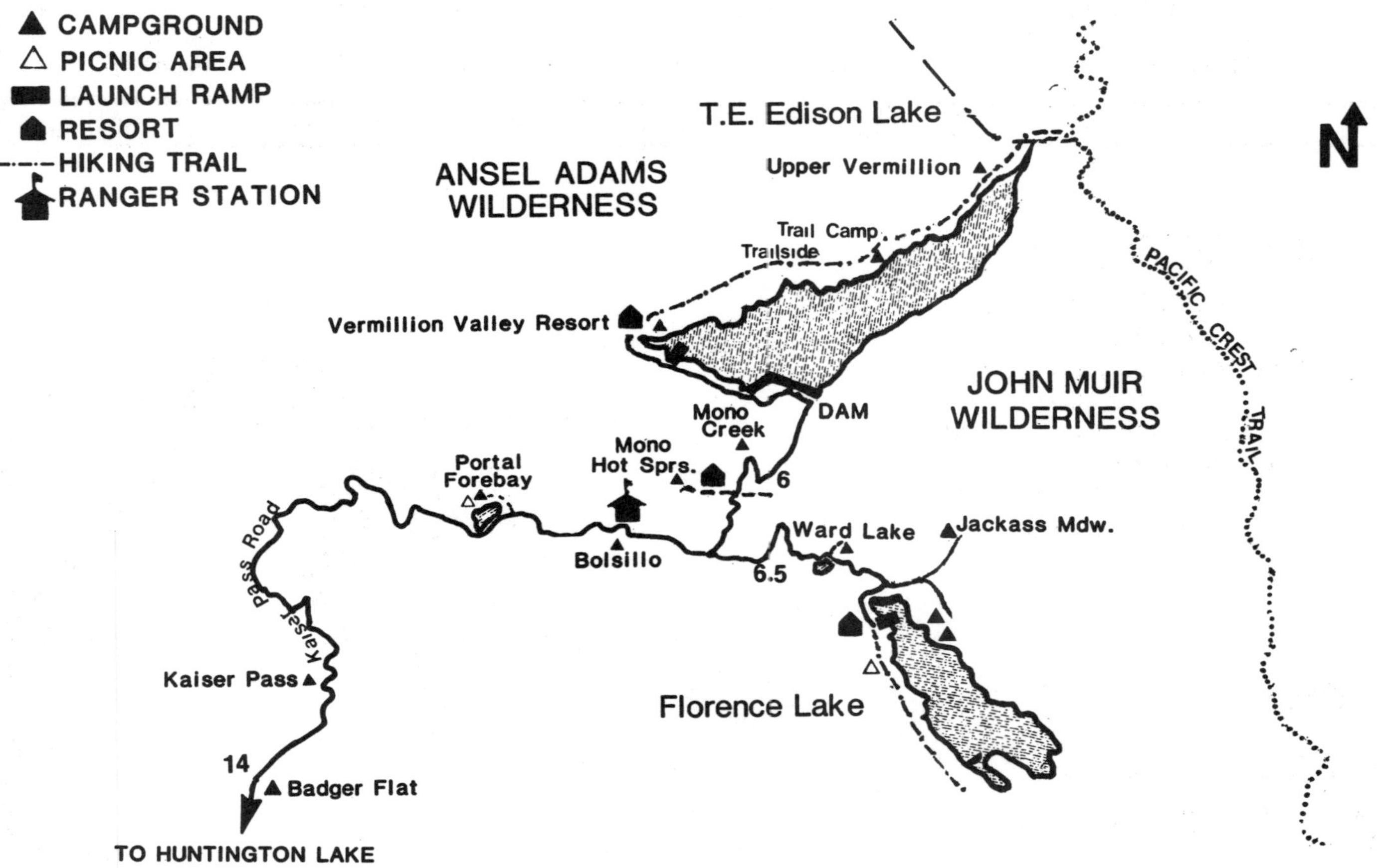

INFORMATION: U. S. F. S., P.O. Box 300, Shaver Lake 93664, Ph: 209-841-3311

CAMPING	BOATING	RECREATION	OTHER
162 Sites for Tents in This Area R.V.s and Trailers Use Caution Due to Narrow One-Lane Winding Rds. Primitive Camping Allowed Anywhere with Campfire Permit Fee: $6	Power, Row, Canoe & Inflatable Speed Limit - 15 MPH Launch Ramps Rentals: Fishing Boats & Canoes	Fishing: Rainbow, Brown & Brook Trout Picnicking Hiking Horseback Riding & Pack Trips Ferry Service for Backpackers Entry Point to John Muir & Ansel Adams Wilderness Permit Required	Cabins Restaurants Grocery Stores Bait & Tackle Gas Station High Sierra Ranger Station (Seasonal) Ph: 209-877-7173

PINE FLAT LAKE AND AVOCADO LAKE PARK

Pine Flat Lake is at an elevation of 961 feet in the Sierra Foothills east of Fresno. This 20 mile long Lake has 67 miles of generally open shoreline. There is a moderate growth of pine and oak trees throughout the area. The U. S. Army Corps of Engineers has jurisdiction over the Lake. In addition to the public campgrounds around the Lake, there are private developments along Trimmer Springs Road which offer overnight lodging and R.V. accommodations. Good marina facilities and warm water are attractive to waterskiers, boaters and swimmers. A variety of fish await the angler at this popular Lake. Avocado Lake Park is on the Kings River below Pine Flat Dam. This small 83 surface acre Lake offers non-powered boating and a warm water fishery. There is no camping permitted but there are nice picnic areas and a swimming beach.

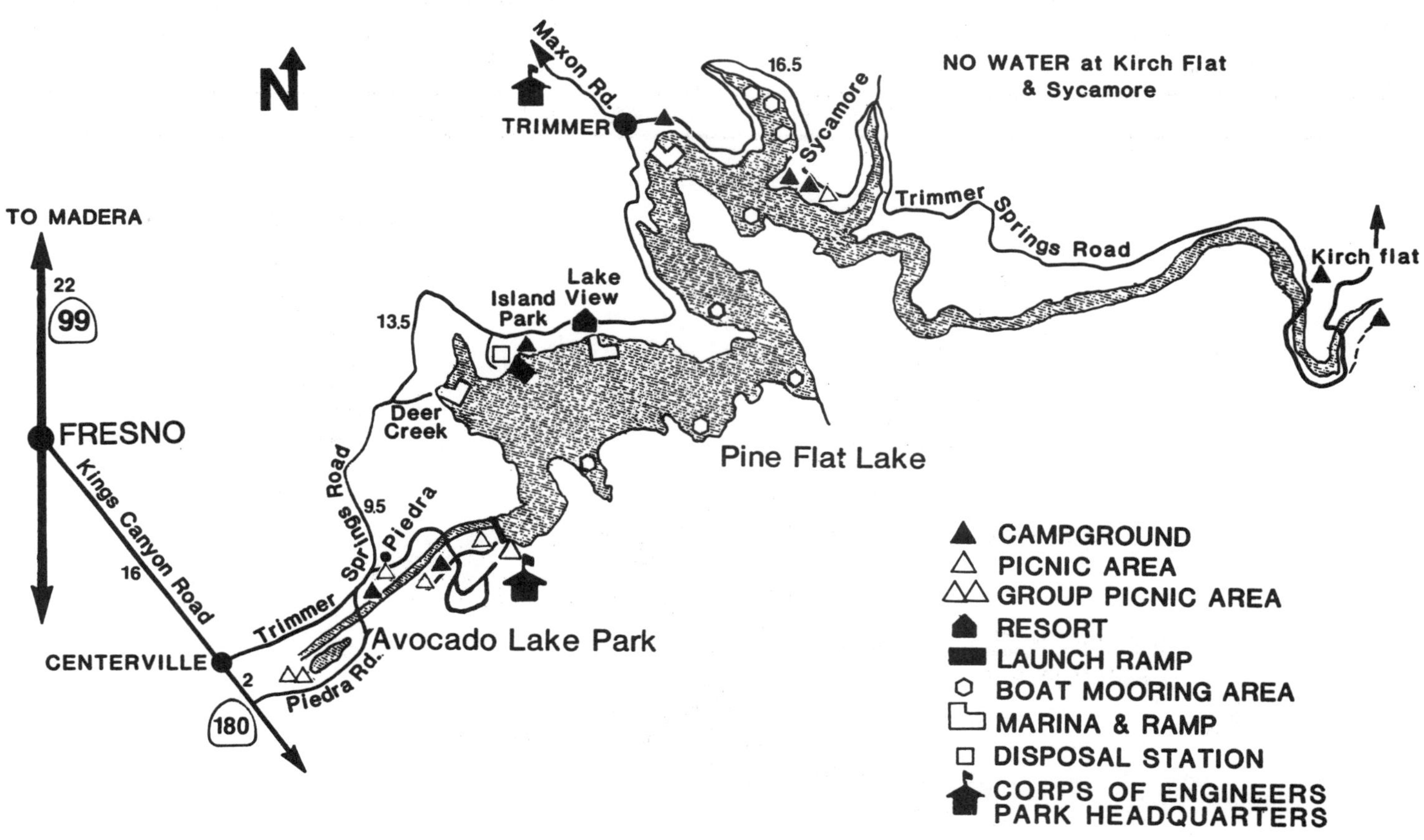

INFORMATION: Pine Flat Lake, P.O. Box 117, Piedra 93649, Ph: 209-787-2589			
CAMPING	BOATING	RECREATION	OTHER
Island Park: 104 Dev. Tent/RV Sites Plus Overflow Fees: 0 - $8 2 Group Campsites: Fee: $25 2 Handicap Sites Sunnyslope Camp: P.O. Box 146 Piedra 93649 Ph: 209-787-2730 95 R.V. Sites Hookups - $10	Pine Flat: Open to All Boats 3 Full Service Marinas Overnight Mooring No Shoreline Camping Rentals: Fishing, Pontoon & Jet Skis Avocado Lake Park: No Gas-Powered Boats Hand Launch	Fishing: Rainbow Trout, Large & Smallmouth Bass, Catfish & Panfish Swimming Picnicking Campfire Program River Raft Trips Hunting: Deer, Quail, Dove, Rabbit & Squirrel Designated Areas Shotguns Only On Corps Land	Motel & Cabins Restaurants-Lounges Snack Bars - Stores Bait, Tackle & Gas Avocado Lake Fresno Co. Parks 2220 Tulare St. Fresno 93721 Ph: 209-488-3004

HUME AND SEQUOIA LAKES

Hume Lake, at 5,200 feet, and Sequoia, at 5,300 feet, are in the beautiful Sequoia National Forest. Hume Lake has 85 surface acres and Sequoia has 88 acres. The angler will find trout, and the boater is restricted to small non-powered crafts; electric motors are allowed at Hume. Sequoia Lake is operated by the YMCA and early reservations are advised at this popular camp. Since Sequoia is a private family camp, there is no day use. Be sure to bring your camera to this beautiful country of the Giant Sequoia Trees (survivors of the Ice Age), and the majestic Kings Canyon National Park.

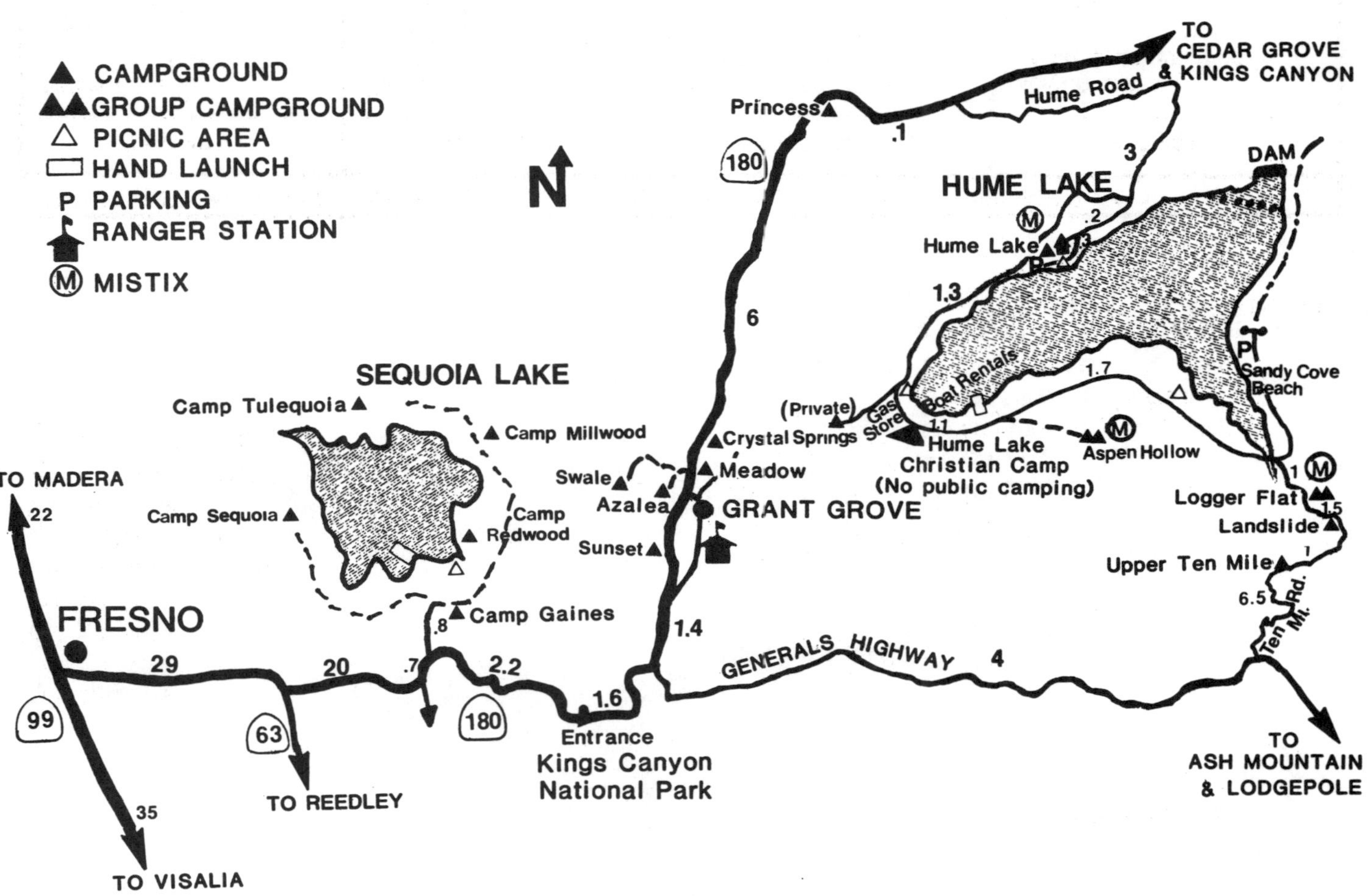

INFORMATION: U. S. F. S., 35860 E. Kings Canyon Rd., Dunlap 93621, Ph: 209-338-2251			
CAMPING	BOATING	RECREATION	OTHER
Hume Lake: 75 Dev. Sites for Tents & R.V.s, Fee: $8 No Hookups 2 Group Camps Reserve MISTIX Ph: 1-800-283-CAMP Nearby Campgrounds: 180 Plus Sites Sequoia Family Camp Central Valley YMCA P.O. Box 5618 Fresno 93755	Hume Lake: Open to All Non-Powered Boats Electric Motors O.K. 5 MPH Speed Limit Hand Launch Boat Rentals at Christian Camp Sequoia: Sail, Canoes & Row Boats Furnished Powered Boats O.K. No Motors	Fishing: Sequoia - Rainbow, Smallmouth Bass & Perch Hume - Rainbow & Brown Trout Picnicking & Swimming Hiking & Backpacking Horseback Riding & Rentals at Hume Lake Christian Camp Hunting: Deer Nature Study Photography	Hume Lake Christian Camp - Gas, Store Restaurant Ph: 209-335-2881 Sequoia Family Camp Meals, Store, Craft Materials, Laundry Before July 1 - Ph: 209-233-5737 After July 1 - Ph: 209-335-2886

DIAZ LAKE AND PLEASANT VALLEY RESERVOIR

Diaz Lake rests at an elevation of 3,700 feet on the eastern slope of the Sierra, 15 miles from the Mt. Whitney Trailhead. This 86 surface acre lake offers varied boating and is popular with waterskiers. A new ramp has been developed along with an 80 foot floating dock. There is both a trout and warm water fishery. Pleasant Valley, at 4,200 feet, is often a good trout lake but boating is not permitted. There is a 15 minute hike to the lake from the campground. Inyo County recently developed more picnic tables, barbecues, and restroom facilities at Pleasant Valley and new handicapped restroom facilities at Diaz Lake. Tinemaha Reservoir is open to trout fishing year round.

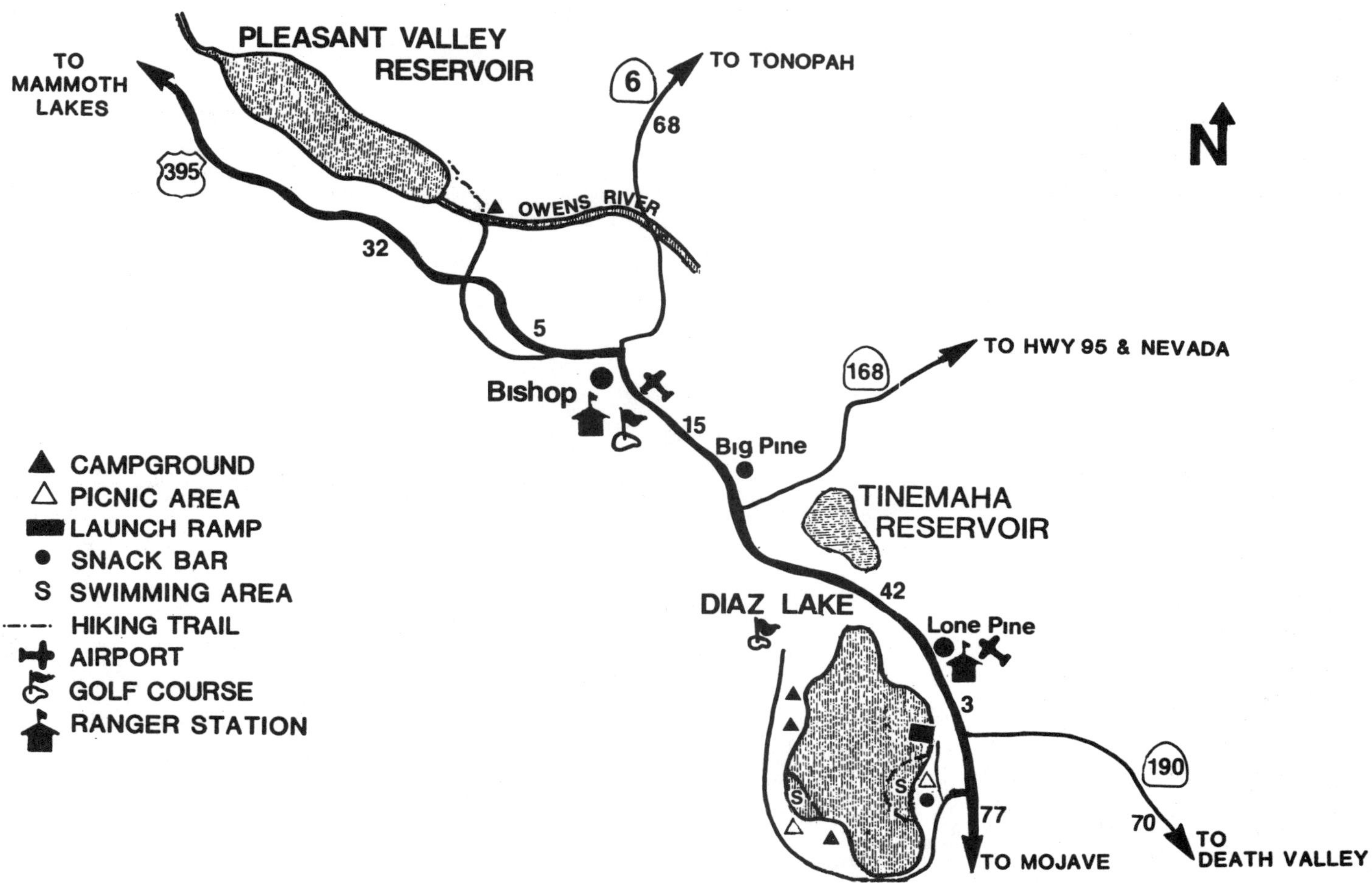

INFORMATION: Inyo County Parks, P.O. Box 237, Independence 93526, Ph: 619-878-2411

CAMPING	BOATING	RECREATION	OTHER
Pleasant Valley: 200 Tent & R.V. Sites No Hookups-Fee: $5 Diaz Lake: 300 Tent & R.V. Sites No Hookups-Fee: $6 Group Camping 2 Week Advance Reservations Required Ph: 619-876-5656	Diaz Lake: Power, Row, Canoe, Sail, Waterski & Inflatables Launch Ramp - $5 Speed Limit - 35 MPH May through Oct. Speed Limit - 15 MPH Nov. through Apr. Noise Level Laws are Strictly Enforced Maximum Boat Size-22'	Fishing: Rainbow & Brown Trout, Small-mouth Bass, Bluegill & Catfish Swimming - Beaches Picnicking Hiking & Backpacking Horse Trips into Back Country Hang Gliding Hunting: Waterfowl No ORV's Allowed	Full Facilities in Bishop & Lone Pine Diaz Lake: P.O. Box 503

SOUTH SECTION

LAKES 149—196

NUMBERS REPRESENT LAKES IN NUMERICAL ORDER IN BOOK

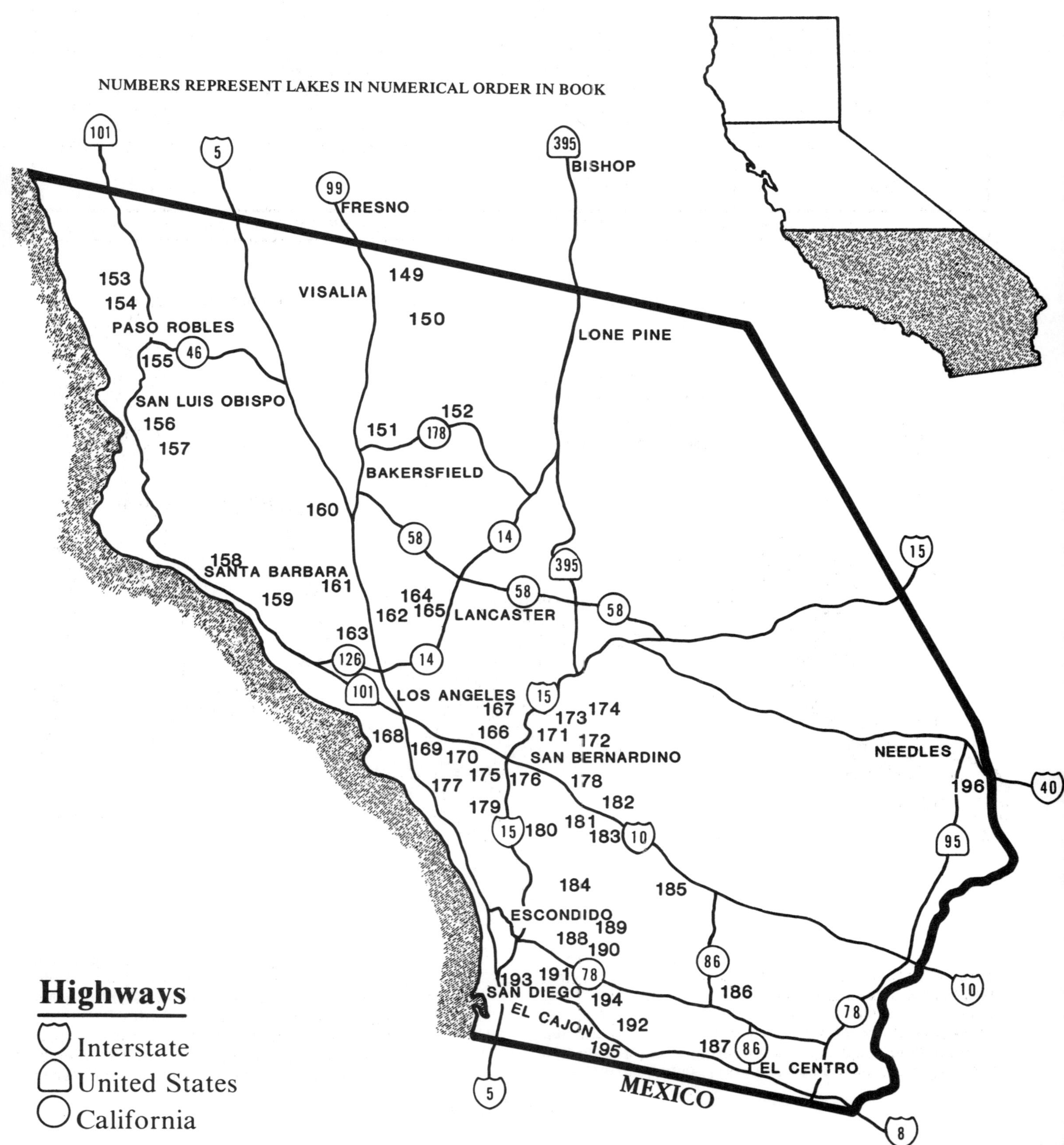

LAKE KAWEAH

Lake Kaweah rests at an elevation of 694 feet in the rolling foothills below Sequoia National Park. It was created with the damming of the Kaweah River about 20 miles upstream from Visalia. The lake is 6 miles long with 22 miles of shoreline surrounded by oak-studded hills. There is a total surface area of 1,945 acres when full but there is often a 100 foot drop late in the season. The U. S. Army Corps of Engineers maintain Termindus Dam, a 250 foot high and 2,375 foot long earth filled dam, along with the nice campgrounds, picnic areas and marina facilities. This is a good boating lake for varied craft including houseboats which are popular along the many coves and inlets. Submerged rocks are a hazard during low water. Fishing can be good for a broad variety of game fish.

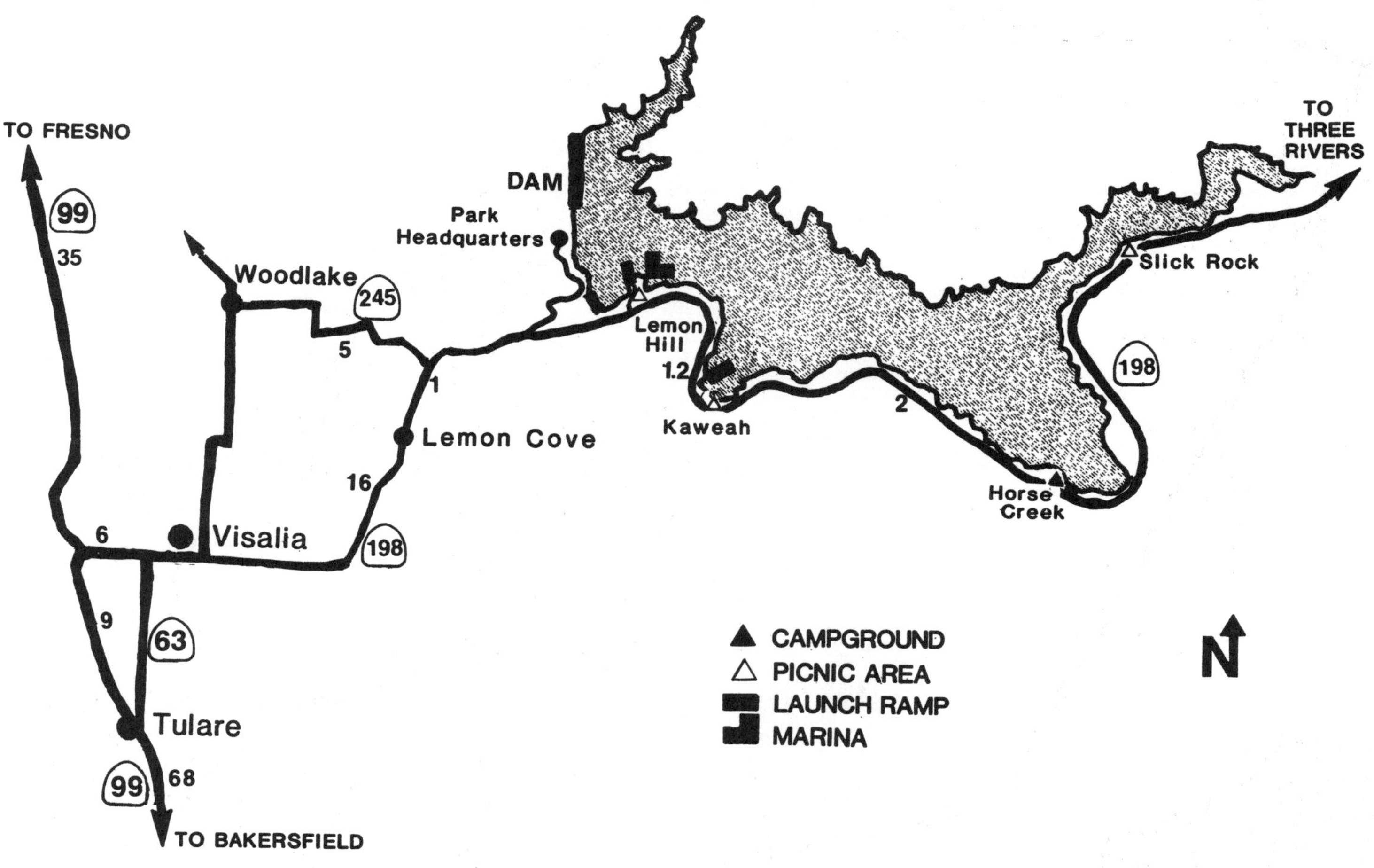

INFORMATION: U. S. Army Corps of Engineers, P.O. Box 346, Lemon Cove 93244, Ph: 209-597-2301

CAMPING	BOATING	RECREATION	OTHER
80 Dev. Sites for Tents & R.V.s (Handicap Site by Reservation) Overnight on Boat Permitted Anywhere Away From Shore	Power, Row, Canoe, Sail, Waterski, Jet Ski Full Service Marina Launch Ramps Rentals: Fishing Boats, Houseboats & Pontoons Docks, Berths, Moorings, Gas Low Water Late in Season Submerged Rock Hazards	Fishing: Florida & Spotted Bass, Bluegill, Channel Catfish, Black & White Crappie, Redear Sunfish - Rainbow Trout in Season Swimming Picnicking Campfire Program	Snack Bar Bait & Tackle Disposal Station Full Facilities at Woodlake and Three Rivers

SUCCESS LAKE

Success Lake rests at an elevation of 640 feet in the southern Sierra foothills. The lake has a surface area of 2,450 acres with 30 miles of shoreline. The U. S. Army Corps of Engineers has jurisdiction over the abundant and well-maintained camping, marine and recreation facilities. There is a Wildlife Area open for public use with hunting allowed, shotguns only, during appropriate seasons. The bird watcher may find several rare or endangered species, such as the Bald Eagle. There is good fishing year round and all types of boating are permitted from houseboats to waterskiing at this complete facility.

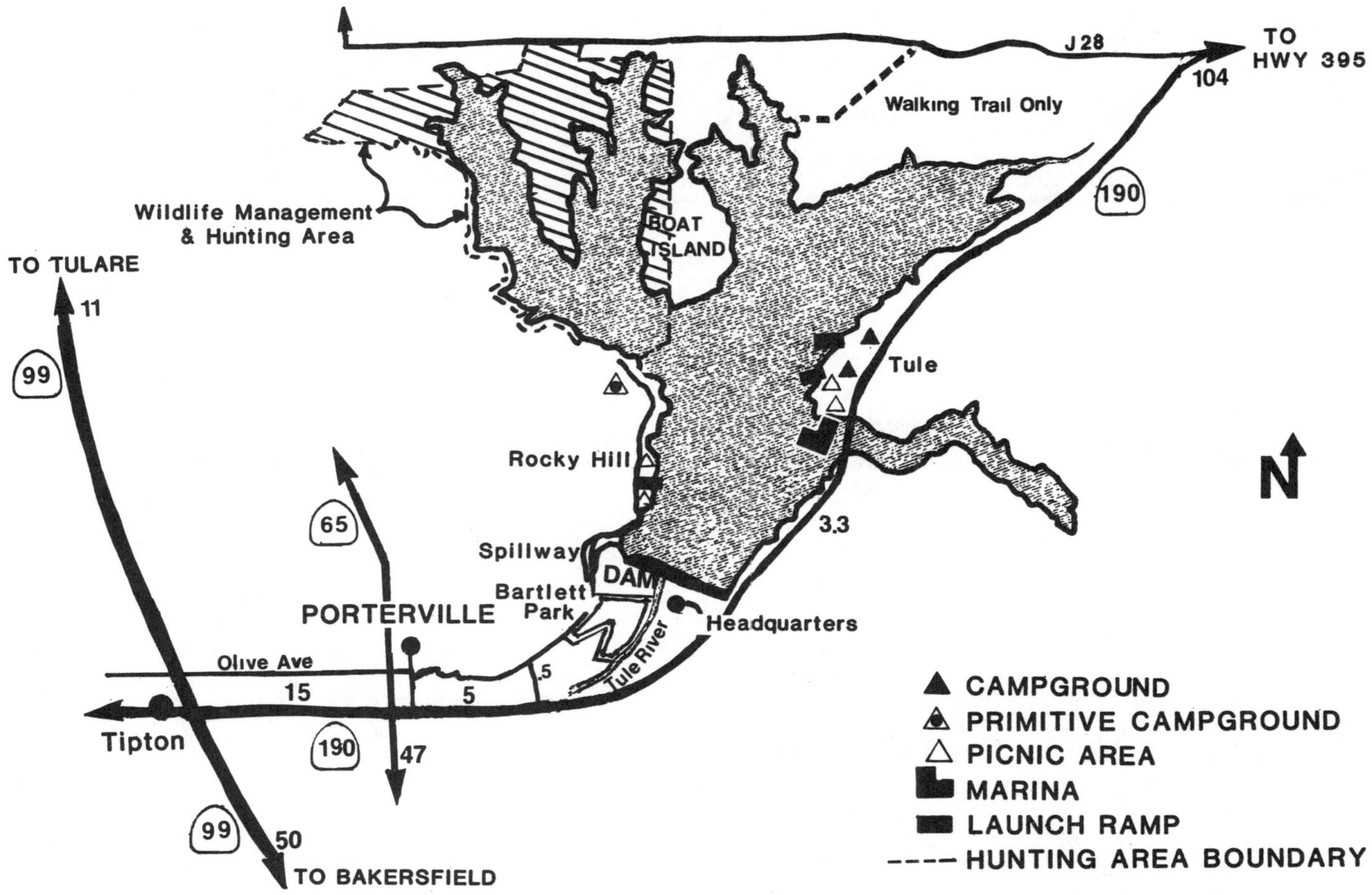

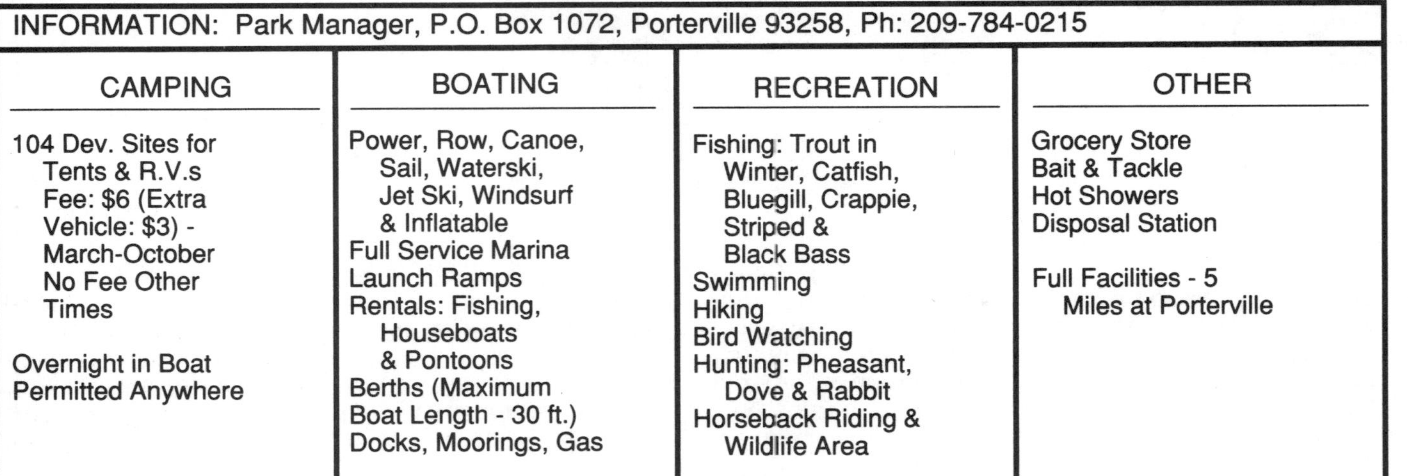

INFORMATION: Park Manager, P.O. Box 1072, Porterville 93258, Ph: 209-784-0215

CAMPING	BOATING	RECREATION	OTHER
104 Dev. Sites for Tents & R.V.s Fee: $6 (Extra Vehicle: $3) - March-October No Fee Other Times Overnight in Boat Permitted Anywhere	Power, Row, Canoe, Sail, Waterski, Jet Ski, Windsurf & Inflatable Full Service Marina Launch Ramps Rentals: Fishing, Houseboats & Pontoons Berths (Maximum Boat Length - 30 ft.) Docks, Moorings, Gas	Fishing: Trout in Winter, Catfish, Bluegill, Crappie, Striped & Black Bass Swimming Hiking Bird Watching Hunting: Pheasant, Dove & Rabbit Horseback Riding & Wildlife Area	Grocery Store Bait & Tackle Hot Showers Disposal Station Full Facilities - 5 Miles at Porterville

WOOLLOMES, HART AND MING LAKES

The nice facilities at Hart, Woollomes and Ming Lakes are under the jurisdiction of Kern County. Lake Woollomes, 300 surface acres, and Hart Lake, 18 surface acres, offer non-powered boating and fishing. Lake Ming, 107 surface acres, is primarily a waterskiing, power boating and drag racing lake but sailing and fishing as scheduled below are added attractions. Brite Valley is under the jurisdiction of the Tehachapi Valley Recreation and Parks Department. This 90 surface acre lake rests at an elevation of 4,000 feet. It is open during the warmer months for non-powered boating and fishing but closed from November through April.

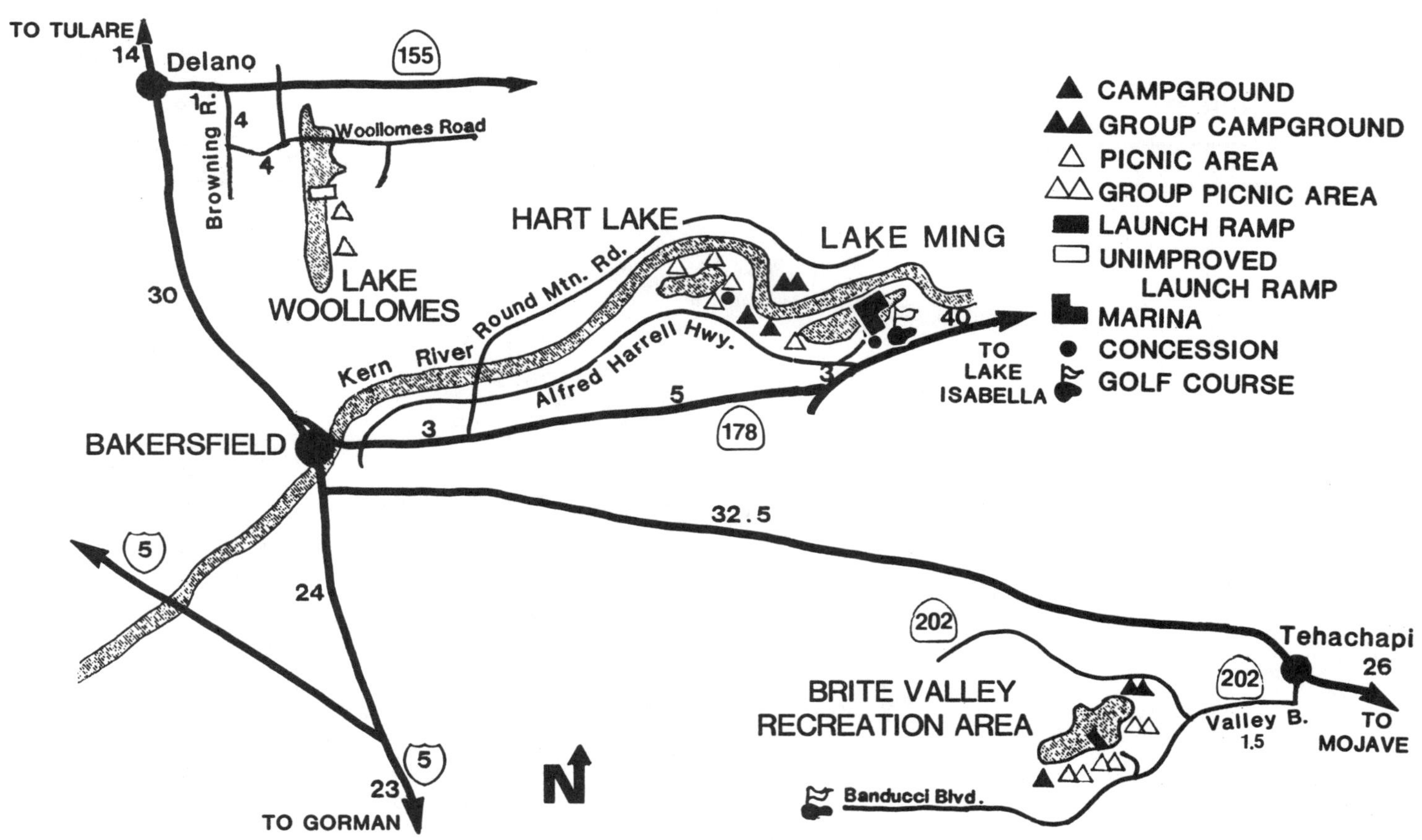

INFORMATION: Kern County Parks, 1110 Golden State, Bakersfield 93301, Ph: 805-861-2345

CAMPING	BOATING	RECREATION	OTHER
Kern River County Park: 50 Dev. Sites for Tents & R.V.s No Hookups Fee: $10 Per Vehicle Per Campsite Maximum 3 Vehicles BriteValley: Unlimited Open Camping Dry Camp: $7 12 Water & Electric Hookups: $9	Woolomes & Hart: Sail, Canoe, Row & Pedal Boats Only Ming: Power Boating & Drag Races Sailing Allowed on Tuesdays & Thursdays After 1:30 pm and the 2nd Weekend of Month Brite Valley: No Power Except Electric Motors	Fishing: Largemouth Bass, Bluegill, Crappie & Catfish Hart & Ming: Trout in Winter Family & Group Picnicking Hiking Swimming at Woollomes Only Golf Course	Brite Valley Aquatic Recreation Area: Information - Tehachapi Valley Recreation & Parks 490 West "D" Tehachapi 93561 Ph: 805-822-3228

ISABELLA LAKE

Isabella Lake lies at an elevation of 2,605 feet in the foothills east of Bakersfield. The surface area of the lake is 11,400 acres with a shoreline of 38 miles. The U. S. Army Corps of Engineers maintains the excellent and ample facilities at this complete recreation lake. The main attractions at Isabella are boating, fishing and waterskiing. Sailing, windsurfing and jet skiing are also popular. Activities range from white water rafting to bird watching. A trap range is available and hunting is allowed in designated areas. Winds can be a hazard so warning lights are located at 5 points around the lake. Lake Patrol, Rescue Service, and Boat Permits are handled by the Kern County Parks Department.

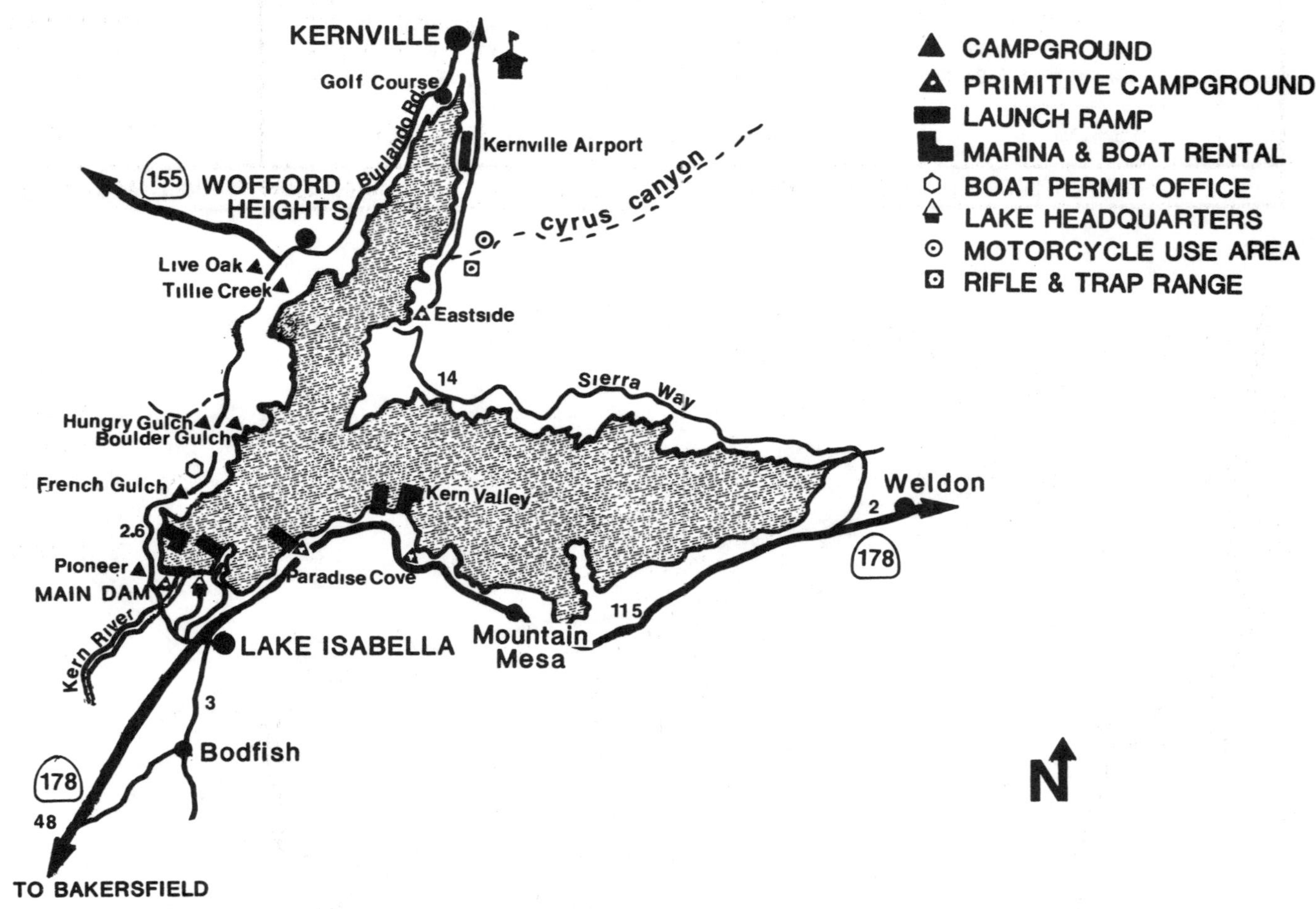

INFORMATION: U. S. Army Corps of Engineers, P.O. Box 997, Lake Isabella 93240, Ph: 619-379-2742

CAMPING	BOATING	RECREATION	OTHER
623 Dev. Sites for Tents & R.V.s Water with "Y" Fee: $8 Group Camp - 25 to 200 People Per Area Call for Fee Info. Plus 1200 Undev. Campsites Disposal Station	Power, Row, Canoe, Sail, Waterski, Jet Ski, Windsurf & Inflatables With Restrictions Boat Permit Fee: $10 Annually Full Service Marinas Launch Ramps Rentals: Fishing & Waterski Boats Docks, Berths, Moorings, Gas	Fishing: Trout, Catfish, Bluegill, Crappie & Florida Bass Swimming Picnicking Hiking White Water Rafting Bird Watching Hunting: Quail & Waterfowl	Full Facilities at Towns Near Lake Airport-Auto Rentals Golf Playgrounds Campfire Programs Nature Study Trailer Rentals & Storage ORV Use Area Rifle & Trap Range

SAN ANTONIO LAKE

San Antonio Lake is at an elevation of 900 feet in the oak-covered rolling hills of Southern Monterey County. The lake has a surface area of 5,500 acres with 60 shoreline miles. There is an abundance of modern campsites, many with full hookups. This is an ideal lake for waterskiing with its mild water temperature, its length of 16 miles, and calm waters protected by the surrounding hills. An excellent warm water fishery makes San Antonio a good year round angler's lake. The facilities are open all year with complete services for vacation activities.

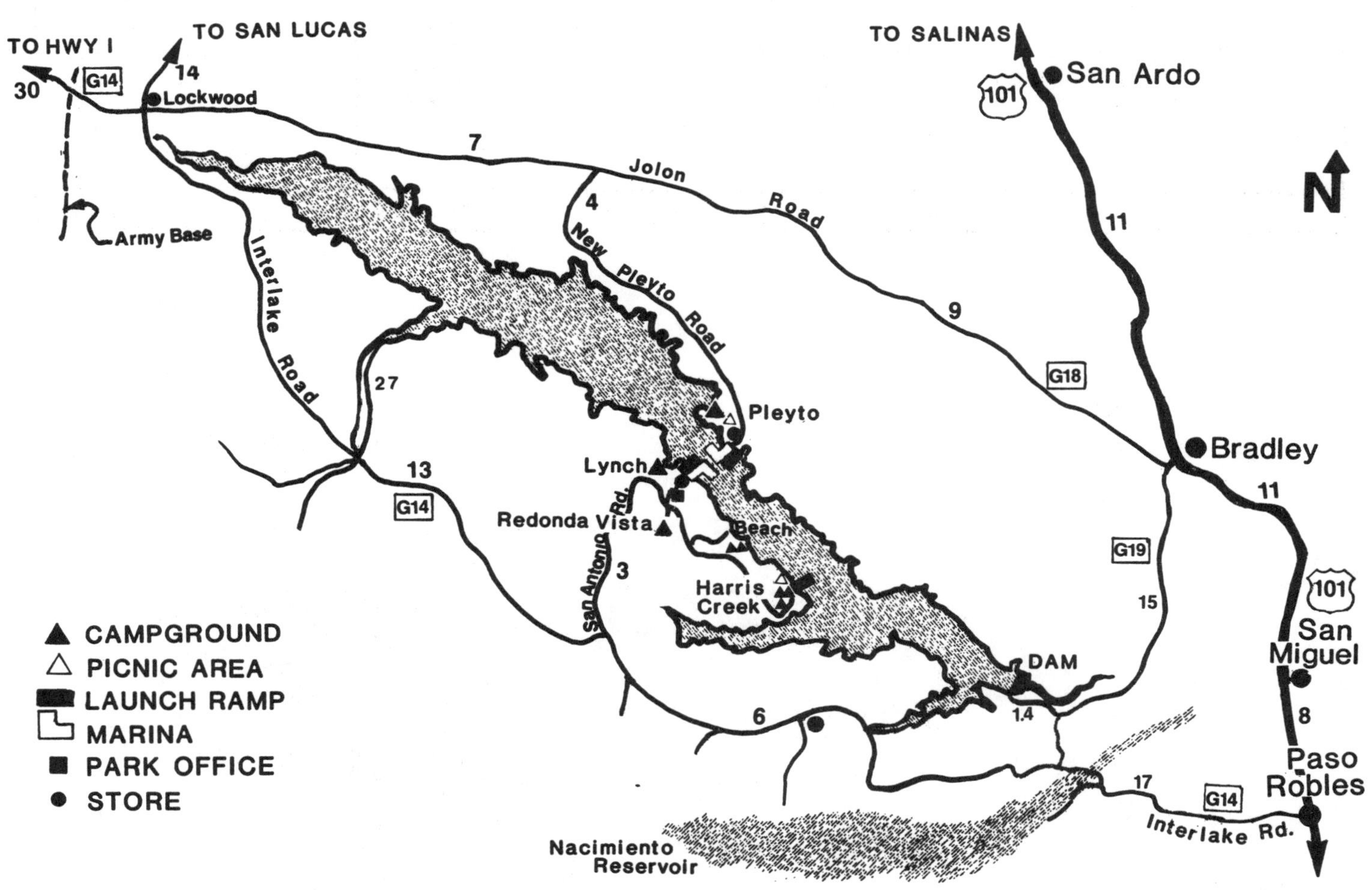

INFORMATION: Monterey Co. Parks Dept., St. Rt. Bx. 2610, Bradley, CA 93426, Ph: 805-472-2311

CAMPING	BOATING	RECREATION	OTHER
650 Dev. Sites for Tents & R.V.s Some With Full Hookups Fees: Winter - $9 - $12 Summer - $10 - $14 Youth Campground to 60 People Disposal Station	Power, Row, Canoe, Sail, Waterski, Jet Ski, Windsurf & Inflatable Full Service Marina Launch Ramps - $3.50 Rentals: Fishing Boats, Pontoons & Houseboats Docks, Mooring, Gas, Dry Storage	Fishing: Catfish, Bluegill, Large & Smallmouth Bass, Striped Bass & Redear Perch Swimming - Beaches Picnicking Hiking Trails Campfire Program Nature Study Birding Exercise Course	Snack Bar Restaurant Grocery Store Bait & Tackle Laundromat Gas Station Game Room Mobile Home Rentals Reservations - Ph: 805-472-2313

LAKE NACIMIENTO

Lake Nacimiento is nestled in a valley of pine and oak trees at an elevation of 800 feet. The surface area is 5,370 acres with 165 miles of shoreline with many delightful coves. Fishing from shore or boat will usually produce bass, either large or smallmouth or the voracious white bass. Crappie, bluegill and catfish are also plentiful. Waterskiing is excellent on the 16-mile long lake with water temperature about 68 degrees. Lake Nacimiento Resort offers an abundance of modern campsites, complete marina facilities and vacation activities, making it an excellent family recreation area. All of these facilities are newly renovated plus the addition of 18 condominiums and a first class restaurant.

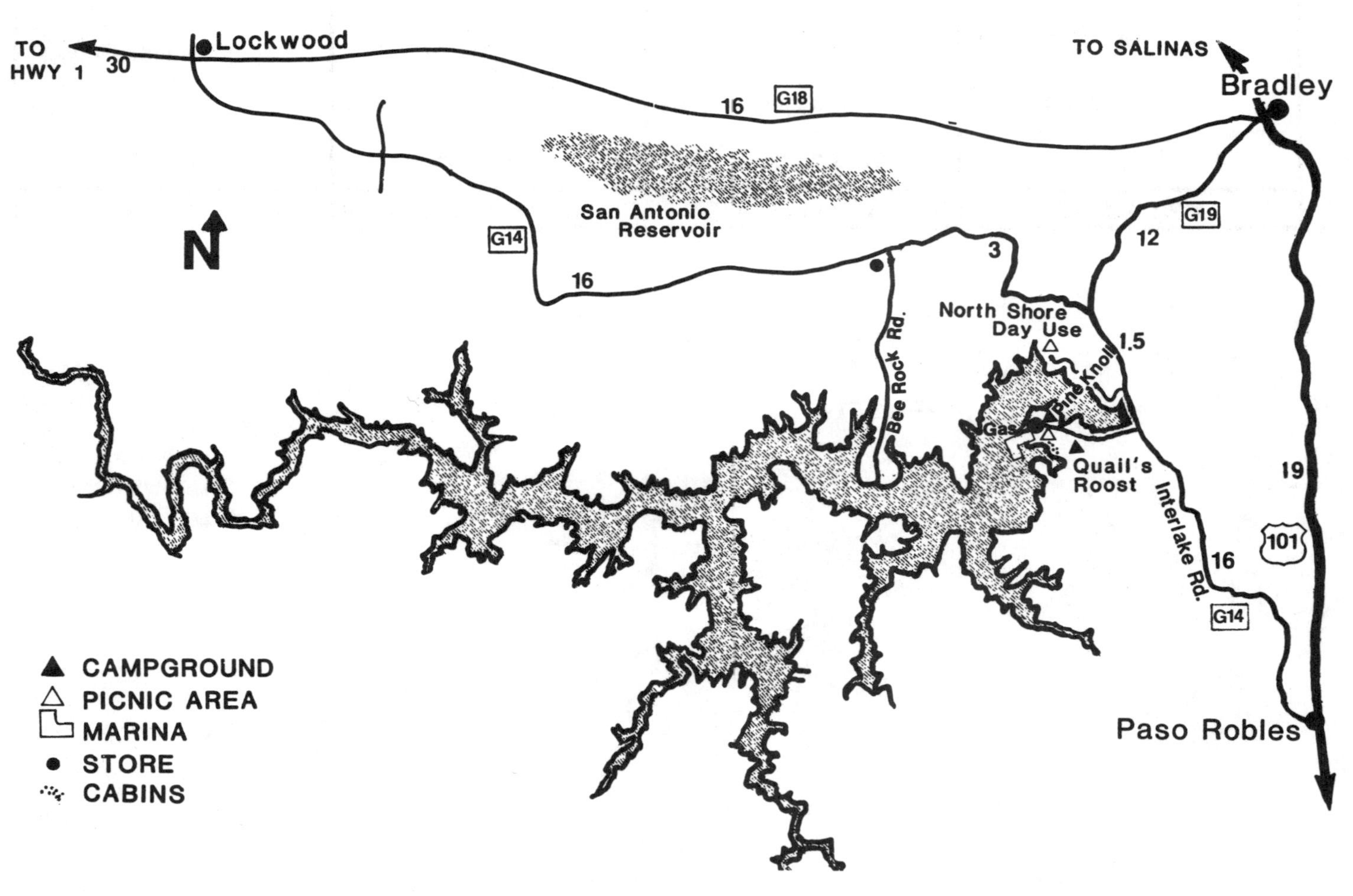

INFORMATION: Lake Nacimiento Resort, Star Route, Bradley 93426, Ph: 805-238-3256			
CAMPING	BOATING	RECREATION	OTHER
350 Dev. Sites for Tents & R.V.s Fees: $16/Night $96/Week 40 R.V. Sites With Full Hookups Fees: $20/Night $120/Week Group Sites to 600 People Winter Rates in Effect 9-14 to 4-1	Power, Row, Canoe, Sail, Waterski, Jet Ski, Windsurf & Inflatable Min. Length - 8 ft. Full Service Marina 3 Launch Ramps Slalom Course Rentals: Fishing Bass Boats, Pontoons, Pleasure Boats County Water Fee: $3.50 a Day	Fishing: Catfish, Bluegill, Crappie, White, Large & Smallmouth Bass Swimming Picnicking Hiking **NO** Motorcycles of Any Type Day Use Fee: $7 - South Shore $5 - North Shore	Cabins Laundry Facility Restaurant Grocery Store Bait & Tackle Hot Showers Disposal Station Gas & Propane Camp Trailer Rental Playgrounds Swimming Pool & Hot Tubs During Summer Only

SANTA MARGARITA LAKE, WHALE ROCK RESERVOIR, AND ATASCADERO LAKE

Nestled amid Central California's coastal range, these lakes vary in recreational opportunities. Santa Margarita, the largest of the three with 1,070 surface acres, is a warm water fisherman's delight with nearby camping facilities. Although waterskiing and windsurfing are not permitted, it is a good boating lake. Atascadero is a small city lake with picnic facilities, a concession and rental boats. Power boating is not allowed. You may fish for trout and bass. The City of San Luis Obispo does not allow boating or any water contact at Whale Rock Reservoir. There is a 3 trout limit per day.

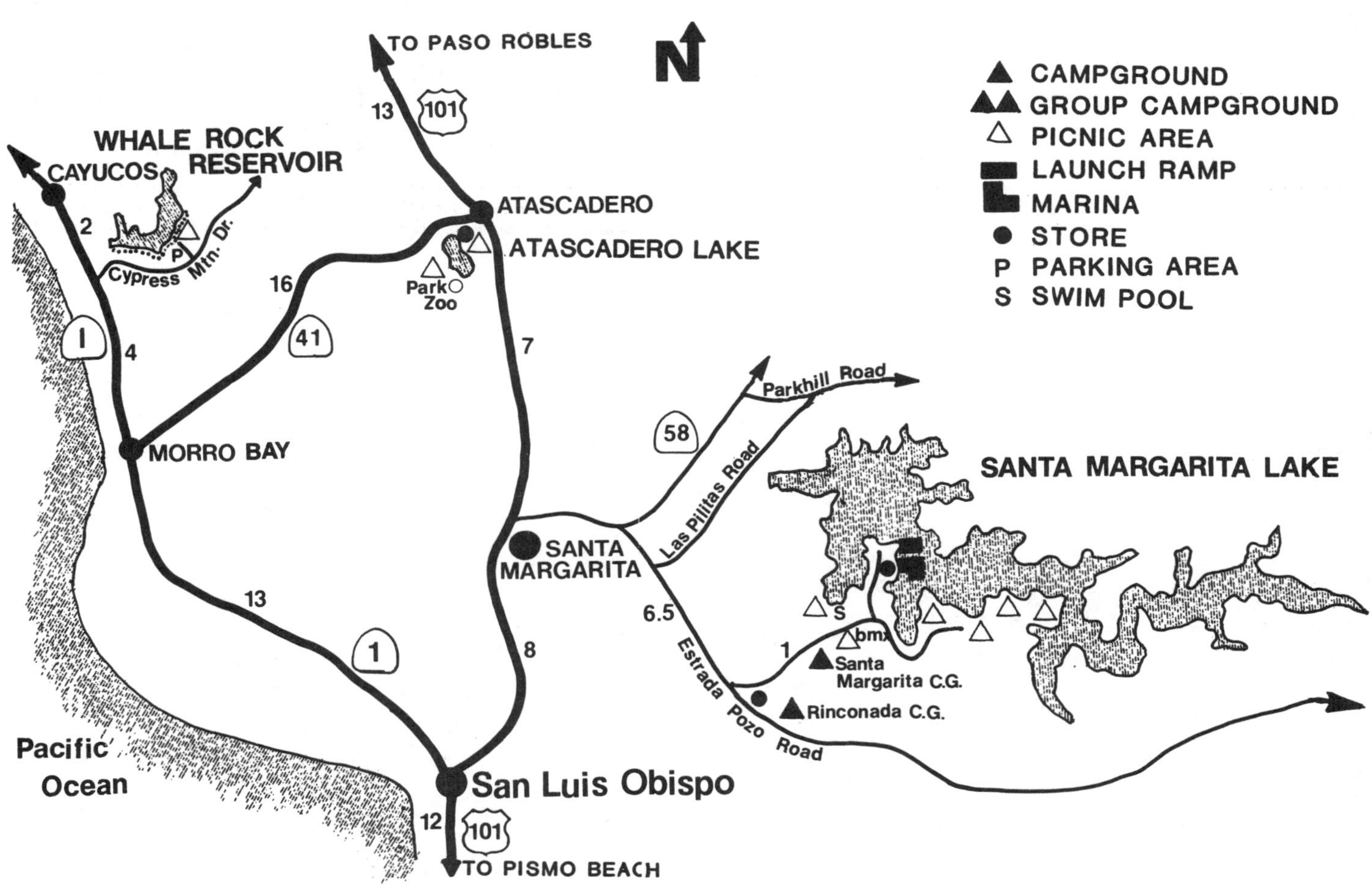

NFORMATION: Santa Margarita Marina, Star Rt. Box 36, Santa Margarita 93453, Ph: 805-438-3474			
CAMPING	BOATING	RECREATION	OTHER
Santa Margarita: Star Rt., Box 34C Santa Margarita Ph: 805-438-5618 100 Tent/R.V. Sites Full & Partial Hookups Fees: $12 - $15 RincondaCamp: Star Rt., Box 36D Santa Margarita Ph: 805-438-5479 60 Tent/R.V. Sites 17 With Full Hookups Fee: $8 - $10.50	Santa Margarita: All Boats Over 10 Feet Allowed **NO** Waterskiing or Windsurfing Approved Inflatable Full Service Marina Rentals: Fishing Boats & Motors, Pontoons Launch: $3.50 Whale Rock: No Boating	Fishing: Rainbow Trout, Bluegill, Catfish, Crappie, Largemouth & Striped Bass Swimming: St. Margarita-Pool Atascadero-Kiddie Pool Only Whale Rock-None Picnicking Hiking & Riding Trails	Santa Margarita: Snacks & Drinks Bait & Tackle Atascadero: Boating: Restricted No Power Boats 5 MPH Speed Limit **NO** Waterskiing or Windsurfing Hand Launch Only

LOPEZ LAKE

Lopez Lake was opened in 1969 and is administered by the San Luis Obispo County Parks and Recreation Department. Its 950 surface acres are favored by westerly breezes coming off the Pacific which make it a popular lake for sailing and windsurfing. There are good marine support facilities and special areas are set aside for sailing, windsurfing, jet skis and waterskiing. The angler will find a variety of game fish. In addition to the well maintained oak-shaded campsites listed below, there are overflow sites. This is a complete recreation facility offering a good naturalist program which can be enjoyed on trails, by boat or at the campfire. The two 600-foot waterslides are popular with the youngsters.

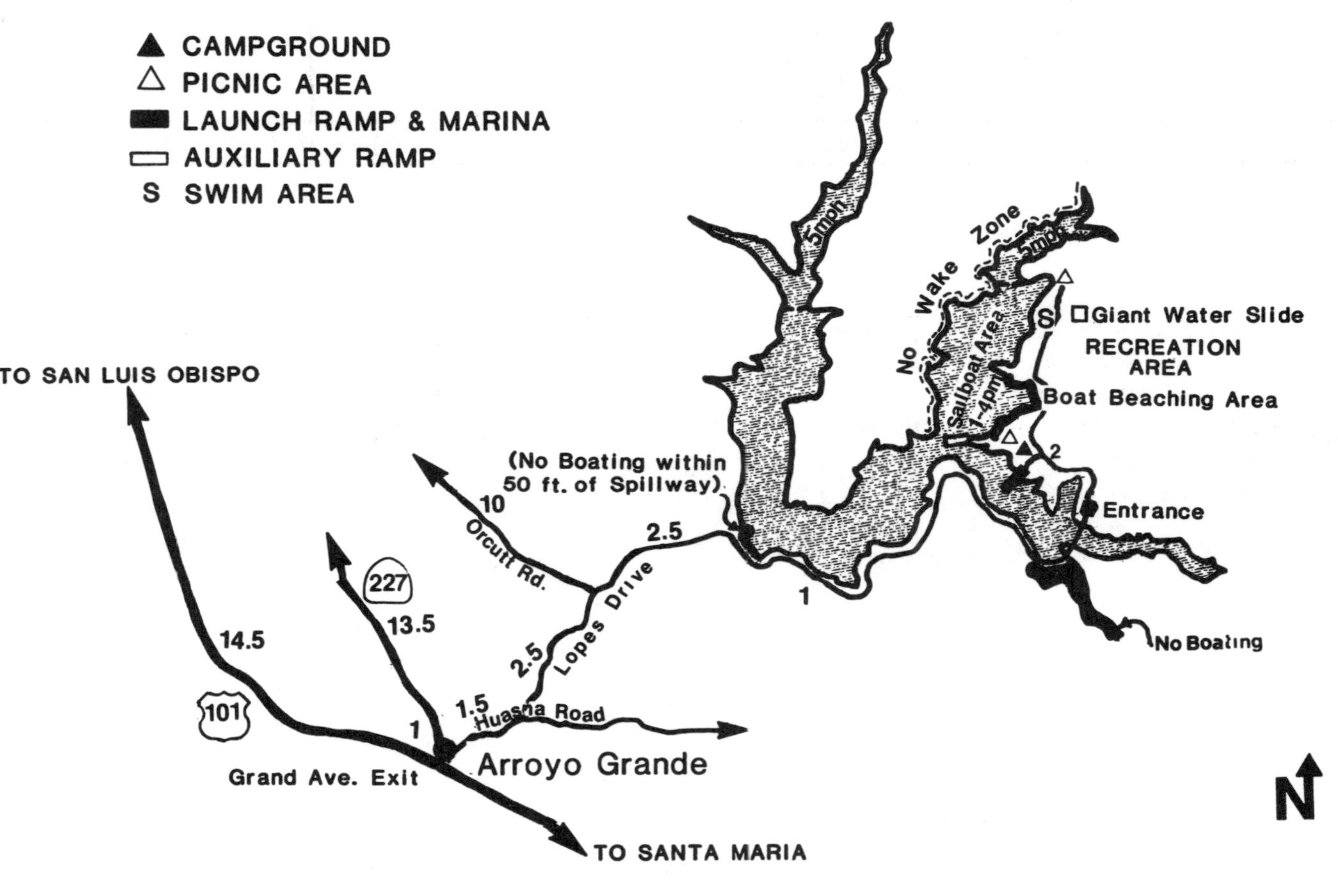

INFORMATION: Lopez Lake, 6800 Lopez Dr., Arroyo Grande 93420, Ph: 805-489-2095

CAMPING	BOATING	RECREATION	OTHER
148 Primitive Sites for Tents & R.V.s Fee: $10 67 Sites with Electric Hookups Fee: $14 135 Sites with Full Hookups Fee: $16 Reservations: Ph: 805-489-8019 Monday-Friday 8 am - 5 pm	Open to All Boating Speed Limit: 40 MPH Full Service Marina Paved Launch: $3.50 per Day $40 per Year Boat/Trailer Storage: $14 per Day $27 per Month $215 per Year Rentals: Fishing, Ski, Patio, Canoe, Sail & Sailboard	Fishing: Trout, Catfish, Bluegill, Crappie, Redear Sunfish & Black Bass Swimming: n Designated Areas Picnicking Hiking & Nature Trails Boat Tours Campfire Programs	Snack Bar General Store Bait & Tackle Laundromat Gas Station Waterslide Hot Spas Pets: $1.50 a Day, Must Have Proof of Current Rabies Vaccination

ZACA LAKE

Zaca Lake is Southern California's only natural mineral lake. Owned and operated by the Human Potential Foundation, this small rustic facility is at an elevation of 2,400 feet in the San Rafael Mountains of the Los Padres National Park. Located 40 miles north of Santa Barbara, this area has an abundance of wildlife and a variety of plants and trees. Although the small 25 surface acre lake is closed to fishing, non-powered boating and swimming are available. There are numerous hiking trails for those so inclined but the prevailing theme here is peace and relaxation. The resort offers a nice restaurant with good food and drink, remodeled cabins with queen-sized beds, fireplaces and tiled jacuzzi tubs. This is where you come to get away from it all.

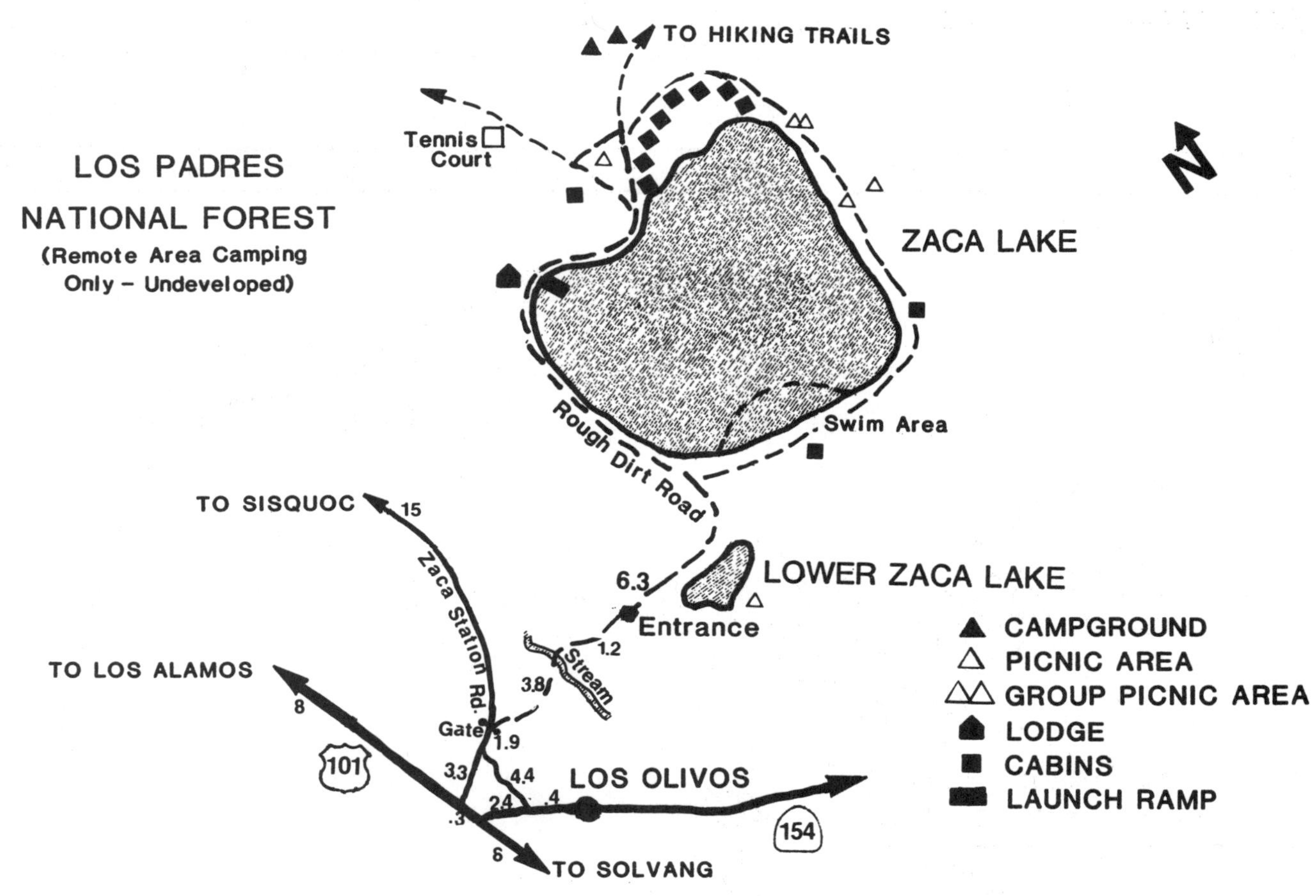

INFORMATION: Zaca Lake, P.O. Box 187, Los Olivos 93441, Ph: 805-688-4891			
CAMPING	BOATING	RECREATION	OTHER
Lodge, Housekeeping Cabins Camping: $10 Los Padres National Forest Remote Camping 100 Sites No Open Fires	Row, Pedal, Canoe, Sail & Sailboards No Motors Unimproved Launch Ramp: $4 Boat Rentals	Hiking & Riding Trails Backpacking Swimming Picnicking Tennis Mineral Baths	Restaurant Snack Bar Cocktail Lounge Game Room Gas

LAKE CACHUMA

Lake Cachuma is nestled at an elevation of 800 feet amid the oak-shaded hills of the Santa Ynez Valley. This is one of the most complete recreation parks in the State providing an abundance of modern camping, marine, recreation and other support facilities. In addition to the campgrounds at the lake, the Cachuma Recreation Area includes the San Marcos Camp which will accommodate large groups to 4,000 people with complete facilities. This 3,200 acre lake is open to most boating. Waterskiing, kayaks, rafts and canoes are not allowed. Fishing can be excellent. There are hiking, nature and riding trails. Swimming pools and bicycle rentals are open from June through Labor Day. Park naturalists conduct a variety of programs. Gibraltar Reservoir is open for trout fishing on a limited permit basis through the City of Santa Barbara.

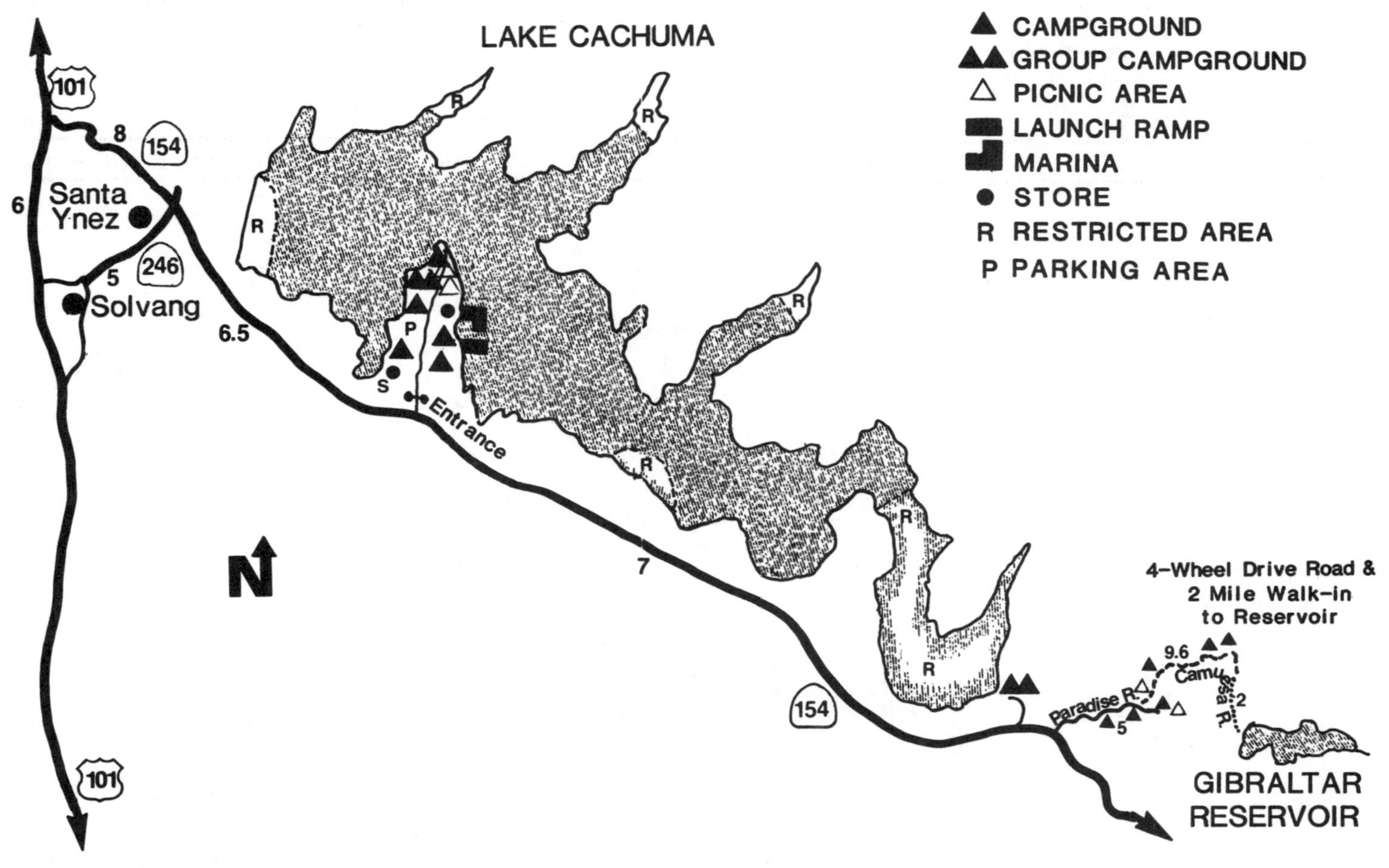

INFORMATION: Cachuma Lake, Star Route, Santa Barbara 93105, Ph: 805-688-8780			
CAMPING	BOATING	RECREATION	OTHER
470 Dev. Sites for Tents & R.V.s Fees: $9 - $11 90 R.V. Sites - Full and Partial Hookups Fee: $15 11 Group Camps - 8 to 30 Units 3 Disposal Stations	Open to Most Boating Contact Above for Restrictions Launch Ramp Full Service Marina Docks, Berths & Moorings Trailer & Boat Storage Rentals: Fishing, Patio & Sail Boats	Fishing: Catfish, Bluegill, Crappie, Large & Smallmouth Bass, Redear Sunfish, Rainbow Trout Birding Swimming: Pools Only Picnicking Hiking & Riding Trails Bicycle Rentals Nature Programs & Tours	Handicap Facilities 5 Restrooms with Hot Showers General Store Bait & Tackle Snack Bar Laundromat Recreation Center Pools Gas Station Riding Stables

LAKE CASITAS

Lake Casitas is at an elevation of 600 feet in the oak-covered rolling hills west of Ojai. This 2,700 surface acre lake is under the jurisdiction of the Casitas Municipal Water District which maintains a strict boating and swimming policy of no body contact with the water. The 32 miles of shoreline has many restricted areas, so please note them on the map. Casitas is famous for big fish and once held the State record for largemouth bass at 21 pounds, 3 ounces. It now holds the State record for redear sunfish at 3 pounds, 7 ounces. You can fish from boat, bank or pier and perhaps catch a World's Record. The 6,200 acre tree-shaded recreation area offers excellent picnicking, camping and boating facilities.

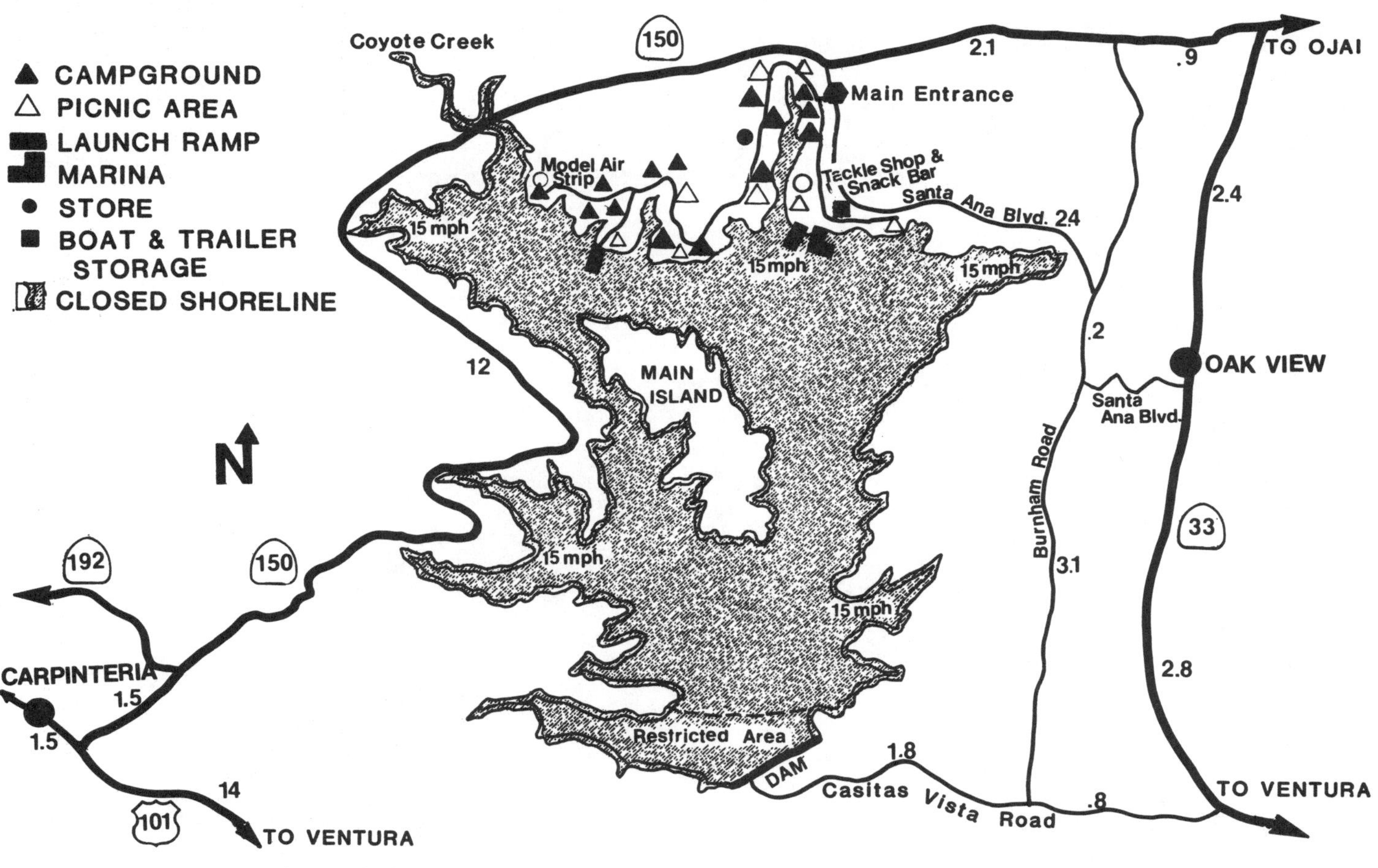

INFORMATION: Casitas Rec. Area, 11311 Santa Ana Rd., Ventura 93001, Ph: 805-649-2233			
CAMPING	**BOATING**	**RECREATION**	**OTHER**
454 Plus Dev. Sites - Tents & R.V.s Plus Overflow Fees: $9 per Night $9 per Night for Extra Vehicle $1 per Day for Pet 2 Large Overflow Areas Disposal Stations Reservations: Groups Only Handicap Facilities	Power, Row, Sail Only - 11 ft. Min. to 24 ft. Max. - Strict Regulations Speed Limit - 40 MPH Boat Permit: $3.50/Day Full Service Marina Launch Ramps Rentals: Fishing & Row Boats, Pontoons Docks, Moorings, Berths, Gas, Storage	Fishing: Trout, Bluegill, Large-mouth & Florida Bass, Redear Sunfish, Perch & Crappie No Swimming Picnicking Hiking Playgrounds Model Airplane Strip	Snack Bar Restaurant Grocery Store Showers - 25 cents Bait & Tackle Ph: 805-649-2043 Trailer Rentals: Ph: 805-649-1202 Trailer & Boat Storage

LAKE EVANS AND LAKE WEBB BUENA VISTA AQUATIC RECREATION AREA

Buena Vista Recreation Area is at an elevation of 293 feet in the semi-arid south San Joaquin Valley. This is Kern County's finest recreation area consisting of 1,586 acres and two lakes with complete modern facilities for camping, picnicking, swimming and boating. Lake Evans has a surface area of 86 acres and Lake Webb has 873 acres. Both lakes are stocked continually with warm water game fish. Trophy trout are stocked in the winter months at Lake Evans. All boating is allowed in both lakes but Lake Evans is restricted to a 5 MPH speed limit. Waterskiing is permitted at Lake Webb in a counterclockwise pattern. There is a no-ski area for sailboats and power boats without skiers.

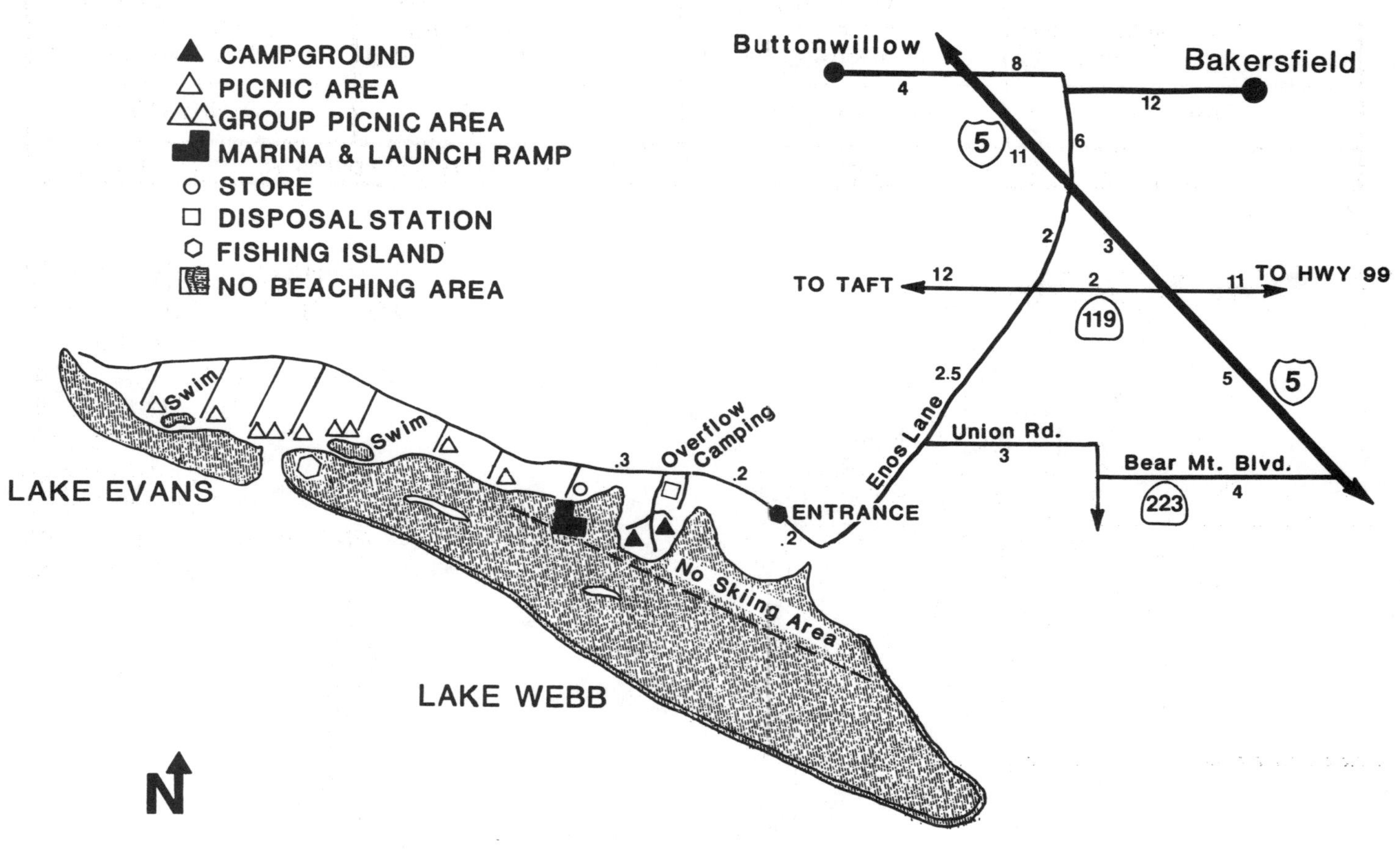

INFORMATION: Kern County Parks, 1110 Golden State, Bakersfield 93301, Ph: 805-861-2345			
CAMPING	BOATING	RECREATION	OTHER
112 Dev. Sites for Tents & R.V.s Fees: No Hookups $12 - $15 Full Hookups $14 - $18 Plus Overflow Area Fee: $6 Pets - $2 a Day No Reservations Buena Vista Recreation Area Ph: 805-763-1526	Power, Row, Canoe, Sail, Windsurf, Jet Ski & Inflatable Meet Requirements Speed Limits: 5 MPH-Lake Evans 45 MPH-Lake Webb Launch Ramps Waterski Beaches Rentals: Fishing & Paddle Boats Docks, Moorings, Gas	Fishing: Trout in Winter, Catfish, Bluegill, Crappie, Largemouth & Striped Bass Swimming: Lagoons Only Picnicking Deep Pit Barbecues Playgrounds	Snack Bar Grocery Store Beer & Wine Bait & Tackle Laundromat Gas Station Propane Waterski & Equipment Rental Full Facilities - 14 Miles at Taft

PYRAMID LAKE

Pyramid Lake is at an elevation of 2,606 feet in the Angeles National Forest in Northwestern Los Angeles County. This popular lake has a surface area of 1,297 acres. Most of its 21 miles of rugged shoreline is accessible only by boat. There are boat-in picnic sites and restrooms scattered around the lake. Spanish Point is a favorite spot with its picnic sites and ski beach. While there is a good trout and warm water fishery, Pyramid is known as one of Southern California's prime striped bass waters. There are good marine and campground facilities under concession from the U. S. Forest Service. Quail Lake, the beginning of the southern portion of the California Aqueduct, offers no facilities. The angler, however, may fish for stripers from the bank.

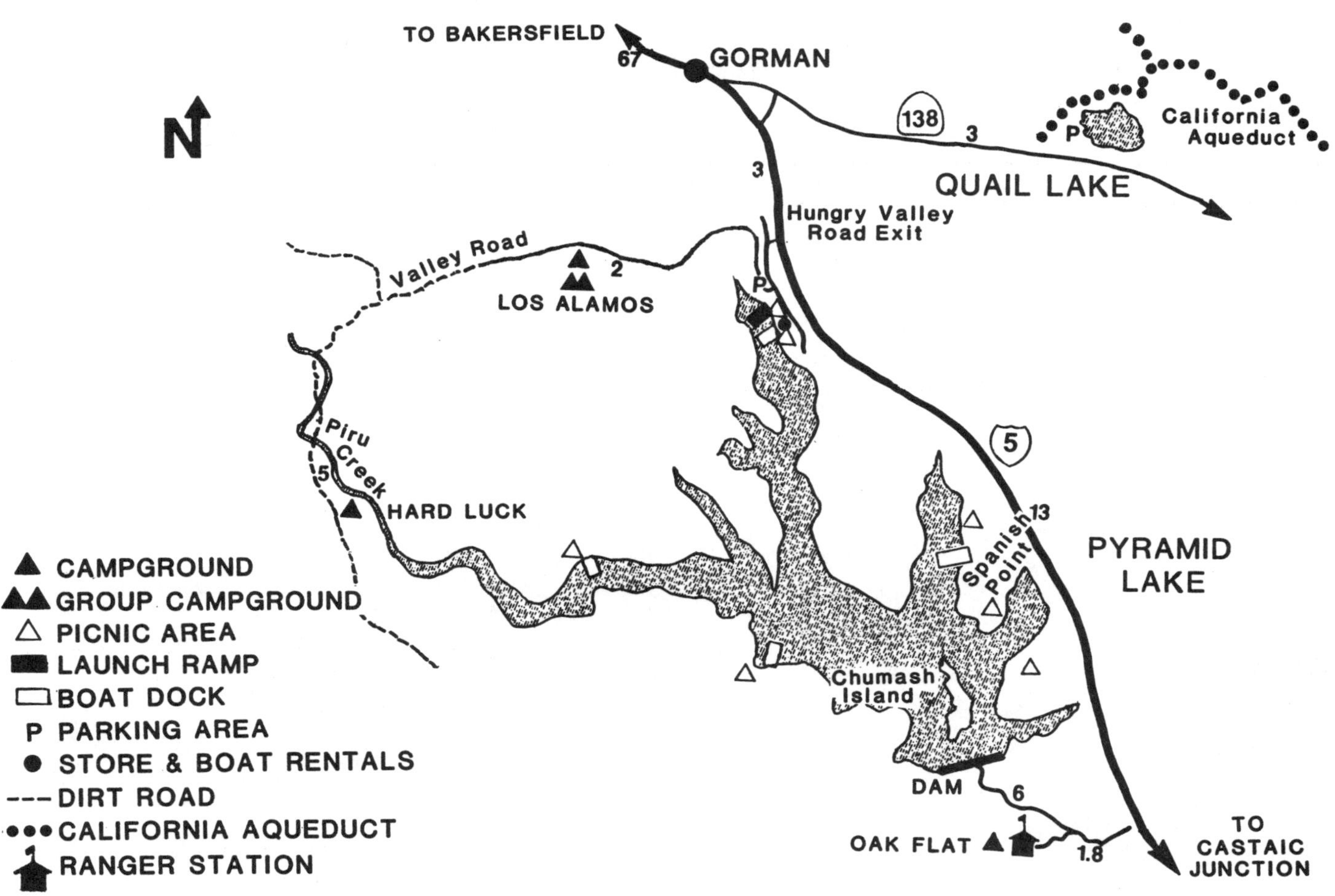

INFORMATION: Pyramid Lake Marina, P.O. Box 102, Gorman 93243, Ph: 805-257-2790

CAMPING	BOATING	RECREATION	OTHER
Los Alamos: 93 Dev. Sites Tents & R.V.s Fee: $5 Group Sites for 6 to 75 People Fee: $50 - $130 Ph: 805-248-6575 Hard Luck: 26 Dev. Sites Tents & R.V.s Fee: $5 First Come, First Served Ph: 805-248-6575	Open to All Boating, Waterskiing & Windsurfing Speed Limit 35 MPH Full Service Marina Docks & Gas Launch Ramp Boat Rentals: Fishing, Ski & Recreational Boats	Fishing: Rainbow Trout, Channel Catfish, Striped & Largemouth Bass, Bluegill, Crappie & Sunfish Swimming Beaches Picnicking Boat-In Picnic Sites	Snack Bar Bait & Tackle

CASTAIC LAKE

Castaic Lake and the Afterbay Lagoon, at an elevation of 1,500 feet, are a part of the California State Water Project and is operated by Los Angeles County. The Castaic Lake facility is Los Angeles County's largest recreation area with 9,000 acres. There are two separate lakes. The Main Reservoir has a surface area of 2,500 acres and the Afterbay Lagoon has 180 surface acres. The Main Reservoir's east arm is open to slower boating, 20 MPH speed limit, while the west arm is for waterskiing and fast boating. The Lagoon is open to non-power boating and swimming daily from mid-June through September and weekends and holidays from October through May. Fishing at the Main Reservoir is from sunrise to sunset, but the Lagoon offers 24-hour fishing on the shoreline of the east side of the lake. There is a good warm water fishery with the primary game fish being the Florida bass. Trout are stocked in the winter months.

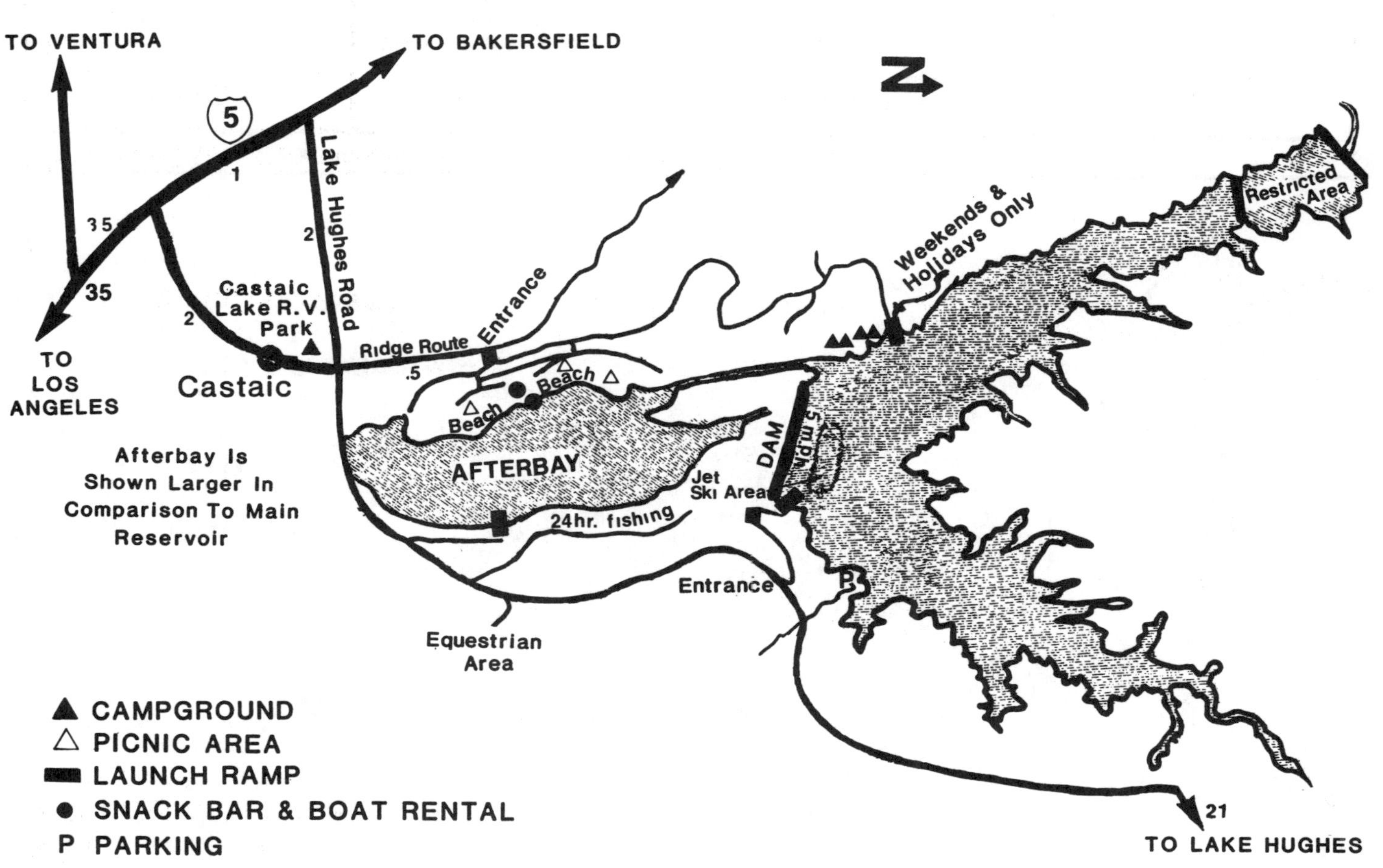

INFORMATION: Castaic Lake, P.O. Box 397, Castaic 91310, Ph: 805-257-4050

CAMPING	BOATING	RECREATION	OTHER
Group Camping - Non-Profit Groups to 200 Plus People 3 Nights Maximum $12.50 - $100.00 Castaic Lake RV Park 31540 Ridge Route Castaic 91318 Ph: 805-257-3340 103 R.V. Sites Full Hookups-to $18	Main Reservoir: All Boating Allowed 35 MPH Speed Limit Launch Ramps, Docks Rentals: Fishing Boats & Windsurfers Afterbay: Non-Power Boats Launch Ramp: $4 Rentals: Sail & Row, Windsurfers, Canoes, Paddleboats	Fishing: Trout, Catfish, Bluegill, Large & Smallmouth Bass Swimming Beaches at Afterbay Only Picnicking Hiking & Riding Trails	Snack Bar Bait & Tackle 24 Hour Fishing Area in Afterbay *Boaters Should Arrive Early as Launch is Closed After 500 Boats & 75 Jet Skis

LAKE PIRU

Lake Piru is at an elevation of 1,055 feet in the Los Padres National Forest near Metropolitan Los Angeles. It is owned and operated by the United Water Conservation District. The surface area of the lake ranges from a maximum of 1,200 acres to a minimum of 750 acres. The water is deep and clear. This is a proven fishing lake with warm water species growing to large sizes. Trout are planted twice a week in season. Although boating restrictions are sharply defined, this is a nice boating and sailing lake with good marina facilities. The campgrounds are located amid oak and olive trees above the launch ramp.

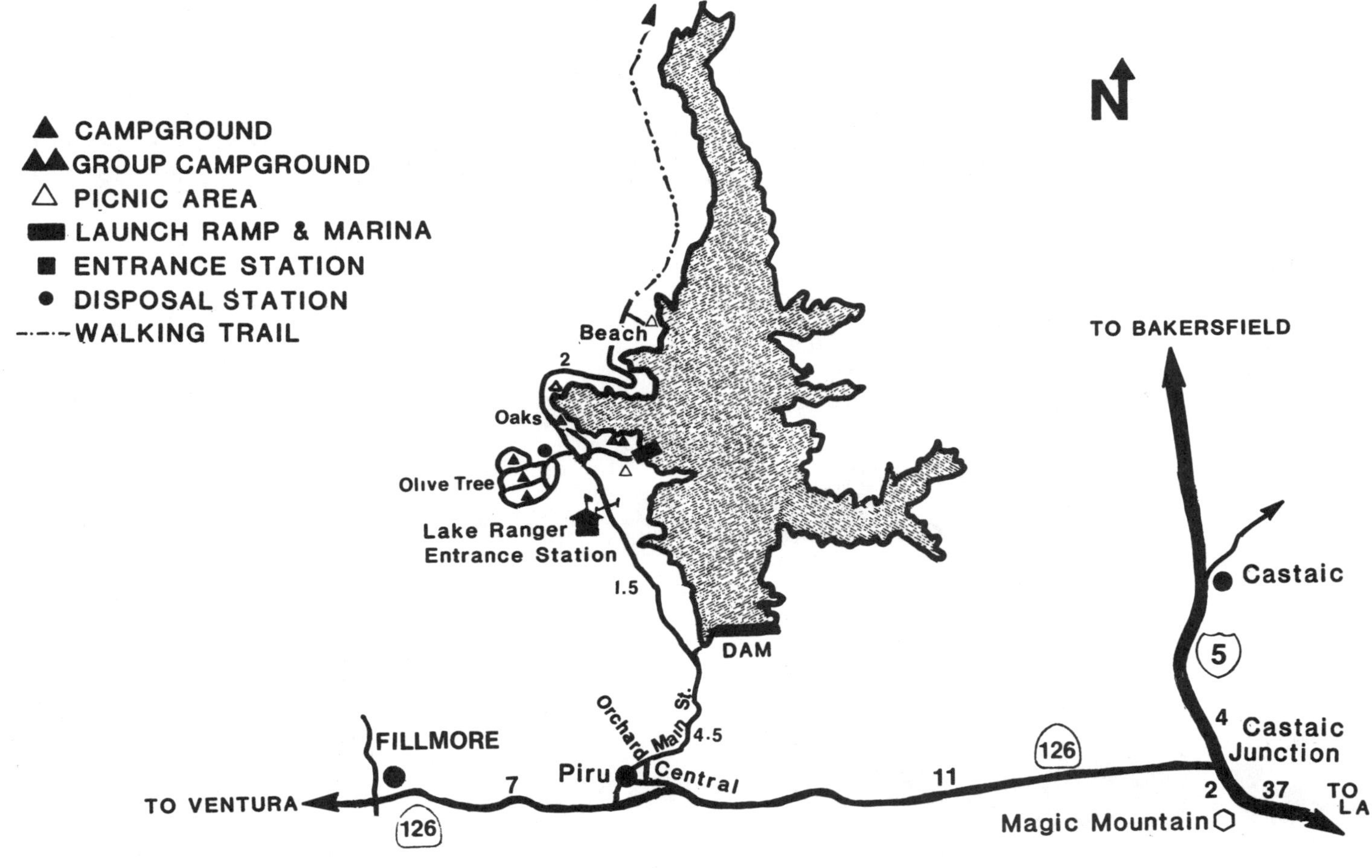

INFORMATION: Park Manager, P.O. Box 202, Piru 93040, Ph: 805-521-1500			
CAMPING	**BOATING**	**RECREATION**	**OTHER**
187 Tent Sites Fee: $10 62 R.V. Sites Electric Hookups Fee: $13 Group Camp: 4 to 12 Sites Day Use Fee: $3.50	Power, Waterskiing, Sail & Inflatables (Must be 12' long with 3 Separate Compartments & 3 HP Minimum) No Windsurfing, Jet Skis, Canoes or Rowboats Full Service Marina 5-Lane Launch Ramp Rentals	Fishing: Rainbow & Brown Trout, Bass, Catfish, Crappie, Bluegill Swim Beach Picnicking Hiking & Riding Trails in Los Padres National Forest Backpacking	Snack Bar Bait & Tackle Disposal Station Marine Supplies Dock, Fuel & Dry Storage Full Facilities in Piru

LAKE HUGHES AND ELIZABETH LAKE

Elizabeth Lake and Lake Hughes are at an elevation of 3,300 feet in the Angeles National Forest north of Los Angeles. These small lakes are within 5 miles of each other and are separated by an even smaller private membership lake. Lake Hughes has a surface area of 35 acres. Access is through a resort which is open to the public year around and offers camping, fishing and all boating. The western half of Elizabeth Lake is owned and operated by the U. S. Forest Service which maintains picnic sites and allows swimming at your own risk in the lake. There are warm water fisheries at both lakes and trout in Elizabeth Lake.

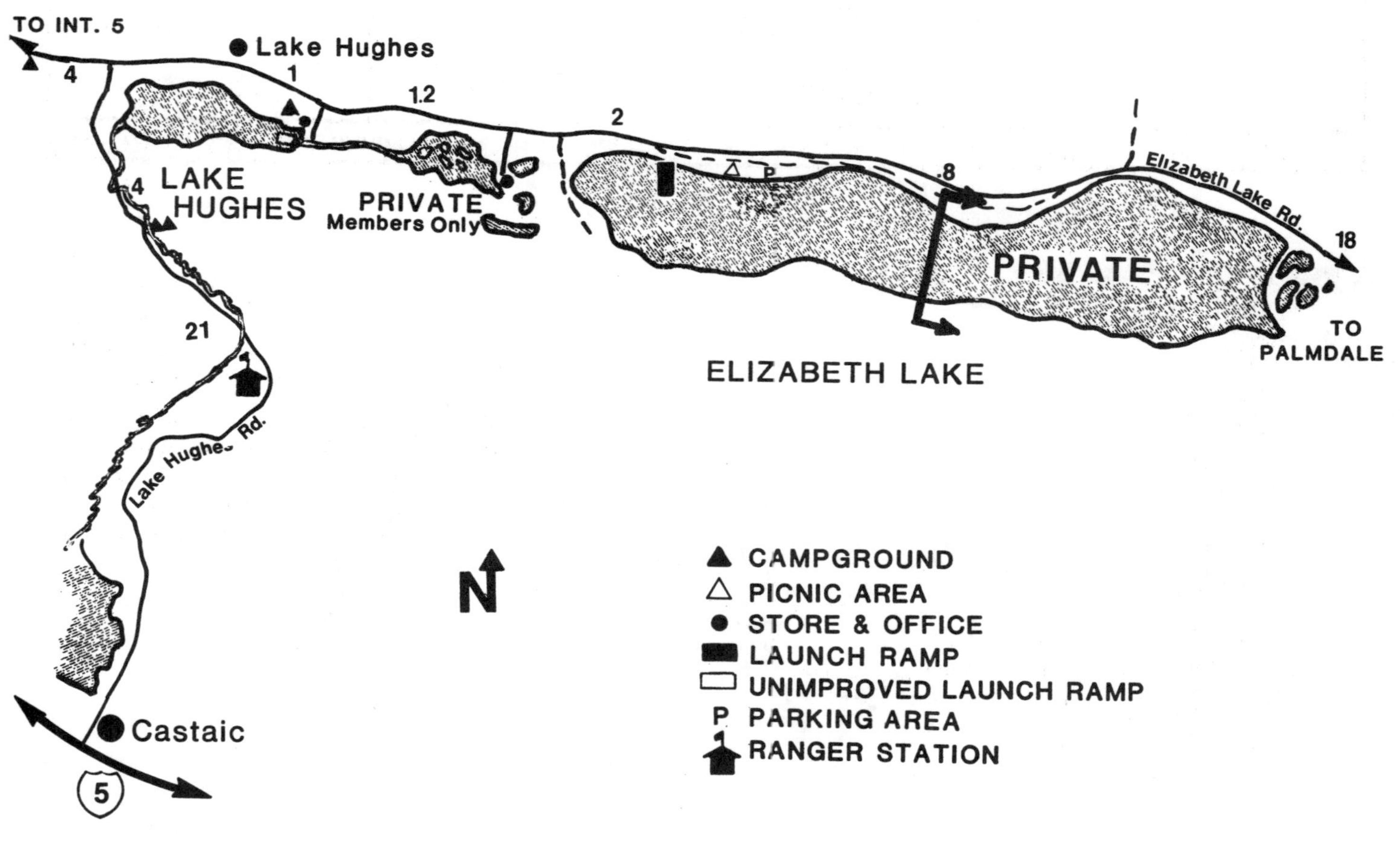

INFORMATION: Saugus Ranger District, 30800 Bouquet Canyon Rd., Saugus 91350, Ph: 805-252-9710			
CAMPING	BOATING	RECREATION	OTHER
Hughes Lakeshore Park Ph: 805-724-1845 Water & Electric Hookups Hot Showers Fee: $10 Weekly & Monthly Rates	Open to Sail & Power Boating 10 HP Motors Max. Paved Launch Ramps Rentals: Row & Paddle Boats at Lake Hughes Check for Current Water Level Conditions	Fishing: Catfish, Bass, Bluegill & Crappie Trout at Lake Elizabeth-Winter Picnicking Hiking	Lake Hughes: Snack Bar Arcade Pool Tables Horseshoes General Store Restaurant Playground

APOLLO PARK, FRAZIER PARK AND LITTLE ROCK RESERVOIR

Little Rock Reservoir, at 3,400 feet elevation, is in the Angeles National Forest. This 150 surface acre lake is usually very low by September. Fishing is often good for rainbow and brown trout, and it is stocked every other week in season. Apollo County Park is a part of the Los Angeles County Regional Park System. There are three lakes, named after the three astronauts of the Apollo flight, providing a recycled water trout fishery. Frazier Lake is a very small fishing lake for trout, bass and catfish.

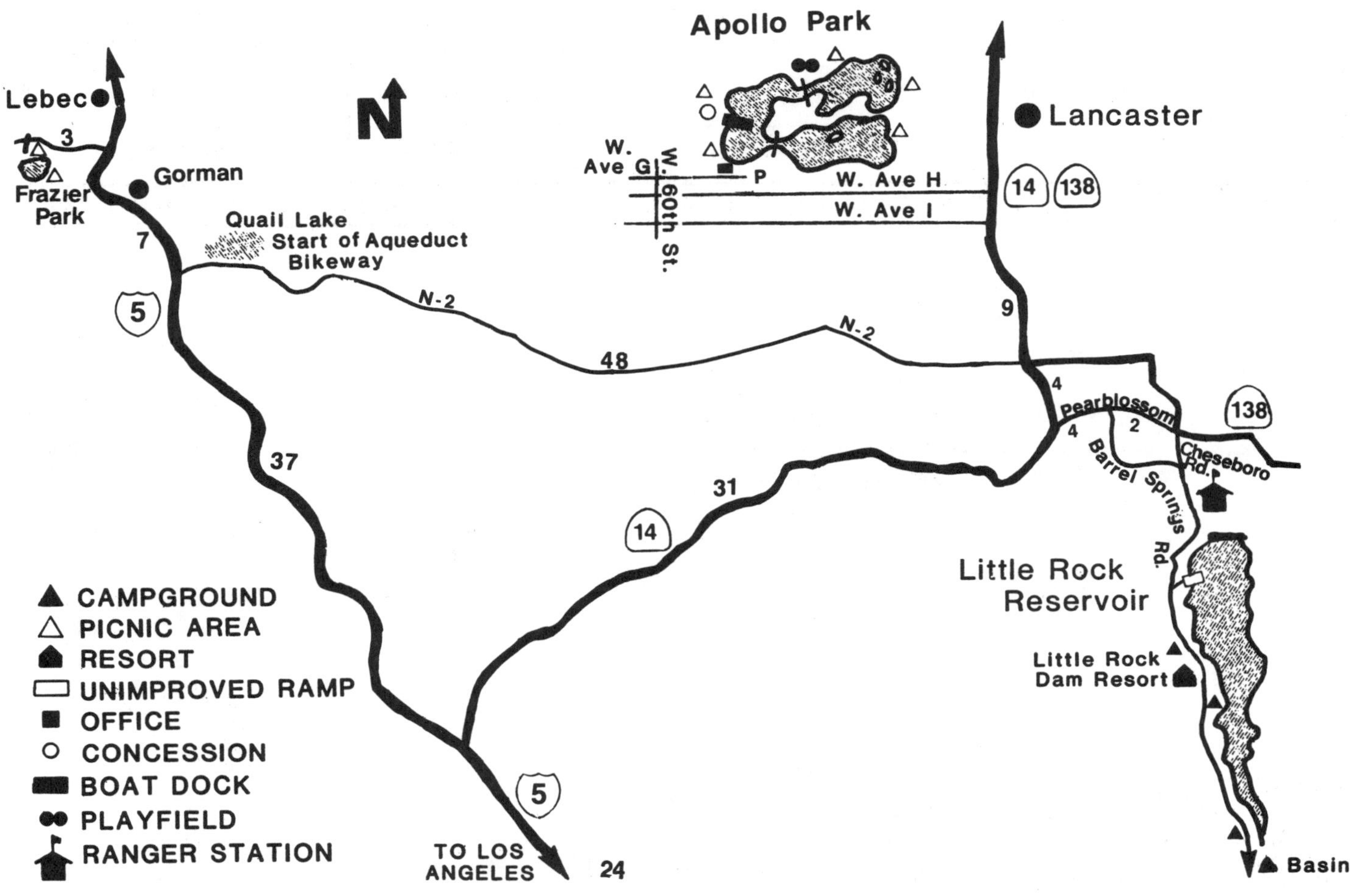

INFORMATION: Valyermo Ranger District, 34146 Longview Rd., Pearblossom 93553, Ph: 805-944-2187			
CAMPING	BOATING	RECREATION	OTHER
Little Rock Reservoir U. S. F. S. 37 Dev. Sites for Tents & R.V.s Fee: $7-$10 Basin Campground Designed for OHV Users	Little Rock Reservoir Fishing Boats Only Speed Limit: 5 MPH Launch Area - No Ramp Rentals at Resort: Rowboats & Motors Apollo Park: No Boating Frazier Park: No Boating	Fishing: Rainbow, German Brown, Kamloop Trout, Catfish Picnicking Hiking Rockhounding Hunting: Deer Children's Play Area Apollo Capsule OHV Trails Below Little Rock	Little Rock Dam Resort 32700 Cheseboro Rd. Palmdale 93550 Ph: 805-944-1923 Grocery Store Cafe, Bait & Tackle Apollo County Park West Ave. G Lancaster 93534 Ph: 805-945-8290

MOJAVE NARROWS PARK, JACKSON LAKE AND GLEN HELEN PARK

Mojave Narrows Regional Park is at an elevation of 2,700 feet in the high desert. Jackson Lake, at an elevation of 6,500 feet, is in the Big Pines Recreation Area. Glen Helen Regional Park is at 1,000 feet elevation just 15 minutes from downtown San Bernardino. These lakes offer many recreational opportunities. Boating is limited, but the angler will find winter trout, bass and channel catfish at Glen Helen and Mojave Narrows. Spring, summer and fall trout will be found at Jackson Lake. Excellent campgrounds, picnic areas, hiking, and riding trails await the visitor.

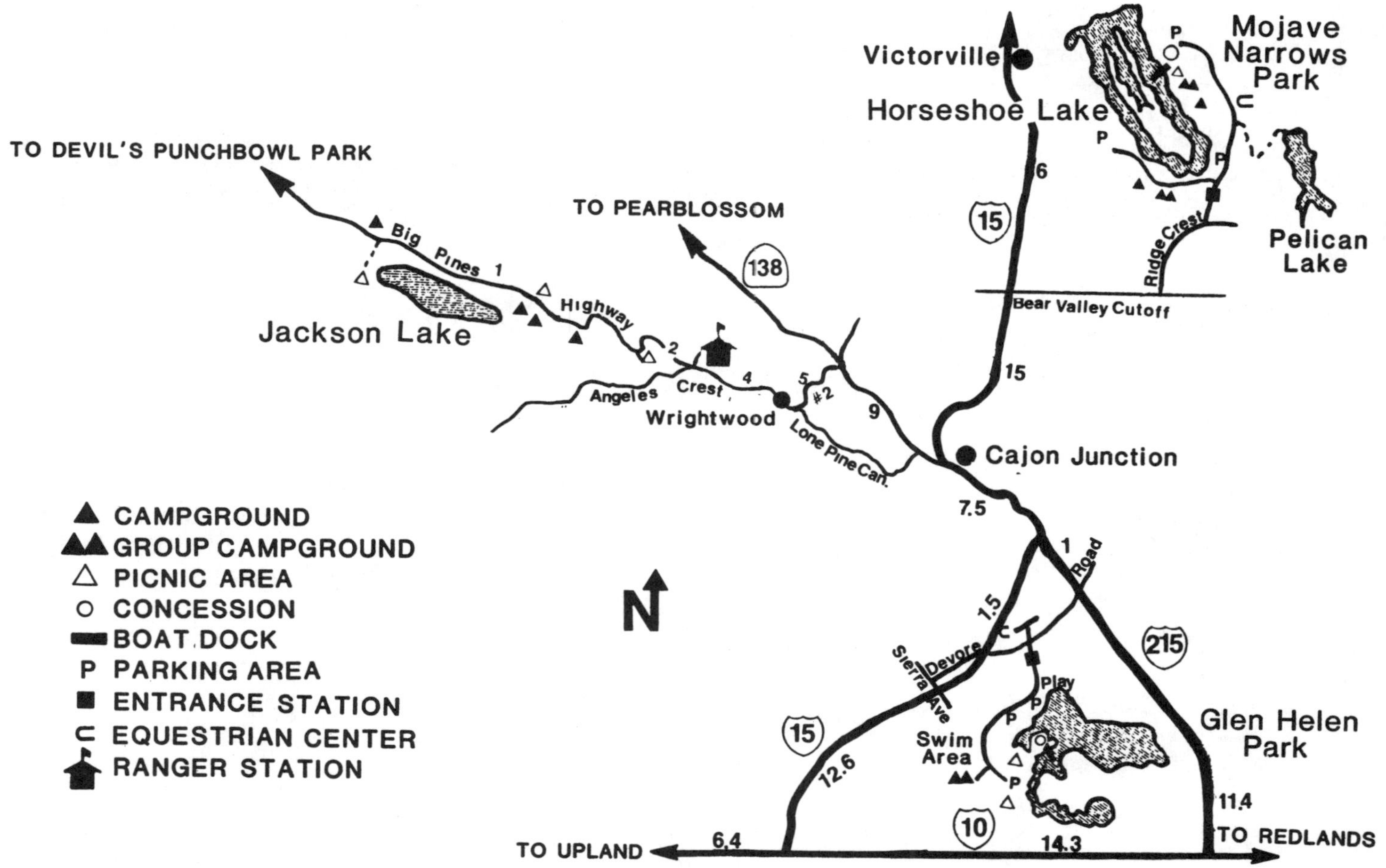

INFORMATION: Regional Parks, 825 E. 3rd, San Bernardino 92415, Ph: 714-387-2594			
CAMPING	**BOATING**	**RECREATION**	**OTHER**
Mojave Narrows: 87 Dev. Sites - No Hookups Group Sites (10+) Disposal Station Fee: $9 Ph: 619-245-2226 Glen Helen: No Hookups Group Sites Only Reserve: Ph: 714-880-2522 Senior Citizens Discounts	Glen Helen and Mojave Narrows: No Private Boats or Rafts Rentals: Paddle Boats Jackson Lake: Hand Launch Non-Power Boats Only	Fishing: Trout, Bass & Catfish Picnicking Jackson Lake: Swimming Glen Helen: Swimming, Waterslides Mojave Narrows: Hiking & Riding Trails Horse Rentals Handicap Nature Trail	Jackson Lake U.S.F.S. Valyermo R.D. 34146 Longview Rd. Pearblossom 93553 Ph: 805-944-2187 Visitor Info. Center Table Mtn. Camping 115 Sites No Hookups - $10 Group Sites Ph: 619-249-3483

CRYSTAL LAKE

Crystal Lake is at an elevation of 5,700 feet in the Crystal Lake Recreation Area of the Angeles National Forest. Located in San Gabriel Canyon, this popular Recreation Area provides an abundance of recreational facilities and opportunities. The small 5 acre lake offers good fishing and limited small craft boating. There are many miles of hiking trails ranging from self-guided nature trails to moderately strenuous hikes along the Pacific Crest Trail. The San Gabriel River's North, East and West Forks lure the dedicated angler. The hunter should check with the Ranger District Office for restrictions prior to scheduling an outing. The San Dimas and San Gabriel Reservoirs are open to shoreline fishing only as there are no boating facilities.

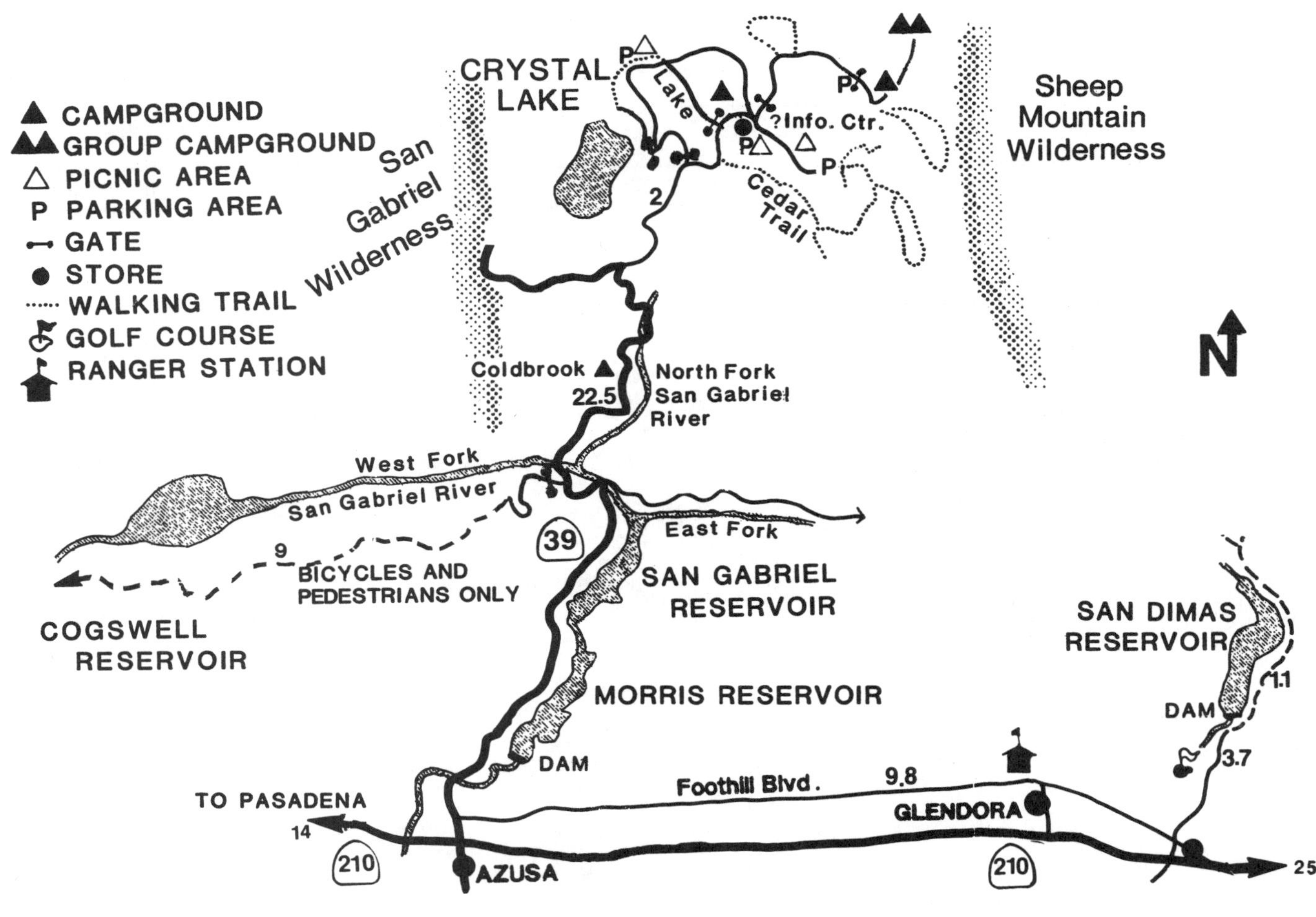

INFORMATION: Mt. Baldy Ranger District, 110 N. Wabash Av., Glendora 91740, Ph: 818-335-1251			
CAMPING	**BOATING**	**RECREATION**	**OTHER**
Crystal Lake: 176 Dev. Sites for Tents & R.V.s-$8 9 Group Sites First Come-First Serve Coldbrook: 24 Dev. Sites for Tents & R.V.s-$8 For Reservations: Ph: 818-910-1113	Crystal Lake Only Small Non-Powered Craft Hand Launch - 200 Yards Down Steps	Fishing: Rainbow Trout Hiking & Nature Trails Backpacking Naturalist Programs No Swimming No Hunting Within The Crystal Lake Recreation Area	General Store Snack Bar Visitor's Center Ph: 818-910-1149 (Weekends) Full Facilities In Azusa

ALONDRA PARK AND HARBOR LAKE

Alondra Park is under the jurisdiction of Los Angeles County. Within this 84 acre urban park is a small 8 acre fishing lake. Boating is not allowed. There are picnic sites, a swimming area, community gardens, paddle tennis courts and a children's play area. There are also group camping areas. Harbor Lake Park is under the jurisdiction of the City of Los Angeles. There is no private boating at this small lake but there are canoe and sailing lessons. The angler will find largemouth bass, bluegill, perch and catfish. There are youth group campgrounds, picnic areas and a playground. Harbor Lake Park is a wildlife sanctuary where a variety of plants, birds and animals may be observed in their natural habitats.

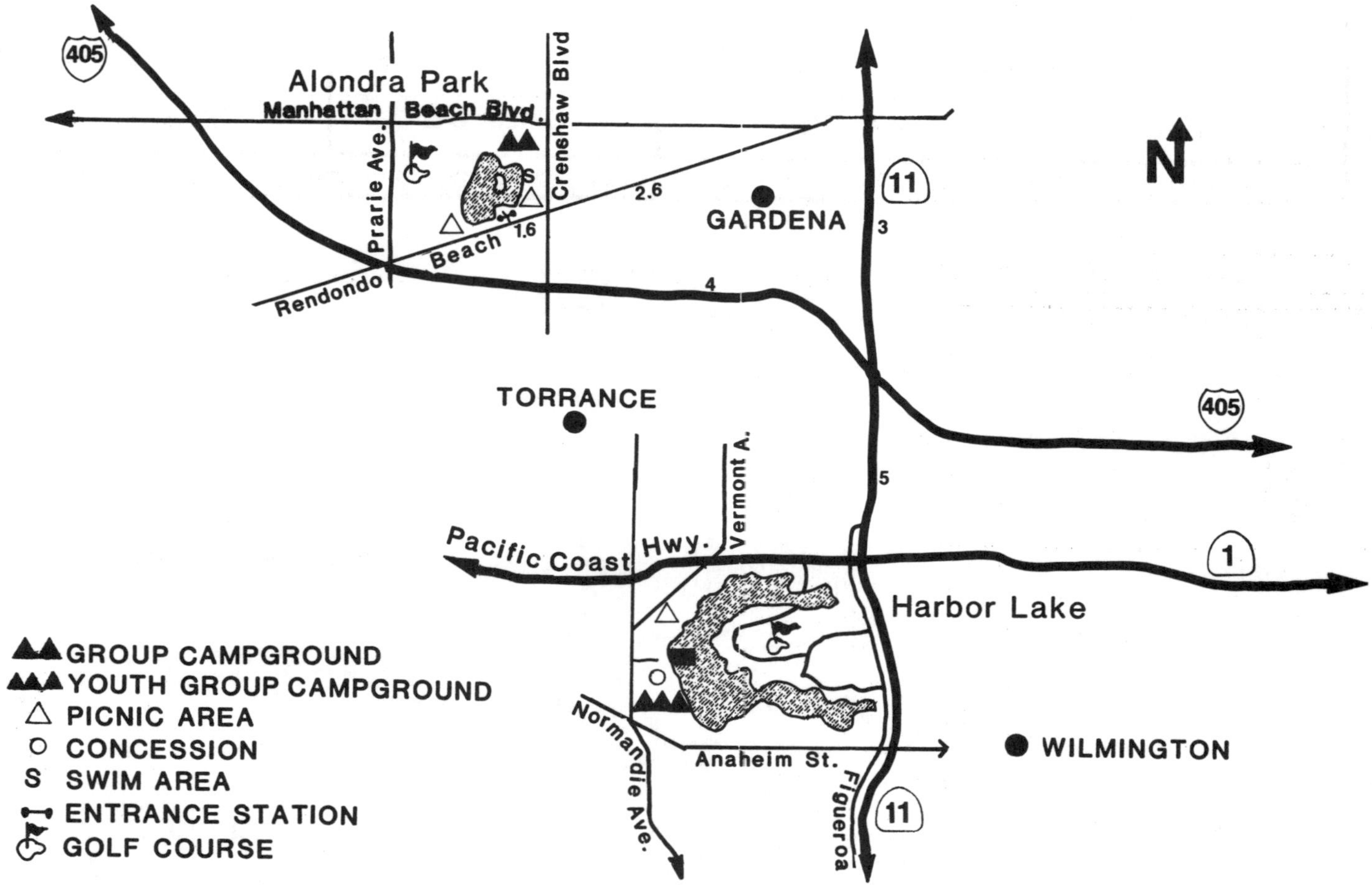

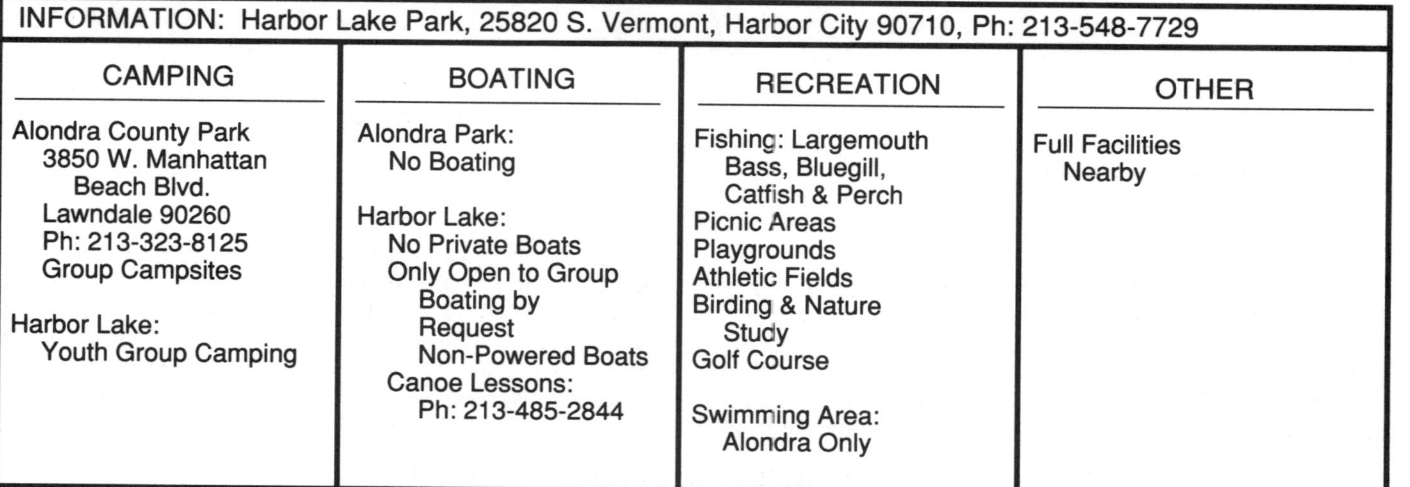

INFORMATION: Harbor Lake Park, 25820 S. Vermont, Harbor City 90710, Ph: 213-548-7729

CAMPING	BOATING	RECREATION	OTHER
Alondra County Park 3850 W. Manhattan Beach Blvd. Lawndale 90260 Ph: 213-323-8125 Group Campsites Harbor Lake: Youth Group Camping	Alondra Park: No Boating Harbor Lake: No Private Boats Only Open to Group Boating by Request Non-Powered Boats Canoe Lessons: Ph: 213-485-2844	Fishing: Largemouth Bass, Bluegill, Catfish & Perch Picnic Areas Playgrounds Athletic Fields Birding & Nature Study Golf Course Swimming Area: Alondra Only	Full Facilities Nearby

EL DORADO EAST REGIONAL PARK

El Dorado East is a 450 acre urban park under the administration of the City of Long Beach. Nestled amid the rolling green hills of the park are 4 small lakes of approximately 40 acres. There is no boating at these lakes except for model boats. Fishing from the shore for trout and warm water species is often rewarding. There are nice family group and company picnic areas. A network of paved trails awaits the bicycler and roller skater. There is a vita course along with a number of running courses for the casual jogger or serious runner. An 85 acre nature center with 2 miles of self-guided nature trails is available for the stroller or hiker. The Olympic Archery Range is the finest in Southern California. Facilities abound at this complete recreation park.

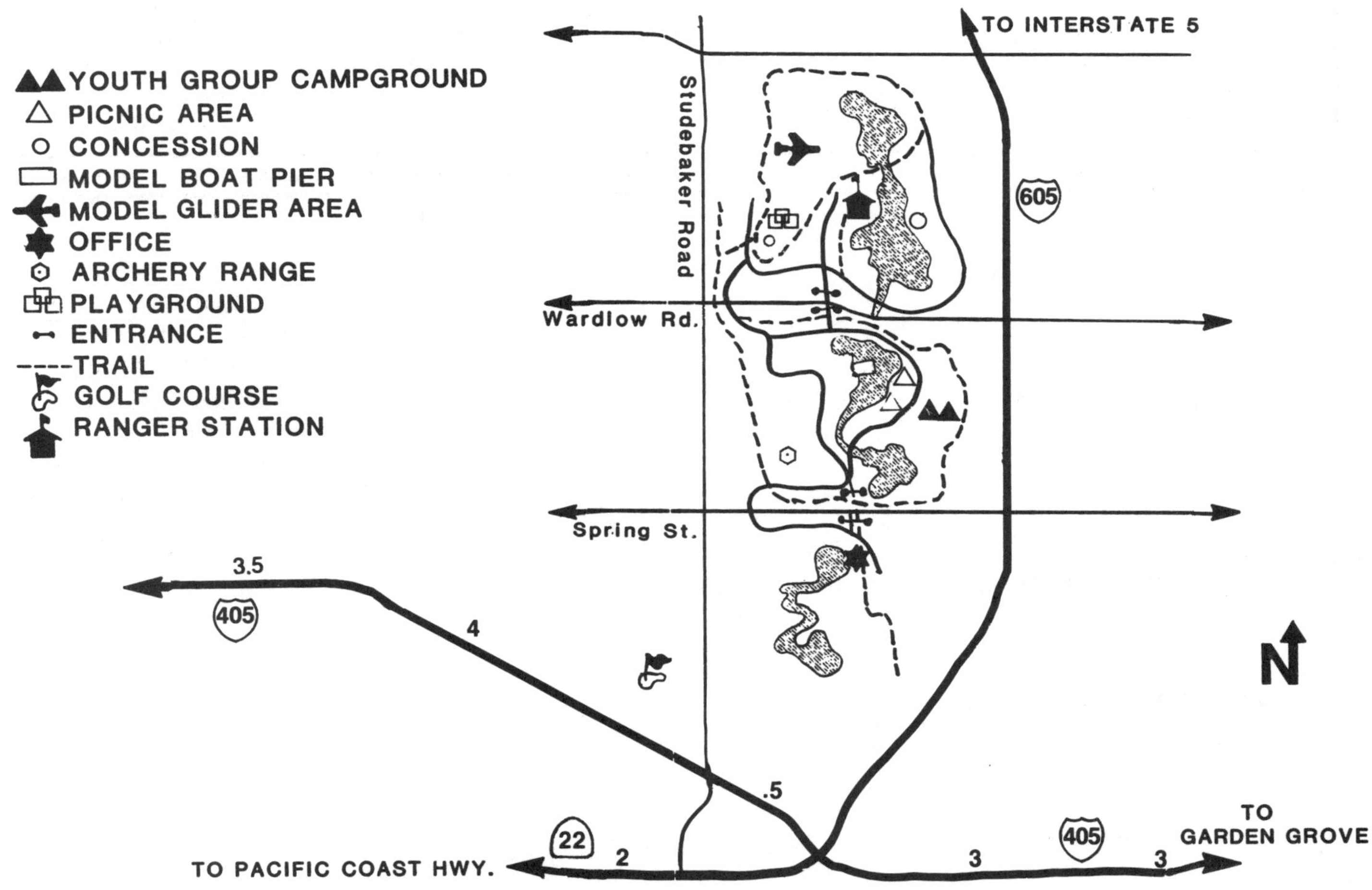

INFORMATION: El Dorado East, 7550 E. Spring St., Long Beach 90815, Ph: 213-421-9431 Ext. 3333			
CAMPING	**BOATING**	**RECREATION**	**OTHER**
Day Use Only Except For: Youth Group Camping Under 18 Years Old 15 Children Minimum Group Picnicking to 400 - Permit Required for 25 or more Ph: 213-432-5931 Ext. 271 or 272	Model Boat Pier Paddle Boats	Fishing: Trout (Winter), Bluegill, Largemouth Bass, Channel, Catfish Picnicking Jogging, Skating & Bicycling Trails Vita Course, Olympic Archery Range Nature Center & Trails No Swimming	Snack Bar Full Facilities Nearby Vehicle Entrance Fees: $2 - Weekdays $3 - Weekends $4 - Buses $5 - Holidays & Special Events Days

PECK ROAD, SANTA FE AND LEGG LAKE

These three Los Angeles County Parks provide picnic areas, hiking and bicycle trails and lakes for fishing. The 80 acre lake at Peck Road Water Conservation Park is closed to boating and swimming. This natural area is open from Wednesday through Sunday. Santa Fe Dam Park has a 70 acre lake open to non-powered boating. There are also swim beaches, an equestrian staging area, a nature center and preserve. Group picnic areas may be rented. Legg Lake, actually three small lakes totaling 76.5 acres, is within the Whittier Narrows Recreation Area. This 1,092 acre multi-purpose Park has a sporting dog area, a skeet and trap shooting range, archery range, model hobby areas, athletic field, horseback riding, golf course and lighted tennis courts. There is no private boating or swimming but you may rent a rowboat. Youth group camping is available at Whittier Narrows and Santa Fe Dam.

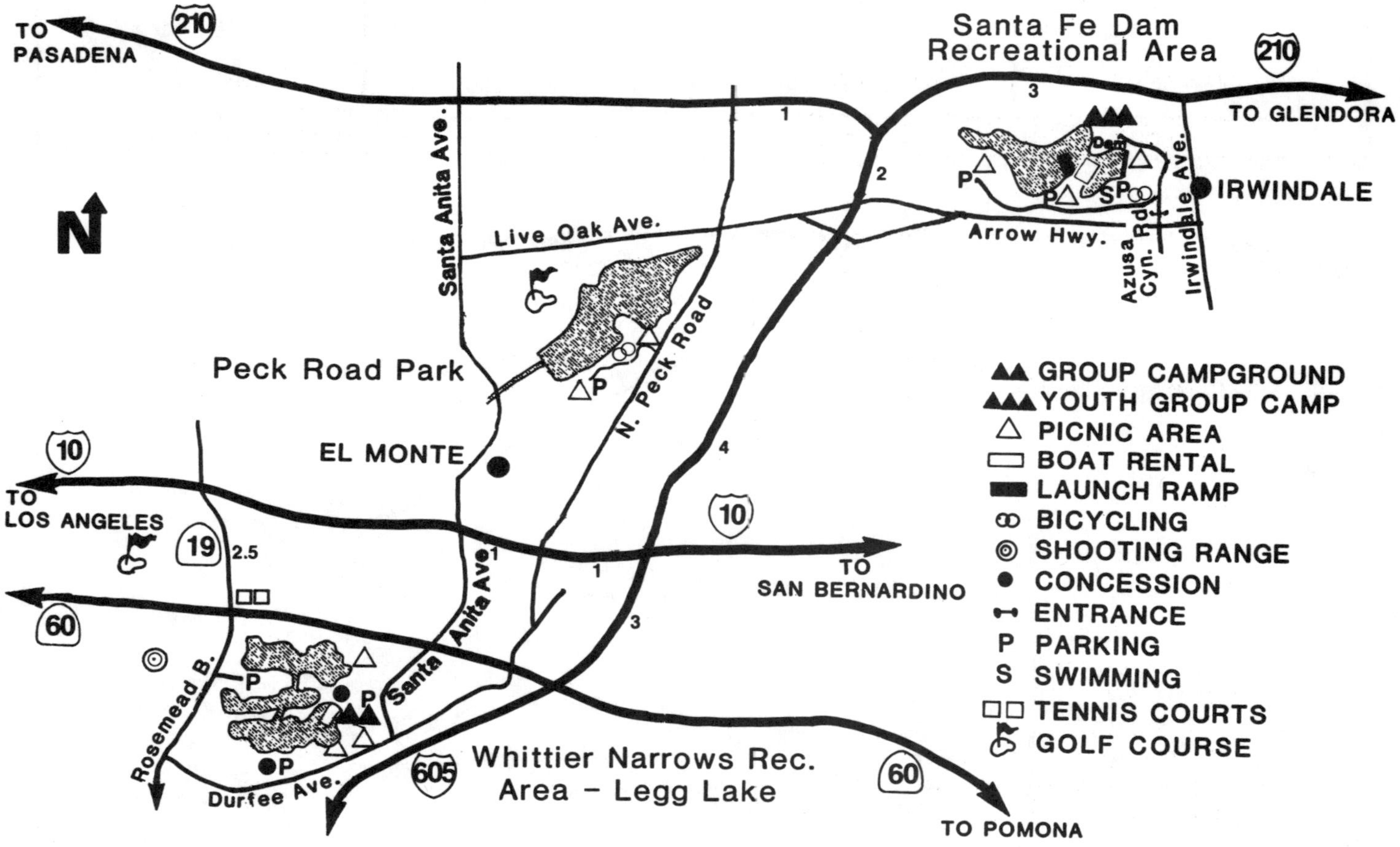

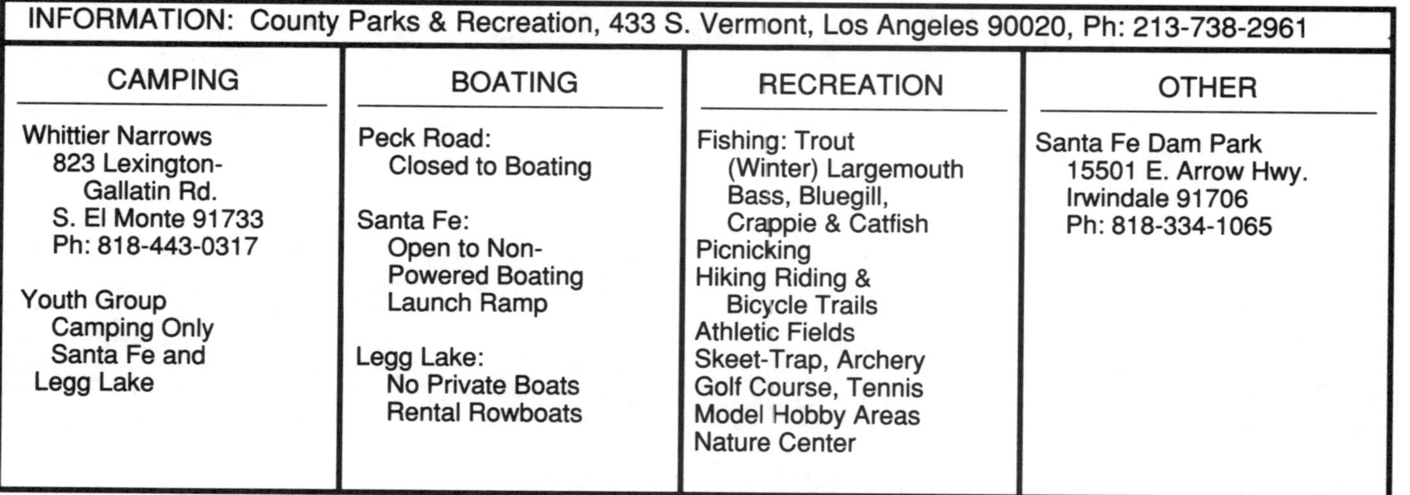

INFORMATION: County Parks & Recreation, 433 S. Vermont, Los Angeles 90020, Ph: 213-738-2961

CAMPING	BOATING	RECREATION	OTHER
Whittier Narrows 823 Lexington- Gallatin Rd. S. El Monte 91733 Ph: 818-443-0317 Youth Group Camping Only Santa Fe and Legg Lake	Peck Road: Closed to Boating Santa Fe: Open to Non- Powered Boating Launch Ramp Legg Lake: No Private Boats Rental Rowboats	Fishing: Trout (Winter) Largemouth Bass, Bluegill, Crappie & Catfish Picnicking Hiking Riding & Bicycle Trails Athletic Fields Skeet-Trap, Archery Golf Course, Tennis Model Hobby Areas Nature Center	Santa Fe Dam Park 15501 E. Arrow Hwy. Irwindale 91706 Ph: 818-334-1065

SILVERWOOD LAKE

The Silverwood State Recreation Area is at an elevation of 3,378 feet in the San Bernardino Mountains just east of Interstate 5 on the edge of the high Mojave Desert. This is a popular recreation lake with a surface area of 1,000 acres and a shoreline of 13 miles. There are good marine support facilities. The lake is open to all types of boating. Several brushy areas were left uncleared when filling the Lake which has provided a natural fish habitat. Although planted trout are the most popular attraction, the angler will find a varied fishery. There are 10 miles of paved trails for the hiker and bicyclist. In addition to the nice oak-shaded campsites at Silverwood, the camper will find a 90 unit modern campground at nearby Mojave River Forks.

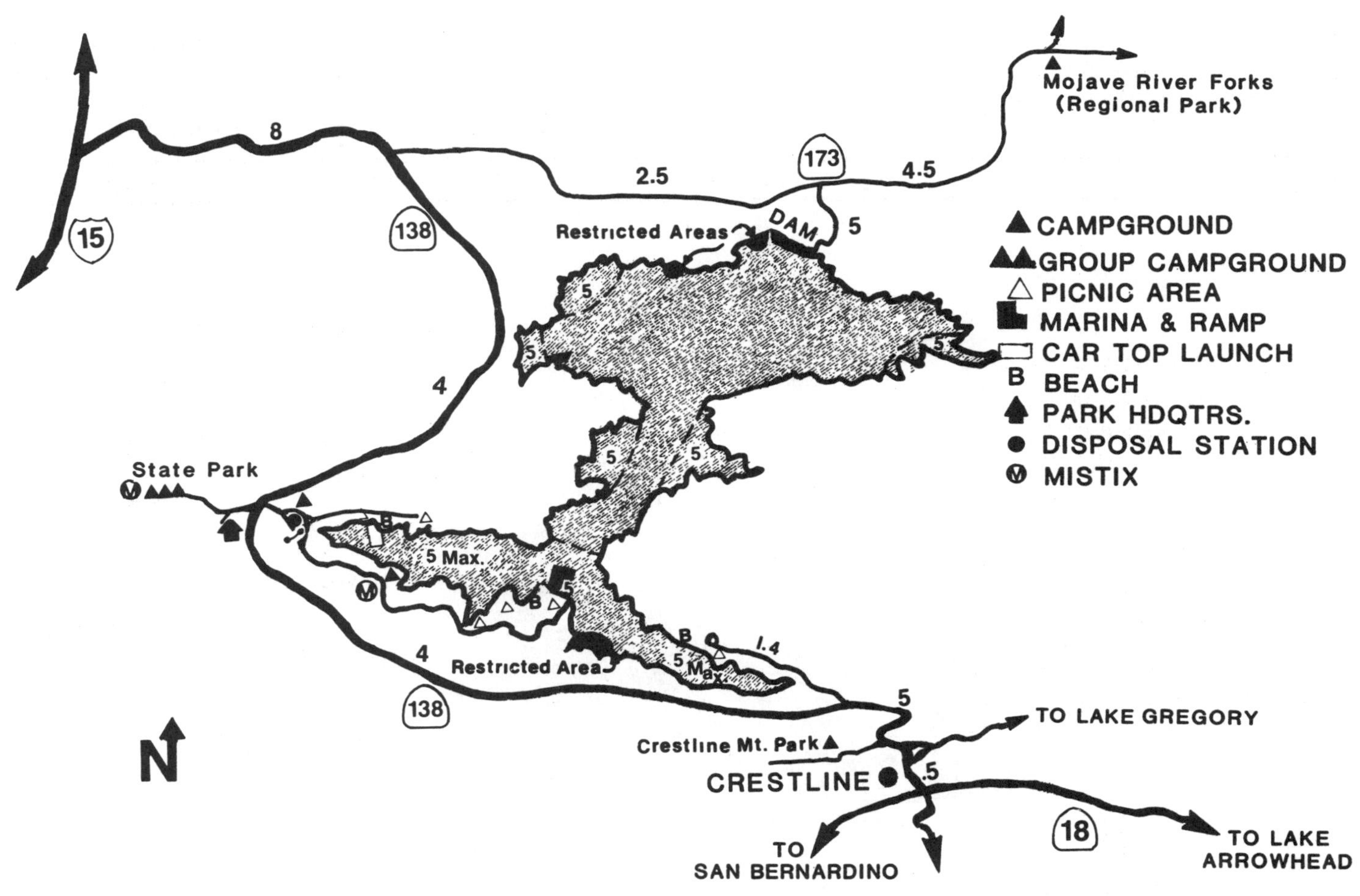

INFORMATION: State Rec. Area, Star Rt., Box 7A, Hesperia 92345, Ph: 619-389-2281/2303

CAMPING	BOATING	RECREATION	OTHER
135 Dev. Sites for Tents & R.V.s Fee: $10 3 Group Sites - 120 People Each 7 Bike-In or Hike-In Sites - Fee: $1 Paved Sites With Ramp for the Handicapped For Reservations: Ph:1-800-444-7275	Power, Row, Canoe, Sail, Waterski, Jet Ski, Windsurf & Inflatables Speed Limit - 35 MPH Launch Ramp Rentals: Fishing Boats & Pontoons Docks, Berths, Gas Hazards: High, Unpredictable Winds	Fishing: Brown & Rainbow Trout, Catfish, Bluegill, Perch, Striped & Largemouth Bass, & Silver Salmon Swimming Picnicking Hiking Campfire Program	Snack Bar Grocery Store Bait & Tackle Disposal Station Mojave River Forks P.O. Box 1005 Hesperia 92345 Ph: 619-389-2322

LAKE GREGORY

Lake Gregory is a part of the San Bernardino County Regional Park System. Located at an elevation of 4,520 feet in the San Bernardino Mountains near Crestline, this popular day use lake offers a variety of water related activities. There are sandy swimming beaches, picnic facilities, snack bars, a 300 foot water slide, and a boat house. Boating is limited to rental fishing and pedal boats. This small 120 surface acre lake offers good fishing either by boat or from the shoreline. The fish habitat is enhanced by an aeration system. In addition to the warm water species and Rainbow trout, Lake Gregory is the only lake in Southern California being stocked with Brown trout. The lake is open to night fishing. This is a nice family park with full facilities in the village and nearby Crestline.

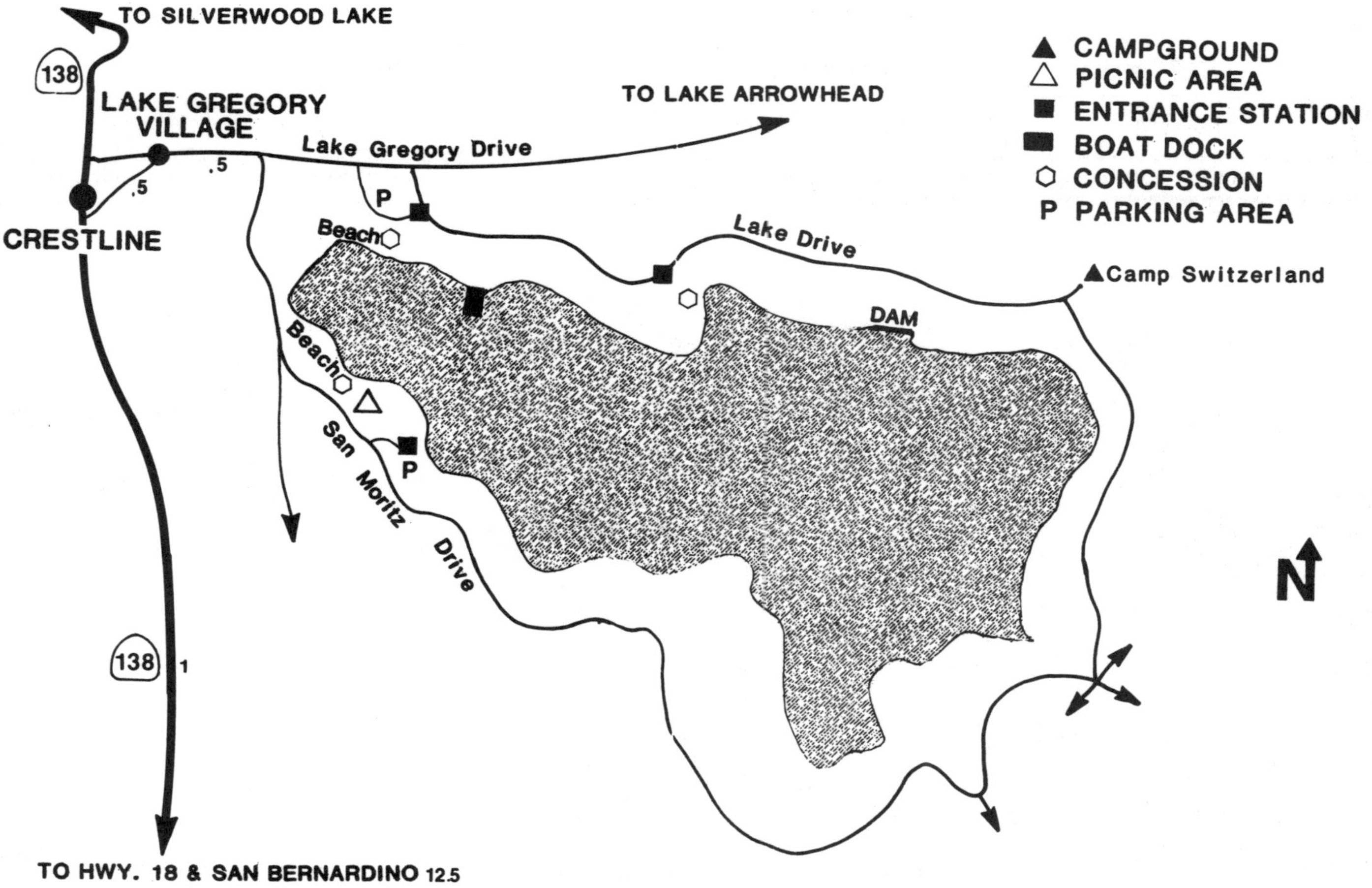

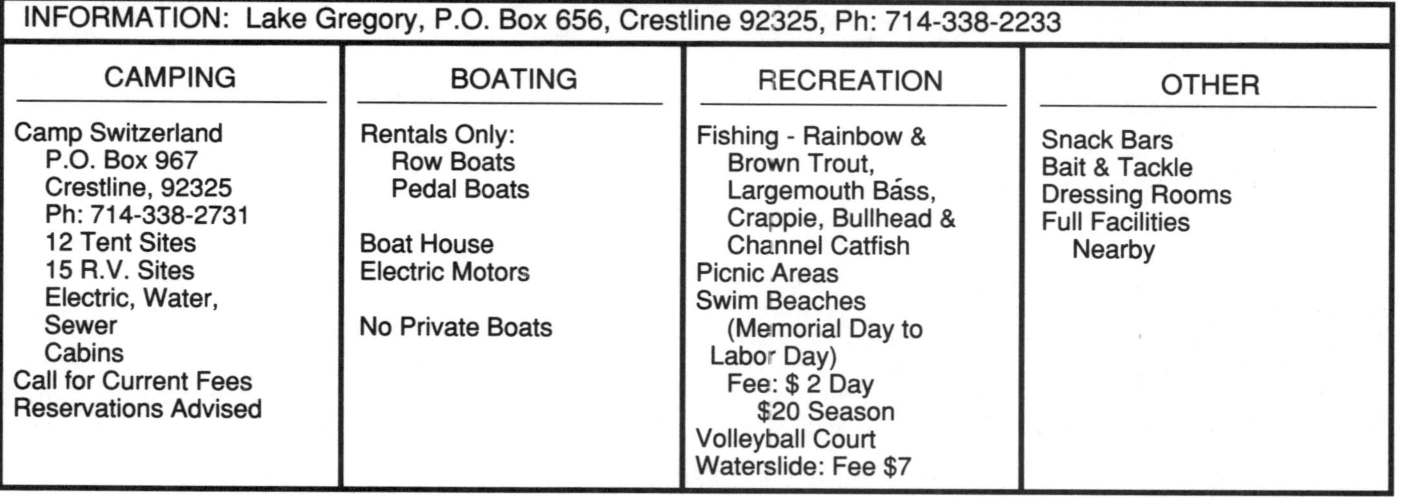

INFORMATION: Lake Gregory, P.O. Box 656, Crestline 92325, Ph: 714-338-2233

CAMPING	BOATING	RECREATION	OTHER
Camp Switzerland P.O. Box 967 Crestline, 92325 Ph: 714-338-2731 12 Tent Sites 15 R.V. Sites Electric, Water, Sewer Cabins Call for Current Fees Reservations Advised	Rentals Only: Row Boats Pedal Boats Boat House Electric Motors No Private Boats	Fishing - Rainbow & Brown Trout, Largemouth Bass, Crappie, Bullhead & Channel Catfish Picnic Areas Swim Beaches (Memorial Day to Labor Day) Fee: $ 2 Day $20 Season Volleyball Court Waterslide: Fee $7	Snack Bars Bait & Tackle Dressing Rooms Full Facilities Nearby

ARROWHEAD, GREEN VALLEY, ARROWBEAR AND JENKS LAKES

Nestled high in the San Bernardino National Forest ranging in elevation from 5,100 feet at Lake Arrowhead to 6,700 feet at Jenks Lake. Each has a trout and warm water fishery. Boating varies as shown below. Lake Arrowhead rests in a pretty Alpine setting but it is privately owned and many restrictions prevail; public use is limited. The Forest Service has a number of nice campgrounds throughout this scenic area. There are many hiking and riding trails, especially near Jenks Lake where the San Gorgonio Wilderness invites the backpacker and equestrian. Green Valley is a small family oriented lake offering fishing, swimming and rental boats. Arrowbear is primarily a small fishing lake.

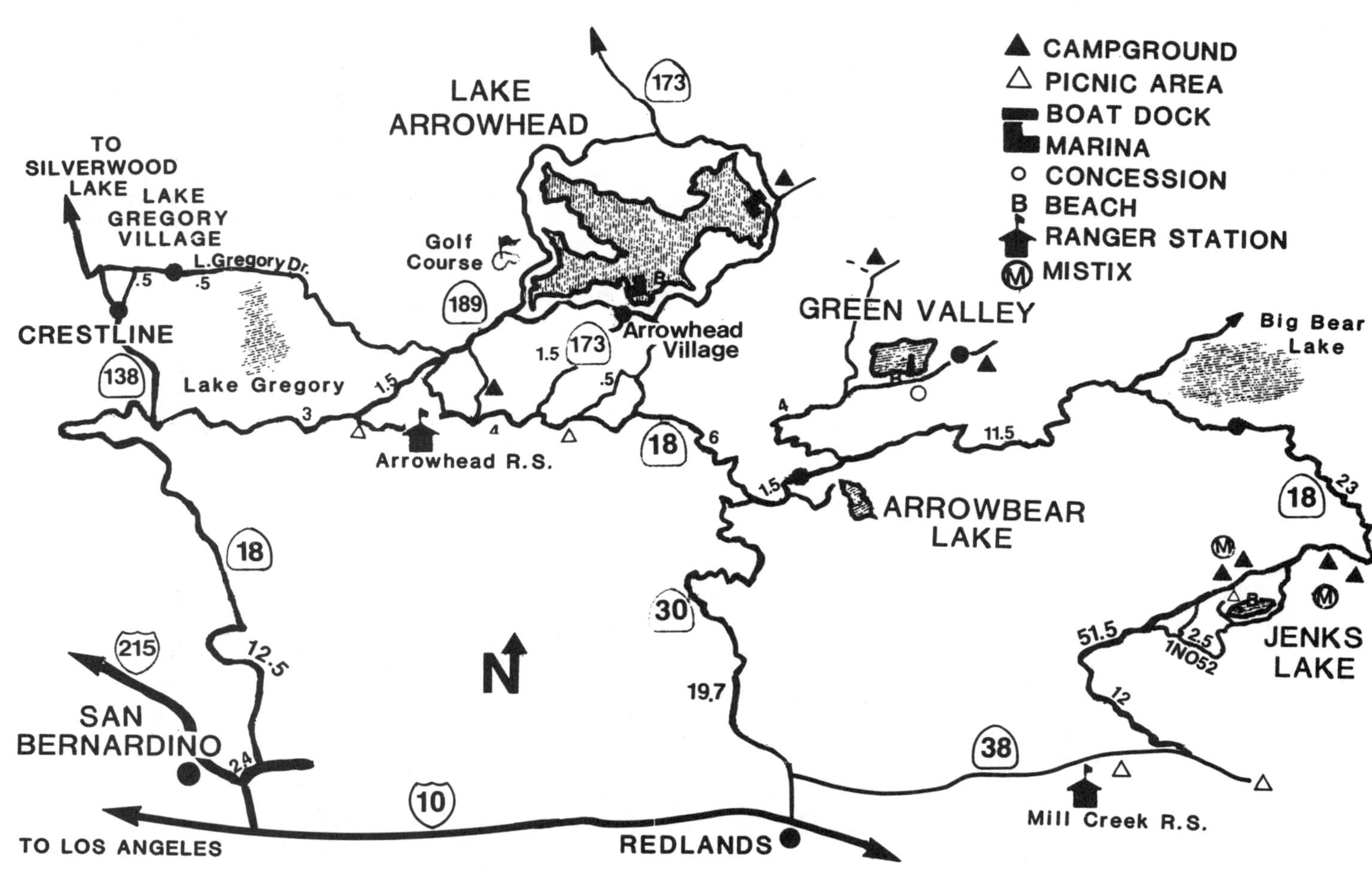

INFORMATION: Arrowhead Lake Assoc., P.O. Box 1119, Lake Arrowhead 92352 Ph: 714-337-2595			
CAMPING	**BOATING**	**RECREATION**	**OTHER**
U. S. F. S. Arrowhead R.S. 26577 Hwy. 18 P.O. Box 7 Rimforest 92378 Ph: 714-337-2444 Mill Creek R.S. 34701 Mill Crk. Rd. Mentone 92359 Ph: 714-794-1123	Arrowhead: No Public Boats Allowed Marina - Ph: 714-337-8451 Rentals: Ski, Fishing, Canoe & Sail Boats Green Valley: Non-Power Rentals Arrowbear: No Boating Jenks: Non-Power Hand Launch No Rentals	Fishing: Rainbow & Brown Trout, Smallmouth Bass, Kokanee Salmon, Catfish & Bluegill Picnicking Hiking & Equestrian Trails - Horse Rentals in Area Swimming Beaches Golf Course	Resorts & Facilities Nearby Green Valley Water District: Ph: 714-867-2912 Arrowbear Water District: Ph: 714-867-2704

BIG BEAR LAKE

Big Bear Lake is one of California's most popular recreation lakes. Located in the San Bernardino National Forest at an elevation of 7,000 feet, this beautiful mountain lake is just two hours from downtown Los Angeles. Originally dammed in 1884, improved by another dam in 1911, Big Bear now has a constant surface area of 3,000 acres. The lake is over 7 miles long, a mile and a half wide and has a shoreline of 24 miles. It is owned and administered by the Big Bear Municipal Water District which regulates the activities on the lake. All types of boating are permitted subject to size restrictions and a valid permit which may be obtained from many of the marinas. There are numerous marine facilities around the lake. In addition to the many Forest Service campsites, there are extensive private facilities at this complete destination resort area.

. . . Continued . . .

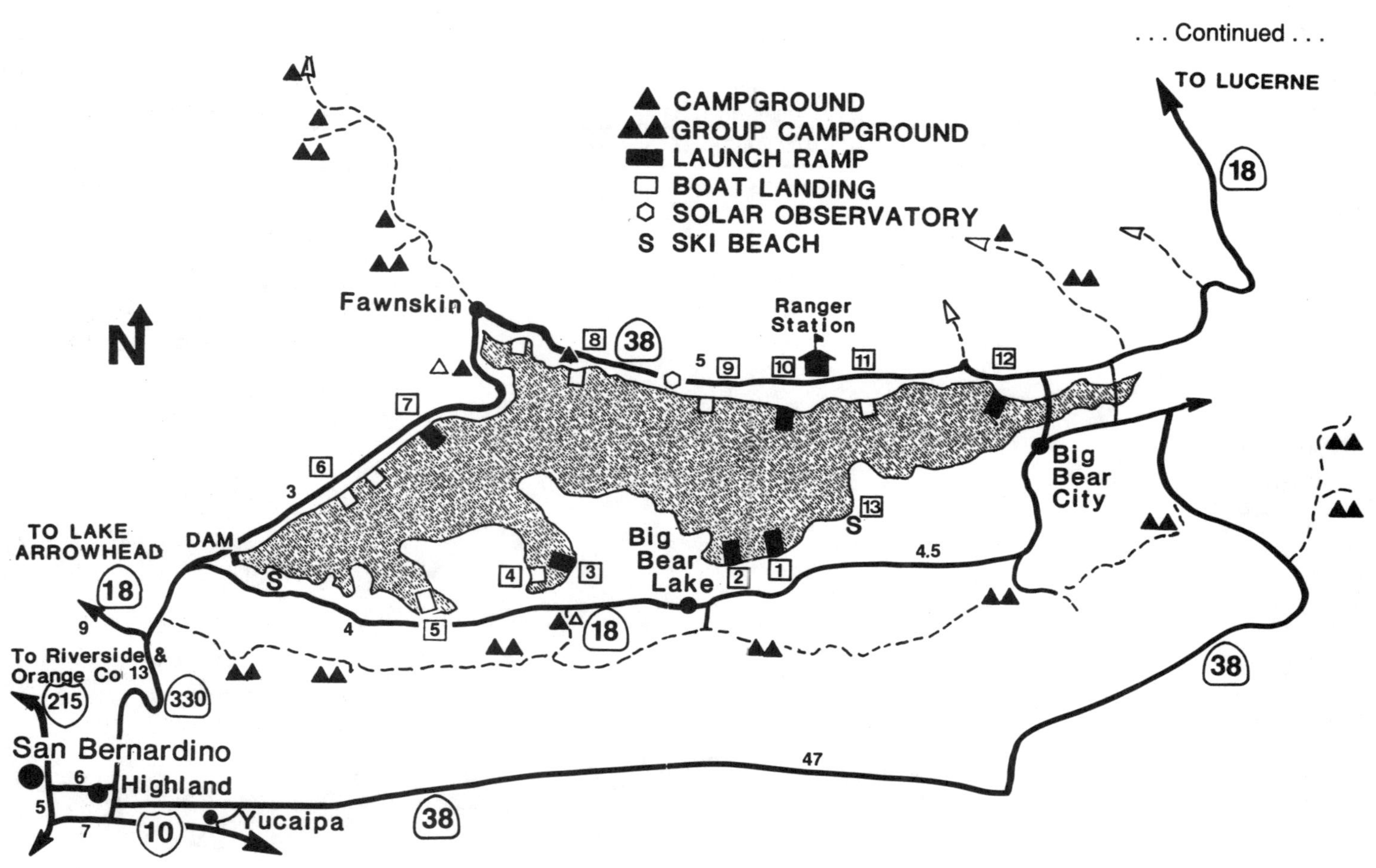

INFORMATION: Chamber of Commerce, P.O. Box 2860, Big Bear Lake 92315, Ph: 714-866-4607			
CAMPING	BOATING	RECREATION	OTHER
U.S.D.A. Forest Service 7 Campgrounds with 254 Dev. Sites for Tents & R.V.s Fee: $7 - $9 Remote Area Camping at No Charge Group Sites See Following Page	Open to All Boating Subject to Length-Maximum 26' Valid Lake Permit Required 35 MPH Speed Limit Full Service Marinas Launch Ramps Rentals: Power, Sail, Fishing, Sailboard, Jet Ski & Surfjet Berths-Docks-Storage	Fishing: Trout, Bass, Channel Catfish, Bluegill, Silver Salmon Swimming - Pools Hiking & Backpacking Horseback Riding: Trails & Rentals Golf & Tennis Picnicking	Complete Resort Facilities See Following Page for Information

BIG BEAR LAKE

GENERAL INFORMATION:	Big Bear Chamber of Commerce, 41647 Big Bear Blvd., Big Bear Lake 92315, Ph: 714-866-4607
LAKE INFORMATION:	Big Bear Municipal Water District, 42169-D Big Bear Blvd., Big Bear Lake 92315, Ph: 714-866-5796
CAMPING/HIKING INFORMATION:	Big Bear Ranger District, Box 290, Fawnskin 92333, Ph: 714-866-3437
LODGING INFORMATION:	Central Reservation Service, P.O. Box 3050, Big Bear Lake 92315, Ph: 714-866-4601

U.S.D.A. FOREST SERVICE CAMPGROUNDS

FAMILY CAMPSITES:

BIG PINE FLAT - 7 Miles NW of Fawnskin on Forest Service Rd. 3N14 - 19 Tent/R.V. Sites, Trailers to 22', Pack-In, Pack-Out, Open 5/20 to 11/15, Fee: $7.

HOLCOMB VALLEY - 4 Miles North on 2N09 to 3N16 East on 3N16 3/4 Mile - 19 Tent/R.V. Sites, Trailers to 15', Pack-In, Pack-Out, Open All Year, May Be Inaccessible During Winter Snow, No Water, No Fee.

HORSE SPRINGS - 10 Miles NW of Fawnskin on 3N14 to 3N17, East on 3N17 - 17 Tent/R.V. Sites, No Trailers, Pack-In, Pack-Out, Open Year Round, May Be Inaccessible During Winter Snow, No Water, No Fee.

GROUP CAMPGROUNDS: - Reservations at Big Bear Ranger Station - Open Year Round

BIG PINE HORSE CAMP - Timber Setting near Big Pine - To 60 People, Water, 15 Vehicles Maximum, Horsemen, Fee: $20.

BLUFF MESA - Timber Setting, off 2N10 - To 40 People, 8 Vehicles Maximum - Tents/R.V.s, Trailers to 15', No Water, Fee: $25.

BOULDER - Timber Setting, off 2N10 - To 40 People, 8 Vehicles Maximum - Tents/R.V.s, Trailers to 15', No Water, Fee: $25.

BUTTERCUP - Timber Setting Near Pine Knot - To 40 People, 8 Vehicles Maximum - Tents/R.V.s, Trailers to 15', Normal Season is 5/15 to 9/30, Fee: $25.

DEER - Timber Setting, off 2N10 - To 40 People, 8 Vehicles Maximum - Tents/R.V.s, Trailers to 15', No Water, Fee: $25.

GREEN CANYON - Timber Setting, off 2N93 - To 40 People, 8 Vehicles Maximum - Tents/R.V.s, Trailers to 15', No Water, Fee: $25.

GRAY'S PEAK - Timber Setting, off 3N14 - To 40 People, 8 Vehicles Maximum - Tents/R.V.s Trailers to 15', No Water, Fee: $25.

PRIVATELY OPERATED CAMPGROUNDS UNDER CONCESSION FROM FOREST SERVICE:

COLDBROOK - 2 Blocks South of Big Bear Blvd. on Tulip Lane - 36 Dev. Tent/R.V. Sites, Trailers to 15', Open All Year (Walk-in - Winter), Fee: $7.

GROUT BAY - 1/4 Mile West of Fawnskin on Hwy. 38 - 23 Tent/R.V. Sites, Trailers to 15', Open 4/1 to 11/1, Fee: $7.

HANNA FLAT - 2 1/2 Miles NW of Fawnskin on Forest Service Rd. 3N14 - 88 Tent/R.V. Sites, Trailers to 15', Open 5/20 - 9/30, Fee: $9.

PINE KNOT - South on Summit Blvd., off Big Bear Blvd. to Wall, Left 1/4 Mile - 52 Tent/R.V. Sites, Trailers to 15', Handicapped Facilities, Open 5/20 - 9/30, Fee: $7.

...Continued...

BIG BEAR LAKE

IRONWOOD - Timber Setting, off 3N97 - To 25 People, 8 Vehicles Maximum - Tents/R.V.s, Trailers to 15', No Water, Fee: $20.

JUNIPER SPRINGS - Desert Setting, off 2N01 - To 40 People, 8 Vehicles Masimum - Tents/R.V.s, Trailers to 15' Water, Fee: $25.

ROUND VALLEY - Desert Setting, off 2No1 - To 15 People, 3 Vehicles Maximum - Tents/R.V.s, Trailers to 15', Water, Fee: $20.

SIBERIA CREEK - Timber Setting - Walk-in, To 40 People, Tent Sites, No Water, No Fee.

TANGLEWOOD - Timber Setting, off 3N15 - To 40 People, 8 Vehicles Maximum - Tents, R.V.s, Trailers to 15', No Water, Fee: $25.

MARINE FACILITIES - See Map for Number Location

1 **PINE KNOT LANDING & MARINE -** Ph: 714-866-2628 - Rentals, Docks, Moorings, Launch Ramp, Storage, Bait & Tackle, Marine Store, Lake Tours.

2 **BIG BEAR MARINA -** Ph: 714-866-3218 - Boat Permit Sales, Rentals, Docks, Moorings, Launch Ramp, Gas, Storage, Bait & Tackle.

3 **HOLLOWAY'S MARINA -** Ph: 714-866-5706 - Boat Permit Sales, Rentals, Docks, Moorings, Launch Ramp, Gas, Bait & Tackle, Grocery Store, R.V. Facilities, Lake Tours.

4 **PLEASURE POINT LANDING -** Ph: 714-866-2455 - Boat & Fishing Permit Sales, Rentals, Docks, Moorings, Launch Ramp, Gas, Bait & Tackle, Picnic Area, Snack Bar.

5 **BOULDER BAY MARINA & LANDING -** Ph: 714-866-7557 - Rentals, Docks, Moorings, Gas, Bait & Tackle.

6 **GRAY'S LANDING -** Ph: 714-866-2443 - Boat Rentals, Bait & Tackle, Fishing Pier.

7 **DUANE BOYER PUBLIC LAUNCH RAMP -** Ph: 714-866-2917 - Boat Permit Sales, Launch Ramp, Boat-Trailer Parking, Day Use Area.

8 **CLUSTER PINES -** Ph: 714-866-2246 - Camping & Docking Facilities, Small Grocery Store.

9 **LIGHTHOUSE LANDING -** Ph: 714-866-9464 - Boat Rentals, Docks, Moorings, R.V. Facilities, Small Store.

10 **BIG BEAR SHORES -** Ph: 714-866-4151 - Camping & R.V. Facilities, Small Store.

11 **JUNIPER MARINA -** Ph: 714-866-2940 - Boat Rentals, Docks, Mooring, Day Use.

12 **EAST LAUNCH RAMP -** Ph: 714-866-2917 - North Shore Drive, West of Stanfield Cutoff, Boat Permit Sales, Launch Ramp, Boat-Trailer Parking, Day Use Area.

13 **MEADOW PARK SWIM BEACH -** Ph: 714-866-3640 or 866-3652 - Park Avenue Near Knight Ave., Public Swimming Area, Sandy Beach, Snack Bar.

PUDDINGSTONE LAKE

Puddingstone Lake is at an elevation of 941 feet within the 2,000 acre Frank G. Bonelli Regional Park. This complete recreation facility is administered by the Department of Parks and Recreation of Los Angeles County. The 250 surface acre lake has good marina facilities and is open to all boating. The angler will find trout and a warm water fishery.

This well landscaped park has turfed picnic areas, a sandy swim beach, multi-purpose trails and a full facility R.V. park and campground. The Equestrian Center complements the riding trails throughout the park. Raging Waters is the largest water theme park west of the Rockies. There is a park entrance fee of $3 for each vehicle towing a boat.

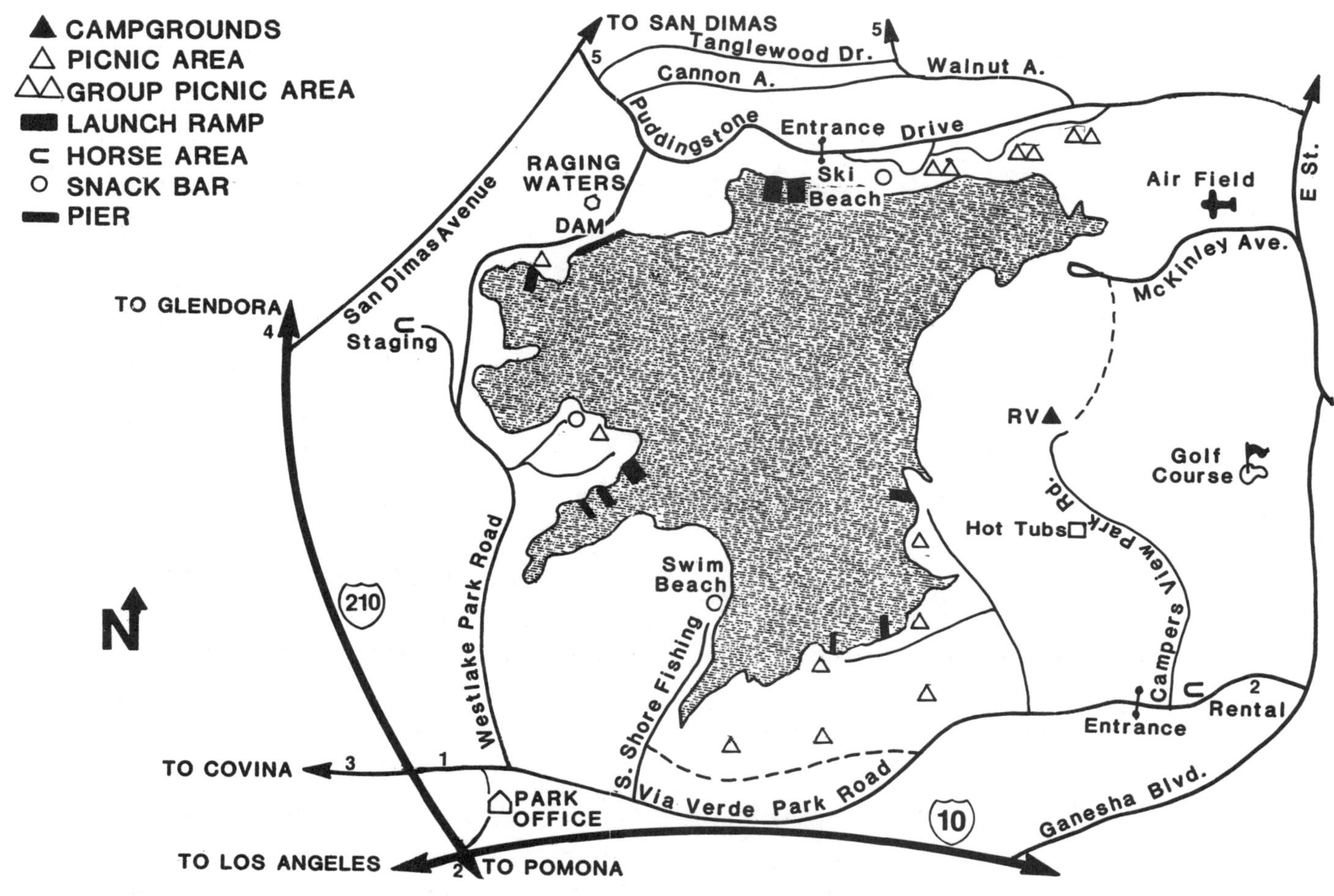

INFORMATION: Bonelli Park, 120 E. Via Verde, San Dimas 91773, Ph: 714-599-8411

CAMPING	BOATING	RECREATION	OTHER
56 Dev. Sites for Tents 487 Dev. Sites for R.V.s - Full Hookups Group Sites, Swim Pool, Spa, Rec. Rm. Volleyball Courts & General Store Disposal Station Fees: $15 - $22 Ph: 714-599-8355	Open to All Boating All Boats Must be Min. 8 ft-Max. 26 ft Power Boats Must be Min. 12 ft. Jet Skis Allowed (M-F) Check at Entrance for All Regulations Boat Rentals: Ph: 714-599-2667 Paved Launch Ramps Fee: $3	Fishing: Trout, Bass, Bluegill, Crappie, Perch & Catfish Swimming at Designated Area Picnicking Group Picnic Areas by Reservation Hiking & Equestrian Trails Tram & Raging Waters	Equestrian Center: Horse Boarding Roping Arena Ph: 714-599-8830 Raging Waters: Water Slides, Wave Pool, Rapids, Kids Pool Ph: 714-592-6453 Restaurants, Snack Bars, Bait & Tackle Gift Shop Hot Tubs: 1 - 100 People Ph: 714-592-2222

LAKE PERRIS

The Lake Perris State Recreation Area is the southern terminus of the California State Water Project. The lake's 2,200 surface acres are surrounded by rocky mountains towering to more than a thousand feet above the water's surface. Alessandro Island provides a popular boat-in picnic area. This island rises 230 feet creating an interesting view of the surrounding area. The complete recreation park provides an abundance of activities and support facilities. The fishing is good from boat or shore. Lake Perris holds the world record for Alabama Spotted bass at 9 pounds 4 ounces caught in 1987. This is a popular lake for waterskiing, sailboarding, sailing and boating. There are specific areas for waterfowl and upland game hunters. The hiker, bicycler and horseback rider will find extensive trails and there is even a rock climbing area.

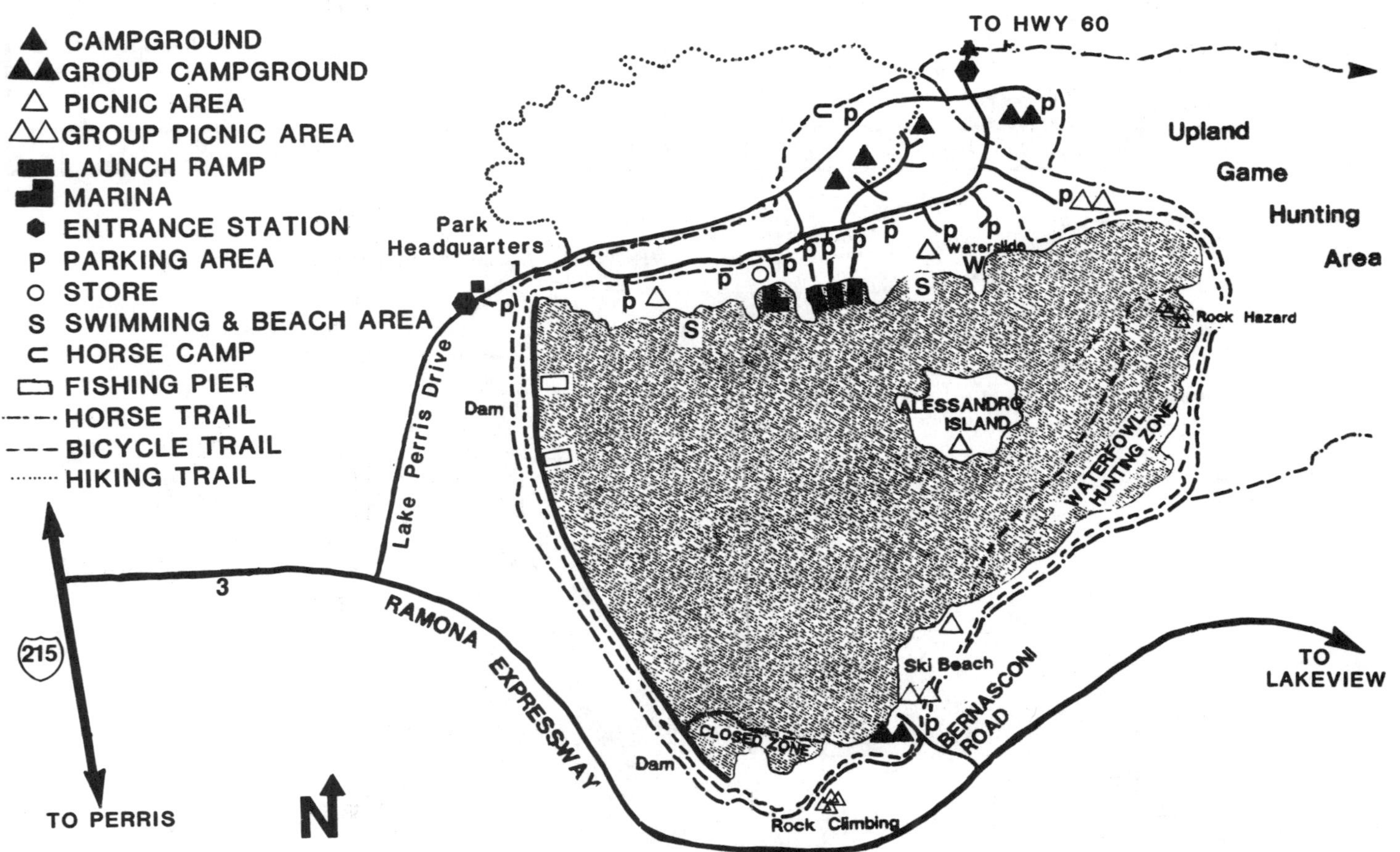

INFORMATION: State Recreation Area, 17801 Lake Perris Dr., Perris 92370, Ph: 714-657-9000			
CAMPING	BOATING	RECREATION	OTHER
167 Dev. Tent Sites Fee: $10 254 R.V. Sites - Hookups-Fee: $16 6 Group Campgrounds 25-100 People & 25-80 People Disposal Station Boat Camping in Slips Only With Prior Approval	Open to All Boating 35 MPH Speed Limit 5 MPH Zoned Areas Full Service Marina Launch Ramps: Motor Vessel: $5 Over 8 Feet: $4 Under 8 Feet: $2 Boat Storage, Slips, Gas Dock Rentals: Fishing Boats Hobie Cats, Jet Skis, Sailboards & Paddle Boats	Fishing: Trout, Alabama Spotted & Largemouth Bass, Bluegill, Channel Catfish, Sunfish Picnicking 3 Group Sites Swimming Beaches & Waterslide Hiking, Bicycle & Riding Trails Rock Climbing Area Hunting: Waterfowl & Upland Game	Regional Indian Museum Horse Camp: Corrals, Water Troughs, Picnic Tables to 50 People Coffee Shop, Snack Bar Restaurant Bait & Tackle Marina Supplies Boat Repairs

ORANGE COUNTY REGIONAL PARKS CARBON CANYON, CRAIG, RALPH P. CLARK, YORBA, IRVINE, MILE SQUARE, WILLIAM R. MASON AND LAGUNA NIGUEL

The millions of residents and visitors to Orange County will find an abundance of regional parks, harbors and beaches. We have included only those regional parks that offer a recreational lake for fishing and perhaps boating. For those who are interested in the many other facilities, contact Orange County as listed below. We have also listed below three private fishing lakes, Anaheim Lake, Irvine Lake and Santa Ana River Lakes. Anaheim and Santa Ana River are not shown on the map so contact these facilities for directions and information.

...Continued...

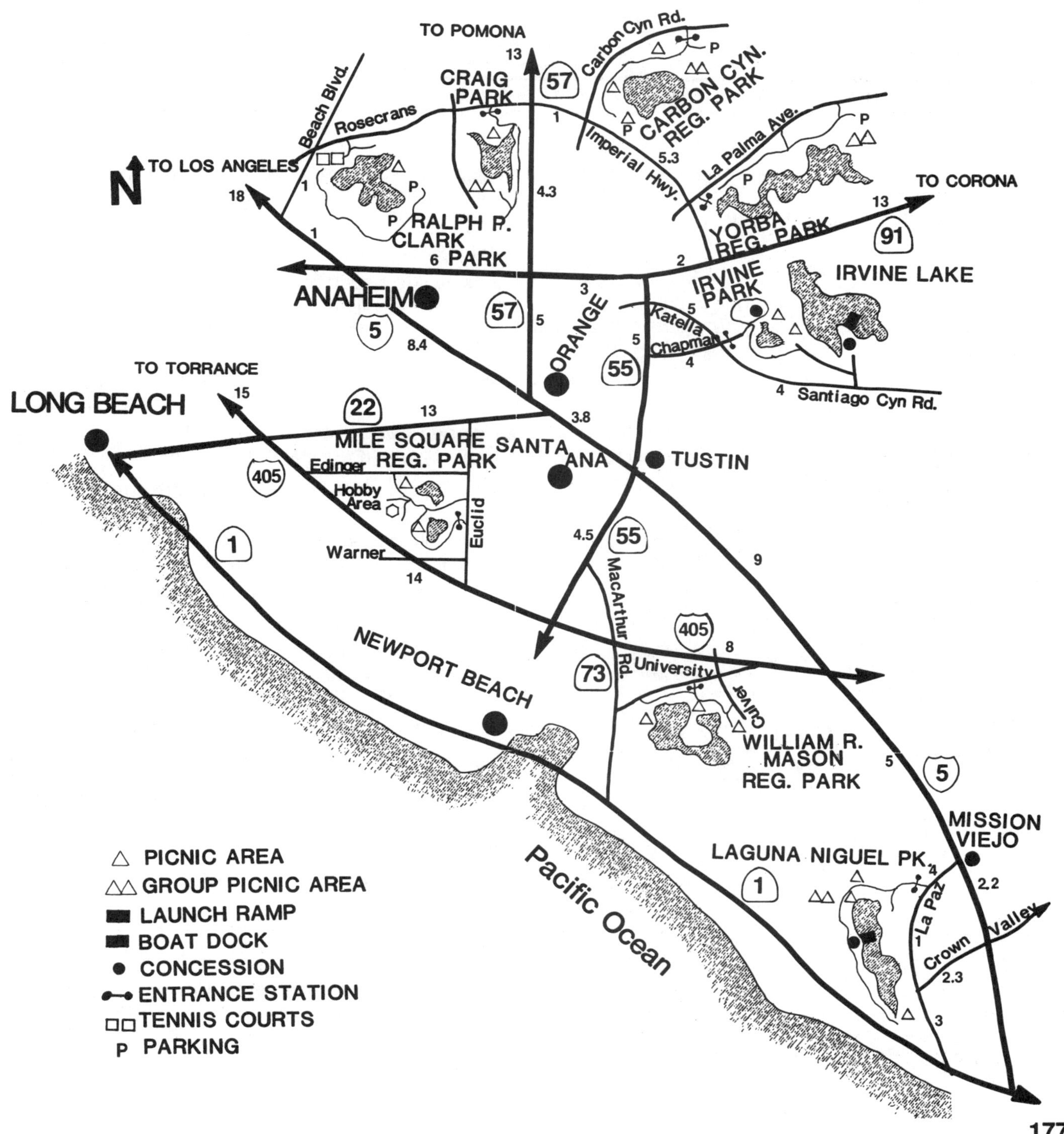

CARBON CANYON REGIONAL, 4442 Carbon Canyon Rd., Brea 92621, Ph: 714-996-5252

This 124 acre park is in the foothills of Chino Hill Range upstream from Carbon Canyon Dam. The park features a 10 acre grove of coastal redwoods amid sycamore, pepper and eucalyptus. There is a 4 acre fishing lake with two piers, bicycle, equestrian and hiking trails, picnic areas, playground, tennis courts and athletic fields.

CRAIG REGIONAL PARK, 3300 North State College Blvd., Fullerton 92635, Ph: 714-990-0271.

There is a natural amphitheater and turfed play area with the park's 124 acres. Horse enthusiasts will find numerous trails through the park. There are also bicycle and hiking trails. Picnic areas and shelters are available along with a multi-purpose sports complex. There is a 3 acre fishing lake.

IRVINE REGIONAL PARK, 21501 E. Chapman, Orange 92669, Ph: 714-633-8072

This park lies amid the coast live oaks and California sycamores in the hillside of Santiago Canyon. This is California's oldest regional park. The 447 acres includes picnic areas throughout the park, a paved bicycle and walking trail which meanders through to playgrounds and athletic fields. There are also group picnic areas, horse rentals, pony rides and bicycle rentals. The park ranger conducts interpretive programs. The Orange County Zoo and barnyard are popular. Anglers will find the nearby Irvine Lake a popular fishing area.

LAGUNA NIGUEL REGIONAL PARK, 28241 La Paz Rd., Laguna Niguel 92656, Ph: 714-831-2791

This 174 turfed park offers eucalyptus, acacia, white alder and California sycamore. There are equestrian and bicycle trails throughout the park along with group and family picnic areas and shelters. The 42 acre lake is stocked with catfish and trout in the cooler months. For fishing information phone 714-831-2790.

MILE SQUARE REGIONAL PARK, 16801 Euclid St., Fountain Valley 92708, Ph: 714-962-5549

This 640 acre former bean field and navy airstrip is now a popular regional park. Opened to the public in 1970, it offers areas for team sports, special events such as archery meets and dog shows. There are four miles of bicycle and jogging trails along with a children's playground. Although swimming is prohibited in the lake, there are refreshing spray pools.

RALPH B. CLARK REGIONAL PARK, 8800 Rosecrans Ave., Buena Park 90621, Ph: 714-670-8045

Orginally acquired by the County of Orange in 1974 to preserve its rich fossil beds, this park features picnic areas, playgrounds and athletic fields along with tennis courts. The lake offers largemouth bass, channel catfish and bluegill.

WILLIAM R. MASON REGIONAL PARK, 18712 University Dr., Irvine 92715, Ph: 714-854-2491

The Irvine Company donated this 345 acre park to Orange County. Originally named University Park, its name was changed to William R. Mason in honor of this former Irvine Company president. There are picnic areas, athletic fields, hiking, jogging and bicycle trails. The 9 acre lake is open to fishing. There are future plans to acquire San Canyon Reservoir increasing the park to 440 acres.

YORBA REGIONAL PARK, 7600 E. La Palma Ave., Anaheim 92807, Ph: 714-970-1460

This 175 acre regional park is bordered on the north side by the Santa Ana River. There are picnic shelters, organized group shelters, tables and barbecue grills. Bicycle, equestrian and hiking trails run the length of the park. There is a ten station exercise course as well as lighted athletic fields. Fishing is also offered in the connecting lakes.

INFORMATION: Orange Co. Recreational Facilities, 10852 Douglas Road, Anaheim 92806, Ph: 714-999-5191

CAMPING	BOATING	RECREATION	OTHER
Orange County: Caspers Wilderness Park 33401 Ortega Way San Juan Capistrano Ph: 714-728-0235 Featherly Reg. Park 24001 Santa Ana Cyn. Anaheim 90808 Ph: 714-637-0210 O'Neill Reg. Park 30892 Trabuco Cyn. Trabuco Canyon 92678 Ph: 714-858-9365 Camping Fee: $10	Small Boats Rentals Only at Irvine & Laguna Niguel Parks	Fishing: Largemouth Bass, Bluegill, Channel Catfish, Trout (Stocked in Winter) Picnic Areas Playgrounds Athletic Fields Hiking & Equestrian Trails Bicycle Paths Interpretive Programs Group Facilities: Permits at Least 15 Days in Advance	Private Fishing Facilities: Anaheim Lake 3451 Miraloma Anaheim 92806 Ph: 714-524-7100 Irvine Lake Star Route 38 Orange 92667 Ph: 714-649-2560 Santa Ana River Lakes 4060 E. La Palma Anaheim 92807 Ph: 714-632-7830

CUCAMONGA-GUASTI, YUCAIPA PARK, PRADO PARK AND FAIRMOUNT PARK

These small lakes offer limited boating but the surrounding parks offer an abundance of recreational opportunities. Cucamonga-Guasti, Yucaipa Park and Prado Park are a part of the San Bernardino County Regional Park System. Fairmont Park is administered by the City of Riverside. Fishing is popular the year round for bass and channel catfish. During the winter months, the angler will find planted trout. In addition to modern campgrounds, Yucaipa and Prado offers horseback riding trails and equestrian centers. There is a variety of activities unique to each park from trap shooting to waterslides.

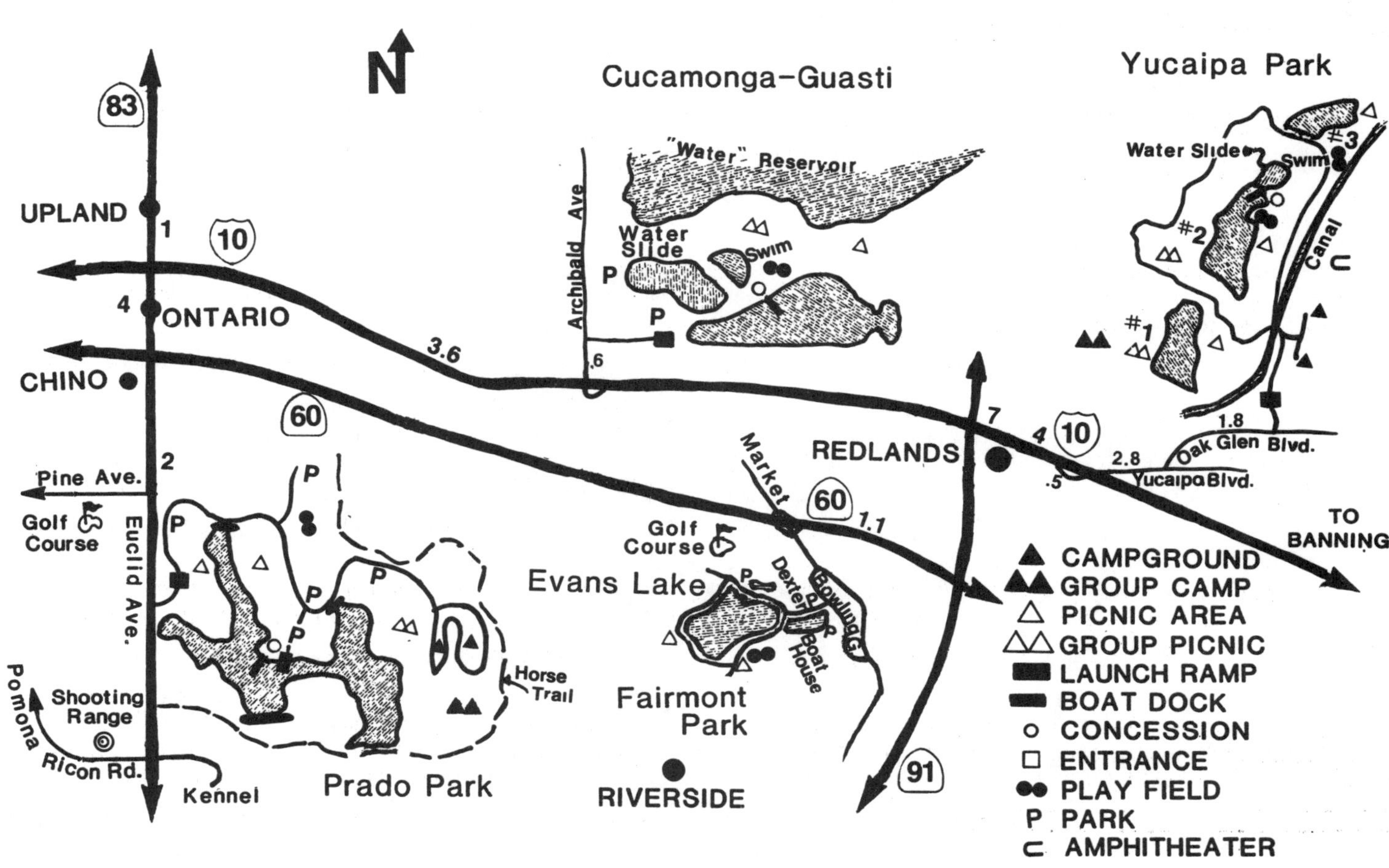

INFORMATION: Regional Parks, 825 3rd Street, San Bernardino 92415, Ph: 714-384-5233			
CAMPING	**BOATING**	**RECREATION**	**OTHER**
Yucaipa Park: Ph: 714-790-3120 26 R.V. Sites to 60 Rigs Overflow Tent Sites 13 Group sites to 35 Rigs No Hookups - Fee: $9 Prado Park: Ph: 714-597-4260 50 R.V. Sites with Full Hookups Fee: $14 Senior Citizen Discounts	Prado: Non-Power Boats Launch Ramp Rentals: Rowboats & Paddle Boats Yucaipa & Cucamonga-Guasti Paddle Boat Rentals Only	Fishing: Trout-Winter, Bass & Catfish Swimming Lagoons Picnic Areas Yucaipa & Guasti: Waterslides Hiking & Riding Trails Prado Park: Equestrian Center & Horse Rentals Athletic Fields Shooting Ranges: Trap Skeet, Pistol, Rifle, Air Gun	Prado Park: Golf Course Cucamonga-Guasti Ph: 714-945-4321 Fairmont Park: City of Riverside Parks & Rec. 3900 Main St. Riverside 92522 Ph: 714-782-5301

LAKE ELSINORE

Lake Elsinore, at an elevation of 1,273 feet, has been described as "one of the most unruly and unpredictable bodies of water in California." In spite of its fickle nature, Lake Elsinore provides an abundance of water sports. This large fluctuating lake offers sailing, boating and waterskiing. It is known as one of the best bass fishing lakes in the West. The State Recreation Area Campground is under concession to the Lake Elsinore Recreation Area, Inc., a private corporation. There are many walnut shaded lawns awaiting the camper at this well maintained facility. There are a number of private campgrounds, resorts and marinas around the lake. Elsinore, long famed for its mineral springs, offers the visitor three spas. Corona, 86 surface acres, is a private fishing lake for stocked trout, catfish, crappie and largemouth bass.

. . . Continued . . .

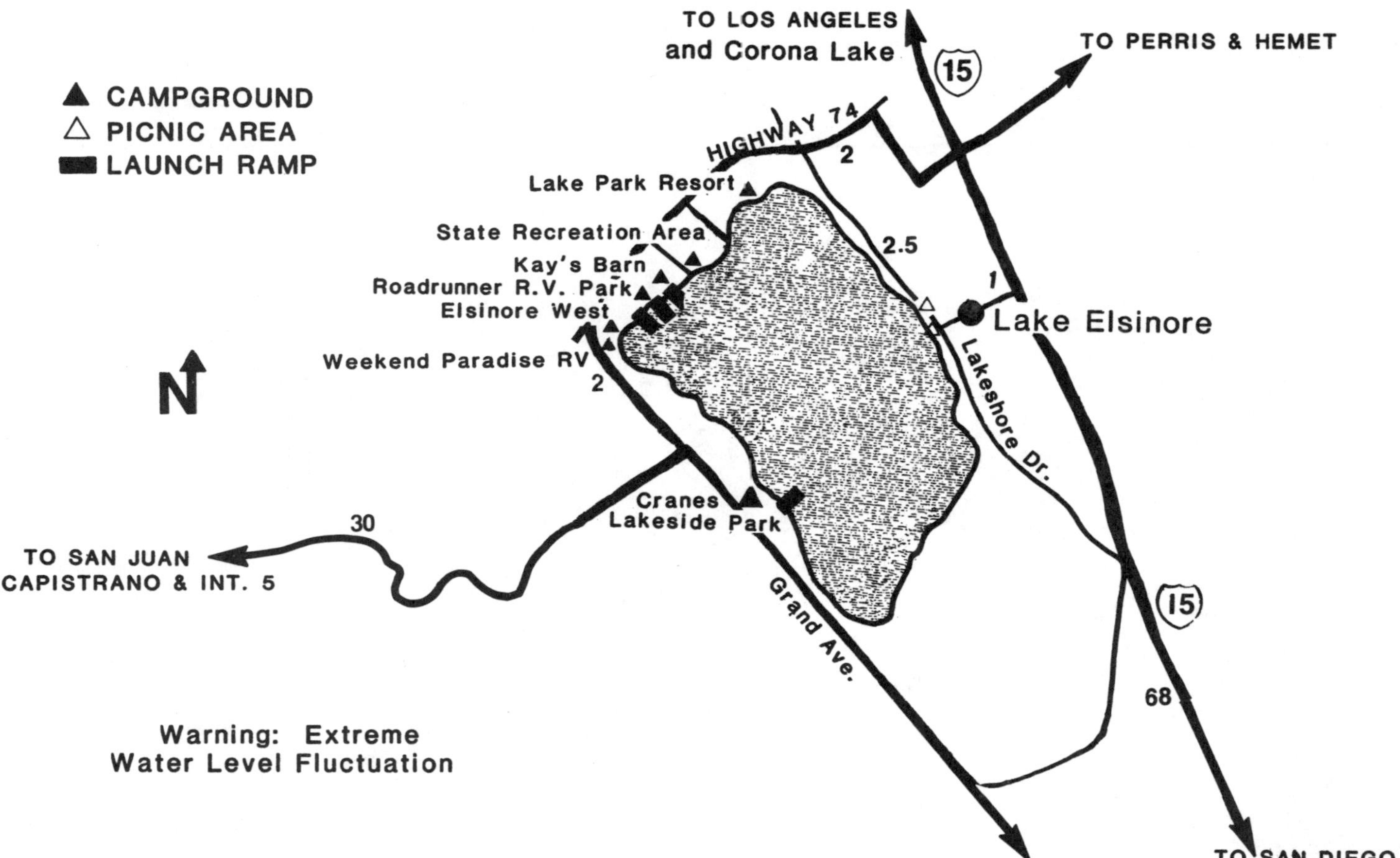

INFORMATION: State Campground, 32040 Riverside Dr., Lake Elsinore 92330, Ph: 714-674-3177

CAMPING	BOATING	RECREATION	OTHER
400 Dev. Sites for Tents & R.V.s Fee: $11.50 for 2 $14.50 with Elec. Hookup Pets: $2 Disposal Station Group Site to 800 People Day Use Only: Fee: $4 for 2 $1 Each Additional Person	Power, Row, Canoe, Sail, Windsurf, Waterski & Jet Ski Boating Fee: $5 Day Annual Permits: $25-$65 Launch Ramps, Marinas Slips, Docks, Gas 35 MPH Speed Limit Rentals: Fishing Boats Kayaks, Paddle Boats Noise Level Restrict.	Fishing: Small & Largemouth Bass, Carp, Crappie, Bluegill & Catfish Swimming: In Pools & Designated Areas Picnicking Hiking, Riding & Bicycle Trails Hang Gliding & Ultra Lite Planes Parachuting Mineral Baths	Full Facilities in Lake Elsinore Corona Lake 12510 Temescal Corona 91720 Ph: 714-735-3556 Boat Rentals See Following Page

LAKE ELSINORE

LAKE PARK RESORT

32000 Riverside Dr., Lake Elsinore 92330, Ph: 714-674-7911
Beach Tent & R.V. Camp Area, 121 R.V. Sites, Full Hookups, Fees: $14 - $16, Cable T.V., Hot Showers, Flush Toilets, Disposal Station, Laundry, Swim Beach & Olympic Size Pool, Recreation Center, Picnic Area, Hand Launch & Dock, Rentals: Fishing Boats & Jet Skis.

KAY JORDAN'S CAMPGROUND

32310 Riverside Dr., Lake Elsinore 92330, Ph: 714-674-9908
Tent/R.V. Sites, No Hookups, Fee: $8, Swimming Beach, Launch Ramp, Lake Use Permits.

ROAD RUNNER R.V. PARK

32500 Riverside Dr., Lake Elsinore 92330, Ph: 714-674-4900
145 R.V. Sites, 100 Full Hookups, Fees: $12 - $17, Hot Showers, Flush Toilets, Disposal Station, Laundry, Launch Ramp, Lake Use Permits.

ELSINORE WEST MARINA

32790 Riverside Dr., Lake Elsinore 92330, Ph: 714-678-1300
Open Tent & R.V. Camp Area, 170 R.V. Sites, Full Hookups, Fees: $12 - $17, Hot Showers, Flush Toilets, Cable T.V., Picnic Area, Launch Ramp, Docks, Lake Use Permits.

WEEKEND PARADISE R.V. PARK

Grand Ave., Lake Elsinore 92330, Ph: 714-678-3715
30 R.V. Sites, Water & Electric Hookups, Fee: $14, Flush Toilets, Hot Showers, Disposal Station, Pavillion, Launch Ramp, Dock.

CRANE LAKESIDE PARK

15980 Grand Ave., Lake Elsinore 92330, Ph: 714-678-2112
21 R.V. Sites, Water & Electric Hookups, Hot Showers, Flush Toilets, Snack Bar, Swim Area, Recreation Center, Laundry.

FOR OTHER FACILITIES AND ACCOMMODATIONS CONTACT:

Lake Elsinore Chamber of Commerce
132 W. Grand Avenue
Lake Elsinore 92330
Ph: 714-674-2577

LAKE SKINNER

Located at an elevation of 1,500 feet in the transitional area between coast and desert, Lake Skinner rests amid semi-arid vegetation, rolling hills of wild flowers and oak trees. The lake has a surface area of 1,200 acres. The 14 miles of irregular shoreline is surrounded by the 6,000 acre Lake Skinner Park. This new and developing facility is operated by Riverside County Parks Department. In addition to the campsites, there is a half-acre swimming pool, beaches, ecology ponds, marine facilities, camp store and fishing areas. There are a number of good riding trails and a primitive equestrian campground where water is piped in for the horses. This is a good sailing lake with moderate winds. Power boating is restricted to 10 MPH with low wake conditions. It is well stocked with trout and warm water fish. The facilities are nicely maintained with grassy areas and sandy beaches.

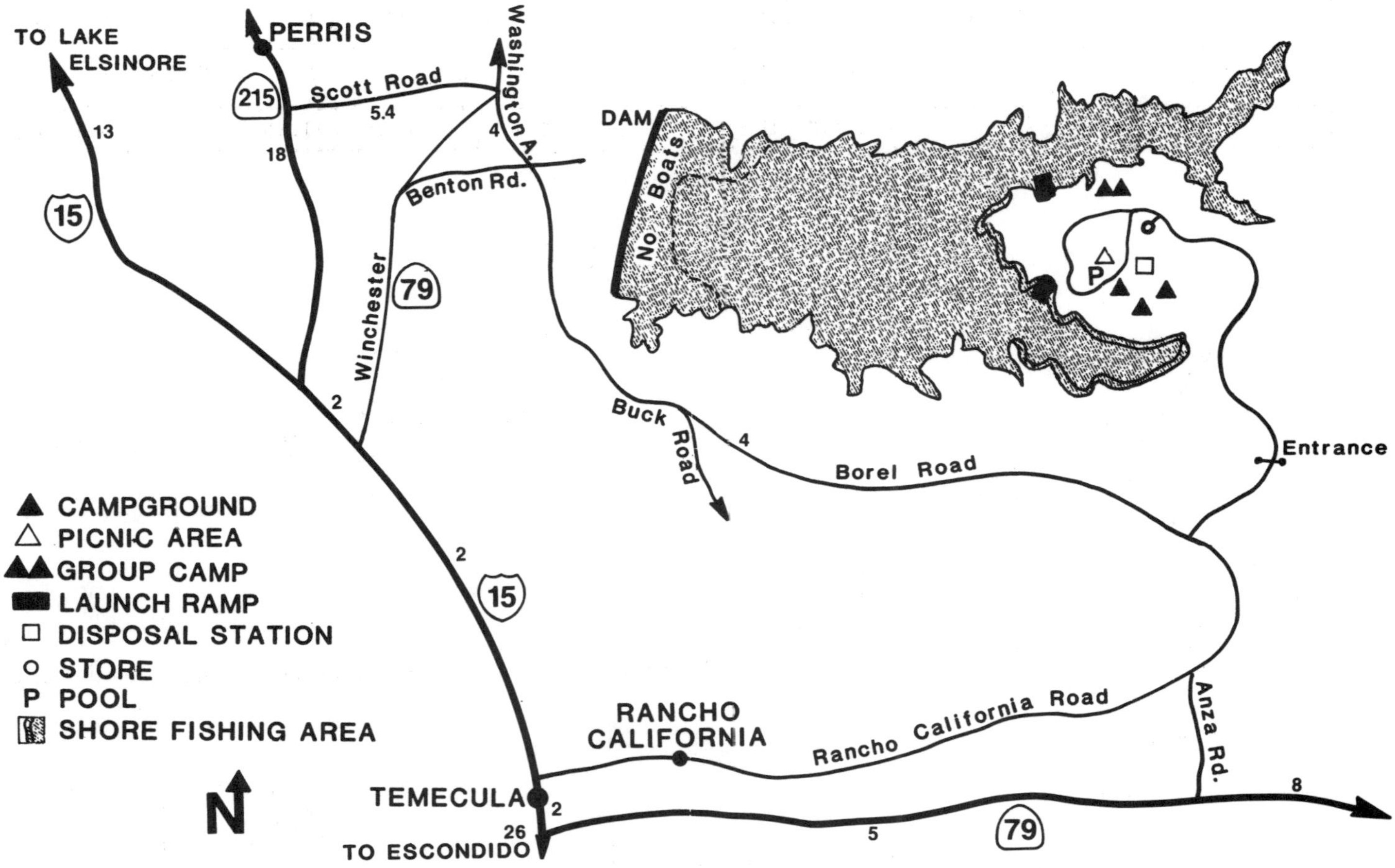

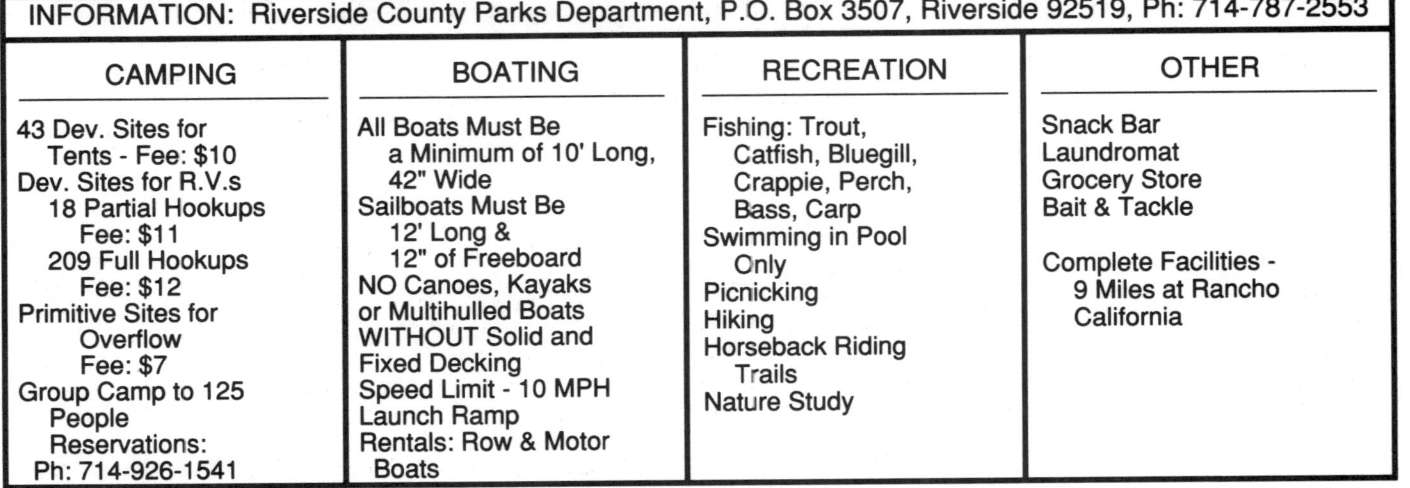

INFORMATION: Riverside County Parks Department, P.O. Box 3507, Riverside 92519, Ph: 714-787-2553			
CAMPING	BOATING	RECREATION	OTHER
43 Dev. Sites for Tents - Fee: $10 Dev. Sites for R.V.s 18 Partial Hookups Fee: $11 209 Full Hookups Fee: $12 Primitive Sites for Overflow Fee: $7 Group Camp to 125 People Reservations: Ph: 714-926-1541	All Boats Must Be a Minimum of 10' Long, 42" Wide Sailboats Must Be 12' Long & 12" of Freeboard NO Canoes, Kayaks or Multihulled Boats WITHOUT Solid and Fixed Decking Speed Limit - 10 MPH Launch Ramp Rentals: Row & Motor Boats	Fishing: Trout, Catfish, Bluegill, Crappie, Perch, Bass, Carp Swimming in Pool Only Picnicking Hiking Horseback Riding Trails Nature Study	Snack Bar Laundromat Grocery Store Bait & Tackle Complete Facilities - 9 Miles at Rancho California

LAKE FULMOR, REFLECTION LAKE AND ANGLER'S LAKE

Lake Fulmor is at an elevation of 5,300 feet near the beautiful mountain resort community of Idyllwild. Although facilities are limited to Day Use at this small trout lake, the visitor is sure to enjoy the relaxed atmosphere in this area of the San Bernardino National Forest. Angler's and Reflection Lakes, at 1,600 feet elevation, are small private fishing facilities. Angler's Lake provides open camping and no limit fishing.

Reflection Lake offers a developed campground with full hookups. Boating is limited to canoes, inflatables and rowboats. Electric motors are allowed. Trout and Channel catfish are planted weekly in season at both Angler's and Reflection Lakes and State fishing licenses are not required at these private facilities.

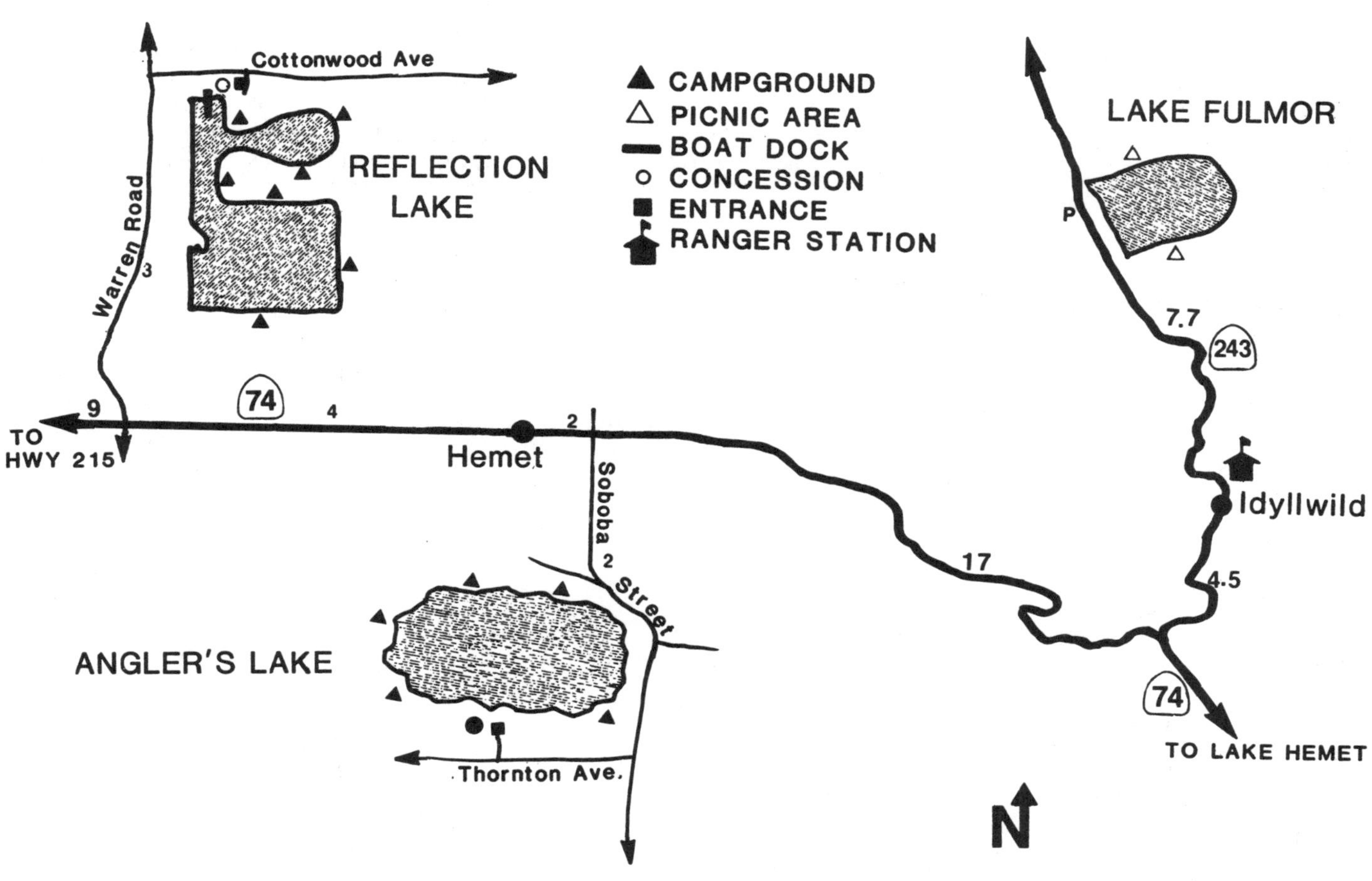

INFORMATION: Reflection Lake, 36151 Cottonwood Rd., San Jacinto 92383, Ph: 714-654-7906			
CAMPING	**BOATING**	**RECREATION**	**OTHER**
Reflection Lake: 121 Sites - Water and Electric Hookups Disposal Station Fees: Tents: $12.50 Hookups: $14.25 Angler's Lake: Open Campsites to 300 People Fee: $9	Reflection Lake: Row, Canoe & Inflatables, Electric Motors Only Rentals: Rowboats Angler's & Fulmor: No Boating Be Certain to Check Status of Current Water Levels	Fishing: Trout, Bass, Bluegill & Catfish Fishing Fees: Angler's Lake: $10 Reflection Lake: Campers $6 Day Use $7 Picnicking Hiking No Swimming	Angler's Lake 42660 Thornton Ave. Hemet 92344 Ph: 714-927-2614 Lake Fulmor: Idyllwild R.S. P.O. Box 518 Idyllwild 92349 Ph: 714-659-2117

LAKE HEMET

Lake Hemet rests at an elevation of 4,400 feet in a pleasant mountain meadow of the San Bernardino National Forest. Surrounded by chaparral covered hills, this 420 acre lake is under the jurisdiction of the Lake Hemet Municipal Water District. Boating is limited to fishing boats. This is primarily a fishing lake. Large trout are caught throughout the year. In addition, the angler will find a good bass and catfish fishery. There is a large developed campground at the lake. Nearby Herkey Creek has a 300-site campground operated by Riverside County. Although swimming is not allowed in Lake Hemet, swimming is permitted at Herkey Creek when water is available.

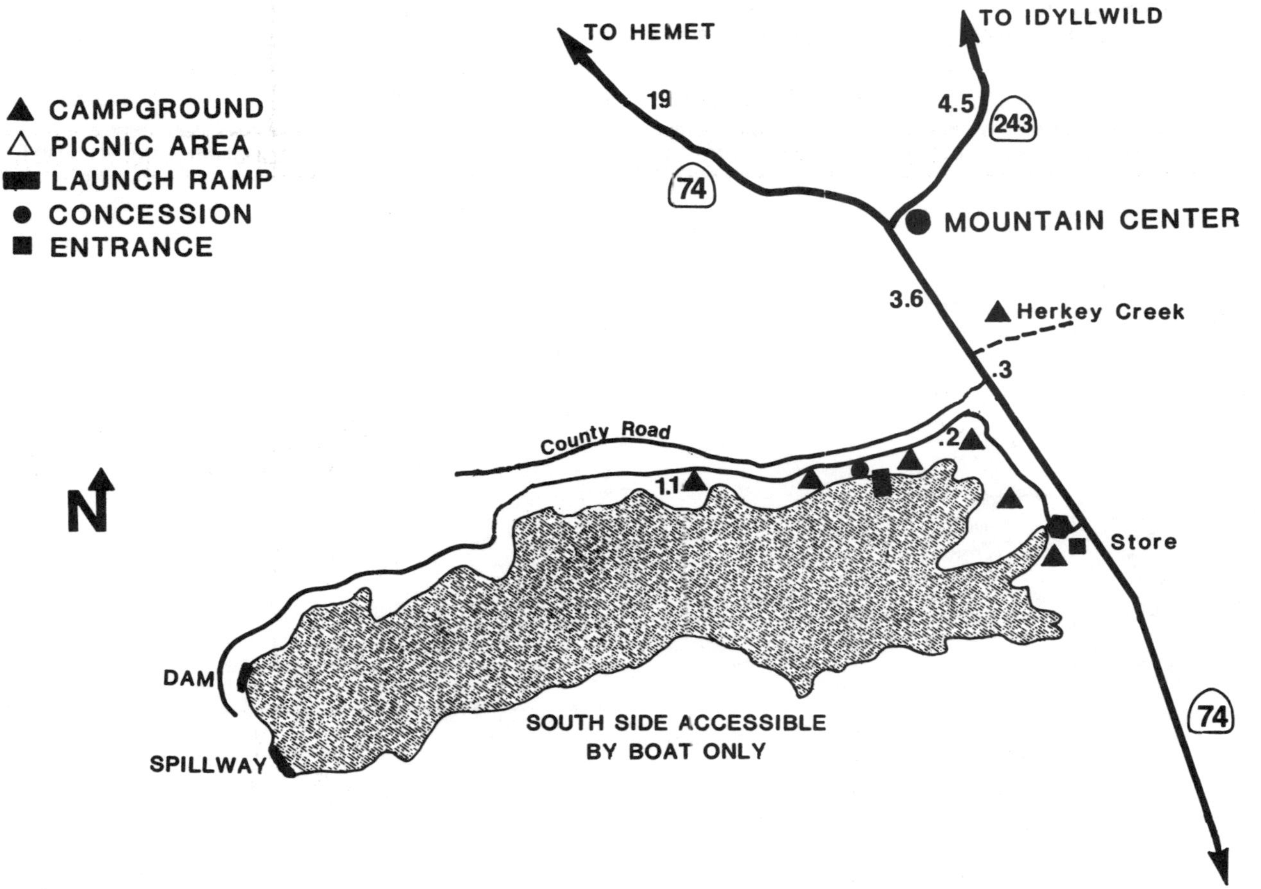

INFORMATION: Lake Hemet, Box 4, Mountain Center 92361, Ph: 714-659-2680

CAMPING	BOATING	RECREATION	OTHER
900 Dev. Sites for Tents & R.V.s Electric & Water Hookups Pay Showers No Generators Fee: $7 Herkey Creek: 310 Sites Tents & R.V.s No Hookups Fee: $6 Group Sites	No Canoes, Kayaks, Sailboats, Inflatables or Boats Less Than 10 Feet in Length Rentals: Rowboats & Motors 10 MPH Speed Limit Cement Launch Ramp Location Depends On Water Level	Fishing: Trout, Bass & Catfish Picnicking Hiking No Swimming No Motorcycles	General Store: Food Camping Supplies Bait & Tackle No Gas Available For Auto or Boats

LAKE CAHUILLA

Lake Cahuilla is at an elevation of 44 feet, 6 miles southwest of Indio. This 135-surface acre lake is owned by the Coachella Valley Water District, and the palm-shaded park is operated by Riverside County. Located in the desert with temperatures up to 100 degrees, Cahuilla offers a pleasant retreat. There is a 10-acre beach for swimming and an adjacent water play area for the children. This oasis offers an abundance of well-maintained campsites along with a secluded group campground and a shady picnic area. The winter months can be delightful with temperatures of 75 degrees luring the camper and fisherman to this nice facility.

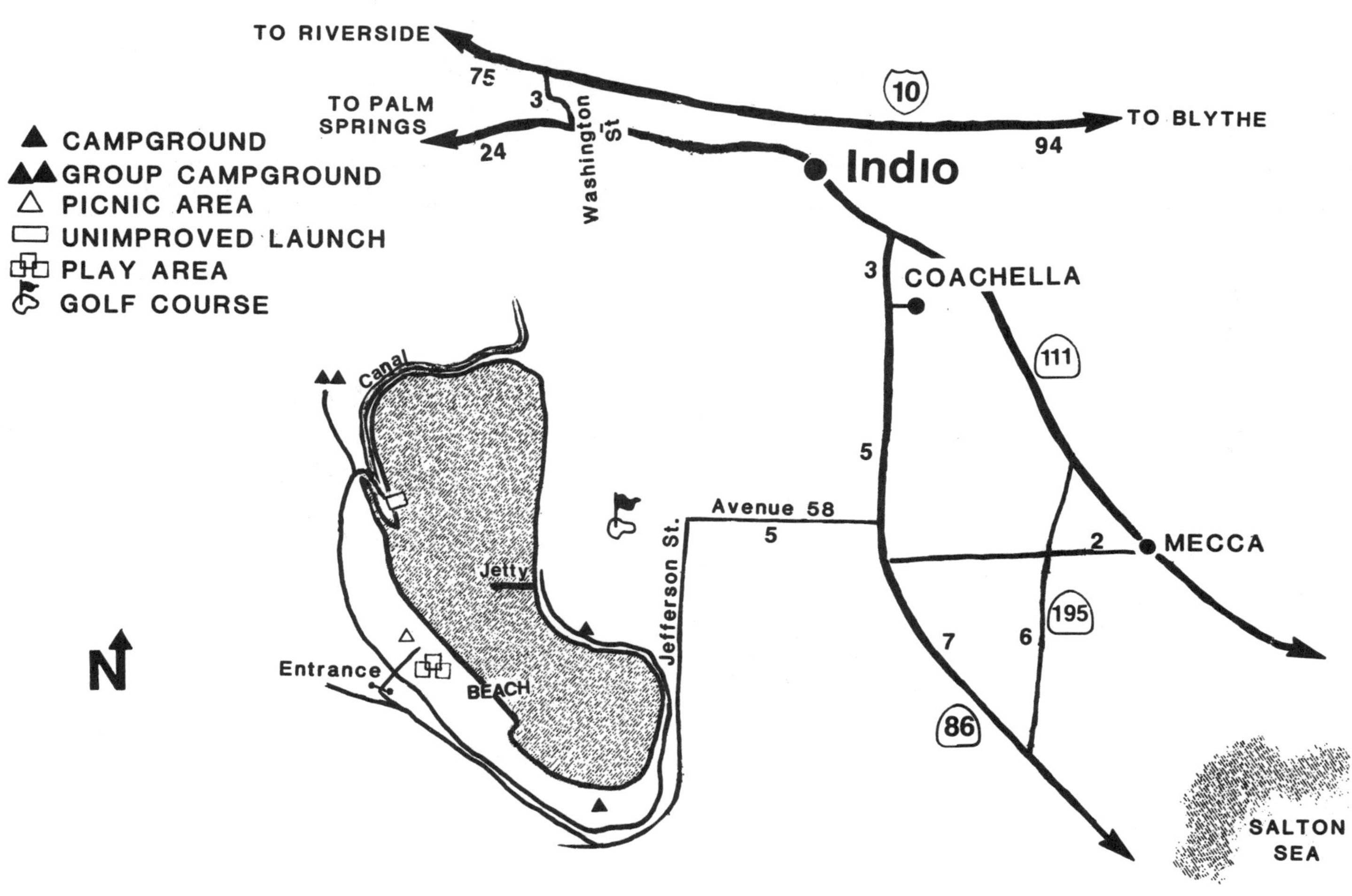

INFORMATION: Riverside County Parks Department, Box 3507, Riverside 92519, Ph: 714-787-2551			
CAMPING	**BOATING**	**RECREATION**	**OTHER**
80 Primitive Sites Fee: $7 Groups: $72 for First 12 Vehicles 60 Developed Sites Water & Electric Hookups - $10 Security Gate - Card Required $10 Deposit Phone Riverside County Parks for Reservations	Sail, Row, Electric Motors Only Speed Limit - 10 MPH Hand Launch Only	Fishing: Rainbow Trout (Winter), Channel Catfish Striped Bass Fishing Pier - Accessible to Handicapped 10-Acre Swim Beach Water Play Area Picnicking Hiking & Backpacking Horseback Trails	Lake Cahuilla Ph: 619-564-4712 Snack Bar Bait & Tackle Disposal Station Security Gate Locked Between 10:00 p.m. and 6:00 a.m. Full Facilities - 6 Miles at Indio

WISTER UNIT, FINNEY AND RAMER LAKES

The 6,127 acres of the Imperial Wildlife Area hosts one of Southern California's most abundant wildlife habitats. This is the home of a rich variety of birds, fish, amphibians, reptiles and mammals. Naturalists, bird watchers, photographers and those who just love nature are drawn to this area. With prime waterfowl hunting available, there are restrictions which apply to the number of hunters and other regulations; contact the Wildlife Headquarters for details. There is also a good warm water fishery. Located below sea level in the hot desert climate of the Imperial Valley, the temperature is often over 100 degress in the summer months. A more temperate climate of 70 degrees prevails in fall, winter and spring to welcome visitors.

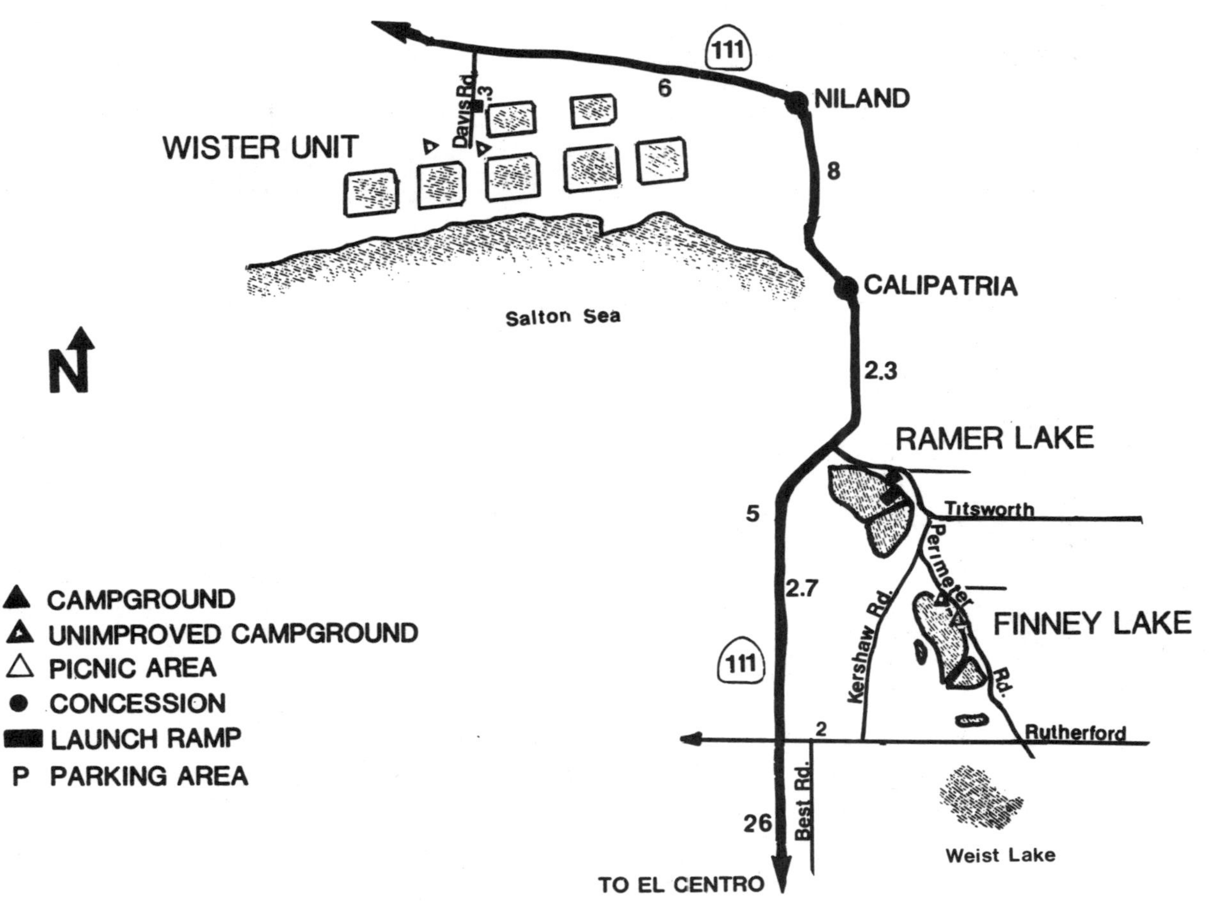

INFORMATION: Imperial Wildlife Area, Rt. 1, Box 6, Niland 92257, Ph: 619-359-0577

CAMPING	BOATING	RECREATION	OTHER
Primitive Open Camping Chemical Toilets Fire Rings	Finney-Ramer: No Power Boats Electric Motors Only Wister Ponds: No Boating	Fishing: Largemouth Bass, Bluegill, Crappie, Catfish & Carp Picnicking Hiking Nature Study Hunting: Duck, Geese, Dove, Quail & Rabbit Frogging	Nearest Facilities in Niland & Brawley

SALTON SEA

The Salton Sea is located in a desert valley 228 feet below sea level surrounded by mountains reaching to 10,000 feet. It is one of the world's largest inland bodies of salt water with a surface area of 360 square miles. Although summer temperatures range well over 100 degrees, fall, winter and spring temperatures are in the 70's. This warm, shallow Sea provides an abundance of food for its game fish. Orangemouth Corvina, Croaker (Bairdiella) and Sargo were introduced from the Gulf of California and the Tilapia was imported from Africa. These fish have flourished and the angler is rewarded with California's richest inland fishery. Numerous marinas, campgrounds and resorts support the recreational abundance of this desert oasis.

. . . Continued . . .

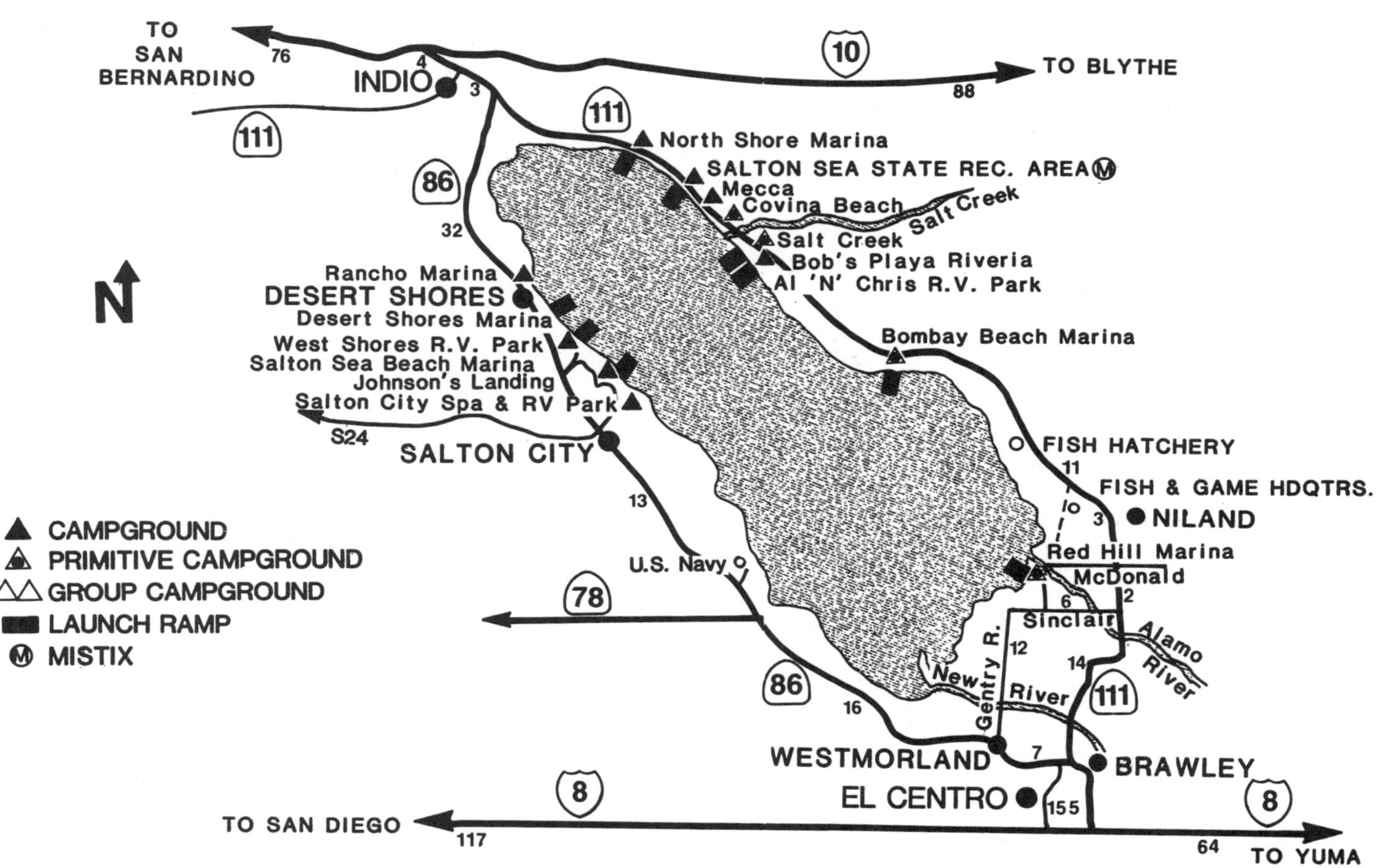

INFORMATION: See Following Page			
CAMPING	BOATING	RECREATION	OTHER
See Following Page for Campgrounds	Open to All Boating Full Service Marinas Launch Ramps Gas, Docks Dry Storage Caution: Sudden Strong Winds Many Unmarked Underwater Hazards Especially at North & South Ends	Fishing: Corvina, Sargo, Gulf Croaker, Tilapia Frogging Swimming Beaches Picnicking - Shade Ramadas Nature Trails Birdwatching Hunting: Waterfowl, Pheasant, Dove & Rabbit	Full Facilities Around the Lake Mineral Spas For Additional Information Contact Westshores Chamber of Commerce P.O. Box 5185 Salton City 92275 Ph: 619-394-4112

SALTON SEA - A PARTIAL LIST OF FACILITIES:

SALTON SEA STATE RECREATION AREA - P.O. Box 3166, North Shore 92254, Ph: 619-393-3052
Headquarters Campground: 25 Tent/R.V. Sites, Wheelchair Accessible, 15 Full Hookups, Disposal Station, Flush Toilets, Solar Showers, Shade Ramadas, Shaded Picnic Area, Fish Cleaning Station, Campfire Programs, Nature Trail to Mecca Beach, Launch Ramp, Mooring, Boat Wash Rack. Fee: $8 - $14. Reservations: Year Around - Mistix System (Senior Citizens Discount)

Mecca Beach Campground: 108 Tent/R.V. Sites, Wheelchair Accessible, Flush Toilets, Solar Showers, Shaded Picnic Area, Fish Cleaning Station, Campfire Programs. Fee: $8

Covina Beach, Salt Creek & Bombay Beach Campgrounds: 800 Primitive Sites on Water's Edge, Chemical Toilets, Water, Beach Launch. Fee: $5

BOB'S PLAYA RIVIERA - 10565 Hwy. 111, North Shore 92254, Ph: 619-354-1835
67 Tent/R.V. Sites, 40 Full Hookups, 7 Electric & Water Hookups, Hot Showers, Flush Toilets, Boat & Trailer Storage, Full Service Marina, Launch Ramp, Bait, Gas, Groceries, Laundry, Row Boat Rentals.

AL 'N' CHRIS R.V. PARK - P.O. Box 3106, North Shore 92254, Ph: 619-354-1272
80 Full Hookups. Season Lease Sites, Flush Toilets, Hot Showers, Full Service Marina, Launch Ramp, Laundry, No Tents.

BOMBAY MARINA - 9518 Avenue B, Niland 92257, Ph: 619-354-1694
50 Tent/R.V. Sites, 16 Full Hookups, Trailer Rentals, 18 Shaded Sites, Open Tent Camping, Hot Showers, Flush Toilets, Snacks, Bait & Tackle, Ice, Drinks, Boat Slips, Launch Ramp, Rental Boats.

RED HILL MARINA - Imperial County Resident Ranger, P.O. Box 1419, Niland 92257, Ph: 619-348-2310
240 Acre Primitive Tent/R.V. Dry Camp, 80 R.V. Sites, Electric & Water Hookups, Showers, Shade Ramadas, Disposal Station, Picnic Tables, Launch, Docks, Dry Storage, Boatwash Rack, Snack Bar, Bait & Tackle, Beer, Ice.

SALTON CITY SPA & R.V. PARK - P.O. Box 5375, Salton City 92275, Ph: 619-394-4333
315 R.V. Sites, Full Hookups, Flush Toilets, Hot Showers, Hot Mineral Spa, Swimming Pool, Pool Tables, Dry Storage.

JOHNSON'S LANDING & R.V. PARK - P.O. Box 5312, Salton City 92275, Ph: 619-394-4755
108 R.V. Sites, Flush Toilets, Hot Showers, Launch Ramp, Bait & Tackle, Restaurant, Bar.

SALTON SEA BEACH MARINA - 288 Coachella, Salton Sea Beach 92274-9517, Ph: 619-395-5212
144 R.V. Full Hookups, Overflow Site for Tents & R.V.s, Water & Electric Hookups, Gas Groceries, Bait & Tackle, Disposal Station, Launch Ramp, Boat Gas.

WEST SHORES R.V. PARK - P.O. Box 5312, Salton City 92275, Ph: 619-394-4755
108 R.V. Sites, Full Hookups, Hot Showers, Flush Toilets, Disposal Station, Launch Ramp, Dock, Bait & Tackle, Restaurant & Bar.

DESERT SHORES MARINA - Desert Shores 92274, Ph: 619-395-5280
Launch Ramp, Tie Ups, Charters, Snacks, Drinks.

RANCHO MARINA - 301 N. Palm Dr., Desert Shores 92274, Ph: 619-395-5410
75 Tent/R.V. Sites, 47 Full Hookups, Flush Toilets, Hot Showers.

NORTH SHORE MARINA - P.O. Box 3108, North Shore 92254, Ph: 619-393-3071
Motel, R.V. Park, Swimming Pool, Boat Storage, Launch Ramp, Bait & Tackle, Restaurant, Tennis Court.

WIEST LAKE

Wiest Lake is located 4 miles north of Brawley off Highway 111. It is 110 feet below sea level in the agriculturally rich Imperial Valley. This 50 surface acre lake is under the jurisdiction of Imperial County which operates the facilities. The Lake is open to all types of boating from fishing boats to waterskis. There is a good warm water fishery. The visitor will find picnic sites, a swimming area and hiking trails. Although there is no shooting within the park, the hunter will find waterfowl, dove and rabbit in the nearby Imperial Wildlife Area. Frogging is also popular. Hot summer temperatures are a burden but a more moderate climate prevails in the fall, winter and spring.

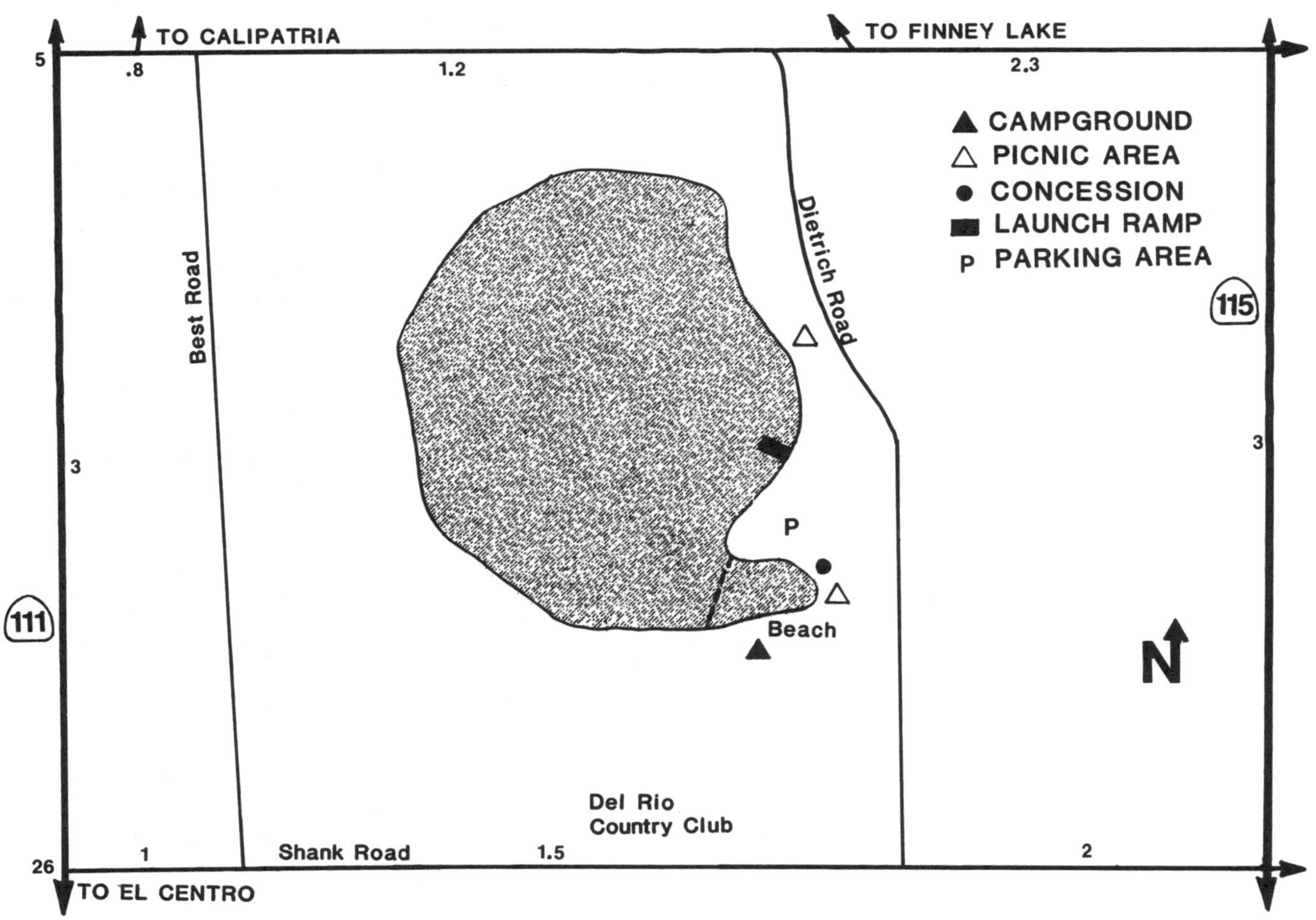

INFORMATION: Wiest Lake, 5351 Dietrich Rd., Brawley 92227, Ph: 619-344-3712			
CAMPING	BOATING	RECREATION	OTHER
20 Tent Sites Fee: $5 25 R.V. Sites Electric & Water Hookups Fee: $8 Handicapped Facilities Disposal Station Flush Toilets	Open to All Boating Paved Launch Ramp Docks Dry Storage	Fishing: Largemouth Bass, Bluegill, Crappie, Catfish & Carp Picnicking Hiking Nature Study Swimming Nearby: Hunting: Duck, Geese, Dove, Quail, Rabbit Frogging	Full Facilities in Brawley & El Centro

SUNBEAM LAKE

Sunbeam Lake is actually two small lakes totaling 14 surface acres. Owned and operated by Imperial County, the park offers a variety of recreational opportunities. Although boating is allowed in both lakes, power boating is limited to only one of the lakes. There is a spring fed swimming lagoon and the fisherman will find a variety of warm water fish.

These lakes are 43 feet below sea level where summer temperatures average over 100 degrees. Fall, winter and spring are in the 70's. Surrounded by palm trees, Sunbeam Lake is a pleasant oasis. The campground is temporarily closed so contact the Imperial County Parks and Recreation for current status.

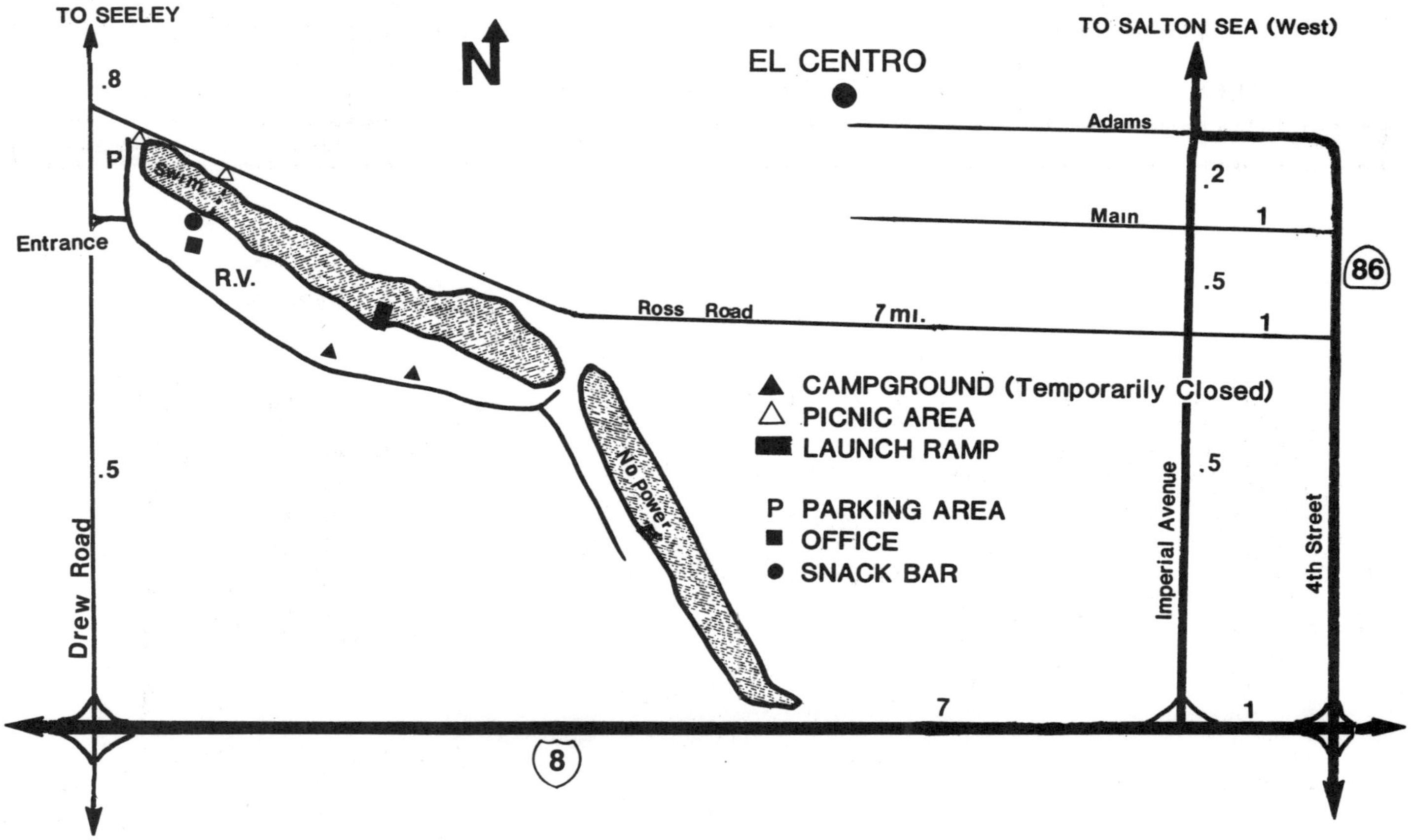

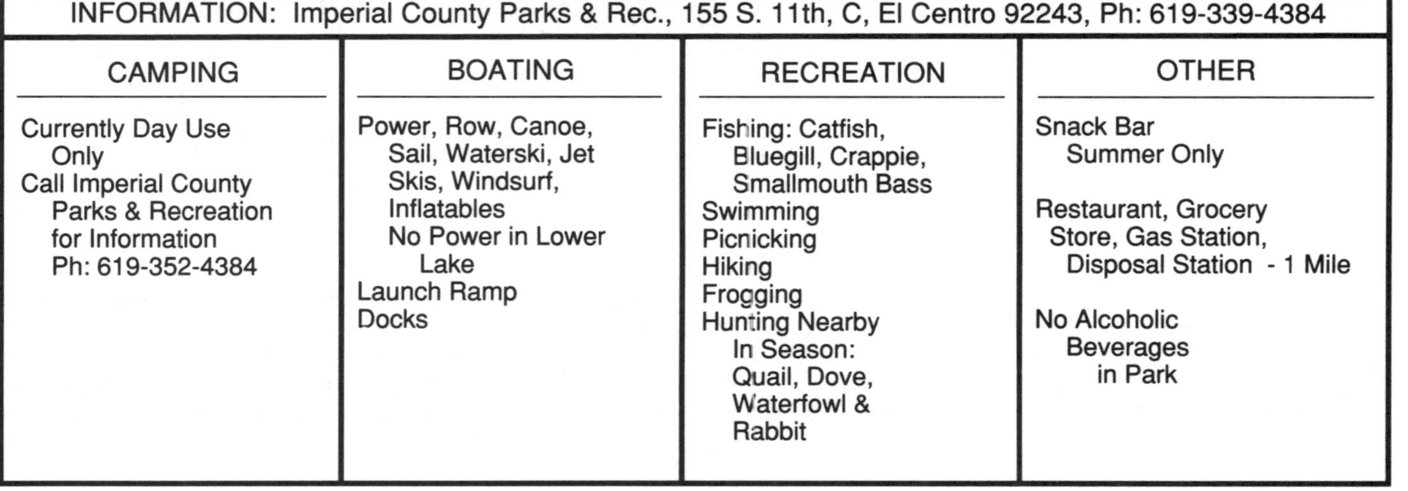

INFORMATION: Imperial County Parks & Rec., 155 S. 11th, C, El Centro 92243, Ph: 619-339-4384			
CAMPING	BOATING	RECREATION	OTHER
Currently Day Use Only Call Imperial County Parks & Recreation for Information Ph: 619-352-4384	Power, Row, Canoe, Sail, Waterski, Jet Skis, Windsurf, Inflatables No Power in Lower Lake Launch Ramp Docks	Fishing: Catfish, Bluegill, Crappie, Smallmouth Bass Swimming Picnicking Hiking Frogging Hunting Nearby In Season: Quail, Dove, Waterfowl & Rabbit	Snack Bar Summer Only Restaurant, Grocery Store, Gas Station, Disposal Station - 1 Mile No Alcoholic Beverages in Park

DIXON LAKE

The Dixon Lake Recreation Area is operated by the City of Escondido Community Services Department. Nestled in chaparral and avocado-covered foothills, Dixon Lake is at an elevation of 1,045 feet. It has a surface area of 70 acres with 2 miles of shoreline within this 527 acre park. The facilities are excellent for camping, fishing and picnicking. Many large bass and catfish await the angler. Trout are stocked from November through May and catfish from June through August.

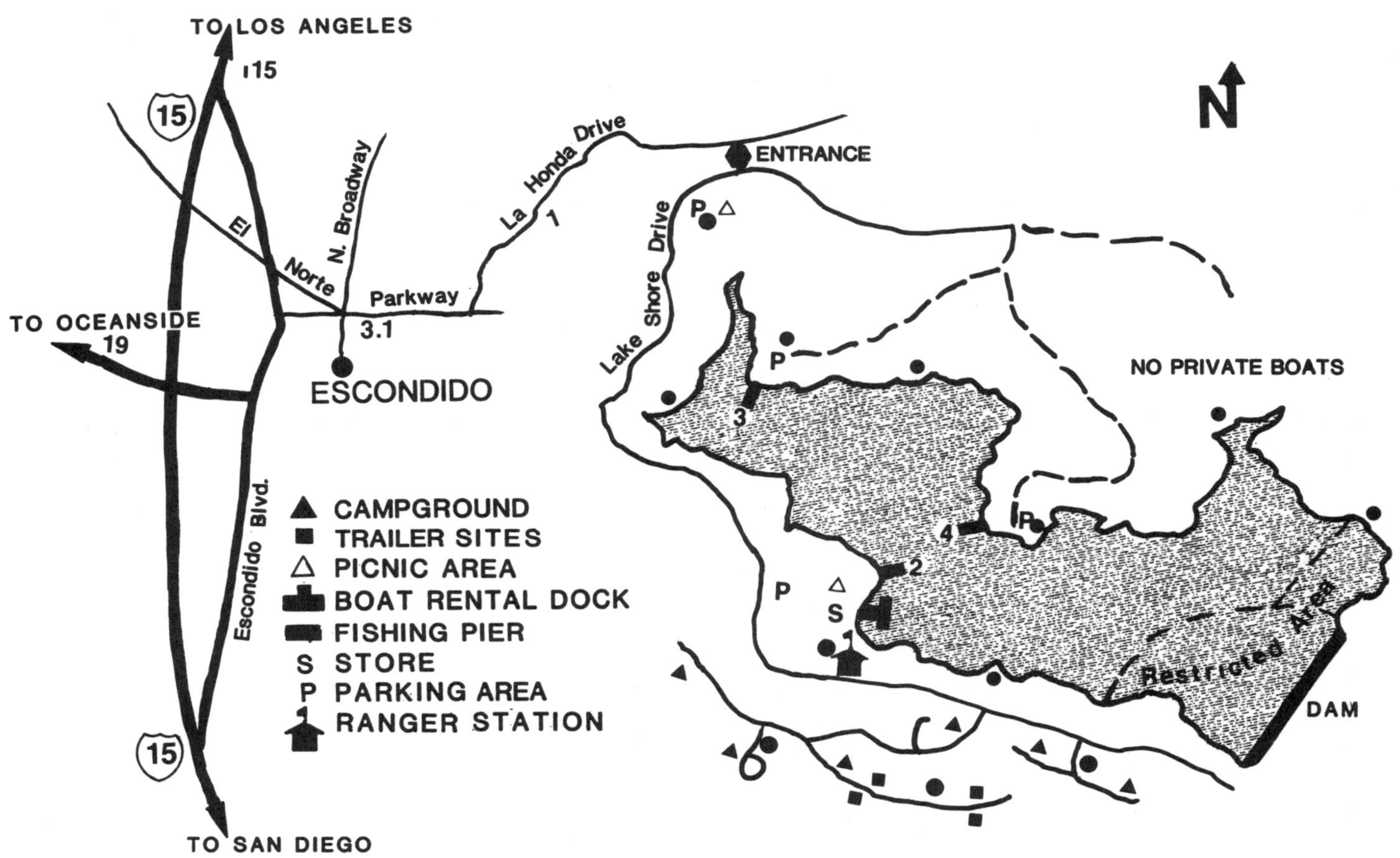

INFORMATION: Community Services, 100 Valley Blvd., Escondido 92025			
CAMPING	BOATING	RECREATION	OTHER
35 Tent & R.V. Sites Fee: $10 2nd Vehicle: $2 10 Full Hookup Sites Fee: $14 2nd Vehicle: $2 Reservations Accepted Fee: $5 Ph: 619-741-3328 8 a.m. - 5 p.m.	No Private Boats Rentals: Rowboats with Electric Motors	Fishing: Trout, Catfish, Bluegill, Crappie, Redear Sunfish, Florida Bass No Swimming or Wading Picnicking: Reservations Ph: 619-741-3328 8 a.m. - 5 p.m.	Hiking - Nature Trails Campfire Programs Snack Bar Bait & Tackle Disposal Station Fishing Pier with Handicapped Facilities Full Facilities in Escondido Ranger Station Ph: 619-741-4680

LAKE HENSHAW

Lake Henshaw is at an elevation of 2,740 feet in a valley on the south slopes of Palomar Mountain. The water level varies with the demands of man and nature. In 1942, the lake reached its highest mark of nearly 25 miles of shoreline. The present shoreline is approximately 5 miles with a surface area of 1,137 acres. The large oak trees around the resort area create a pleasant contrast to the surrounding semi-arid mountains. The resort offers a nice campground with excellent support facilities. Lake Henshaw is long known for its good fishing for bass, crappie, bluegill and channel catfish.

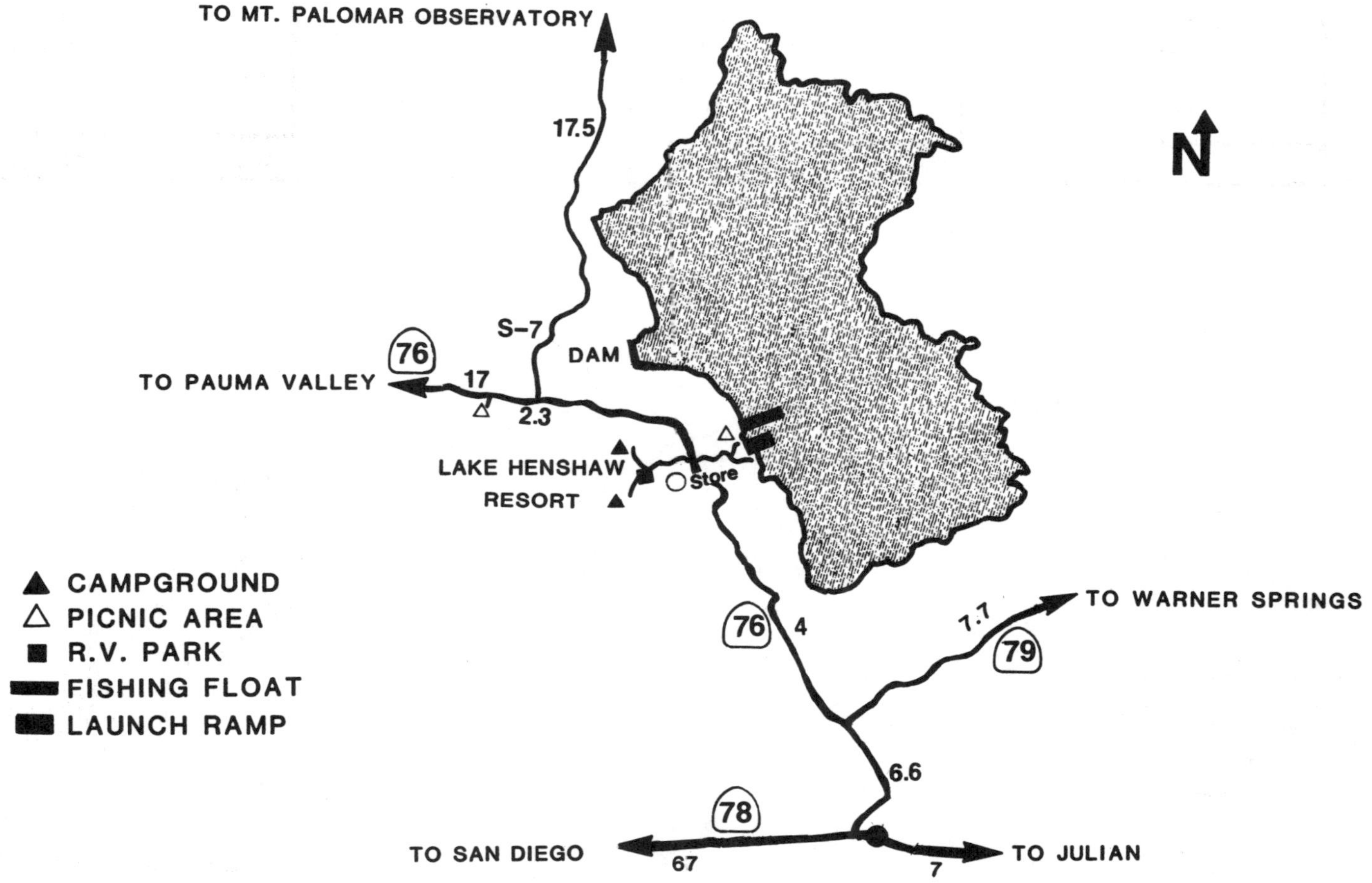

INFORMATION: Lake Henshaw Resort, 26439 Hwy. 76, Santa Ysabel 92070, Ph: 619-782-3501

CAMPING	BOATING	RECREATION	OTHER
200 Dev. Sites for Tents Fee: $10 100 Dev. Sites for R.V.s Full Hookups Fee: $12 Available at Times - Several Permanent Residents Disposal Station Fee: $4	Power & Row 10 Feet Minimum Length 10 MPH Speed Limit Launch Ramp Rentals: Fishing Boats	Fishing: Catfish, Bluegill, Crappie & Bass Fishing Float Swimming - Pool Only Picnicking Hiking Playgrounds Club House	Cabins Restaurant Grocery Store Bait & Tackle Hot Showers Laundromat Propane Therapy Pool

AGUA HEDIONDA LAGOON, LAKE WOHLFORD, AND PALOMAR PARK (DOANE POND)

From a saltwater lagoon to a coniferous mountain meadow pond at 5,500 feet, the lakes on this page offer a striking contrast. Doane Pond is in the Palomar State Park with hiking and nature trails, picnic sites and a campground. The Palomar Observatory is also nearby. Trout are caught seasonally; November through June are the best months. Wohlford, at 1,500 feet, is a good fishing lake with trout (in season), Florida bass, channel catfish and pan fish. Sailboats, canoes, kayaks, rafts and collapsible boats are not permitted. Agua Hedionda Lagoon is a large saltwater lagoon off Interstate Highway 5 which offers all types of boating. This is a popular waterskiing and jet ski facility. There are also waterski and jet ski schools, a 3-lane paved launch ramp, dry storage and a concession.

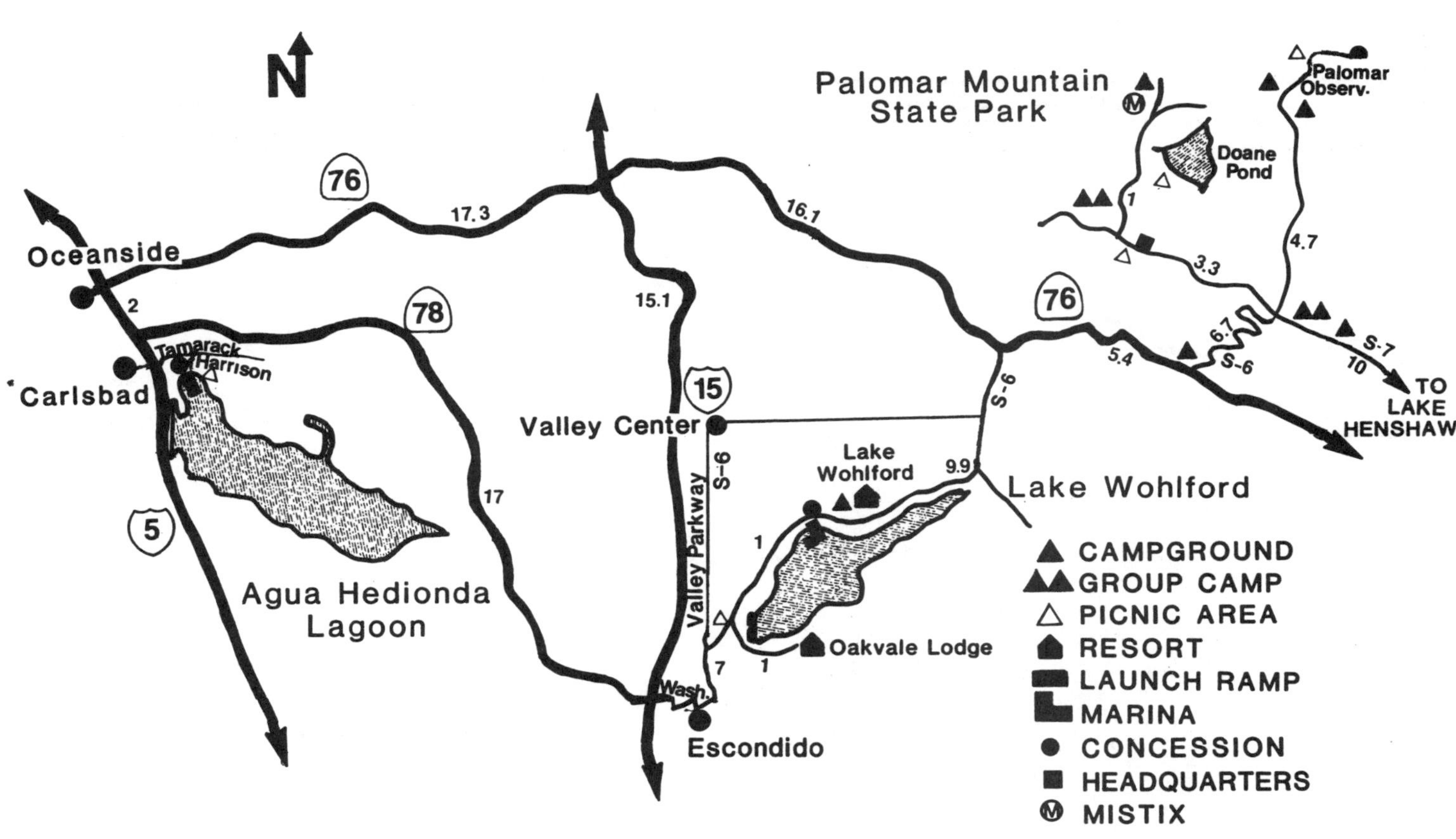

INFORMATION: Palomar Mountain State Park (Only), Palomar 92060, Ph: 619-742-3462

CAMPING	BOATING	RECREATION	OTHER
Doane Valley Campground: 31 Dev. Sites Reservations Advised Ph: 619-765-0755 Agua Hedionda Lagoon (No Camping) 4215 Harrison St. Carlsbad 92008 Ph: 619-434-3089	Agua Hedionda: Open to All Boats With $300,00 Insurance Launch Fee Not Allowed: Windsurfers Speed Limit: 45 MPH Jet Ski Rentals Water Ski School Lake Wohlford: 18 Feet Max. Length Speed Limit: 5 MPH Rental Fishing Boats	Doane Pond: No Boating No Swimming Fishing: Trout, Florida Bass Catfish, Crappie & Bluegill Picnicking Hiking Nature Study	Lake Wohlford Resort: 25484 Lake Wohlford Rd. Escondido 92027 Ph: 619-749-2755 7 R.V. Sites with Full Hookups Cabins with Kitchens Concessions Cafe

LAKE POWAY AND SANTEE LAKE

These lakes in the San Diego area provide a popular warm water fishery. In addition, the angler will find trout planted during the winter months at Poway and Santee. The Lake Poway Recreation Area provides a primitive camping area, picnic sites, nature and equestrian trails. The 60 acre lake is open to row and electrical boating and night fishing is allowed. The Santee Lakes Recreational Area offers a large number of modern campsites with a swimming pool, picnic facilities, playgrounds, volleyball courts and horseshoe pits. The seven small lakes are closed to private boating but rentals are available.

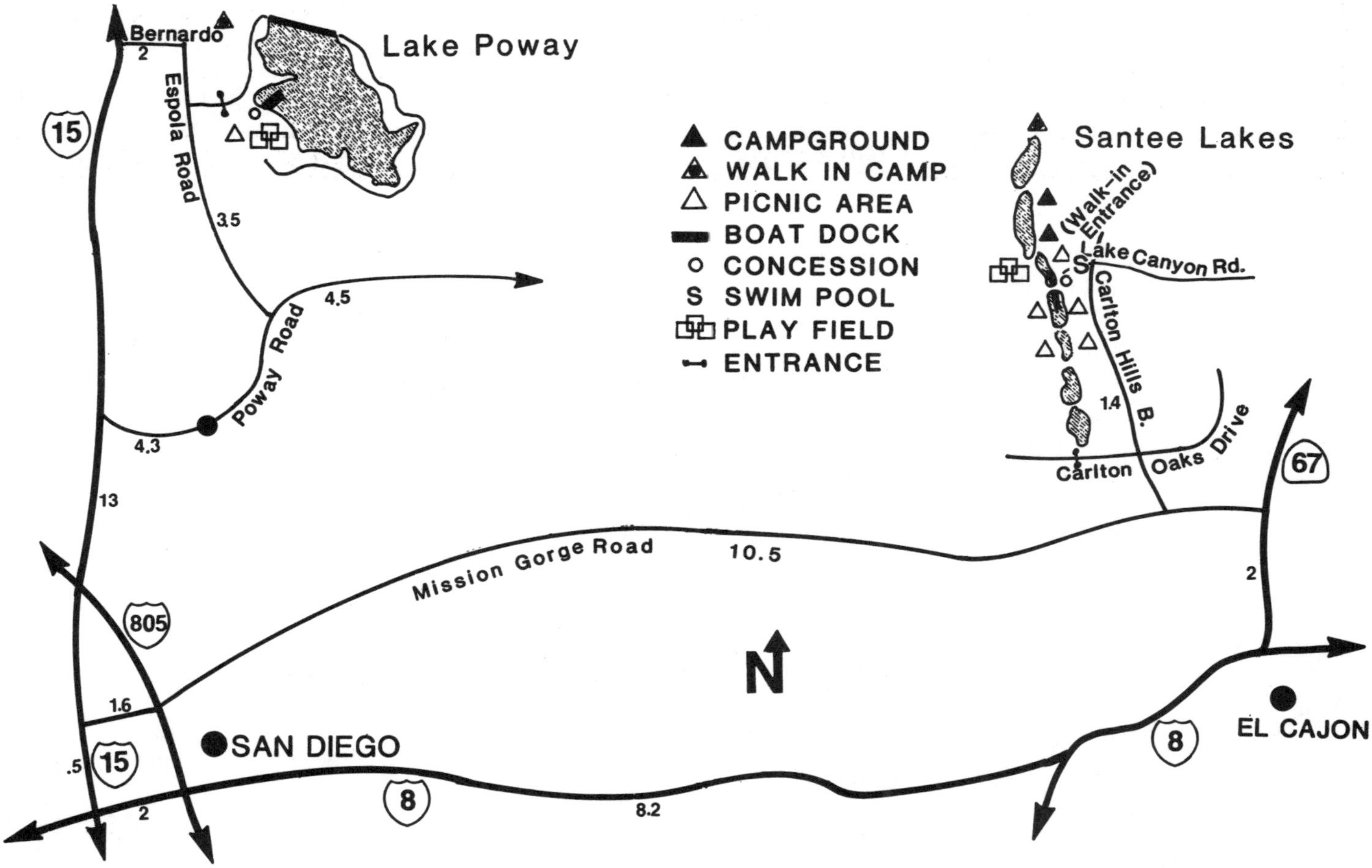

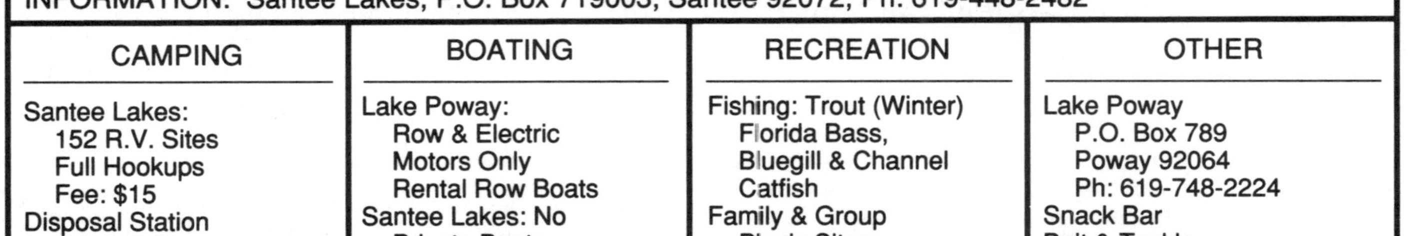

INFORMATION: Santee Lakes, P.O. Box 719003, Santee 92072, Ph: 619-448-2482

CAMPING	BOATING	RECREATION	OTHER
Santee Lakes: 152 R.V. Sites Full Hookups Fee: $15 Disposal Station Laundry & Groceries	Lake Poway: Row & Electric Motors Only Rental Row Boats Santee Lakes: No Private Boats Rentals: Row, Paddle & Canoe	Fishing: Trout (Winter) Florida Bass, Bluegill & Channel Catfish Family & Group Picnic Sites Hiking, Riding & Nature Trails-Poway Playgrounds Volleyball Courts Horseshoe Pits	Lake Poway P.O. Box 789 Poway 92064 Ph: 619-748-2224 Snack Bar Bait & Tackle 2 Playgrounds Tournament Volleyball Courts, Horseshoes Softball-Night Lights 15 Acre Grass Picnic Area - Group Reservations

LAKE CUYAMACA

Lake Cuyamaca is at an elevation of 4,650 feet in a mountain setting of oak, pine and cedar forests. The dam was originally built in 1887. Thanks to a dedicated group of residents and sportsmen, the minimum pool is 110 surface acres. Normally this is the only lake in San Diego County that has trout all year. Cuyamaca stocks 40,000 pounds of rainbow trout each year. It offers excellent fishing for warm water fish as well. Cuyamaca Rancho State Park has over 100 miles of scenic horseback riding and hiking trails. Los Caballos Campground offers 16 developed sites including corrals for families with horses. In addition, Los Vaqueros Campground is for equestrian groups with facilities for 80 people and 50 horses.

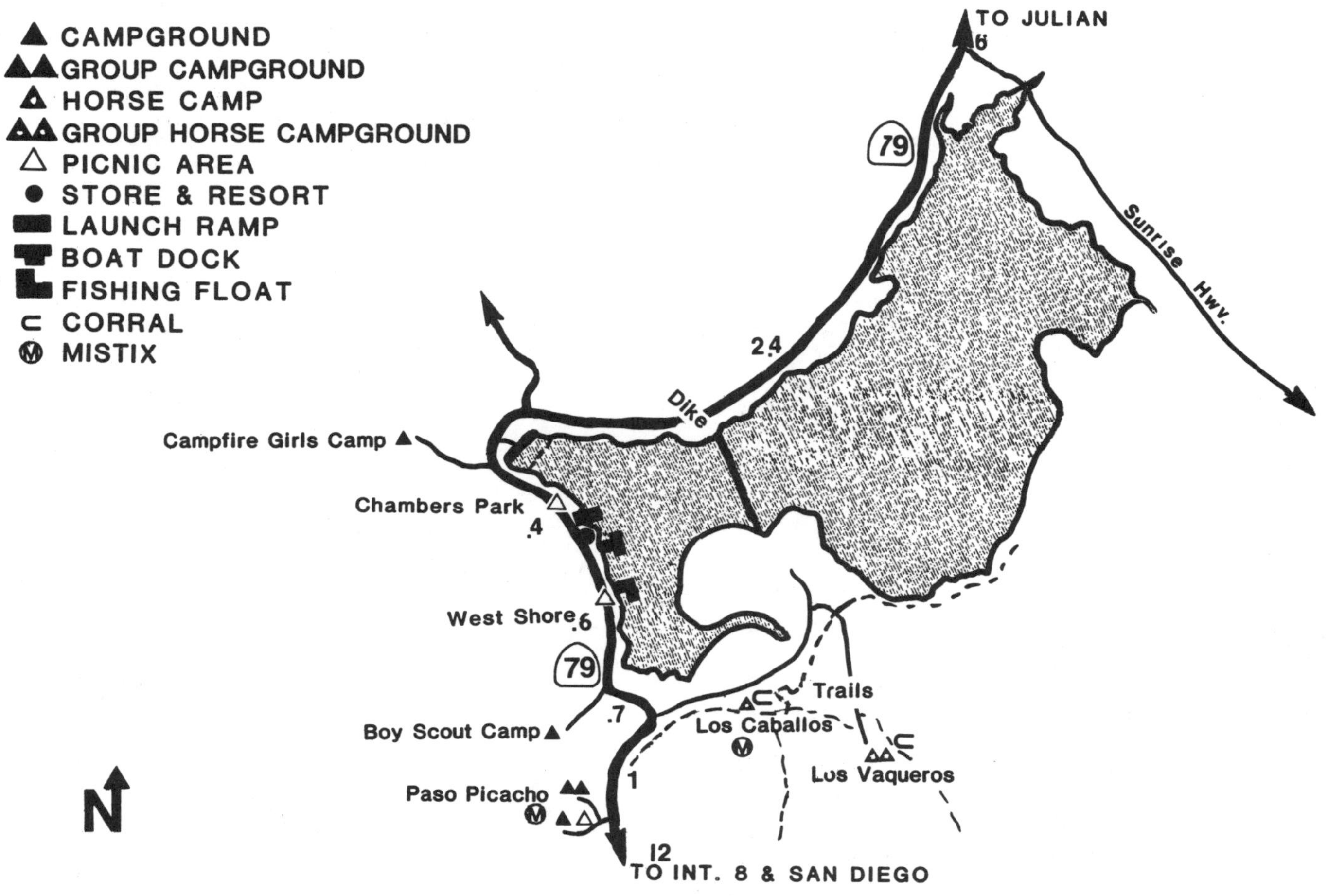

INFORMATION: Park Ranger, 15027 Highway 79, Julian 92036, Ph: 619-765-0515			
CAMPING	BOATING	RECREATION	OTHER
At Lake For R.V.s Only 23 Sites with Hookups Fee: $12 27 Sites without Hookups Fee: $ 8 Cuyamaca Rancho State Park: Paso Picacho: 85 Dev. Sites for Tents & R.V.s Group Camp - 160 People Maximum Reserve - MISTIX	Power & Row Boats Between 10 Ft. & 18 Ft. Only Inflatables Must Have Discernible Bow & Stern, 9-18 Ft. Wood Bottom and Multiple Inflatable Compartments Speed Limit - 10 MPH Launch Ramp Rentals: Boat & Motor, Canoes	Fishing: Trout, Perch, Catfish, Bluegill & Bass No Swimming or Body Contact with Water Hiking Backpacking-Parking Hunting: Duck - Wed. & Sun. a.m. in Season	Snack Bar Restaurant Grocery Store Bait & Tackle Disposal Station Gas Station

SAN DIEGO CITY LAKES: HODGES, SUTHERLAND, MIRAMAR, SAN VICENTE, EL CAPITAN, AND LOWER OTAY

These popular lakes provide some of the best bass fishing in America. They are operated by the City of San Diego. The lakes are open from sunrise to sunset but the days each one is open varies and is subject to change. It is advisable to call for current schedules. The Water Utilities Department provides a daily Hot Line with fishing and hunting information. Phone 619-465-3474.

. . . Continued . . .

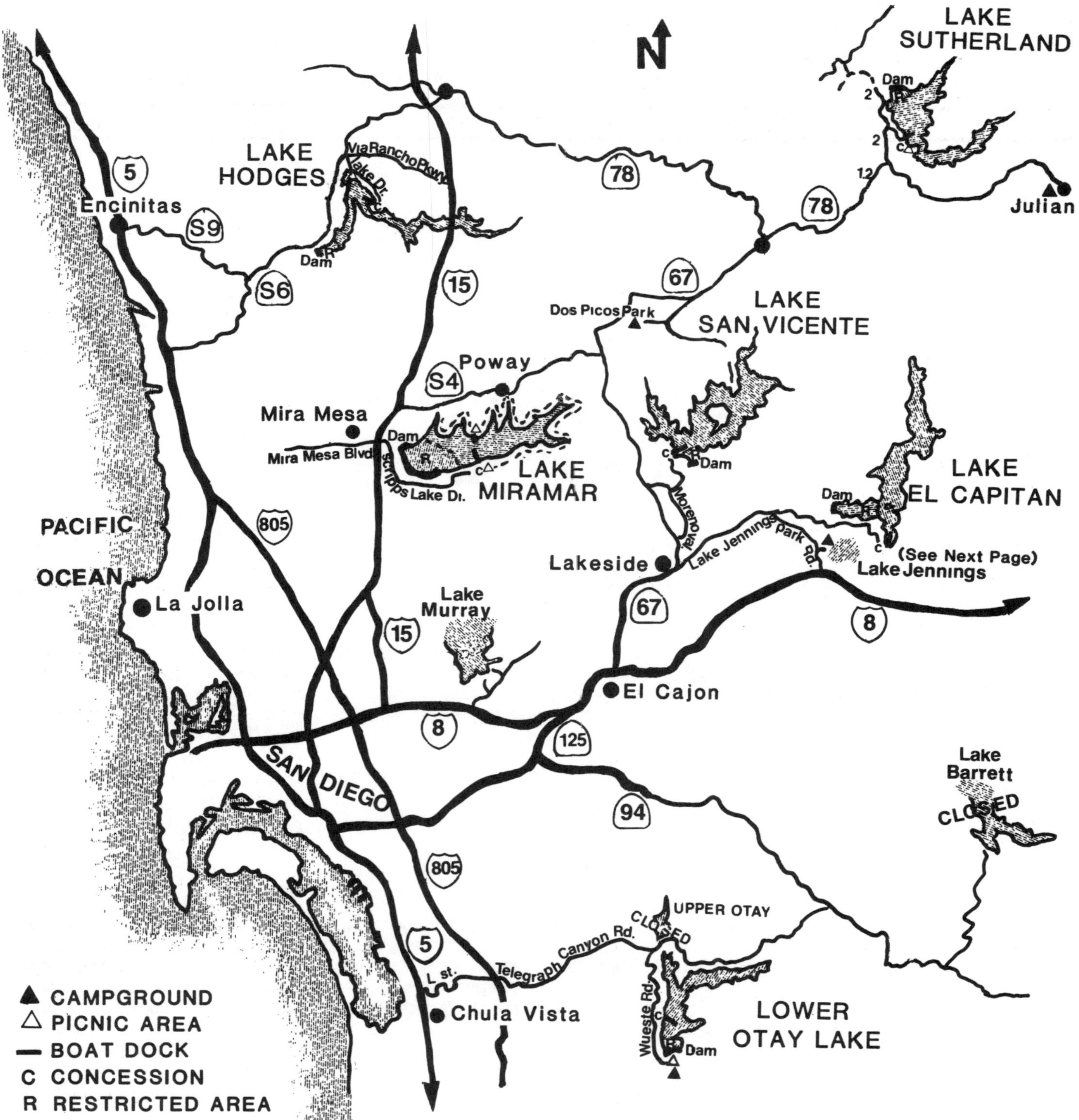

LAKE HODGES is at an elevation of 330 feet 5 miles south of Escondido. This lake has a maximum surface area of 1,234 acres with 12 miles of chaparral covered shoreline. The nearest accommodations are in Escondido. Season: Spring - Fall on Wednesday, Thursday, Saturday and Sunday.

LAKE SUTHERLAND is at an elevation of 2,074 feet northeast of Ramona. There are 557 surface acres at capacity with 11 miles of oak and chaparral covered shoreline. Nearest campgrounds are at Dos Picos Park in Ramona and William Heise Park in Julian, both operated by the County of San Diego. The angler will find Florida bass, bluegill, and channel catfish. Season: Spring - Fall on Friday, Saturday and Sunday. Waterfowl Season: October - January, Open to hunting on Wednesday and Saturday.

LAKE MIRAMAR is at an elevation of 714 feet in the rolling hills below Poway. This small lake has 162 surface acres with 4 miles of shoreline. Nearest facilities are in Mira Mesa. Trout season is normally November through May and there is a year round fishery (except for 3 weeks in late fall) of Florida bass, bluegill, channel catfish and redear sunfish. Open on Monday, Tuesday, Saturday, and Sunday. Holds State record for largemouth bass at 21 lbs, 10 oz. caught March 14, 1988.

LAKE SAN VICENTE is at elevation of 659 feet in the low mountains east of El Cajon. The lake has a maximum surface area of 1,069 acres and 14 miles of shoreline. The County operates Dos Picos Park Campground to the north and Lake Jennings Campground nearby. There are trout in season along with Florida bass, bluegill and channel catfish. Season: Winter - Memorial Day on Thursday, Saturday and Sunday. Waterskiing Program from May to October.

LAKE EL CAPITAN is at elevation of 750 feet in the foothills east of Lakeside. There is a maximum surface area of 1,574 acres with 20 miles of bushy shoreline. The angler will find Florida bass, bluegill, bullhead, channel catfish, and crappie. Nearest camping facilities are at Lake Jennings County Park. Other accommodations in Lakeside and El Cajon. Season: Spring - Labor Day on Friday, Saturday and Sunday.

LAKE MURRAY is the "in town" reservoir located in a suburban area between San Diego and La Mesa at the base of Cowles Mountain. The lake is open from November through September and planted weekly with rainbow trout from fall to spring. Open Wednesday, Saturday and Sunday.

LAKE LOWER OTAY is in the rolling chaparral covered hills east of Chula Vista at an elevation of 492 feet. The maximum surface area of the lake is 1,266 acres with 13 miles of shoreline. There is a county campground nearby and full facilities in Chula Vista. Florida bass, channel and white catfish, bullhead, crappie and bluegill are in the lake. Season: Spring - Fall on Wednesday, Saturday and Sunday.

LAKE BARRETT is closed to fishing but open for waterfowl hunting on Thursdays and Sundays in season.

INFORMATION: Water Utilities, Lake Recreation, 5520 Kiowa Dr., La Mesa 92041			
CAMPING	BOATING	RECREATION	OTHER
Lower Otay County Park: 22 Tent Sites: $8 26 R.V. Sites with Full Hookups: $12 Lake Jennings County Park: See Page on Lake Jennings for Detailed Information	Power, Row, Sail & Inflatables Subject to Inspection Speed Limit 10 MPH Launch Ramps Fee: $4 Launch Ramps Rentals: Fishing Boats Row: $8 Per Day Motor: $22 Per Day Reservations- Ph: 619-390-0222	Fishing: For Species See Above for Lake Fishing Hot Line - Ph: 619-465-3474 Fishing Permits: $2 - $4 Hunting as Shown Above Hiking Picnicking	Privately Operated Concessions at Each Lake: Food & Beverages Bait & Tackle Fishing Licenses

LAKE JENNINGS

Lake Jennings is east of El Cajon at an elevation of 690 feet. It is owned by the Helix Water District which administers strict sanitation standards for this domestic water supply reservoir of 180 surface acres. The 5 miles of fairly steep shoreline is semi-arid dotted with sumac trees and a few pine trees. The primary recreation is fishing. Lake Jennings is open year round for fishing on Fridays, Saturdays and Sundays. Trout season runs from October through May. Catfish season runs from June through September. The lake remains open until midnight on Fridays and Saturdays during catfish season only. This is the lake for big channel or blue catfish; the largest was a 46 pound blue catfish. A 190 foot handicapped accessible fishing float has been added to the lake.

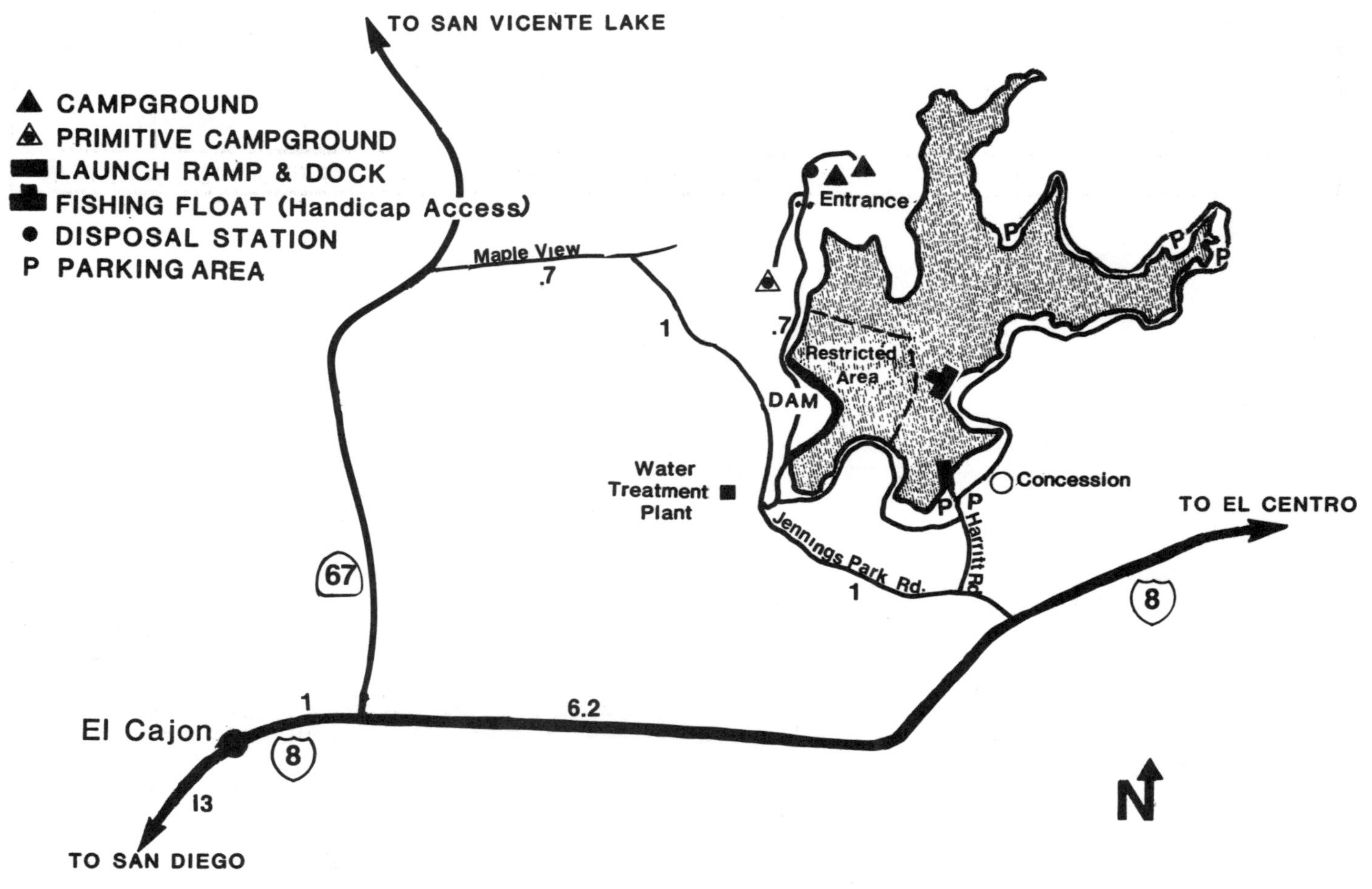

INFORMATION: County Parks, 5201 Ruffin Road, Ste. P, San Diego 92123, Ph: 619-565-3600			
CAMPING	BOATING	RECREATION	OTHER
27 Dev. Sites-Tents Fee: $10 31 Dev. Sites-R.V.s Electric & Water Hookups, Fee: $14 29 Dev. Sites-R.V.s Full Hookups Fee: $16 Pets - $1 Per Night 10 Primitive Sites for Tents Only Fee: $7	Fishing Boats Only Speed Limit - 10 MPH Launch Ramp - $3 Rentals: Fishing Boats & Motors Open Year Round Fridays, Saturdays & Sundays Only	Fishing: Trout, Catfish, Bluegill, Bass Fridays, Saturdays & Sundays - Permit Required Fish Plants Weekly No Swimming	Snack Bar - Open In Season Bait & Tackle Full Facilities in El Cajon Campers Only Can Fish From Shore In Campgrounds Year Round

LAKE MORENA

Lake Morena is at an elevation of 3,000 feet in the Cleveland National Forest east of San Diego. San Diego County maintains a nice lake front park in a setting of live oak trees amid the rocky foothills. In addition to the developed campground, there is an undeveloped open camping area on the north end of the lake. This 80 year old lake has a surface area of over 1,000 acres. Morena has an abundant population of warm water fish including the Florida strain of bass. There are trout planted during the winter months and fishing is the primary activity. Boating is limited to 10 MPH and inflatables are subject to rigid standards. The nearby Pacific Crest Trail invites the hiker, backpacker and equestrian.

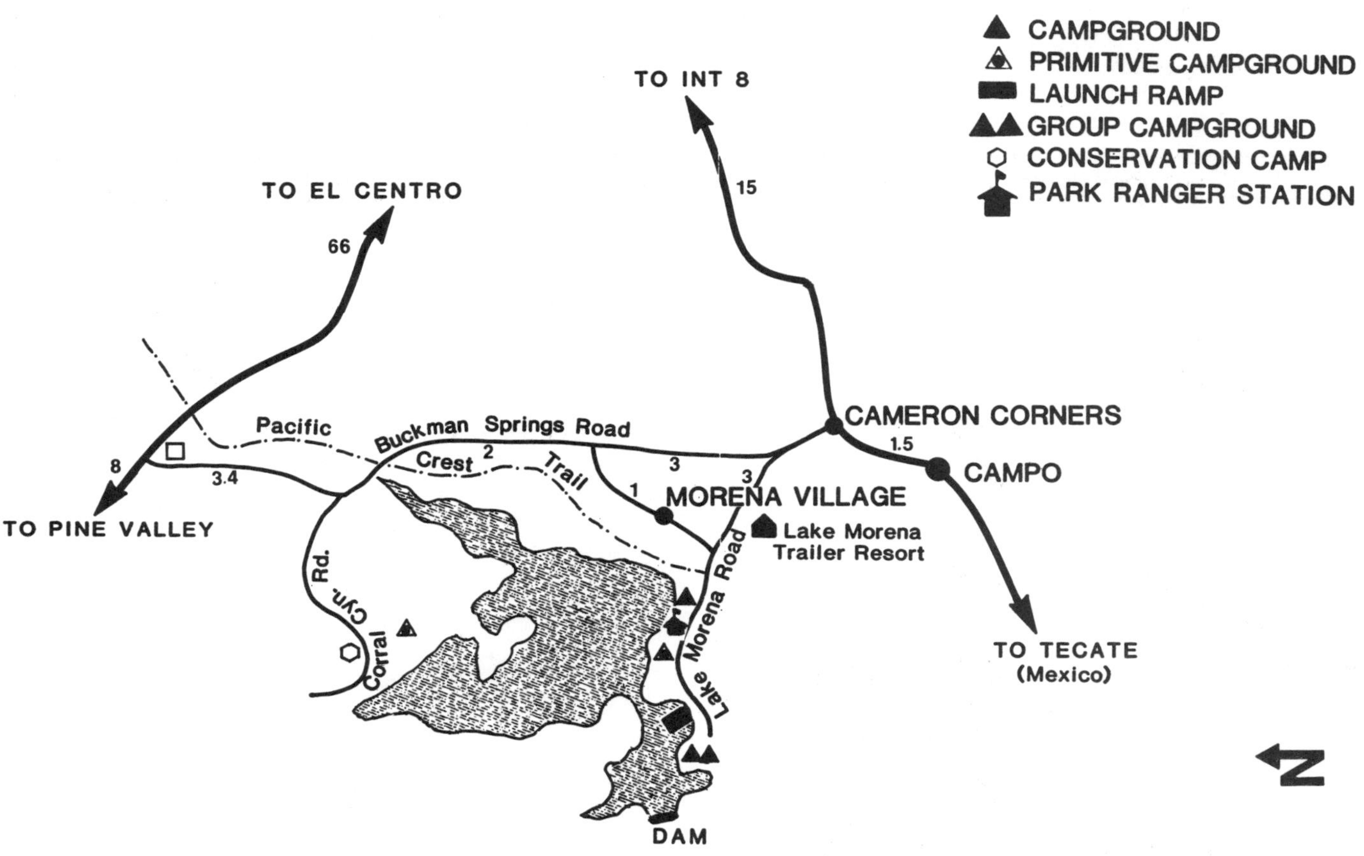

INFORMATION: County Parks, 5201 Ruffin Rd., San Diego 92123, Ph: 619-565-3600			
CAMPING	BOATING	RECREATION	OTHER
28 Dev. Sites for Tents & R.V.s Fee: $10 58 Sites with Water & Electric Hookups Fee: $12 Undeveloped Open Camping Fee: $7 1 Group Camp to 35 People Maximum Reservations Accepted	Power, Row, Sail & Inflatables (Strict Regulations) 10 MPH Speed Limit Unimproved Launch Ramp Rentals: Fishing, Motor & Row Boats	Fishing: Florida Bass, Bluegill, Catfish & Crappie - Trout in Winter Picnicking Hiking Backpacking Riding Trails Nature Study Environmental Education Nature Interpretive Programs	Lake Morena Trailer Resort Rt. 1, Box 137 Campo 92006 Ph: 619-478-5677 42 R.V. Sites Full Hookups Fee: $12 Disposal Station LP Gas Morena Village: Gas, Restaurant & Store

LAKE HAVASU

Lake Havasu is at an elevation of 482 feet in the desert between Arizona and California. Flowing out of Topock Gorge, the Colorado River becomes Lake Havasu. This 19,300 acre lake of secluded coves, quiet inlets and open water backs up 45 miles behind Parker Dam. Famed for its outstanding fishery and excellent boating, Lake Havasu attracts thousands of visitors. Major fishing, powerboating and waterskiing tournaments are held yearly. Numerous campgrounds, resorts and marinas are located around the lake. The hub of the area is Lake Havasu City and Pittsburg Point which offer complete facilities. The boat camper and houseboater will find the 13,000 acres of Lake Havasu State Park a pleasant retreat.

. . . Continued . . .

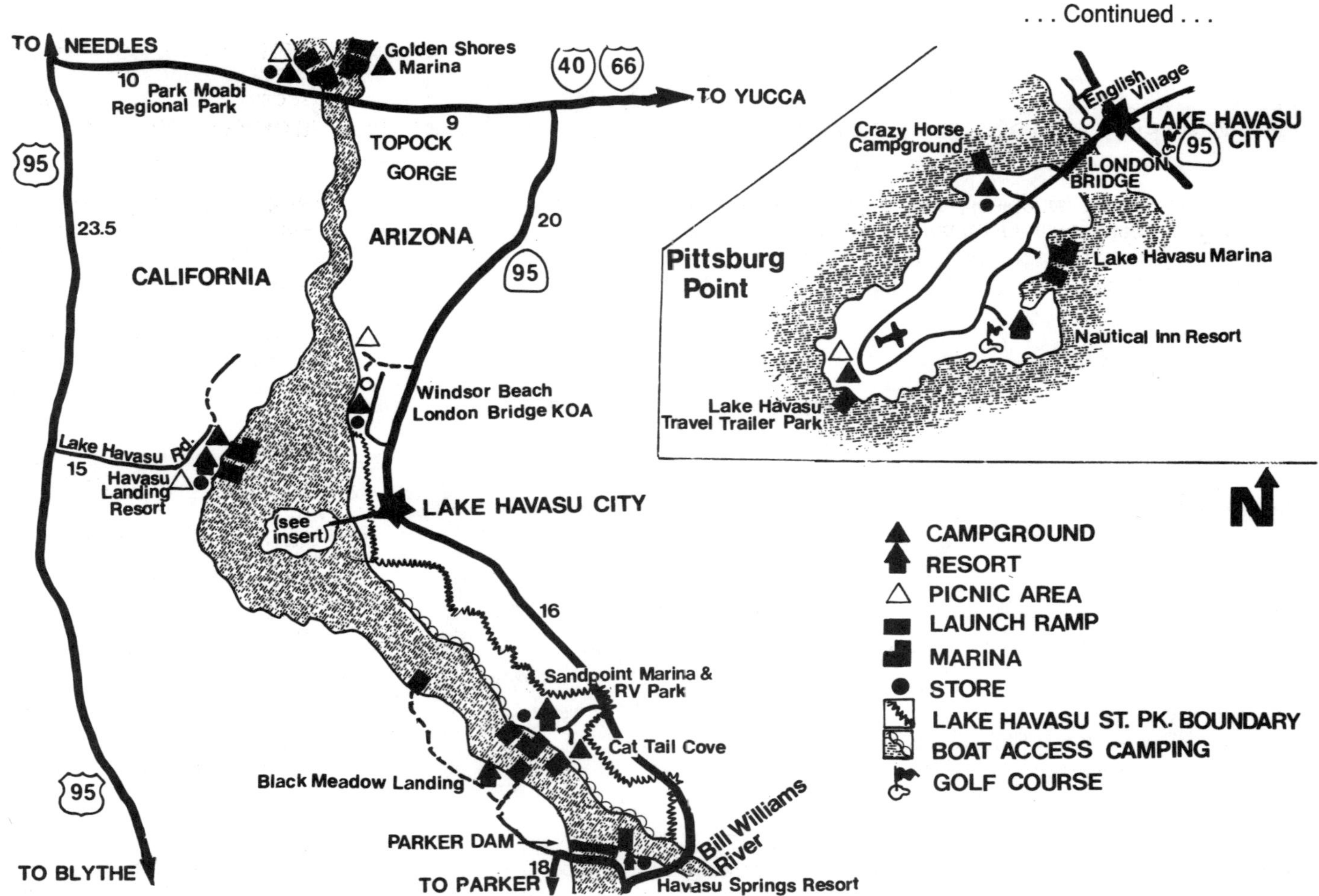

INFORMATION: Lake Havasu Area Chamber of Commerce, Visitor & Convention Bureau

CAMPING	BOATING	RECREATION	OTHER
Chamber of Commerce 1930 Mesquite Ave. Suite 3 Lake Havasu City AZ 86403 Ph: 602-855-4115 or 602-453-3444 Numerous Campgrounds Around Lake - See Following Pages	Power, Row, Canoe, Sail, Waterski, Jet Ski, Windsurf & Inflatable Full Service Marinas Rentals: Fishing, Power, Pontoons & Houseboats High Winds Can be A Hazard in Fall & Spring Each Year	Fishing: Catfish, Bluegill, Crappie, Largemouth & Striped Bass Swimming Picnicking Hiking Backpacking Nature Study Hunting: Waterfowl, Quail & Dove	Full Resort Facilities Airport Golf Courses Tennis Courts Boat Excursions Casino Trips Home of the London Bridge See Recreation on the Colorado River for Full Details

LAKE HAVASU

CAMPGROUNDS & RESORTS AS SHOWN ON MAP - NUMEROUS OTHER FACILITIES - CONTACT THE CHAMBER OF COMMERCE FOR FURTHER DETAILS.

PARK MOABI REGIONAL PARK, Park Moabi Rd., Needles 92363, Ph: 619-326-3831. 648 T/R.V. Sites, Full & Partial Hookups - Fee: $9-$14 - Hot Showers, Laundromat, Flush Toilets, Picnic Sites with Tables & Barbecues, Disposal Station, Swim Beach, 5-Lane Launch Ramp, Waterfront Cabanas, Fishing Area, Dry Storage, Recreation Hall & Arcade, General Store, Ice, Full Service Marina, Gas Docks, Rentals: Houseboats and Fishing Boats, Courtesy Dock, 37 Boat Slips, Bait & Tackle.

GOLDEN SHORES MARINA, HC-12, Box 502, Topock, AZ 86436, Ph: 602-768-2325. R.V. sites, Full Hookups - Fee: $10, Store, Restaurant, Gas, Fuel Dock, Slips & Launch Ramp.

HAVASU LANDING RESORT, P.O. Box 1975, Chemehuevi Valley 92363, Ph: 619-858-4593. Owned by the Chemehuevi Tribe. 1,500 Tent Sites, 175 R.V. & Trailer Sites, Full Hookups. Fees: $13 a Day in Season, $10 a Day Off Season. Plus Unlimited Boat Access, Camping Along the Shoreline of the Reservation. Complete Destination Campground with Hot Showers, Flush Toilets, Laundromat, Snack Bars, Grocery Store, Restaurant & Lounge. Full Service Marina - Two Launch Ramps, 202 Slips, Courtesy Dock & Houseboat Rentals. 5 Star Mobile Home Park - 500 Spaces.

BLACK MEADOW LANDING, P.O. Box 98, Parker Dam 92267, Ph: 619-663-3811. 150 sites for Tents - Fee: $5 for 2 Adults. 31 Sites for R.V.s - Full Hookups, Disposal Station. Hot Showers, Flush Toilets, Laundromat. Ice, Restaurant, Boat Ramp. Boat Rentals: Fishing Boats & Pontoons. Grocery Store, Tackle Shop, Motel with 32 Rooms and 20 Kitchen Cabins.

LONDON BRIDGE KOA, 3405 London Bridge Drive, Lake Havasu, AZ 86403. 84 R.V. Sites, Full & Partial Hookups, Tents allowed - Fee: $13, Hot Showers, Swim Pool, Store, & Cafe.

HAVASU SPRINGS RESORT, Route 2, Box 624, Parker AZ 85344, Ph: 602-667-3361. Fee: $5, 100 R.V. Sites with Full Hookups, Cable TV - Fee: $11.50 Plus $1 for Electricity. Hot Showers, Flush Toilets, Laundromat. Restaurant & Lounge, Motel, Grocery Store, Swimming Pool & Beach, Boat Ramp, 250 Slips, Boat Rentals: Fishing, Waterski, Patio, Jet Ski, Camp-a-Float, Houseboats, Dry Storage, Gas, Ski Beach, Video Game Room.

CAT TAIL COVE, Lake Havasu State Park, 1350 W. McCulloch Blvd., Lake Havasu City, AZ 86403, Ph: 602-855-1223. 40 Sites for Tents & R.V.s, Fee: $7 for Residents, $8 for Non-Residents. Electrical & Water Hookups, Disposal Station, Hot Showers, Flush Toilets. Boat Ramp. 12 Miles South of Lake Havasu City.

The Lake Havasu State Park has provided miles of shoreline for boat access camping and picnicking. 200 Boat Access Only Sites are scattered along the Arizona Shore South of Lake Havasu City. The campgrounds are all named and range from "Solitude" with 1 site to "Hi Isle" with 14 sites. Most have a table, trash barrel, firepit and vault-type toilets nearby. Fees: $4 for Residents, $5 for Non-Resident per Night. Day Use Only: $2 for Residents, $3 for Non-Residents.

SANDPOINT MARINA AND R.V. PARK, P.O. Box 1469, Lake Havasu City, AZ 86403, Ph: 602-855-0549. 170 Sites for Tents & R.V.s - Full Hookups, Disposal Station. Hot Showers, Flush Toilets, 2 Laundromats, 24-Hour Ice Service, Snack Bar, Game Room, Grocery Store & Tackle Shop, Gas Pumps Available on Land and Water. Playground, Swim Beach, Launch Ramp, Boat Slips with Electrical Hookups, Cable T.V., Rentals: Fishing Boats, Houseboats, Pontoons and Travel Trailers.

. . . Continued . . .

LAKE HAVASU

PITTSBURG POINT

CRAZY HORSE CAMPGROUND, 1534 Beachcomber Dr., Lake Havasu City, AZ 86403, Ph: 602-855-2127. At State Park: 590 Sites for Tents & R.V.s with Full Hookups. R.V.: $15 per Night for 4 People, Car, Truck or Van: $13 per Night for 4 People. $3 Extra Charge for Air During In Season - Apr. to Oct. Disposal Station, Hot Showers, Flush Toilets, Laundromat. Grocery Store, Ice. Boat Ramp, Swim Beach, Arcade (In Season). Pets Welcome.

LAKE HAVASU MARINA, 1100 McCulloch Blvd., Lake Havasu City, AZ 86403, Ph: 602-855-2159. 6-Lane Launch Ramp, Permanent Docks, Gas Dock, Temporary Slips, Pumpouts for Boats. Boat Rentals: Fishing, Waterski & Pontoons, OMC, Mercury and Volvo Repairs, Boat Cleaning, Fiberglass Repairs. Grocery Store, Beer & Wine, Ice, Bait & Tackle, Waterski Equipment, Dry Storage.

NAUTICAL INN RESORT, P.O. Box 1885, Lake Havasu City, AZ 86403, Ph: 602-855-2141. Lake Havasu's Only Lake Front Resort, 120 Rooms & Suites Overlooking the Lake, Private Beach & Dock, Swimming Pool, Lighted Tennis Courts, 18-Hole Executive Golf Course, Conference Center, Restaurants & Cocktail Lounges, Rental Boats: Catamarans, Windsurfers, Sail Lessons, Para Sailing. Gift Shops, Beauty Salon, Convenience Store.

LAKE HAVASU TRAVEL TRAILER PARK, P.O. Box 100, Lake Havasu City, AZ 86403, Ph: 602-855-2322. 167 R.V. & Trailer Sites with Full Hookups. Fee: Winter—$12.96 (Summer—$15.67) per Night for 2 People, Monthly Rates. Parking Area for Self-Contained Units. Hot Showers, Flush Toilets, Laundromat, Ice. Launch Ramp. Swimming Pool, Therapy Pool, Recreation Hall, Docks (Free to Guests).

FOR ADDITIONAL ACCOMMODATIONS AND FACILITIES CONTACT:

Lake Havasu Area Chamber of Commerce
VCB Division
1930 Mesquite Avenue, #3, AZ 86403
Ph: 602-855-4115 or 602-453-3444

For a complete guide to the Colorado River, order "RECREATION ON THE COLORADO RIVER." Order form on back page of this book.

CALIFORNIA

OREGON
NATIONAL FORESTS OF CALIFORNIA
STATE PARKS LOCATED AT LAKES
KLAMATH
Yreka
KLAMATH
MODOC
Alturas
SIX RIVERS
SHASTA
Eureka
LASSEN
Redding
TRINITY
Susanville
PLUMAS
Quincy
MENDOCINO
Reno
Willows
TAHOE
Nevada City
Placerville
ELDORADO
Sacramento
TOIYABE
STANISLAUS
Sonora
San Francisco
INYO
Bishop
SIERRA
Fresno
SEQUOIA
Monterey
LOS
Porterville
SEQUOIA
PADRES
ANGELES
SAN BERNARDINO
Santa Barbara
Pasadena
San Bernardino
CLEVELAND
San Diego
MEXICO

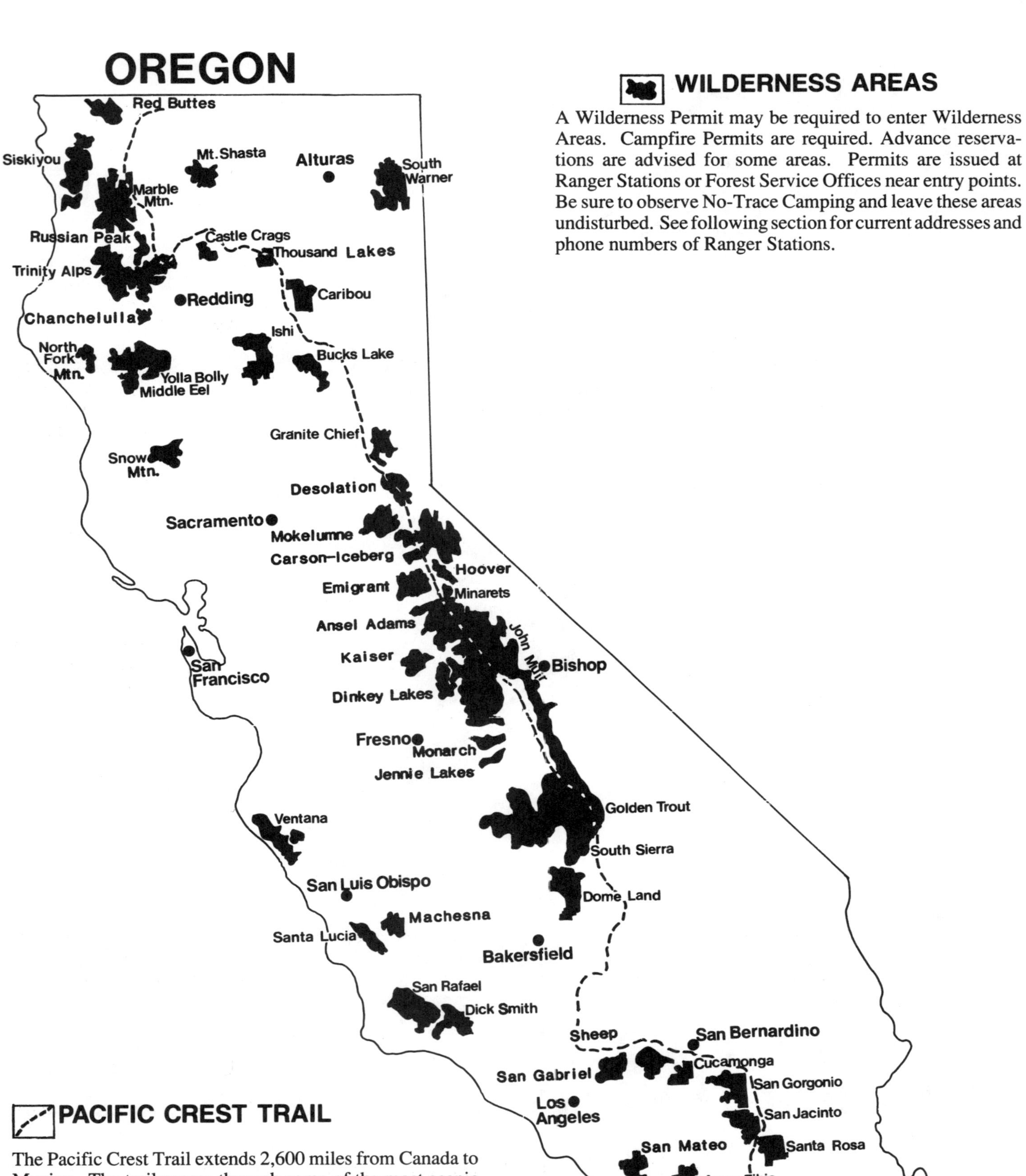

WILDERNESS AREAS

A Wilderness Permit may be required to enter Wilderness Areas. Campfire Permits are required. Advance reservations are advised for some areas. Permits are issued at Ranger Stations or Forest Service Offices near entry points. Be sure to observe No-Trace Camping and leave these areas undisturbed. See following section for current addresses and phone numbers of Ranger Stations.

PACIFIC CREST TRAIL

The Pacific Crest Trail extends 2,600 miles from Canada to Mexico. The trail passes through some of the most scenic areas of California. While some marathon hikers have challenged its entire length, most enter at trailheads as noted in the narratives of this book. Be sure to check with the nearest Ranger Stations for Permits and information.

RANGER STATIONS AND FOREST SERVICE OFFICES

CALIFORNIA REGION OF THE U.S.FOREST SERVICE

General Information, Maps and Wilderness Permits may be obtained at the following locations:

ANGELES NATIONAL FOREST

Head Office
701 N. Santa Anita Ave.
Arcadia 91006
Ph: 818-574-1613

Saugus Ranger District
30800 Bouquet Canyon Rd.
Saugus 91350
Ph: 805-296-9710

Arroyo-Seco Ranger District
Oak Grove Park
Flintridge 91011
Ph: 818-790-4522

Tujunga Ranger District
12371 N. Little Tujunga Cyn. Rd.
San Fernando 91342
Ph: 818-899-1900

Mt. Baldy Ranger District
110 N. Wabash Ave.
Glendora 91740
Ph: 818-335-1251

Valyermo Ranger District
34146 Longview Rd.
P.O. Box 589
Pearblossom 93553
Ph: 805-944-2187

CLEVELAND NATIONAL FOREST

Head Office
880 Front St., Rm. 5-N-14
San Diego 92188
Ph: 619-557-5050

Trabuco Ranger District
1147 E. Sixth Street
Corona 91719
Ph: 714-736-1811

Decanso Ranger District
3348 Alpine Blvd.
Alpine 92001
Ph: 619-445-6235 or
619-286-9882

Palomar Ranger District
332 S. Juniper
Escondido 92025
Ph: 619-566-0130 or
619-788-0250

ELDORADO NATIONAL FOREST

Head Office
100 Forni Rd.
Placerville 95667
Ph: 916-622-5061

Information Center
3070 Camino Heights Dr.
Camino 95709
Ph: 916-644-6048

Placerville Ranger District
3491 Carson Court
Placerville 95667
Ph: 916-644-2324

Amador Ranger District
26820 Silver Dr.
Star Route 3, Hwy. 88
Pioneer 95666
Ph: 209-295-4251

Georgetown Ranger District
7600 Wentworth Springs Rd.
Georgetown 95634
Ph: 916-333-4312

Pacific Ranger District
Pollock Pines 95726
Ph: 916-644-2324

Placerville Nursery
2375 Fruitridge Rd.
Camino 95709
Ph: 916-622-9600

...Continued...

INYO NATIONAL FOREST

Head Office
873 No. Main St.
Bishop 93514
Ph: 619-873-5841

Mammoth Ranger District
P.O. Box 148
Mammoth Lakes 93546
Ph: 619-934-2505

Mono Lake Ranger District
P.O. Box 10
Lee Vining 93541
Ph: 619-647-6525

Mt. Whitney Ranger District
P.O. Box 8
Lone Pine 93545
Ph: 619-876-5542

White Mountain Ranger District
798 No. Main Street
Bishop 93514
Ph: 619-873-4207

KLAMATH NATIONAL FOREST

Head Office
1312 Fairlane Road
Yreka 96097
Ph: 916-842-6131

Goosenest Ranger District
37805 Hwy. 97
Macdoel 96058
Ph: 916-398-4391

Happy Camp Ranger District
P.O. Box 377
Happy Camp 96039
Ph: 916-493-2243

Oak Knoll Ranger District
22541 Hwy. 96
Klamath River 96050
Ph: 916-465-2241

Salmon River Ranger District
P.O. Box 280
Etna 96027
Ph: 916-467-5757

Scott River Ranger District
11263 S. Hwy. 3
Fort Jones 96032
Ph: 916-468-5351

Ukonom Ranger District
P.O. Drawer 410
Orleans 95556
Ph: 916-627-3291

LAKE TAHOE BASIN MANAGEMENT UNIT

This Unit covers parts of Eldorado, Tahoe and Toiyabe National Forests.

Head Office
P.O. Box 731002
870 Emerald Bay Rd.
South Lake Tahoe 95731-7302
Ph: 916-573-2600

Tahoe Visitor Center
1/2 Mile from Camp Richardson
Ph: 916-541-0209
Open Summers Only

William Kent Info. Station
William Kent Campground
West Shore
Ph: 916-583-3642
Open Summers Only

LASSEN NATIONAL FOREST

Head Office
55 South Sacramento St.
Susanville 96130
Ph: 916-257-2151

Almanor Ranger District
P.O. Box 767
Chester 96020
Ph: 916-258-2141

Eagle Lake Ranger District
55 So. Sacramento St.
Susanville 96130
Ph: 916-257-2595

Hat Creek Ranger District
P.O. Box 220
Fall River Mills 96028
Ph: 916-336-5521

...Continued...

LOS PADRES NATIONAL FOREST

Head Office
6144 Calle Real
Goleta 93117
Ph: 805-683-6711

Ojai Ranger District
1190 E. Ojai Ave.
Ojai 93023
Ph: 805-646-4348

Monterey Ranger District
406 S. Mildred
King City 93930
Ph: 408-385-5434

Santa Lucia Ranger District
1616 N. Carlotti Dr.
Santa Maria 93454
Ph: 805-925-9538

Mt. Pinos Ranger District
Star Route, Box 400
Frazier Park 93225
Ph: 805-245-3731

Santa Barbara Ranger District
Star Route, Los Prietos
Santa Barbara 93105
Ph: 805-967-3481

MENDOCINO NATIONAL FOREST

Head Office
420 E. Laurel St.
Willows 95988
Ph: 916-934-3316

Stonyford Ranger District
Stites-Ladoga Rd.
Star Rt. Box 12
Stonyford 95979
Ph: 916-963-3128

Corning Ranger District
22000 Corning Rd.
P.O. Box 1019
Corning 96021
Ph: 916-824-5196

Upper Lake Ranger District
Middlecreek Rd.
P.O. Box 96
Upper Lake 95485
Ph: 707-275-2361

Covelo Ranger District
78150 Covelo Rd.
Covelo 95428
Ph: 707-983-6118

Chico Tree Improvement Center
2741 Cramer Lane
Chico 95926
Ph: 916-895-2276

MODOC NATIONAL FOREST

Head Office
441 N. Main St.
Alturas 96101
Ph: 916-233-5811

Doublehead Ranger District
P.O. Box 818
Tulelake 96134
Ph: 916-667-2246

Big Valley Ranger District
P.O. Box 159
Adin 96006
Ph: 916-299-3210

Warner Mountain Ranger District
P.O. Box 220
Cedarville 96104
Ph: 916-279-6116

Devil's Garden Ranger District
P.O. Box 5
Canby 96015
Ph: 916-233-4611

PLUMAS NATIONAL FOREST

Head Office
159 Lawrence
P.O. Box 1500
Quincy 95971
Ph: 916-283-2050

La Porte Ranger District
Challenge Ranger Station
P.O. Box 369
Challenge 95925
Ph: 916-675-2462

Quincy Ranger District
1400 E. Main, Box 69
Quincy 95971
Ph: 916-283-0555

Beckworth Ranger District
Mohawk Ranger Station
P.O. Box 7
Blairsden 96013
Ph: 916-836-2575

Milford Ranger District
Laufman Ranger Station
Milford 96121
Ph: 916-253-2223

Greenville Ranger District
P.O. Box 329
Greenville 95947
Ph: 916-284-7126

Oroville Ranger District
875 Mitchell Ave.
Oroville 95965
Ph: 916-534-6500

...Continued...

SAN BERNADINO NATIONAL FOREST

Head Office
1824 Commercenter Circle
San Bernadino 92408-3430
Ph: 714-383-5588

Cajon Ranger District
Star Route, Box 100
Fontana 92335
Ph: 714-887-2576

Arrowhead Ranger District
26577 Highway 18
P.O. Box 7
Rimforest 92378
Ph: 714-337-2444

San Gorgonio Ranger District
Mill Creek Station
34701 Mill Creek Rd.
Mentone 92359
Ph: 714-794-1123

Big Bear Ranger District
P.O. Box 290
Fawnskin 92333
Ph: 714-866-3437

San Jacinto Ranger District
Idyllwild Ranger Station
P.O. Box 518
Idyllwild 92349
Ph: 714-659-2117

SEQUOIA NATIONAL FOREST

Head Office
900 W. Grand Ave.
Porterville 93257-2035
Ph: 209-784-1500

Hot Springs Ranger District
Route 4, Box 548
Calif. Hot Springs 93207
Ph: 805-548-6503

Cannell Meadow Ranger District
P.O. Box 6
Kernville 93238
Ph: 619-376-3781

Hume Lake Ranger District
35860 E. Kings Canyon Rd.
Dunlap 93621
Ph: 209-338-2251

Greenhorn Ranger District
Federal Bldg., Rm. 322
800 Truxton Ave.
Bakersfield 93301
Ph: 805-861-4212

Tule Ranger District
32588 Highway 190
Springville 93265
Ph: 209-539-2607

SHASTA-TRINITY NATIONAL FOREST

Head Office
2400 Washington Ave.
Redding 96001
Ph: 916-246-5222

McCloud Ranger District
P.O. Box 1620
McCloud 96057
Ph: 916-964-2184

Weaverville Ranger District
P.O. Box 1190
Weaverville 96093
Ph: 916-623-2121

Big Bar Ranger District
Star Route 1, Box 10
Big Bar 96010
Ph: 916-623-6106

Mt. Shasta Ranger District
204 West Alma
Mt. Shasta 96067
Ph: 916-926-4511

Yolla Bolla Ranger District
Platina 96076
Ph: 916-352-4211

Hayfork Ranger District
P.O. Box 159
Hayfork 96041
Ph: 916-628-5227

Shasta Lake Ranger District
6543 Holiday Drive
Redding 96003
Ph: 916-275-1587

NCSC (FTS)
6106 Airport Rd.
Redding 96002
Ph: 916-246-5285

SIERRA NATIONAL FOREST

Head Office
Federal Building
1130 "O" St., Room 3009
Fresno 93721
Ph: 209-487-5155

Mariposa Ranger District
41969 Highway 41
Oakhurst 93644
Ph: 209-683-4665

Kings River Ranger District
34849 Maxon Rd.
Sanger 93657
Ph: 209-855-8321

Minarets Ranger District
North Fork 93643
Ph: 209-877-2218

Pineridge Ranger District
P.O. Box 300
Shaver Lake 93664
Ph: 209-841-3311

Kings River Ranger District
Dinkey Ranger Station, Dinkey Rte.
Shaver Lake 93664
Ph: 209-841-3404
(Summers Only)

...Continued...

SIX RIVERS NATIONAL FOREST

Head Office
507 "F" Street
Eureka 95501
Ph: 707-442-1721

Mad River Ranger District
Star Route, Box 300
Bridgeville 95526
Ph: 707-574-6233

Zenia Fire Station
General Delivery
Zenia 95495
Ph: 707-922-6069

Gasquet Ranger District
P.O. Box 228
Gasquet 95543
Ph: 707-457-3131

Orleans Ranger District
Drawer B
Orleans 95556
Ph: 916-627-3291

Big Flat Station
Gasquet Ranger District
(Summer Station Only)
No Phone or Mail Service

Lower Trinity Ranger District
P.O. Box 668
Willow Creek 95573
Ph: 916-629-2118

Salyer Fire Station
Lower Tr. Rd.
(No Mail Service)
Salyer 95563
Ph: 916-629-2114

Humboldt Nursery
4886 Cottage Grove
McKinleyville 95521
Ph: 707-839-3256

STANISLAUS NATIONAL FOREST

Head Office
19777 Greenley Rd.
Sonora 95370
Ph: 209-532-3671

Mi-Wok Ranger District
Highway 108E
P.O. Box 100
Mi-Wok Village 95346
Ph: 209-586-3234

Calaveras Ranger District
Highway 4
P.O. Box 500
Hathaway Pines 95233
Ph: 209-795-1381

Summit Ranger District
Highway 108 at Pinecrest
Star Route, Box 1295
Sonora 95370
Ph: 209-965-3434

Groveland Ranger District
Highway 120 - Star Route
P.O Box 75G
Groveland 95321
Ph: 209-962-7825

TAHOE NATIONAL FOREST

Head Office
Highway 49 & Coyote St.
Nevada City 95959
Ph: 916-265-4531

Nevada City Ranger District
Highway 49 & Coyote St.
Nevada City 95959
Ph: 916-265-4538

Downieville Ranger District
N. Yuba Ranger Station
15924 Highway 49
Camptonville 95922

Sierraville Ranger District
P.O. Box 95, Hwy. 89
Sierraville 96126
Ph: 916-994-3401

Foresthill Ranger District
22830 Auburn-Foresthill Rd.
Foresthill 95631
Ph: 916-367-2224

Truckee Ranger District
P.O. Box 909
Truckee 95734
Ph: 916-587-3558

NATIONAL PARKS

Lassen Volcanic National Park
Mineral 96063
Ph: 916-595-4444

Sequoia-Kings Canyon
National Park
Three Rivers 93271
Ph: 209-565-3341

Yosemite National Park
P.O. Box 577
Yosemite National Park 95389
Ph: 209-372-0265

CALIFORNIA STATE PARKS SYSTEM
P.O. Box 94296
Sacramento, CA 94296-0001
Information Ph: 916-445-6477

Publications Office - 1st Floor
1416 Ninth Street
Sacramento, CA 95814
Information Ph: 916-322-7000

CALIFORNIA OFFICE OF TOURISM
1121 "L" Street, Suite 103
Sacramento, CA 95814
Information Ph: 1-800-862-2543

DEPARTMENT OF FISH & GAME OFFICES

HEADQUARTERS:

1416 Ninth Street
Sacramento, CA 95814
Ph: 916-445-3531

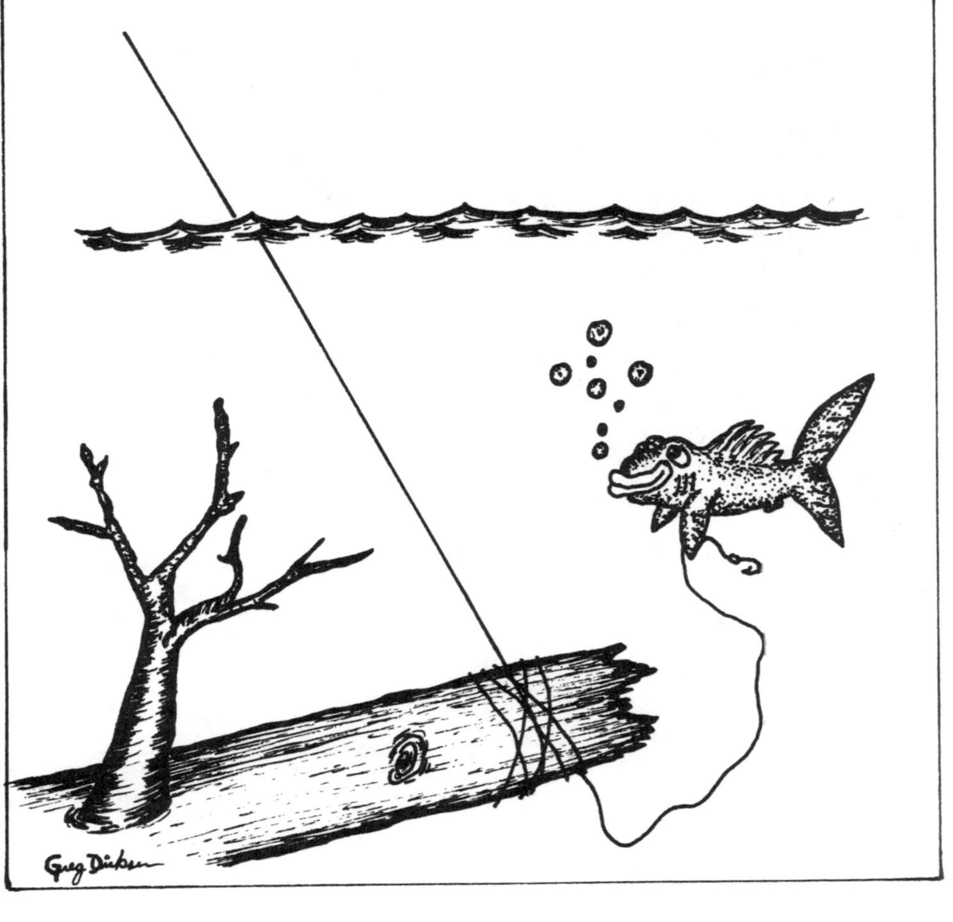

REGIONAL OFFICES:

Region 1
601 Lucust Street
Redding, CA 96001
Ph: 916-225-2300

Region 2
1701 Nimbus Rd.
Rancho Cordova 95670
Ph: 916-355-0978

Region 3
7329 Silverado Trail
Napa
Ph: 707-944-5500
Mailing Address:
P.O. Box 47
Yountville, 94599

Region 4
1234 E. Shaw Ave.
Fresno 93710
Ph: 209-222-3761

Region 5
330 Golden Shore, Suite 50
Long Beach 90802
Ph: 213-590-5132

LEAVE ONLY
FOOTPRINTS
TAKE ONLY MEMORIES